Conference of the North American Chapter of the Association for Computational Linguistics: Human Language Technologies (NAACL HLT 2019)

Industry Papers

Minneapolis, Minnesota, USA
2 – 7 June 2019

ISBN: 978-1-5108-8755-8

NAACL HLT 2019

**The 2019 Conference of the
North American Chapter of the
Association for Computational Linguistics:
Human Language Technologies**

**Proceedings of the Conference
Vol. 2 (Industry Papers)**

June 2 - June 7, 2019

Introduction

We welcome you to the second installment of the NAACL-HLT Industry Track.

Introduced at NAACL-HLT 2018 in New Orleans, the industry track provides a forum for researchers, engineers and application developers to exchange ideas, share results and discuss use cases of successful deployment of language technologies in real-world settings. The inaugural Industry track was very successful in terms of both participation during the conference and feedback received through the post-conference survey.

Continuing the industry track into its second year, we took stock of the opinions that participants and organizers shared about the separate industry track. Many recognized the need to reflect the shift in contemporary NLP work which has grown substantially outside academic and research organizations into industry. On the other hand, there was a concern that the industry track unfairly advantaged industry-affiliated participants. This year we have taken small steps towards integrating the industry track more into the conference by adhering to the same standards as the main track of the conference in terms of timelines and acceptance ratios. At the same time, we have made conscious attempts to welcome all constituents of the NAACL conferences to this new track.

Submissions to the industry track were solicited from all members of the NAACL community including but not limited to students, practitioners and researchers. The call for papers focused on advances and challenges in the deployment of language processing technologies in real-world systems. Following the same deadlines and policies as the main track of the NAACL-HLT 2019 conference, we have aimed to eliminate the perceptions of unfair advantages to papers submitted to the industry track.

Despite moving the submission deadline to over a month earlier and requiring that the authors choose the most suitable track for their papers, we received 124 abstracts and 114 paper submissions, a 25% year-over-year increase. Twelve percent of the submissions were rejected without review due to incompleteness, non-compliance with format requirements or submission policies (such as the double submission policy). We saw a remarkable increase in papers that were co-authored by researchers in academia and industry labs: 48% vs. 29% in 2018.

Submitted papers were reviewed by our program committee with rich representation of the present spectrum of NLP researchers and professionals. Each submission was reviewed by at least three members of the program committee. Reviews solicited committee opinions along two primary aspects: focus on real-world applications and lessons offered by the paper. Reviews also took into consideration clarity, methodological rigor, ethical use of datasets and compliance with conference guidelines. Thanks to the enthusiastic and diligent efforts of the industry track program committee, the reviews were completed on time. We accepted 28 papers based on committee recommendations as well as alignment of the papers with the goals of industry track. The acceptance rate reduced from 33% to 28% compared to NAACL-HLT 2018.

The Industry Track program this year will consist of two oral sessions (5 papers each) and one poster session (18 posters). The presentation format was determined based on reviewer recommendations as well as a paper's overall score. The first oral session will address various challenges of using language technologies in real-world applications. One of the common themes for many papers in this session is ensuring system robustness towards new domains, locales or user inputs in a variety of different applications. The second oral session showcases several deployed systems. In addition to discussing the choices made for system architecture and standard evaluation metrics, these papers also report the impact on end users, the ultimate test of a system's usefulness. Work presented in the poster session paints a rich picture of the many real-world applications of NLP and speech technologies and the challenges associated with these applications.

NAACL-HLT 2019 Industry Track also features the "Careers in NLP" panel discussion. The rebranded edition of this panel discussion recognizes the diversity of NLP careers today. Traditional career paths have typically led NLP researchers into academia, industrial labs, and government agencies. Today, we also see an increase in roles at startup companies and an emerging NLP practitioner role in industry that intersects with software, data, and product. As last year, the panel will be moderated by Philip Resnik, professor at the University of Maryland, and we expect the conversation to include trends in NLP careers, emerging skills, prominent challenges and opportunities for cross-functional collaboration as NLP professionals in today's organizations, and more.

The NAACL-HLT 2019 industry track program is the culmination of the small steps we have taken towards elevating and integrating this track further into the conference. We hope the program we have put together will strengthen the community's resolve to continue to organize and attend a similar track at future conferences.

On a personal note, we recognize the privilege of chairing the NAACL-HLT 2019 Industry Track. We thank the conference general chair, Jill Burstein, for inviting us to the organizing committee. Thanks also to Program Chairs Christy, Ted and Thamar as well as all members of the organizing committee. We were generously helped by every member of this committee over the past year and organizing this track was possible only with their advice and efforts. We once again recognize and thank every member of the industry track program committee for volunteering their time. Finally, thanks to the authors and attendees of the industry track for embracing this initiative and offering a reason to continue the industry track at NAACL-HLT conferences.

Anastassia, Michelle, Rohit

Industry Track Co-chairs:

Rohit Kumar
Anastassia Loukina, Educational Testing Service
Michelle Morales, IBM

Program Committee:

Nitin Agarwal, Microsoft
Sachin Agarwal, Apple
Hua Ai, Delta Airlines
Alan Akbik, Zalando Research
Miguel Ballesteros, IBM Research AI
Nikoletta Basiou, SRI International
Frederic Bechet, Aix-Marseille Université
Trung Bui, Adobe Research
Donna Byron, IBM Cognitive Applications
Vitor Carvalho, Intuit AI
Francisco Casacuberta, Universitat Politècnica de València
Praveen Chandar, Spotify
Sourish Chaudhuri, Google Inc
Ciprian Chelba, Google
Wei Chen, Google
John Chen, Interactions LLC
Laura Chiticariu, IBM Watson
Justin Chiu, Avrio AI
Brooke Cowan, Expedia Group
Deborah Dahl, Conversational Technologies
Lingjia Deng, Bloomberg L.P.
Giuseppe Di Fabbrizio, VUI Inc.
Matthew Dunn, LivePerson
Keelan Evanini, Educational Testing Service
Oliver Ferschke, M*Modal
Michael Flor, Educational Testing Service
Rashmi Gangadharaiah, AWS AI Amazon
Anna Lisa, Gentile IBM Research Almaden
Rahul Goel, Amazon Alexa
Anuj Goyal, Amazon Alexa
Dilek Hakkani-Tur, Amazon Alexa AI
Sanjika Hewavitharana, eBay
Derrick Higgins, American Family Insurance
Lynette Hirschman, MITRE
Yufang Hou, IBM Research
Javid Huseynov, IBM
Rahul Jha, Microsoft Corporation
Mahesh Joshi, LinkedIn
Adi Kalyanpur, Elemental Cognition
Kartikay Khandelwal, Facebook
Saurabh Khanwalkar, Bose Corporation

Doo Soon Kim, Adobe Research
Sun Kim, National Center for Biotechnology Information (NCBI)
Jared Kramer, Amazon
Sanjeev Kumar, Quark.ai
Gakuto Kurata, IBM Research
Constantine Lignos, University of Southern California Information Sciences Institute
Bing Liu, University of Illinois at Chicago
Alexander Loeser, Beuth-University of Applied Sciences Berlin
Xiaoqiang Luo, LinkedIn
Nitin Madnani, Educational Testing Service
Arindam Mandal, Amazon.com
Yuji Matsumoto, NAIST / Riken AIP
Florian Metze, Carnegie Mellon University
Lisa Michaud, Aspect Software
Isabelle Moulinier, Capital One
Matthew Mulholland, Educational Testing Service
Udhyakumar Nallasamy, Apple
Elnaz Nouri, Microsoft Research
Mari Olsen, Lionbridge - Machine Intelligence
Stefano Pacifico, Epistemic AI
Aasish Pappu, Spotify Research
Youngja Park, IBM T. J. Watson Research Center
Ioannis Partalas, Expedia Group
Siddharth Patwardhan, Apple
Alexandros Potamianos, Behavioral Signals
John Prager, IBM Research
Rashmi Prasad, Interactions Corporation
Long Qin, Singsound Inc
Elio Querze, Bose Corp
Owen Rambow, Elemental Cognition LLC
Meghana Ravikumar, SigOpt
Sravana Reddy, Spotify
Ehud Reiter, University of Aberdeen
Steve Renals, University of Edinburgh
Giuseppe Riccardi, University of Trento
Brian Riordan, Educational Testing Service
Salim Roukos, IBM
Nicholas Ruiz, Interactions LLC
Alicia Sagae, Consulting Scientist
Avneesh Saluja, Netflix
Stefan Scherer, Embodied Inc.
Frank Schilder, Thomson Reuters
Frank Seide, Microsoft Research
Ethan Selfridge, Interactions LLC
Rushin Shah, Facebook
Michal Shmueli-Scheuer, IBM Research
Sunayana Sitaram, Microsoft Research India
Kazoo Sone, Google
Biplav Srivastava, IBM
Svetlana Stoyanchev, Interactions Corporation
David Suendermann-Oeft, Modality

Isabel Trancoso, INESC-ID / IST
Keith Trnka, 98point6 Inc.
Ling Tsou, SDL
Gokhan Tur, Uber
Ngoc Phuoc An Vo, IBM Research
Xinhao Wang, Educational Testing Service
Yi-Chia Wang, Uber AI
Jason D Williams, Apple

Careers in NLP Panel:

Judith L. Klavans, Independent
Yunyao Li, IBM Research
Owen Rambow, Elemental Cognition
Philip Resnik (Moderator), University of Maryland
Joel Tetreault, Grammarly

Conference Program

Monday, June 3, 2019

13:00–14:30 *Careers in NLP Panel*

Tuesday June 4, 2019

09:00–10:30 ***Oral Sessions (long papers) and Posters (long and short papers)***

Session 4E (Industry): Real world challenges

09:00–09:18 *Enabling Real-time Neural IME with Incremental Vocabulary Selection*
Jiali Yao, Raphael Shu, Xinjian Li, Katsutoshi Ohtsuki and Hideki Nakayama

09:18–09:36 *Locale-agnostic Universal Domain Classification Model in Spoken Language Understanding*
Jihwan Lee, Ruhi Sarikaya and Young-Bum Kim

09:36–09:54 *Practical Semantic Parsing for Spoken Language Understanding*
Marco Damonte, Rahul Goel and Tagyoung Chung

09:54–10:12 *Fast Prototyping a Dialogue Comprehension System for Nurse-Patient Conversations on Symptom Monitoring*
Zhengyuan Liu, Hazel Lim, Nur Farah Ain Suhaimi, Shao Chuen Tong, Sharon Ong, Angela Ng, Sheldon Lee, Michael R. Macdonald, Savitha Ramasamy, Pavitra Krishnaswamy, Wai Leng Chow and Nancy F. Chen

10:12–10:30 *Graph Convolution for Multimodal Information Extraction from Visually Rich Documents*
Xiaojing Liu, Feiyu Gao, Qiong Zhang and Huasha Zhao

15:30–17:00 ***Oral sessions (long papers) and Posters (long and short papers)***

Session 6E (Industry): Deployed systems

15:30–15:48   *Diversifying Reply Suggestions Using a Matching-Conditional Variational Autoencoder*
Budhaditya Deb, Peter Bailey and Milad Shokouhi

15:48–16:06   *Goal-Oriented End-to-End Conversational Models with Profile Features in a Real-World Setting*
Yichao Lu, Manisha Srivastava, Jared Kramer, Heba Elfardy, Andrea Kahn, Song Wang and Vikas Bhardwaj

16:06–16:24   *Detecting Customer Complaint Escalation with Recurrent Neural Networks and Manually-Engineered Features*
Wei Yang, Luchen Tan, Chunwei Lu, Anqi Cui, Han Li, Xi Chen, Kun Xiong, Muzi Wang, Ming Li, Jian Pei and Jimmy Lin

16:24–16:42   *Multi-Modal Generative Adversarial Network for Short Product Title Generation in Mobile E-Commerce*
Jianguo Zhang, Pengcheng Zou, Zhao Li, Yao Wan, Xiuming Pan, Yu Gong and Philip S. Yu

16:42–17:00   *A Case Study on Neural Headline Generation for Editing Support*
Kazuma Murao, Ken Kobayashi, Hayato Kobayashi, Taichi Yatsuka, Takeshi Masuyama, Tatsuru Higurashi and Yoshimune Tabuchi

Wednesday June 5, 2019

15:30–16:30   ***Oral Sessions (short papers) and Posters (Industry)***

Session 9F: Industry posters

15:30–16:30   *Neural Lexicons for Slot Tagging in Spoken Language Understanding*
Kyle Williams

15:30–16:30   *Active Learning for New Domains in Natural Language Understanding*
Stanislav Peshterliev, John Kearney, Abhyuday Jagannatha, Imre Kiss and Spyros Matsoukas

15:30–16:30   *Scaling Multi-Domain Dialogue State Tracking via Query Reformulation*
Pushpendre Rastogi, Arpit Gupta, Tongfei Chen and Mathias Lambert

15:30–16:30   *Are the Tools up to the Task? an Evaluation of Commercial Dialog Tools in Developing Conversational Enterprise-grade Dialog Systems*
Marie Meteer, Meghan Hickey, Carmi Rothberg, David Nahamoo and Ellen Eide Kislal

15:30–16:30   *Development and Deployment of a Large-Scale Dialog-based Intelligent Tutoring System*
Shazia Afzal, Tejas Dhamecha, Nirmal Mukhi, Renuka Sindhgatta, Smit Marvaniya, Matthew Ventura and Jessica Yarbro

15:30–16:30   *Learning When Not to Answer: a Ternary Reward Structure for Reinforcement Learning Based Question Answering*
Fréderic Godin, Anjishnu Kumar and Arpit Mittal

15:30–16:30   *Extraction of Message Sequence Charts from Software Use-Case Descriptions*
Girish Palshikar, Nitin Ramrakhiyani, Sangameshwar Patil, Sachin Pawar, Swapnil Hingmire, Vasudeva Varma and Pushpak Bhattacharyya

15:30–16:30   *Improving Knowledge Base Construction from Robust Infobox Extraction*
Boya Peng, Yejin Huh, Xiao Ling and Michele Banko

15:30–16:30   *A k-Nearest Neighbor Approach towards Multi-level Sequence Labeling*
Yue Chen and John Chen

15:30–16:30   *Train One Get One Free: Partially Supervised Neural Network for Bug Report Duplicate Detection and Clustering*
Lahari Poddar, Leonardo Neves, William Brendel, Luis Marujo, Sergey Tulyakov and Pradeep Karuturi

15:30–16:30   *Robust Semantic Parsing with Adversarial Learning for Domain Generalization*
Gabriel Marzinotto, Geraldine Damnati, Frederic Bechet and Benoit Favre

15:30–16:30   *TOI-CNN: a Solution of Information Extraction on Chinese Insurance Policy*
Lin Sun, Kai Zhang, Fule Ji and Zhenhua Yang

15:30–16:30   *Cross-lingual Transfer Learning for Japanese Named Entity Recognition*
Andrew Johnson, Penny Karanasou, Judith Gaspers and Dietrich Klakow

15:30–16:30   *Neural Text Normalization with Subword Units*
Courtney Mansfield, Ming Sun, Yuzong Liu, Ankur Gandhe and Bjorn Hoffmeister

15:30–16:30   *Audio De-identification - a New Entity Recognition Task*
Ido Cohn, Itay Laish, Genady Beryozkin, Gang Li, Izhak Shafran, Idan Szpektor, Tzvika Hartman, Avinatan Hassidim and Yossi Matias

15:30–16:30   *In Other News: a Bi-style Text-to-speech Model for Synthesizing Newscaster Voice with Limited Data*
Nishant Prateek, Mateusz Łajszczak, Roberto Barra-Chicote, Thomas Drugman, Jaime Lorenzo-Trueba, Thomas Merritt, Srikanth Ronanki and Trevor Wood

15:30–16:30   *Generate, Filter, and Rank: Grammaticality Classification for Production-Ready NLG Systems*
Ashwini Challa, Kartikeya Upasani, Anusha Balakrishnan and Rajen Subba

15:30–16:30   *Content-based Dwell Time Engagement Prediction Model for News Articles*
Heidar Davoudi, Aijun An and Gordon Edall

Enabling Real-time Neural IME with Incremental Vocabulary Selection

Jiali Yao
Microsoft
jiayao@microsoft.com

Raphael Shu
The University of Tokyo
shu@nlab.ci.i.u-tokyo.ac.jp

Xinjian Li
Carnegie Mellon University
xinjianl@andrew.cmu.edu

Katsutoshi Ohtsuki
Microsoft
Katsutoshi.Ohtsuki@microsoft.com

Hideki Nakayama
The University of Tokyo
nakayama@ci.i.u-tokyo.ac.jp

Abstract

Input method editor (IME) converts sequential alphabet key inputs to words in a target language. It is an indispensable service for billions of Asian users. Although the neural-based language model is extensively studied and shows promising results in sequence-to-sequence tasks, applying a neural-based language model to IME was not considered feasible due to high latency when converting words on user devices. In this work, we articulate the bottleneck of neural IME decoding to be the heavy softmax computation over a large vocabulary. We propose an approach that incrementally builds a subset vocabulary from the word lattice. Our approach always computes the probability with a selected subset vocabulary. When the selected vocabulary is updated, the stale probabilities in previous steps are fixed by recomputing the missing logits. The experiments on Japanese IME benchmark shows an over 50x speedup for the softmax computations comparing to the baseline, reaching real-time speed even on commodity CPU without losing conversion accuracy[1]. The approach is potentially applicable to other incremental sequence-to-sequence decoding tasks such as real-time continuous speech recognition.

1 Introduction

Input Method Editors (IME) run on every desktop and mobile devices that allows users to type the scripts in their language. Though Latin users can type directly without conversion as a second step, some common languages such as Chinese and Japanese require users to convert the keyboard input sequence as there are thousands of characters in these languages. The conversion task of an IME takes a key sequence and converts it to a sequence of words in the target language. In the ideal case, the conversion results shall fit the intention of users. The accuracy of the conversion task directly affects the typing efficiency and user experiences.

The conversion task is a sequence decoding task similar to speech recognition, machine translation, and optical character recognition. Conventionally, an n-gram language model toolkit is used to evaluate the path probability during decoding (Stolcke, 2002; Heafield, 2011). Due to the ability of leveraging context information without hitting data sparsity issue, neural language models as an alternative option have been extensively studied in the past (Bengio et al., 2003; Schwenk, 2007; Mikolov et al., 2010; Mikolov and Zweig, 2012), which achieve state-of-the-art performance on many tasks (Sundermeyer et al., 2012; Luong et al., 2015; Jozefowicz et al., 2016). With emerging dedicated hardware processing unit such as custom ASIC (Jouppi and Young, 2017), neural-based models are promising to be even more widely applied to user devices.

However, neural-based language models were not considered feasible for the IME conversion task. The main reason is that an IME has to run interactively on various user devices, whereas speech recognition and machine translation services are normally provided on servers. Furthermore, the neural model has to meet following requirements in order to be adopted in practice: 1) **low-latency incremental conversion**; 2) **word lattice post-editing**. First, the conversion task for IME is an incremental process that needs to return the best paths immediately when receiving each key input. Existing speed optimization methods (Deoras et al., 2011; Hori et al., 2014) normally increase the speed of processing sequences in batch. Some methods incorporate prefix tree (Si et al., 2013), which doesn't ensure the worse

---

[1]The source code of the implementation is available from https://github.com/jiali-ms/JLM

Proceedings of NAACL-HLT 2019, pages 1–8
Minneapolis, Minnesota, June 2 - June 7, 2019. ©2019 Association for Computational Linguistics

case latency still meets the real-time requirement. Second, IME allows users to post-edit the converted results at word lattice by manually selecting candidates. It limits the choice of many end-to-end neural network architectures (Cho et al., 2014; Vaswani et al., 2017) as they do not provide a way for users to select partial conversion results.

In this work, we enhance a neural language model tailored for IMEs to meet real-time inference speed requirements on the conversion task. Our baseline model is composed of a LSTM-based language model (Hochreiter and Schmidhuber, 1997) with a Viterbi decoder (Forney, 1973) as Figure 1 shows. We articulate the bottleneck of run-time speed as the heavy linear transformation in the softmax layer. We propose an incremental vocabulary selection approach that builds a subset vocabulary V_t at each decoding step t. By only computing softmax over V_t, the cost of softmax significantly drops since $|V_t|$ is usually a small number that is less than 1% of the original vocabulary size. We evaluate the speedup comparing to other softmax optimizations on a Japanese benchmark. The contributions of this work can be summarized as:

1. We propose a novel incremental vocabulary selection approach, which significantly reduces the latency of lattice decoding in IME conversion task.

2. We provide an extensive comparison among different approaches for speeding up the softmax computation in lattice decoding.

3. We demonstrate that with our proposed acceleration method helps the neural models to meet the requirement for real-world applications.

2   Related Work

Applying a neural-based model for input method is studied in a few previous works. Chen et al. (2015) proposed a MLP architecture for Chinese Pinyin input method to re-score the n-best list of n-gram decoded results similar to speech recognition solutions (Deoras et al., 2011; Si et al., 2013). Though not in literature, we have found the implementation of RNN-based input method[2]. The

---

[2]Yoh Okuno. Neural ime: Neural input method engine. https://github.com/yohokuno/neural_ime, 2016

decoding results on Japanese corpus show promising accuracy improvement comparing to the n-gram model. Huang et al. (2018) treats the Chinese input conversion as machine translation and apply sequence-to-sequence models with attention mechanism. The conversion and other features are served as cloud services. Our work focus on enabling real-time neural-based models on devices with limited computation resources.

The softmax layer with a large vocabulary size is the most computational-heavy operation of a neural-based language model. Differentiated softmax (Chen et al., 2016) and its variation (Joulin et al., 2017) decrease the amount of computation by reducing the embedding size of long tail words in the vocabulary with frequency based segmentation. For prediction tasks where only top-k words are necessary, softmax approximation such as SVD softmax (Shim et al., 2017) uses a low-rank matrix in the softmax layer for a first pass fast ranking. Zhang et al. (2018) proposes a word graph traverse approach to find top-k hypothesis in logarithmic complexity. In a word lattice decoder, where the target words are given, structured output layer (Mnih and Hinton, 2009; Le et al., 2011; Shi et al., 2013) is often applied to avoid calculating probability distributions from the full vocabulary. Character-based RNN (Mikolov et al., 2010) is a good alternative for word-based language models that can significantly reduce the vocabulary size. However, there are still tens of thousands of Chinese characters.

Another approach to solving the softmax bottleneck is vocabulary manipulation. In machine translation, given a source sentence, the vocabulary of target words can be largely limited before translation. It is possible to compute the softmax on a subset of the full vocabulary (Jean et al., 2015; Mi et al., 2016). However, for the input method, the conversion task takes user input incrementally. Our proposed incremental vocabulary selection can work without predicting the full vocabulary beforehand, which is designed for reducing the latency for incremental sequence decoding tasks with a large vocabulary.

3   Neural-based Input Method Editor

Our proposed approach for neural-based IME is illustrated in Figure 1. We use a neural-based language model to predict the word probabilities in the lattice decoder. Although there are

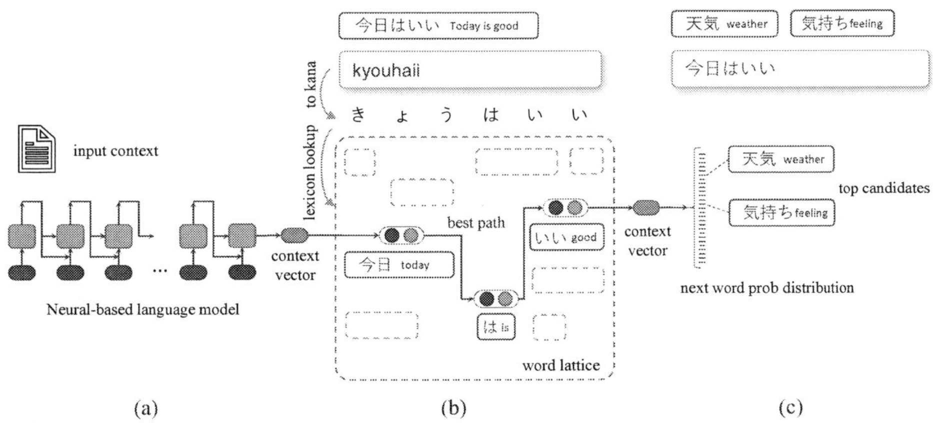

Figure 1: Illustration of a neural-based IME with LSTM language model and word lattice decoder. (a) Input context. (b) Conversion with a LSTM-based language model and Viterbi lattice decoder. (c) Word prediction.

various choices for the model architecture, we choose a single layer LSTM (Hochreiter and Schmidhuber, 1997) model considering the run-time speed constraint. Other model architectures such as sequence-to-sequence models (Cho et al., 2014) and the bi-directional LSTM-based models (Huang et al., 2015) are not considered as they cannot generate conversion results incrementally.

Conversion task is illustrated in Figure 1(b). User key inputs are first converted into Japanese Kana (also known as "fifty sounds") with pre-defined rules. Given a partial observed Kana character input sequence $(x_1, ..., x_t)$, we search for a set of words in the dictionary that match any suffix of the observation as lattice words at step t:

$$D_t = \bigcup_{i=1}^{t} \mathrm{match}(x_i, ..., x_t), \qquad (1)$$

where the function $\mathrm{match}(\cdot)$ returns all lexicon items matching the partial sequence. For example, given the observation "ha ru ka", the lexicon set D_t contains all words matching "ha ru ka" or "ru ka" or "ka".

Given a word $w_t \in D_t$, to construct a hypothesis π_t ending with w_t, previous hypotheses π_{t-l} are used as the context to evaluate $p(w_t|\pi_{t-l})$, where l is the length of the Kana representation of w_t. Since l is a variable for w_t, only aligned hypotheses can be connected. To find the best hypotheses, we use a Viterbi decoder to decode with a beam size B.

We use a LSTM-based language model directly here to evaluate $p(w_t|\pi_{t-l})$. The conversion task

has to compute $B \times |V| \times T$ steps of LSTM computation for one input sequence, where $|V|$ is the vocabulary size, T is the sequence length. Heavy computation cost of LSTM model comes from two operations: the matrix operations inside the LSTM cell and the matrix projection at softmax. In the case of a LSTM model with a vocabulary size of 100K, a hidden size of 512, and an embedding size of 256, estimated by simple matrix multiplication, the number of multiplication operations for LSTM cell is about 1.5M, while the softmax has 50M operations. In practice, the softmax occupies 97% of the total computation cost, which is the bottleneck for the conversion task with large vocabulary size.

4 Incremental Vocabulary Selection

To solve the challenges, we propose an incremental vocabulary selection algorithm, which significantly reduces the amount of softmax computation during decoding. The algorithm of *incremental vocabulary selection* is given in Alg. 1. Let Π be the hypothesis dictionary that stores the best hypotheses at each step with LSTM states. We define $\Pi[\cdot]$ as the dictionary lookup operation to get the best hypotheses at a specified step. Π is initialized with a start hypothesis that contains the LSTM state carried over from the previously converted sequence.

In current conversion step, when a new input character x_t arrives, we construct a subset vocabulary V_t that covers all possible output words for

Algorithm 1 Incremental vocabulary selection

1: **Initialize:**
    $B \leftarrow$ beam size
    $\Pi \leftarrow$ hypothesis dictionary
    $\tilde{V} \leftarrow$ samples from vocabulary
    $t \leftarrow$ current step t
2: $V_t \leftarrow$ sub vocabulary with Eq. 2
3: $V_t \leftarrow V_t \cup \tilde{V}$
4: $V_{\text{fix}} \leftarrow$ empty set
5: **for** $k \leftarrow t - 1$ to 1 **do**
6:     $V_{\text{fix}} \leftarrow V_{\text{fix}} \cup (V_t \setminus V_k)$
7:     $V_k \leftarrow V_t$
8: Re-compute the logits on V_{fix} for all past hyps
9: Evaluate $\Pi[t]$
10: $\Pi[t] \leftarrow$ best B hyps in $\Pi[t]$
11: Update LSTM state for $\Pi[t]$
12: **output** $\Pi[t]$

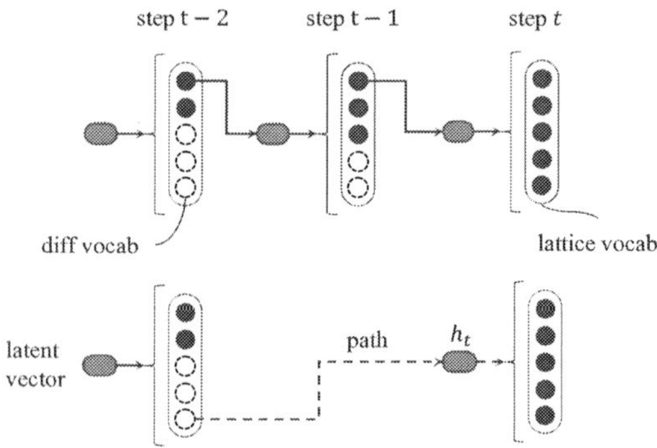

Figure 2: Previously aligned hypotheses have missing vocabulary to evaluate words in current step.

the sequence until step t as:

$$V_t = \bigcup_{i=1}^{t} D_i. \qquad (2)$$

To evaluate a newly formed hypothesis (π_{t-l}, w_t), we need to query the probability $p(w_t|\pi_{t-l})$, which is already calculated and cached in $\Pi[t - l]$. However, as Figure 2 illustrates, since the V_t is built incrementally, the softmax distribution calculated in previous steps may not contain the word w_t. To evaluate $\Pi[t]$, we need to fix the missing vocabulary items in previously calculated softmax distributions. In principle, we can correct a stale probability in step k by adding the logits of missing vocabulary to the denominator as:

$$P(y_k = i|h_k)$$
$$= \frac{\exp(h_k^\top W_i)}{\sum\limits_{j \,\in\, V_k} \exp(h_k^\top W_j) + \sum\limits_{j \,\in\, d} \exp(h_k^\top W_j)}. \qquad (3)$$

where W is the projection matrix of the output layer. h_k is the cached LSTM state for a hypothesis π_k that can be re-used to calculate missing logits. d is the difference of vocabulary between steps $V_t \setminus V_k$. In practice, as each path has different missing vocabularies, we compute a union of all missing vocabularies V_{fix} and then re-compute the logits of them in one batch.

As the vocabulary in initial steps is fairly small, we introduce $\tilde{V}$ as a subset vocabulary sampled from the full vocabulary. In contrast to the beam search in machine translation, we have to rank paths that contain a different number of words. We use V_t jointly with $\tilde{V}$ to make the word probabilities closer to their original probabilities.

After the best hypotheses are decided, we immediately update the LSTM state for B hypotheses in $\Pi[t]$. The single best hypothesis in $\Pi[t]$ is finally returned to the IME engine as the output of the conversion task.

5 Experiments

5.1 Dataset

We use BCCWJ (Balanced Corpus of Contemporary Written Japanese) corpus (Maekawa et al., 2014) for evaluating our model. The corpus is well balanced with various sources of text representing contemporary written Japanese. This corpus contains 5.8M sentences, which are segmented into 127M tokens. In our experiments, all words are further segmented into short unit words. Each word has a format of "display/reading/POS". The reading and part-of-speech (POS) attributes are attached to indicate different usages of the same word. Among the 611K unique words, we choose top 50K frequent ones which cover 97.3% of the token appearances as an appropriate vocabulary size for the IME task. The words in the vocabulary are ranked with frequency. Most frequent words are at the top.

5.2 Experiment Settings

The BCCWJ dataset is split into training, valid and test set. The ratio is 70%, 20%, and 10% respectively. We randomly sample 2000 sentences from the test set for evaluating the conversion accuracy.

For input method task, we evaluate the conversion accuracy using a Viterbi decoder with a beam size of 10. In Japanese, there are often more than one correct conversion results. For instance, a verb may have two acceptable styles, one in original Japanese Kana, the other in Chinese characters. To better evaluate the model performance, we also report the top-10 conversion accuracy in addition to top-1 conversion accuracy.

We implement using TensorFlow[3]. We use a batch size of 384. A dropout with a drop rate of 0.9 is applied before the LSTM layer. Adam is used with a fixed learning rate of 0.001. The hyper-parameters are shared for all experiments.

A replica of the same model is written in numpy to work with a Viterbi decoder in python. It uses the weights learned with TensorFlow model. The inference performance is measure with numpy on a single Intel E5 CPU. We also apply the underline BLAS library to accelerate matrix operation.

5.3 Evaluation of Neural-based Input Method Editor

We first compared the neural model performance with a conventional n-gram model. We evaluate the perplexity of the n-gram model with SRILM package (Stolcke, 2002). We choose modified Kneser Ney (Kneser and Ney, 1995; James, 2000) as the smoothing algorithm when learning the n-gram model. No cut-offs or pruning is applied. The learned language model is plugged into our input method pipeline for evaluating the sentence conversion accuracy. The prediction accuracy is not provided as the perplexity directly reflects it.

The LSTM baseline model has a standard architecture. The embedding size is 256, and the hidden size is 256. The size of LSTM cells is selected empirically on a validation dataset. In practice, using a network size bigger than 256 cannot gain significant improvement over perplexity. In all the following experiments, we bind the input embedding and output embedding according to (Press and Wolf, 2017). The idea is proven to save space and almost loss-less. We treat it as the baseline model in the following experiments.

As shown in Table 1, the LSTM baseline achieved significant improvement on perplexity, comparing to conventional n-gram based models. The top-1 and top-10 path conversion accuracy

---

[3]We implement a standard LSTM cell to avoid any unexpected customization from published version

model	pp	top1 hit %	top10 hit %
uni-gram	833.55	26.95	45.85
bi-gram KN	99.30	51.15	78.10
tri-gram KN	68.11	55.60	79.65
LSTM baseline	**41.39**	**61.20**	**88.30**

Table 1: Performance comparison of baseline LSTM model with conventional n-gram model.

were increased by 5.6% and 8.65% respectively comparing to tri-gram KN. In real products, bi-gram is often used for decoding while tri-gram is only used for re-ranking the best paths. Please note that in this evaluation, we did not apply any pruning for n-gram. In practice, the n-gram model takes over 1GB storage size.

5.4 Evaluation of Run-time Speed

In this section, we compare the inference speed of various methods for accelerating the computation. We measure the execution speed only for the component that computes the language model probabilities. For neural-based methods, the component includes the LSTM and softmax layers. For the n-gram model, the computation of probability is only a lookup in the hash tables. Other components such as lattice construction are not included as they heavily depend on implementation.

We report the decoding time in each step receiving a key input, as the per-step latency is critical for the real-time user experience. The computation cost for decoding the whole sequence is linear to the number of steps. For comparison, we also report the computation time of the softmax alone.

As Table 2 shows, our proposed incremental vocabulary selection (IVS) achieves an 84x speedup for softmax computation comparing to the LSTM baseline. The lattice vocabulary in our experiments contains only a few hundred words, while the full vocabulary has 50k words. IVS only takes 3 ms to handle a new coming key. Such a high processing speed meets the real-time latency requirement even on low-end devices. In contrast, the non-incremental vocabulary selection is less efficient since it recalculates from the beginning of each step. After solving the speed bottleneck of computing the softmax layer, the majority of the computational cost comes from the LSTM cells.

We also evaluate various sampling methods with IVS. We find top sampling help close the ac-

model	total time (ms)	softmax time (ms)	top-1 hit (%)	top-10 hit (%)
tri-gram Kneser-Ney	0.0025	-	55.6	79.6
LSTM baseline w/o batch	526	513	61.2	88.3
LSTM baseline w/ batch	87	84	61.2	88.3
Char LSTM	63	21	53.2	79.8
Char LSTM w/ large beam[4]	152	55	54.4	85.2
D-Softmax	38	35	60.8	86.8
D-Softmax*	37	35	60.9	87.5
IVS	3	1	58.8	86.9
w/ top sampling	**4**	**2**	**60.1**	**88.2**
w/ uniform sampling	4	2	58.9	87.2
w/ self-norm	3	1	60.1	88.2
non-incremental VS	11	2	58.8	86.9

Table 2: Evaluation of different model acceleration approaches in terms of computation time and resultant accuracy. The computation time is reported for each step.

curacy gap between the baseline and softmax approximation. In our experiments, the number of samples used in top sampling and uniform sampling methods is both 400.

If we are able to train the neural language model from scratch, then the self-normalization (Devlin et al., 2014) approach can be applied as a softmax approximation. When applying self-normalization, the model is trained with additional normalization terms, which force the exponential logits to sum up to 1. Therefore, it eliminates the necessity of performing vocabulary sampling. However, if one only has access to a pre-trained language model, then applying self-normalization is not an option.

Differentiated softmax (D-Softmax) (Chen et al., 2016) and its variation (D-softmax*) (Joulin et al., 2017) can also reduce the amount of softmax computation by over a half depending on the segmentation strategy. However, since the vocabulary size is still large, the room for speedup is limited. For character-based LSTM models, we use a hidden size of 1024 and embedding size of 512. Since there is no direct mapping between a single Kana and a single Chinese character, we use the word lattice and evaluate the path probability by character-based LSTM. It reduces the vocabulary size from 50K to 3717 in this experiment. However, the amount of vocabulary is still non-trivial. Furthermore, the integration of character-based models is not as efficient as word-based

models in this task. Consequently, we have to use a large beam size to improve accuracy.

The cost to loop previous steps during fixing the vocabulary is not given here due to the implementation detail. In a real scenario, users do not type the full sentence in one effort. Instead, they type and convert in fragments, where each fragment contains a few words. It is trivial compared to softmax computation.

We confirmed that batching is critical for accelerating matrix operations on CPU. The LSTM computation without batching is almost 7x slower with a beam size 10. Therefore, we batch all the softmax computations when fixing the vocabulary in the second pass to achieve the best speed.

6 Conclusion

IME plays an important role in improving typing efficiency and user experience. It has to work on various devices with extremely low latency. We study the key challenges to apply neural-based input method on real commodity devices. The proposed incremental vocabulary selection approach reduces the cost of computing the softmax layer without losing accuracy. Our proposed method sets a strong baseline in a real-time IME conversion task. More importantly, as the computation has low latency, the model is production-ready to be used on real devices.

---

[4]The large beam size is set to 50 in our experiments.

References

Yoshua Bengio, Réjean Ducharme, Pascal Vincent, and Christian Jauvin. 2003. A neural probabilistic language model. *Journal of machine learning research*, 3(Feb):1137–1155.

Shenyuan Chen, Hai Zhao, and Rui Wang. 2015. Neural network language model for chinese pinyin input method engine. In *Proceedings of the 29th Pacific Asia Conference on Language, Information and Computation*, pages 455–461.

Wenlin Chen, David Grangier, and Michael Auli. 2016. Strategies for training large vocabulary neural language models. In *Proceedings of the 54th Annual Meeting of the Association for Computational Linguistics (Volume 1: Long Papers)*, volume 1, pages 1975–1985.

Kyunghyun Cho, Bart van Merrienboer, Caglar Gulcehre, Dzmitry Bahdanau, Fethi Bougares, Holger Schwenk, and Yoshua Bengio. 2014. Learning phrase representations using rnn encoder–decoder for statistical machine translation. In *Proceedings of the 2014 Conference on Empirical Methods in Natural Language Processing (EMNLP)*, pages 1724–1734.

Anoop Deoras, Tomas Mikolov, and Kenneth Church. 2011. A fast re-scoring strategy to capture long-distance dependencies. In *EMNLP*.

Jacob Devlin, Rabih Zbib, Zhongqiang Huang, Thomas Lamar, Richard M. Schwartz, and John Makhoul. 2014. Fast and robust neural network joint models for statistical machine translation. In *ACL*.

G David Forney. 1973. The viterbi algorithm. *Proceedings of the IEEE*, 61(3):268–278.

Kenneth Heafield. 2011. Kenlm: Faster and smaller language model queries. In *WMT@EMNLP*.

Sepp Hochreiter and Jürgen Schmidhuber. 1997. Long short-term memory. *Neural computation*, 9(8):1735–1780.

Takaaki Hori, Yotaro Kubo, and Atsushi Nakamura. 2014. Real-time one-pass decoding with recurrent neural network language model for speech recognition. *2014 IEEE International Conference on Acoustics, Speech and Signal Processing (ICASSP)*, pages 6364–6368.

Yafang Huang, Zuchao Li, Zhuosheng Zhang, and Hai Zhao. 2018. Moon ime: Neural-based chinese pinyin aided input method with customizable association. In *Proceedings of ACL 2018, System Demonstrations*, pages 140–145. Association for Computational Linguistics.

Zhiheng Huang, Wei Xu, and Kai Yu. 2015. Bidirectional lstm-crf models for sequence tagging. *arXiv preprint arXiv:1508.01991*.

Frankie James. 2000. Modified kneser-ney smoothing of n-gram models. Technical report.

Sebastien Jean, Kyunghyun Cho, Roland Memisevic, and Yoshua Bengio. 2015. On using very large target vocabulary for neural machine translation. In *53rd Annual Meeting of the Association for Computational Linguistics and the 7th International Joint Conference on Natural Language Processing of the Asian Federation of Natural Language Processing, ACL-IJCNLP 2015*, pages 1–10. Association for Computational Linguistics (ACL).

Armand Joulin, Moustapha Cissé, David Grangier, Hervé Jégou, et al. 2017. Efficient softmax approximation for gpus. In *International Conference on Machine Learning*, pages 1302–1310.

Norman P. Jouppi and Cliff Young. 2017. In-datacenter performance analysis of a tensor processing unit. *2017 ACM/IEEE 44th Annual International Symposium on Computer Architecture (ISCA)*, pages 1–12.

Rafal Jozefowicz, Oriol Vinyals, Mike Schuster, Noam Shazeer, and Yonghui Wu. 2016. Exploring the limits of language modeling. *arXiv preprint arXiv:1602.02410*.

Reinhard Kneser and Hermann Ney. 1995. Improved backing-off for m-gram language modeling. In *icassp*, volume 1, page 181e4.

Hai Son Le, Ilya Oparin, Alexandre Allauzen, Jean-Luc Gauvain, and Franois Yvon. 2011. Structured output layer neural network language model. *2011 IEEE International Conference on Acoustics, Speech and Signal Processing (ICASSP)*, pages 5524–5527.

Thang Luong, Hieu Pham, and Christopher D. Manning. 2015. Effective approaches to attention-based neural machine translation. In *EMNLP*.

Kikuo Maekawa, Makoto Yamazaki, Toshinobu Ogiso, Takehiko Maruyama, Hideki Ogura, Wakako Kashino, Hanae Koiso, Masaya Yamaguchi, Makiro Tanaka, and Yasuharu Den. 2014. Balanced corpus of contemporary written japanese. *Language resources and evaluation*, 48(2):345–371.

Haitao Mi, Zhiguo Wang, and Abe Ittycheriah. 2016. Vocabulary manipulation for neural machine translation. In *Proceedings of the 54th Annual Meeting of the Association for Computational Linguistics (Volume 2: Short Papers)*, volume 2, pages 124–129.

Tomáš Mikolov, Martin Karafiát, Lukáš Burget, Jan Černocký, and Sanjeev Khudanpur. 2010. Recurrent neural network based language model. In *Eleventh Annual Conference of the International Speech Communication Association*.

Tomas Mikolov and Geoffrey Zweig. 2012. Context dependent recurrent neural network language model. *2012 IEEE Spoken Language Technology Workshop (SLT)*, pages 234–239.

Andriy Mnih and Geoffrey E Hinton. 2009. A scalable hierarchical distributed language model. In *Advances in neural information processing systems*, pages 1081–1088.

Ofir Press and Lior Wolf. 2017. Using the output embedding to improve language models. In *Proceedings of the 15th Conference of the European Chapter of the Association for Computational Linguistics: Volume 2, Short Papers*, volume 2, pages 157–163.

Holger Schwenk. 2007. Continuous space language models. *Computer Speech & Language*, 21:492–518.

Yongzhe Shi, Weiqiang Zhang, Jia Liu, and Michael T. Johnson. 2013. Rnn language model with word clustering and class-based output layer. *EURASIP J. Audio, Speech and Music Processing*, 2013:22.

Kyuhong Shim, Minjae Lee, Iksoo Choi, Yoonho Boo, and Wonyong Sung. 2017. Svd-softmax: Fast softmax approximation on large vocabulary neural networks. In *Advances in Neural Information Processing Systems*, pages 5463–5473.

Yujing Si, Qingqing Zhang, Ta Li, Jielin Pan, and Yonghong Yan. 2013. Prefix tree based n-best list re-scoring for recurrent neural network language model used in speech recognition system. In *INTERSPEECH*.

Andreas Stolcke. 2002. Srilm-an extensible language modeling toolkit. In *Seventh international conference on spoken language processing*.

Martin Sundermeyer, Ralf Schlüter, and Hermann Ney. 2012. Lstm neural networks for language modeling. In *INTERSPEECH*.

Ashish Vaswani, Noam Shazeer, Niki Parmar, Jakob Uszkoreit, Llion Jones, Aidan N. Gomez, Lukasz Kaiser, and Illia Polosukhin. 2017. Attention is all you need. In *NIPS*.

Minjia Zhang, Xiaodong Liu, Wenhan Wang, Jianfeng Gao, and Yuxiong He. 2018. Navigating with graph representations for fast and scalable decoding of neural language models. *CoRR*, abs/1806.04189.

Locale-agnostic Universal Domain Classification Model in Spoken Language Understanding

Jihwan Lee
Amazon Alexa AI
jihwl@amazon.com

Ruhi Sarikaya
Amazon Alexa AI
rsarikay@amazon.com

Young-Bum Kim
Amazon Alexa AI
youngbum@amazon.com

Abstract

In this paper, we introduce an approach for leveraging available data across multiple locales sharing the same language to 1) improve domain classification model accuracy in Spoken Language Understanding and user experience even if new locales do not have sufficient data and 2) reduce the cost of scaling the domain classifier to a large number of locales. We propose a locale-agnostic universal domain classification model based on selective multi-task learning that learns a joint representation of an utterance over locales with different sets of domains and allows locales to share knowledge selectively depending on the domains. The experimental results demonstrate the effectiveness of our approach on domain classification task in the scenario of multiple locales with imbalanced data and disparate domain sets. The proposed approach outperforms other baselines models especially when classifying locale-specific domains and also low-resourced domains.

1 Introduction

Recent success of intelligent personal digital assistants (IPDA) such as Amazon Alexa, Google Assistant, Apple Siri, Microsoft Cortana (Sarikaya, 2017; Sarikaya et al., 2016) in USA has led to their expansion to multiple locales and languages. Some of those virtual assistant systems have been released in the United States (US), the United Kingdom (GB), Canada (CA), India (IN), and so on. Such expansion typically leads to building a separate domain classification model for each new locale, and it brings two challenging issues: 1) having a separate model per locale becomes a bottleneck for rapid scaling of virtual assistant due to the resource and maintenance costs that grow linearly with the number of locales, and 2) new locales typically comes without much training data and cannot take full advantage of useful data available in other mature locales to achieve the high model accuracy.

In this study, we propose a new approach that reduces the cost of scaling natural language understanding to a large number of locales, given the sufficient amount of data in one of the locales of that language, while achieving high domain classification accuracy over all locales. The approach is based on a multi-task learning framework that aims to share available data to learn a joint representation, and we introduce a way to selectively share knowledge across locales while considering locale-specificity in the joint learning. Multi-task learning has been widely used to tackle the problem of low-resource tasks or leveraging data between correlated targets (Liu et al., 2017; Ruder and Plank, 2018; Augenstein et al., 2018; Peters et al., 2017; Kim et al., 2017b), but none of them consider locale-specificity when sharing knowledge to learn a joint representation.

We evaluate our proposed approach on the real-world utterance data spoken by customers to an intelligent personal digital assistant across different locales. The experimental results empirically demonstrate that the proposed universal model scales to multiple locales, while achieving higher domain classification accuracy compared to competing locale-unified models as well as per-locale separate models. The proposed model named universal model is able to successfully predict domains for locale-specific utterances while sharing common knowledge across locales without sacrificing the accuracy of predicting locale-independent domains.

The paper is organized as follows. In Section 2, we discuss several design considerations that motivate our model design. In Section 3, we define the problem of domain classification with multiple locales that have different domain sets, and then introduce a novel universal domain classifi-

Proceedings of NAACL-HLT 2019, pages 9–15
Minneapolis, Minnesota, June 2 - June 7, 2019. ©2019 Association for Computational Linguistics

cation model with several technical details. We present our experimental observations over different approaches on the Amazon Alexa dataset in Section 4. Finally, we conclude the paper in Section 5.

2   Motivations

2.1   Locale/Domain-Maturity

Let the term *maturity* be defined by how long it has been since a service or model was deployed in a locale and/or how much data have been collected. Every locale has different degrees of maturity. That is, while some locales have spent time long enough to collect sufficient data to train models, others may suffer from the lack of data (see more details of data statistics in Section 4). In addition to that, domains that are commonly available in multiple locales have different levels of maturity for each locale. Those two dimensions of maturity are not always aligned with each other. In other words, there could exist domains that have more data in immature locales than in mature locales, depending on targeted users, regional properties of domains, and so forth.

2.2   Locale-Specificity

When an SLU service is deployed in multiple locales, each of the locales has its own domain set and there can exist overlapping domains between locales. Such domains may share the same schema including intents and slots and thus they should be able to handle the same patterns of utterances regardless of locales. It allows locales to share the knowledge of common domains with each other, which eventually helps immature locales to overcome the lack of data. A special case that needs to be carefully considered is that a domain could be locale-specific. Even though a domain is common across different locales, it may be defined with different intents/slots. For example, the domain `OpenTable`, which is capable of restaurant reservation, is available in both US and GB, but the slot values including restaurant names are totally different between the two locales. That is, the utterance *"Make a reservation for The Fox Club London"* can be handled by `OpenTable` in GB locale, but probably not in US locale, because the restaurant *The Fox Club London* is located in London. If we have different locales share the same utterance patterns between them even for such locale-specific domains, then it will cause confusion on the models. We thus identify locale-specific domains in advance of model training and do not allow input utterances of such domain to be shared by different locales. We need to handle domains in a similar way that are available only in a particular locale.

3   Universal Model

In this section, we describe our proposed model illustrated in Figure 1 in detail. Suppose that given k locales, $\{l_i | i = 1, 2, \ldots, k\}$, each locale l_i is associated with its own domain set $D_i = \{d_{ij} | j = 1, 2, \ldots, |D_i|\}$. There could exist overlapping domains between locales and some of the overlapping domains may share exactly the same intents/slots while others may have different intents/slots across locales. The main task is that given an input utterance from locale l_i the model should be able to correctly classify the utterance into a domain $d_{ij} \in D_i$ that can best handle the utterance. Here we assume that all locales use the same language, English, but have different domain sets. Our deep neural model, as a proposed solution to the task, is comprised of two layers. The first layer includes a BiLSTM shared encoder and k BiLSTM locale-specific encoders. The second layer consists of a set of k locale-specific prediction layers.

3.1   Shared and Locale-specific Encoders

Given an input utterance that forms a word sequence, an encoder makes a vector representation of the entire utterance by using word embeddings for English language in general. We use Bidirectional LSTM (BiLSTM) to encode an input utterance and consider it to be a mapping function $\mathcal{F}$ that consumes a sequence of word embeddings and then produces an embedding vector given by concatenating the outputs of the ends of the word sequences from the forward LSTM and the backward LSTM. While different locales share common domains and utterances, each of them also should be able to learn certain patterns observed from domains available only in the locale. In other words, there exist both global and local patterns in the entire domain set. In order to effectively capture both patterns and avoid confusion between locales, we use a shared encoder $\mathcal{F}_s$ and multiple locale-specific encoders $\mathcal{F}_{l_i}$ for $\forall i = 1, 2, \ldots, k$, each of which corresponds to a particular locale l_i, as similarly adopted in (Kim et al., 2017a, 2016c). While the shared encoder $\mathcal{F}_s$ learns global patterns of utterances commonly observable across

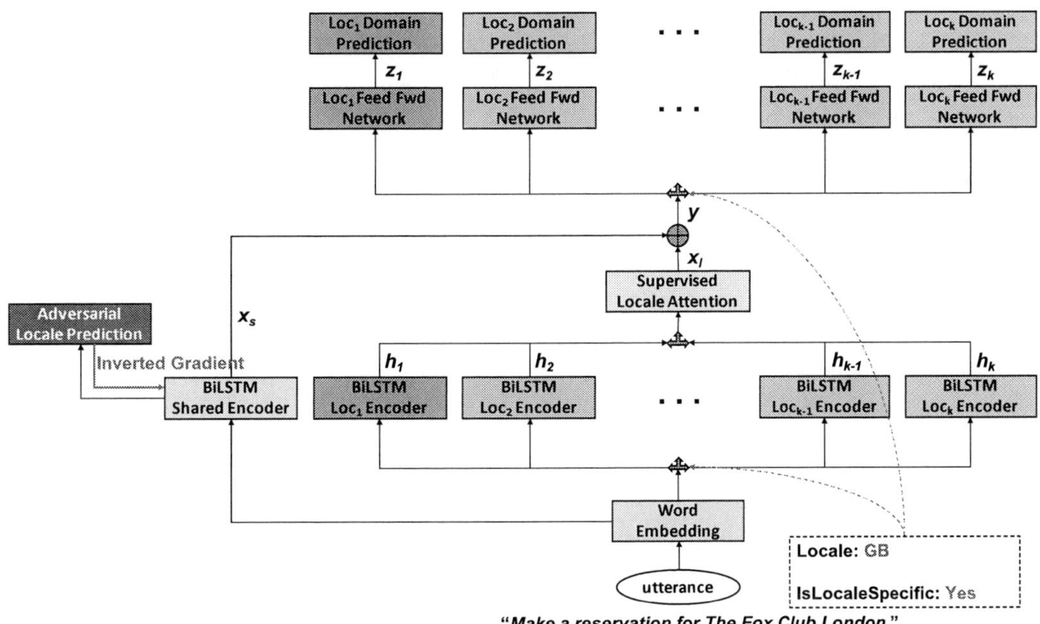

Figure 1: Model architecture of the universal model.

different locales, each of the locale-specific encoders $\mathcal{F}_{l_i}$, which corresponds to one of the locales l_i, learns local patterns of utterances that are observed specifically in the locale l_i.

3.2 Adversarial Locale Prediction Loss

Intuitively, the shared encoder $\mathcal{F}_s$ is expected to be able to better capture common utterance patterns over all locales rather than to learn patterns that are seen in only some particular locales. Thus, $\mathcal{F}_s$ can be further tuned to be locale-invariant by adding a locale prediction layer with negative gradient flow, as similarly proposed in (Kim et al., 2017c; Ganin et al., 2016; Liu et al., 2017). Let $\mathbf{x_s}$ denote an encoded vector for an input utterance produced by the shared encoder $\mathcal{F}_s$. $\mathbf{x_s}$ is then fed into a single-layer neural network to make a prediction for its corresponding locale l_i. Formally,

$$\mathbf{z}_{adv} = softmax(\mathbf{W}_{adv} \cdot \mathbf{x_s} + \mathbf{b}_{adv}) \quad (1)$$

where $\mathbf{W}_{adv}$ and $\mathbf{b}_{adv}$ are a weight matrix and a bias term for the locale prediction layer of the feed-forward network. Since we aim to make the shared encoder $\mathcal{F}_s$ to be locale-invariant, the adversarial locale prediction loss is given by the *positive* log-likelihood:

$$\mathcal{L}_{adv} = \sum_{i=1}^{k} t_i \log[\mathbf{z}_{adv}]^i \quad (2)$$

where t_i is a binary indicator if locale l_i is the correct prediction or not.

3.3 Supervised Locale Attention

In order to allow the locale-specific encoders to share knowledge about common domains across locales, we give a chance to learn an input utterance to any locale-specific encoders $\mathcal{F}_{l_i}$ as long as its associated domain is in D_i, except the case of locale-specific domains (i.e., `OpenTable`). Suppose $S_{d_{ij}} = \{l_w | d_{ij} \in D_w, \forall w = 1, 2, \cdots, k\}$ if d_{ij} is not locale-specific, otherwise $S_{d_{ij}} = \{l_i\}$. That is, depending on which locales a given domain is available in and whether or not it is locale-specific, its utterance needs to be selectively routed to locale-specific encoders $\mathcal{F}_{l_i}$ where $l_i \in S_{d_{ij}}$. However, we do not know a ground-truth domain associated with an input utterance during inference and it means that there is no way to do such selective routing unfortunately. Instead, we can use supervised attention mechanism to approximate the locales in which a domain is available. During training, we have each of the locale-specific encoder outputs attend each other and provide them with information about which locales should be highly attended, as explained in the following.

Let $\mathbf{H} = [\mathbf{h}_{l_1}, \mathbf{h}_{l_2}, \ldots, \mathbf{h}_{l_k}] \in \mathbb{R}^{d_h \times k}$ denote a matrix of encoded vectors generated by $\mathcal{F}_{l_i}$ for $\forall i = 1, 2, \ldots, k$. Then, the attention weights are obtained as follows,

$$\mathbf{a} = logistic(\mathbf{w} \cdot tanh(\mathbf{V} \cdot \mathbf{H})) \qquad (3)$$

where $\mathbf{w} \in \mathbb{R}^{d_a}$ and $\mathbf{V} \in \mathbb{R}^{d_a \times d_h}$ are learnable weight parameters, and d_a is a hyperparameter we can set arbitraily. The resulted vector $\mathbf{a}$ contains attention weights in the range between 0 and 1 over the encoded vectors $\mathbf{h}_{l_1}, \ldots, \mathbf{h}_{l_k}$. Then a locale-aware encoded vector $\mathbf{x}_l$ can be achieved by taking a weighted linear combination of $\mathbf{h}_{l_1}, \ldots, \mathbf{h}_{l_k}$:

$$\mathbf{x}_l = \mathbf{a} \cdot \mathbf{H}^{\top} \qquad (4)$$

The final vector representation $\mathbf{y} \in \mathbb{R}^{2 \cdot d_h}$ for the input utterance is the concatenation of two encoded vectors $\mathbf{x}_s$ and $\mathbf{x}_l$ that are produced from $\mathcal{F}_s$ and $\mathcal{F}_l$, respectively. Note we have to make sure that the proper encoders that correspond to $S_{d_{ij}}$ always get high attention weights. Thus, instead of just letting $\mathbf{V}$ and $\mathbf{w}$ be optimized during training the model, we can optimize them in a supervised way. That is, in training time, the model is aware of locales where a ground-truth domain is available. In other words, we can reward or penalize the attention weights depending on whether or not their corresponding locales have the domain of an input utterance. Therefore, the loss function for the attention weights is defined as,

$$\mathcal{L}_{loc} = -\left(\sum_{l \in S_{d_{ij}}} \log(a_l) + \sum_{l' \notin S_{d_{ij}}} \log(1 - a_{l'}) \right) \qquad (5)$$

3.4 Domain Classification

Once we obtain an encoded vector $\mathbf{y}$ that represents an input utterance, we feed it into prediction layers, consisting of feed forward networks, to make predictions. Since the availability of domains depends on locales, the prediction layers use the locale information associated with the utterance to route the encoded vector to only a subset of prediction layers in which the domain of the utterance is available. Then, the output vector produced by the prediction layer specifically for the locale l_i is

$$\mathbf{z}_i = \mathbf{W}_i^2 \cdot \sigma(\mathbf{W}_i^1 \cdot \mathbf{y} + \mathbf{b}_i^1) + \mathbf{b}_i^2 \qquad (6)$$

where $\mathbf{W}_i$ and $\mathbf{b}_i$ are the weight and bias parameters used by the l_i specific prediction layer, and σ is an activation function for non-linearity. Since our model is structured with a multi-task learning framework to learn a joint representation across locales, we calculate $\mathbf{z}_i$ for all $l_i \in S_{d_{ij}}$ and then the predictions are made independently. Then the prediction loss is

$$\mathcal{L}_{pos} = -\log p(d_{ij}|z_i) \qquad (7)$$

$$\mathcal{L}_{neg} = -\sum_{\substack{\hat{d}_{ij} \in D_i \\ \hat{d}_{ij} \neq d_{ij}}} \log p(\hat{d}_{ij}|z_i) \qquad (8)$$

$$\mathcal{L}_{pred} = \frac{1}{|S_{d_{ij}}|} \sum_{l_i \in S_{d_{ij}}} (\mathcal{L}_{pos} + \mathcal{L}_{neg}) \qquad (9)$$

Note that the prediction loss must be normalized by the number of locales in $S_{d_{ij}}$ because the size of the set changes depending on how many locales has the domain associated with an input utterance and thus the number of the final prediction layer Then, the final objective function looks as follows,

$$\underset{\theta_{\mathcal{F}_s}, \theta_{\mathcal{F}_l}, \mathbf{V}, \mathbf{w}, \mathbf{W}, \mathbf{b}}{\arg \min} \quad \mathcal{L}_{adv} + \mathcal{L}_{loc} + \mathcal{L}_{pred} \qquad (10)$$

where $\theta_{\mathcal{F}_s}$ and $\theta_{\mathcal{F}_l}$ are the LSTM weight parameters in the shared encoder and the locale-specific encoders, respectively.

4 Experiments

4.1 Dataset

We use a subset of the Amazon Alexa dataset that consists of utterances spoken to Alexa by real customers over four different English locales including US (United States), GB (United Kingdom), CA (Canda), IN (India). Each of the utterances is labeled with a ground-truth domain. The main objective of this experiment should be to show the effectiveness of various approaches on domain classification task under the situation where there exist multiple locales that have imbalanced data and disparate domain sets. Thus, we consider the following two aspects: 1) how differently various domain classification approaches behave depending

Locale	Train	Validation	Test	No. domains
US	173,258	24,653	122,931	177
GB	85,539	10,378	53,226	240
CA	7,113	887	4,487	51
IN	4,821	637	2,990	41

Table 1: Data statistics

Locale	Overall	Locale-specific	Locale-independent	Single-locale	Small
US	177	15	162	0	35
GB	240	16	224	82	100
CA	51	3	48	6	33
IN	41	4	37	12	20

Table 2: Test set breakdown

	US	GB	CA	IN
US	177	155	44	26
GB		240	27	23
CA			51	10
IN				41

Table 3: Domain overlaps between locales

on domains and 2) how well they can overcome the challenging issues discussed in Section 1. To this end, we categorize all domains in the dataset into four different groups.

- **Locale-specific** A set of domains which are defined with different intents/slots across locales.

- **Locale-independent** A set of domains which have exactly the same intent/slot lists across locales.

- **Single-locale** A set of domains which are available in only a single locale.

- **Small** A set of domains that lack data in a locale but have sufficient data in other locales.

Table 1 shows its brief statistics per locale, Table 2 presents the number of domains for each of four different domain categories, and Table 3 shows how many domains are overlapping between locales.

4.2 Competing Models

We compare the performances of the following five models.

- **single** A standard BiLSTM based encoder trained with only data in a particular locale.

- **union** An extension of 'single' trained with US data additionally.

- **constrained** A BiLSTM encoder trained with all locales data. It uses the locale information associated with the utterance to route the encoded utterance to only a subset of domains available in the constrained output space for the locale to make prediction (Kim et al., 2016b,a).

- **universal** This is our main contribution model described throughout the paper.

- **universal + adv** An extension of 'universal' incorporating the adversarial locale prediction loss as discussed in Section 3.2.

4.3 Domain Classification

To demonstrate the effectiveness of our model architecture especially on domains with insufficient data and/or locale-dependency, we report the classification performances of all competing models on several subsets of the dataset (four different groups presented in Section 4.1) as well as the entire data. We use classification accuracy as our main evaluation metric. The experimental results in Table 4 clearly show two major points: 1) our proposed universal model outperforms all other baselines over all locales and all domain sets, and 2) the baseline models achieve very poor accuracy especially when leveraging available data in other locales is of critical importance or when there needs to selectively share knowledge depending on the locale-specificity of a domain. If a model that shares knowledge across locales does not handle locale-specific domains carefully, its performance would deteriorate due to confusion on locale-specific patterns. The 'constrained' model uses a shared encoder and allows locales to shares its prediction layer, but it does not determine whether or not to share knowledge for each domain. As a result, its classification accuracy is only 44% for locale-specific domains and 25% for single-locale domains in the IN dataset with lack of data. Also, 'single' and 'union' models do not have any chance to learn a joint representation while sharing knowledge and thus they totally fail to make predictions correctly for locale-specific, single-locale, and small domains. In contrast, our universal model is very robust to domains with insufficient data and domains with locale-specific patterns over all locales. It proves that our approach is very effective for capturing both global and local patterns by selectively sharing domain knowledge across locales. Also, the adversarial locale prediction is only helpful for

Locale	Model	Overall	Locale-specific	Locale-independent	Single-locale	Small
US	single	70.21	54.39	69.90	–	8.18
	union	70.21	54.39	69.90	–	8.18
	constrained	74.25	76.08	74.02	–	38.30
	universal	**82.64**	88.20	**81.92**	–	**61.79**
	universal + adv	11.13	**97.51**	0.00	–	5.38
GB	single	56.02	62.81	55.09	37.81	0.00
	union	66.61	78.74	64.96	48.19	36.54
	constrained	67.82	76.83	66.60	50.51	38.04
	universal	80.06	**88.37**	78.93	**83.60**	57.96
	universal + adv	**80.52**	85.88	**79.79**	82.22	**59.52**
CA	single	43.43	3.57	43.68	0.00	0.24
	union	61.04	10.71	61.35	0.65	30.78
	constrained	76.46	67.85	76.51	39.17	55.66
	universal	**94.00**	**75.00**	**94.12**	97.74	**77.09**
	universal + adv	35.21	71.42	34.98	**98.87**	36.69
IN	single	56.25	0.00	60.46	0.00	0.00
	union	45.93	0.00	49.38	0.00	17.96
	constrained	62.64	44.71	63.98	25.94	58.64
	universal	**88.09**	**87.01**	**88.17**	80.00	**68.47**
	universal + adv	22.30	**87.01**	17.46	**82.97**	10.50

Table 4: Domain classification accuracy over different domain categories and different locales.

locale-specific and single-locale domains. That is probably because the effect of adversarial loss paradoxically makes the model rely on only the locale-specific encoders which are well-optimized for locale-specific/single-locale domains. There needs deep analysis about why it does not affect the GB locale, and we leave it as future works.

4.4 Implementation Details

All the models were optimized using a minibatch size of 64 and trained for 20 epochs by the Adam optimizer (Kingma and Ba, 2014) with initial parameter values $\eta = 1 \times 10^{-3}, \beta_1 = 0.9, \beta_2 = 0.999$. We picked the weight parameter values that achieved the best classification accuracy on the validation set to report the test set accuracy presented in Table 4. We used pre-trained word embeddings with 100 dimensionality, generated by GloVe (Pennington et al., 2014). The dimensionality of each hidden output of LSTMs is 100 for both the shared encoder $\mathcal{F}_s$ and the locale-specific encoder $\mathcal{F}_{l_i}$, and the hidden outputs of both forward LSTM and backward LSTM are concatenated, thereby the output of each BLSTM for each time step is 200. The inputs and the outputs of the BLSTMs are regularized with dropout rate 0.5 (Pham et al., 2014).

5 Conclusion

In this paper, we propose a multi-task learning based locale-agnostic universal model for domain classification task that dynamically chooses subsets of locale-specific components depending on input data. It leverages available data across locales sharing the same language to reduce the cost of scaling the domain classification model to a larger number of locales and maximize model performance even for new locales without sufficient data. The experimental results show that the universal model effectively exploits both global and local patterns and allows locales selectively share knowledge with each other. Especially, its classification performance is notable on immature locales/domains with insufficient data and locale-specific domains.

For future work, we consider adopting the proposed model architecture to multi-lingual scenario as well. The proposed model architecture is limited to supporting multiple locales using the same language only (e.g.., English in our experiments). However, voice-driven virtual assistant systems are becoming more and more popular around the world while expanding to non-English locales such as France, Italy, Spain and so on, and there could be a lot of domains built with multiple supported languages. It will definitely make the rapid scaling of a domain classification model to a large number of locales much more challenging in the future. We plan to address several issues, including but not limited to: 1) how can we capture and share knowledge of common patterns of utterances belonging to the same domain but written in different languages across different locales? 2) how can we prevent a locale from interfering with other locales using different language for learning linguistic context of utterances?

References

Isabelle Augenstein, Sebastian Ruder, and Anders Søgaard. 2018. Multi-task learning of pairwise sequence classification tasks over disparate label spaces. In *In Proceedings of the Conference of the North American Chapter of the Association for Computational Linguistics: Human Language Technologies (NAACL-HLT)*.

Yaroslav Ganin, Evgeniya Ustinova, Hana Ajakan, Pascal Germain, Hugo Larochelle, François Laviolette, Mario Marchand, and Victor Lempitsky. 2016. Domain-adversarial training of neural networks. *The Journal of Machine Learning Research*, 17(1):2096–2030.

Joo-Kyung Kim, Young-Bum Kim, Ruhi Sarikaya, and Eric Fosler-Lussier. 2017a. Cross-lingual transfer learning for pos tagging without cross-lingual resources. In *Proceedings of the 2017 Conference on Empirical Methods in Natural Language Processing*, pages 2832–2838.

Young-Bum Kim, Sungjin Lee, and Karl Stratos. 2017b. Onenet: Joint domain, intent, slot prediction for spoken language understanding. In *Automatic Speech Recognition and Understanding Workshop (ASRU), 2017 IEEE*, pages 547–553. IEEE.

Young-Bum Kim, Alexandre Rochette, and Ruhi Sarikaya. 2016a. Natural language model reusability for scaling to different domains. In *Proceedings of the 2016 Conference on Empirical Methods in Natural Language Processing*, pages 2071–2076.

Young-Bum Kim, Karl Stratos, and Dongchan Kim. 2017c. Adversarial adaptation of synthetic or stale data. In *Proceedings of the 55th Annual Meeting of the Association for Computational Linguistics (Volume 1: Long Papers)*, volume 1, pages 1297–1307.

Young-Bum Kim, Karl Stratos, and Ruhi Sarikaya. 2016b. Domainless adaptation by constrained decoding on a schema lattice. In *Proceedings of COLING 2016, the 26th International Conference on Computational Linguistics: Technical Papers*, pages 2051–2060.

Young-Bum Kim, Karl Stratos, and Ruhi Sarikaya. 2016c. Frustratingly easy neural domain adaptation. In *Proceedings of COLING 2016, the 26th International Conference on Computational Linguistics: Technical Papers*, pages 387–396.

Diederik P Kingma and Jimmy Ba. 2014. Adam: A method for stochastic optimization. *arXiv preprint arXiv:1412.6980*.

Pengfei Liu, Xipeng Qiu, and Xuanjing Huang. 2017. Adversarial multi-task learning for text classification. In *Proceedings of the 55th Annual Meeting of the Association for Computational Linguistics*.

Jeffrey Pennington, Richard Socher, and Christopher Manning. 2014. Glove: Global vectors for word representation. In *Proceedings of the 2014 conference on empirical methods in natural language processing (EMNLP)*, pages 1532–1543.

Matthew E Peters, Waleed Ammar, Chandra Bhagavatula, and Russell Power. 2017. Semi-supervised sequence tagging with bidirectional language models. *arXiv preprint arXiv:1705.00108*.

Vu Pham, Théodore Bluche, Christopher Kermorvant, and Jérôme Louradour. 2014. Dropout improves recurrent neural networks for handwriting recognition. In *Frontiers in Handwriting Recognition (ICFHR), 2014 14th International Conference on*, pages 285–290. IEEE.

Sebastian Ruder and Barbara Plank. 2018. Strong baselines for neural semi-supervised learning under domain shift. In *Proceedings of the 56th Annual Meeting of the Association for Computational Linguistics*.

Ruhi Sarikaya. 2017. The technology behind personal digital assistants: an overview of the system architecture and key components. *IEEE Signal Processing Magazine*, 34(1):67–81.

Ruhi Sarikaya, Paul A Crook, Alex Marin, Minwoo Jeong, Jean-Philippe Robichaud, Asli Celikyilmaz, Young-Bum Kim, Alexandre Rochette, Omar Zia Khan, Xiaohu Liu, et al. 2016. An overview of end-to-end language understanding and dialog management for personal digital assistants. In *2016 IEEE Spoken Language Technology Workshop (SLT)*, pages 391–397. IEEE.

Practical Semantic Parsing for Spoken Language Understanding

Marco Damonte[*]
University of Edinburgh
m.damonte@sms.ed.ac.uk

Rahul Goel   Tagyoung Chung
Amazon Alexa AI
{goerahul,tagyoung}@amazon.com

Abstract

Executable semantic parsing is the task of converting natural language utterances into logical forms that can be directly used as queries to get a response. We build a transfer learning framework for executable semantic parsing. We show that the framework is effective for Question Answering (Q&A) as well as for Spoken Language Understanding (SLU). We further investigate the case where a parser on a new domain can be learned by exploiting data on other domains, either via multitask learning between the target domain and an auxiliary domain or via pre-training on the auxiliary domain and fine-tuning on the target domain. With either flavor of transfer learning, we are able to improve performance on most domains; we experiment with public data sets such as Overnight and NLmaps as well as with commercial SLU data. The experiments carried out on data sets that are different in nature show how executable semantic parsing can unify different areas of NLP such as Q&A and SLU.

1 Introduction

Due to recent advances in speech recognition and language understanding, conversational interfaces such as Alexa, Cortana, and Siri are becoming more common. They currently have two large uses cases. First, a user can use them to complete a specific task, such as playing music. Second, a user can use them to ask questions where the questions are answered by querying knowledge graph or database back-end. Typically, under a common interface, there exist two disparate systems that can handle each use cases. The system underlying the first use case is known as a spoken language understanding (SLU) system. Typical commercial SLU systems rely on predicting a coarse user intent and then tagging each word in the utterance to

the intent's slots. This architecture is popular due to its simplicity and robustness. On the other hand, Q&A, which need systems to produce more complex structures such as trees and graphs, requires a more comprehensive understanding of human language.

One possible system that can handle such a task is an executable semantic parser (Liang, 2013; Kate et al., 2005). Given a user utterance, an executable semantic parser can generate tree or graph structures that represent logical forms that can be used to query a knowledge base or database. In this work, we propose executable semantic parsing as a common framework for both uses cases by framing SLU as executable semantic parsing that unifies the two use cases. For Q&A, the input utterances are parsed into logical forms that represent the machine-readable representation of the question, while in SLU, they represent the machine-readable representation of the user intent and slots. One added advantage of using parsing for SLU is the ability to handle more complex linguistic phenomena such as coordinated intents that traditional SLU systems struggle to handle (Agarwal et al., 2018). Our parsing model is an extension of the neural transition-based parser of Cheng et al. (2017).

A major issue with semantic parsing is the availability of the annotated logical forms to train the parsers, which are expensive to obtain. A solution is to rely more on distant supervisions such as by using question–answer pairs (Clarke et al., 2010; Liang et al., 2013). Alternatively, it is possible to exploit annotated logical forms from a different domain or related data set. In this paper, we focus on the scenario where data sets for several domains exist but only very little data for a new one is available and apply transfer learning techniques to it. A common way to implement transfer learning is by first pre-training the model on a

---

Proceedings of NAACL-HLT 2019, pages 16–23
Minneapolis, Minnesota, June 2 - June 7, 2019. ©2019 Association for Computational Linguistics

domain on which a large data set is available and subsequently fine-tuning the model on the target domain (Thrun, 1996; Zoph et al., 2016). We also consider a multi-task learning (MTL) approach. MTL refers to machine learning models that improve generalization by training on more than one task. MTL has been used for a number of NLP problems such as tagging (Collobert and Weston, 2008), syntactic parsing (Luong et al., 2015), machine translation (Dong et al., 2015; Luong et al., 2015) and semantic parsing (Fan et al., 2017). See Caruana (1997) and Ruder (2017) for an overview of MTL.

A good Q&A data set for our domain adaptation scenario is the Overnight data set (Wang et al., 2015b), which contains sentences annotated with Lambda Dependency-Based Compositional Semantics (Lambda DCS; Liang 2013) for eight different domains. However, it includes only a few hundred sentences for each domain, and its vocabularies are relatively small. We also experiment with a larger semantic parsing data set (NLmaps; Lawrence and Riezler 2016). For SLU, we work with data from a commercial conversational assistant that has a much larger vocabulary size. One common issue in parsing is how to deal with rare or unknown words, which is usually addressed by either delexicalization or by implementing a copy mechanism (Gulcehre et al., 2016). We show clear differences in the outcome of these and other techniques when applied to data sets of varying sizes. Our contributions are as follows:

- We propose a common semantic parsing framework for Q&A and SLU and demonstrate its broad applicability and effectiveness.

- We report parsing baselines for Overnight for which exact match parsing scores have not been yet published.

- We show that SLU greatly benefits from a copy mechanism, which is also beneficial for NLmaps but not Overnight.

- We investigate the use of transfer learning and show that it can facilitate parsing on low-resource domains.

2 Transition-based Parser

Transition-based parsers are widely used for dependency parsing (Nivre, 2008; Dyer et al., 2015)

and they have been also applied to semantic parsing tasks (Wang et al., 2015a; Cheng et al., 2017).

In syntactic parsing, a transition system is usually defined as a quadruple: $T = \{S, A, I, E\}$, where S is a set of states, A is a set of actions, I is the initial state, and E is a set of end states. A state is composed of a buffer, a stack, and a set of arcs: $S = (\beta, \sigma, A)$. In the initial state, the buffer contains all the words in the input sentence while the stack and the set of subtrees are empty: $S_0 = (w_0|\ldots|w_N, \emptyset, \emptyset)$. Terminal states have empty stack and buffer: $S_T = (\emptyset, \emptyset, A)$.

During parsing, the stack stores words that have been removed from the buffer but have not been fully processed yet. Actions can be performed to advance the transition system's state: they can either consume words in the buffer and move them to the stack (SHIFT) or combine words in the stack to create new arcs (LEFT-ARC and RIGHT-ARC, depending on the direction of the arc)[1]. Words in the buffer are processed left-to-right until an end state is reached, at which point the set of arcs will contain the full output tree.

The parser needs to be able to predict the next action based on its current state. Traditionally, supervised techniques are used to learn such classifiers, using a parallel corpus of sentences and their output trees. Trees can be converted to states and actions using an oracle system. For a detailed explanation of transition-based parsing, see Nivre (2003) and Nivre (2008).

2.1 Neural Transition-based Parser with Stack-LSTMs

In this paper, we consider the neural executable semantic parser of Cheng et al. (2017), which follows the transition-based parsing paradigm. Its transition system differs from traditional systems as the words are not consumed from the buffer because in executable semantic parsing, there are no strict alignments between words in the input and nodes in the tree. The neural architecture encodes the buffer using a Bi-LSTM (Graves, 2012) and the stack as a Stack-LSTM (Dyer et al., 2015), a recurrent network that allows for push and pop operations. Additionally, the previous actions are also represented with an LSTM. The output of these networks is fed into feed-forward layers and softmax layers are used to predict the next action

---

[1]There are multiple different transition systems. The example we describe here is that of *arc-standard* system (Nivre, 2004) for projective dependency parsing.

given the current state. The possible actions are REDUCE, which pops an item from the stack, TER, which creates a terminal node (i.e., a leaf in the tree), and NT, which creates a non-terminal node. When the next action is either TER or NT, additional softmax layers predict the output token to be generated. Since the buffer does not change while parsing, an attention mechanism is used to focus on specific words given the current state of the parser.

We extend the model of Cheng et al. (2017) by adding character-level embeddings and a copy mechanism. When using only word embeddings, out-of-vocabulary words are usually mapped to one embedding vector and do not exploit morphological features. Our model encodes words by feeding each character embedding onto an LSTM and concatenate its output to the word embedding:

$$x = \{e_w; h_c^M\}, \tag{1}$$

where e_w is the word embedding of the input word w and h_c^M is the last hidden state of the character-level LSTM over the characters of the input word $w = c_0, \ldots, c_M$.

Rare words are usually handled by either delexicalizing the output or by using a copy mechanism. Delexicalization involves substituting named entities with a specific token in an effort to reduce the number of rare and unknown words. Copy relies on the fact that when rare or unknown words must be generated, they usually appear in the same form in the input sentence and they can be therefore copied from the input itself. Our copy implementation follows the strategy of Fan et al. (2017), where the output of the generation layer is concatenated to the scores of an attention mechanism (Bahdanau et al., 2015), which express the relevance of each input word with respect to the current state of the parser. In the experiments that follow, we compare delexicalization with copy mechanism on different setups. A depiction of the full model is shown in Figure 1.

3 Transfer learning

We consider the scenario where large training corpora are available for some domains and we want to bootstrap a parser for a new domain where little training data is available. We investigate the use of two transfer learning approaches: pre-training and multi-task learning.

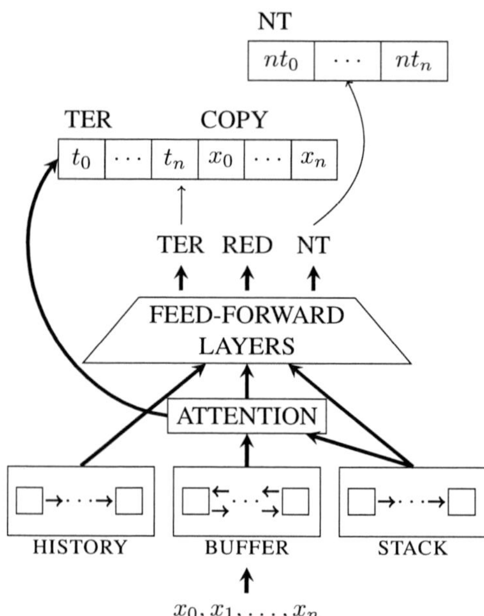

Figure 1: The full neural transition-based parsing model. Representations of stack, buffer, and previous actions are used to predict the next action. When the TER or NT actions are chosen, further layers are used to predict (or copy) the token.

For MTL, the different tasks share most of the architecture and only the output layers, which are responsible for predicting the output tokens, are separate for each task. When multi-tasking across domains of the same data set, we expect that most layers of the neural parser, such as the ones responsible for learning the word embeddings and the stack and buffer representation, will learn similar features and can, therefore, be shared. We implement two different MTL setups: a) when separate heads are used for both the TER classifier and the NT classifier, which is expected to be effective when transferring across tasks that do not share output vocabulary; and b) when a separate head is used only for the TER classifier, more appropriate when the non-terminals space is mostly shared.

4 Data

In order to investigate the flexibility of the executable semantic parsing framework, we evaluate models on Q&A data sets as well as on commercial SLU data sets. For Q&A, we consider Overnight (Wang et al., 2015b) and NLmaps (Lawrence and Riezler, 2016).

Overnight It contains sentences annotated with Lambda DCS (Liang, 2013). The sentences are divided into eight domains: *calendar, blocks, housing, restaurants, publications, recipes, socialnetwork,* and *basketball.* As shown in Table 1, the number of sentences and the terminal vocabularies are small, which makes the learning more challenging, preventing us from using data-hungry approaches such as sequence-to-sequence models. The current state-of-the-art results, to the best of our knowledge, are reported by Su and Yan (2017). Previous work on this data set use denotation accuracy as a metric. In this paper, we use logical form exact match accuracy across all data sets.

NLmaps It contains more than two thousand questions about geographical facts, retrieved from OpenStreetMap (Haklay and Weber, 2008). Unfortunately, this data set is not divided into subdomains. While NLmaps has comparable sizes with some of the Overnight domains, its vocabularies are much larger: containing 160 terminals, 24 non-terminals and 280 word types (Table 1). The current state-of-the-art results on this data set are reported by Duong et al. (2017).

SLU We select five domains from our SLU data set: *search, recipes, cinema, bookings,* and *closet.* In order to investigate the use case of a new low-resource domain exploiting a higher-resource domain, we selected a mix of high-resource and low-resource domains. Details are shown in Table 1. We extracted shallow trees from data originally collected for intent/slot tagging: intents become the root of the tree, slot types are attached to the roots as their children and slot values are in turn attached to their slot types as their children. An example is shown in Figure 2. A similar approach to transform intent/slot data into tree structures has been recently employed by Gupta et al. (2018b).

5 Experiments

We first run experiments on single-task semantic parsing to observe the differences among the three different data sources discussed in Section 4. Specifically, we explore the impact of an attention mechanism on the performance as well as the comparison between delexicalization and a copy mechanism for dealing with data sparsity. The metric used to evaluate parsers is the exact match accuracy, defined as the ratio of sentences correctly parsed.

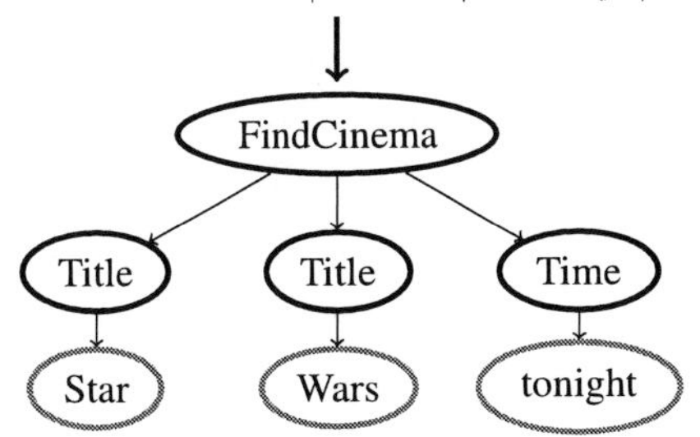

Figure 2: Conversion from intent/slot tags to tree for the sentence *Which cinemas screen Star Wars tonight?*

DOMAIN	#	TER	NT	Words
Q&A				
calendar	535	31	13	114
blocks	1276	30	13	99
housing	601	34	13	109
restaurants	1060	40	13	144
publications	512	24	12	80
recipes	691	30	13	121
social	2828	56	16	225
basketball	1248	40	15	148
NLmaps	1200	160	24	280
SLU				
search	23706	1621	51	1780
recipes	18721	530	40	643
cinema	13180	806	36	923
bookings	1280	10	19	42
closet	943	63	13	107

Table 1: Details of training data. # is the number of sentences, *TER* is the terminal vocabulary size, *NT* is the non-terminal vocabulary size and *Words* is the input vocabulary size.

rectly parsed.

5.1 Attention

Because the buffer is not consumed as in traditional transition-based parsers, Cheng et al. (2017) use an additive attention mechanism (Bahdanau et al., 2015) to focus on the more relevant words in the buffer for the current state of the stack.

In order to find the impact of attention on the different data sets, we run ablation experiments, as shown in Table 2 (left side). We found that attention between stack and buffer is not always beneficial: it appears to be helpful for larger data sets while harmful for smaller data sets. Attention is, however, useful for NLmaps, regardless of the

DOMAIN	BL	−Att	+Delex	+Copy
calendar	38.1	**43.5**	4.20	32.1
blocks	22.6	**25.1**	24.3	22.8
housing	19.0	**29.6**	6.90	21.2
restaurants	32.2	**37.3**	21.7	33.7
publications	27.3	**32.9**	11.8	26.1
recipes	47.7	**58.3**	24.1	48.1
social	44.9	**51.2**	47.7	50.9
basketball	65.2	**69.6**	38.6	66.5
NLmaps	44.9	43.5	46.4	**60.7**
search	35.6	34.9	29.2	**52.7**
recipes	40.9	37.9	37.7	**47.6**
cinema	31.5	35.5	35.7	**56.9**
bookings	72.3	77.7	72.3	**77.7**
closet	17.6	35.9	29.2	**44.1**

Table 2: Left side: Ablation experiments on attention mechanism. Right side: Comparison between delexicalization and copy mechanism. *BL* is the model of Section 2.1, *−Att* refers to the same model without attention, *+Delex* is the system with delexicalization and in *+Copy* we use a copy mechanism instead. The scores indicate the percentage of correct parses.

data size. Even though NLmaps data is similarly sized to some of the Overnight domains, its terminal space is considerably larger, perhaps making attention more important even with a smaller data set. On the other hand, the high-resource SLU's *cinema* domain is not able to benefit from the attention mechanism. We note that the performance of this model on NLmaps falls behind the state of the art (Duong et al., 2017). The hyper-parameters of our model were however not tuned on this data set.

5.2 Handling Sparsity

A popular way to deal with the data sparsity problem is to delexicalize the data, that is replacing rare and unknown words with coarse categories. In our experiment, we use a named entity recognition system[2] to replace names with their named entity types. Alternatively, it is possible to use a copy mechanism to enable the decoder to copy rare words from the input rather than generating them from its limited vocabulary.

We compare the two solutions across all data sets on the right side of Table 2. Regardless of the data set, the copy mechanism generally outperforms delexicalization. We also note that delexi-

calization has unexpected catastrophic effects on exact match accuracy for *calendar* and *housing*. For Overnight, however, the system with copy mechanism is outperformed by the system without attention. This is unsurprising as the copy mechanism is based on attention, which is not effective on Overnight (Section 5.1). The inefficacy of copy mechanisms on the Overnight data set was also discussed in Jia and Liang (2016), where answer accuracy, rather than parsing accuracy, was used as a metric. As such, the results are not directly comparable.

For NLmaps and all SLU domains, using a copy mechanism results in an average accuracy improvement of 16% over the baseline. It is worth noting that the copy mechanism is unsurprisingly effective for SLU data due to the nature of the data set: the SLU trees were obtained from data collected for slot tagging, and as such, each leaf in the tree has to be copied from the input sentence.

Even though Overnight often yields different conclusions, most likely due to its small vocabulary size, the similar behaviors observed for NLmaps and SLU is reassuring, confirming that it is possible to unify Q&A and SLU under the same umbrella framework of executable semantic parsing.

In order to compare the NLmaps results with Lawrence and Riezler (2016), we also compute F1 scores for the data set. Our baseline outperforms previous results, achieving a score of 0.846. Our best F1 results are also obtained when adding the copy mechanism, achieving a score of 0.874.

5.3 Transfer Learning

The first set of experiments involve transfer learning across Overnight domains. For this data set, the non-terminal vocabulary is mostly shared across domains. As such, we use the architecture where only the TER output classifier is not shared. Selecting the best auxiliary domain by maximizing the overlap with the main domain was not successful, and we instead performed an exhaustive search over the domain pairs on the development set. In the interest of space, for each main domain, we report results for the best auxiliary domain (Table 3). We note that MTL and pre-training provide similar results and provide an average improvement of 4%. As expected, we observe more substantial improvements for smaller domains.

We performed the same set of experiments on

---

[2]https://spacy.io

DOMAIN	BL	MTL	PRETR.
calendar	43.5	**48.8**	48.2
blocks	25.1	24.1	**25.1**
housing	29.6	38.1	**38.1**
restaurants	37.3	**39.2**	36.7
publications	32.9	37.3	**40.4**
recipes	58.3	**63.4**	63.0
social	51.2	52.4	**54.5**
basketball	69.6	69.1	**71.1**

Table 3: Transfer learning results for the Overnight domains. *BL − Att* is the model without transfer learning. *PRETR.* stands for pre-training. Again, we report exact match accuracy.

DOMAIN	BL + Copy	MTL	PRETR.
search	52.7	52.3	**53.1**
cinema	56.9	**57.7**	56.4
bookings	77.7	**81.2**	78.0
closet	44.1	**52.5**	50.8

Table 4: Transfer learning results for SLU domains. *BL + Copy* is the model without transfer learning. *PRETR.* stands for pre-training. Again, the numbers are exact match accuracy.

the SLU domains, as shown in Table 4. In this case, the non-terminal vocabulary can vary significantly across domains. We therefore choose to use the MTL architecture where both TER and NT output classifiers are not shared. Also for SLU, there is no clear winner between pre-training and MTL. Nevertheless, they always outperform the baseline, demonstrating the importance of transfer learning, especially for smaller domains.

While the focus of this transfer learning framework is in exploiting high-resource domains annotated in the same way as a new low-resource domain, we also report a preliminary experiment on transfer learning across tasks. We selected the *recipes* domain, which exists in both Overnight and SLU. While the SLU data set is significantly different from Overnight, deriving from a corpus annotated with intent/slot labels, as discussed in Section 4, we found promising results using pre-training, increasing the accuracy from 58.3 to 61.1. A full investigation of transfer learning across domains belonging to heterogeneous data sets is left for future work.

The experiments on transfer learning demonstrate how parsing accuracy on low-resource domains can be improved by exploiting other domains or data sets. Except for the Overnight's *blocks* domain, which is one of the largest in Overnight, all domains in Overnight and SLU were shown to provide better results when either MTL or pre-training was used, with the most significant improvements observed for low-resource domains.

6 Related work

A large collection of logical forms of different nature exist in the semantic parsing literature: semantic role schemes (Palmer et al., 2005; Meyers et al., 2004; Baker et al., 1998), syntax/semantics interfaces (Steedman, 1996), executable logical forms (Liang, 2013; Kate et al., 2005), and general purpose meaning representations (Banarescu et al., 2013; Abend and Rappoport, 2013). We adopt executable logical forms in this paper. The Overnight data set uses Lambda DCS, the NLmaps data set extracts meaning representations from OpenStreetMap, and the SLU data set contains logical forms reminiscent of Lambda DCS that can be used to perform actions and query databases. State-of-the-art results are reported in Su and Yan (2017) for Overnight and Duong et al. (2017) for NLmaps.[3]

Our semantic parsing model is an extension of the executable semantic parser of Cheng et al. (2017), which is inspired by Recurrent Neural Network Grammars (Dyer et al., 2016). We extend the model with ideas inspired by Gulcehre et al. (2016) and Luong and Manning (2016).

We build our multi-task learning architecture upon the rich literature on the topic. MTL was first introduce in Caruana (1997). It has been since used for a number of NLP problems such as tagging (Collobert and Weston, 2008), syntactic parsing (Luong et al., 2015), and machine translation (Dong et al., 2015; Luong et al., 2015). The closest to our work is Fan et al. (2017), where MTL architectures are built on top of an attentive sequence-to-sequence model (Bahdanau et al., 2015). We instead focus on transfer learning across domains of the same data sets and employ a different architecture which promises to be less data-hungry than sequence-to-sequence models.

---

[3]The results on Overnight are not computed on the logical form they produce but on the answer they obtain using the logical form as a query. As such, their results are not directly comparable to ours.

Typical SLU systems rely on domain-specific semantic parsers that identify intents and slots in a sentence. Traditionally, these tasks were performed by linear machine learning models (Sha and Pereira, 2003) but more recently jointly-trained DNN models are used (Mesnil et al., 2015; Hakkani-Tür et al., 2016) with differing contexts (Gupta et al., 2018a; Vishal Ishwar Naik, 2018). More recently there has been work on extending the traditional intent/slot framework using targeted parsing to handle more complex linguistic phenomenon like coordination (Gupta et al., 2018c; Agarwal et al., 2018).

7 Conclusions

We framed SLU as an executable semantic parsing task, which addresses a limitation of current commercial SLU systems. By applying our framework to different data sets, we demonstrate that the framework is effective for Q&A as well as for SLU. We explored a typical scenario where it is necessary to learn a semantic parser for a new domain with little data, but other high-resource domains are available. We show the effectiveness of our system and both pre-training and MTL on different domains and data sets. Preliminary experiment results on transfer learning across domains belonging to heterogeneous data sets suggest future work in this area.

Acknowledgments

The authors would like to thank the three anonymous reviewers for their comments and the Amazon Alexa AI team members for their feedback.

References

Omri Abend and Ari Rappoport. 2013. Universal conceptual cognitive annotation (ucca). In *Proceedings of ACL*.

Sanchit Agarwal, Rahul Goel, Tagyoung Chung, Abhishek Sethi, Arindam Mandal, and Spyros Matsoukas. 2018. Parsing coordination for spoken language understanding. *arXiv preprint arXiv:1810.11497*.

Dzmitry Bahdanau, Kyunghyun Cho, and Yoshua Bengio. 2015. Neural machine translation by jointly learning to align and translate.

Collin F Baker, Charles J Fillmore, and John B Lowe. 1998. The berkeley framenet project. In *Proceedings of COLING*.

Laura Banarescu, Claire Bonial, Shu Cai, Madalina Georgescu, Kira Griffitt, Ulf Hermjakob, Kevin Knight, Philipp Koehn, Martha Palmer, and Nathan Schneider. 2013. Abstract meaning representation for sembanking. *Linguistic Annotation Workshop*.

Rich Caruana. 1997. Multitask learning. *Machine learning*, 28(1):41–75.

Jianpeng Cheng, Siva Reddy, Vijay Saraswat, and Mirella Lapata. 2017. Learning structured natural language representations for semantic parsing. In *Proceedings of the 55th Annual Meeting of the Association for Computational Linguistics (Volume 1: Long Papers)*, volume 1, pages 44–55.

James Clarke, Dan Goldwasser, Ming-Wei Chang, and Dan Roth. 2010. Driving semantic parsing from the world's response. In *Proceedings of CoNLL*. Association for Computational Linguistics.

Ronan Collobert and Jason Weston. 2008. A unified architecture for natural language processing: Deep neural networks with multitask learning. In *Proceedings of ICML*.

Daxiang Dong, Hua Wu, Wei He, Dianhai Yu, and Haifeng Wang. 2015. Multi-task learning for multiple language translation. In *Proceedings of ACL*.

Long Duong, Hadi Afshar, Dominique Estival, Glen Pink, Philip Cohen, and Mark Johnson. 2017. Multilingual semantic parsing and code-switching. In *Proceedings of CoNLL 2017*.

Chris Dyer, Miguel Ballesteros, Wang Ling, Austin Matthews, and Noah A Smith. 2015. Transition-based dependency parsing with stack long short-term memory. In *Proceedings of ACL*.

Chris Dyer, Adhiguna Kuncoro, Miguel Ballesteros, and Noah A Smith. 2016. Recurrent neural network grammars. In *Proceedings of NAACL*.

Xing Fan, Emilio Monti, Lambert Mathias, and Markus Dreyer. 2017. Transfer learning for neural semantic parsing. In *Proceedings of the 2nd Workshop on Representation Learning for NLP*.

Alex Graves. 2012. Supervised sequence labelling. In *Supervised sequence labelling with recurrent neural networks*, pages 5–13. Springer.

Caglar Gulcehre, Sungjin Ahn, Ramesh Nallapati, Bowen Zhou, and Yoshua Bengio. 2016. Pointing the unknown words. *Proceedings of ACL*.

Raghav Gupta, Abhinav Rastogi, and Dilek Hakkani-Tur. 2018a. An efficient approach to encoding context for spoken language understanding. *arXiv preprint arXiv:1807.00267*.

Sonal Gupta, Rushin Shah, Mrinal Mohit, and Anuj Kumar. 2018b. Semantic parsing for task oriented dialog using hierarchical representations. In *Proceedings of EMNLP*.

Sonal Gupta, Rushin Shah, Mrinal Mohit, Anuj Kumar, and Mike Lewis. 2018c. Semantic parsing for task oriented dialog using hierarchical representations. *arXiv preprint arXiv:1810.07942*.

Dilek Hakkani-Tür, Gökhan Tür, Asli Celikyilmaz, Yun-Nung Chen, Jianfeng Gao, Li Deng, and Ye-Yi Wang. 2016. Multi-domain joint semantic frame parsing using bi-directional rnn-lstm. In *Interspeech*, pages 715–719.

Mordechai Haklay and Patrick Weber. 2008. Openstreetmap: User-generated street maps. *Ieee Pervas Comput*, 7(4):12–18.

Robin Jia and Percy Liang. 2016. Data recombination for neural semantic parsing. In *Proceedings of the 54th Annual Meeting of the Association for Computational Linguistics (Volume 1: Long Papers)*, volume 1, pages 12–22.

Rohit J Kate, Yuk Wah Wong, and Raymond J Mooney. 2005. Learning to transform natural to formal languages. In *Proceedings of the National Conference on Artificial Intelligence*, volume 20, page 1062. Menlo Park, CA; Cambridge, MA; London; AAAI Press; MIT Press; 1999.

Carolin Lawrence and Stefan Riezler. 2016. Nlmaps: A natural language interface to query openstreetmap. In *Proceedings of COLING*.

Percy Liang. 2013. Lambda dependency-based compositional semantics. *arXiv preprint arXiv:1309.4408*.

Percy Liang, Michael I Jordan, and Dan Klein. 2013. Learning dependency-based compositional semantics. *Computational Linguistics*, 39(2):389–446.

Minh-Thang Luong, Quoc V Le, Ilya Sutskever, Oriol Vinyals, and Lukasz Kaiser. 2015. Multi-task sequence to sequence learning. *arXiv preprint arXiv:1511.06114*.

Minh-Thang Luong and Christopher D Manning. 2016. Achieving open vocabulary neural machine translation with hybrid word-character models. In *Proceedings of the ACL*.

Grégoire Mesnil, Yann Dauphin, Kaisheng Yao, Yoshua Bengio, Li Deng, Dilek Hakkani-Tur, Xiaodong He, Larry Heck, Gokhan Tur, Dong Yu, et al. 2015. Using recurrent neural networks for slot filling in spoken language understanding. *IEEE/ACM Transactions on Audio, Speech, and Language Processing*, 23(3):530–539.

Adam Meyers, Ruth Reeves, Catherine Macleod, Rachel Szekely, Veronika Zielinska, Brian Young, and Ralph Grishman. 2004. Annotating noun argument structure for nombank. In *Proceedings of LREC*.

Joakim Nivre. 2003. An efficient algorithm for projective dependency parsing. In *Proceedings of the 8th International Workshop on Parsing Technologies (IWPT*. Citeseer.

Joakim Nivre. 2004. Incrementality in deterministic dependency parsing. In *Proceedings of the Workshop on Incremental Parsing: Bringing Engineering and Cognition Together*, pages 50–57. Association for Computational Linguistics.

Joakim Nivre. 2008. Algorithms for deterministic incremental dependency parsing. *Computational Linguistics*, 34(4):513–553.

Martha Palmer, Daniel Gildea, and Paul Kingsbury. 2005. The proposition bank: An annotated corpus of semantic roles. *Computational linguistics*, 31(1):71–106.

Sebastian Ruder. 2017. An overview of multi-task learning in deep neural networks. *arXiv preprint arXiv:1706.05098*.

Fei Sha and Fernando Pereira. 2003. Shallow parsing with conditional random fields. In *Proceedings of the 2003 Conference of the North American Chapter of the Association for Computational Linguistics on Human Language Technology-Volume 1*, pages 134–141. Association for Computational Linguistics.

Mark Steedman. 1996. Surface structure and interpretation.

Yu Su and Xifeng Yan. 2017. Cross-domain semantic parsing via paraphrasing. In *Proceedings of EMNLP*.

Sebastian Thrun. 1996. Is learning the n-th thing any easier than learning the first? In *Proceedings of NIPS*.

Rahul Goel Vishal Ishwar Naik, Angeliki Metallinou. 2018. Context aware conversational understanding for intelligent agents with a screen.

Chuan Wang, Nianwen Xue, and Sameer Pradhan. 2015a. A transition-based algorithm for amr parsing. In *Proceedings of NAACL*.

Yushi Wang, Jonathan Berant, and Percy Liang. 2015b. Building a semantic parser overnight. In *Proceedings of ACL*.

Barret Zoph, Deniz Yuret, Jonathan May, and Kevin Knight. 2016. Transfer learning for low-resource neural machine translation. In *Proceedings of EMNLP*.

Fast Prototyping a Dialogue Comprehension System for Nurse-Patient Conversations on Symptom Monitoring

Zhengyuan Liu*, Hazel Lim*, Nur Farah Ain Binte Suhaimi*, Shao Chuen Tong[†],
Sharon Ong[‡], Angela Ng[‡], Sheldon Lee[⊤], Michael R. Macdonald[⊤],
Savitha Ramasamy*, Pavitra Krishnaswamy*, Wai Leng Chow[†] and Nancy F. Chen*

*Institute for Infocomm Research, A*STAR, Singapore
[†]Health Services Research, Changi General Hospital, Singapore
[‡]Health Management Unit, Changi General Hospital, Singapore
[⊤]Department of Cardiology, Changi General Hospital, Singapore
{liu_zhengyuan, nfychen}@i2r.a-star.edu.sg

Abstract

Data for human-human spoken dialogues for research and development are currently very limited in quantity, variety, and sources; such data are even scarcer in healthcare. In this work, we investigate fast prototyping of a dialogue comprehension system by leveraging on minimal nurse-to-patient conversations. We propose a framework inspired by nurse-initiated clinical symptom monitoring conversations to construct a simulated human-human dialogue dataset, embodying linguistic characteristics of spoken interactions like thinking aloud, self-contradiction, and topic drift. We then adopt an established bidirectional attention pointer network on this simulated dataset, achieving more than 80% F1 score on a held-out test set from real-world nurse-to-patient conversations. The ability to automatically comprehend conversations in the healthcare domain by exploiting only limited data has implications for improving clinical workflows through red flag symptom detection and triaging capabilities. We demonstrate the feasibility for efficient and effective extraction, retrieval and comprehension of symptom checking information discussed in multi-turn human-human spoken conversations.

1 Introduction

1.1 Problem Statement

Spoken conversations still remain the most natural and effortless means of human communication. Thus a lot of valuable information is conveyed and exchanged in such an unstructured form. In telehealth settings, nurses might call discharged patients who have returned home to continue to monitor their health status. Human language technology that can efficiently and effectively extract key information from such conversations is clinically useful, as it can help streamline workflow processes and digitally document patient medical information to increase staff productivity. In this work, we design and prototype a dialogue comprehension system in the question-answering manner, which is able to comprehend spoken conversations between nurses and patients to extract clinical information[1].

1.2 Motivation of Approach

Machine comprehension of written passages has made tremendous progress recently. Large quantities of supervised training data for reading comprehension (e.g. SQuAD (Rajpurkar et al., 2016)), the wide adoption and intense experimentation of neural modeling (Seo et al., 2017; Wang et al., 2017), and the advancements in vector representations of word embeddings (Pennington et al., 2014; Devlin et al., 2018) all contribute significantly to the achievements obtained so far. The first factor, the availability of large scale datasets, empowers the latter two factors. To date, there is still very limited well-annotated large-scale data suitable for modeling human-human spoken dialogues. Therefore, it is not straightforward to directly port over the recent endeavors in reading comprehension to dialogue comprehension tasks.

In healthcare, conversation data is even scarcer due to privacy issues. Crowd-sourcing is an ef-

---

[1]N.F.C., P.K., R.S. and C.W.L. conceptualized the overall research programme; N.F.C. and L.Z. proposed and developed the proposed approach; L.Z. and N.F.C. developed methods for data analysis; L.Z., L.J.H., N.F.S., and N.F.C. constructed the corpus; T.S.C, S.O., A.N. S.L.G, and M.R.M acquired, prepared, and validated clinical data; L.Z., N.F.C., P.K., S.L.G., M.R.M and C.W.L interpreted results; L.Z., N.F.C., L.J.H, N.F.S., P.K. and C.W.L wrote the paper.

Proceedings of NAACL-HLT 2019, pages 24–31
Minneapolis, Minnesota, June 2 - June 7, 2019. ©2019 Association for Computational Linguistics

ficient way to annotate large quantities of data, but less suitable for healthcare scenarios, where domain knowledge is required to guarantee data quality. To demonstrate the feasibility of a dialogue comprehension system used for extracting key clinical information from symptom monitoring conversations, we developed a framework to construct a simulated human-human dialogue dataset to bootstrap such a prototype. Similar efforts have been conducted for human-machine dialogues for restaurant or movie reservations (Shah et al., 2018). To the best of our knowledge, no one to date has done so for human-human conversations in healthcare.

1.3 Human-human Spoken Conversations

Human-human spoken conversations are a dynamic and interactive flow of information exchange. While developing technology to comprehend such spoken conversations presents similar technical challenges as machine comprehension of written passages (Rajpurkar et al., 2018), the challenges are further complicated by the interactive nature of human-human spoken conversations:

(1) Zero anaphora is more common: Coreference resolution of spoken utterances from multiple speakers is needed. For example, in Figure 1(a) *headaches, the pain, it, head bulging* all refer to the patient's headache symptom, but they were uttered by different speakers and across multiple utterances and turns. In addition, anaphors are more likely to be omitted (see Figure 1(a) A4) as this does not affect the human listeners understanding, but it might be challenging for computational models.

(2) Thinking aloud more commonly occurs: Since it is more effortless to speak than to type, one is more likely to reveal her running thoughts when talking. In addition, one cannot retract what has been uttered, while in text communications, one is more likely to confirm the accuracy of the information in a written response and revise if necessary before sending it out. Thinking aloud can lead to self-contradiction, requiring more context to fully understand the dialogue; e.g., in A6 in Figure 1(a), the patient at first says he has none of the symptoms asked, but later revises his response saying that he does get dizzy after running.

(3) Topic drift is more common and harder to detect in spoken conversations: An example is shown in Figure 1(a) in A3, where *No* is actu-

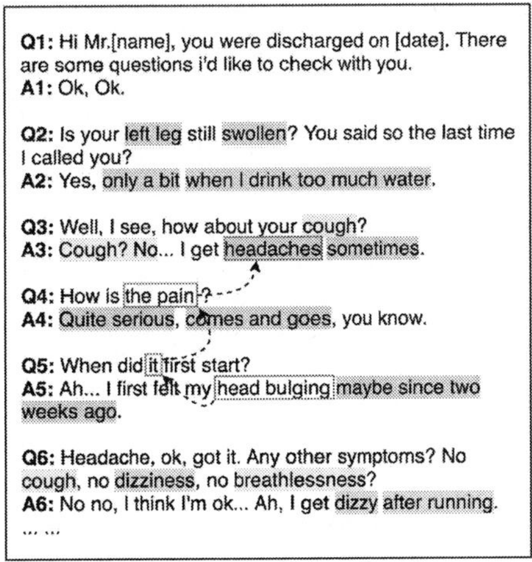

(a) Multi-Turn Spoken Dialogue Example

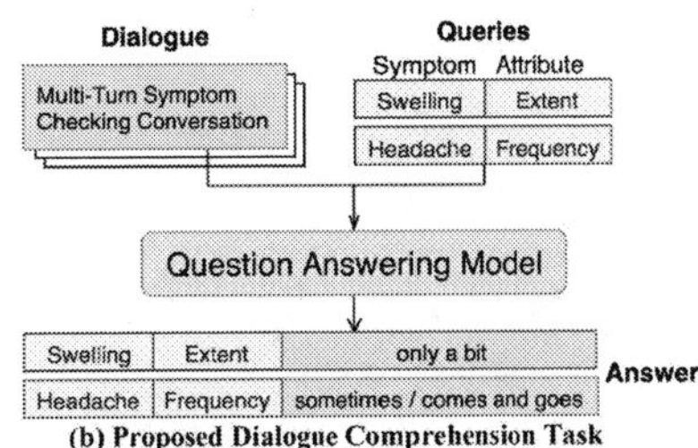

(b) Proposed Dialogue Comprehension Task

Symptom	Activity	Extent	Time	Frequency	Location
Swelling	when drink too much water	only a bit			left leg
Headache		quite serious	since two weeks ago	sometimes / comes and goes	
Dizziness	after running				
No Symptom:					
Cough, Breathlessness.					

(c) Clinical Use Case: Extractive Summary of Symptom Checking Dialogues

Figure 1: Dialogue comprehension of symptom checking conversations.

ally referring to *cough* in the previous question, and then the topic is shifted to *headache*. In spoken conversations, utterances are often incomplete sentences so traditional linguistic features used in written passages such as punctuation marks indicating syntactic boundaries or conjunction words suggesting discourse relations might no longer exist.

1.4 Dialogue Comprehension Task

Figure 1(b) illustrates the proposed dialogue comprehension task using a question answering (QA) model. The input are a multi-turn symptom checking dialogue D and a query Q specifying a *symptom* with one of its *attributes*; the output is the extracted answer A from the given dialogue. A training or test sample is defined as $S = \{D, Q, A\}$. Five attributes, specifying certain details of clinical significance, are defined to characterize the answer types of A: (1) the *time* the patient has been experiencing the symptom, (2) *activities* that trigger the symptom (to occur or worsen), (3) the *extent* of seriousness, (4) the *frequency* occurrence of the symptom, and (5) the *location* of symptom. For each symptom/attribute, it can take on different linguistic expressions, defined as *entities*. Note that if the queried symptom or attribute is not mentioned in the dialogue, the groundtruth output is "No Answer", as in (Rajpurkar et al., 2018).

2   Related Work

2.1   Reading Comprehension

Large-scale reading comprehension tasks like SQuAD (Rajpurkar et al., 2016) and MARCO (Nguyen et al., 2016) provide question-answer pairs from a vast range of written passages, covering different kinds of factual answers involving entities such as location and numerical values. Furthermore, HotpotQA (Yang et al., 2018) requires multi-step inference and provides numerous answer types. CoQA (Reddy et al., 2018) and QuAC (Choi et al., 2018) are designed to mimic multi-turn information-seeking discussions of the given material. In these tasks, contextual reasoning like coreference resolution is necessary to grasp rich linguistic patterns, encouraging semantic modeling beyond naive lexical matching. Neural networks contribute to impressive progress in semantic modeling: distributional semantic word embeddings (Pennington et al., 2014), contextual sequence encoding (Sutskever et al., 2014; Gehring et al., 2017) and the attention mechanism (Luong et al., 2015; Vaswani et al., 2017) are widely adopted in state-of-the-art comprehension models (Seo et al., 2017; Wang et al., 2017; Devlin et al., 2018).

While language understanding tasks in dialogue such as domain identification (Ravuri and Stolcke, 2015), slot filling (Kurata et al., 2016) and user intent detection (Wen et al., 2016) have attracted much research interest, work in dialogue comprehension is still limited, if any. It is labor-intensive and time-consuming to obtain a critical mass of annotated conversation data for computational modeling. Some propose to collect text data from human-machine or machine-machine dialogues (Li et al., 2016; Shah et al., 2018). In such cases, as human speakers are aware of current limitations of dialogue systems or due to predefined assumptions of user simulators, there are fewer cases of zero anaphora, thinking aloud, and topic drift, which occur more often in human-human spoken interactions.

2.2   NLP for Healthcare

There is emerging interest in research and development activities at the intersection of machine learning and healthcare[2][3], of which much of the NLP related work are centered around social media or online forums (e.g., (Wallace et al., 2014; Lyles et al., 2013)), partially due to the world wide web as a readily available source of information. Other work in this area uses public data sources such as MIMIC[4] in electronic health records: text classification approaches have been applied to analyze unstructured clinical notes for ICD code assignment (Baumel et al., 2017) and automatic intensive emergency prediction (Grnarova et al., 2016). Sequence-to-sequence textual generation has been used for readable notes based on medical and demographic recordings (Liu, 2018). For mental health, there has been more focus on analyzing dialogues. For example, sequential modeling of audio and text have helped detect depression from human-machine interviews (Al Hanai et al., 2018). However, few studies have examined human-human spoken conversations in healthcare settings.

3   Real-World Data Analysis

3.1   Data Preparation

We used recordings of nurse-initiated telephone conversations for congestive heart failure patients undergoing telemonitoring, post-discharge from the hospital. The clinical data was acquired by the Health Management Unit at Changi General Hospital. This research study was approved by the SingHealth Centralised Institutional Review Board (Protocol 1556561515). The patients were recruited during 2014-2016 as part of their routine care delivery, and enrolled into the telemonitoring health management program with consent for use of anonymized versions of their data for research.

The dataset comprises a total of 353 conversations from 40 speakers (11 nurses, 16 patients, and 13 caregivers) with consent to the use of anonymized data for research. The speakers are

---

[2]ML4H: Machine Learning for Health, Workshop at NeurIPS 2018 https://ml4health.github.io/2018/

[3]2018 Workshop on Health Intelligence (W3PHIAI 2018) http://w3phiai2018.w3phi.com/

[4]https://mimic.physionet.org/

Utterance Type	%
Open-ended Inquiry	31.8
Detailed Inquiry	33.0
Multi-Intent Inquiry	15.5
Reconfirmation Inquiry	21.3
Inquiry with Transitional Clauses	8.5
Yes/No Response	52.1
Detailed Response	29.4
Response with Revision	5.1
Response with Topic Drift	11.1
Response with Transitional Clauses	9.5
Sampled Turn Number	1200

Table 1: Linguistic characterization of inquiry-response types and their occurrence frequency from the seed data in Section 3.2.

38 to 88 years old, equally distributed across gender, and comprise a range of ethnic groups (55% Chinese, 17% Malay, 14% Indian, 3% Eurasian, and 11% unspecified). The conversations cover 11 topics (e.g., medication compliance, symptom checking, education, greeting) and 9 symptoms (e.g., chest pain, cough) and amount to 41 hours.

Data preprocessing and anonymization were performed by a data preparation team, separate from the data analysis team to maintain data confidentiality. The data preparation team followed standard speech recognition transcription guidelines, where words are transcribed verbatim to include false starts, disfluencies, mispronunciations, and private self-talk. Confidential information were marked and clipped off from the audio and transcribed with predefined tags in the annotation. Conversation topics and clinical symptoms were also annotated and clinically validated by certified telehealth nurses.

3.2 Linguistic Characterization on Seed Data

To analyze the linguistic structure of the inquiry-response pairs in the entire 41-hour dataset, we randomly sampled a seed dataset consisting of 1,200 turns and manually categorized them to different types, which are summarized in Table 1 along with the corresponding occurrence frequency statistics. Note that each given utterance could be categorized to more than one type. We elaborate on each utterance type below.

Open-ended Inquiry: Inquiries about general well-being or a particular symptom; e.g., *"How are you feeling?"* and *"Do you cough?"*

Detailed Inquiry: Inquiries with specific details that prompt yes/no answers or clarifications; e.g., *"Do you cough at night?"*

Multi-Intent Inquiry: Inquiring more than one symptom in a question; e.g., *"Any cough, chest pain, or headache?"*

Reconfirmation Inquiry: The nurse reconfirms particular details; e.g., *"Really? At night?"* and *"Serious or mild?"*. This case is usually related to explicit or implicit coreferencing.

Inquiry with Transitional Clauses: During spoken conversations, one might repeat what the other party said, but it is unrelated to the main clause of the question. This is usually due to private self-talk while thinking aloud, and such utterances form a transitional clause before the speaker starts a new topic; e.g., *"Chest pain... no chest pain, I see... any cough?"*.

Yes/No Response: Yes/No responses seem straightforward, but sometimes lead to misunderstanding if one does not interpret the context appropriately. One case is tag questions: *A:"You don't cough at night, do you?" B:'Yes, yes" A:"cough at night?" B:"No, no cough"*. Usually when the answer is unclear, clarifying inquiries will be asked for reconfirmation purposes.

Detailed Response: Responses that contain specific information of one symptom, like *"I felt tightness in my chest"*.

Response with Revision: Revision is infrequent but can affect comprehension significantly. One cause is thinking aloud so a later response overrules the previous one; e.g., *"No dizziness, oh wait... last week I felt a bit dizzy when biking"*.

Response with Topic Drift: When a symptom/topic like headache is inquired, the response might be: *"Only some chest pain at night"*, not referring to the original symptom (headache) at all.

Response with Transitional Clauses: Repeating some of the previous content, but often unrelated to critical clinical information and usually followed by topic drift. For example, *"Swelling... swelling... I don't cough at night"*.

4 Simulating Symptom Monitoring Dataset for Training

We divide the construction of data simulation into two stages. In Section 4.1, we build templates and expression pools using linguistic analysis followed by manual verification. In Section 4.2, we present our proposed framework for generating simulated training data. The templates and framework are verified for logical correctness and clinical soundness.

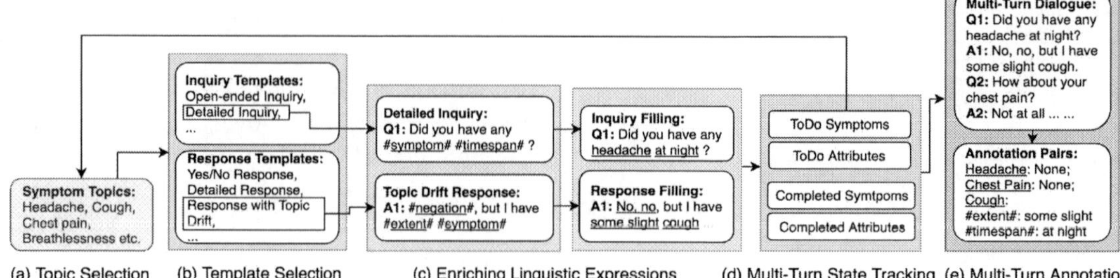

Figure 2: Simulated data generation framework.

4.1 Template Construction

4.1.1 Linguistically-Inspired Templates

Each utterance in the seed data is categorized according to Table 1 and then abstracted into templates by replacing entity phrases like *cough* and *often* with respective placeholders *"#symptom#"* and *"#frequency#"*. The templates are refined through verifying logical correctness and injecting expression diversity by linguistically trained researchers. As these replacements do not alter the syntactic structure, we interchange such placeholders with various verbal expressions to enlarge the simulated training set in Section 4.2. Clinical validation was also conducted by certified telehealth nurses.

4.1.2 Topic Expansion & Symptom Customization

For the 9 symptoms (e.g. chest pain, cough) and 5 attributes (e.g., extent, frequency), we collect various expressions from the seed data, and expand them through synonym replacement. Some attributes are unique to a particular symptom; e.g., *"left leg"* in *#location#* is only suitable to describe the symptom *swelling*, but not the symptom *headache*. Therefore, we only reuse general expressions like *"slight"* in *#extent#* across different symptoms to diversify linguistic expressions.

4.1.3 Expression Pool for Linguistic Diversity

Two linguistically trained researchers constructed expression pools for each symptom and each attribute to account for different types of paraphrasing and descriptions. These expression pools are used in Section 4.2 (c).

4.2 Simulated Data Generation Framework

Figure 2 shows the five steps we use to generate multi-turn symptom monitoring dialogue samples.

(a) Topic Selection: While nurses might prefer to inquire the symptoms in different orders depending on the patient's history, our preliminary analysis shows that modeling results do not differ noticeably if topics are of equal prior probabilities. Thus we adopt this assumption for simplicity.

(b) Template Selection: For each selected topic, one inquiry template and one response template are randomly chosen to compose a turn. To minimize adverse effects of underfitting, we redistributed the frequency distribution in Table 1: For utterance types that are below 15%, we boosted them to 15%, and the overall relative distribution ranking is balanced and consistent with Table 1.

(c) Enriching Linguistic Expressions: The placeholders in the selected templates are substituted with diverse expressions from the expression pools in Section 4.1.3 to characterize the symptoms and their corresponding attributes.

(d) Multi-Turn Dialogue State Tracking: A greedy algorithm is applied to complete conversations. A "completed symptoms" list and a "to-do symptoms" list are used for symptom topic tracking. We also track the "completed attributes" and "to-do attributes". For each symptom, all related attributes are iterated. A dialogue ends only when all possible entities are exhausted, generating a multi-turn dialogue sample, which encourages the model to learn from the entire discussion flow rather than a single turn to comprehend contextual dependency. The average length of a simulated dialogue is 184 words, which happens to be twice as long as an average dialogue from the real-world evaluation set. Moreover, to model the roles of the respondents, we set the ratio between patients and caregivers to 2:1; this statistic is inspired by the real scenarios in the seed dataset. For both the caregivers and patients, we assume equal probability of both genders. The corresponding pronouns in the conversations are thus determined by the role and gender of these settings.

(e) Multi-Turn Sample Annotation: For each multi-turn dialogue, a query is specified by a symptom and an attribute. The groundtruth output of the QA system is automatically labeled based on the template generation rules, but also manually verified to ensure annotation quality. Moreover, we adopt the unanswerable design in (Rajpurkar et al., 2018): when the patient does not mention a particular symptom, the answer is defined as *"No Answer"*. This process is repeated until all logical permutations of symptoms and attributes are exhausted.

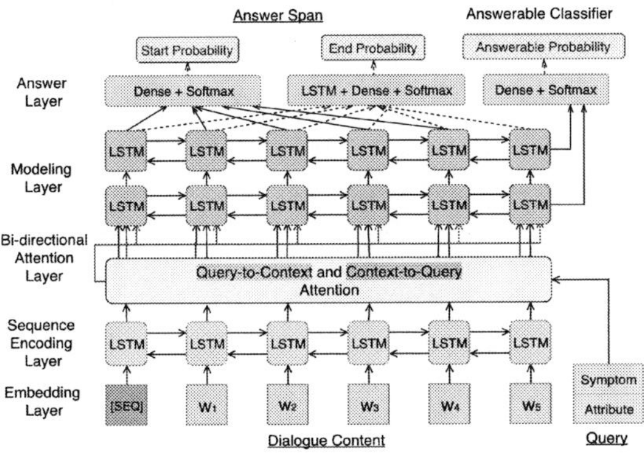

Figure 3: Bi-directional attention pointer network with an answerable classifier for dialogue comprehension.

5 Experiments

5.1 Model Design

We implemented an established model in reading comprehension, a bi-directional attention pointer network (Seo et al., 2017), and equipped it with an answerable classifier, as depicted in Figure 3. First, tokens in the given dialogue D and query Q are converted into embedding vectors. Then the dialogue embeddings are fed to a bi-directional LSTM encoding layer, generating a sequence of contextual hidden states. Next, the hidden states and query embeddings are processed by a bi-directional attention layer, fusing attention information in both context-to-query and query-to-context directions. The following two bi-directional LSTM modeling layers read the contextual sequence with attention. Finally, two respective linear layers with softmax functions are used to estimate token i's p_i^{start} and p_i^{end} probability of the answer span A.

In addition, we add a special tag "[SEQ]" at the head of D to account for the case of *"No answer"* (Devlin et al., 2018) and adopt an answer-

Training Samples	10k	50k	100k	150k
Base Evaluation Set:				
EM Score	15.41	80.33	89.68	**91.45**
F1 Score	50.63	89.18	92.27	**94.17**
Augmented Evaluation Set:				
EM Score	11.59	57.22	**78.29**	72.12
F1 Score	49.36	74.53	**85.69**	82.75
Real-World Evaluation Set:				
EM Score	38.81	42.93	**78.23**	75.41
F1 Score	46.29	52.68	**80.18**	78.09

Table 2: QA model evaluation results. Each sample is a simulated multi-turn conversation.

able classifier as in (Liu et al., 2018). More specifically, when the queried symptom or attribute is not mentioned in the dialogue, the answer span should point to the tag "[SEQ]" and answerable probability should be predicted as 0.

5.2 Implementation Details

The model was trained via gradient backpropagation with the cross-entropy loss function of answer span prediction and answerable classification, optimized by Adam algorithm (Kingma and Ba, 2015) with initial learning rate of 0.001. Pretrained GloVe (Pennington et al., 2014) embeddings (size = 200) were used. We re-shuffled training samples at each epoch (batch size = 16). Out-of-vocabulary words ($<$ 0.05%) were replaced with a fixed random vector. L2 regularization and dropout (rate = 0.2) were used to alleviate overfitting (Srivastava et al., 2014).

5.3 Evaluation Setup

To evaluate the effectiveness of our linguistically-inspired simulation approach, the model is trained on the simulated data (see Section 4.2). We designed 3 evaluation sets: (1) **Base Set** (1,264 samples) held out from the simulated data. (2) **Augmented Set** (1,280 samples) built by adding two out-of-distribution symptoms, with corresponding dialogue contents and queries, to the Base Set (*"bleeding"* and *"cold"*, which never appeared in training data). (3) **Real-World Set** (944 samples) manually delineated from the the symptom checking portions (approximately 4 hours) of real-world dialogues, and annotated as evaluation samples.

5.4 Results

Evaluation results are in Table 2 with exact match (EM) and F1 score in (Rajpurkar et al., 2016) metrics. To distinguish the correct answer span from the plausible ones which contain the same words, we measure the scores on the position indices of

	EM	F1
Augmented Evaluation Set:		
Best-trained Model	**78.29**	**85.69**
w/o Bi-Attention	72.08	78.57
w/o Pre-trained Embedding	56.98	72.31
Real-World Evaluation Set:		
Best-trained Model	**78.23**	**80.18**
w/o Bi-Attention	70.52	74.09
w/o Pre-trained Embedding	60.88	66.47

Table 3: Ablation experiments on 100K training size.

tokens. Our results show that both EM and F1 score increase with training sample size growing and the optimal size in our setting is 100k. The best-trained model performs well on both the Base Set and the Augmented Set, indicating that out-of-distribution symptoms do not affect the comprehension of existing symptoms and outputs reasonable answers for both in- and out-of-distribution symptoms. On the Real-World Set, we obtained 78.23 EM score and 80.18 F1 score respectively.

Error analysis suggests the performance drop from the simulated test sets is due to the following: 1) sparsity issues resulting from the expression pools excluding various valid but sporadic expressions. 2) nurses and patients occasionally chitchat in the Real-World Set, which is not simulated in the training set. At times, these chit-chats make the conversations overly lengthy, causing the information density to be lower. These issues could potentially distract and confuse the comprehension model. 3) an interesting type of infrequent error source, caused by patients elaborating on possible causal relations of two symptoms. For example, a patient might say "*My giddiness may be due to all this cough*". We are currently investigating how to close this performance gap efficiently.

5.5 Ablation Analysis

To assess the effectiveness of bi-directional attention, we bypassed the bi-attention layer by directly feeding the contextual hidden states and query embeddings to the modeling layer. To evaluate the pre-trained GloVe embeddings, we randomly initialized and trained the embeddings from scratch. These two procedures lead to 10% and 18% performance degradation on the Augmented Set and Real-World Set, respectively (see Table 3).

6 Conclusion

We formulated a dialogue comprehension task motivated by the need in telehealth settings to extract key clinical information from spoken conversations between nurses and patients. We analyzed linguistic characteristics of real-world human-human symptom checking dialogues, constructed a simulated dataset based on linguistically inspired and clinically validated templates, and prototyped a QA system. The model works effectively on a simulated test set using symptoms excluded during training and on real-world conversations between nurses and patients. We are currently improving the model's dialogue comprehension capability in complex reasoning and context understanding and also applying the QA model to summarization and virtual nurse applications.

Acknowledgements

Research efforts were supported by funding for Digital Health and Deep Learning I2R (DL2 SSF Project No: A1718g0045) and the Science and Engineering Research Council (SERC Project No: A1818g0044), A*STAR, Singapore. In addition, this work was conducted using resources and infrastructure provided by the Human Language Technology unit at I2R. The telehealth data acquisition was funded by the Economic Development Board (EDB), Singapore Living Lab Fund and Philips Electronics Hospital to Home Pilot Project (EDB grant reference number: S14-1035-RF-LLF H and W).

We acknowledge valuable support and assistance from Yulong Lin, Yuanxin Xiang, and Ai Ti Aw at the Institute for Infocomm Research (I2R); Weiliang Huang at the Changi General Hospital (CGH) Department of Cardiology, Hong Choon Oh at CGH Health Services Research, and Edris Atikah Bte Ahmad, Chiu Yan Ang, and Mei Foon Yap of the CGH Integrated Care Department.

We also thank Eduard Hovy and Bonnie Webber for insightful discussions and the anonymous reviewers for their precious feedback to help improve and extend this piece of work.

References

Tuka Al Hanai, Mohammad Ghassemi, and James Glass. 2018. Detecting depression with audio/text sequence modeling of interviews. In *Proc. of INTERSPEECH*, pages 1716–1720.

Tal Baumel, Jumana Nassour-Kassis, Raphael Cohen, Michael Elhadad, and Noemie Elhadad. 2017. Multi-label classification of patient notes a case study on ICD code assignment. In *Workshop on Health Intelligence, AAAI*.

Eunsol Choi, He He, Mohit Iyyer, Mark Yatskar, Wentau Yih, Yejin Choi, Percy Liang, and Luke Zettlemoyer. 2018. Quac: Question answering in context. In *Proc. of EMNLP*, pages 2174–2184.

Jacob Devlin, Ming-Wei Chang, Kenton Lee, and Kristina Toutanova. 2018. BERT: Pre-training of deep bidirectional transformers for language understanding. *arXiv preprint arXiv:1810.04805*.

Jonas Gehring, Michael Auli, David Grangier, Denis Yarats, and Yann N Dauphin. 2017. Convolutional sequence to sequence learning. *arXiv preprint arXiv:1705.03122*.

Paulina Grnarova, Florian Schmidt, Stephanie L Hyland, and Carsten Eickhoff. 2016. Neural document embeddings for intensive care patient mortality prediction. *arXiv preprint arXiv:1612.00467*.

Diederik P Kingma and Jimmy Ba. 2015. Adam: A method for stochastic optimization. In *Proc. of ICLR*.

Gakuto Kurata, Bing Xiang, Bowen Zhou, and Mo Yu. 2016. Leveraging Sentence-level Information with Encoder LSTM for Semantic Slot Filling. In *Proc. of EMNLP*, pages 2077–2083.

Xiujun Li, Zachary C Lipton, Bhuwan Dhingra, Lihong Li, Jianfeng Gao, and Yun-Nung Chen. 2016. A user simulator for task-completion dialogues. *arXiv preprint arXiv:1612.05688*.

Peter J Liu. 2018. Learning to write notes in electronic health records. *arXiv preprint arXiv:1808.02622*.

Xiaodong Liu, Wei Li, Yuwei Fang, Aerin Kim, Kevin Duh, and Jianfeng Gao. 2018. Stochastic answer networks for squad 2.0. *arXiv preprint arXiv:1809.09194*.

Minh-Thang Luong, Hieu Pham, and Christopher D Manning. 2015. Effective approaches to attention-based neural machine translation. In *Proc. of EMNLP*, pages 1412–1421.

Courtney R Lyles, Andrea López, Rena Pasick, and Urmimala Sarkar. 2013. 5 mins of uncomfyness is better than dealing with cancer 4 a lifetime: an exploratory qualitative analysis of cervical and breast cancer screening dialogue on twitter. *Journal of Cancer Education*, 28(1):127–133.

Tri Nguyen, Mir Rosenberg, Xia Song, Jianfeng Gao, Saurabh Tiwary, Rangan Majumder, and Li Deng. 2016. MS MARCO: A human generated machine reading comprehension dataset. *arXiv preprint arXiv:1611.09268*.

Jeffrey Pennington, Richard Socher, and Christopher Manning. 2014. GloVe: Global vectors for word representation. In *Proc. of EMNLP*, pages 1532–1543.

Pranav Rajpurkar, Robin Jia, and Percy Liang. 2018. Know What You Don't Know: Unanswerable Questions for SQuAD. In *Proc. of ACL*, pages 784–789.

Pranav Rajpurkar, Jian Zhang, Konstantin Lopyrev, and Percy Liang. 2016. SQuAD: 100,000+ questions for machine comprehension of text. In *Proc. of EMNLP*, pages 2383–2392.

Suman Ravuri and Andreas Stolcke. 2015. Recurrent neural network and lstm models for lexical utterance classification. In *Proc. of INTERSPEECH*.

Siva Reddy, Danqi Chen, and Christopher D Manning. 2018. CoQA: A conversational question answering challenge. *arXiv preprint arXiv:1808.07042*.

Minjoon Seo, Aniruddha Kembhavi, Ali Farhadi, and Hannaneh Hajishirzi. 2017. Bidirectional attention flow for machine comprehension. In *Proc. of ICLR*.

Pararth Shah, Dilek Hakkani-Tür, Gokhan Tür, Abhinav Rastogi, Ankur Bapna, Neha Nayak, and Larry Heck. 2018. Building a conversational agent overnight with dialogue self-play. *arXiv preprint arXiv:1801.04871*.

Nitish Srivastava, Geoffrey Hinton, Alex Krizhevsky, Ilya Sutskever, and Ruslan Salakhutdinov. 2014. Dropout: a simple way to prevent neural networks from overfitting. *The Journal of Machine Learning Research*, 15(1):1929–1958.

Ilya Sutskever, Oriol Vinyals, and Quoc V Le. 2014. Sequence to sequence learning with neural networks. In *NIPS*, pages 3104–3112.

Ashish Vaswani, Noam Shazeer, Niki Parmar, Jakob Uszkoreit, Llion Jones, Aidan N Gomez, Łukasz Kaiser, and Illia Polosukhin. 2017. Attention is all you need. In *NIPS*, pages 5998–6008.

Byron C Wallace, Michael J Paul, Urmimala Sarkar, Thomas A Trikalinos, and Mark Dredze. 2014. A large-scale quantitative analysis of latent factors and sentiment in online doctor reviews. *Journal of the American Medical Informatics Association*, 21(6):1098–1103.

Wenhui Wang, Nan Yang, Furu Wei, Baobao Chang, and Ming Zhou. 2017. Gated self-matching networks for reading comprehension and question answering. In *Proc. of ACL*, volume 1, pages 189–198.

Tsung-Hsien Wen, David Vandyke, Nikola Mrksic, Milica Gasic, Lina M Rojas-Barahona, Pei-Hao Su, Stefan Ultes, and Steve Young. 2016. A network-based end-to-end trainable task-oriented dialogue system. In *Proc. of ACL*, pages 438–449.

Zhilin Yang, Peng Qi, Saizheng Zhang, Yoshua Bengio, William W Cohen, Ruslan Salakhutdinov, and Christopher D Manning. 2018. HotpotQA: A Dataset for Diverse, Explainable Multi-hop Question Answering. In *Proc. of EMNLP*, pages 2369–2380.

Graph Convolution for Multimodal Information Extraction from Visually Rich Documents

Xiaojing Liu, Feiyu Gao, Qiong Zhang, Huasha Zhao
Alibaba Group
{huqiang.lxj,feiyu.gfy,qz.zhang,huasha.zhao}@alibaba-inc.com

Abstract

Visually rich documents (VRDs) are ubiquitous in daily business and life. Examples are purchase receipts, insurance policy documents, custom declaration forms and so on. In VRDs, visual and layout information is critical for document understanding, and texts in such documents cannot be serialized into the one-dimensional sequence without losing information. Classic information extraction models such as BiLSTM-CRF typically operate on text sequences and do not incorporate visual features. In this paper, we introduce a graph convolution based model to combine textual and visual information presented in VRDs. Graph embeddings are trained to summarize the context of a text segment in the document, and further combined with text embeddings for entity extraction. Extensive experiments have been conducted to show that our method outperforms BiLSTM-CRF baselines by significant margins, on two real-world datasets. Additionally, ablation studies are also performed to evaluate the effectiveness of each component of our model.

1 Introduction

Information Extraction (IE) is the process of extracting structured information from unstructured documents. IE is a classic and fundamental Natural Language Processing (NLP) task, and extensive research has been made in this area. Traditionally, IE research focuses on extracting entities and relationships from plain texts, where information is primarily expressed in the format of natural language text. However, a large amount of information remains untapped in VRDs.

VRDs present information in the form of both text and vision. The semantic structure of the document is not only determined by the text within it but also the visual features such as layout, tabular structure and font size of the document. Examples

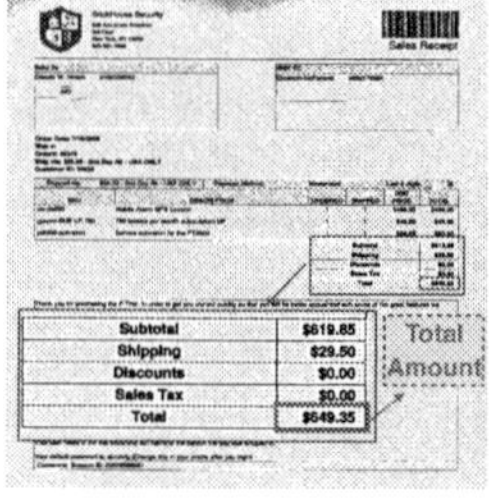 

(a) Purchase receipt   (b) Value-added tax invoice

Figure 1: Examples of VRDs and example entities to extract.

of VRDs are purchase receipts, insurance policy documents, custom declaration forms and so on. Figure 1 shows example VRDs and example entities to extract.

VRDs can be represented as a graph of *text segments* (Figure 2), where each text segment is comprised of the position of the segment and the text within it. The position of the text segment is determined by the four coordinates that generate the bounding box of the text. There are other potentially useful visual features in VRDs, such as fonts and colors, which are complementary to the position of the text. They are out of the scope of this paper, and we leave them to future works.

The problem we address in this paper is to extract the values of pre-defined entities from VRDs. We propose a graph convolution based method to combine textual and visual information presented in VRDs. The graph embeddings produced by graph convolution summarize the context of a text segment in the document, which are further combined with text embeddings for entity extraction using a standard BiLSTM-CRF model. The following paragraphs summarize the challenges of the task and the contributions of our work.

Proceedings of NAACL-HLT 2019, pages 32–39
Minneapolis, Minnesota, June 2 - June 7, 2019. ©2019 Association for Computational Linguistics

1.1 Challenges

IE from VRDs is a challenging task, and the difficulties mainly arise from how to effectively incorporate visual cues from the document and the scalability of the task.

First, text alone is not adequate to represent the semantic meaning in VRDs, and the contexts of the texts are usually expressed in visual cues. For example, there might be multiple dates in the purchase receipts. However, it is up to the visual part of the model to distinguish between the Invoice Date, Transaction Date, and Due Date. Another example is the tax amount in value-added tax invoice, as shown in Figure 1(b). There are multiple "money" entities in the document, and there is a lack of any textual context to determine which one is tax amount. To extract the tax amount correctly, we have to leverage the (relative) position of the text segment and visual features of the document in general.

Template matching based algorithms (Chiticariu et al., 2013; Dengel and Klein, 2002; Schuster et al., 2013) utilize visual features of the document to extract entities; however, we argue that they are mostly not scalable for the task in real-world business settings. There are easily thousands of vendors on the market, and the templates of purchase receipts from each vendor are not the same. Thousands of templates need to be created and maintained in this single scenario. It requires substantial efforts to update the template and make sure it's not conflicting with the rest every time a new template comes in, and the process is error-prone. Besides, user uploaded pictures introduce another dimension of variance from the template. An example is shown in Figure 1(b). Value-added tax invoice is a nation-wide tax document, and the layout is fixed. However, pictures taken by users are usually distorted, often blurred and sometimes contain interfering objects in the image. A simple template-based system performs poorly in such a scenario, while sophisticated rules require significant engineering efforts for each scenario, which we believe is not scalable.

1.2 Contributions

In this paper, we present a novel method for IE from VRDs. The method first computes graph embeddings for each text segment in the document using graph convolution. The graph embeddings represent the context of the current text segment where the convolution operation combines both textual and visual features of the context. Then the graph embeddings are combined with text embeddings to feed into a standard BiLSTM for information extraction.

Extensive experiments have been conducted to show our method outperforms BiLSTM-CRF baselines by significant margins, on two real-world datasets. Additionally, ablation studies are also performed to evaluate the effectiveness of each component of our model. Furthermore, we also provide analysis and intuitions on why and how individual components work in our experiments.

2 Related Works

Our work is inspired by recent research in the area of graph convolution and information extraction.

2.1 Graph Convolution Network

Neural network architectures such as CNN and RNNs have demonstrated huge success on many artificial intelligence tasks where the underlying data has grid-like or sequential structure (Krizhevsky et al., 2012; Kim et al., 2016; Kim, 2014). Recently, there is a surge of interest in studying the neural network structure operating on graphs (Kipf and Welling, 2016; Hamilton et al., 2017), since much data in the real world is naturally represented as graphs. Many works attempt to generalize convolution on the graph structure. Some use a spectrum based approach where the learned model depends on the structure of the graph. As a result, the approach does not work well on dynamic graph structures. The others define convolution directly on the graph (Veličković et al., 2017; Hamilton et al., 2017; Xu et al., 2018; Johnson et al., 2018; Duvenaud et al., 2015). We follow the latter approach in our work to model the text segment graph of VRDs.

Different from existing works, this paper introduces explicit edge embeddings into the graph convolution network, which models the relationship between vertices directly. Similar to (Veličković et al., 2017), we apply self-attention (Vaswani et al., 2017) to define convolution on variable-sized neighbors, and the approach is computationally efficient since the operation is parallelizable across node pairs.

2.2 Information Extraction

Recently, significant progress has been made in information extraction from unstructured or semi-structured text. However, most works focus on plain text documents (Peng et al., 2017; Lample et al., 2016; Ma and Hovy, 2016; Chiu and Nichols, 2016). For information extraction from VRDs, (Palm et al., 2017) which uses a recurrent neural network (RNN) to extract entities of interest from VRDs (invoices) is the closest to our work, but does not take visual features into account. Besides, some of the studies (d'Andecy et al., 2018; Medvet et al., 2011; Rusinol et al., 2013) in the area of document understanding deal with a similar problem to our work, and explore using visual features to aid text extraction from VRDs; however, approaches they proposed are based on a large amount of heuristic knowledge and human-designed features, as well as limited in known templates, which are not scalable in real-world business settings. We also acknowledge a concurrent work of (Katti et al., 2018), which models 2-D document using convolution networks. However, there are several key differences. Our neural network architecture is graph-based, and our model operates on text segments instead of characters as in (Katti et al., 2018).

Besides, information extraction based on the graph structure has been developed most recently. (Peng et al., 2017; Song et al., 2018) present a graph LSTM to capture various dependencies among the input words and (Wang et al., 2018) designs a novel graph schema to extract entities and relations jointly. However, their models are not concerned with visual information directly.

3 Model Architecture

This section describes the document model and the architecture of our proposed model. Our model first encodes each text segment in the document into graph embedding, using multiple layers of graph convolution. The embedding represents the information in the text segment given its visual and textual context. By visual context, we refer to the layout of the document and relative positions of the individual segment to other segments. Textual context is the aggregate of text information in the document overall; our model learns to assign higher weights on texts from neighbor segments. Then we combine the graph embeddings with text embeddings and apply a standard BiLSTM-CRF

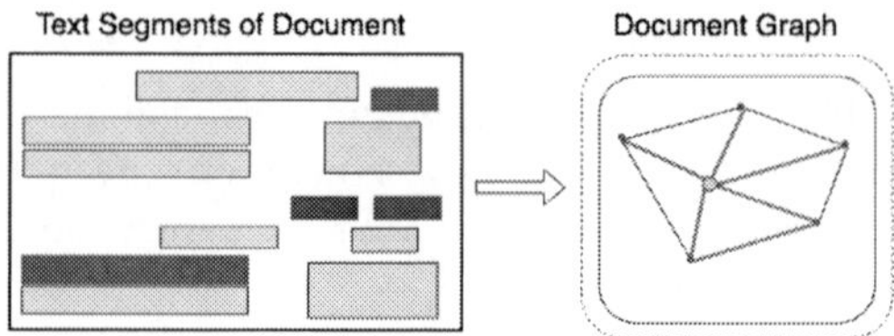

Figure 2: Document graph. Every node in the graph is fully connected to each other.

model for entity extraction.

3.1 Document Modeling

We model each document as a graph of text segments (see Figure 2), where each text segment is comprised of the position of the segment and the text within it. The graph is comprised of nodes that represent text segments, and edges that represent visual dependencies, such as relative shapes and distance, between two nodes. Text segments are generated using an in-house Optical Character Recognition (OCR) system.

Mathematically, a document $\mathcal{D}$ is a tuple (T, E), where $T = \{t_1, t_2, \cdots, t_n\}, t_i \in \mathcal{T}$ is a set of n text boxes/nodes, $R = \{r_{i1}, r_{i2}, \cdots, r_{ij}\}, r_{ij} \in \mathcal{R}$ is a set of edges, and $E = T \times R \times T$ is a set of directed edges of the form (t_i, r_{ij}, t_j) where $t_i, t_j \in T$ and $r_{ij} \in R$. In our experiments, every node is connected to each other.

3.2 Feature Extraction

For node t_i, we calculate node embedding $\mathbf{t}_i$ using a single layer Bi-LSTM (Schuster and Paliwal, 1997) to extract features from the text content in the segment.

Edge embedding between node t_i and node t_j is defined as follows,

$$\mathbf{r}_{ij} = [x_{ij}, y_{ij}, \frac{w_i}{h_i}, \frac{h_j}{h_i}, \frac{w_j}{h_i}], \tag{1}$$

where x_{ij} and y_{ij} are horizontal and vertical distance between the two text boxes respectively, and w_i and h_i are the width and height of the corresponding text box. The third, fourth and fifth value of the embedding are the aspect ratio of node t_i, relative height, and width of node t_j respectively. Empirically, a visual distance between two segments is an important feature. For example, in general, the positions of relevant information are

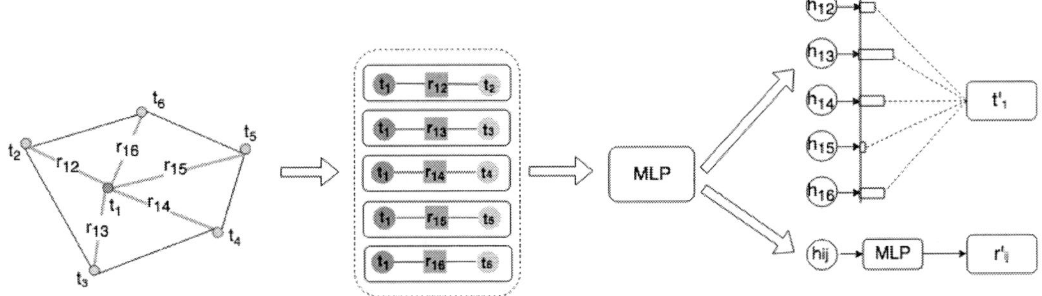

Figure 3: Graph convolution of document graph. Convolution is defined on node-edge-node triplets (t_i, r_{ij}, t_j). Each layer produces new embeddings for both nodes and edges.

closer in one document, such as the key and value of an entity. Moreover, the shape of the text segment plays a critical role in representing semantic meanings. For example, the length of the text segment which has address information is usually longer than that of one which has a buyer name. Therefore, we use edge embedding to encode information regarding the visual distance between two segments, the shape of the source node, and the relative size of the destination node.

To summarize, node embedding encodes textual features, while edge embedding primarily represents visual features.

3.3 Graph Convolution

Graph convolution is applied to compute visual text embeddings of text segments in the graph, as shown in Figure 3. Different from existing works, we define convolution on the node-edge-node triplets (t_i, r_{ij}, t_j) instead of on the node alone. We compare the performances of the models using nodes only and node-edge-node triplets in Section 5.3. For node t_i, we extract features $\mathbf{h}_{ij}$ for each neighbour t_j using a multi-layer perceptron (MLP) network,

$$\mathbf{h}_{ij} = g(\mathbf{t}_i, \mathbf{r}_{ij}, \mathbf{t}_j) = \text{MLP}([\mathbf{t}_i \| \mathbf{r}_{ij} \| \mathbf{t}_j]), \quad (2)$$

where $\|$ is the concatenate operation. There are several benefits of using this triplet feature set. First, it combines visual features directly into the neighbor representation. Furthermore, the information of the current node is copied across the neighbors. As a result, the neighbor features can potentially learn where to attend given the current node.

In our model, graph convolution is defined based on the self-attention mechanism. The idea is to compute the output hidden representation of each node by attending to its neighbors. In its most general form, each node can attend to all the other nodes, assuming a fully connected graph.

Concretely the output embedding $\mathbf{t}'_i$ of the layer for node t_i is computed by,

$$\mathbf{t}'_i = \sigma(\sum_{j \in \{1, \cdots, n\}} \alpha_{ij} \mathbf{h}_{ij}), \quad (3)$$

where α_{ij} are the attention coefficients, and σ is an activation function. In our experiments, the attention mechanism is designed as the follows,

$$\alpha_{ij} = \frac{\exp(\text{LeakyRelu}(\mathbf{w}_a^T \mathbf{h}_{ij}))}{\sum_{j \in \{1, \cdots, n\}} \exp(\text{LeakyRelu}(\mathbf{w}_a^T \mathbf{h}_{ij}))}, \quad (4)$$

where $\mathbf{w}_a$ is a shared attention weight vector. We apply the LeakyRelu activation function to avoid the "dying Relu" problem and to increase the "contrast" of the attention coefficients potentially.

The edge embedding output of the graph convolution layer is defined as,

$$\mathbf{r}'_{ij} = \text{MLP}(\mathbf{h}_{ij}). \quad (5)$$

Outputs $\mathbf{t}'_i, \mathbf{r}'_{ij}$ are fed as inputs to the next layer of graph convolution (as computed in equation 2) or network modules for downstream tasks.

3.4 BiLSTM-CRF with Graph Embeddings

We combine graph embeddings with token embeddings and feed them into standard BiLSTM-CRF for entity extraction. As illustrated in Figure 4, visual text embedding generated from the graph convolution layers of the current text segment is

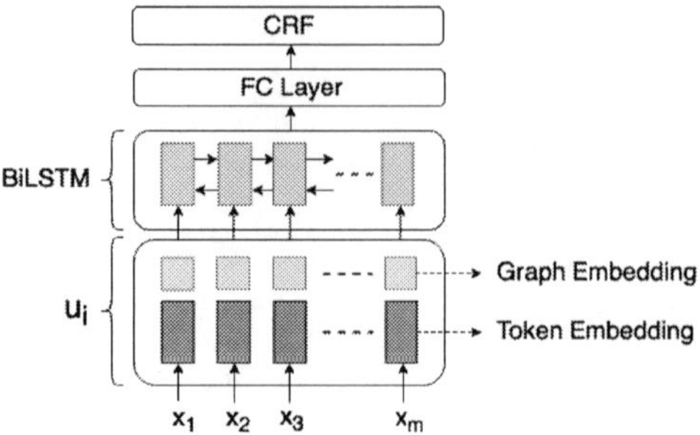

Figure 4: BiLSTM-CRF with graph embeddings.

concatenated to each token embedding of the input sequence; Intuitively, graph embedding adds contextual information to the input sequence.

Formally, assume for node t_i, the input token sequence of the text segment is $x_1, x_2, \cdots, x_m$, and the graph embedding of the node is $\mathbf{t}'_i$. The input embedding $\mathbf{u}_i$ is defined as,

$$\mathbf{u}_i = e(x_i) \| \mathbf{t}'_i \tag{6}$$

where e is token embedding lookup function, and Word2Vec vectors are used as token embeddings in our experiments.

Then the input embeddings are fed into a Bi-LSTM network to be encoded, and the output is further passed to a fully connected network and then a CRF layer.

4 Model Supervision and Training

We build an annotation system to facilitate the labeling of the ground truth data. For each document, we label the values for each pre-defined entity, and their locations (bounding boxes). To generate training data, we first identify the text segment each entity belongs to, and then we label the text in the segment according to IOB tagging format (Sang and Veenstra, 1999). We assign label O to all tokens in empty text segments.

Since human annotated bounding boxes cannot match OCR detected box exactly, we apply a simple heuristic to determine which text segment an entity belongs to based on overlap area. A text segment is considered to contain an entity if $A_{overlap}/\min(A_{annotator}, A_{ocr})$ is bigger than a manually set threshold; Here $A_{annotator}, A_{ocr}, A_{overlap}$ are the area of the annotated box of the corresponding entity, the area of the ocr detected box and the area of the overlap between the two boxes respectively.

In our experiments, the graph convolution layers and BiLSTM-CRF extractors are trained jointly. Furthermore, to improve prediction accuracy, we add the segment classification task which classifies each text segment into a pre-defined tag as an auxiliary task and discuss the effect of multi-task learning in Section 5.4.3. We feed the graph embedding of each text segment into a sigmoid classifier to predict the tag. Since the parameters of the graph convolution layers are shared across the extraction task and segment classification task, we employ a multi-task learning approach for model training. In multi-task training, the goal is to optimize the weighted sum of the two losses. In our experiments, the weight is determined using a principled approach as described in (Kendall et al., 2017). The idea is to adjust each task's relative weight in the loss function by considering task-dependant uncertainties.

5 Experiments

We apply our model for information extraction from two real-world datasets. They are Value-Added Tax Invoices (VATI) and International Purchase Receipts (IPR).

5.1 Datasets Description

VATI consists of 3000 user-uploaded pictures and has 16 entities to exact. Example entities are the names of buyer/seller, date and tax amount. The invoices are in Chinese, and it has a fixed template since it is national standard invoice. However, there are many noises in the documents which include distracting objects in the image and skewed document orientation to name a few. IPR is a data set of 1500 scanned receipt documents in English which has 4 entities to exact (Invoice Number, Vendor Name, Payer Name and Total Amount). There exist 146 templates for the receipts. Variable templates introduce additional difficulties to the IPR dataset. For both datasets, we assign 70% of each dataset for training, 15% for validation and 15% for the test. The number of text segments varies per document from 100 to 300.

5.2 Baselines

We compare the performance of our system with two BiLSTM-CRF baselines. Baseline I applies BiLSTM-CRF to each text segment, where each text segment is an individual sentence. Baseline II applies the tagging model to the concatenated

Model	VATI	IPR
Baseline I	0.745	0.747
Baseline II	0.854	0.820
BiLSTM-CRF + GCN	0.873	0.836

Table 1: F_1 score. Performance comparisons.

Entities	Baseline I	Baseline II	Our model
Invoice #	0.952	0.961	0.975
Date	0.962	0.963	0.963
Price	0.527	0.910	0.943
Tax	0.584	0.902	0.924
Buyer	0.402	0.797	0.833
Seller	0.681	0.731	0.782

Table 2: F_1 score. Performance comparisons for individual entities from VATI dataset.

document. Text segments in a document are concatenated from left to right and from top to bottom according to (Palm et al., 2017). Baseline II incorporates a one-dimensional textual context to the model.

5.3 Results

We use the F_1 score to evaluate the performances of our model in all experiments. The main results are shown in Table 1. As we can see, our proposed model outperforms both baselines by significant margins. Capturing patterns from VRDs with one-dimensional text sequence is difficult. More specifically, we present performance comparisons of six entities from VATI dataset in Table 2. It can be seen that compared with two baselines, our model performs almost identical on "simple" entities which can be distinguished by the text segment's text feature alone (*i.e.*, Invoice Number and Date) where visual features and context information are not necessary. However, our proposed model clearly outperforms baselines on entities which can not be represented by text alone, such as Price, Tax, Buyer, and Seller.

To further examine the contributions made by each sub-component of the graph convolution network, we perform the following ablation studies. In each study, we exclude visual features (edge embeddings), textual features (node embeddings) and the use of attention mechanism respectively, to see their impacts on F_1 scores on both two datasets. As presented in Table 3, it can be seen that visual features play a critical role in the performance of our model; they lead to more than

Configurations/Datasets	VATI	IPR
Full model	0.873	0.836
w/o vis. features	0.808	0.775
w/o text features	0.871	0.817
w/o attention	0.872	0.821

Table 3: F_1 score. Ablation studies of individual component of graph convolution.

5% performance drop in both datasets. Intuitively, visual features provide more information about contexts of the text segments, so it improves the performance by discriminating between text segments with similar semantic meanings. Moreover, textual features make similar contributions. Furthermore, the attention mechanism shows more effectiveness on variable template datasets, which results in 1.5% performance gains. However, it makes no contribution to fixed layout datasets. We make further discussions on attention in the next section.

5.4 Discussions
5.4.1 Attention Analysis

To better understand how attention works in our model, we study the attention weights (on all other text segments) of each text segment in the document graph. Interestingly, for the VATI dataset, we find that attention weights are usually concentrated on a fixed text segment with strong textual features (the segment contains address information) regardless of the text segment studied. The reason behind that may be attention mechanism tries to find an anchor point of the document, and one anchor is enough as VATI documents all share the same template. Strong textual features help locate the anchor more accurately.

For variable layout documents, more attention is paid to nearby text segments, which reflects the local structure of the document. Specifically, attention weights of the left and upper segments are even higher. Furthermore, segments that contain slot keywords such as "address", "amount" and "name" receive higher attention weights.

5.4.2 The Number of Graph Convolution Layers

Here we evaluate the impact of different numbers of graph convolution layers. In theory, a higher number of layers encodes more information and therefore can model more complex relationships. We perform the experiments on selected entity

Entities	1 layer	2 layer	3 layer
Invoice #	0.959	0.975	0.964
Date	0.960	0.963	0.960
Price	0.931	0.943	0.931
Tax	0.915	0.924	0.917
Buyer	0.829	0.833	0.827
Seller	0.772	0.782	0.775

Table 4: F_1 score. Performance comparisons of different graph convolution layers for individual entities from VATI dataset.

Model	VATI	IPR
BiLSTM-CRF + GCN	0.873	0.836
+ Multi-task	0.881	0.849

Table 5: F_1 score. Effectiveness of multi-task learning approach.

types of the VATI dataset, and the results are presented in Table 4. As we can see, additional layers in the network do not help simple tasks. By simple task, we mean that task achieves high accuracy with single layer graph convolution. However, more layers indeed improve the performances of more difficult tasks. As shown in the table, the optimal number of layers is two for our task, as three layers overfit the model. Ideally, the number of graph convolution layers used should be adaptive to the specific task, of which we leave the study to future works.

5.4.3 Multi-Task Learning

As shown in Table 5, our task benefits from the segment classification task and multi-task learning method in both datasets. The two tasks in our experiments are complementary, and compared with the single task model, the multi-task learning model may have better generalization performance by adopting more information. Furthermore, we find that the multi-task learning helps the training converge much faster.

6 Conclusions and Future Works

This paper studies the problem of entity extraction from VRDs. A graph convolution architecture is proposed to encode text embeddings given visually rich context. BiLSTM-CRF is applied to extract the final results. We manually annotated two real-world datasets of VRDs, and perform comprehensive experiments and analysis. Our system outperforms BiLSTM baselines and presents a novel method for IE from VRDs. Furthermore, we plan to extend the graph convolution framework to other tasks in VRDs, such as document classification.

Acknowledgments

We thank the OCR team of Alibaba Group for providing us OCR service support and anonymous reviewers for their helpful comments.

References

Laura Chiticariu, Yunyao Li, and Frederick R Reiss. 2013. Rule-based information extraction is dead! long live rule-based information extraction systems! In *Proceedings of the 2013 conference on empirical methods in natural language processing*, pages 827–832.

Jason PC Chiu and Eric Nichols. 2016. Named entity recognition with bidirectional lstm-cnns. *Transactions of the Association for Computational Linguistics*, 4:357–370.

Vincent Poulain d'Andecy, Emmanuel Hartmann, and Marçal Rusiñol. 2018. Field extraction by hybrid incremental and a-priori structural templates. In *2018 13th IAPR International Workshop on Document Analysis Systems (DAS)*, pages 251–256. IEEE.

Andreas R Dengel and Bertin Klein. 2002. smartfix: A requirements-driven system for document analysis and understanding. In *International Workshop on Document Analysis Systems*, pages 433–444. Springer.

David K Duvenaud, Dougal Maclaurin, Jorge Iparraguirre, Rafael Bombarell, Timothy Hirzel, Alán Aspuru-Guzik, and Ryan P Adams. 2015. Convolutional networks on graphs for learning molecular fingerprints. In *Advances in neural information processing systems*, pages 2224–2232.

Will Hamilton, Zhitao Ying, and Jure Leskovec. 2017. Inductive representation learning on large graphs. In *Advances in Neural Information Processing Systems*, pages 1024–1034.

Justin Johnson, Agrim Gupta, and Li Fei-Fei. 2018. Image generation from scene graphs. *arXiv preprint*.

Anoop Raveendra Katti, Christian Reisswig, Cordula Guder, Sebastian Brarda, Steffen Bickel, Johannes Höhne, and Jean Baptiste Faddoul. 2018. Chargrid: Towards understanding 2d documents. *arXiv preprint arXiv:1809.08799*.

Alex Kendall, Yarin Gal, and Roberto Cipolla. 2017. Multi-task learning using uncertainty to weigh losses for scene geometry and semantics. *arXiv preprint arXiv:1705.07115*, 3.

Yoon Kim. 2014. Convolutional neural networks for sentence classification. *arXiv preprint arXiv:1408.5882*.

Yoon Kim, Yacine Jernite, David Sontag, and Alexander M Rush. 2016. Character-aware neural language models. In *AAAI*, pages 2741–2749.

Thomas N Kipf and Max Welling. 2016. Semi-supervised classification with graph convolutional networks. *arXiv preprint arXiv:1609.02907*.

Alex Krizhevsky, Ilya Sutskever, and Geoffrey E Hinton. 2012. Imagenet classification with deep convolutional neural networks. In *Advances in neural information processing systems*, pages 1097–1105.

Guillaume Lample, Miguel Ballesteros, Sandeep Subramanian, Kazuya Kawakami, and Chris Dyer. 2016. Neural architectures for named entity recognition. *arXiv preprint arXiv:1603.01360*.

Xuezhe Ma and Eduard Hovy. 2016. End-to-end sequence labeling via bi-directional lstm-cnns-crf. *arXiv preprint arXiv:1603.01354*.

Eric Medvet, Alberto Bartoli, and Giorgio Davanzo. 2011. A probabilistic approach to printed document understanding. *International Journal on Document Analysis and Recognition (IJDAR)*, 14(4):335–347.

Rasmus Berg Palm, Ole Winther, and Florian Laws. 2017. Cloudscan-a configuration-free invoice analysis system using recurrent neural networks. *arXiv preprint arXiv:1708.07403*.

Nanyun Peng, Hoifung Poon, Chris Quirk, Kristina Toutanova, and Wen-tau Yih. 2017. Cross-sentence n-ary relation extraction with graph lstms. *arXiv preprint arXiv:1708.03743*.

Marçal Rusinol, Tayeb Benkhelfallah, and Vincent Poulain dAndecy. 2013. Field extraction from administrative documents by incremental structural templates. In *Document Analysis and Recognition (ICDAR), 2013 12th International Conference on*, pages 1100–1104. IEEE.

Erik F Sang and Jorn Veenstra. 1999. Representing text chunks. In *Proceedings of the ninth conference on European chapter of the Association for Computational Linguistics*, pages 173–179. Association for Computational Linguistics.

Daniel Schuster, Klemens Muthmann, Daniel Esser, Alexander Schill, Michael Berger, Christoph Weidling, Kamil Aliyev, and Andreas Hofmeier. 2013. Intellix–end-user trained information extraction for document archiving. In *2013 12th International Conference on Document Analysis and Recognition*, pages 101–105. IEEE.

Mike Schuster and Kuldip K Paliwal. 1997. Bidirectional recurrent neural networks. *IEEE TRANSACTIONS ON SIGNAL PROCESSING*, 45(11):2673.

Linfeng Song, Yue Zhang, Zhiguo Wang, and Daniel Gildea. 2018. N-ary relation extraction using graph state lstm. *arXiv preprint arXiv:1808.09101*.

Ashish Vaswani, Noam Shazeer, Niki Parmar, Jakob Uszkoreit, Llion Jones, Aidan N Gomez, Łukasz Kaiser, and Illia Polosukhin. 2017. Attention is all you need. In *Advances in Neural Information Processing Systems*, pages 5998–6008.

Petar Veličković, Guillem Cucurull, Arantxa Casanova, Adriana Romero, Pietro Liò, and Yoshua Bengio. 2017. Graph attention networks. *arXiv preprint arXiv:1710.10903*.

Shaolei Wang, Yue Zhang, Wanxiang Che, and Ting Liu. 2018. Joint extraction of entities and relations based on a novel graph scheme. In *IJCAI*, pages 4461–4467.

Kun Xu, Lingfei Wu, Zhiguo Wang, and Vadim Sheinin. 2018. Graph2seq: Graph to sequence learning with attention-based neural networks. *arXiv preprint arXiv:1804.00823*.

Diversifying Reply Suggestions using a Matching-Conditional Variational Autoencoder

Budhaditya Deb　　　　　**Peter Bailey**　　　　　**Milad Shokouhi**

Microsoft Search, Assistance and Intelligence
{budeb, pbailey, milads}@microsoft.com

Abstract

We consider the problem of diversifying automated reply suggestions for a commercial instant-messaging (IM) system (Skype). Our conversation model is a standard matching based information retrieval architecture, which consists of two parallel encoders to project messages and replies into a common feature representation. During inference, we select replies from a fixed response set using nearest neighbors in the feature space. To diversify responses, we formulate the model as a generative latent variable model with Conditional Variational Auto-Encoder (M-CVAE). We propose a constrained-sampling approach to make the variational inference in M-CVAE efficient for our production system. In offline experiments, M-CVAE consistently increased diversity by $\sim 30 - 40\%$ without significant impact on relevance. This translated to a 5% gain in click-rate in our online production system.

1 Introduction

Automated reply suggestions or smart-replies (SR) are increasingly becoming common in many popular applications such as Gmail (2016), Skype (2017), Outlook (2018), LinkedIn (2017), and Facebook Messenger.

Given a message, the problem that SR solves is to suggest short and relevant responses that a person may select with a click to avoid any typing. For example, for a message such as Want to meet up for lunch? an SR system may suggest the following three responses {Sure; No problem!; Ok}. While these are all relevant suggestions, they are semantically equivalent. In this paper, we consider how we can diversify the suggestions such as with {Sure; Sorry I can't; What time?} without losing any relevance. Our hypothesis is that encompassing greater semantic variability and intrinsic diversity will lead to higher click-rates for suggestions.

Smart-reply has been modeled as an sequence-to-sequence (S2S) process (Li et al., 2016; Kannan et al., 2016; Vinyals and Le, 2015) inspired by their success in machine translation. It has also been modeled as an Information Retrieval (IR) task (Henderson et al., 2017). Here, replies are selected from a fixed list of responses, using two parallel *Matching* networks to encode messages and replies in a common representation. Our production system uses such a Matching architecture.

There are several practical factors in favor of the *Matching-IR* approach. Production systems typically maintain a curated response-set (to have better control on the feature and to prevent inappropriate responses) due to which they rarely require a generative model. Moreover, inference is efficient in the matching architecture as vectors for the fixed response set can be pre-computed and hashed for fast lookup. Qualitatively, S2S also tends to generate generic, and sometimes incorrect responses due to label and exposure bias. Solutions for S2S during training (Wiseman and Rush, 2016) and inference (Li et al., 2016) have high overhead. Matching architectures on the other hand, can incorporate a global normalization factor during training to mitigate this issue (Sountsov and Sarawagi, 2016).

In practice we found that the Matching model retrieves responses which are semantically very similar in lexical content and underlying intent as shown in (Table 1). This behavior is not surprising and even expected since we optimize the model as a point estimation on golden message-reply (m-r) pairs. In fact, it illustrates the effectiveness of encoding similar intents in the common feature space. While this leads to individual responses being highly relevant, the model needs to diversify the responses to improve the overall relevance of the set by covering a wider variety of intents. We hypothesize that diversity would improve the click rates in our production system. This is the

Proceedings of NAACL-HLT 2019, pages 40–47
Minneapolis, Minnesota, June 2 - June 7, 2019. ©2019 Association for Computational Linguistics

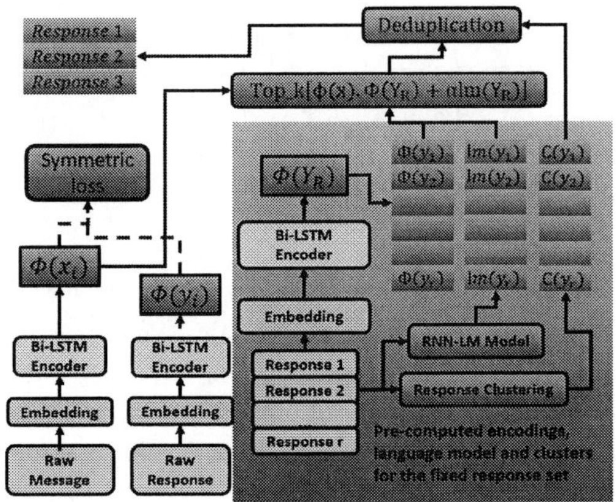

Figure 1: Training and inference graph for *Matching*. During inference, the response side stack is pre-computed (shaded grey).

Message	Matching	M-CVAE
I'm betting on snow tomorrow.	I hope so I hope so too I hope so! I hope so too. I hope so.	I hope so too . As am I. I bet you are. You will not I might too
It's time for me to go to bed.	Go to sleep Go to sleep! Wake up Goodnight Wake up!	Goodnight Night! Same lol Sweet dreams Goodnight!

Table 1: The top responses (without de-duplication) for Matching and M-CVAE.

2 Matching Model

Our training data consists of message reply (m-r) pairs $[x_i, y_i]$ from one-on-one IM conversations[1]. A parallel stack of embedding and bi-directional LSTM layers encodes the raw text of m-r by concatenating the last hidden state of the backward and forward recurrences as $\Phi_X(x_i)$ and $\Phi_Y(y_i)$ (Figure 1). The encodings are trained to map to a common feature representation using the *symmetric-loss*: a probabilistic measure of the similarity as a normalized dot product $\Theta_{x_i y_i} = \Phi_X(x_i) \cdot \Phi_Y(y_i)$ in equation 1. We maximize the $-\ln p(\Theta)$ during training.

Note the denominator in the *symmetric-loss* is different from a softmax (where the marginalization is usually over the y terms) to approximate $p(y_i|x_i)$. Instead, it the sums over each message w.r.t. all responses and vice-versa. This normalization (analogous to a Jaccard index) in both directions enforces stronger constraints for a dialog pair[2]. Thus, it is more appropriate for a conversational model where the goal is *conversation compatibility* rather than *content similarity*. Symmetric loss improved the relevance in our model. We omit the results here, to focus on diversity.

$$p(\Theta_{x_i y_i}) = \frac{e^{\Theta_{x_i y_i}}}{\sum_{y_j} e^{\Theta_{x_i y_j}} + \sum_{x_j} e^{\Theta_{x_j y_i}} - e^{\Theta_{x_i y_i}}} \quad (1)$$

$$S_k(x) = \text{softmax}_k[top_k[\Phi_X(x) \cdot \Phi_Y(Y_R) + \alpha lm(Y_R)]] \quad (2)$$

During inference, we pre-compute the response vectors $\Phi_Y(Y_R)$ for a fixed response set Y_R. We encode an input x as $\Phi_X(x)$, and find the K nearest responses Y_{R_k}, using a score composed of the dot product of $\Phi_X(x)$ and $\Phi_Y(Y_R)$ and a

main focus of this paper. We provide two baselines approaches using lexical clustering and maximal marginal relevance (MMR) for diversification in the Matching model.

Since we typically do not have multiple responses in one-on-one conversational data (and thus cannot train for multiple-intents), we consider a generative Latent Variable Model (LVM) to learn the hidden intents from individual m-r pairs. Our key hypothesis is that intents can be encoded through a latent variable, which can be then be utilized to generate diverse responses.

To this end, we propose the Matching-CVAE (M-CVAE) architecture, which introduces a generative LVM on the Matching-IR model using the neural variational autoencoder (VAE) framework (Kingma and Welling, 2014). M-CVAE is trained to generate the vector representation of the response conditioned on the input message and a stochastic latent variable. During inference we sample responses for a message and use voting to rank candidates. To reduce latency, we propose a constrained sampling strategy for M-CVAE which makes variational inference feasible for production systems. We show that the Matching architecture maintains the relevance advantages and inference-efficiency required for a production system while CVAE allows diversification of responses.

We first describe our current production model and diversification approaches. Next, we present our key contribution: Matching-CVAE. Finally we report on our results from offline and online experiments, including production system performance.

---

[1] Multi-user conversations were difficult to align reliably, given highly restricted access to preserve our users privacy.

[2] Li et al. (2016) made a similar argument with Mutual Information penalty during inference.

language-model penalty $lm(Y_R)^3$ in equation 2. The $lm(Y_R)$ is intended to suppress very specific responses similar to (Henderson et al., 2017). The α parameter is tuned separately on an evaluation set. We de-duplicate the Y_{R_k} candidates and select top three as suggested replies. The training and inference graph is shown in Figure 1.

2.1 Response Diversification

The matching model by itself, retrieves very similar responses as shown in Table 1. Clearly, the responses need to be de-duplicated to improve the quality of suggestions. We present two baseline approaches to increase diversity.

Lexical Clustering (LC): Table 1, motivates the use of simple lexical rules for de-duplication. We cluster responses which only differ in punctuations (`Thanks!`, `Thanks.`), contractions (`cannot:can't`, `okay:ok`), synonyms (`yeah`, `yes`, `ya`) etc. We further refine the clusters by joining responses with one-word edit distance between them (`Thank you so much.` `Thank you very much`) except for negations. During inference, we de-duplicate candidates belonging to the same clusters.

Maximal Marginal Relevance (MMR): As a way to increase the diversity in IR, (Carbonell and Goldstein, 1998) introduced the MMR criterion to penalize the query-document similarity with inter-document similarity to rank candidates using *marginal* relevance.

In the context of the SR, we apply the MMR principle as follows. First, we select the K candidates, (with scores $S_k(x)$ and response vectors $\Phi_Y(Y_{R_k})$) using equation 2. Next, we compute the the novelty N_k (or marginal relevance) of the kth response with respect to the other $K-1$ candidates using equation 3. Finally, we re-rank the candidates using the MMR score computed from equation 4. Our MMR implementation is an approximation of the original (which is iterative). Nevertheless, it allows the ranking in one single forward pass and thus is very efficient in terms of latency.

$$N_k = \frac{1}{K-1} \sum_{j \neq k}^{K} CosSim(\Phi_Y(Y_{R_k}), \Phi_Y(Y_{R_j})) \quad (3)$$

$$MMR_k(x) = \beta S_k(x) - (1-\beta)N_k \quad (4)$$

Table 3 shows that LC and MMR are quite effective at reducing duplicates. We have also ex-plored other clustering approaches using embeddings from unsupervised models, but they were not as effective as LC or MMR.

3 Matching-CVAE (M-CVAE)

Neither MMR nor LC solves the core issue with diversification i.e., learning to suggest diverse responses from individual m-r pairs. Privacy restrictions prevent any access to the underlying training data for explicit annotation and modeling for intents. Instead, we model the hidden intents in individual m-r pairs using a latent variable model (LVM) in M-CVAE.

In M-CVAE we generate a response vector conditioned on the message vector and a stochastic latent vector. The generated response vector is then used to select the corresponding raw response text.

M-CVAE relies on two hypotheses. First, the encoded vectors are accurate distributional indexes for raw text. Second, the latent variable encodes intents (i.e. a manifold assumption that similar intents have the same latent structure). Thus, samples from different latent vectors can be used to generate and select diverse responses within the Matching-IR framework.

We start with a base Matching model which encodes an m-r pair as $\Phi_X(x_i)$ and $\Phi_Y(y_i)$. We assume a stochastic vector z which encodes a latent intent, such that $\Phi_Y(y_i)$ is generated conditioned on $\Phi_X(x_i)$ and z. The purpose of learning the LVM is to maximize the probability of observations Φ_X, Φ_Y by marginalizing over z. This is typically infeasible in a high dimensional space.

Instead, the variational framework seeks to learn a posterior $Q_\phi(z|\Phi_X, \Phi_Y)$ and a generating $p_\varphi(\Phi_Y|\Phi_X, z)$ function to directly approximate the marginals. In the neural variational framework (Kingma and Welling, 2014) and the conditional variant CVAE (Sohn et al., 2015), the functionals Q_ϕ and p_φ are approximated using non-linear neural layers[4], and trained using Stochastic Gradient Variational Bayes (SGVB).

We use two feed forward layers for Q_ϕ and p_φ as shown in equations 5 and 7. Here, $\leftrightarrow$ denotes the concatenation of two vectors. To sample from Q_ϕ, we use the re-parameterization trick of Kingma (2014). First, we encode the input vectors interpreted as mean and variance $[\mu, \sigma^2]$. Next, we transform to a multivariate Gaussian form by

---

[3]We train an LSTM language model on the training data.

[4]Also referred as inference/recognition and reconstruction networks, they appear like an auto-encoder network.

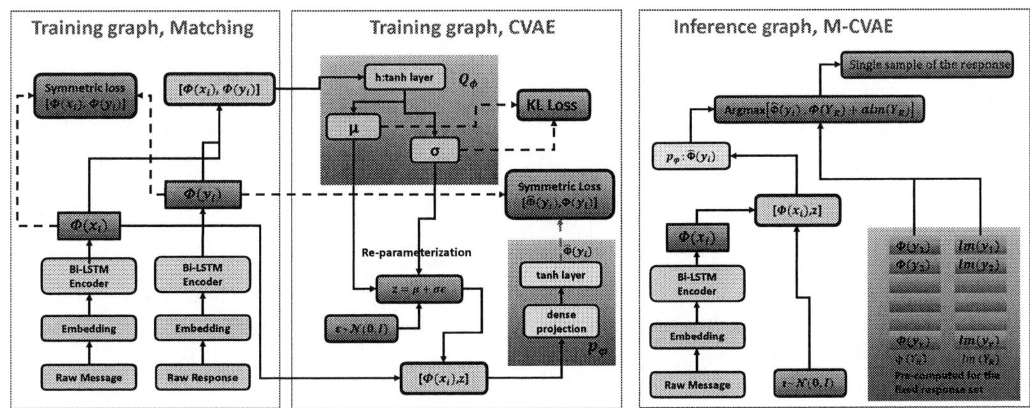

Figure 2: Matching (left) and CVAE (center) training models. Dotted arrows show the inputs to the loss functions. Right side shows the M-CVAE inference network where the shaded region shows the pre-computed values of the fixed response set..

sampling $\varepsilon \sim \mathcal{N}(0, I)$, and apply the linear transformation in equation 6. We reconstruct the response vector as $\hat{\Phi}_Y$ with p_φ (equation 7). Figure 2 shows the complete M-CVAE architecture.

The network is trained with the evidence lower bound objective (ELBO) by conditioning the standard VAE loss with message vector Φ_X in equation 8. The first term can be computed in closed form as it is the KL Divergence between two Normal distributions. The second term denotes the reconstruction loss for the response vector. We compute the reconstruction error using the symmetric loss, $p(\hat{\Phi}_Y(y_i), \Phi_Y(y_i))$ from equation 1 in the training minibatch. As is standard in SGVB, we use only one sample per item during training.

$$h = \tanh\left(w^\phi_{\mu_1} \cdot \overleftrightarrow{\Phi_X \Phi_Y} + b^\phi_{\mu_1}\right)$$
$$\mu = w^\phi_{\mu_2} \cdot h + b^\phi_{\mu_2} \quad (5)$$
$$\sigma = \exp\left((w^\phi_{\sigma_2} \cdot h + b^\phi_{\sigma_2})/2\right)$$

$$z \sim Q_\phi = \mu + \sigma \cdot \varepsilon, \; where \; \varepsilon \sim \mathcal{N}(0, I) \quad (6)$$

$$\hat{\Phi}_Y : p_\varphi = w^\varphi_2 \cdot \tanh\left(w^\varphi_1 \cdot \overleftrightarrow{z\Phi_X} + b^\varphi_1\right) + b^\varphi_2 \quad (7)$$

$$ELBO = -D_{KL}\left[Q_\phi\left(z|\Phi_X, \Phi_Y\right) \| p\left(z|\Phi_X, \Phi_X\right)\right]$$
$$+ E\left[\ln p_\varphi(\Phi_Y|z, \Phi_X)\right] \quad (8)$$

$$Predict : Argmax_{Y_R}[\hat{\Phi}_Y(y_i) \cdot \Phi_Y(Y_R) + lm(Y_R)] \quad (9)$$

3.1 Inference in CVAE

During inference, We pre-compute the response vectors $\Phi_Y(Y_R)$ and $lm(Y_R)$ scores as before. However, instead of matching the message vector with the response vectors, we find the nearest-neighbors of the *generated* response vector, $\hat{\Phi}_Y$ with $\Phi_Y(Y_R)$. We use a sampling and voting strategy to rank the response candidates.

Sampling Responses: To generate $\hat{\Phi}_Y$, we first sample $z \sim \mathcal{N}(0, I)$, concatenate with $\Phi(x)$ and generate $\hat{\Phi}(y)$ with the decoder p_φ from equation 7. The sampling process is shown Figure 2 (right).

Voting Responses: The predicted response sample for a given input and a z sample is given by equation 9. In each sample, a candidate response (argmax) gets the winning vote. We generate a large number of such samples and use the total votes accumulated by responses as a proxy to estimate the likelihood $p(y|x)$. Finally, we use the voting-score to rank the candidates in M-CVAE.

3.2 Constrained sampling in CVAE

To deploy M-CVAE in production we needed to solve two issues. First, generating a large number of samples significantly increased the latency compared to Matching. Reducing the number of samples leads to higher variance where M-CVAE can sometimes select diverse but irrelevant responses (compared to Matching which selects relevant but duplicate responses). We propose a *constrained sampling* strategy which solves both these problems by allowing better trade off between diversity and relevance at a reduced cost.

We note that the latency bottleneck is essentially in the large dot product with pre-computed response vectors (our response set size is ~30k) in equation 9. Here, the number of matrix multiplications for N samples is $600 * 30000 * N$ (with encoding dimension size of 600). However, during the sampling process, only a few relevant candidates actually get a vote. Thus, we can reduce this cost by pre-selecting top K candidates using the Matching score (eq. 2) and then pruning the response vector to the selected K candidates. This *constrains* the dot-product in each sampling step to only K vectors, and reduces the number of matrix multiplications for N samples to $600 * K * N$, where $K \ll 30000$.

By pruning the response set, we are able to fit all the sampling vectors within a single matrix, and apply the entire sampling and voting step as matrix operations in one forward pass through the network. This leads to an extremely efficient graph and allows us to deploy the model in production.

Sampling with MMR: As seen in Table 1, the candidates selected using Matching score can have very low diversity to begin with and can reduce the effectiveness of M-CVAE. To diversify the initial candidates, we can use our MMR ranking approach as follows. We first select top $2K$ responses using Matching and compute the MMR scores from equation 4. Next, we use the MMR scores to select the top K diverse responses for use in constrained sampling in M-CVAE.

All the inference components (Matching, MMR, and constrained sampling), when applied together requires just one forward pass through the network. Thus, we can not only trade-off diversity and relevance, but also control the latency at the same time. Constrained sampling was critical for deploying to production systems.

4 Experiments and Results

Our current production model in Skype is a parallel Matching stack (Figure 1) with embedding size of 320 and 2 Bi-LSTM layers with hidden size of 300 for both messages and replies. The token vocabulary is ~100k (tokens with a minimum frequency of 50 in the training set), and the response set size is ~30k. It selects top 15 candidates and de-duplicates using lexical clustering to suggest three responses. The entire system is implemented on the Cognitive Toolkit (CNTK) which provides efficient training and run-time libraries, particularly suited to RNN based architectures.

We analyze the M-CVAE model in comparison to this production model [5]. The production model is also used as the control for online A/B

---

[5]Since the production model has gone through numerous parameter tuning and flights, we assume it to be a strong baseline to compare with.

testing, so it is natural to use the same model for offline analysis. To train the M-CVAE, we use the base Matching model, freeze its parameters, and then train the CVAE layers on top. We apply a dropout rate of 0.2 after the initial embedding layer (for both Matching and M-CVAE) and use the Adadelta learner for training. We use the loss on a held out validation set for model selection.

Training data: We sample ~100 million pairs of m-r pairs from one-on-one IM conversations. We filter out multi-user and multi-turn conversations since they were difficult to align reliably. We set aside 10% of the data to compute validation losses for model selection. The data is completely eyes-off i.e., neither the training nor the validation set is accessible for eyes-on analysis.

Response set: To generate the response set, we filter replies from the m-r pairs with spam, offensive, and English vocabulary filters and clean them of personally identifiable information. Next, we select top 100k responses based on frequency and then top 30k based on lm-scores. We pre-compute the lm-scores, lexical-clusters and encodings for the response set and embed them inside the inference graphs as shown in Figure 1 and 2.

Evaluation metrics and set: The model predicts three responses per message for which we compute two metrics: *Defects* (a response is deemed incorrect) and *Duplicates* (at least 2 out of 3 responses are semantically similar). We use crowd sourced human judgments with at least 5 judges per sample. Judges are asked to provide a binary *Yes/No* answer on defects and duplicates. Judge consensus (inter annotator agreement) of 4 and above is considered for metrics, with 3 deemed as *no-consensus* (around 5%). Since training/validation sets are not accessible for analysis, we created an *evaluation* set of 2000 messages using crowd sourcing for reporting our metrics.

M-CVAE parameters: We consider three parameters for ablation studies in M-CVAE: size of latent vector z, number of samples s and the response pruning size k for constrained sampling. The results are shown in Table 2. The M-CVAE numbers (row 2 onwards) are relative to the base Matching model in row 1. First, row 2 shows that latent vector size of 256 provides a suitable balance between defects and duplicates, but in general, the size of the latent variable is not a significant factor in performance. Next, in row 3, we see that the response-pruning size k, is an effective

	Fixed params	Ablation	Defects	Duplicates
1. Matching	2-layer BiLSTM	-	7.76	31.66
2. M-CVAE	k=15, s=300 different latent vector size	z = 64	+2.46	-13.39
		z = 128	+0.71	-14.48
		z = 256	+0.24	-11.72
		z = 512	+1.74	-12.62
3. M-CVAE	z=256, s=300 different top k constraint size	k = 15	+0.24	-11.72
		k = 30	+2.82	-14.55
		k = 50	+2.97	-14.93
		k = 100	+3.2	-15.32
		Un-const	+3.26	-15.71
4. M-CVAE	k=15, z=256 different # samples	s = 100	+1.64	-15.77
		s = 200	+1.15	-14.42
		s = 300	+0.24	-11.72
		s = 1000	+0.15	-11.62

Table 2: Relative change in *Defect* and *Duplicate* metrics for different hyper-parameters of M-CVAE w.r.t. to the baseline Matching (row 1). In all cases, M-CVAE significantly reduces duplicates with minor increase in defects w.r.t. to the baseline model. Row highlighted in green is the configuration chosen for online A/B test.

		Matching		M-CVAE	
		Defects	Duplicates	Defects	Duplicates
w/o LC		7.18	48.57	7.46	24.32
+ LC		7.76	31.66	8.00	19.94
+ LC, MMR, β: 0.01		8.33	29.72	9.80	16.98
+ LC, MMR, β: 0.05		9.97	23.29	9.65	15.76
+ LC, MMR, β: 0.1		12.03	19.43	10.18	15.05
+ LC, MMR, β: 0.2		13.25	16.08	11.13	13.64
+ LC, MMR, β: 0.5		13.57	13.25	11.68	12.12

Table 3: Contribution of baseline diversification techniques, LC and MMR on duplicate reduction.

	Common params	Defects	Duplicates
S2S	2 layers LSTM	13.27	22.1
Matching	3 layers, FF	8.70	36.77
Matching	2 layers, BiLSTM	**7.76**	31.66
M-CVAE	S=300, k=15, z=256	8.00	**19.94**

Table 4: Summary metrics comparing architectures.

Architecture	Samples	Top K	Latency (ms)
S2S beam search	-	15 (beam)	207.5
Matching (FF)	-	-	7.12
Matching (BiLSTM)	-	-	9.08
Matching + MMR	-	15	9.6
M-CVAE (un-const)	300	-	99.12
M-CVAE (const)	300	15	10.03
M-CVAE(const)+ MMR	300	30/15	10.67

Table 5: Latency (in ms) in production servers.

control to trade-off defects and duplicates. Thus, constrained sampling not only reduces the latency but also provides quality control required in a production system. In row 4, we see that more samples lead to better metrics but the improvements are marginal beyond 300 samples. In all cases, M-CVAE significantly reduces duplicates (by as much as 40%) without any major increase in defects. We select the model with hyper-parameters $[k = 15, z = 256, s = 300]$ for further analysis.

Diversification with LC: The first two rows of Table 3 analyzes the impact of LC based de-duplication. LC can significantly reduce the duplicates in the base matching model. However, M-CVAE (even without LC) reduces the rates by almost 50% as shown in column 4 in row 1. Using LC as a post processing step after M-CVAE, can give further boosts in diversity (row 2).

Diversification with MMR: Table 3 also reports the impact of MMR re-ranking. For Matching+MMR, duplicates can reduce significantly as we increase the β parameter, but at the cost of increased defects. With MMR+M-CVAE, further diversification can be achieved, and typically at a lower defect rate. This shows the advantage of using M-CVAE which conditions the responses on the message and hence has stronger controls on the relevance than MMR.

Comparison with other architectures: We have considered two other architectures for our SR system. First is a standard S2S with attention (Bahdanau et al., 2014) with equivalent parameters for embedding and LSTMs as our base model, and inference using beam search decoding with width 15. Second, is a feed-forward (instead of an LSTM) based Matching encoder architecture which is equivalent to the one in (Henderson et al., 2017). All models use LC for de-duplication after 15 candidate responses are selected. Table 4 validates our architectural preference towards Matching/Bi-LSTM which has a superior performance in terms of defects.

Inference latency: Architecture choices were also driven by latency requirements in our production system. The results are summarized in Table 5 for different architectures. S2S and unconstrained sampling in M-CVAE were unsuitable for production due to their high latencies. With constrained sampling (including MMR), the latency increases marginally compared to the base model, and allows us to put the model in production.

Online experiments: Offline metrics were used principally for selecting the best candidate models for online A/B experiments. We selected M-CVAE model with parameters [z=256, k=15, s=300] from Table 2. Using our existing production model as the control, and a treatment group consisting of 10% of our IM client users (with

	% Change	P-Value
Overall Click Rate (user level)	+4.71%	0.0003
Position 1 Click Rate	+1.01%	0.5558
Position 2 Click Rate	+10.32%	0.0001
Position 3 Click Rate	+6.71%	0.019

Table 6: Click rates for the M-CVAE flighted model. The control is the Matching model in production.

the same population properties as the control), we conducted an online A/B test for two weeks. Table 6 shows that the click-rate for M-CVAE compared to the Matching model increased by ~5% overall.

Gains were driven by the increase in the 2nd (10.3%) and 3rd (6.7%) suggested reply positions with virtually no impact in the 1st position. This correlates with our offline analysis since M-CVAE typically differs from the base model at these two positions. Intuitively, the three positions point to the *head, torso and tail* intents of responses[6]. Gains at these positions show that M-CVAE extracts diverse responses without sacrificing the relevance of these tail intents.

Driven by these gains, we have switched our production system in Skype to use M-CVAE for 100% of users.

5   Related work

Several researchers have used CVAEs (Sohn et al., 2015) for generating text (Miao et al., 2016; Guu et al., 2018; Bowman et al., 2016), modeling conversations (Park et al., 2018), diversifying responses in dialogues (Zhao et al., 2017; Shen et al., 2017) and improving translations (Schulz et al., 2018). These papers use S2S architectures which we found impractical for production. We demonstrate similar objectives without having to rely on any sequential generative process, in an IR setting.

VAE has been also used in IR (Chaidaroon and Fang, 2017) to generate hash maps for semantically similar documents and top-n recommendation systems (Chen and de Rijke, 2018). In contrast, we demonstrate semantic-diversity in intents in a conversational IR model with M-CVAE.

Novelty and diversity are well-studied problems in IR (Yue and Joachims, 2008; Clarke et al., 2008) where it is assumed that document topics are available (and not latent) during training. Diversification effect as shown in (Chen and Karger, 2006) relies on relevance (click) data, and thus is not

directly applicable in our system. MMR (Carbonell and Goldstein, 1998) is a relevant prior work which we use as a baseline.

6   Conclusions

We formulate the IR-based conversational model as a generative LVM, optimized with the CVAE framework. M-CVAE learns to diversify responses from single m-r pairs without any supervision. Online results show that diversity increases the click rates in our system. Using efficient constrained sampling approach, we have successfully shipped the M-CVAE model to production.

Increase in click rates over millions of users is incredibly hard. We have also experimented with the M-CVAE model trained for suggesting replies to emails in Outlook Web App (significantly different characteristics than IM) and seen similar gains. The results across domains suggests strong generalization properties of the M-CVAE model and validates our hypothesis that increased diversity leads to higher click-rates by encompassing greater semantic variability of intents.

Perhaps the most important quality of the M-CVAE is that response vector can be flexibly conditioned on the input and thus a transduction process. In contrast, in the Matching IR model, response vectors are pre-computed and independent of the input. M-CVAE thus opens up new avenues to improve the quality of responses further through personalization and stylization. This is the subject of future work.

Acknowledgments

We gratefully acknowledge the contributions of Lei Cui, Shashank Jain, Pankaj Gulhane and Naman Mody in different parts of our production system on which this work builds upon. We also thank Chris Quirk and Kieran McDonald for their insightful feedback during the initial development of this work. Finally, we thank our partner teams (Skype, infrastructure, and online experimentation) for their support.

References

Dzmitry Bahdanau, Kyunghyun Cho, and Yoshua Bengio. 2014. Neural Machine Translation by Jointly Learning to Align and Translate. *CoRR*, abs/1409.0473.

Samuel R. Bowman, Luke Vilnis, Oriol Vinyals, Andrew M. Dai, Rafal Józefowicz, and Samy Ben-

---

[6]which was validated by the absolute click rates for each of these positions but not shown in the table

gio. 2016. Generating sentences from a continuous space. In *CoNLL*.

Jaime Carbonell and Jade Goldstein. 1998. The Use of MMR, Diversity-based Reranking for Reordering Documents and Producing Summaries. In *SIGIR*.

Suthee Chaidaroon and Yi Fang. 2017. Neural Variational Inference for Text Processing. In *SIGIR*.

Harry Chen and David R. Karger. 2006. Less is more. Probabilistic models for retrieving fewer relevant documents. In *SIGIR*.

Yifan Chen and Maarten de Rijke. 2018. A Collective Variational Autoencoder for Top-N Recommendation with Side Information. *CoRR*, abs/1807.05730.

Charles L.A. Clarke, Maheedhar Kolla, Gordon V. Cormack, Olga Vechtomova, Azin Ashkan, Stefan Büttcher, and Ian MacKinnon. 2008. Novelty and Diversity in Information Retrieval Evaluation. In *SIGIR*.

CNTK. The Microsoft Cognitive Toolkit. https://www.microsoft.com/en-us/cognitive-toolkit/.

Kelvin Guu, Tatsunori B. Hashimoto, Yonatan Oren, and Percy Liang. 2018. Generating Sentences by Editing Prototypes. *Transactions of the Association of Computational Linguistics*, 6:437–450.

Matthew Henderson, Rami Al-Rfou', Brian Strope, Yun-Hsuan Sung, László Lukács, Ruiqi Guo, Sanjiv Kumar, Balint Miklos, and Ray Kurzweil. 2017. Efficient Natural Language Response Suggestion for Smart Reply. *CoRR*, abs/1705.00652.

Anjuli Kannan, Karol Kurach, Sujith Ravi, Tobias Kaufmann, Andrew Tomkins, Balint Miklos, Gregory S. Corrado, László Lukács, Marina Ganea, Peter Young, and Vivek Ramavajjala. 2016. Smart Reply: Automated Response Suggestion for Email. In *KDD*.

Diederik P. Kingma and Max Welling. 2014. Auto-Encoding Variational Bayes. *ICLR*.

Jiwei Li, Michel Galley, Chris Brockett, Jianfeng Gao, and William B. Dolan. 2016. A Diversity-Promoting Objective Function for Neural Conversation Models. In *HLT-NAACL*.

Yishu Miao, Lei Yu, and Phil Blunsom. 2016. Neural Variational Inference for Text Processing. In *ICML*.

Microsoft. 2018. Designed to be fast - The Outlook on the web user experience gets simpler and more powerful.

Yookoon Park, Jaemin Cho, and Gunhee Kim. 2018. A Hierarchical Latent Structure for Variational Conversation Modeling . In *NAACL*.

Jeff Pasternack and Nimesh Chakravarthi. 2017. Building Smart Replies for Member Messages.

Philip Schulz, Wilker Aziz, and Trevor Cohn. 2018. A Stochastic Decoder for Neural Machine Translation. In *ACL*.

Xiaoyu Shen, Hui Su, Yanran Li, Wenjie Li, Shuzi Niu, Yang Zhao, Akiko Aizawa, and Guoping Long. 2017. A Conditional Variational Framework for Dialog Generation. In *ACL*.

Skype-Team. 2017. Introducing Cortana in Skype.

Kihyuk Sohn, Honglak Lee, and Xinchen Yan. 2015. Learning Structured Output Representation using Deep Conditional Generative Models. In *NIPS*.

Pavel Sountsov and Sunita Sarawagi. 2016. Length bias in Encoder Decoder Models and a Case for Global Conditioning. In *EMNLP*.

Oriol Vinyals and Quoc V. Le. 2015. A Neural Conversational Model. In *ICML Deep Learning Workshop*.

Sam Wiseman and Alexander M. Rush. 2016. Sequence-to-Sequence Learning as Beam-Search Optimization. In *EMNLP*.

Yisong Yue and Thorsten Joachims. 2008. Predicting Diverse Subsets Using Structural SVMs. In *ICML*.

Tiancheng Zhao, Ran Zhao, and Maxine Eskénazi. 2017. Learning Discourse-level Diversity for Neural Dialog Models using Conditional Variational Autoencoders. In *ACL*.

Goal-Oriented End-to-End Conversational Models with Profile Features in a Real-World Setting

Yichao Lu   Manisha Srivastava   Jared Kramer
Heba Elfardy   Andrea Kahn   Song Wang   Vikas Bhardwaj
Amazon
Seattle, WA, USA
{yichaolu,mansri,jaredkra,helfardy,kahna,sonwang,vikab}
@amazon.com

Abstract

End-to-end neural models for goal-oriented conversational systems have become an increasingly active area of research, though results in real-world settings are few. We present real-world results for two issue types in the customer service domain. We train models on historical chat transcripts and test on live contacts using a human-in-the-loop research platform. Additionally, we incorporate customer profile features to assess their impact on model performance. We experiment with two approaches for response generation: (1) sequence-to-sequence generation and (2) template ranking. To test our models, a customer service agent handles live contacts and at each turn we present the top four model responses and allow the agent to select (and optionally edit) one of the suggestions or to type their own. We present results for turn acceptance rate, response coverage, and edit rate based on approximately 600 contacts, as well as qualitative analysis on patterns of turn rejection and edit behavior. Top-4 turn acceptance rate across all models ranges from 63%-80%. Our results suggest that these models are promising for an agent-support application.

1 Introduction

While interest in training conversational models has been steadily increasing, recent research has largely focused on how algorithmic improvements help model performance on fabricated datasets. In this work, we explore how two general approaches to conversational modeling perform on real-world data in a customer service setting, with the goal of developing an application that provides customer service agents with recommended responses to enable them to help customers more quickly.

Conversational systems are typically divided into two broad categories: chit-chat systems (Zhang et al., 2018b; Du et al., 2018) and goal-oriented systems, with the latter designed to accomplish specific tasks such as restaurant reservations (Gupta et al., 2018; Peng et al., 2017). Many of these systems use separate components for dialog state (belief) tracking and natural language generation (Bordes et al., 2016; Liu and Lane, 2017; Wen et al., 2016), while others are end-to-end.

Recent work in end-to-end approaches can be further categorized into sequence-to-sequence models that generate responses word by word (Vinyals and Le, 2015; Serban et al., 2016), and template-based approaches that score pairs of conversation history and candidate response (Liu et al., 2018; Zhou et al., 2018; Kannan et al., 2016). Sequence-to-sequence models are easily scaled to new domains but tend to generate safe, generic responses that may not be effective in helping the user achieve their goal (Baheti et al., 2018; Shao et al., 2017; Zhang et al., 2018a; Li et al., 2016). End-to-end templated models are less expensive to develop than belief tracking systems, but still require domain knowledge and may not cover all situations. As a result, some research has focused on hybrid approaches (Qiu et al., 2017; Serban et al., 2017).

Regardless of the approach, there is a shortage of work investigating the performance of task-oriented conversational systems in a real-world setting. The majority of the literature on task-oriented models describes performance on fabricated datasets, which may not translate to real-world data (Gangadharaiah et al., 2018). Furthermore, research on sequence-to-sequence models often borrows automated evaluation metrics from the Machine Translation literature such as BLEU score (Papineni et al., 2002), which have been shown to correlate only weakly with human judgment (Liu et al., 2016; Novikova et al., 2017). In addition, there has been only limited research

48

Proceedings of NAACL-HLT 2019, pages 48–55
Minneapolis, Minnesota, June 2 - June 7, 2019. ©2019 Association for Computational Linguistics

on using customer profile information to augment textual features in end-to-end conversational models (Zhang et al., 2018b).

In this work, we seek to address these gaps by training task-oriented, multi-turn conversational models for the customer service domain and reporting results on interactions with real customers. Our use case is an agent-support application that recommends responses, similar to the smart reply feature in Gmail (Kannan et al., 2016) and LinkedIn (Pasternack et al., 2017). We incorporate user profile information as features to enable our models to generate relevant, personalized responses. Our research goals are to explore the effect of customer profile features in two different model formulations, and to present a practical comparison of these two general approaches in a real-world setting.

In Section 2, we describe the training data used to develop these models. In Section 3, we describe the end-to-end models we developed, which include both sequence-to-sequence and template-based models. In Section 4, we introduce a research platform for testing our models in a real-world, human-in-the-loop setting, and in Section 5, we report results on conversations with real customers. In Section 6, we describe the impact of profile features, conduct an analysis of rejected and edited turns, and comment on the performance of each type of model. In Section 7, we summarize the conclusions drawn from this work and propose future directions.

2   Data

Our training data consists of historical transcripts from customer service chats handled in English. When a customer begins a chat contact, they are prompted for an initial description of their issue and are then connected to a customer service agent (CSA). We classify these initial utterances into specific customer issues (e.g., *order tracking*, *payment questions*) before connecting the customer to a CSA. These two conversational participants work together to diagnose and resolve the customer's issue(s). Throughout this process, the CSA has access to a wide variety of customer information, such as order status, and internal APIs to execute actions such as canceling or refunding an order. For our experiments, we select the customer issue types *cancel order* and *return refund status*.

Raw text:

Customer: I want to cancel the shoes I ordered yesterday.

Agent: Welcome to Customer Service.

Agent: I am here to help you.

Agent: Give me a moment to look into this.

Training Sample:

Input: **CUSTOMER** I want to cancel the shoes I ordered yesterday. **AGENT** Welcome to Customer Service. **AGENT** I am here to help you. **PROFILE** cancellable, carrier, membership-status. **Output**: Give me a moment to look into this.

Figure 1: Training sample for generative model with profile features. Given raw text and recorded profile features, the training instance is created by appending the turns and profile features while the label is the next agent turn.

In addition to chat transcripts, we experiment with adding particular pieces of customer profile information to our data for the *cancel order* experiments. These data points are similar to the information a CSA accesses when handling a contact. For the *cancel order* related contacts only, we incorporate data points extracted from a customer's profile and details about their orders that are relevant for order cancellation. Specifically, we include the customer's membership status, the order fulfillment method, the shipping carrier, whether the order is a single or multi-item order, and whether the order was eligible for cancellation at the time of contact.

3   Approach

As noted above, our motivation for these experiments is to report real-world results for existing response generation methods and to assess the impact of augmenting our training data with customer profile information. To this end, we train models representing two established response generation strategies: sequence-to-sequence response generation and response ranking. Each model is trained on approximately 5M conversation-response pairs from roughly 350K historical chats related to the specific customer service issue. In this section, we describe our model design and how we incorporate profile information into the system. We train both types of models for the *return refund status* and *cancel order* issue types, but we only add profile information for the latter.

3.1 Response Generation Model

Our response generation models use a transformer-based encoder-decoder model (Vaswani et al., 2017) to create responses. When generating a response at the t-th turn, the encoder takes as input the conversation history $U_t = (u_1, u_2, \ldots, u_t)$, where $u_k = (w_1, w_2, \ldots, w_{n_k})$ is the utterance k with n_k words.

Additionally, since customer profile information is crucial for correctly diagnosing and solving a customer's issue, we incorporate profile features for the *cancel order* response generation model. We do so by appending the profile features to the conversation history and thus the input to the encoder is of the form $[U_t|P]$, where P represents the profile features and $|$ is the concatenation operator.

Figure 1 shows an example of how the conversation is processed for training. Each turn in the conversation history is prepended by a special token to indicate whether it is an agent or a customer turn, and another token is used to separate profile features from dialogue turns. The embeddings of both words in the turns and customer profile features as in Figure 1 are used as an input to the transformer encoder. The output of the encoder, $S = (s_1, s_2, \ldots, s_t)$ where each s_k is a vector of size equal to the dimension of the hidden state of the encoder, is then fed as an input to the decoder together with the target sequence shifted by one word.

3.2 Response Ranking Model

For our response ranking models, the input to the model is a pair consisting of the conversation history with customer profile features and a candidate response. The model outputs a probability of how appropriate a candidate response is given the conversation history. Candidate responses are pulled from a predefined pool of utterances–templates– and ranked based on the probability score. To develop these templates, we use historical chat transcripts between customers and CSAs to come up with a list of approximately 100 templates–50 for each domain–that cover the most common use cases. The advantage of this approach is that it gives us control over how diverse and informative we want our responses to be and allows us to add new templates without having to retrain the model.

This approach uses a hierarchical encoder to encode the context and a separate encoder to encode the response. Each of: (1) last turn, (2)

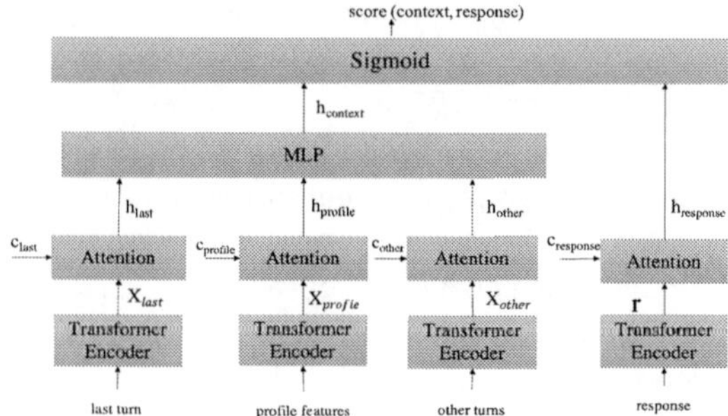

Figure 2: Response Ranking Model Architecture

profile features and (3) the rest of the conversation history are encoded using transformer encoders. The outputs of the transformer encoders ($\mathbf{X}_{last}, \mathbf{X}_{profile}, \mathbf{X}_{other}$) are then passed through a cross attention layer. A separate word context vector ($\mathbf{c}_{last}$, $\mathbf{c}_{profile}$, $\mathbf{c}_{other}$) is passed to each of the cross attention layers. The word context vector can be seen as a high-level representation of a fixed query *"What is the informative word?"* (Yang et al., 2016). Each word context vector is randomly initialized and jointly learned during the training process. The final context encoded vector, given in Equation 1, is the concatenation of the output of the three attention layers passed through a multilayer perceptron.

$$h_{context} = MLP([h_{last}; h_{profile}; h_{other}]) \quad (1)$$

Similar to the context, we use a transformer encoder to encode the candidate response and pass the output through a cross attention layer together with a response context vector c_r. The response context vector is randomly initialized and jointly learned. The classification layer is simply the dot product of the context vector and the response vector followed by a sigmoid activation layer. The output of this layer, given in Equation 2, can be interpreted as how appropriate the candidate response is given the context.

$$score = sigmoid(h_{context} \cdot h_{response}) \quad (2)$$

To create positive training samples, we pair a conversation history with the next agent response. For negative samples, we randomly pick a different conversation history and pair it with the same agent response. Figure 2 shows the architecture of this model.

4 Experimental Setup

We trained response generation and response ranking models using only the conversation history for

Repeat until the contact is resolved:

Every time the customer types into their chat window:

1. E2E model suggests four responses.

   CSA may wait for customer if still typing.

2. CSA selects best response & may choose:

   - to edit response
   - *"None of the above"* & create custom response

3. CSA sends best response

4. CSA may choose to repeat steps 1-3 to send multiple responses before the next customer utterance is issued.

Figure 3: Contact Flow

return refund status. For *cancel order* we trained both model types with and without profile information, giving us a total of 6 experiments. Our experiments were carried out using a human-in-the-loop research platform that CSAs used to resolve live customer contacts. This platform presents the CSA with the standard chat interface but replaces the CSA's text box with a list of suggested responses from a given model. Every time the customer or the CSA enters text into their chat window, our model refreshes the top four recommended next CSA utterances. Because our goal is to make agents more efficient without degrading the customer experience, we allowed agents to edit suggested turns before sending them. Figure 3 shows the conversational flow for each chat contact.

5   Results

We describe the results of our experiments in terms of turn acceptance, defined as the percentage of agent turns for which a model-generated response was accepted by the CSA. We present results for *cancel order* and *return refund status* separately because the issues do not have the same resolution difficulty. Qualitative analysis on reasons for turn rejection and patterns of edit behavior are included in Section 6.

In Table 1, we present results for 613 contacts handled by our models with a human in the loop (approximately 100 contacts per experiment). In each of our experiments, the CSA was shown the top 4 model suggestions at each turn; turn acceptance at 4 refers to the frequency with which the CSA chose one of the suggestions, and turn acceptance at 1 refers to the frequency with which

the CSA chose the highest ranked suggestion. The average number of CSA turns is roughly equal for all experiments.

Turn acceptance at 4 ranges from 63.0% to 80.1%, with the generative+profile model achieving the best performance for *cancel order* and the generative model performing best for *return refund status*. Turn acceptance at 1 ranges from 27.1% to 38.8%, with the ranking+profile model performing best for *cancel order* and the ranking model performing best for *return refund status*. It is possible that turn acceptance at 1 would be higher in a setting where agents were not given 4 choices.

We also look at our models' ability to handle contacts start to finish and report the percentage of contacts for which all or all but one of the agent turns were model-generated. For these metrics, the top performing models are generative+profile for *cancel order* (14.9%) and generative for *return refund status* (26.3%). For both issue types, only a very small number of contacts (<10) had the top recommendation selected for all turns. The average depth of the first rejection (the percentage of turns in the conversation that occurred before the first rejection) was also highest for the generative+profile model for *cancel order* (68%) and the generative model for *return refund status* (48%). We also found that, on average, accepted turns are 4-5 words shorter than rejected ones, suggesting that longer, more complex turns are less likely to be accepted.

6   Analysis & Discussion

In this section, we describe qualitative analysis on observed patterns in edit behavior and turn rejection for each experiment. We also compare the performance of the generative vs. the ranking models and describe the impact of adding profile features to the models.

6.1   Edited Turns

Since we allowed CSAs to edit suggested turns before sending them, we calculated the edit rate and analyzed the nature of edits they performed. Our goals in this analysis were to 1) estimate the percentage of accepted turns that require only minor, stylistic changes, vs. those that require more substantial edits and 2) understand the nature of major edits so we can improve model recommendations in these cases.

	Cancel Order				Check R/R Status	
	Exp.1	Exp.2	Exp.3	Exp.4	Exp.5	Exp.6
	Gen	Gen+profile	Rank	Rank+profile	Gen	Rank
Total contacts	123	74	124	79	114	99
Average number of CSA turns	12.7	9.9	11.2	10.2	11.4	11.4
%Contacts: all turns accepted	8.5	**14.9**	8.9	12.7	**26.3**	11.1
%Contacts: all but 1 turn accepted	21.1	**39.2**	21.8	29.1	**21.9**	16.2
%Contacts: all turns accepted with top recommendation	0.0	**5.4**	0.0	1.3	0.9	**2.0**
Turn acceptance at 4	74.7	**80.1**	63.0	76.3	**75.5**	70.7
Turn acceptance at 1	33.3	37.2	33.7	**38.8**	27.1	**33.2**
Average depth of first rejection (% of contact)	53	**68**	55	60	**48**	47
Median depth of first rejection (% of contact)	50	**67**	50	60	**46**	45
Avg. no. of words in rejected turns	15.5	12.0	14.5	11.0	10.3	13.4
Avg. no. of words in accepted turns	8.5	7.7	7.6	7.3	9.3	7.8

Table 1: Results of the different experiments on both *cancel order* and *return refund status* domains.

We calculated token-level edit distance[1] between suggested and sent turns (see Table 2). We then grouped the accepted turns into three buckets with edit distances of 0, 1-5, and >5, respectively, based on observations that edits of length <5 were more often stylistic and edits of length >5 more often changed the fundamental message.

We further analyzed a random sample of 100 turns with edits of length >5 and found that they fell into four broad categories:

1. The CSA replaced a conversation filler with a more informative response. The suggestion that was edited would not have derailed the conversation, but it also did not directly progress toward the customer's goal. This was particularly common for the generative models. We observe a similar trend in the rejected turns (see Section 6.2).

2. The recommended text provided extra information (which may have been incorrect or redundant) that the CSA deleted. This was observed only for the ranking models and suggests that these models would benefit from shorter templates.

3. The recommended text provided some information but not all, and the CSA needed to edit it to add something. This was observed only for the generative models.

4. The CSA replaced a conversational filler with a different conversational filler. This was ob-

served across both types of models.

One surprising observation was that the number of accepted turns with no edits was greater for the models that did not incorporate profile information. This requires deeper analysis.

6.2 Rejected Turns

We performed a manual analysis of 200 rejected turns across all experiments to understand how we can improve the performance of our models. We found that turn rejections were occasionally caused by real-world constraints that our models were not prepared to handle. For example, in 7% of the cases the CSA needed to reject the model's suggestions in order to send an idle message asking if the customer was still present. In future work, this could be addressed by incorporating idle time as a contextual feature.

Both generative and ranking models were able to handle greetings and closings fairly well. However, the models struggled at times with the crucial turns in our goal-oriented setting: those where the bot must suggest an actual resolution to the customer's issue. As noted above, the average depth of rejection was roughly halfway through the contact. Given that the first quarter of a contact is primarily greetings and the second quarter is typically diagnosis, our models seem to fail most often during the solution phase of the contact. In our analysis, we found that issue breadth is a common cause of turn rejection, with 24% of turn rejection coming from cases such as canceling subscriptions or gift cards instead of physical orders.

---

[1]We use a token-level version of Levenshtein edit distance between the two case-normalized strings after stripping punctuation. Additions, deletions, and substitutions are all counted equally.

	Cancel Order				Check R/R Status	
	Exp.1	Exp.2	Exp.3	Exp.4	Exp.5	Exp.6
	Gen	Gen+profile	Rank	Rank+profile	Gen	Rank
Accept. with no edits (%)	45.5	39.0	42.4	34.5	34.3	42.2
Accept. with edit distance >1 and <5 (%)	26.3	29.4	25.5	22.1	20.7	17.3
Accept. with edit distance >5 (%)	28.2	31.6	32.1	43.5	45.0	40.5

Table 2: Rate of edit distances between accepted and sent turns

An additional 4% of turn rejections occurred when the contact needed to be transferred to a specialist. Providing additional order-specific profile features could help the model navigate these edge cases.

Agent behavior and training was also a major factor in turn acceptance. We found that 16% of rejected turns occurred when the CSA decided to reject the model suggestions in favor of a stylistically different but semantically similar message. We also found that 34% of the turn rejections could have potentially been avoided if the agent had been willing to take sequential turns. For example, the models frequently suggest turns such as *Thanks, just a moment* or *I see*, which the agent rejected in favor of a more goal-oriented statement. However, accepting one of these suggestions would not have interrupted the conversation flow and would have given the model another chance to produce the appropriate suggestion.

6.3 Generative vs. Ranking Models

Across all experiments, the generative models outperformed the ranking models in terms of top-4 turn acceptance rate. The best performing models in terms of per-contact response coverage (all turns accepted and all but 1 turn accepted) and depth of first rejection were also generative models. The ranking models, however, performed best in terms of top-1 turn acceptance. A closer analysis of rejected turns from the generative and ranking models showed that the relatively higher acceptance rate of the generative models came from both greetings/closings and resolution-specific turns. Suggestions from the generative models did lack semantic diversity compared to the ranking models. This is because the generative models perform beam search at the word level as opposed to utterance level for the ranking models. We expected that this would give the ranking models an advantage in turn acceptance rate, but this was not borne out. This may be due to the fact that CSAs seem to reject messages that are too specific or too long; rejecting the entire message and writing a new one is more appealing than editing for longer model suggestions.

6.4 Profile Features

Adding profile features improved both top-1 and top-4 turn acceptance rate for both generative and ranking models. As one would expect, we observed that these features altered the models' suggested responses. When the membership-status feature was positive, the models consistently suggested appropriate greetings such as *Thanks for being a member, how can I help you.* When the cancel-eligible feature was positive, the model was more likely to suggest *Sure. I can cancel the order for you*, and when this feature was negative the model made suggestions such as *I am sorry I cannot cancel your order since your order has shipped and entered the shipping process.*

6.5 User Feedback

Since our goal is to help agents resolve customers' issues more efficiently, we asked agents to provide us with their feedback on the system. The feedback was overwhelmingly positive, with almost all agents reporting that having personalized response recommendations saved them time and that customers were also impressed by how quickly the agents were able to fix their issues. Some agents also reported that they liked that they did not have to type, which suggests that the proposed system could be used as an accessibility tool.

7 Conclusion & Future Work

In this paper, we present experimental results for generative and ranking end-to-end models for real-world goal-oriented conversations. We trained our models using both transcript and customer profile data. Our models achieve a top-4 turn acceptance rate ranging from 63% to 80%, suggesting that these models can be effective in assisting CSAs by recommending text responses as they handle customer chats. Agent feedback on the recommendations from these models has been overwhelmingly positive, and such an agent-support application has the potential to improve customers' experience by enabling agents to assist them more efficiently.

We believe that additional investment in contextual and profile features would improve performance for both model types. In addition, we could improve the performance of the ranking models by modifying their template pools, primarily by adding shorter utterances or splitting longer utterances. In future work, combining output from the generative and the ranking models in a single system could improve overall performance.

Lastly, this work highlights the need for a more mature rubric for analysis of turn rejection and edit reasons. We observed CSAs rejecting and editing turns to add and remove information, and to avoid particular conversational fillers. We also observed model failures due to real-world constraints like customers going idle and issue-specific edge cases. In future work, we plan to develop a more comprehensive annotation guide for error analysis in real-world goal-oriented systems.

References

Ashutosh Baheti, Alan Ritter, Jiwei Li, and Bill Dolan. 2018. Generating more interesting responses in neural conversation models with distributional constraints. In *Proceedings of the 2018 Conference on Empirical Methods in Natural Language Processing.*

Antoine Bordes, Y-Lan Boureau, and Jason Weston. 2016. Learning end-to-end goal-oriented dialog. In *arXiv preprint arXiv:1605.07683.*

Jiachen Du, Wenjie Li, Yulan He, Ruifeng Xu, Lidong Bing, and Xuan Wang. 2018. Variational autoregressive decoder for neural response generation. In *Proceedings of the 2018 Conference on Empirical Methods in Natural Language Processing.*

Rashmi Gangadharaiah, Balakrishnan Narayanaswamy, and Charles Elkan. 2018. What we need to learn if we want to do and not just talk. In *Proceedings of the 2018 Conference of the North American Chapter of the Association for Computational Linguistics: Human Language Technologies, Volume 3 (Industry Papers)*, pages 25–32. Association for Computational Linguistics.

Sonal Gupta, Rushin Shah, Mrinal Mohit, Anuj Kumar, and Mike Lewis. 2018. Semantic parsing for task oriented dialog using hierarchical representations. In *Proceedings of the 2018 Conference on Empirical Methods in Natural Language Processing*, pages 2787–2792.

Anjuli Kannan, Karol Kurach, Sujith Ravi, Tobias Kaufmann, Andrew Tomkins, Balint Miklos, Greg Corrado, Laszlo Lukacs, Marina Ganea, Peter Young, et al. 2016. Smart reply: Automated response suggestion for email. In *Proceedings of the 22nd ACM SIGKDD International Conference on Knowledge Discovery and Data Mining*, pages 955–964. ACM.

Jiwei Li, Michel Galley, Chris Brockett, Jianfeng Gao, and Bill Dolan. 2016. A diversity-promoting objective function for neural conversation models. In *Proceedings of the 2016 Conference of the North American Chapter of the Association for Computational Linguistics: Human Language Technologies*, pages 110–119.

Bing Liu and Ian Lane. 2017. An end-to-end trainable neural network model with belief tracking for task-oriented dialog. In *Interspeech.*

Bing Liu, Gokhan Tur, Dilek Hakkani-Tur, Pararth Shah, and Larry Heck. 2018. Dialogue learning with human teaching and feedback in end-to-end trainable task-oriented dialogue systems. In *Proceedings of the 2018 Conference of the North American Chapter of the Association for Computational Linguistics: Human Language Technologies, Volume 1 (Long Papers)*, pages 2060–2069.

Chia-Wei Liu, Ryan Lowe, Iulian Serban, Mike Noseworthy, Laurent Charlin, and Joelle Pineau. 2016. How not to evaluate your dialogue system: An empirical study of unsupervised evaluation metrics for dialogue response generation. In *Proceedings of the 2016 Conference on Empirical Methods in Natural Language Processing.*

Jekaterina Novikova, Ondřej Dušek, Amanda Cercas Curry, and Verena Rieser. 2017. Why we need new evaluation metrics for NLG. In *Proceedings of the 2017 Conference on Empirical Methods in Natural Language Processing*, pages 2241–2252.

Kishore Papineni, Salim Roukos, Todd Ward, and Wei-Jing Zhu. 2002. BLEU: a method for automatic evaluation of machine translation. In *Proceedings of the 40th annual meeting on association for computational linguistics*, pages 311–318. Association for Computational Linguistics.

Jeff Pasternack, Nimesh Chakravarthi, Adam Leon, Nandeesh Rajashekar, Birjodh Tiwana, and Bing Zhao. 2017. Building smart replies for member messages.

Baolin Peng, Xiujun Li, Lihong Li, Jianfeng Gao, Asli Celikyilmaz, Sungjin Lee, and Kam-Fai Wong. 2017. Composite task-completion dialogue policy learning via hierarchical deep reinforcement learning. In *Proceedings of the 2017 Conference on Empirical Methods in Natural Language Processing.*

Minghui Qiu, Feng-Lin Li, Siyu Wang, Xing Gao, Yan Chen, Weipeng Zhao, Haiqing Chen, Jun Huang, and Wei Chu. 2017. Alime chat: A sequence to sequence and rerank based chatbot engine. In *Proceedings of the 55th Annual Meeting of the Association for Computational Linguistics (Volume 2: Short Papers)*, pages 498–503.

Iulian V Serban, Chinnadhurai Sankar, Mathieu Germain, Saizheng Zhang, Zhouhan Lin, Sandeep Subramanian, Taesup Kim, Michael Pieper, Sarath Chandar, Nan Rosemary Ke, et al. 2017. A deep reinforcement learning chatbot. *arXiv preprint arXiv:1709.02349*.

Iulian Vlad Serban, Alessandro Sordoni, Yoshua Bengio, Aaron C Courville, and Joelle Pineau. 2016. Building end-to-end dialogue systems using generative hierarchical neural network models. In *AAAI*, volume 16, pages 3776–3784.

Yuanlong Shao, Stephan Gouws, Denny Britz, Anna Goldie, Brian Strope, and Ray Kurzweil. 2017. Generating high-quality and informative conversation responses with sequence-to-sequence models. In *Proceedings of the 2017 Conference on Empirical Methods in Natural Language Processing*.

Ashish Vaswani, Noam Shazeer, Niki Parmar, Jakob Uszkoreit, Llion Jones, Aidan N Gomez, Łukasz Kaiser, and Illia Polosukhin. 2017. Attention is all you need. In *Advances in Neural Information Processing Systems*, pages 5998–6008.

Oriol Vinyals and Quoc Le. 2015. A neural conversational model. *arXiv preprint arXiv:1506.05869*.

Tsung-Hsien Wen, David Vandyke, Nikola Mrksic, Milica Gasic, Lina M. Rojas-Barahona, Pei-Hao Su, Stefan Ultes, and Steve Young. 2016. A network-based end-to-end trainable task-oriented dialogue system. In *arXiv preprint arXiv:1604.04562*.

Zichao Yang, Diyi Yang, Chris Dyer, Xiaodong He, Alex Smola, and Eduard Hovy. 2016. Hierarchical attention networks for document classification. In *Proceedings of the 2016 Conference of the North American Chapter of the Association for Computational Linguistics: Human Language Technologies*, pages 1480–1489.

Ruqing Zhang, Jiafeng Guo, Yixing Fan, Yanyan Lan, Jun Xu, and Xueqi Cheng. 2018a. Learning to control the specificity in neural response generation. In *Proceedings of the 56th Annual Meeting of the Association for Computational Linguistics (Volume 1: Long Papers)*.

Saizheng Zhang, Emily Dinan, Jack Urbanek, Arthur Szlam, Douwe Kiela, and Jason Weston. 2018b. Personalizing dialogue agents: I have a dog, do you have pets too? In *Proceedings of the 56th Annual Meeting of the Association for Computational Linguistics (Volume 1: Long Papers)*.

Xiangyang Zhou, Lu Li, Daxiang Dong, Yi Liu, Ying Chen, Wayne Xin Zhao, Dianhai Yu, and Hua Wu. 2018. Multi-turn response selection for chatbots with deep attention matching network. In *Proceedings of the 56th Annual Meeting of the Association for Computational Linguistics (Volume 1: Long Papers)*.

Detecting Customer Complaint Escalation with Recurrent Neural Networks and Manually-Engineered Features

Wei Yang,[1,2] **Luchen Tan,**[2] **Chunwei Lu,**[2] **Anqi Cui,**[2] **Han Li,**[3] **Xi Chen,**[3]
Kun Xiong,[2] **Muzi Wang,**[5] **Ming Li,**[1,2] **Jian Pei,**[3,4] and **Jimmy Lin**[1,2]

[1]University of Waterloo   [2]RSVP.ai   [3]JD.com Inc.
[4]Simon Fraser University   [5]Tsinghua University

Abstract

Consumers dissatisfied with the normal dispute resolution process provided by an e-commerce company's customer service agents have the option of escalating their complaints by filing grievances with a government authority. This paper tackles the challenge of monitoring ongoing text chat dialogues to identify cases where the customer expresses such an intent, providing triage and prioritization for a separate pool of specialized agents specially trained to handle more complex situations. We describe a hybrid model that tackles this challenge by integrating recurrent neural networks with manually-engineered features. Experiments show that both components are complementary and contribute to overall recall, outperforming competitive baselines. A trial online deployment of our model demonstrates its business value in improving customer service.

1   Introduction

Customers today demand a high-quality online shopping experience, which includes prompt redress of their complaints if they are dissatisfied with any aspect of their purchase or feel their rights have been violated. Addressing such complaints is critical to building brand loyalty and preserving a company's online reputation. In most cases, complaints are first expressed to a company's customer service agents. If their dispute resolution efforts are not satisfactory, customers may seek to further escalate the complaint *beyond* the company's representatives: two common escalation scenarios are to publicly complain about their experiences on social media or to file a formal grievance with a government authority such as a consumer protection bureau. Both are obviously detrimental to an e-commerce company.

In this work, we aim to identify cases of the latter, where the customer remains dissatisfied after initial dispute resolution attempts and intends to file a formal grievance with a governmental agency. This is formulated as an online classification problem over text chat dialogues, where our goal is to preempt the escalation of the complaint by connecting the customer with a specialized service agent to intervene and provide a higher level of attention.

Our work makes the following contributions: To our knowledge, we are the first to formalize and examine this problem of identifying complaint escalation. This problem is more challenging than just performing sentiment analysis: plenty of unhappy customers express negative affect in their dialogues without escalating and filing additional grievances. Tackling this challenge requires identifying the *intent* of the customer. Our explorations began with Hierarchical Attention Networks (Yang et al., 2016), which we have adapted and simplified for our task. As with most real-world systems, our final model integrates manually-engineered features, and we show that such explicit features complement latent representations learned by recurrent neural networks. We evaluated our models both on retrospective data and in a trial online deployment. Controlled ablation studies show the contributions of neural as well as non-neural signals, and confirm that our model outperforms competitive baselines. For the academic audience, we discuss factors that impact production deployment: one important message is that despite the effectiveness of neural networks in addressing many NLP tasks, production systems often still depend on hybrid approaches that integrate manual feature engineering.

2   Background and Model Framework

The context of our problem is chat-based customer service for JD.com, a major Chinese e-commerce company. We focus on text chat initially for a

Proceedings of NAACL-HLT 2019, pages 56–63
Minneapolis, Minnesota, June 2 - June 7, 2019. ©2019 Association for Computational Linguistics

A: 您好, 京东客服1234号很高兴为您服务!
(Hi, agent id 1234 from JD.com, happy to assist you!)

C: 我再三和你们说了地址, 结果你们还让我跑去原来的
地址, 这要耽误我多少天
(I've told you the address several times already, but you've
wasted my time by making me go back to the original
address.)

A: 您好, 还麻烦您提供下订单号, 妹子这边给您查询哦～
(Hi, can you please provide me with the order number? I'll
look into this for you!)

C: 有很多单都这样, 问题一直都在. 我们消费者还能不能
维权了.
(The same problem has happened on many orders. I want to
protect my rights as a consumer.)

...

Figure 1: Sample chat dialogue between a service agent
(A) and a customer (C).

few reasons: Many customers, especially younger
ones, prefer text-based interactions as opposed to
speaking with customer service agents. Text chat
avoids confounding errors due to imperfect speech
recognition and provides an easier starting point to
tackle this challenge.

We aim to deploy an automated monitoring system that continuously scans all ongoing chat dialogues in (near) real time to identify customers
who intend to escalate their complaints. Separately, the company has an additional pool of
specialized service agents trained to handle these
more complex cases—these can be viewed as a
finite resource where the monitoring system provides triage, prioritizing the attention of these
agents. An angry customer, for example, might be
contacted separately in an attempt to address his
or her complaint to preempt the filing of additional
grievances. Detecting complaint escalation intents
can be viewed as a prediction problem over dialogue sequences, and our task can be modeled in
terms of maximizing recall at a fixed cutoff, where
the cutoff corresponds to available resources (e.g.,
the number of calls that these specialized service
agents can make in a day).

As a result of this setup, the input to our model
is a moving window of the most recent dialogue
between the customer and the service agent. A
sample is shown in Figure 1, along with English
translations. An obvious starting point is the Hierarchical Attention Network (HAN) of Yang et al.
(2016), originally developed for document classification. The model uses two separate layers of
RNNs with attention mechanisms to encode con-

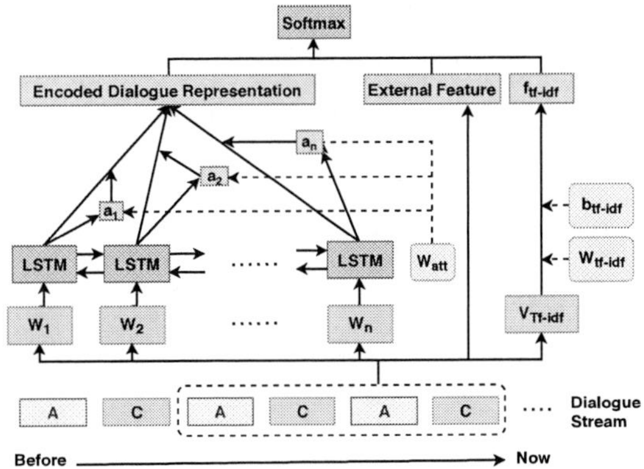

Figure 2: Our full hybrid model for detecting complaint
escalation intents.

text at the word- and sentence-levels, on top of
which a softmax is applied for classification. This
architecture was designed to capture signals at the
sentence level (with the word encoder) and then
integrate evidence across sentences (with the sentence encoder) to model document structure in a
hierarchical manner.

Starting with the HAN architecture, preliminary
experiments revealed an interesting observation—
for our task, hierarchical modeling did not increase classification accuracy, as compared to an
alternative, single-layer architecture. In other
words, we found that a "flat" architecture that
takes as input the concatenation of recent dialogue
(with a special end-of-utterance token) performed
just as well as HAN.

We explain this finding as follows: the sentence-
level encoder attempts to learn from the sequence
of utterances that comprise the chat history, which
does not help in our case since most of the useful signal is concentrated at the end of the dialogue sequence. Thus, the hierarchical structure introduces more parameters without bringing
much benefit. In a production environment, simpler models are preferable to more complex alternatives given comparable accuracy, and thus as a
result, we use this single-layered variant of HAN
as our base model. This is shown on the left side of
Figure 2. However, in a slight tweak from the original HAN design, we use a bidirectional LSTM instead of a bidirectional GRU as the word encoder.
We dub our model "Flat" Attention Network, or
FAN for short.

The base FAN model is then augmented
with several sources of additional signal from

No.	Feature	Mean	λ
1	# of emojis	0.0188	10
2	# of ellipsis marks	0.0001	10
3	# of question marks	0.1348	10
4	# of exclamation marks	0.0152	10
5	# of sentences	0.5577	10
6	# of words	0.3664	100
7	Sentiment score	0.3486	-
8	# of words in TD1	0.0051	10
9	# of words in TD2	0.0834	100

Table 1: Statistics of external textual features used in our complete model. TD1 and TD2 are two term dictionaries.

manually-engineered features. The integration of neural networks with external features in hybrid systems is common in real-world production settings for a few reasons: neural networks are often introduced to improve upon existing solutions, and hence it makes sense to reuse existing components. Manually-engineered features capture aspects of the domain that usually provide an "easy" boost in terms of accuracy. In total, we use nine features, described in Table 1.

Features 1 through 6 are self-explanatory and represent counts of various token types and simple statistics. Feature 7 is the sentiment score from a logistic regression classifier that we have separately trained on social media data. The training data contains 6.981 million Chinese microblog messages (Weibo) with at least one emoji or emoticon. The emojis and emoticons are used as (noisy) sentiment labels, e.g., happy face for positive and sad face for negative. This distant supervision method is widely used in social media (Pak and Paroubek, 2010; Lin and Kolcz, 2012). In our task, all emojis and emoticons are removed from the text during training as they only serve as the labels.

Features 8 and 9 are counts from two term dictionaries, called TD1 and TD2. TD1 contains 121 terms and was manually gathered by examining customer dialogues. TD2 contains $8,712$ terms and was extracted by computing the pointwise KL-divergence (Tan et al., 2016) between the term distributions of positive vs. negative training examples, and then selecting the top words according to this measure. TD1 is a subset of TD2.

All features (except for Feature 7) are normalized by $\min(1, f_{\text{raw}}/\lambda)$, with λ shown in the final column of Table 1. The mean values of the normalized features are shown in the third column.

In addition, we compute the tf-idf representa-

tion of the chat dialogue using only the terms from TD2 as features. From this, we wish to learn an attentive weight for each dimension (i.e., terms in TD2) and a bias parameter as follows:

$$f_{\text{tf-idf}} = W_{\text{tf-idf}} \cdot V_{\text{tf-idf}} + b_{\text{tf-idf}}$$

Finally, the nine external features in Table 1 and $f_{\text{tf-idf}}$ are concatenated to the encoded sentence representation from the base FAN model that is fed into the fully-connected layer and softmax for classification (shown in the right portion of Figure 2). The parameters $W_{\text{tf-idf}}$ and $b_{\text{tf-idf}}$ for $f_{\text{tf-idf}}$ are trained via backpropagation along with the rest of the network.

3 Experimental Setup

3.1 Dataset

For training, we gathered from the enterprise data warehouse chat logs and records of escalated complaints from February 1st to July 10th, 2018. There are approximately three million chat logs (one per customer) per day. For some complaints, we have no record of chat dialogues with the customer; these are cases where, for example, all interactions occurred over the phone. These cases comprise approximately 30% of the complaints, which we removed. This yielded a total of 21k complaints that serve as positive training examples. Of these, 45% were filed within a day after the last contact with customer service, 84% were filed within a week, and 96% within a month. From these numbers, we can see that detecting complaint escalation intents is a very hard problem, since the number of complaints is very small compared to the total volume of customer interactions; we are trying to detect a very rare event.

3.2 Model Training

Applying FAN to our problem requires making a few more design choices, since we are dealing with a dialogue between two parties: Do we take as input only the customer's text, the service agent's text, or both? Preliminary experiments show that, predictably, considering only the agent's text yields low accuracy—but somewhat surprisingly, little is gained from taking *both* the agent's text and the customer's text. We believe that this is because the agent's text contains fewer signals (since they are usually following a script), and given a fixed window size as input, it is better to maximize the amount of text from the customer that the model considers.

For positive training instances we selected the last 100 words from the customer dialogue for each complaint, under the assumption that the last interaction with the customer is the source of the complaint escalation. The window size was determined based on preliminary exploration, and we apply Jieba[1] for word segmentation. In total, we have 21k positive examples. For negative training instances, we randomly sampled dialogue data from customers who did not file a complaint. As we show in our experiments, negative sampling has an impact on the quality of our results.

We pretrained a 300-dimensional embedding for all models using fastText (Bojanowski et al., 2017) on the dialogue data in the training set with ten million negative samples. To regularize the network, we applied a dropout of 0.1 on the normalized attention weights. We used sigmoid cross entropy loss and the Adam optimizer (Kingma and Ba, 2014) to train our model. The dimension of the hidden layer in the final fully-connected network was set to 100. We reserved 10% training data for validation and found that our model reached the best recall on the validation data after three epochs of training, at which point we stopped training.

Our models were evaluated in two different ways: first, retrospectively with dialogue data extracted from the enterprise data warehouse, and second, from an online deployment.

3.3 Baselines

We compared variants of our neural model against a number of baselines:

Logistic Regression (LR): We deployed two variants, one where all tokens (about 40 million) serve as features (called LR-all) and the other where only tokens from our dictionaries (TD1 and TD2) are used (called LR-dict). In both cases, the feature vectors are weighted using tf-idf, and the model was learned using scikit learn[2] with default hyperparameters.

LightGBM:[3] We also tried a tree-based algorithm, using exactly the feature vectors as the LR-dict setting. We set the number of leaves to 32 and the maximum depth to 8. Learning rate is set to 0.2 and the number of iterations is set to 100.

---

[1] https://github.com/fxsjy/jieba
[2] https://scikit-learn.org/
[3] https://github.com/Microsoft/LightGBM

Finally, we evaluated three previous neural network models, using as input the final 100 words from the customer dialogue (the same as our FAN model): fastText (Joulin et al., 2017), CNN (Kim, 2014), and LSTM (Lai et al., 2015).

3.4 Evaluation Metrics

Our classification models are evaluated as follows: We begin by gathering all the complaints filed on a particular evaluation date. The size of this set is denoted as $|C|$, which forms the ground truth for computing recall. Recall at "T-0" is computed by running our model on each customer's chat data on the day the complaint was filed at a particular cutoff K, which we refer to as R_0. Similarly, we run our model on chat data from the day before ("T-1"), two days before ("T-2"), etc. What we call "Total" recall, or R_{tot}, is computed over the union of all these $7 \cdot K$ predictions. The timespan of a week for measuring recall balances the complexity of the calculations with our observation that 84% of escalated complaints are filed within a week from last contact with the customer (See Section 3.1).

Note that our approach of selecting a particular day and looking "backwards" in time for evaluation may seem a bit counter-intuitive. A slightly more natural alternative would be to consider customer dialogues on a particular day and look "forward" in time to see if a complaint has been filed within a week. This, however, does not allow us to accurately compute the ground truth (i.e., the denominator for the recall calculation), because the customer dialogue from "today" might not be the source of the complaint. For example, the customer and the agent might have had a friendly interaction "today", and it was not until "tomorrow" that the customer became dissatisfied with some aspect of the service.

4 Results

4.1 Overall Model Effectiveness

Our main results are shown in Table 2 for data from July 17th, where each row shows the effectiveness of a model. For this evaluation, we ran our model on the last 100 words of customer dialogue at the end of the day, also extracted from the enterprise data warehouse. Here, we measure recall at $K = 3000$. The number of complaints filed on that day, or $|C|$, was 169. As we have discussed before, detecting escalation intents is a

Models	R_0	R_{tot}
LR-dict	25 (14.8%)	49 (29.0%)
LR-all	22 (13.0%)	44 (26.4%)
LightGBM	22 (13.0%)	41 (24.3%)
fastText	12 (7.1%)	24 (14.2%)
CNN	27 (16.0%)	44 (26.0%)
LSTM	25 (14.8%)	52 (30.8%)
FAN_{base}	28 (16.6%)	60 (35.5%)
$FAN_{tf\text{-}idf}$	36 (21.3%)	69 (40.8%)
FAN_{full}	41 (24.3%)	75 (44.4%)

Table 2: Comparisons with baselines on July 17th, where $|C| = 169$.

# Neg	R_0	R_{tot}
10M	43 (25.4%)	73 (43.2%)
5M	42 (24.9%)	73 (43.2%)
1M	37 (21.9%)	72 (42.6%)
0.1M	31 (18.3%)	67 (39.6%)

Table 3: Effects of negative sampling on July 17th data.

Date	R_0	R_{tot}	$|C|$
Jul 17th	41 (24.3%)	75 (44.4%)	169
Jul 18th	30 (17.1%)	57 (32.5%)	175
Jul 19th	43 (23.1%)	87 (46.7%)	186
Jul 20st	34 (24.1%)	65 (46.1%)	141
Jul 21st	37 (38.1%)	46 (47.4%)	97
Jul 22nd	33 (24.6%)	58 (43.3%)	134
Jul 23rd	32 (20.3%)	67 (42.4%)	158
Average	36 (23.6%)	65 (43.0%)	151

Table 4: Recall results over an entire week.

difficult problem because the events are quite rare. The absolute recall numbers are difficult to interpret when attempting to answer the basic question, "Is the classifier good?" The answer to this question, however, becomes very clear when we compare FAN to the other baselines.

We evaluated three separate variants of our model: FAN_{base} contains only the recurrent neural network component, $FAN_{tf\text{-}idf}$ adds the single $f_{tf\text{-}idf}$ feature (which entails learning the weights $W_{tf\text{-}idf}$ for terms in the TD2 term dictionary), and FAN_{full} denotes the complete model (learning $W_{tf\text{-}idf}$ as well as taking advantage of the nine external features). In all model variants, we used 5M negative examples. The FAN base model alone beats all the other models, both those that use neural networks and those that do not. Consistent with the literature on text classification prior to the advent of neural networks, logistic regression is a simple yet strong baseline, especially coupled with feature selection: we see that using terms from the TD2 dictionary as the feature space is better than using all terms.

Looking at the recall of the neural network models, we see that fastText alone does not perform very well, and a generic CNN achieves comparable recall to logistic regression. The biggest difference between the LSTM and the FAN_{base} model is incorporation of attention, and so these results show, consistent with the literature, that attention is very important. Beyond FAN_{base}, we see that other aspects of our model also contribute to its effectiveness. Learning the weights $W_{tf\text{-}idf}$ for terms in our TD2 dictionary alongside the recurrent neural network in an end-to-end fashion boosts recall, and manually-engineered features provide yet another boost on top of that.

4.2 Effects of Negative Sampling

Table 3 shows the impact of negative sampling on recall: Here, we fixed the positive samples and all hyperparameters, and varied the number of negative training examples. Results show that increasing the number of negative examples from 100k to 5M has a noticeable impact on recall; however, there appears to be little gained beyond 5M negative examples. From a practical perspective, the amount of negative sampling determines the training time of the model in a roughly linear manner. For this particular task, it appears that 5M represents a "sweet spot" that balances model quality and training time.

Note that the results of using 5M negative samples in Table 3 are from a different trial than the figures reported in Table 2, thus explaining small differences in results for models trained with the same settings.

4.3 Online Deployment

In Table 4, we report the recall of our model over an entire week (evaluated retrospectively). Other than outliers on July 18th and July 21st, we are able to identify approximately a quarter of all escalated complaints on that day (i.e., R_0), and the recall seems relatively stable.

In moving towards online deployment, we ran a simulation study on the July 17th data, where our classifier was run every 20 minutes on *all* ongoing customer chat dialogues. At each time step, the

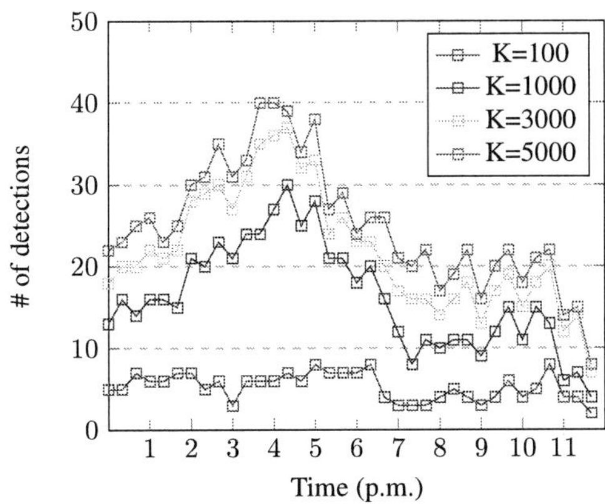

Figure 3: Simulated deployment on July 17th data.

Date	R_0	$|C|$
Oct 8th	52 (21.76%)	239
Oct 9th	59 (21.00%)	281
Oct 10th	54 (25.59%)	211
Oct 11th	63 (25.93%)	243
Oct 12th	50 (28.41%)	176
Oct 13th	30 (25.00%)	120
Oct 14th	43 (27.22%)	158
Average	50 (24.50%)	204

Table 5: Results from the online deployment.

classifier returns $K \in [100, 1000, 3000, 5000]$ results. Simulation output is presented in Figure 3 for the afternoon to evening hours, where the y axis shows the number of *detected* escalated complaints at that time, using all complaints filed over the next week as the ground truth. Note that as we explained above, it is not possible to compute recall because a complaint filed (for example) three days later may be based on a customer interaction that has not happened yet.

Two more caveats are necessary to properly interpret these results: First, classification output at different time steps include duplicates if a dialogue persists over a long period of time, and second, the number of successfully detected cases follows general shopping trends (e.g., late afternoon is when customer service is most active anyway). Although these results are somewhat difficult to interpret, it most closely matches our deployment scenario, since the output of our classifier at regular intervals would feed a priority queue for further enhanced customer service (and this queue would obviously remove duplicates).

Satisfied with the effectiveness of our model, it was deployed on live data starting in October 2018. We present results from a week's worth of data in Table 5. It should be emphasized that these are "real" in-the-wild results from actual online dialogues (whereas all previous results were on retrospective data extracted from the data warehouse). These result are compiled by running our classifier every 20 minutes with $K = 5000$, but R_0 is computed with respect to the union of all results after deduplication (so these values are not directly comparable to previous tables). Also, note that while R_{tot} is useful as a retrospective metric,

it does not make sense to measure in an online setting. In terms of R_0 as a business metric, we estimate that we have improved recall by 12–15% over the previous model, based on comparable reports in July.

5 Related Work and Discussion

Detection of complaint escalation intents is straightforwardly formulated as a text classification problem, which of course has been studied for decades. Prior to the neural wave, popular techniques include Naive Bayes (McCallum and Nigam, 1998) and Support Vector Machines (Joachims, 1998) with feature engineering. There is plethora of work based on CNNs (LeCun et al., 1998; Kim, 2014; Johnson and Zhang, 2015; Conneau et al., 2017) and RNNs (Johnson and Zhang, 2016; Zhou et al., 2015; Socher et al., 2013); attention mechanisms have also been found to be effective (Yang et al., 2016; Du et al., 2017; Du and Huang, 2018).

We readily concede that there are at best minor modeling advances in this work and thus little novelty from a purely academic perspective. However, our primary contribution is to provide a case study to the broader community of how NLP solutions are deployed in production settings. In this respect, we make two points:

First, we feel that many models discussed in the academic literature are too complex for operational deployment: model complexity increases training time, inference latency, and sensitivity to hyperparameters, which can make models unstable, particularly to incoming data that is changing and evolving. This is why we are constantly trying to simplify models without compromising quality—for example, this led to our observation that for our task, hierarchical modeling (Yang et al., 2016) does not seem to contribute tangible value. In production deployments, there are important tradeoffs between complexity, accuracy, and inference latency that need to be considered, and we do not see much discussion along these lines in the academic literature. As an example of the last consideration, taking the last N words of customer dialogue represents a compromise, since our model needs to monitor *all* ongoing dialogues at a particular moment in time (numbering in the tens of thousands).

Second, our deployed model is a mishmash of manually-engineered features, external dictionaries, and multiple neural components. It certainly lacks the "elegance" of end-to-end neural solutions that dominate the literature, but we dare say that most deployed "real world" systems are complex hybrids like ours. Most important business problems are not solved *de novo*: there are usually already-deployed solutions we are trying to improve upon, in which case it makes no sense to ignore existing features and models and start from scratch. In the academic literature, hybrid approaches are under-explored relative to their real-world impact. It would be desirable to see more papers that examine the evolution of approaches from, for example, rule-based systems to manual feature engineering to neural models.

6   Conclusion

There is often a chasm between research and practice, and this is certainly the case for many NLP applications. Through this work, we hope to build a bridge between academic researchers and industrial practitioners by sharing some of our experiences in designing and deploying hybrid models combining neural networks and feature engineering. For the specific problem of detecting customer complaint escalation intents, we have shown that while neural networks have indeed advanced the state of the art, manual feature engineering still contributes to effectiveness and still has its place in the "toolbox" of the practitioner.

References

Piotr Bojanowski, Edouard Grave, Armand Joulin, and Tomas Mikolov. 2017. Enriching word vectors with subword information. *Transactions of the Association for Computational Linguistics*, 5:135–146.

Alexis Conneau, Holger Schwenk, Loïc Barrault, and Yann LeCun. 2017. Very deep convolutional networks for text classification. In *Proceedings of the 15th Conference of the European Chapter of the Association for Computational Linguistics: Volume 1, Long Papers*, pages 1107–1116.

Changshun Du and Lei Huang. 2018. Text classification research with attention-based recurrent neural networks. *International Journal of Computers Communications & Control*, 13(1):50–61.

Jiachen Du, Lin Gui, Ruifeng Xu, and Yulan He. 2017. A convolutional attention model for text classification. In *Proceedings of the National CCF Conference on Natural Language Processing and Chinese Computing*, pages 183–195.

Thorsten Joachims. 1998. Text categorization with support vector machines: Learning with many relevant features. In *Proceedings of the 10th European Conference on Machine Learning*, pages 137–142.

Rie Johnson and Tong Zhang. 2015. Effective use of word order for text categorization with convolutional neural networks. In *Proceedings of the Conference of the North American Chapter of the Association for Computational Linguistics: Human Language Technologies*, pages 103–112.

Rie Johnson and Tong Zhang. 2016. Supervised and semi-supervised text categorization using LSTM for region embeddings. In *Proceedings of the 33rd International Conference on International Conference on Machine Learning*, pages 526–534.

Armand Joulin, Edouard Grave, Piotr Bojanowski, and Tomas Mikolov. 2017. Bag of tricks for efficient text classification. In *Proceedings of the 15th Conference of the European Chapter of the Association for Computational Linguistics: Volume 2, Short Papers*, pages 427–431.

Yoon Kim. 2014. Convolutional neural networks for sentence classification. In *Proceedings of the 2014 Conference on Empirical Methods in Natural Language Processing (EMNLP 2014)*, pages 1746–1751, Doha, Qatar.

Diederik P. Kingma and Jimmy Ba. 2014. Adam: a method for stochastic optimization. *arXiv:1412.6980*.

Siwei Lai, Liheng Xu, Kang Liu, and Jun Zhao. 2015. Recurrent convolutional neural networks for text classification. In *Proceedings of the 29th AAAI Conference on Artificial Intelligence*, pages 2267–2273.

Yann LeCun, Léon Bottou, Yoshua Bengio, and Patrick Haffner. 1998. Gradient-based learning applied to document recognition. *Proceedings of the IEEE*, 86(11):2278–2324.

Jimmy Lin and Alek Kolcz. 2012. Large-scale machine learning at Twitter. In *Proceedings of the ACM SIGMOD International Conference on Management of Data*, pages 793–804.

Andrew McCallum and Kamal Nigam. 1998. A comparison of event models for naive bayes text classification. In *Proceedings of the AAAI Workshop on Learning for Text Categorization*, pages 41–48.

Alexander Pak and Patrick Paroubek. 2010. Twitter as a corpus for sentiment analysis and opinion mining. In *Proceedings of the Seventh Conference on International Language Resources and Evaluation (LREC 2010)*, pages 1320–1326.

Richard Socher, Alex Perelygin, Jean Wu, Jason Chuang, Christopher D. Manning, Andrew Ng, and Christopher Potts. 2013. Recursive deep models for semantic compositionality over a sentiment treebank. In *Proceedings of the 2013 Conference on Empirical Methods in Natural Language Processing*, pages 1631–1642.

Luchen Tan, Adam Roegiest, Charles L.A. Clarke, and Jimmy Lin. 2016. Simple dynamic emission strategies for microblog filtering. In *Proceedings of the 39th International ACM SIGIR conference on Research and Development in Information Retrieval*, pages 1009–1012.

Zichao Yang, Diyi Yang, Chris Dyer, Xiaodong He, Alex Smola, and Eduard Hovy. 2016. Hierarchical attention networks for document classification. In *Proceedings of the Conference of the North American Chapter of the Association for Computational Linguistics: Human Language Technologies*, pages 1480–1489.

Chunting Zhou, Chonglin Sun, Zhiyuan Liu, and Francis Lau. 2015. A C-LSTM neural network for text classification. *arXiv:1511.08630*.

Multi-Modal Generative Adversarial Network for Short Product Title Generation in Mobile E-Commerce

Jian-Guo Zhang,[1] Pengcheng Zou,[2] Zhao Li,[2] Yao Wan,[3]
Xiuming Pan,[2] Yu Gong,[2] Philip S. Yu[1]

[1] University of Illinois at Chicago, USA; [2]Alibaba Group; [3]Zhejiang University, China

{jzhan51,psyu}@uic.edu, wanyao@zju.edu.cn
{xuanwei.zpc,lizhao.lz}@alibaba-inc.com
{xuming.panxm,gongyu.gy}@alibaba-inc.com

Abstract

Nowadays, more and more customers browse and purchase products in favor of using mobile E-Commerce Apps such as Taobao and Amazon. Since merchants are usually inclined to describe redundant and over-informative product titles to attract attentions from customers, it is important to concisely display short product titles on limited screen of mobile phones. To address this discrepancy, previous studies mainly consider textual information of long product titles and lacks of human-like view during training and evaluation process. In this paper, we propose a Multi-Modal Generative Adversarial Network (MM-GAN) for short product title generation in E-Commerce, which innovatively incorporates image information and attribute tags from product, as well as textual information from original long titles. MM-GAN poses short title generation as a reinforcement learning process, where the generated titles are evaluated by the discriminator in a human-like view. Extensive experiments on a large-scale E-Commerce dataset demonstrate that our algorithm outperforms other state-of-the-art methods. Moreover, we deploy our model into a real-world online E-Commerce environment and effectively boost the performance of click through rate and click conversion rate by 1.66% and 1.87%, respectively.

1 Introduction

E-commerce companies such as TaoBao and Amazon put many efforts to improve the user experience of their mobile Apps. For the sake of improving retrieval results by search engines, merchants usually write lengthy, over-informative, and sometimes incorrect titles, e.g., the original product title in Fig. 1 contains more than 20 Chinese words, which may be suitable for PCs. However, these titles are cut down and no more than 10 words can be displayed on a mobile phone with limited screen size varying from 4 to 5.8 inches. Hence, to properly

Figure 1: A product with original long titles (green box), cutoff short titles (red box), the main image (blue box), and attribute tags (yellow box).

display products in mobile screen, it is important to produce succinct short titles to preserve important information of original long titles and accurate descriptions of products.

This problem is related to text summarization, which can be categorized into two classes: extractive (Cao et al., 2016; Miao and Blunsom, 2016; Nallapati et al., 2017) and abstractive (Chen et al., 2016; Chopra et al., 2016; See et al., 2017; Wan et al., 2018) methods. The extractive methods select important words from original titles, while the abstractive methods generate titles by extracting words from original titles or generating new words from data corpus. They usually approximate such goals by predicting the next word given previous predicted words using maximum likelihood estimation (MLE) objective. Despite their successes to a large extent, they suffer from the issue of *exposure bias* (Ranzato et al., 2016). It may cause the models to behave in undesired ways, e.g., generating repetitive or truncated outputs. In addition, predicting next word based on previously generated words will make the learned model lack of human-like

Proceedings of NAACL-HLT 2019, pages 64–72
Minneapolis, Minnesota, June 2 - June 7, 2019. ©2019 Association for Computational Linguistics

holistic view of the whole generated short product titles.

More recent state-of-the-art methods (Gong et al., 2018; Wang et al., 2018) treat short product titles generation as a sentence compression task following attention-based extractive mechanism. They extract key characteristics mainly from original long product titles. However, in real E-Commerce scenario, product titles are usually redundant and over-informative, and sometimes even inaccurate, e.g., long titles of a cloth may include both "å»å|çé (hip-pop|wild)" and "æèº|æ·å (artsy|delicate)" simultaneously. It is a tough task to generate succinct and accurate short titles merely relying on the original titles. Therefore, it is insufficient to regard short title generation as traditional text summarization problem in which original text has already contained complete information.

In this paper, we propose a novel **Multi-Modal Generative Adversarial Network**, named **MM-GAN**, to better generate short product titles. It contains a generator and a discriminator. The generator generates a short product title based on original long titles, with additional information from the corresponding visual image and attribute tags. On the other hand, the discriminator tries to distinguish whether the generated short titles are human-produced or machine-produced in a human-like view. The task is treated as a reinforcement learning problem, in which the quality of a machine-generated short product title depends on its ability to fool the discriminator into believing it is generated by human, and output of the discriminator is a reward for the generator to improve generated quality. The main contributions of this paper can be summarized as follows:

- In this paper, we focus on a fundamental problem existing in the E-Commerce industry, i.e., generating short product titles for mobile E-Commerce Apps. We formulate the problem as a reinforcement learning task;
- We design a multi-modal generative adversarial network to consider multiple modalities of inputs for better short product titles generation in E-commerce;
- To verify the effectiveness of our proposed model, we deploy it into a mobile E-commerce App. Extensive experiments on a large-scale real-world dataset with A/B testing show that our proposed model outperforms state-of-the-art methods.

2   Related Work

Our work is related to text summarization tasks and generative adversarial networks (GANs).

Text Summarization. In terms of text summarization, it mainly includes two categories of approaches: extractive and abstractive methods. Extractive methods produce a text summary by extracting and concatenating several words from original sentence. Whereas abstractive methods generate a text summary based on the original sentence, which usually generate more readable and coherent summaries. Traditional extractive methods such as graphic models (Mihalcea, 2005) and optimization-based models (Woodsend and Lapata, 2010) usually rely on human-engineered features. Recent RNN-based methods (Chopra et al., 2016; Gong et al., 2018; Nallapati et al., 2017; Wang et al., 2018) have become popular in text summarization tasks. Among them, (Gong et al., 2018; Wang et al., 2018) design attention-based neural networks for short product titles generation in E-commerce. (Gong et al., 2018) considers rich semantic features of long product titles. (Wang et al., 2018) designs a multi-task model and uses user searching log data as additional task to facilitate key words extraction from original long titles. However, they mainly consider information from textual long product titles, which sometimes are not enough to select important words and filter out over-informative and irrelevant words from long product titles. In addition, these methods mainly apply MLE objective and predict next word based on previous words. As a consequence, these models usually suffer from *exposure bias* and lack of human-like view.

Generative Adversarial Networks (GANs). GAN is firstly proposed in (Goodfellow et al., 2014), which is designed for generating real-valued, continuous data, and has gained great success in computer vision tasks (Dai et al., 2017; Isola et al., 2017; Ledig et al., 2017). However, applying GANs to discrete scenarios like natural language has encountered many difficulties, since the discrete elements break the differentiability of GANs and prohibit gradients backpropagating from the discriminator to generator. To mitigate these above mentioned issues, SeqGan (Yu et al., 2017) models sequence generation procedure as a sequential decision making process. It applies a policy gradient method to train the generator and discriminator, and shows improvements on multiple generation task such as poem generation and music generation. MaskGan (Fedus et al., 2018) designs a actor-critic reinforcement learning based GAN to improve qualities of text generation through filling in missing texts conditioned on the surrounding context. There are also some other RL based GANs for text generation such as LeakGan (Guo et al., 2017), RankGan (Lin et al., 2017), SentiGan (Wang and Wan, 2018), etc. All above methods are designed for unsupervised text generation tasks. (Li et al., 2017) designs an adversarial learning method for neural dialogue generation. They train a seq2seq model to produce responses and use a discriminator to distinguish whether the responses are human-generated and machine-generated, and showing promising results. It should be noticed that our work differs from other similar tasks such as image captioning (Dai et al., 2017) and visual question answering (Antol et al., 2015). The image captioning can be seen as generating caption from a single modality of input, while the visual question answering mainly focuses on aligning the input image and question to generate a correct answer. In our task, we put more attention on learning more information from the multi-modal input sources (i.e., long product titles, product image and attribute tags) to generate a short product title.

3 Multi-Modal Generative Adversarial Network

In this section, we describe in details the proposed MM-GAN. The problem can be formulated as follows: given an original long product title $L = \{l_1, l_2, ..., l_K\}$ consisted of K Chinese or English words, a single word can be represented in a form like "skirt" in English or "半身裙" in Chinese. With an additional image I and attribute tags $A = \{a_1, a_2, ..., a_M\}$, the model targets at generating a human-like short product title $S = \{s_1, s_2, ..., s_N\}$, where M and N are the number of words in A and S, respectively.

3.1 Multi-Modal Generator

The multi-modal generative model defines a policy of generating short product titles S given original long titles L, with additional information from product image I and attribute tags A. Fig. 2 illustrates the architecture of our proposed multi-modal generator which follows the seq2seq (Sutskever et al., 2014) framework.

Multi-Modal Encoder. As we mentioned be-

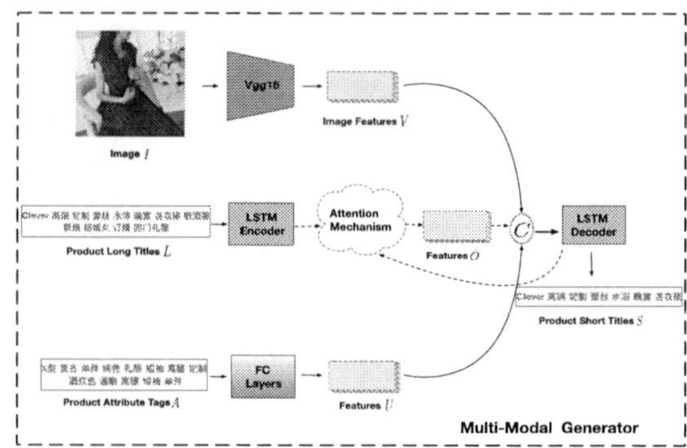

Figure 2: Overall Framework of MM-GAN.

fore, our model tries to incorporate multiple modalities of a product (i.e., product image, attribute tags and long title). To learn the multi-modal embedding of a product, we first adopt a pre-trained VGG16 (Simonyan and Zisserman, 2015) as the CNN architecture to extract features $V = [v_1, v_2, ..., v_Z]$ of an image I from the condensed fully connected layers, where Z is the number of latent features. In order to get more descriptive features, we fine-tune the last 3 layers of VGG16 based on a supervised classification task given classes of products images. Second, we encode the attribute tags A into a fixed-length feature vector $U = [u_1, u_2, \ldots, u_{M'}]$, and $U = f_1(A)$, where f_1 denotes fully connected layers, M' is the output size of f_1. Third, we apply a recurrent neural network to encode the original long titles L as $O = [o_1, o_2, \ldots, o_K]$, where $o_t = f_2(o_{t-1}, l_t)$. Here f_2 represents a non-linear function, and in this paper the LSTM unit (Hochreiter and Schmidhuber, 1997) is adopted.

Decoder. The hidden state h_t for the t-th target word s_t in short product titles S can be calculated as $h_t = f_2(h_{t-1}, s_{t-1}, \hat{o}_t)$. Here we adopt an attention mechanism (Bahdanau et al., 2015) to capture important words from original long titles L. The context vector $\hat{o}_t$ is a weighted sum of hidden states O, which is represented as:

$$\hat{o}_t = \sum_{k=1}^{K} \alpha_{t,k} o_k, \tag{1}$$

where $\alpha_{t,k}$ is the contribution of an input word l_k to the t-th target word using an alignment model g (Bahdanau et al., 2015):

$$\alpha_{t,k} = \frac{\exp(g(h_{t-1}, o_k))}{\sum_{k'=1}^{K} \exp(g(h_{t-1}, o_{k'}))}. \tag{2}$$

After obtaining all features U, V, $\hat{O}$ from A, I and L, respectively, we then concatenate them into the final feature vector:

$$C = \tanh(W[\hat{O}; V; U]), \qquad (3)$$

where W are learnable weights and $[;]$ denotes the concatenation operator.

Finally, C is fed into the LSTM based decoder to predict the probability of generating each target word for short product titles S. As the sequence generation problem can be viewed as a sequence decision making process (Bachman and Precup, 2015), we denote the whole generation process as a policy $\pi(S|C)$.

3.2 Discriminator

The discriminator model D is a binary classifier which takes an input of a generated short product titles S and distinguishes whether it is human-generated or machine-generated. The short product titles are encoded into a vector representation through a two-layer LSTM model, and then fed into a sigmoid function, which returns the probability of the input short product titles being generated by human:

$$R_\phi(S) = sigmoid(W_d\,[LSTM(S)] + b_d), \quad (4)$$

where ϕ are learnable parameters for D, W_d is a weight matrix and b_d is a bias vector.

3.3 End-to-End Training

The multi-modal generator G tries to generate a sequence of tokens S under a policy π and fool the discriminator D via maximizing the reward signal received from D. The objective of G can be formulated as follows:

$$J(\theta) = \mathbb{E}_{S \sim \pi_\theta(S|C)}\left[R_\phi(S)\right], \qquad (5)$$

where θ are learnable parameters for G.

Conventionally, GANs are designed for generating continuous data and thus G is differentiable with continuous parameters guided by the objective function from D (Yu et al., 2017). Unfortunately, it has difficulty in updating parameters through back-propagation when dealing with discrete data in text generation. To solve the problem, we adopt the REINFORCE algorithm (Williams, 1992). Specifically, once the generator reaches the end of a sequence (i.e., $S = S_{1:T}$), it receives a reward $R_\phi(S)$ from D based on the probability of being real.

In text generation, D will provide a reward to G only when the whole sequence has been generated, and no intermediate reward is obtained before the final token of S is generated. This may cause the discriminator to assign a low reward to all tokens in the sequence though some tokens are proper results. To mitigate the issue, we evaluate the reward function by aggregating the N'-time Monte-Carlo simulations (Yu et al., 2017) at each decoding step:

$$R'_\phi(S_{1:t-1}, a' = s_t) \approx \qquad (6)$$

$$\begin{cases} \frac{1}{N'} \sum_{n=1}^{N'} R(S_{1:t}, S_{t+1:N}^{(n)}), & t < N \\ R(S_{1:t-1}, s_t), & t = N, \end{cases}$$

where $\{S_{t+1:N}^{(1)}, \ldots, S_{t+1:N}^{(N')}\}$ is the set of generated short titles, which are sampled from the $t+1$-th decoding step based current state and action. Now we can compute the gradient of the objective function for the generator G:

$$\nabla_\theta J(\theta) \approx \qquad (7)$$

$$\mathbb{E}_{S \sim \pi_\theta(S|C)} \left[\sum_{t=1}^{N} \nabla_\theta \log(\pi_{\theta(s_t|C)}) R'_\phi(S_{1:t-1}, s_t) \right],$$

where ∇_θ is the partial differentiable operator for θ in G, and the reward R'_ϕ is fixed during updating of generator.

The objective function for the discriminator D can be formulated as:

$$\mathbb{E}_{S \sim \mathcal{P}_\theta(S|C)} \left[\log R'_\phi(S|C)\right] - \mathbb{E}_{S \sim \pi_\theta(S|C)} \left[\log R'_\phi(S|C)\right],$$
$$(8)$$

where $S \sim \mathcal{P}_\theta$ and $S \sim \pi_\theta$ denote that S is from human-written sentences and synthesized sentences, respectively.

On training stage, we first pre-train G and D for several steps. Due to the large size of searching space of possible sequences, it is also very important to feed human-generated short product titles to the generator for model updates. Specifically, we follow the Teacher Forcing mechanism (Lamb et al., 2016). In each training step, we first update the generator using machine-generated data with rewards gained from the discriminator, then sample some data from human-generated short product titles and assign a reward of 1 to them, where the generator uses this reward to update parameters. Alg. 1 summarizes the training procedure, where D-steps and G-steps are both set to 1 in this paper.

Algorithm 1: Multi-Modal Generative Adversarial Network

Input: Long product titles L, short titles S, images I, attribute tags A. Multi-modal generator G, discriminator D.

1. Fine-tune last 3 layers of pretrained VGG16 network to get image features V based on a classification task
2. Pretrain G on human-generated data using MLE
3. Pretrain D on human-generated data and machine-generated data
4. **for** *number of training iterations* **do**
5.   **for** $i \leftarrow 1$ **to** *D-steps* **do**
6.   Sample S from human-generated data
7.   Sample $\hat{S} \sim \pi_\theta(\cdot|C)$
8.   Update D on both S and $\hat{S}$
9.   **for** $i \leftarrow 1$ **to** *G-steps* **do**
10.   Sample (L, V, A, S) from human-generated data
11.   Sample $(L, V, A, \hat{S}) \sim \pi_\theta(\cdot|C)$ based on MC search
12.   Compute reward R'_ϕ for $(L, V, A, \hat{S})$ using D
13.   Update G using R'_ϕ based on Eq. (7)
14.   Teacher-Forcing: Update G on (L, V, A, S) using MLE

Data set size	2,403,691
Avg. length of long Titles	13.7
Avg. length of Short Titles	4.5
Avg. length of Attributes Tags	18.3
Avg. number of Image	1

Table 1: Statistics of the crawled dataset. Here all the lengths are counted by Chinese or English words.

4 Experiments

4.1 Experimental Setup

Dataset. The dataset used in our experiment is crawled from a module named 有好货 (Youhaohuo) of the well-known 淘宝 (TAOBAO) platform in China. Every product in the dataset includes a long product title and a short product title written by professional writers, along with product several high quality visual images and attributes tags, here for each product we use its main image. This Youhaohuo module includes more than 100 categories of products, we crawled top 7 categories of them in the module, and exclude the products with original long titles shorter than 10 Chinese characters. We further tokenize the original long tittles and short titles into Chinese or English words, e.g. "skirt" is a word in English and 半身裙 is a word in Chinese. Table 1 shows some details of the dataset. We randomly select 1.6M samples for training, 0.2M samples for validation, and test our proposed model on 5000 samples.

Baselines. We compare our proposed model with the following four baselines: (a) Pointer Network (**Ptr-Net**) (See et al., 2017) which is a seq2seq based framework with pointer-generator network copying words from the source text via *pointing*. (b) Feature-Enriched-Net (**FE-Net**) (Gong et al., 2018) which is a deep and wide model based on attentive RNN to generate the textual long product titles. (c) Agreement-based MTL (**Agree-MTL**) (Wang et al., 2018) which is a multi-task learning approach to improve product title compression with user searching log data. (d) Generative Adversarial Network (**GAN**) (Li et al., 2017) which is a generative adversarial method for text generation with only one modality of input.

Implementation Details. We first pre-train the multi-modal generative model given human-generated data via maximum likelihood estimation (MLE), and we transfer the pretrained model weights for the multi-modal encoder and decoder modules. Then we pre-train the discriminator using human-generated data and machine-generated data. To get training samples for the discriminator, we sample half of data from multi-modal generator and another half from human-generated data. After that, we perform normal training process based on pre-trained MM-GAN.

Specifically, we create a vocabulary of 35K words for long product titles and short titles, and another vocabulary of 35k for attribute tags in training data with size of 1.6M. Words appear less than 8 times in the training set are replaced as <UNK>. We implement a two-layer LSTM with 100 hidden states to encoder attribute tags, and all other LSTMs in our model are two layers with 512 hidden states. The last 3 layers of the pre-trained VGG16 network are fine tuned based on the products visual images with 7 classes. The Adam optimizer (Kingma and Ba, 2015) is initialized with a learning rate 10^{-3}. The multi-modal generator and discriminator are pre-trained for 10000 steps, the normal training steps are set to 13000, the batch size is set to 512 for the discriminator and 256 for the generator, the MC search time is set to 7.

4.2 Automatic Evaluation

To evaluate the quality of generated product short titles, we follow (Wang et al., 2018; Gong et al., 2018) and use standard recall-oriented ROUGE metric (Lin, 2004), which measures the generated quality by counting the overlap of N-grams be-

Models	Ptr-Net	FE-Net	Agree-MTL	GAN	MM-GAN
ROUGE-1	59.21	61.07	66.19	60.67	**69.53**
ROUGE-2	42.01	44.16	49.39	46.46	**52.38**
ROUGE-L	57.12	58.00	64.04	60.27	**65.80**

Table 2: ROUGE performance of different models on the test set.

	Data	Methods	Results
Product Long Titles	Artka 阿卡 夏新 花边 镂空 荷叶边 抽绳 民族 狂野 复古 衬衫 S110061Q (Artka Artka summer lace hollow-out flounce drawstring nation wild retro shirt S110061Q)	FE-Net	阿卡 花边 镂空 荷叶边 衬衫 (Artka lace hollow-out flounce shirt)
Image Attributes Tags	修身 常规款 圆领 Artka 米白 长袖 套头 复古 通勤 纯色 夏季 喇叭袖 棉 (slim common round-neck Artka off-white long-sleeve pullover retro commuting plain summer flare-sleeve cotton)	Agree-MTL	Artka 阿卡 夏新 花边 镂空 荷叶边 衬衫 (Artka Artka summer lace hollow-out flounce shirt)
		GAN	Artka 荷叶边 抽绳 衬衫 (Artka lace flounce drawstring shirt)
		MM-GAN	Artka 花边 荷叶边 镂空 复古 衬衫 (Artka lace flounce hollow-out retro shirt)

Table 3: The comparison of generated short titles among different methods.

tween the machine-generated and human- generated titles. Here we consider ROUGE-1 (1-gram), ROUGE-2 (bi-grams), ROUGE-L (longest common subsequence). Experimental results on the test set are shown in Table 2. From this table, we note that our proposed MM-GAN achieves best performance on three metrics. Furthermore, when comparing MM-GAN with GAN, we can see that our proposed MM-GAN achieves an improvement of 8.86%, 5.92%, 5.53%, in terms of ROUGE-1, ROUGE-2, ROUGE-3, respectively. This verifies that additional information such as image and attribute tags from product can absolutely facilitate our model to generate better short titles. In addition, compared with the best model Agree-MTL, MM-GAN improves ROUGE-1, ROUGE-2, ROUGE-L by 3.34%, 2.99%, 1.76%, respectively. We attribute the outperformance of MM-GAN to two facts: (a) it incorporates multiple sources, containing more information than other single-source based models. (b) it applies a discriminator to distinguish whether a product short titles are human-generated or machine-generated, which makes the model evaluate the generated sequence in a human-like view, and naturally avoid exposure bias in other methods.

4.3 Online A/B Testing

In order to further verify the effectiveness of MM-GAN, we test our method in the real-world online environment of the TaoBao App.

We perform A/B testing in seven categories of products in the E-commerce App, i.e., "连衣裙| (one-piece)", "男士T恤| (Man T-shirt), "衬衫| (shirt)", "休闲裤| (Casual pants)", "女士T恤 | (Woman T-shirt)", "半身裙| (skirt)", "毛针织衫| (Sweaters)". During online A/B testing, users (3×10^6 users per day) are split equally into two groups and are directed into a baseline bucket and an experimental bucket. For users in the baseline bucket, product short titles are generated by the default online system, following an ILP based method (Clarke and Lapata, 2008). While for users in the experimental bucket, product short titles are generated by MM-GAN. All conditions in the two buckets are identical except for short titles generation methods. We apply Click Through Rate (CTR) and Click Conversion Rate (CVR) to measure the performance. $CTR = \frac{\#click\_of\_product}{\#pv\_of\_product}$, and $CVR = \frac{\#trade\_of\_product}{\#click\_of\_product}$, where $\#click\_of\_product$ indicates clicking times of a product, $\#pv\_of\_product$ is the number of page views of the product and $\#trade\_of\_product$ is the number of purchases of the product.

We deploy A/B testing for 7 days and calculate overall CTR for all products in the baseline bucket and experimental bucket. MM-GAN improves CTR by 1.66% and CVR by 1.87% in the experimental bucket over the default online system in the baseline bucket. It verifies the effectiveness of our proposed method. Moreover, through online A/B testing, we find that with more readable, informative product short titles, users are more likely to click, view and purchase corresponding products, which indicates good short product titles can help improving the product sales on E-commerce Apps.

4.4 Qualitative Analysis

Table 3 shows a sample of product short titles generated by MM-GAN and baselines.

From this table, we can note that (a) product

Figure 3: Some samples generated by MM-GAN.

short titles generated by our model are more fluent, informative than baselines, and core product words (e.g., "Artka| (阿卡)", "复古| (retro)", "衬衫| (shirt)") can be recognized. (b) There are over-informative words (e.g., 阿卡| (Artka)", "S110061Q") and irrelevant words (e.g., "狂野| (wild)") in product long titles. Over-informative words may disturb model's generation process, irrelevant words may give incorrect information to the model. These situations could happen in real E-commerce environment. FE-Net misses the English brand name "Artka" and gives its Chinese name '阿卡" instead. Agree-MTL using user searching log data performs better than GAN. However, Agree-MTL still generates the over-informative word '阿卡". MM-GAN outperforms all baselines, information in additional attribute tags such as "复古| (retro)", "Artka"), and other information from the product main image are together considered by the model and help the model select core words and filter out irrelevant words in generated product short titles. It shows that MM-GAN using different types of inputs can help generate better product short titles. To leave a deeper impression on the performance of our proposed model, we also put more online samples generated by the MM-GAN in a module of the TaoBao App, as shown in Fig. 3. From all generated samples we also find few bad cases which are not shown online (e.g., repetitive words in the generated short titles, wrong generated words which are not related to the product at all), leaving a great space for further improvement.

5 Conclusion

In this paper, we propose a multi-modal generative adversarial network for short product title generation in E-commerce. Different from conventional methods which only consider textual information from long product titles, we design a multi-modal generative model to incorporate additional information from product image and attribute tags. Extensive experiments on a large real-world E-commerce dataset verify the effectiveness of our proposed model when comparing with several state-of-the-art baselines. Moreover, the online deployment in a real environment of an E-commerce app shows that our method can improve the click through rate and click conversion rate.

6 Acknowledgement

This work is supported in part by NSF through grants IIS-1526499, IIS-1763325, and CNS-1626432, and NSFC 61672313. We thank the anonymous reviewers for their valuable comments.

References

Stanislaw Antol, Aishwarya Agrawal, Jiasen Lu, Margaret Mitchell, Dhruv Batra, C Lawrence Zitnick, and Devi Parikh. 2015. Vqa: Visual question answering. In *ICCV*.

Philip Bachman and Doina Precup. 2015. Data generation as sequential decision making. In *NIPS*.

Dzmitry Bahdanau, Kyunghyun Cho, and Yoshua Bengio. 2015. Neural machine translation by jointly learning to align and translate. In *ICLR*.

Ziqiang Cao, Wenjie Li, Sujian Li, Furu Wei, and Yanran Li. 2016. Attsum: Joint learning of focusing and summarization with neural attention. In *COLING*.

Qian Chen, Xiaodan Zhu, Zhenhua Ling, Si Wei, and Hui Jiang. 2016. Distraction-based neural networks for document summarization. In *IJCAI*.

Sumit Chopra, Michael Auli, and Alexander M Rush. 2016. Abstractive sentence summarization with attentive recurrent neural networks. In *NAACL-HLT*.

James Clarke and Mirella Lapata. 2008. Global inference for sentence compression: An integer linear programming approach. *Journal of Artificial Intelligence Research*.

Bo Dai, Sanja Fidler, Raquel Urtasun, and Dahua Lin. 2017. Towards diverse and natural image descriptions via a conditional gan. In *ICCV*.

William Fedus, Ian Goodfellow, and Andrew M Dai. 2018. Maskgan: Better text generation via filling in the _. In *ICLR*.

Yu Gong, Xusheng Luo, Kenny Q Zhu, Shichen Liu, and Wenwu Ou. 2018. Automatic generation of chinese short product titles for mobile display. In *IAAI*.

Ian Goodfellow, Jean Pouget-Abadie, Mehdi Mirza, Bing Xu, David Warde-Farley, Sherjil Ozair, Aaron Courville, and Yoshua Bengio. 2014. Generative adversarial nets. In *NIPS*.

Jiaxian Guo, Sidi Lu, Han Cai, Weinan Zhang, Yong Yu, and Jun Wang. 2017. Long text generation via adversarial training with leaked information. In *AAAI*.

Sepp Hochreiter and Jürgen Schmidhuber. 1997. Long short-term memory. *Neural computation*.

Phillip Isola, Jun-Yan Zhu, Tinghui Zhou, and Alexei A Efros. 2017. Image-to-image translation with conditional adversarial networks. In *ICCV*.

Diederik P Kingma and Jimmy Ba. 2015. Adam: A method for stochastic optimization. In *ICLR*.

Alex M Lamb, Anirudh Goyal ALIAS PARTH GOYAL, Ying Zhang, Saizheng Zhang, Aaron C Courville, and Yoshua Bengio. 2016. Professor forcing: A new algorithm for training recurrent networks. In *NIPS*.

Christian Ledig, Lucas Theis, Ferenc Huszár, Jose Caballero, Andrew Cunningham, Alejandro Acosta, Andrew P Aitken, Alykhan Tejani, Johannes Totz, Zehan Wang, et al. 2017. Photo-realistic single image super-resolution using a generative adversarial network. In *CVPR*.

Jiwei Li, Will Monroe, Tianlin Shi, Sébastien Jean, Alan Ritter, and Dan Jurafsky. 2017. Adversarial learning for neural dialogue generation. In *EMNLP*.

Chin-Yew Lin. 2004. Rouge: A package for automatic evaluation of summaries. *Text Summarization Branches Out*.

Kevin Lin, Dianqi Li, Xiaodong He, Zhengyou Zhang, and Ming-Ting Sun. 2017. Adversarial ranking for language generation. In *NIPS*.

Yishu Miao and Phil Blunsom. 2016. Language as a latent variable: Discrete generative models for sentence compression. In *EMNLP*.

Rada Mihalcea. 2005. Language independent extractive summarization. In *ACL*.

Ramesh Nallapati, Feifei Zhai, and Bowen Zhou. 2017. Summarunner: A recurrent neural network based sequence model for extractive summarization of documents. In *AAAI*.

Marc'Aurelio Ranzato, Sumit Chopra, Michael Auli, and Wojciech Zaremba. 2016. Sequence level training with recurrent neural networks. In *ICLR*.

Abigail See, Peter J Liu, and Christopher D Manning. 2017. Get to the point: Summarization with pointer-generator networks. In *ACL*.

Karen Simonyan and Andrew Zisserman. 2015. Very deep convolutional networks for large-scale image recognition. In *ICLR*.

Ilya Sutskever, Oriol Vinyals, and Quoc V Le. 2014. Sequence to sequence learning with neural networks. In *NIPS*.

Yao Wan, Zhou Zhao, Min Yang, Guandong Xu, Haochao Ying, Jian Wu, and Philip S Yu. 2018. Improving automatic source code summarization via deep reinforcement learning. In *Proceedings of the 33rd ACM/IEEE International Conference on Automated Software Engineering*, pages 397–407. ACM.

Jingang Wang, Junfeng Tian, Long Qiu, Sheng Li, Jun Lang, Luo Si, and Man Lan. 2018. A multi-task learning approach for improving product title compression with user search log data. In *AAAI*.

Ke Wang and Xiaojun Wan. 2018. Sentigan: Generating sentimental texts via mixture adversarial networks. In *IJCAI*.

Ronald J Williams. 1992. Simple statistical gradient-following algorithms for connectionist reinforcement learning. *Machine learning*.

Kristian Woodsend and Mirella Lapata. 2010. Automatic generation of story highlights. In *ACL*.

Lantao Yu, Weinan Zhang, Jun Wang, and Yong Yu. 2017. Seqgan: Sequence generative adversarial nets with policy gradient. In *AAAI*.

A Case Study on Neural Headline Generation for Editing Support

Kazuma Murao[*†], **Ken Kobayashi**[*†], **Hayato Kobayashi**[†‡],

Taichi Yatsuka[†], **Takeshi Masuyama**[†], **Tatsuru Higurashi**[†], **Yoshimune Tabuchi**[†]

[†]Yahoo Japan Corporation   [‡]RIKEN AIP

{kmurao,kenkoba,hakobaya}@yahoo-corp.jp

{tyatsuka,tamasuya,thiguras,yotabuch}@yahoo-corp.jp

Abstract

There have been many studies on neural headline generation models trained with a lot of (article, headline) pairs. However, there are few situations for putting such models into practical use in the real world since news articles typically already have corresponding headlines. In this paper, we describe a practical use case of neural headline generation in a news aggregator, where dozens of professional editors constantly select important news articles and manually create their headlines, which are much shorter than the original headlines. Specifically, we show how to deploy our model to an editing support tool and report the results of comparing the behavior of the editors before and after the release.

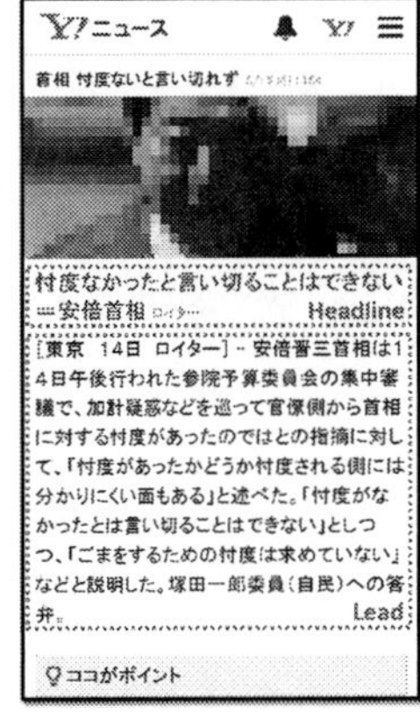

(a) List of news topics including short titles.

(b) Page of news entry including headline and lead.

Figure 1: News-aggregator of Yahoo! JAPAN.

1 Introduction

A news-aggregator is a website or mobile application that aggregates a large amount of web content, e.g., online newspapers provided by different publishers. The main purpose of such a service is to help users obtain important news out of vast amounts of information quickly and easily. Therefore, it is critical to consider how to compactly show news, as well as what type of news to select, to improve service quality. In fact, the news-aggregator of Yahoo! JAPAN[1], the largest Japanese portal site, is supported by dozens of professional editors who constantly select important news articles and manually create their new headlines called *short titles*, which are much shorter than the original headline, to construct a news-topic list. Note that we use the term "title" to avoid confusion with the original news headline, although they are similar concepts.

Figure 1 shows screenshots of the news-aggregator of Yahoo! JAPAN, where the English translations of the short title, headline and lead are listed in Table 1. The left figure (a) shows the list of news topics (important news articles), which includes short titles, and the right figure (b) shows the entry page of the first topic in the list, which consists of a headline and lead. The lead is a short version of the article and can be used by users to decide whether to read the whole article. The editors' job is to create a short title from news content including the headline and lead. A short title has two advantages over a normal headline; one is quick understandability of the content and the other is saving display space by using a single line. This means that short titles can increase a user's chances of reaching interesting articles. Since the click-through rate of news articles is directly related to ad revenue, even a small improvement in short titles has a significant impact on business.

We tackle an automatic-generation task of such short titles for a news aggregator to support the

---

[*]Both authors contributed equally to this work.

[1]https://www.yahoo.co.jp/

Proceedings of NAACL-HLT 2019, pages 73–82

Minneapolis, Minnesota, June 2 - June 7, 2019. ©2019 Association for Computational Linguistics

	Japanese	English translation
Short title	首相 忖度ないと言い切れず	The prime minister cannot say that there is no surmise.
Headline	忖度なかったと言い切ることはできない＝加計問題で安倍首相	It cannot be said that there is no "sontaku (surmise)" with absolute certainty. The prime minister Abe said about the problem of "Kake Gakuen (Kake school)".
Lead	安倍晋三首相は１４日午後行われた参院予算委員会の集中審議で、加計疑惑などを巡り、官僚側から首相に対する忖度（そんたく）があったのではとの指摘に対して「忖度があったかどうか、忖度される側には分かりにくい面もある」と述べた。「忖度がなかったと言い切ることはできない」としつつ、「ごまをするための忖度は求めていない」などと説明した。塚田一郎委員（自民）への答弁。	Prime Minister Shinzo Abe said, in an intensive deliberation with the House of Councilors Budget Committee held on the afternoon of the 14th, as an answer to a question about whether bureaucrats surmised to the prime minister regarding the Kake suspicion, "It is difficult to understand whether there is a sontaku (surmise)". He said "It cannot be said that there was nothing wrong," while explaining that "I do not need to be obsequious". An answer to Ichiro Tsukada (LDP).

Table 1: Short title, headline, and lead in Figure 1(b) with English versions.

editorial process. Our task is a variant of news-headline generation, which has been extensively studied, as described in Section 6. A clear difference between their task and ours is that we need to generate short titles from news content including headlines. Thus, we formulate our task as an abstractive summarization from multiple information sources, i.e., headlines and leads, based on an encoder-decoder model (Section 2).

There are roughly three approaches for handling multiple information sources. The first approach is to merge all sources with some weights based on the importance of each source, which can be achieved by a weighted average of the context vectors, as in multimodal summarization (Hori et al., 2017). This is the most general approach since the other two can also be regarded as special cases of the weighted average. The second approach is to use one source as the main source and others as secondary ones. This is effective when the main source can be clearly determined, such as query-focused summarization (Nema et al., 2017), where the target document is main and a query is secondary. The third approach is to find the salient components of the sources. This is suitable when there are many sources including less informative ones (redundant sources), such as lengthy-document summarization that outputs a multi-sentence summary (Tan et al., 2017), where each sentence can be regarded as one source. We addressed an extension of the weighted average approach and compared our proposed model with a multimodal model (Hori et al., 2017) from the first approach and a query-based model (Nema et al., 2017) from the second approach, as well as the normal encoder-decoder model. Since we have only two sources (headlines and leads), where the

headline source is clearly salient for generating a short title, the third approach can be reduced to the normal encoder-decoder model.

Our contributions are as follows.

- We report on a case study of short-title generation of news articles for a news aggregator as a real-world application of neural headline generation. This study supports previous studies based on the encoder-decoder model from a practical standpoint since most real-world news articles basically already have headlines, which means that there has been little direct application of these previous studies.

- We propose an encoder-decoder model with multiple encoders for separately encoding news headlines and leads (Section 3). Our comparative experiments with several baselines involving evaluations done by crowdsourcing workers showed the effectiveness of our model, especially using the "usefulness" measure (Section 4).

- We describe how to deploy our model to an editing support tool and show the results of comparing the editors' behavior before and after releasing the tool (Section 5), which imply that the editors began to refer to generated titles after the release.

2 Encoder-Decoder Model

An encoder-decoder model (Bahdanau et al., 2015) is a conditional language model that predicts the correct output sequence from an input sequence, which is learned from many correct pairs of input and output sequences, e.g., news articles and their headlines. To train this model, we calculate the following conditional likelihood

$$p(y \mid x) = \prod_{t=1}^{T-1} p(y_{t+1} \mid y_{\leq t}, x) \qquad (1)$$

with respect to each pair (x, y) of an input sequence $x = x_1 \cdots x_S$ and output sequence $y = y_1 \cdots y_T$, where $y_{\leq t} = y_1 \cdots y_t$, and maximize its mean. The model $p(y \mid x)$ in Eq. (1) is computed by a combination of two recurrent neural networks (RNNs): an encoder and decoder. The encoder reads an input sequence x to recognize its content, and the decoder predicts an output sequence y corresponding to the content.

More formally, an encoder calculates a hidden state h_s for each element x_s in a x by using the state transition function f_{enc} of the encoder: $h_s = f_{\text{enc}}(x_s, h_{s-1})$. In a similar fashion, a decoder calculates a hidden state $\hat{h}_t$ for each element y_t in a y by using the state transition function f_{dec} of the decoder after setting the last hidden state of the encoder as the initial state of the decoder ($\hat{h}_0 = h_S$): $\hat{h}_t = f_{\text{dec}}(y_t, \hat{h}_{t-1})$. Then, a prediction of outputs for each $\hat{h}_t$ is calculated using the output function g_{dec} with an attention mechanism:

$$p(y_{t+1} \mid y_{\leq t}, x) = g_{\text{dec}}(\hat{h}_t, c_t), \qquad (2)$$

where c_t is a weighted average of the encoder hidden states $\{h_1, \cdots, h_S\}$, defined by

$$c_t = \sum_{s=1}^{S} a_t(s) h_s, \qquad (3)$$

where $a_t(s)$ represents a weight of an encoder hidden state h_s with respect to a decoder hidden state $\hat{h}_t$. c_t represents a soft alignment (or attention weight) to the source sequence at the target position t, so it is called a *context*.

3 Proposed Method

We propose an encoder-decoder model with multiple encoders. For simplicity, we describe our model assuming two encoders for news headlines and leads. Let d_t and d'_t be contexts calculated with Eq. (3) with the headline encoder and lead encoder, respectively. Our model combines the two context vectors inspired by a gating mechanism in long-short term memory networks (Hochreiter and Schmidhuber, 1997) as follows:

$$w_t = \sigma(W[d_t; d'_t; \hat{h}_t]), \qquad (4)$$
$$w'_t = \sigma(W'[d_t; d'_t; \hat{h}_t]), \qquad (5)$$
$$\bar{c}_t = w_t \odot d_t + w'_t \odot d'_t, \qquad (6)$$

where function σ represents the sigmoid function, i.e., $\sigma(x) = 1/(1 + e^{-x})$, and the operator $\odot$ represents the element-wise product. Eq. (4) calculates a gating weight w_t for d_t, where W represents a weight matrix for a concatenated vector $[d_t; d'_t; \hat{h}_t]$. Similarly, Eq. (5) calculates a gating weight w'_t for d'_t. Eq. (6) calculates a mixed context $\bar{c}_t$ made from the two contexts, d_t and d'_t. Finally, the output function in our model is constructed by substituting c_t with $\bar{c}_t$ in Eq. (2).

Our model can be regarded as an extension of the multimodal fusion model (Hori et al., 2017), where multiple contexts are mixed using scalar weights, i.e., $\bar{c}_t = \alpha d_t + \beta d'_t$, where α and β are positive scalar weights calculated using an attention mechanism such as $a_t(s)$ in Eq. (3). Our model can obtain a more sophisticated mixed context than their model since that model only takes into account which encoder to weigh at a time step, while our model adjusts weights on the element level.

4 Experiments

4.1 Dataset

We prepared a dataset extracted from the news-aggregator of Yahoo! JAPAN by Web crawling. The dataset included 263K (headline, lead, short title) triples, and was split into three parts, i.e., for training (90%), validation (5%), and testing (5%). We preprocessed them by separating characters for training since our preliminary experiments showed that character-based training clearly performed better than word-based training.

The statistics of our dataset are as follows. The average lengths of headlines, leads, and short titles are 24.87, 128.49, and 13.05 Japanese characters, respectively. The dictionary sizes (for characters) of headlines, leads, and short titles are 3618, 4226, and 3156, respectively. Each news article has only one short title created by a professional editor. The percentage of short titles equal to their headlines is only 0.13%, while the percentage of extractively solvable instances, in which the characters in each short title are completely matched by those in the corresponding headline, was about 20%. However, the average edit distance (Levenshtein, 1966) between short titles and headlines was 23.74. This means that short titles cannot be easily created from headlines.

Hyper-parameter	Value
# of layers (RNN, CNN)	3
# of units (embedding)	200
# of units (RNN, CNN)	400
# of units (context)	400
Window width of CNN	7
Dropout rate	0.3
Learning rate	0.05
Momentum rate	0.8
Learning_decay rate	0.85
# of epochs	20
Batch size	64
Beam width	5

Table 2: Hyper-parameter settings.

	Readablity	Usefulness	Average
Editor	3.62	3.18	3.40
Prefix	2.72	2.38	2.55
OpenNMT	3.53	3.16	3.35
MultiModal	3.51	3.12	3.32
QueryBased	3.52	3.11	3.32
GateFusion	3.50	†3.22	3.36
HybridFusion	†3.55	†3.22	†3.39

Table 3: Mean scores of readability (r), usefulness (u), and their average $\frac{r+u}{2}$ based on crowdsourcing. The "†" mark shows a statistical significance from all three baselines OpenNMT, MultiModal, and QueryBased on a one-tailed, paired t-test ($p < 0.01$).

4.2 Training

We implemented our model on the OpenNMT[2] toolkit. We used a convolutional neural network (CNN) (Kim, 2014), instead of an RNN, to construct the lead encoder since leads are longer than headlines and require much more computational time. Since the CNN encoder outputs all hidden states for an input sequence in the same format as the RNN encoder, we can easily apply these states to Eq. (3). Our headline encoder still remains as an RNN (i.e., bidirectional LSTM) for fair comparison with the default implementation. We used a stochastic gradient descent algorithm with Nesterov momentum (Nesterov, 1983) as an optimizer, after initializing parameters by uniform sampling on $(-0.1, 0.1)$. Table 2 lists the details of the hyper-parameter settings in our experiment. Other settings were basically the same as the default implementation of OpenNMT.

4.3 Evaluation

We conducted two crowdsourcing tasks to separately measure readability and usefulness. The readability task asked ten workers how readable each short title was on a four-point scale (higher is better), while the usefulness task asked them how useful the short title was compared to the corresponding article. The score of each generated short title was calculated by averaging the scores collected from the ten workers.

4.4 Compared Models

We prepared four models, our model GateFusion and three baselines MultiModal, QueryBased, and OpenNMT, listed below. We implemented the fusion mechanisms of MultiModal and

---

[2]`https://github.com/OpenNMT/OpenNMT-py`

QueryBased on OpenNMT using an RNN encoder for headlines and CNN encoder for leads (see Appendix A for detailed definitions).

- GateFusion: Our model with a gating mechanism described in Section 3. This is a fusion based on vector weights.

- MultiModal: A multimodal model proposed by (Hori et al., 2017), which can handle multimodal information such as image and audio as well as text by using separate encoders. The model combines contexts obtained from the encoders via an attention mechanism such as $a_t(s)$ in Eq. (3). This is a fusion based on scalar weights.

- QueryBased: A query-based model proposed by (Nema et al., 2017), which can finetune the attention on a document by using a query for query-focused summarization. We regard a headline as a document and a lead as a query since the headline is more similar to its short title. Specifically, the model finetunes an attention weight $a_t(s)$ for calculating a headline context d_t by using a pre-computed lead context d'_t. This is a fusion based on cascade connection.

- OpenNMT: An encoder-decoder model with a single encoder implemented in OpenNMT, whose input is a headline only, because a variant using a lead did not perform better than this setting.

4.5 Results

Table 3 lists the results from the crowdsourcing tasks for readability and usefulness (see Appendix B for the details of these scores). Editor and Prefix in the top block of rows show the results of correct short titles created by editors and a naive model using the first 13.5 Japanese characters[3], respectively. The middle and bottom blocks represent the three baselines and our models, respectively. We explain our hybrid model `HybridFusion` later. Each model was prepared as an ensemble of ten models by random initialization, aiming for robust performance. Our `GateFusion` clearly performed better than the three baselines regarding usefulness and interestingly outperformed even `Editor`. This implies that `GateFusion` tends to aggressively copy elements from source sequences. However, this seemed to result in complicated expressions; thus, `GateFusion` performed the worst with respect to readability. To overcome this weakness, we developed a hybrid model `HybridFusion` that consists of `GateFusion` and another fusion model `QueryBased`, which performed relatively well in terms of readability. The results indicate that `HybridFusion` performed the best regarding readability and usefulness. It can be considered that `QueryBased` helps `GateFusion` generate headline-style outputs since `QueryBased` mainly uses the headline source.

Table 4 lists output examples generated by the best model `OpenNMT` from the three baselines and our best model `HybridFusion` (see Appendix C for more examples). In this case, the difference between `OpenNMT` and `HybridFusion` is easily comprehensible. The former selected "進化 (evolution)", and the latter selected "ダルビッシュ (Darvish)" from the headline. In Japanese headlines, the last word tends to be important, so using the last word is basically a good strategy. However, the lead indicates that "Darvish" is more important than "evolution" (actually, there is no word "evolution" in the lead); thus, `HybridFusion` was able to correctly select the long name "Darvish" and abbreviate it to "ダル (Dar)". In addition, it forcibly changed the style to the short title's style by putting the name into the forefront to easily get users' attention. This suggests that our neural-headline-generation model `HybridFusion` can successfully work even in this real-world application.

5 Deployment to Editing Support Tool

We deployed our short-title-generation model to an editing support tool in collaboration with the

---

[3]13.5 is the limit in the news-aggregator, where space, numbers, and alphabet characters are counted as 0.5.

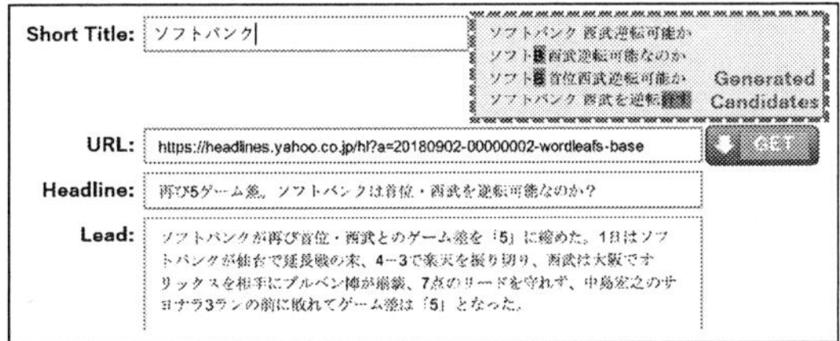

Figure 2: Screenshot of editing support tool displaying generated candidates for creating a short title.

news service, as shown in Figure 2. In the tool, when an editor enters the URL of an article, the tool can automatically fetch the headline and lead of the article and display up to five candidates next to the edit form of a short title, as shown in the dotted box in the figure. These candidates are hypotheses (with high probabilities) generated by the beam search based on the model. Then, the editor can effectively create a short title by referring to the generated candidates. This supporting feature is expected to be useful especially for inexperienced editors since the quality of short titles is heavily dependent on editors' experience.

From now on, we briefly describe three features of the tool to improve its usability when displaying candidates: cutoff of unpromising candidates, skipping redundant candidates, and highlighting unknown characters. After that, we discuss the effect of the deployment analyzing user behavior before and after releasing the tool.

5.1 Cutoff of Unpromising Candidates

The quality of displayed candidates is one of the main factors that affect the usability of the tool. If the tool frequently displays unpromising candidates, editors will gradually start ignoring them. Therefore, we cutoff unpromising candidates whose perplexity scores are higher than a certain threshold, where the perplexity score of a candidate is calculated by the inverse of the geometric mean of the generation probabilities for all characters in the candidate. We set the threshold considering the results of the editors' manual evaluation, where they checked if each candidate was acceptable or not. Specifically, we used 1.47 (=1/0.68) as the threshold, which means that the (geometric) mean character likelihood in the candidate should be higher than 0.68. If all candidates are judged as unpromising, the tool displays a message like "No promising candidates."

	Input and generated title (Japanese)	English translation
`Headline`	逆境をチャンスに変えたダルビッシュの進化	Evolution of Darvish; turning adversity into opportunity.
`Lead`	レンジャーズのダルビッシュ有（29）が28	Yu Darvish (29) in Rangers took a mound for the first time
	日、本拠地で行われたパイレーツ戦で [...]	in 1 year and 9 months with Pirates [...]
`Editor`	術前より進化 ダルの肉体改造	Dar sculpted his body better than before surgery.
`OpenNMT`	逆境をチャンスに変えた進化	Evolution; turning adversity into opportunity.
`HybridFusion`	ダル 逆境をチャンスに変えた	Dar turned adversity into opportunity.

Table 4: Examples of generated titles. `Headline` and `Lead` denote headline and lead as input. `Editor` is reference title created by an editor. `OpenNMT` and `HybridFusion` are the OpenNMT model and our hybrid model.

5.2 Skipping Redundant Candidates

The purpose of the tool is to give editors some new ideas for creating short titles, so it is not useful to display redundant candidates similar to others. Therefore, we skip candidates whose edit distance (Levenshtein, 1966) to the other candidates is lower than a threshold when selecting hypotheses in descending order of probability. Formally, the edit distance between two texts is defined as the minimum number of single-character edits (insertions, deletions, or substitutions) required to change one text into the other. We set the threshold to 2 so as to restrict variations of Japanese particles as there are many particles with a similar meaning in Japanese[4], e.g., "は (ha)" and "が (ga)". Although we used a unit cost for the edit distance, we can adjust the cost of each edit operation so that the tool can ignore variations of prepositions if we want to use English texts.

5.3 Highlighting Unknown Characters

One difficulty of neural models is that there is a possibility of generating incorrect or fake titles, which do not correspond to the article. This is a serious issue for news editing support since displayed candidates can mislead editors. For example, if the tool displays "藤波 (Fujinami)" for the news about "藤浪 (Fujinami)", where they are different names with the same pronunciation, editors might choose the incorrect one. As a simple solution, we highlighted unknown characters that do not appear in both headline and lead in red. In Figure 2, two phrases ("B" and "許す") are highlighted since they do not appear in the headline and lead. When a candidate includes highlighted characters, editors can carefully check if the candidate is semantically correct. Note that we did not exclude candidates with unknown characters so that the model can aggressively generate paraphrases and abbreviations. For example, the tool

[4]`https://en.wikipedia.org/wiki/`
`Japanese_particles`

	ROUGE-L ($\pm$ SE)	# articles
Before	52.71% ($\pm$ 0.56)	1773
After	57.65% ($\pm$ 0.53)	1959

Table 5: Sequence matching rates (ROUGE-L) of editors' titles and generated titles, which are averaged over articles over three weeks before/after releasing tool.

suggests "ソフト B(Soft B.)" as an abbreviation of "ソフトバンク (Softbank)" in the figure.

5.4 Effect of Deployment

To investigate the effect of the deployment, we compared the sequence matching rates between editors' correct titles and generated candidates before and after releasing the tool. The sequence matching rate is basically calculated by ROUGE-L (Lin, 2004), which is defined as the rate of the length of the longest common subsequence between two sequences, i.e., a correct title and a generated candidate. Because we have multiple candidates for each article, we calculate the sequence matching rate as the maximum of their ROUGE-L scores, assuming that editors may refer to the most promising candidate. Note that the candidates were filtered by the aforementioned features, so we omitted a few articles without candidates.

Table 5 shows the results of the sequence matching rates averaged over the articles over three weeks before and after releasing the tool. The results indicate that the ROUGE-L score increased by about 5 percentage points after the release. This implies that editors created their titles by referring to the displayed candidates to some extent. In fact, the ratio of the exact matched titles (ROUGE-L = 100%) in all articles (before/after the release) increased after the release by a factor of 1.62(i.e., from 3.78% to 6.13%). Similarly, the ratio of the 80% matched titles (ROUGE-L $\geq$ 80%) also increased by a factor of 1.32 (i.e., from 14.04% to 18.53%). This suggests that professional editors obtained new ideas from generated titles of the tool.

6 Related Work

We briefly review related studies from three aspects: news headline generation, editing support, and application of headline generation. In summary, our work is the first attempt to deploy a neural news-headline-generation model to a real-world application, i.e., news editing support tool.

News-headline-generation tasks have been extensively studied since early times (Wang et al., 2005; Soricut and Marcu, 2006; Woodsend et al., 2010; Alfonseca et al., 2013; Sun et al., 2015; Colmenares et al., 2015). In this line of research, Rush et al. (2015) proposed a neural model to generate news headlines and released a benchmark dataset for their task, and consequently this task has recently received increasing attention (Chopra et al., 2016; Takase et al., 2016; Kiyono et al., 2017; Zhou et al., 2017; Suzuki and Nagata, 2017; Ayana et al., 2017; Raffel et al., 2017; Cao et al., 2018; Kobayashi, 2018). However, their approaches were basically based on the encoder-decoder model, which is trained with a lot of (article, headline) pairs. This means that there are few situations for putting their models into the real world because news articles typically already have corresponding headlines, and most editors create a headline before its content (according to a senior journalist). Therefore, our work can strongly support their approaches from a practical perspective.

Considering technologies used for editing support, there have been many studies for various purposes, such as spelling error correction (Farra et al., 2014; Hasan et al., 2015; Etoori et al., 2018), grammatical error correction (Dahlmeier and Ng, 2012; Susanto et al., 2014; Choshen and Abend, 2018), fact checking (Baly et al., 2018; Thorne and Vlachos, 2018; Lee et al., 2018), fluency evaluation (Vadlapudi and Katragadda, 2010; Heilman et al., 2014; Kann et al., 2018), and so on. However, when we consider their studies on our task, they are only used after editing (writing a draft). On the other hand, the purpose of our tool is different from theirs since our tool can support editors before or during editing. The usage of (interactive) machine translation systems (Denkowski et al., 2014; González-Rubio et al., 2016; Wuebker et al., 2016; Ye et al., 2016; Takeno et al., 2017) for supporting manual post-editing are similar to our purpose, but their task is completely different from ours. In other words, their task is a translation without information loss, whereas our task

is a summarization that requires information compression. We believe that a case study on summarization is still important for the summarization community.

There have been several studies reporting case studies on headline generation for different real services: (a) question headlines on question answering service (Higurashi et al., 2018), (b) product headlines on e-commerce service (Wang et al., 2018), and (c) headlines for product curation pages (Mathur et al., 2018; Camargo de Souza et al., 2018). The first two (a) and (b) are extractive approaches, and the last one (c) is an abstractive approach, where the input is a set of slot/value pairs, such as "color/white." That is, our task is more difficult to use in the real-world. In addition, application to news services tends to be sensitive since news articles contain serious contents such as incidents, accidents, and disasters. Thus, our work should be valuable as a rare case study applying a neural model to such a news service.

7 Conclusion

We addressed short-title generation from news articles for a news aggregator to support the editorial process. We proposed an encoder-decoder model with multiple encoders for separately encoding multiple information sources, i.e., news headlines and leads. Comparative experiments using crowdsourcing showed that our hybrid model performed better than the baselines, especially using the usefulness measure. We deployed our model to an editing support tool and empirically confirmed that professional editors began to refer to the generated titles after the release. Future research will include verifying how much our headline generation model can affect practical performance indicators, such as click-through rate. In this case, we need to develop a much safer model since our model sometimes yields erroneous outputs or fake news titles, which cannot be directly used in the commercial service.

Acknowledgements

We would like to thank editors and engineers in the news service who continuously supported our experiments. We are also in debt to Chahine Koleejan who helped with proofreading. Finally, special thanks go to the anonymous reviewers for their insightful comments.

References

Enrique Alfonseca, Daniele Pighin, and Guillermo Garrido. 2013. HEADY: News headline abstraction through event pattern clustering. In *Proceedings of the 51st Annual Meeting of the Association for Computational Linguistics (ACL 2013)*, pages 1243–1253. Association for Computational Linguistics.

Ayana, Shi-Qi Shen, Yan-Kai Lin, Cun-Chao Tu, Yu Zhao, Zhi-Yuan Liu, and Mao-Song Sun. 2017. Recent Advances on Neural Headline Generation. *Journal of Computer Science and Technology*, 32(4):768–784.

Dzmitry Bahdanau, Kyunghyun Cho, and Yoshua Bengio. 2015. Neural machine translation by jointly learning to align and translate. In *Proceedings of the 3rd International Conference on Learning Representations (ICLR 2015)*.

Ramy Baly, Mitra Mohtarami, James Glass, Lluís Màrquez, Alessandro Moschitti, and Preslav Nakov. 2018. Integrating Stance Detection and Fact Checking in a Unified Corpus. In *Proceedings of the 2018 Conference of the North American Chapter of the Association for Computational Linguistics: Human Language Technologies (NAACL-HLT 2018))*, pages 21–27. Association for Computational Linguistics.

Ziqiang Cao, Furu Wei, Wenjie Li, and Sujian Li. 2018. Faithful to the Original: Fact Aware Neural Abstractive Summarization. In *Proceedings of the Thirty-Second AAAI Conference on Artificial Intelligence (AAAI 2018)*, pages 4784–4791. AAAI Press.

Sumit Chopra, Michael Auli, and Alexander M. Rush. 2016. Abstractive Sentence Summarization with Attentive Recurrent Neural Networks. In *Proceedings of the 2016 Conference of the North American Chapter of the Association for Computational Linguistics: Human Language Technologies (NAACL-HLT 2016)*, pages 93–98. Association for Computational Linguistics.

Leshem Choshen and Omri Abend. 2018. Automatic Metric Validation for Grammatical Error Correction. In *Proceedings of the 56th Annual Meeting of the Association for Computational Linguistics (ACL 2018)*, pages 1372–1382. Association for Computational Linguistics.

Carlos A. Colmenares, Marina Litvak, Amin Mantrach, and Fabrizio Silvestri. 2015. HEADS: Headline Generation as Sequence Prediction Using an Abstract Feature-Rich Space. In *Proceedings of the 2015 Conference of the North American Chapter of the Association for Computational Linguistics: Human Language Technologies (NAACL-HLT 2015)*, pages 133–142. Association for Computational Linguistics.

Daniel Dahlmeier and Hwee Tou Ng. 2012. Better Evaluation for Grammatical Error Correction. In *Proceedings of the 2012 Conference of the North American Chapter of the Association for Computational Linguistics (NAACL-HLT 2012)*, pages 568–572. Association for Computational Linguistics.

Michael Denkowski, Alon Lavie, Isabel Lacruz, and Chris Dyer. 2014. Real Time Adaptive Machine Translation for Post-Editing with cdec and TransCenter. In *Proceedings of the EACL 2014 Workshop on Humans and Computer-assisted Translation*, pages 72–77. Association for Computational Linguistics.

Pravallika Etoori, Manoj Chinnakotla, and Radhika Mamidi. 2018. Automatic Spelling Correction for Resource-Scarce Languages using Deep Learning. In *Proceedings of ACL 2018, Student Research Workshop*, pages 146–152. Association for Computational Linguistics.

Noura Farra, Nadi Tomeh, Alla Rozovskaya, and Nizar Habash. 2014. Generalized Character-Level Spelling Error Correction. In *Proceedings of the 52nd Annual Meeting of the Association for Computational Linguistics (ACL 2014)*, pages 161–167. Association for Computational Linguistics.

Jesús González-Rubio, Daniel Ortiz Martinez, Francisco Casacuberta, and Jose Miguel Benedi Ruiz. 2016. Beyond Prefix-Based Interactive Translation Prediction. In *Proceedings of The 20th SIGNLL Conference on Computational Natural Language Learning (CoNLL 2016)*, pages 198–207. Association for Computational Linguistics.

Saša Hasan, Carmen Heger, and Saab Mansour. 2015. Spelling Correction of User Search Queries through Statistical Machine Translation. In *Proceedings of the 2015 Conference on Empirical Methods in Natural Language Processing (EMNLP 2015)*, pages 451–460. Association for Computational Linguistics.

Michael Heilman, Aoife Cahill, Nitin Madnani, Melissa Lopez, Matthew Mulholland, and Joel Tetreault. 2014. Predicting Grammaticality on an Ordinal Scale. In *Proceedings of the 52nd Annual Meeting of the Association for Computational Linguistics (ACL 2014)*, pages 174–180. Association for Computational Linguistics.

Tatsuru Higurashi, Hayato Kobayashi, Takeshi Masuyama, and Kazuma Murao. 2018. Extractive headline generation based on learning to rank for community question answering. In *Proceedings of the 27th International Conference on Computational Linguistics (COLING 2018)*, pages 1742–1753. Association for Computational Linguistics.

Sepp Hochreiter and Jürgen Schmidhuber. 1997. Long short-term memory. *Neural Computation*, 9(8):1735–1780.

Chiori Hori, Takaaki Hori, Teng-Yok Lee, Ziming Zhang, Bret Harsham, John R. Hershey, Tim K. Marks, and Kazuhiko Sumi. 2017. Attention-based multimodal fusion for video description. In *ICCV*.

Katharina Kann, Sascha Rothe, and Katja Filippova. 2018. Sentence-Level Fluency Evaluation: References Help, But Can Be Spared! In *Proceedings of the 22nd Conference on Computational Natural Language Learning (CoNLL 2018)*, pages 313–323. Association for Computational Linguistics.

Yoon Kim. 2014. Convolutional neural networks for sentence classification. In *Proceedings of the 2014 Conference on Empirical Methods in Natural Language Processing (EMNLP)*, pages 1746–1751. Association for Computational Linguistics.

Shun Kiyono, Sho Takase, Jun Suzuki, Naoaki Okazaki, Kentaro Inui, and Masaaki Nagata. 2017. Source-side Prediction for Neural Headline Generation . *CoRR*, abs/1712.08302.

Hayato Kobayashi. 2018. Frustratingly Easy Model Ensemble for Abstractive Summarization. In *Proceedings of the 2018 Conference on Empirical Methods in Natural Language Processing (EMNLP 2018)*, pages 4165–4176. Association for Computational Linguistics.

Nayeon Lee, Chien-Sheng Wu, and Pascale Fung. 2018. Improving Large-Scale Fact-Checking using Decomposable Attention Models and Lexical Tagging. In *Proceedings of the 2018 Conference on Empirical Methods in Natural Language Processing (EMNLP 2018)*, pages 1133–1138. Association for Computational Linguistics.

Vladimir Iosifovich Levenshtein. 1966. Binary Codes Capable of Correcting Deletions, Insertions and Reversals. *Soviet Physics Doklady*, 10(8):707–710.

Chin-Yew Lin. 2004. ROUGE: A Package for Automatic Evaluation of Summaries. In *Proceedings of the ACL Workshop on Text Summarization Branches Out*.

Prashant Mathur, Nicola Ueffing, and Gregor Leusch. 2018. Multi-lingual neural title generation for e-Commerce browse pages. In *Proceedings of the 2018 Conference of the North American Chapter of the Association for Computational Linguistics: Human Language Technologies (NAACL-HLT 2018)*, pages 162–169. Association for Computational Linguistics.

Preksha Nema, Mitesh M. Khapra, Anirban Laha, and Balaraman Ravindran. 2017. Diversity driven attention model for query-based abstractive summarization. In *ACL*, pages 1063–1072.

Yurii Nesterov. 1983. A method of solving a convex programming problem with convergence rate o(1/k2). *Soviet Mathematics Doklady*, 27.

Colin Raffel, Minh-Thang Luong, Peter J. Liu, Ron J. Weiss, and Douglas Eck. 2017. Online and Linear-Time Attention by Enforcing Monotonic Alignments. In *Proceedings of the 34th International Conference on Machine Learning (ICML 2017)*, pages 2837–2846.

Alexander M. Rush, Sumit Chopra, and Jason Weston. 2015. A Neural Attention Model for Abstractive Sentence Summarization. In *Proceedings of the 2015 Conference on Empirical Methods in Natural Language Processing (EMNLP 2015)*, pages 379–389. Association for Computational Linguistics.

Radu Soricut and Daniel Marcu. 2006. Stochastic Language Generation Using WIDL-Expressions and its Application in Machine Translation and Summarization. In *Proceedings of the 21st International Conference on Computational Linguistics and 44th Annual Meeting of the Association for Computational Linguistics (COLING-ACL 2006)*, pages 1105–1112. Association for Computational Linguistics.

José G. Camargo de Souza, Michael Kozielski, Prashant Mathur, Ernie Chang, Marco Guerini, Matteo Negri, Marco Turchi, and Evgeny Matusov. 2018. Generating E-Commerce Product Titles and Predicting their Quality. In *Proceedings of the 11th International Conference on Natural Language Generation*, pages 233–243. Association for Computational Linguistics.

Rui Sun, Yue Zhang, Meishan Zhang, and Donghong Ji. 2015. Event-Driven Headline Generation. In *Proceedings of the 53rd Annual Meeting of the Association for Computational Linguistics and the 7th International Joint Conference on Natural Language Processing (ACL-IJCNLP 2015)*, pages 462–472. Association for Computational Linguistics.

Raymond Hendy Susanto, Peter Phandi, and Hwee Tou Ng. 2014. System Combination for Grammatical Error Correction. In *Proceedings of the 2014 Conference on Empirical Methods in Natural Language Processing (EMNLP 2014)*, pages 951–962. Association for Computational Linguistics.

Jun Suzuki and Masaaki Nagata. 2017. Cutting-off redundant repeating generations for neural abstractive summarization. In *Proceedings of the 15th Conference of the European Chapter of the Association for Computational Linguistics (EACL 2017)*, pages 291–297. Association for Computational Linguistics.

Sho Takase, Jun Suzuki, Naoaki Okazaki, Tsutomu Hirao, and Masaaki Nagata. 2016. Neural Headline Generation on Abstract Meaning Representation. In *Proceedings of the 2016 Conference on Empirical Methods in Natural Language Processing (EMNLP 2016)*, pages 1054–1059. Association for Computational Linguistics.

Shunsuke Takeno, Masaaki Nagata, and Kazuhide Yamamoto. 2017. Controlling target features in neural machine translation via prefix constraints. In *Proceedings of the 4th Workshop on Asian Translation (WAT2017)*, pages 55–63. Asian Federation of Natural Language Processing.

Jiwei Tan, Xiaojun Wan, and Jianguo Xiao. 2017. Abstractive Document Summarization with a Graph-Based Attentional Neural Model. In *Proceedings of the 55th Annual Meeting of the Association for Computational Linguistics (ACL 2017)*, pages 1171–1181. Association for Computational Linguistics.

James Thorne and Andreas Vlachos. 2018. Automated Fact Checking: Task Formulations, Methods and Future Directions. In *Proceedings of the 27th International Conference on Computational Linguistics (COLING 2018)*, pages 3346–3359. Association for Computational Linguistics.

Ravikiran Vadlapudi and Rahul Katragadda. 2010. On Automated Evaluation of Readability of Summaries: Capturing Grammaticality, Focus, Structure and Coherence. In *Proceedings of the NAACL HLT 2010 Student Research Workshop*, pages 7–12. Association for Computational Linguistics.

Jingang Wang, Junfeng Tian, Long Qiu, Sheng Li, Jun Lang, Luo Si, and Man Lan. 2018. A Multi-Task Learning Approach for Improving Product Title Compression with User Search Log Data. In *Proceedings of the Thirty-Second AAAI Conference on Artificial Intelligence (AAAI 2018)*, pages 451–458.

Ruichao Wang, John Dunnion, and Joe Carthy. 2005. Machine Learning Approach to Augmenting News Headline Generation. In *Proceedings of the Second International Joint Conference on Natural Language Processing (IJCNLP 2005)*. Association for Computational Linguistics.

Kristian Woodsend, Yansong Feng, and Mirella Lapata. 2010. Title Generation with Quasi-Synchronous Grammar. In *Proceedings of the 2010 Conference on Empirical Methods in Natural Language Processing (EMNLP 2010)*, pages 513–523. Association for Computational Linguistics.

Joern Wuebker, Spence Green, John DeNero, Sasa Hasan, and Minh-Thang Luong. 2016. Models and Inference for Prefix-Constrained Machine Translation. In *Proceedings of the 54th Annual Meeting of the Association for Computational Linguistics (ACL 2016)*, pages 66–75. Association for Computational Linguistics.

Na Ye, Guiping Zhang, and Dongfeng Cai. 2016. Interactive-predictive machine translation based on syntactic constraints of prefix. In *Proceedings of the 26th International Conference on Computational Linguistics (COLING 2016)*, pages 1797–1806. The COLING 2016 Organizing Committee.

Qingyu Zhou, Nan Yang, Furu Wei, and Ming Zhou. 2017. Selective encoding for abstractive sentence summarization. In *Proceedings of the 55th Annual Meeting of the Association for Computational Linguistics (ACL 2017)*, pages 1095–1104. Association for Computational Linguistics.

Neural Lexicons for Slot Tagging in Spoken Language Understanding

Kyle Williams
Microsoft
One Microsoft Way
Redmond, Washington, 98052
`kyle.williams@microsoft.com`

Abstract

We explore the use of lexicons in neural models for slot tagging in spoken language understanding. We develop models that encode lexicon information as features for use in a Long-short term memory neural network. Experiments are performed on data from 4 domains from an intelligent assistant under conditions that often occur in an industry setting, where there may be: 1) large amounts of training data, 2) limited amounts of training data for new domains, and 3) cross domain training. Results show that the use of neural lexicon information leads to a significant improvement in slot tagging, with improvements in the F-score of up to 12%.

1 Introduction

Spoken language understanding (SLU) is an important component of systems that interface with users, such as intelligent assistants. These systems are becoming increasingly popular as a means for people to accomplish tasks in their homes and on mobile devices. These tasks might include switching on the lights or booking a taxi. Typically, an SLU system detects the domain, intent, and semantic slots of an utterance (Li et al., 2017) and uses the information to perform actions.

It is common to use lexicons (also known as gazettes or dictionaries) to improve the performance of SLU systems (Ratinov and Roth, 2009). Lexicons are typically collections of phrases that are semantically related and thus provide knowledge that can aid the SLU system. For instance, a lexicon called *holidays* might contain the phrases *Thanksgiving, Christmas Eve, Labor Day.* Similarly, a lexicon called *days of the week* would contain *Monday, Tuesday, Wednesday*, etc. There are many ways lexicons can be built, such as by using domain experts or by harvesting information from knowledge graphs, such as DBPedia[1]. In an industry setting, it is also possible that lexicons already exist for other natural language applications.

Previous work has shown how lexicons can be used to improve slot tagging with Conditional Random Fields (Ratinov and Roth, 2009), where slot tagging refers to the process of identifying semantic entities of interest in an utterance. For instance, given the utterance *"book a taxi to the airport"*, a slot tagging model might identify *taxi* as a *transport_type* and *airport* as a *destination*. In this paper, we investigate the effect of integrating these types of lexicons into Long-Short Term Memory (LSTM) neural models in an industry setting. We focus on LSTM models since they have been shown to produce state-of-the-art results in many natural language tasks. We consider integrating lexicon features into a Long-short term memory neural network in two ways: 1) by considering lexicon membership as binary features and 2) by embedding the lexicons and allowing the model to learn the representation as part of the end-to-end training of the neural network.

To evaluate these approaches, we measure the performance of models on data from four domains belonging to an intelligent assistant under three data scenarios that commonly occur in production SLU systems. The first scenario is when there is a considerable amount of training data available to train a SLU system, as may occur if a sizeable investment has been made to collect data. The second scenario is when there is only a small amount of training data available, as may be the case when the SLU is expanded to cover new domains for which very little training data exists. The third scenario is cross domain slot prediction, where we use a model trained on utterances from one domain to identify entities in utterances belonging to another

---

[1]https://wiki.dbpedia.org/

83

Proceedings of NAACL-HLT 2019, pages 83–89
Minneapolis, Minnesota, June 2 - June 7, 2019. ©2019 Association for Computational Linguistics

domain. This setting commonly occurs when one attempts to leverage existing SLU models for use in a new domain.

2 Related Work

There have been many previous studies involving spoken language understanding for the slot tagging problem. Yao et al. (2014) investigate the use of LSTMs for slot tagging and compare the performance of the LSTM-based model to a standard RNN and a Conditional Random Field. Their results show the LSTM to outperform the two other models. Mesnil et al. (2015) evaluate several RNN-based models for slot tagging and show the RNN-based models to outperform the CRF-based model. Ma and Hovy (2016) propose a LSTM-CNN-CRF model, which induces character representations using a convolutional neural network. The character representations are then combined with word embeddings and fed into an LSTM, and lastly the output of the LSTM is fed into a CRF decoder. In Kurata et al. (2016), the authors use an encoder-labeler approach to first encode sentences into fixed size vectors and then use the encoded state as the initial state for a labeling LSTM.

The reason that many researchers have been using LSTMs for natural language understanding is due to their ability to model long-term dependencies. However, some researchers have proposed other architectures. For instance, Shi et al. (2016) propose the Recurrent Support Vector Machine (RSVM), which uses a recurrent neural network to induce a feature representation and a structured support vector machine to perform structured prediction on the output of the RNN.

Dugas and Nichols (2016) use lexicon embedding features for named entity recognition in tweets. They produce lexicon embeddings that are concatenated with word embeddings; however, our work differs in the inclusion of the additional neural lexicon models, experiments comparing them under varying data conditions that commonly occur in an industry setting, and our evaluation is based on spoken utterances from an intelligent assistant rather than tweets. Furthermore, we analyze cases where lexicons are useful and cases where they are not.

3 Neural Lexicon Models

Our proposed neural lexicon models are based on an Long Short-Term Memory (LSTM) architecture. The architecture is shown visually in Figure 1 and described in detail below.

In each of our models we induce a feature representation based on the characters and words that appear in an input sequence of words. We closely follow the approach of previous studies (Kim et al., 2017; Lample et al., 2016) and induce both character and word embeddings using bidirectional LSTMs. As in Kim et al. (2017), for a given sequence of words $W = w_1, w_2, ..., w_n$ where word w_i has character $w_i(j)$ at position j. We define the following:

- Character embedding: e_c for each $c \in C$
- Character LSTM: ϕ_f^C, ϕ_b^C
- Word embedding: e_w for each $w \in W$
- Word LSTM: ϕ_f^W, ϕ_b^W,

where $\phi_f^C, \phi_b^C, \phi_f^W, \phi_b^W$ refer to the forward and backward character and word LSTMs. A character sensitive word representation v_i is computed as:

$$f_j^C = \phi_f^C(e_{w_i(j)}, f_{j-1}^C), \forall j = 1...|w_i| \quad (1)$$
$$b_j^C = \phi_b^C(e_{w_i(j)}, b_{j+1}^C), \forall j = |w_i|...1 \quad (2)$$
$$v_i = f_{|w_i|}^C \oplus b_1^C \oplus e_{w_i}, \quad (3)$$

where $\oplus$ represents the vector concatenation operation whereby the final states of the forward and backward LSTMs are concatenated with the word embedding. Next the model computes:

$$f_i^W = \phi_f^W(v_i, f_{i-1}^W), \forall i = 1...n \quad (4)$$
$$b_i^W = \phi_b^W(v_i, b_{i+1}^W), \forall i = n...1 \quad (5)$$

In other words, the forward and backward word LSTMs are used to induce character and context sensitive word representations. Finally, the states of the forward and backward LSTMs are concatenated to induce the final word representation r_i:

$$r_i = f_i^W \oplus b_i^W, \quad (6)$$

for each word $w_i, i = 1...n$. These r_i are the word representations that we use for slot prediction.

In this study we focus on slot tagging and predict the tag of each word $w_i, i = 1...n$ using $r_i, i = 1...n$. To do this we add a feed forward layer g, which takes as input the r_i at each timestep. We take the softmax of the the output of g to produce probabilities of semantic tags for each word w_i. We then minimize the cross entropy loss:

$$Loss^{\text{tag}} = -\sum_i p_i \log q_i, \quad (7)$$

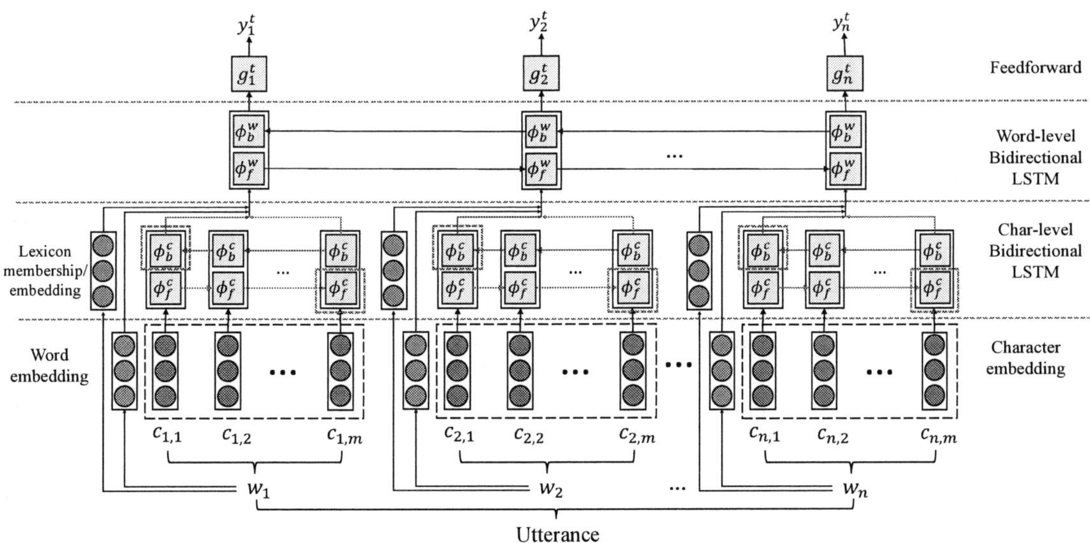

Figure 1: Overall network architecture

where p_i is the distribution of the true labels and q_i is the distribution of the predicted labels.

3.1 Lexicon Membership Model

Having described the basic form of our slot tagging model, we now describe how we extend the model to include lexicon features.

Assume that we have a collection of L lexicons, with each lexicon containing a collection of words and phrases belonging to that lexicon. For instance, a lexicon called *holidays* might contain: *Thanksgiving, Christmas, Labor Day*. Similarly, a lexicon called *days of the week* would contain *Monday, Tuesday, Wednesday*, etc. For each word w_i in an utterance we generate the uni-gram, bi-gram, and tri-gram beginning at word w_i, and we refer to this triple as t_i. For instance, for the utterance *"book a taxi to the airport"*, t_1 = ["book", "book a", "book a taxi"], t_2 = ["a", "a taxi", "a taxi to"], etc. We use $t_i^j, j = 1, 2, 3$, to refer to the j-th element of t_i, i.e., the uni-gram, bi-gram, or tri-gram.

For each word w_i in the input utterance, we define a membership lexicon feature vector lex_i of length $|L|$, where each element $\text{lex}_i(l), l = 1, 2, ..., |L|$, is defined as:

$$\text{lex}_i(l) = \begin{cases} 1 & \text{if } t_i^j \text{ in lexicon } l, j = 1, 2, 3 \\ 0 & \text{otherwise} \end{cases} \quad (8)$$

In other words, every word w_i has an associated feature vector lex_i of length $|L|$. The k-th element of lex_i is 1 if a uni-gram, bi-gram, or tri-gram rooted at w_i exists in the k-th lexicon and is zero otherwise.

The word representation (Eq. 3) for each word is modified to include lexicon information:

$$v_i^{\text{lex}} = f_{|w_i|}^C \oplus b_1^C \oplus e_{w_i} \oplus \text{lex}_i. \quad (9)$$

The effect of this is to append a binary feature lexicon membership feature vector to the word representation. We then input the v_i^{lex} into the word LSTM layer to induce the character, lexicon, and context sensitive word representation. This can be seen visually in Figure 1 where the lexicon membership features are appended to the word embeddings and output of the character-level LSTM before being fed into the word-level LSTM. We refer to this model as the Lexicon Membership Model (M^{Member}).

3.2 Lexicon Embeddings Model

In the next model we propose to embed the lexicon information. Similar to the case of the word embeddings, we define lexicon embeddings as follows:

- Lexicon embedding: e_l for each $l \in L$,
- No Lexicon embedding: e_o,

that is, each of the $|L|$ lexicons is represented by an embedding and e_o represent an additional embedding, which is used in cases where a uni-gram, bi-gram, or tri-gram rooted at a word does not belong to any lexicon. We then define the embedded lexicon feature vector as:

$$\text{ELex}_i = \begin{cases} e_l & \text{if } t_i^j \text{ in lexicon } l, j = 1, 2, 3, l \in L \\ e_o & \text{otherwise.} \end{cases} \tag{10}$$

In other words, if a uni-gram, bi-gram, or tri-gram rooted at w_i appears in a lexicon l, we assign the embedding of lexicon l to ELex_i. If two or more of the n-grams rooted at a word w_i match a lexicon, we use the longest match.

We then adapt Eq. 9 to use the lexicon embeddings instead of the lexicon membership feature:

$$v_i^{\text{ELex}} = f_{|w_i|}^C \oplus b_1^C \oplus e_{w_i} \oplus \text{ELex}_i. \tag{11}$$

The effect of this is to append a lexicon embedding to the word representation. As was the case with before, we input the v_i^{ELex} into the word LSTM layer to induce the character, lexicon, and context sensitive word representation as in Eq. 4-6. This can be seen visually in Figure 1 where the lexicon embedding features are appended to the word embeddings and output of the character-level LSTM before being fed into the word-level LSTM. We refer to this model as the Lexicon Embeddings Model (M^{Embed}).

4 Experiments

We conduct experiments under three settings in order to evaluate how the lexicon models affect slot tagging performance.

- **All Training Data:** In this setting we use all of the available training data for each domain when training the slot tagging models.
- **Limited Training Data:** In this setting we simulate the constrained data scenario that often occurs when expanding an SLU system to support new domains and limit the amount of training data available.
- **Cross Domain:** In this setting we consider cross domain prediction and train on one domain and then predict common slots in other domains.

4.1 Data

We conduct all of our experiments on data from four domains belonging to an intelligent assistant. The source of the data is user utterances, which

Domain	Slots	Train	Validation	Test
Recipes	10	20,000	6,809	1,186
Services	10	1800	194	500
Location	4	136,783	34,954	51,976
Time	4	129,340	34,644	46,803

Table 1: Description of datasets.

were transcribed by a speech-to-text system and then had their semantic slots labeled by trained annotators. The domains that we use are *Recipes*, *Services*, *Location*, and *Time*. The *Recipes* domain focuses on assisting users with recipes. The *Services* domain is used to help users find services, such as car repairs. The *Location* and *Time* domains identify location and time information in user utterances. These four domains differ in terms of the types of queries they contain, as well as their data sizes and the size of their lexicons. Table 1 shows details on the slots and amount of data available for each domain. As can be seen from the table, the results differ with the *Location* and *Time* domains having large amounts of training data available, while the *Services* domain has very limited data.

4.2 Lexicon Descriptions

We now describe the lexicons associated with each domain. The lexicons were created as part of the data pipeline for an intelligent assistant. Table 2 lists the domains and the number of lexicons associated with each of them. For the *Recipes* domain there are 3 lexicons: ingredients, recipe names, and cocktail names, with members such as: *banana pudding* and *mojito*. For the *Services* domain there is only 1 lexicon, which contains types of services, such as: *pet sitting*. The *Location* domain has 13 lexicons for countries, cities, schools, etc. Finally, the *Time* domain contains 20 lexicons for days of the week, holidays, etc.

The size of the lexicons also varies. For instance, the lexicons in the *Time* domain usually have tens of members. By contrast, in the *Location* domain, there are over 300,000 city names and only about 400 airport names. There are almost 30,000 recipes compared to about 300 cocktails and ingredients in the *Recipes* domain. Lastly, for the *Services* domain there are about 2,300 services types. As this analysis has shown, the properties of the lexicons vary largely among the datasets.

We also analyze the lexicon prevalence in the

Domain	Number of Lexicons	Prevalence
Recipes	3	28.95%
Services	1	29.78%
Location	13	99.13%
Time	20	81.63%

Table 2: Prevalence of lexicon features in training data.

Method	Recipes	Services	Location	Time
LSTM BL	91.20	78.11	84.79	94.05
CRF	90.21	74.51	86.07	93.43
CRF+Lex	90.69	75.47	**87.72**	93.55
M^{Embed}	**91.27**	77.37	86.01†	**94.28**†
M^{Member}	91.16	**78.13**	85.42	94.15

Table 3: F1 score for different models using full training set.

training data. For the training data we compute how many utterances have a sequence of words that belongs to at least one lexicon. These results are shown in the last column of Table 2, where it can be seen that the prevalence of lexicons differs vastly across the domains. For instance, 99.13% of the training utterances in the *Location* domain contain a word or phrase that belongs to a lexicon. By comparison, for the *Recipes* domain, only 28.95% of utterances contain a word or phrase that belongs to a lexicon. As will be seen later, we generally see larger improvements in domains with larger lexicon coverage.

4.3 Methodology

Having described our models and data, we now describe our experimental methodology. For all experiments we randomly initialize all model parameters and shuffle the training dataset for each epoch. To account for randomization, we repeat each experiment 10 times and report the mean of the F-1 metric. To test for significance we make use of the Wilcoxon signed-rank test.

For each experiment, we allow for up to 30 epochs of training and employ early stopping when there is no improvement in the lowest loss on the validation set for 5 epochs. We use a batch size of 10 and set the learning rate to 5×10^{-4}. We set the dropout probability to 0.5. To train the network, we make use of stochastic gradient descent and the Adam optimization algorithm (Kingma and Ba, 2014). We train the network end-to-end to predict the slot tags for each utterance, thus allowing the network to learn the character, word and lexicon representations automatically.

Following previous studies, we set the size of the character and lexicon embeddings to 25 and the size of the word embeddings to 100. The character and lexicon LSTMs have 25 units and the word LSTMs have 100 units.To evaluate our model we report the F-1 score as adapted for entity recognition (Tjong Kim Sang and De Meulder, 2003).

4.3.1 Baselines

We consider three baselines:

LSTM Baseline (LSTM BL): We consider a baseline LSTM model that does not include any lexicon information. This model is described by Equations 1-7.

Conditional Random Field (CRF): Linear chain CRF where we make use of n-gram features and brown cluster-based features.

Conditional Random Field + Lexicon Features (CRF+Lex): The same CRF as above, except we include binary features indicating lexicon membership.

4.4 Results

4.4.1 Full Dataset

This experiment uses all of the available training data. The results are shown in Table 3. For the *Recipes* domain, the highest F1 score is achieved by the M^{Embed} model; however, the difference is not statistically significant compared to the baseline LSTM. For this domain, the LSTM models all outperform the CRF models. For the *Services* domain, we observe that the M^{Member} model achieves the highest F1 score; however, it is also not statistically significant compared to the baseline LSTM. Once again, the LSTM models outperform the CRF models. For the *Location* domain we observe a statistically significant improvement in performance for the M^{Embed} model compared to the baseline LSTM. This improvement exceeds 1%. However, the CRF model outperforms the LSTM models. Lastly, for the the *Time* domain we observe a significant improvement in the F1 score compared to the baseline LSTM for the M^{Embed} model. Furthermore, all LSTM models outperform the CRF baselines.

The results in this experiment show that the M^{Embed} model achieves a statistically significant improvement over the baseline in two of the four

Method	Recipes	Services	Location	Time
Baseline	52.74	46.83	40.01	68.75
M^{Loss}	48.11	41.08	31.75	67.69
M^{Embed}	57.86	**52.54**[†]	51.40	**74.09**[†]
M^{Member}	**58.97**[†]	48.98	**52.78**[†]	70.97

Table 4: F1 score for different models using 1,000 samples during each training iteration.

Method	Location-Services	Time-Services
Baseline	20.09	84.91
M^{Loss}	20.24	85.42
M^{Embed}	19.98	**86.84**[†]
M^{Member}	**20.88**	86.65

Table 5: F1 score for models trained on LOCATION and TIME and tested on SERVICES.

datasets. As was previously discussed, these are datasets where the lexicons cover a majority proportion of the training data. Thus, the results indicate that the inclusion of lexicon information is useful if there is large lexicon coverage in the training data. As a general observation, the LSTM-based models tend outperform the CRF models in 3 of the 4 domains, which is similar to the findings of previous studies (Yao et al., 2014)

4.4.2 Limited Training Data

In this experiment, we investigate how the proposed models perform in the case of limited training data. We follow a similar methodology as before with the following changes: 1) during each training epoch we randomly sample 1,000 training samples; 2) we use a batch size of 1; 3) we lower the learning rate to 5×10^{-5}. The results of this experiment are shown in Table 4.

As can be seen from the table, there are large improvements in all domains when the lexicon-based models are used. In the *Recipes* domain the F1 score is 52.74% for the baseline and is 58.97% for the best performing M^{Member} model. For the *Services* model, the M^{Embed} model achieves an F1 score of 52.54% compared to 46.83% for the baseline. In the *Location* domain the F1 score is 12.77% higher than the baseline using the M^{Member} model, and for the *Time* domain the improvement is 5.34% better using the highest performing M^{Embed} model. The M^{Member} and M^{Embed} models thus achieve the highest F1 score on two domains each. However, it is interesting to note that when the M^{Embed} model outperforms the M^{Member} model is it usually by about 3-4%. By contrast, when the M^{Member} model performs best it usually only performs better than the M^{Embed} model by around 1%.

The results on these smaller datasets suggests that lexicons can have a significant effect on slot tagging performance when training data is limited. In these cases, the additional knowledge provided by the lexicons leads to large improvement in performance. This is an encouraging result for SLU systems that are being extended to new domains as it is sometimes possible to acquire lexicons at a low cost via sources such as DBPedia.

4.4.3 Cross Domain

In this experiment, we use the models trained for the *Location* and *Time* domains to predict common slots in the *Services* domain. Since some of the labels in the *Services* domain do not exist in the *Location* and *Time* models, we assign those labels a tag of Other. The results of this experiment are shown in Table 5. When training on *Location* and predicting *Services* the highest precision and F1 scores are achieved by the M^{Member} model; however, the improvement is not significant. When training on *Time* and predicting *Services* the highest performance is achieved by the M^{Embed} model and is statistically significant.

5 Discussion and Conclusion

Our results show that the M^{Embed} model, which represents lexicon information with embeddings, performs well across domains and experiments. For instance, it achieves a significantly better performance than the baselines in the *Location* and *Time* domains when all available training data is used. In that experiment, the *Location* and *Time* domains had relatively large lexicon coverage. The results suggest that lexicons can help improve performance when large amounts of training data are available and when lexicon coverage is high. For the *Services* and *Recipes* domains, where lexicon coverage was low, the lexicon-based models led to no significant improvement in performance.

When the training data was limited, the M^{Embed} model achieved significantly better performance than the baseline on 2 of the 4 domains. In the other 2 domains, the M^{Member} model performed best. The experiments showed that, when training data is small, the use of lexicons can lead to large improvement in slot tagging performance. For instance, Table 4 shows improvements in the F1 score of about 12% for the *Location* domain and of around 6% for the other domains.

These findings have strong implications for an industry setting. The experiments clearly show that lexicons can be very useful to improve slot tagging when training data is limited, as is the case when expanding to new domains. In these cases, practitioners can benefit greatly by acquiring lexicons from online sources, such as knowledge bases, or using existing lexicons that may have been previously collected. Lexicons can also be beneficial in cases where there are large amounts of training data, but only if the lexicon coverage is high. Our experiments show that using lexicons as embedding features generally leads to good improvements in a variety of situations.

References

Fabrice Dugas and Eric Nichols. 2016. DeepNNNER: Applying BLSTM-CNNs and Extended Lexicons to Named Entity Recognition in Tweets. In *Proceedings of the 2nd Workshop on User Generated Text*, pages 138–144.

Young-Bum Kim, Karl Stratos, and Dongchan Kim. 2017. Domain Attention with an Ensemble of Experts. In *Proceedings of the 55th Annual Meeting of the Association for Computational Linguistics*, pages 643–653.

Diederik Kingma and Jimmy Ba. 2014. Adam: A Method for Stochastic Optimization. *arXiv preprint arXiv:1412.6980*.

Gakuto Kurata, Bing Xiang, Bowen Zhou, and Mo Yu. 2016. Leveraging sentence-level information with encoder lstm for semantic slot filling. In *Proceedings of the 2016 Conference on Empirical Methods in Natural Language Processing*, pages 2077–2083.

Guillaume Lample, Miguel Ballesteros, Sandeep Subramanian, Kazuya Kawakami, and Chris Dyer. 2016. Neural Architectures for Named Entity Recognition. *arXiv preprint arXiv:1603.01360*.

Xiujun Li, Yun-Nung Chen, Lihong Li, Jianfeng Gao, and Asli Celikyilmaz. 2017. Investigation of Language Understanding Impact for Reinforcement Learning Based Dialogue Systems. *arXiv preprint arXiv:1703.07055*.

Xuezhe Ma and Eduard Hovy. 2016. End-to-end Sequence Labeling via Bi-directional LSTM-CNNS-CRF. *arXiv preprint arXiv:1603.01354*.

Grégoire Mesnil, Yann Dauphin, Kaisheng Yao, Yoshua Bengio, Li Deng, Dilek Hakkani-Tur, Xiaodong He, Larry Heck, Gokhan Tur, Dong Yu, et al. 2015. Using Recurrent Neural Networks for Slot Filling in Spoken Language Understanding. *IEEE/ACM Transactions on Audio, Speech and Language Processing (TASLP)*, 23(3):530–539.

Lev Ratinov and Dan Roth. 2009. Design challenges and misconceptions in named entity recognition. In *Proceedings of the Thirteenth Conference on Computational Natural Language Learning*, pages 147–155.

Yangyang Shi, Kaisheng Yao, Hu Chen, Dong Yu, Yi-Cheng Pan, and Mei-Yuh Hwang. 2016. Recurrent Support Vector Machines For Slot Tagging In Spoken Language Understanding. In *Annual Conference of the North American Chapter of the Association for Computational Linguistics*, pages 393–399.

Erik F Tjong Kim Sang and Fien De Meulder. 2003. Introduction to the conll-2003 shared task: Language-independent named entity recognition. In *Proceedings of the seventh conference on Natural language learning at HLT-NAACL 2003-Volume 4*, pages 142–147.

Kaisheng Yao, Baolin Peng, Yu Zhang, Dong Yu, Geoffrey Zweig, and Yangyang Shi. 2014. Spoken Language Understanding Using Long Short-term Memory Neural Networks. In *Spoken Language Technology Workshop (SLT), 2014 IEEE*, pages 189–194. IEEE.

Active Learning for New Domains in Natural Language Understanding

Stanislav Peshterliev, John Kearney, Abhyuday Jagannatha, Imre Kiss, Spyros Matsoukas
Alexa Machine Learning, Amazon.com
`{stanislp,jkearn,abhyudj,ikiss,matsouka}@amazon.com`

Abstract

We explore active learning (AL) for improving the accuracy of new domains in a natural language understanding (NLU) system. We propose an algorithm called Majority-CRF that uses an ensemble of classification models to guide the selection of relevant utterances, as well as a sequence labeling model to help prioritize informative examples. Experiments with three domains show that Majority-CRF achieves 6.6%-9% relative error rate reduction compared to random sampling with the same annotation budget, and statistically significant improvements compared to other AL approaches. Additionally, case studies with human-in-the-loop AL on six new domains show 4.6%-9% improvement on an existing NLU system.

1 Introduction

Intelligent voice assistants (IVA) such as Amazon Alexa, Apple Siri, Google Assistant, and Microsoft Cortana, are becoming increasingly popular. For IVA, natural language understanding (NLU) is a main component (De Mori et al., 2008), in conjunction with automatic speech recognition (ASR) and dialog management (DM). ASR converts user's speech to text. Then, the text is passed to NLU for classifying the action or "intent" that the user wants to invoke (e.g., PlayMusicIntent, TurnOn-Intent, BuyItemIntent) and recognizing named-entities (e.g., Artist, Genre, City). Based on the NLU output, DM decides the appropriate response, which could be starting a song playback or turning off lights. NLU systems for IVA support functionality in a wide range of domains, such as music, weather, and traffic. Also, an important requirement is the ability to add support for new domains.

The NLU models for Intent Classification (IC) and Named Entity Recognition (NER) use machine learning to recognize variation in natural language.

Diverse, annotated training data collected from IVA users, or "annotated live utterances," are essential for these models to achieve good performance. As such, new domains frequently exhibit suboptimal performance due to a lack of annotated live utterances. While an initial training dataset can be bootstrapped using grammar generated utterances and crowdsourced collection (Amazon Mechanical Turk), the performance that can be achieved using these approaches is limited because of the unexpected discrepancies between anticipated and live usage. Thus, a mechanism is required to select live utterances to be manually annotated for enriching the training dataset.

Random sampling is a common method for selecting live utterances for annotation. However, in an IVA setting with many users, the number of available live utterances is vast. Meanwhile, due to the high cost of manual annotation, only a small percentage of utterances can be annotated. As such, in a random sample of live data, the number of utterances relevant to new domains may be small. Moreover, those utterances may not be informative, where informative utterances are those that, if annotated and added to the training data, reduce the error rates of the NLU system. Thus, for new domains, we want a sampling procedure which selects utterances that are both relevant and informative.

Active learning (AL) (Settles, 2009) refers to machine learning methods that can interact with the sampling procedure and guide the selection of data for annotation. In this work, we explore using AL for live utterance selection for new domains in NLU. Authors have successfully applied AL techniques to NLU systems with little annotated data overall (Tur et al., 2003; Shen et al., 2004). The difference with our work is that, to the best of our knowledge, there is little published AL research that focuses on data selection explicitly targeting new domains.

Proceedings of NAACL-HLT 2019, pages 90–96
Minneapolis, Minnesota, June 2 - June 7, 2019. ©2019 Association for Computational Linguistics

We compare the efficacy of least-confidence (Lewis and Catlett, 1994) and query-by-committee (Freund et al., 1997) AL for new domains. Moreover, we propose an AL algorithm called Majority-CRF, designed to improve both IC and NER of an NLU system. Majority-CRF uses an ensemble of classification models to guide the selection of relevant utterances, as well as a sequence labeling model to help prioritize informative examples. Simulation experiments on three different new domains show that Majority-CRF achieves 6.6%-9% relative improvements in-domain compared to random sampling, as well as significant improvements compared to other active learning approaches.

2 Related Work

Expected model change (Settles et al., 2008) and expected error reduction (Roy and McCallum, 2001) are AL approaches based on decision theory. Expected model change tries to select utterances that cause the greatest change on the model. Similarly, expected error reduction tries to select utterances that are going to maximally reduce generalization error. Both methods provide sophisticated ways for ascertaining the value of annotating an utterance. However, they require computing an expectation across all possible ways to label the utterance, which is computationally expensive for NER and IC models with many labels and millions of parameters. Instead, approaches to AL for NLU generally require finding a proxy, such as model uncertainty, to estimate the value of getting specific points annotated.

Tur et al. studied least-confidence and query-by-committee disagreement AL approaches for reducing the annotation effort (Tur et al., 2005, 2003). Both performed better than random sampling, and the authors concluded that the overall annotation effort could be halved. We investigate both of these approaches, but also a variety of new algorithms that build upon these basic ideas.

Schutze et al. (Schütze et al., 2006) showed that AL is susceptible to the missed cluster effect when selection focuses only on low confidence examples around the existing decision boundary, missing important clusters of data that receive high confidence. They conclude that AL may produce a suboptimal classifier compared to random sampling with a large budget. To solve this problem Osugi et al. (Osugi et al., 2005) proposed an AL algorithm

that can balance exploitation (sampling around the decision boundary) and exploration (random sampling) by reallocating the sampling budget between the two. In our setting, we start with a representative seed dataset, then we iteratively select and annotate small batches of data that are used as feedback in subsequent selections, such that extensive exploration is not required.

To improve AL, Hong-Kwang and Vaibhava (Kuo and Goel, 2005) proposed to exploit the similarity between instances. Their results show improvements over simple confidence-based selection for data sizes of less than 5,000 utterances. A computational limitation of the approach is that it requires computing the pairwise utterance similarity, an $\mathcal{O}(N^2)$ operation that is slow for millions of utterances available in production IVA. However, their approach could be potentially sped-up with techniques like locality-sensitive hashing.

3 Active Learning For New Domains

We first discuss random sampling baselines and standard active learning approaches. Then, we describe the Majority-CRF algorithm and the other AL algorithms that we tested.

3.1 Random Sampling Baselines

A common strategy to select live utterances for annotation is random sampling. We consider two baselines: uniform random sampling and domain random sampling.

Uniform random sampling is widespread because it provides unbiased samples of the live utterance distribution. However, the samples contain fewer utterances for new domains because of their low usage frequency. Thus, under a limited annotation budget, accuracy improvements on new domains are limited.

Domain random sampling uses the predicted NLU domain to provide samples of live utterances more relevant to the target domains. However, this approach does not select the most informative utterances.

3.2 Active Learning Baselines

AL algorithms can select relevant and informative utterances for annotation. Two popular AL approaches are least-confidence and query-by-committee.

Least-confidence (Lewis and Catlett, 1994) involves processing live data with the NLU models and prioritizing selection of the utterances with the least confidence. The intuition is that utterances with low confidence are difficult, and "teaching" the models how they should be labeled is informative. However, a weakness of this method is that out-of-domain or irrelevant utterances are likely to be selected due to low confidence. This weakness can be alleviated by looking at instances with medium confidence using measures such as least margin between the top-n hypotheses (Scheffer et al., 2001) or highest Shannon entropy (Settles and Craven, 2008).

Query-by-committee (QBC) (Freund et al., 1997) uses different classifiers (e.g., SVMs, MaxEnt, Random Forests) that are trained on the existing annotated data. Each classifier is applied independently to every candidate and the utterances assigned the most diverse labels are prioritized for annotation. One problem with this approach is that, depending on the model and the size of the committee, it could be computationally expensive to apply on large datasets.

3.3 Majority-CRF Algorithm

Majority-CRF is a confidence-based AL algorithm that uses models trained on the available NLU training set but does not rely on predictions from the full NLU system. Its simplicity compared to a full NLU system offers several advantages. First, fast incremental training with the selected annotated data. Second, fast predictions on millions of utterances. Third, the selected data is not biased to the current NLU models, which makes our approach reusable even if the models change.

Algorithm 1 shows a generic AL procedure that we use to implement Majority-CRF, as well as other AL algorithms that we tested. We train an ensemble of models on positive data from the target domain of interest (e.g., Books) and negative data that is everything not in the target domain (e.g., Music, Videos). Then, we use the models to filter and prioritize a batch of utterances for annotation. After the batch is annotated, we retrain the models with the new data and repeat the process.

To alleviate the tendency of the least-confidence approaches to select irrelevant data, we add unsupported utterances and sentence fragments to the negative class training data of the AL models. This helps keep noisy utterances on the negative side of the decision boundary, so that they can be eliminated during filtering. Note that, when targeting

several domains at a time, we run the selection procedure independently and then deduplicate the utterances before sending them for annotation.

Algorithm 1 Generic AL procedure that selects data for a target domain

---

Inputs:

$D \leftarrow$ positive and negative training data

$P \leftarrow$ pool of unannotated live utterances

$i \leftarrow$ iterations, $m \leftarrow$ mini-batch size

Parameters:

$\{\mathcal{M}^k\} \leftarrow$ set of selection models

$\mathcal{F} \leftarrow$ filtering function

$\mathcal{S} \leftarrow$ scoring function

Procedure:

1: **repeat** i iterations
2:     Train selection models $\{\mathcal{M}^k\}$ on D
3:     $\forall\ x_i \in P$ obtain prediction scores $y_i^k = \mathcal{M}^k(x_i)$
4:     $P' \leftarrow \{x_i \in P : \mathcal{F}(y_i^0..y_i^k)\}$
5:     $C \leftarrow \{x_i \in P' : m$ with the smallest score $\mathcal{S}(y_i^0..y_i^k)\}$
6:     Send C for manual annotation
7:     After annotation is done $D \leftarrow D \cup C$ and $P \leftarrow P \setminus C$
8: **until**

Models. We experimented with n-gram linear binary classifiers trained to minimize different loss functions: $\mathcal{M}^{lg} \leftarrow$ logistic, $\mathcal{M}^{hg} \leftarrow$ hinge, and $\mathcal{M}^{sq} \leftarrow$ squared. Each classifier is trained to distinguish between positive and negative data and learns a different decision boundary. Note that we use the raw unnormalized prediction scores $\{y_i^{lg}, y_i^{hg}, y_i^{sq}\}$ (no sigmoid applied) that can be interpreted as distances between the utterance x_i and the classifiers decision boundaries at $y = 0$. The classifiers are implemented in Vowpal Wabbit (Langford et al., 2007) with $\{1, 2, 3\}$-gram features. To directly target the NER task, we used an additional $\mathcal{M}^{cf} \leftarrow$ CRF, trained on the NER labels of the target domain.

Filtering function. We experimented with $\mathcal{F}^{maj} \leftarrow \sum \text{sgn}(y^k) > 0$, i.e., keep only majority positive prediction from the binary classifiers, and $\mathcal{F}^{dis} \leftarrow \sum \text{sgn}(y^k) \in \{-1, 1\}$, i.e., keep only prediction where there is at least one disagreement.

Scoring function. When the set of models $\{\mathcal{M}^k\}$ consists of only binary classifiers, we combine the classifier scores using either the sum of

Algorithm	Models $\{\mathcal{M}^i\}$	Filter $\mathcal{F}$	Scoring $\mathcal{S}$
AL-Logistic	lg	$\operatorname{sgn}(y^{lg}) > 0$	y^{lg}
QBC-SA	lg, sq, hg	$\sum \operatorname{sgn}(y^k) \in \{-1, 1\}$	$\sum |y^k|$
QBC-AS	lg, sq, hg	$\sum \operatorname{sgn}(y^k) \in \{-1, 1\}$	$|\sum y^k|$
Majority-SA	lg, sq, hg	$\sum \operatorname{sgn}(y^k) > 0$	$\sum |y^k|$
Majority-AS	lg, sq, hg	$\sum \operatorname{sgn}(y^k) > 0$	$|\sum y^k|$
QBC-CRF	lg, sq, hg, CRF	$\sum \operatorname{sgn}(y^k) \in \{-1, 1\}$	$p^{lg} \times p^{crf}$
Majority-CRF	lg, sq, hg, CRF	$\sum \operatorname{sgn}(y^k) > 0$	$p^{lg} \times p^{crf}$

Table 1: AL algorithms evaluated. lg, sq, hg refer to binary classifiers (committee members) trained with logistic, squared and hinge loss functions, respectively. y^i denotes the score of committee member i, p^{crf} denotes the confidence of the CRF model and $p^{lg} = (1 + e^{-y^{lg}})^{-1}$ denotes the confidence of the logistic classifier. In all cases, we prioritize by smallest score $\mathcal{S}$.

absolutes $\mathcal{S}^{sa} \leftarrow \sum |y_i^k|$ or the absolute sum $\mathcal{S}^{as} \leftarrow |\sum y_i^k|$. $\mathcal{S}^{sa}$ prioritizes utterances where all scores are small (i.e., close to all decision boundaries), and $\mathcal{S}^{as}$ prioritizes utterances where either all scores are small or there is large disagreement between classifiers (e.g., one score is large negative, another is large positive, and the third is small). Both $\mathcal{S}^{sa}$ and $\mathcal{S}^{as}$ can be seen as generalization of least-confidence to a committee of classifiers. When the set of models $\{\mathcal{M}^k\}$ includes a CRF model $\mathcal{M}^{cf}$, we compute the score with $\mathcal{S}^{cg} \leftarrow P_{cf}(i) \times P_{lg}(i)$, i.e., the CRF probability $P_{cf}(i)$ multiplied by the logistic classifier probability $P_{lg}(i) = \sigma(y_i^{lg})$, where σ is the sigmoid function. Note that we ignore the outputs of the squared and hinge classifiers for scoring, though they are still be used for filtering.

The full set of configurations we evaluated is given in Table 1, which specifies the choice of parameters $\{\mathcal{M}^k\}, \mathcal{F}, \mathcal{S}$ used in Algorithm 1.

AL-Logistic and QBC serve as baseline AL algorithms. The QBC-CRF and Majority-CRF models combine the IC focused binary classifier scores with the NER focused sequence labeling scores and use filtering by disagreement and majority (respectively) to select informative utterances. To the best of our knowledge, this is a novel architecture for active learning in NLU.

Mamitsuka et al. (Mamitsuka et al., 1998) proposed bagging to build classifier committees for AL. Bagging refers to random sampling with replacement of the original training data to create diverse classifiers. We experimented with bagging but found that it is not better than using different classifiers.

4 Experimental Results

4.1 Evaluation Metrics

We use Slot Error Rate (SER) (Makhoul et al., 1999), including the intent as slot, to evaluate the overall predictive performance of the NLU models. SER as the ratio of the number of slot prediction errors to the total number of reference slots. Errors are insertions, substitutions and deletions. We treat the intent misclassifications as substitution errors.

4.2 Simulated Active Learning

AL requires manual annotations which are costly. Therefore, to conduct multiple controlled experiments with different selection algorithms, we simulated AL by taking a subset of the available annotated training data as the unannotated candidate pool, and "hiding" the annotations. As such, the NLU system and AL algorithm had a small pool of annotated utterances for simulated "new" domains. Then, the AL algorithm was allowed to choose relevant utterances from the simulated candidate pool. Once an utterance is selected, its annotation is revealed to the AL algorithm, as well as to the full NLU system.

Dataset. We conducted experiments using an internal test dataset of 750K randomly sampled live utterances, and a training dataset of 42M utterances containing a combination of grammar generated and randomly sampled live utterances. The dataset covers 24 domains, including Music, Shopping, Local Search, Sports, Books, Cinema and Calendar.

NLU System. Our NLU system has one set of IC and NER models per domain. The IC model predicts one of its in-domain intents or a special out-of-domain intent which helps with domain classification. The IC and NER predictions are ranked into a single n-best list based on model confidences (Su et al., 2018). We use MaxEnt (Berger et al., 1996) models for IC and the CRF models for NER (Lafferty et al., 2001).

Experimental Design. We split the training data into a 12M utterances initial training set for IC and NER, and a 30M utterance candidate pool for selection. We choose Books, Local Search, and Cinema as target domains to simulate the AL al-

Domain	Train	Test	Examples
Books	290K	13K	"search in mystery books" "read me a book"
Local Search	260K	16K	"mexican food nearby" "pick the top bank"
Cinema	270K	9K	"more about hulk" "what's playing in theaters"

Table 2: Simulated "new" target domains for AL experiments. The target domain initial training datasets are 90% grammar generated data. The other 21 "non-new" domains have on average 550k initial training datasets with 60% grammar generated data and 40% live data.

gorithms, see Table 2. Each target domain had 550-650K utterances in the candidate pool. The rest of the 21 non-target domains have 28.5M utterances in the candidate pool. We also added 100K sentence fragments and out-of-domain utterances to the candidate pool, which allows us to compare the susceptibility of different algorithms to noisy or irrelevant data. This experimental setup attempts to simulate the production IVA use case where the candidate pool has a large proportion of utterances that belong to different domains.

We employed the different AL algorithms to select 12K utterances per domain from the candidate pool, for a total 36K utterance annotation budget. Also, we evaluated uniform (Rand-Uniform) and domain (Rand-Domain) random sampling with the same total budget. We ran each AL configuration twice and average the SER scores to account for fluctuations in selection caused by the stochasticity in model training. For random sampling, we ran each selection five times.

4.2.1 Simulated Active Learning Results

Table 3 shows the experimental results for the target domains Books, Local Search, and Cinema. For each experiment, we add all AL selected data (in- and out-of-domain), and evaluate SER for the full NLU system.

We test for statistically significant improvements using the Wilcoxon test (Hollander et al., 2013) with 1000 bootstrap resamples and p-value < 0.05.

Random Baselines. As expected, Rand-Uniform selected few relevant utterances for the target domains due to their low frequency in the candidate pool. Rand-Domain selects relevant utterances for the target domains, achieving statistically significant SER improvements compared to Rand-Uniform. However, the overall gains are

small, around 1% relative per target domain. A significant factor for Rand-Domain's limited improvement is that it tends to capture frequently-occurring utterances that the NLU models can already recognize without errors. As such, all AL configurations achieved statistically significant SER gains compared to the random baselines.

Single Model Algorithms. AL-Logistic, which carries out a single iteration of confidence-based selection, exhibits a statistically significant reduction in SER relative to Rand-Domain. Moreover, using six iterations (i.e., $i=6$) further reduced SER by a statistically significant 1%-2% relative to AL-Logistic($i=1$), and resulted in the selection of 200 fewer unsupported utterances. This result demonstrates the importance of incremental selection for iteratively refining the selection model.

Committee Algorithms. AL algorithms incorporating a committee of models outperformed those based on single models by a statistically significant 1-2% ΔSER. The *majority* algorithms performed slightly better than the QBC algorithms and were able to collect more in-domain utterances. The absolute sum scoring function $\mathcal{S}^{as}$ performed slightly better than the sum of absolutes $\mathcal{S}^{sa}$ for both QBC and Majority. Amongst all committee algorithms, Majority-AS performed best, but the differences with the other committee algorithms are not statistically significant.

Committee and CRF Algorithms. AL algorithms incorporating a CRF model tended to outperform purely classification-based approaches, indicating the importance of specifically targeting the NER task. The Majority-CRF algorithm achieves a statistically significant SER improvement of 1-2% compared to Majority-AS (the best configuration without the CRF). Again, the disagreement-based QBC-CRF algorithm performed worse that the majority algorithm across target domains. This difference was statistically significant on Books, but not on Cinema and Local Search.

In summary, AL yields more rapid improvements not only by selecting utterances relevant to the target domain but also by trying to select the most informative utterances. For instance, although the AL algorithms selected 40-50% false positive utterances from non-target domains, whereas Rand-Domain selected only around 20% false positives, the AL algorithms still outperformed Rand-Domain. This indicates that labeling ambiguous false positives helps resolve existing confusions

Algorithm Group	Algorithm ($i = 6$)	Overall	Books		Local Search		Cinema		Non-Target
		#Utt	#Utt	ΔSER	#Utt	ΔSER	#Utt	ΔSER	#Utt
Random	Rand-Uniform	35.8K	747	1.20	672	3.37	547	0.57	33.8K
	Rand-Domain	35.7K	9853	1.52	9453	4.23	9541	1.75	06.8K
Single Model	AL-Logistic(i=1)	34.9K	5405	4.76	7092	6.54	5224	6.09	17.1K
	AL-Logistic	35.1k	5524	6.77	7709	7.24	5330	7.29	16.5K
Committee Models	QBC-AS	35.0K	4768	7.18	7869	8.57	4706	8.72	17.6K
	QBC-SA	35.0K	4705	7.12	7721	8.96	4790	7.52	17.7K
	Majority-AS	35.1K	5389	<u>7.66</u>	8013	9.07	5526	8.98	16.1K
	Majority-SA	35.1K	5267	7.35	8196	8.46	5193	8.42	16.4K
Committee and CRF	QBC-CRF	35.1K	3653	7.44	6593	<u>9.78</u>	4064	<u>10.26</u>	20.7K
	Majority-CRF	35.1K	6541	**8.42**	8552	**9.92**	6951	**11.05**	13.0K

Table 3: Simulation experimental results with 36K annotation budget. ΔSER is % relative reduction is SER compared to the initial model: Books SER 30.59, Local Search SER 39.09, Cinema SER 38.71. Higher ΔSER is better. The best result is in bold, and the second best is underlined. The $i = 1$ means selection in a single iteration, otherwise if not specified selection is in six iterations ($i = 6$). Overall #Utt shows the remaining from the 36K selected after removing the sentence fragments and out-of-domain utterances. Both target and non-target domains IC and NER models are re-retrained with the new data.

between domains. Another important observation is that majority filtering $\mathcal{F}^{maj}$ performs better than QBC disagreement filtering $\mathcal{F}^{dis}$ across all of our experiments. A possible reason for this is that majority filtering selects a better balance of boundary utterances for classification and in-domain utterances for NER. Finally, the Majority-CRF results show that incorporating the CRF model improves the performance of the committee algorithms. We assume this is because incorporation of a CRF-based confidence directly targets the NER task.

4.3 Human-in-the-loop Active Learning

We also performed AL for six new NLU domains with human-in-the-loop annotators and live user data. We used the Majority-SA configuration for simplicity in these case studies. We ran the AL selection for 5-10 iterations with varying batch sizes between 1000-2000.

Domain	ΔSER	#Utt Selected	#Utt Testset
Recipes	8.97	24.1K	4.7K
LiveTV	6.92	11.6K	1.8K
OpeningHours	7.05	6.8K	583
Navigation	4.67	6.7K	6.4K
DropIn	9.00	5.3K	7.2K
Membership	7.13	4.2K	702

Table 4: AL with human annotator results. ΔSER is % relative gain compared to the existing model. Higher is better.

Table 4 shows the results from AL with human annotators. On each feature, AL improved our existing NLU model by a statistically significant 4.6%-9%. On average 25% of utterances are false positive. This is lower than the 50% in the simulation because the initial training data exhibits more examples of the negative class. Around 10% of the AL selected data is lost due to being unactionable or out-of-domain, similar to the frequency with which these utterances are collected by random sampling.

While working with human annotators on new domains, we observed two challenges that impact the improvements from AL. First, annotators make more mistakes on AL selected utterances as they are more ambiguous. Second, new domains may have a limited amount of test data, so the impact of AL cannot be fully measured. Currently, we address the annotation mistakes with manual data clean up and transformations, but further research is needed to develop an automated solution. To improve the coverage of the test dataset for new domains we are exploring test data selection using stratified sampling.

5 Conclusions

In this work, we focused on AL methods designed to select live data for manual annotation. The difference with prior work on AL is that we specifically target new domains in NLU. Our proposed Majority-CRF algorithm leads to statistically significant performance gains over standard AL and random sampling methods while working with a limited annotation budget. In simulations, our Majority-CRF algorithm showed an improvement of 6.6%-9% SER relative gain compared to random sampling, as well as improvements over other AL algorithms with the same annotation budget. Similarly, results with live annotators show statistically significant improvements of 4.6%-9% compared to the existing NLU system.

References

Adam L Berger, Vincent J Della Pietra, and Stephen A Della Pietra. 1996. A maximum entropy approach to natural language processing. *Computational linguistics*.

Renato De Mori, Frédéric Bechet, Dilek Hakkani-Tur, Michael McTear, Giuseppe Riccardi, and Gokhan Tur. 2008. Spoken language understanding.

Yoav Freund, H Sebastian Seung, Eli Shamir, and Naftali Tishby. 1997. Selective sampling using the query by committee algorithm. *Machine learning*.

Myles Hollander, Douglas A Wolfe, and Eric Chicken. 2013. *Nonparametric statistical methods*. John Wiley & Sons.

Hong-Kwang Jeff Kuo and Vaibhava Goel. 2005. Active learning with minimum expected error for spoken language understanding. In *INTERSPEECH*.

John Lafferty, Andrew McCallum, Fernando Pereira, et al. 2001. Conditional random fields: Probabilistic models for segmenting and labeling sequence data. In *Proceedings of the eighteenth international conference on machine learning, ICML*.

John Langford, Lihong Li, and Alex Strehl. 2007. Vowpal Wabbit.

David D Lewis and Jason Catlett. 1994. Heterogeneous uncertainty sampling for supervised learning. In *Proceedings of the eleventh international conference on machine learning*.

John Makhoul, Francis Kubala, Richard Schwartz, and Ralph Weischedel. 1999. Performance measures for information extraction. In *In Proceedings of DARPA Broadcast News Workshop*.

Naoki Abe Hiroshi Mamitsuka et al. 1998. Query learning strategies using boosting and bagging. In *Machine learning: proceedings of the fifteenth international conference (ICML'98)*, volume 1. Morgan Kaufmann Pub.

Thomas Osugi, Deng Kim, and Stephen Scott. 2005. Balancing exploration and exploitation: A new algorithm for active machine learning. In *Data Mining, Fifth IEEE International Conference on*.

Nicholas Roy and Andrew McCallum. 2001. Toward optimal active learning through monte carlo estimation of error reduction. *ICML, Williamstown*.

Tobias Scheffer, Christian Decomain, and Stefan Wrobel. 2001. Active hidden markov models for information extraction. In *International Symposium on Intelligent Data Analysis*.

Hinrich Schütze, Emre Velipasaoglu, and Jan O Pedersen. 2006. Performance thresholding in practical text classification.

Burr Settles. 2009. Active learning literature survey. Computer sciences technical report, University of Wisconsin–Madison.

Burr Settles and Mark Craven. 2008. An analysis of active learning strategies for sequence labeling tasks. In *Proceedings of the conference on empirical methods in natural language processing*.

Burr Settles, Mark Craven, and Soumya Ray. 2008. Multiple-instance active learning. In *Advances in neural information processing systems*.

Dan Shen, Jie Zhang, Jian Su, Guodong Zhou, and Chew-Lim Tan. 2004. Multi-criteria-based active learning for named entity recognition. In *Proceedings of the 42Nd Annual Meeting on Association for Computational Linguistics*.

Chengwei Su, Rahul Gupta, Shankar Ananthakrishnan, and Spyros Matsoukas. 2018. A re-ranker scheme for integrating large scale nlu models. *arXiv preprint arXiv:1809.09605*.

Gokhan Tur, Dilek Hakkani-Tür, and Robert E Schapire. 2005. Combining active and semi-supervised learning for spoken language understanding. *Speech Communication*.

Gokhan Tur, Robert E Schapire, and Dilek Hakkani-Tur. 2003. Active learning for spoken language understanding. In *Acoustics, Speech, and Signal Processing, 2003. Proceedings.(ICASSP'03). 2003 IEEE International Conference on*.

Scaling Multi-Domain Dialogue State Tracking via Query Reformulation

Pushpendre Rastogi
prastogi@amazon.com
Alexa AI
Amazon.com, Inc., USA

Arpit Gupta
arpgup@amazon.com
Alexa AI
Amazon.com, Inc., USA

Tongfei Chen *
tongfei@jhu.edu
Johns Hopkins University
Baltimore, MD,USA

Lambert Mathias
mathiasl@amazon.com
Alexa AI
Amazon.com, Inc., USA

Abstract

We present a novel approach to dialogue state tracking and referring expression resolution tasks. Successful contextual understanding of multi-turn spoken dialogues requires resolving referring expressions across turns and tracking the entities relevant to the conversation across turns. Tracking conversational state is particularly challenging in a multi-domain scenario when there exist multiple spoken language understanding (SLU) sub-systems, and each SLU sub-system operates on its domain-specific meaning representation. While previous approaches have addressed the disparate schema issue by learning candidate transformations of the meaning representation, in this paper, we instead model the reference resolution as a dialogue context-aware user query reformulation task —the dialog state is serialized to a sequence of natural language tokens representing the conversation. We develop our model for query reformulation using a pointer-generator network and a novel multi-task learning setup. In our experiments, we show a significant improvement in absolute F1 on an internal as well as a, soon to be released public corpora respectively.

1 Introduction

Dialogue *assistants* are used by millions of people today to fulfill a variety of tasks. Such assistants also serve as a digital marketplace[1] (Kumar et al., 2017) where any developer can build a domain-specific, task-oriented, dialogue *agent* offering a service such as booking cabs, ordering food, listening to music, shopping etc. Also, these agents may interact with each other, when completing a task on behalf of the user. Figure 1 shows one such interaction where the agent – ShopBot – must interpret the output of the agent – WikiBot. Often

---

* Work done while the author was at Alexa AI
[1] https://dialogflow.com

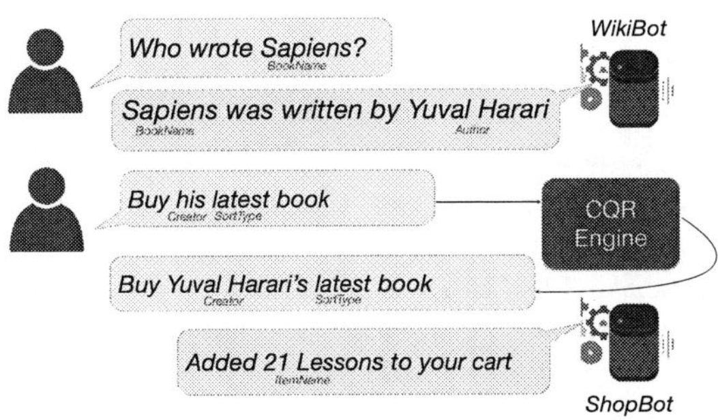

Figure 1: An example dialog where the second utterance by the user BUY HIS LATEST BOOK is reformulated as BUY YUVAL HARARI 'S LATEST BOOK. This reformulated user query is then input to SHOPBOT so that it can understand the user's request using its existing SLU logic for handling single-turn queries. This approach does not require any changes to the agent itself and can be scaled to multiple heterogeneous domains.

accomplishing this task requires understanding the context of a dialogue, communicating the conversational state to multiple agents and updating the state as the conversation proceeds.

Tracking the dialogue state across multiple agents is challenging because agents are typically built for single-turn experiences, and must be laboriously updated to handle the context provided by other agents into their respective domain specific meaning representation. (Naik et al., 2018) proposed *context carryover*, a scalable approach to handle disparate schemas by learning mappings across the meaning representations, thereby eliminating the need to update the agents. However, the challenge of the agent's domain-specific SLU accuracy and choice of meaning representation remains. For example, in Figure 1 the SHOPBOT cannot handle pronominal anaphora and instead incorrectly labels HIS as the mention type CREATOR. Separately solving this problem for each agent, imposes

Proceedings of NAACL-HLT 2019, pages 97–105
Minneapolis, Minnesota, June 2 - June 7, 2019. ©2019 Association for Computational Linguistics

a burden on the developer to relabel their data and update their SLU models, and is expensive and unscalable. Moreover, this approach cannot leverage the syntactic regularities imposed across agents by the natural language itself.

In this work, we propose a novel approach for enabling seamless interaction between agents developed by different developers by using natural language as the API. We build upon the pointer-generator network (PGN) proposed by (See et al., 2017) – originally for news article summarization – to rewrite user utterances and disambiguate them. Furthermore, we describe a new Multi-task Learning (MTL) objective to directly influence the attention of the PGN without requiring any extra manually annotated training data. Our results show that the new MTL objective reduces the error by 3.2% on slots coming from distances ≥ 3, compared to the basic PGN by (See et al., 2017).

2   Technical Details

Task We define a sequence of D dialogue turns, $\mathbf{x_t} = (u_{t-D+1}, r_{t-D+1}, \ldots, u_{t-1}, r_{t-1}, u_t)$, where u_t is the user utterance at time t and r_t is the corresponding system response. $\mathbf{x_t}$ is the total information that our system has at time t. For example, the first row in Figure 2 shows $\mathbf{x_2}$ encoded as a single token sequence corresponding to the dialogue in Figure 1. The query rewriting task is to learn a function f_θ, with parameters θ, which maps $\mathbf{x_t}$ to its *rewrite* $\mathbf{y_t}$ which is another string, i.e. $\mathbf{y_t} = f_\theta(\mathbf{x_t})$. $\mathbf{y_t}$ should contain all the information needed by the agent to fulfill the user's request and it should be understandable by the agent as a standalone user request.

Model We use the pointer-generator (PGN) architecture (See et al., 2017) to construct f_θ. The PGN is a hybrid architecture which combines sequence-to-sequence model with pointer networks. This combination allows the PGN to summarize an input sequence by either *copying* from the input sentence, or *generating* a new word with a decoder RNN. We now describe the operation of the PGN in detail and focus on a single input sequence $\mathbf{x}$ with the subscript t omitted for simplicity. Let us slightly abuse notation and consider $\mathbf{x}, \mathbf{y}$ as sequences of tokens. We index the tokens of $\mathbf{x}, \mathbf{y}$ by l, k respectively. The PGN uses a two-layer Bi-Directional LSTM (BiLSTM) encoder to compute the hidden state vector h_l for $\mathbf{x}_l$.[2]

We now describe how y_k is generated. At time k, the probability of copying a token from the input p^{copy} is computed via a softmax over the attention weights computed using non-linear function of the encoder-LSTM hidden states $\mathbf{h}$ and the decoder LSTM's hidden state h_k^{decoder}. p^{mix} – a soft switch to decide between copying and generating – is computed using another non-linear function of h_k^{dec} and the final output distribution is given by

$$p(y_k) = p^{\text{mix}}p^{\text{gen}}(y_k) + (1 - p^{\text{mix}})p^{\text{copy}}(y_k) \quad (1)$$

At decoding time, we can use either beam-search or greedily pick the token with the highest probability and move on to the next step. This is our baseline architecture for utterance rewriting.

Evaluation Ideally $\mathbf{y_t}$ should be judged as a correct rewrite if the downstream SLU system can parse $\mathbf{y_t}$, invoke the correct agent with the correct slots, and the agent can then take the right action. However, evaluating this notion of correctness would have required probing and instrumenting thousands of downstream agents and is not scalable to implement. Therefore, we used a simpler notion of correctness based on a manually collected set of *golden rewrites*, $\mathcal{Y}_{i,t}^*$, in this paper. Section 4.3 describes the metrics we use to evaluate our model's prediction $y_{i,t}$ against the golden set $\mathcal{Y}_{i,t}^*$.

Learning For training the model, we have a rewrites-corpus $\{\mathbf{x}_{it}, \mathbf{y}_{itj}^*\}_{i=1,t=1,j=1}^{I,T,J}$. I is the number of dialogs, T is the maximum number of turns in a dialog and J is the number of gold rewrites at a turn in a dialog. $\mathbf{y}_{i,t,j}^*$ denotes the jth optimal rewrite for the user utterance at turn t in the ith dialogue – $\mathbf{x}_{ti}$; $y_{i,t,j,k}^*$ is the kth token in $\mathbf{y}_{i,t,j}^*$. Our training objective is to maximize the log-likelihood:

$$\arg\max_\theta \sum_{i,t,j,k} \log p_\theta(y_{i,t,j,k}^*). \quad (2)$$

2.1   Multi Task Learning (MTL): Entity-Copy Auxiliary Objective

In Figure 2, both the references $y_{2,1}^*, y_{2,2}^*$ contain the same subset of entities – U3, and S1 – even though their order, and other tokens, in the gold rewrites have changed. This implies that for the task of rewriting utterances, the subset of entities that should be copied from the input dialog remains the same, irrespective of the dynamics of the decoder LSTM. Based on this observation we define

---

[2]For sake of brevity, we omit the update equations for the LSTM. Please refer to (See et al., 2017) for these details.

Input $x_{t=2}$	BOOKQUERY$_{l=1}$ Who wrote $\frac{\textit{Entity}\text{U1:BookName}}{\text{Sapiens}}$ $_{l=4}$ $\frac{\text{SYSTEM}}{\text{INFORMINTENT}}$ $\frac{\textit{Entity}\text{U1:Sapiens}}{\text{Title}}$ was written by $\frac{\textit{Entity}\text{S1:Author}}{\text{Yuval Harari}}$ $_{l=10}$ $\frac{\text{USER}}{\text{UNKINTENT}}$ Buy $\frac{\textit{Entity}\text{U2:Entity}}{\text{his}}$ $\frac{\textit{Entity}\text{U3:Entity}}{\text{latest}}$ book END$_{l=16}$
Refer. $\mathcal{Y}^*_{t=2}$	$\left\{ y^*_{2,j=1}= \text{Buy}_{k=1}\ \textit{Entity}\text{S1}\ \textit{Entity}\text{U3 book}_{k=4},\ \ y^*_{2,2}= \text{Buy}\ \textit{Entity}\text{U3 book by}\ \textit{Entity}\text{S1} \right\}$

Figure 2: An example of sequential input received by our utterance disambiguation seq2seq model and a list of reference outputs. The words in short-caps denote the domain and intent predicted by the SLU system which are concatenated to the beginning of the sequence. Words beginning with *Entity* are placeholders used to delexicalize names of entities. Both references 1 and 2 are input to the SLU system during training. We explicitly named the indices at a few locations to aid the reader.

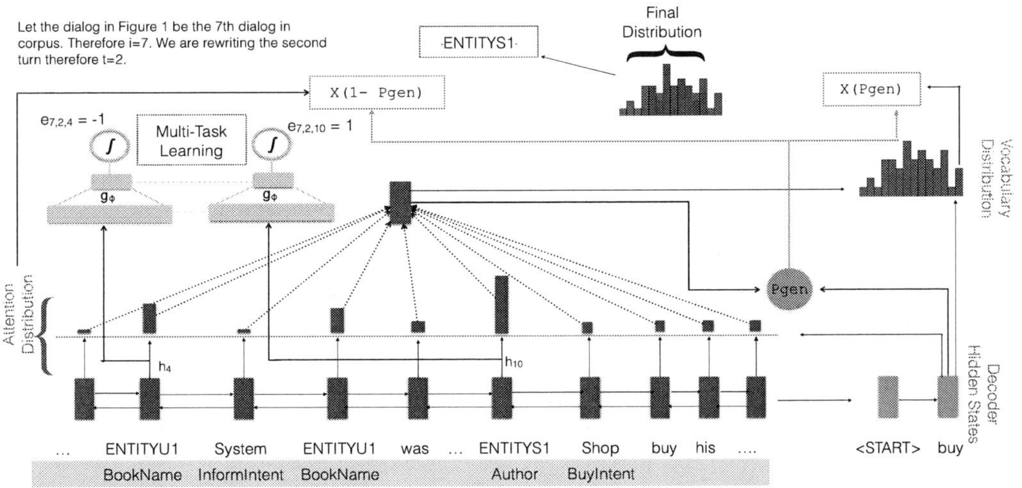

Figure 3: Model Architecture of the CQR Model which performs Multi-Task Learning for Pointer-Generator Networks. We show a snapshot just before decoder generates the word ENTITYS1 or *Yuval Harari*. Also, we show for MTL ENTITYU1 gets the label -1 as it is not one of the final slots, and ENTITYS1 gets a label of 1

an auxiliary task and augment the learning objective as shown in Figure 3.

As mentioned earlier, the copy distribution p_k^{copy} is a function of the encoder hidden state $\mathbf{h} = (h_1, \ldots, h_l, \ldots, h_{|x|})$ which does not change with k. If x_l was an entity token then h_l should be informative enough to decide whether that token should be copied or not. Therefore, we add a two layer feed-forward neural network, g_ϕ, that takes h_l as input and predicts whether the lth token should be copied or not. Given the probability $g_\phi(h_l)$ we minimize the binary cross-entropy loss, and backpropagate through h_l which influences θ. The auxiliary objective should improve the generalization because it forces the encoders representation to become more informative about whether an entity should be copied or not. At inference time g_ϕ is not used. Formally, let $e_{i,t,l}$ take the following value:

$$
e_{i,t,l} = \begin{cases} 1 & \text{if } x_{i,t,l} \text{ is an entity and } x_{i,t,l} \in \mathcal{Y}^*_{i,t} \\ -1 & \text{if } x_{i,t,l} \text{ is an entity and } x_{i,t,l} \notin \mathcal{Y}^*_{i,t} \\ 0 & \text{Otherwise} \end{cases}
$$

Let $\lambda > 0$ be a hyperparameter. We add a binary log-likelihood objective to objective 2 to create objective 3. We refer to the PGN model trained with objective 3 as **CQR** in Table 4.

$$
\sum_{i,t,j,k} \log p(y^*_{i,t,j,k}) + \lambda \sum_{i,t} \sum_{l=1}^{|x_{i,t}|} e_{i,t,l} \log g_\phi(h_{i,t,l}) \quad (3)
$$

3 DataSet and Preprocessing

In this section we will describe how we created the golden rewrites $\{\mathcal{Y}^*_t \mid \forall t\}$ for each of the above datasets and our pre-processing steps that we found crucial to our success.

3.1 Generating gold rewrites

We used two separate approaches to generate gold rewrites for the INTERNAL and INCAR datasets. For the INCAR dataset we collected 6 rewrites for each utterance that had a reference to a previously mentioned entity.[3] For the INTERNAL dataset, which has over 100K sentences the above approach would be prohibitively expensive. Therefore, instead of gathering completely new manual annotation we used a semi-manual process. We utilized a template dataset that is keyed by the *Domain, Intent* and *Slots* present in that utterance and contains the top-5 most common and unambiguous phrasing for that key. For example to create the rewrite in Figure 1 we filled the template:

Buy <u>Creator</u> 's <u>SortType</u> <u>ItemType</u>

This template was chosen randomly from other valid alternatives such as Buy SortType ItemType by Creator . These valid alternatives were determined on the basis of existing manual *domain, intent,* and *schema* SLU annotations which indicated which slots were required to answer the user's utterance.

3.2 Role-based Entity Indexing

In this step, the entity words in x_t are replaced with their canonical versions. Our results show that this significantly improved both BLEU and Entity F1 measures. To replace entity words we use string matching methods to extract tokens for dialogue. We maintain two separate namespaces for user entities and system entities respectively. However, if an entity appears again in dialogue, we do ***not*** assign it a new canonical token but used already assigned one. Also, as seen in Figure 2 we also add the entity tag to slot representation. Lastly, as re-writing happens before any SLU component we do not have this information for u_t. In u_t we only replace entities with canonical tokens, but do not add any information about entity. Table 1 show how to transform dialogue from Figure 1.

Before	After Pre-Processing
Who wrote Sapiens	who wrote U_1‖BookName
Sapiens was written by Yuval Harari	U_1‖Author was written by S_1‖BookName
Buy his most recent book	Buy U_3‖UNK U_4‖UNK book

Table 1: Replacing entities with the role-based canonical versions.

3.3 Abstractified Possessives

Generalizing on rare words and rare contexts is the true test of any NLP system, and linguists have long argued in favor of syntactically motivated models that abstract away from lexical entries as much as possible (Klein and Manning, 2003). In this preprocessing step, we show the benefit of such abstraction. While testing the PGN architecture we noticed that the sequence decoder would sometimes generate an off-topic rewrite if the input sequence contained a rare word. In order to avoid this problem we augmented the input sequence with additional features to mark the syntactic function of words. Specifically we used the Google Syntactic N-gram Corpus (Goldberg and Orwant, 2013) to add syntactic features to each word in the dialogue. We harvested a list of top 1000 words that appear most frequently after possessive pronouns. We concatenated three types of extra features to the words in a dialogue. The first feature was the QUESTION feature which was concatenated to the 7 question words. The second feature was the $PRP\$$ tag which we concatenated to specific possessive pronouns. Finally we added a tag called PSBL – short for possessible – for the top 1000 words that we found from the Syntactic N-Gram Corpus.

We decided not to use POS tags because we did not have manually POS tagged data on our domain and off-the-shelf POS tagger[4] did not perform well on our dataset.

4 Experiments

4.1 Dataset

We used two datasets to evaluate our method. The first is a public dataset (Regan et al., 2019) we call INCAR, which is an extension to (Eric and Manning, 2017). The dataset consists of $3,031$ dialogues from three domains: Calendar Scheduling, Weather, and Navigation, that are useful for an in-car conversational assistant. We crowd-sourced six

---

[3] https://github.com/alexa/
alexa-dataset-contextual-query-rewrite

[4] https://spacy.io/

rewrites for each utterance in the corpus that had a reference to previously mentioned entities. The second dataset, called INTERNAL, is an internal benchmark dataset we collected over six domains – weather, music, video, local business search, movie showtimes and general question answering. Table 2 describes the data statistics for this internal collection. About 40% of the dialogues in this corpus are cross-domain, which makes it much harder than the INCAR dataset.

Context Length	Train	Dev	Test
1	125K	42K	21K
2	8K	3k	1K
>=3	4K	1K	700

Table 2: INTERNAL data statistics. Each turn consists of a user and a system turn i.e context length = 2 implies two turns.

4.2 Training

We used OpenNMT (Klein et al., 2017) toolkit for all our experiments. We modified it to include the multi-task loss function as described in Section 2.1. Unless explicitly mentioned here, we used the default parameters defined in OpenNMT recipe. Various hyper-parameters were tuned on a reduced training set and the development set. Our encoder was a 128-dimensional bi-directional LSTM. We used the Adagrad optimizer with a learning rate of 0.15, and we randomly initialized 128-dimensional word embeddings. The word embeddings were shared between the encoder LSTM and the decoder LSTM. λ in Eq.3 was set to 0.01. We trained the model for 20 epochs with early stopping on a validation set.

4.3 Evaluation Metrics

BLEU: has been widely used in machine translation tasks (Papineni et al., 2002), dialogue tasks (Eric and Manning, 2017), and chatbots (Ritter et al., 2011). It gives us an intrinsic measure to evaluate quality of re-writes without caring about downstream SLU evaluation.

Response Entity F1 (ResF1): We measure this metric for the INCAR dataset, following the approach outlined by (Madotto et al., 2018)[5]. The Response Entity F1 micro-averages over the entire set of system responses and compare the entities in plain text. The entities in each gold system response are selected by a predefined entity list. This

metric evaluates the ability to generate relevant entities and to capture the semantics of the dialogue. We reimplemented the *Mem2SeqH1* architecture in (Madotto et al., 2018)[6] and we refer to our implementation as *Mem2Seq**. We use utterances produced by our proposed **(CQR)** system in the dialogue instead of original utterances while evaluating using Mem2Seq*. Note that our reimplementation, Mem2Seq*, achieves a Response Entity F1 of 33.6 which is higher than the best overall Entity F1 score of 33.4 reported in (Madotto et al., 2018).

Entity F1: This measures micro F1 between entities in the hypothesized rewrite and gold rewrite. This is different from F1 reported by (Madotto et al., 2018) as they evaluate F1 over system entities, whereas here we evaluate the entities over the user turn. We employ a recent state-of-art bi-directional LSTM with CRF decoding (Ma and Hovy, 2016) to implement our SLU system.

5 Results

5.1 INTERNAL Dataset Results

On INTERNAL dataset we show CQR significantly improves over (Naik et al., 2018) in Table 4. **CQR** also improves F1 for current turn slots as it can leverage context and distill necessary information to improve SLU. Further, we can see that most improvements upon the baseline PGN model (M0) come from pre-processing steps like canonicalizing entities. In the baseline model, it has to learn to generate entity tokens individually, whereas in **M1** the model only has to learn to copy tokens like *USER_ENT_1*. Finally, our proposed multi-task learning model (CQR) improves both BLEU and EntityF1 at most distances. Specifically, we see an improvement of 4.2% over **M2** for slots at distances $\geq$3. In Table 4 distance is measured differently from Table 2, here we count User and System turns individually to showcase how distance affects **EntityF1**. If an entity is repeated multiple times in the context, we consider its closest occurrence to report results.

5.2 INCAR Dataset Results

For INCAR dataset we pick the best model **CQR** from Table 4 and re-train on the respective dataset. On the navigation domain we observe significant

---

[5]Evaluation script available at https://github.com/HLTCHKUST/Mem2Seq

[6]The *Mem2Seq H1* was the best performing system in terms of ResF1, in two out of three domains in the InCar dataset, and it was the fastest Mem2Seq model. Therefore, we used *Mem2SeqH1* and not *Mem2SeqH3*

Dialogue	U: Find me a Starbucks in Redmond S: I found a Starbucks in Redmond WA. It's 15.7 miles away on NE 76th St. It's open now until 9:00 PM. U: How do I get there?
PGN	how can i get to redmond
CQR	how do i get to the starbucks on NE 76th St WA
Gold	how do i get to the starbucks on NE 76th St
Dialogue	U: How is the weather tomorrow? S: In Chicago there will be mostly sunny weather U: What about saturday?
PGN	what is the weather in chicago on saturday ?
CQR	what is the weather in chicago on saturday ?
Gold	what is the weather in chicago on saturday ?

Table 3: Examples of generated responses for Internal Dataset

improvement. We believe this is because there are on average 2.3 slots were referred from history in rewrites requiring copy from dialog as compared to 1.3 and 1.1 in schedule and weather domain respectively. Also, we compare with an oracle CQR (i.e., gold-rewrite from our data collection, instead of predicted re-write) to measure the potential of query-rewriting and motivate further research on this topic. We can see that the CQR model performs better than the Mem2Seq* model, indicating that query rewriting is a viable alternative to dialogue state tracking. This is important in environments where changing the NLU systems to leverage memory structures is not always feasible. We claim that query rewriting is a simpler approach in such situations, with no loss in performance.

6   Related Work

Probabilistic methods for task-oriented dialogue systems typically divide an automatic dialogue agent into modules such as automatic speech recognition(ASR) for converting speech to text, spoken language understanding(SLU) for classifying the domain and intent of the current utterance and tagging the slots in the current utterance, dialogue state tracking(DST) for tracking what has happened in the dialogue so far, and dialogue policy for deciding what actions to take next (Young, 2000). In this traditional framework, SLU is seen as a low-level task that interprets the user's current utterance in isolation, without accounting for the dialogue history. For example, in Figure 1 the platform system parses the utterance WHO WROTE SAPIENS, to infer that the user intends to query for information about a book, and then the platform performs

BIO style tagging with an intent-specific schema to label the mentionSAPIENS as the slot key BOOK-NAME. Most SLU systems perform this without any context information. Some recent work focussed on contextual SLU (Shi et al., 2015; Liu et al., 2015; Chen et al., 2016) propose memory architectures to incorporate contextual information while performing the SLU step. However because their task was restricted to domain-intent classification and slot tagging for the current utterance only, a higher level DST module is still required to combine information from previous turns with the current utterance to create a single dialogue state.

DST is considered to be a higher-level module as it has to combine information from previous user utterances and system responses with the current utterance to infer its full meaning. Many deep-learning based methods have recently been proposed for DST such as neural belief tracker (Mrkšić et al., 2017), and self-attentive dialogue state tracker (Zhong et al., 2018) which are suitable for small-scale domain-specific dialogue systems; as well as more scalable approaches such as (Rastogi et al., 2017; Xu and Hu, 2018) that solve the problem of an infinite number of slot values and (Naik et al., 2018) who additionally solve the problem of huge number of disparate schemas in each domain. End-to-End approaches based on deep learning have also been proposed recently to replace such modular architectures, like (Madotto et al., 2018; Eric and Manning, 2017).

Unfortunately, all of the above approaches fail to address the problem that, as the number of domain-specific chatbots on a dialogue platform grows larger, the DST module becomes increasingly complex as it tries to handle the interactions between different chatbots and their different schemas. For example, consider the scenario shown in Figure 1. Chatbot A, the BOOK chatbot, can understand domain-specific utterances like "who wrote X ?" annotated with a special schema with slot keys such as BOOKNAME, AUTHOR. In order to disambiguate utterance u_2 the DST in the conversational platform must know that the CREATOR slot-key in the SHOPPING chatbot co-refers to the AUTHOR slot-key. However, this leads to a quadratic explosion in the number of possible transitions that the platform has to learn, thereby significantly increasing the learning problem for DST. Additionally, the problem is more challenging than just disambiguating pronouns because in some situations there may

System	Entity F1												BLEU
	d=0			d=1			d=2			d≥3			
	P	R	F1	P	R	F1	P	R	F1	P	R	F1	
(Naik et al., 2018)	95.1	**95.1**	95.1	74.9	78.4	76.6	72.2	82.2	76.9	10.4	46.3	17.0	N/A
PGN (M0)	**99.0**	78.1	87.4	**95.9**	62.1	75.4	**95.2**	57.3	71.5	87.3	65.5	74.9	83.4
+Canonical Ent. (M1)	98.7	93.9	**96.3**	92.9	93.5	93.2	94.4	96.9	95.6	69.8	78.5	73.9	89.9
+Syntax Info (M2)	98.6	93.9	96.2	92.9	93.5	93.2	94.3	96.9	95.6	69.8	78.5	73.9	89.9
+MTL (CQR)	98.5	**94.0**	96.2	93.7	**93.8**	**93.7**	94.2	**97.4**	**95.8**	**75.2**	**79.0**	**77.1**	**90.3**
% Relative Improv.	3.6	-1.2	1.2	25.1	19.6	22.3	30.5	18.5	24.6	623.1	70.6	353.5	N/A

Table 4: Comparison of Pointer-Generator variants to traditional state tracking approach on the INTERNAL dataset. We measure entity F1 across slots from different distances separately. Slot distance is counted per utterance starting from the current user utterance. Therefore, slots at d=0 are slots from the current user utterance that should have been copied. d=1 refers to slots from system response in the last turn, d=2 refers to slots from the user in last turn and d≥3 aggregates all other turns. $d \geq 3$ is the most challenging test-subset where **CQR** has the highest benefit.

System	E2E	ResF1			
	BLEU	All	Schedule	Weather	Navigation
Mem2Seq*	11.4	33.6	**48.4**	47.2	19.4
CQR	**11.6**	**36.1**	**48.4**	**47.9**	**23.8**
% Relative Improv.	1.8	7.4	0.0	1.5	22.7
CQR-Oracle	11.8	38.0	48.9	48.9	26.9

Table 5: Comparison of PGN variants proposed in this paper on the INCAR dataset in comparison to the state tracking approach. Our proposed CQR model outperforms the MemSeq* system, which is a stronger baseline than the Mem2Seq results published in Madotto et al. (2018).

be no co-referent pronouns in the current utterance. For example, a user may say "what's the address" instead of saying "what is its address", creating a case of zero-anaphora.

Finally, we will mention that Seq2Seq models with Attention (Sutskever et al., 2014; Bahdanau et al., 2014) have seen rapid adoption in automatic summarisation (See et al., 2017; Rush et al., 2015). Exploring black-box methods like query re-writing allow us to benefit from the progress made in these fields and apply them to state tracking and reference resolution tasks in dialogue.

7 Conclusion

In this work we made three fundamental contributions. First, we proposed *contextual query rewriting*(CQR) as a novel way to interpret an input utterance in context given a dialogue history. For example, we can rewrite BUY HIS LATEST BOOK as BUY YUVAL HARARI'S MOST RECENT BOOK, given the dialogue history, as shown in Figure 1. The output of CQR can directly be fed to the domain-specific downstream SLU system which drastically simplifies the construction of task-specific dialogue *agents*. Since we do not need to change either the spoken language understanding or the dialogue state tracker downstream, our approach is a black-box approach that improves the modularity of industrial-scale, dialogue-asistants. Second, we investigated how to optimally use a Pointer-Generator Network for the CWR task using Multi-Task Learning and task-specific preprocessing. Finally, we demonstrated the efficacy of our approach on two datasets. On INCAR dataset released by (Eric and Manning, 2017), we were able to show that re-writing of the user utterance can benefit end-to-end models. On a proprietary INTERNAL dataset we showed that our approach can greatly improve the experience when referring to entities from much further away in a dialogue history, resulting in relative improvements in Entity F1 of greater than 20% on the most challenging subset of the test-data.

We hope that our approach of directly using natural language as an api will motivate other researchers to conduct work in this direction.

References

Dzmitry Bahdanau, Kyunghyun Cho, and Yoshua Bengio. 2014. Neural machine translation by jointly learning to align and translate. *arXiv preprint arXiv:1409.0473*.

Yun-Nung Vivian Chen, Dilek Hakkani-Tr, Gokhan Tur, Jianfeng Gao, and Li Deng. 2016. End-to-end memory networks with knowledge carryover for multi-turn spoken language understanding. In *17th Annual Meeting of the International Speech Communication Association*. ISCA.

Mihail Eric and Christopher D Manning. 2017. Key-value retrieval networks for task-oriented dialogue. *arXiv preprint arXiv:1705.05414*.

Yoav Goldberg and Jon Orwant. 2013. A dataset of syntactic-ngrams over time from a very large corpus of english books. In *Second Joint Conference on Lexical and Computational Semantics (* SEM), Volume 1: Proceedings of the Main Conference and the Shared Task: Semantic Textual Similarity*, volume 1, pages 241–247.

Dan Klein and Christopher D Manning. 2003. Accurate unlexicalized parsing. In *Proceedings of the 41st Annual Meeting on Association for Computational Linguistics-Volume 1*, pages 423–430. Association for Computational Linguistics.

Guillaume Klein, Yoon Kim, Yuntian Deng, Jean Senellart, and Alexander M. Rush. 2017. OpenNMT: Open-source toolkit for neural machine translation. In *Proc. ACL*.

Anjishnu Kumar, Arpit Gupta, Julian Chan, Sam Tucker, Bjorn Hoffmeister, Markus Dreyer, Stanislav Peshterliev, Ankur Gandhe, Denis Filiminov, Ariya Rastrow, et al. 2017. Just ask: building an architecture for extensible self-service spoken language understanding. *arXiv preprint arXiv:1711.00549*.

Chunxi Liu, Puyang Xu, and Ruhi Sarikaya. 2015. Deep contextual language understanding in spoken dialogue systems. In *Sixteenth annual conference of the international speech communication association*.

Xuezhe Ma and Eduard Hovy. 2016. End-to-end sequence labeling via bi-directional lstm-cnns-crf. In *Proceedings of the 54th Annual Meeting of the Association for Computational Linguistics (Volume 1: Long Papers)*, volume 1, pages 1064–1074.

Andrea Madotto, Chien-Sheng Wu, and Pascale Fung. 2018. Mem2seq: Effectively incorporating knowledge bases into end-to-end task-oriented dialog systems. *arXiv preprint arXiv:1804.08217*.

Nikola Mrkšić, Diarmuid Ó Séaghdha, Tsung-Hsien Wen, Blaise Thomson, and Steve Young. 2017. Neural belief tracker: Data-driven dialogue state tracking. In *Proceedings of the 55th Annual Meeting of the Association for Computational Linguistics (Volume 1: Long Papers)*, pages 1777–1788, Vancouver, Canada. Association for Computational Linguistics.

Chetan Naik, Arpit Gupta, Hancheng Ge, Lambert Mathias, and Ruhi Sarikaya. 2018. Contextual slot carryover for disparate schemas. In *19th Annual Meeting of the International Speech Communication Association*.

Kishore Papineni, Salim Roukos, Todd Ward, and Wei-Jing Zhu. 2002. Bleu: a method for automatic evaluation of machine translation. In *Proceedings of the 40th annual meeting on association for computational linguistics*, pages 311–318. Association for Computational Linguistics.

Abhinav Rastogi, Dilek Hakkani-Tür, and Larry Heck. 2017. Scalable multi-domain dialogue state tracking. In *Automatic Speech Recognition and Understanding Workshop (ASRU), 2017 IEEE*, pages 561–568. IEEE.

Michael Regan, Pushpendre Rastogi, Arpit Gupta Gupta, and Lambert Mathias. 2019. A dataset for resolving referring expressions in spoken dialogue via contextual query rewrites (cqr). *arXiv preprint arXiv:1903.11783*.

Alan Ritter, Colin Cherry, and William B Dolan. 2011. Data-driven response generation in social media. In *Proceedings of the conference on empirical methods in natural language processing*, pages 583–593. Association for Computational Linguistics.

Alexander M. Rush, Sumit Chopra, and Jason Weston. 2015. A neural attention model for abstractive sentence summarization. In *Proceedings of the 2015 Conference on Empirical Methods in Natural Language Processing*, pages 379–389, Lisbon, Portugal. Association for Computational Linguistics.

Abigail See, Peter J. Liu, and Christopher D. Manning. 2017. Get to the point: Summarization with pointer-generator networks. In *Proceedings of the 55th Annual Meeting of the Association for Computational Linguistics (Volume 1: Long Papers)*, pages 1073–1083. Association for Computational Linguistics.

Yangyang Shi, Kaisheng Yao, Hu Chen, Yi-Cheng Pan, Mei-Yuh Hwang, and Baolin Peng. 2015. Contextual spoken language understanding using recurrent neural networks. In *ICASSP 2015*.

Ilya Sutskever, Oriol Vinyals, and Quoc V. Le. 2014. Sequence to Sequence Learning with Neural Networks. In *NIPS*, page 9.

Puyang Xu and Qi Hu. 2018. An end-to-end approach for handling unknown slot values in dialogue state tracking. In *Proceedings of the 56th Annual Meeting of the Association for Computational Linguistics (Volume 1: Long Papers)*, pages 1448–1457, Melbourne, Australia. Association for Computational Linguistics.

Steve J Young. 2000. Probabilistic methods in spoken–dialogue systems. *Philosophical Transactions of the Royal Society of London A: Mathematical, Physical and Engineering Sciences*, 358(1769):1389–1402.

Victor Zhong, Caiming Xiong, and Richard Socher. 2018. Global-locally self-attentive encoder for dialogue state tracking. In *Proceedings of the 56th Annual Meeting of the Association for Computational Linguistics (Volume 1: Long Papers)*, pages 1458–1467, Melbourne, Australia. Association for Computational Linguistics.

Are the Tools up to the Task? An evaluation of commercial dialog tools in developing conversational enterprise-grade dialog systems

Marie Meteer, Meghan Hickey, Ellen Eide Kislal, David Nahamoo, Carmi Rothberg
Pryon, Inc.
mmeteer, mhickey, ekislal, dnahamoo, crothberg@pryoninc.com

Abstract

There has been a significant investment in dialog systems (tools and runtime) for building conversational systems by major companies including Google, IBM, Microsoft, and Amazon. The question remains whether these tools are up to the task of building conversational, task-oriented dialog applications at the enterprise level. In our company, we are exploring and comparing several toolsets in an effort to determine their strengths and weaknesses in meeting our goals for dialog system development: accuracy, time to market, ease of replicating and extending applications, and efficiency and ease of use by developers. In this paper, we provide both quantitative and qualitative results in three main areas: natural language understanding, dialog, and text generation. While existing toolsets were all incomplete, we hope this paper will provide a roadmap of where they need to go to meet the goal of building effective dialog systems.

1 Introduction

With the explosion of smart devices and the significant improvement in speech recognition over the past few years, the demand for intelligent, conversational dialog systems is rising quickly. At our company we are working to meet that demand in the enterprise market to provide secure and natural means for accessing information and improving business processes. Essential to meeting this demand is getting dialog systems into the hands of customers as quickly as possible while ensuring accurate interpretation of utterances as well as conversational means of handling ambiguity, error, and out of domain/out of scope utterances.

In this paper we explore whether the dialog tools available from a number of companies are up to the task of creating complete systems efficiently. We provide both quantitative and qualitative results in three main areas:

- Natural language understanding: intent and entity accuracy, out-of-domain and out-of-scope identification, and anaphora and coreference resolution.

- Dialog management: frame-based and contextual dialog control, dialog structure, and digression.

- Response generation: text generation, error correction and clarification.

We provide results and examples across multiple domains to illustrate the challenges in developing a truly conversational dialog system. As we will show, there is considerable progress in accuracy of intents and entities in constrained domains across all of the toolsets. However, capturing subtle differences in in-scope vs. out-of-scope utterances is still difficult, as is partial understanding, which is important for clarification. For dialog management, all of the tools offer some ability to use frames, however they differ in how robust they are to context. Similarly, for error correction and clarification, the ability to react based on context is limited. Finally, in text generation, we found there was no support beyond template-based generation, which impacts not only naturalness, but the ability to interpret a user's follow-on utterance.

There has been other work comparing just the accuracy of these tools (e.g.(Braun et al., 2017)). as well as the ability of applications built with them to handle particular dialog structures, such as subdialogs (Larsson, 2017) and question answering behavior (Larsson, 2015). Our focus is on the tools themselves and our goal is to not just look at what they do, but what we need them to do.

2 Natural Language Understanding

The most mature component of dialog tools is natural language understanding (NLU). The field has

Proceedings of NAACL-HLT 2019, pages 106–113
Minneapolis, Minnesota, June 2 - June 7, 2019. ©2019 Association for Computational Linguistics

settled on the notion that understanding comprises recognizing the user's intent and extracting the entities in the utterance required to fulfill the intent. While the terms harken back to Barbara Grosz and Candy Sidner's seminal paper "Intentional and Attentional Structure" 1986, the implementation can be more closely tied to work at AT&T, which combined statistical classification used for call routing in applications like HMIHY (How May I Help You) with mainly rule-based extraction of entities (Gupta et al., 2006). Nuance 9 tools allowed both utterance classification ("Statistical Semantic Models") and partial parsing for information extraction ("Robust Parsing Grammars") commercially over a decade ago (Nuance, 2002), though a single utterance could only be processed by one or the other, not both, which significantly limited effectiveness compared to today's systems.

In addition to being fairly mature, NLU performance can also be evaluated quantitatively. We compared three tools, Google's Dialogflow[1] (previously api.ai), IBM Watson Assistant[2], and Microsoft LUIS[3].

We choose two domains to compare. The first is a tech support IT FAQ system which initially included a fairly limited set of questions with answers designed by the customer. Some of these questions had multiple answers based on information such as what kind of computer the user had. The second lets users ask questions about their own financial statements, so the questions are limited by the information available on the account and the answers are user-dependent. Both are currently in trial with customers.

We report results on our regression tests rather than the live application. All of the questions in the test sets were "fully specified" in that there was no missing information that needed to be filled in through dialog.

<hr>

[1] https://dialogflow.com
[2] https://www.ibm.com/watson/ai-assistant/
[3] https://www.luis.ai

Domains	IT V1	IT V2	Finance
Intents	23	51	14
Entities	30	44	15
Training	1164	14525	426
In domain test	267	450	113
OOD test		150	100

Table 1: Test domain numbers

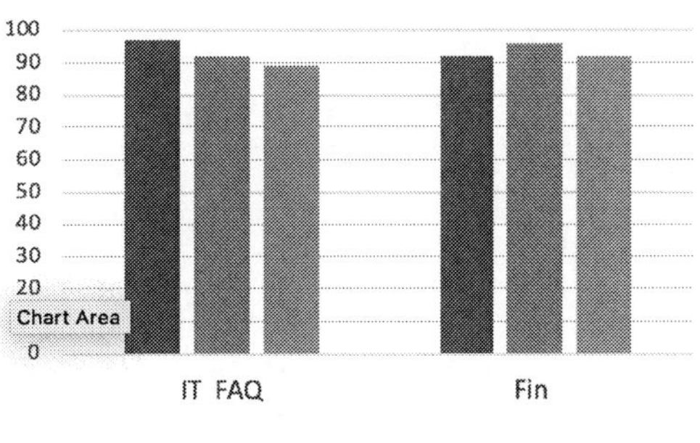

Figure 1: Intent Accuracy

Our first set of tests compared performance between LUIS, Watson and Dialogflow on the two domains. Details of size, training and test are shown in Table 1. We were able to do a direct comparison of intent recognition across the three systems, since we wrote acripts that translated a single source of intents, examples, and entities into the formats required for the tools. Figure 1 shows the performance across the three tools on for IT FAQ V1 and FIN. They were relatively close, with LUIS and Watson each taking first place depending on the domain.

2.1 Intents and Training

In this section, we discuss the effects of increase in scope and increase in training data. Due to time constraints we focused this work on just the IT domain tested on LUIS and Watson. We has more than doubled the scope of the IT application and used both data collection and automatic paraphrasing to increase the amount of training data.

Collecting data when operating in a rapid production mode is challenging. We used Google forms and other tools to collect "paraphrases" from SMEs (subject matter experts) internally and from the customer. One of our first discoveries was that not not everyone knows what a paraphrase is and many of the samples were related questions, for example "How do I disable automatic software updates?" was given as a paraphrase of "How do I get automatic software updates?"

2.1.1 Augmented Training Data

In order to further increase the training data, we used a grammar-based data augmentation technique for generating additional paraphrases for the

Training	Training	LUIS	Watson
V1: Human	1164	63.2%	70.2%
V2: V1+Auto	14525	73.0%	75.5%

Table 2: Intent accuracy comparing training amounts

IT domain. The grammar contained 58 equivalencies, where each equivalency consisted of two or more synonymous words or phrases.

An example of an equivalency is shown here, with alternatives separated by semi-colons:

> **should i**: is it ok to;am i allowed to;do i have permission to;is it bad to;is it against company policy to;is it okay to

In order to generate paraphrases, we create two copies of each sentence, the unaltered input and a processed version of the sentence, each labeled with the intents and entities from the original. The script looks for instances of entries in each equivalence class. If one is found, it randomly replaces that entry with one of the other entries in that class. If no entries of any equivalence class are found in a particular sentence, the paraphrase is identical to the original. After running the script the desired number of times, we take the set of unique sentences in the output as our augmented dataset. Table 2 shows performance of LUIS and Watson on V1 (human created training only) and V2 (human plus automatic paraphrases).

2.1.2 How much is enough?

We also experimented with running the script between one and four times, giving us the potential for up to 16 times the amount of data in our original set. After eliminating duplicates, though, the amount of data is smaller, as shown Table 3 [4]:

We built models in Luis for each of these training sets and test on a common test set of 600 sentences. Results are shown in the third column of the table.

Because the test set is generated from the same methodology as the training set, it lacks some variability which we expect to see in a deployed system. As an attempt to model that variability, we experimented with also passing the test set through the same paraphrase generation module as the training set. Doing so resulted in a new test set

---

[4]While results within a table are consistent, different sets of results may differ given the evolving nature of commercial systems.

with 3005 sentences. Results on that augmented test set are shown in the 4th column of Table 3.

By looking at results on the unaugmented test together with the results on the augmented test, we decided that the set of 7528 training utterances resulted in a desirable model in that it did not degrade the performance on the original test set and resulted more robust performance on the augmented test set.

2.2 Out of Domain and Scope

A significant challenge in a deployed system is recognizing when an utterance is out of domain (OOD), and thus can't be answered. This includes questions:

- Questions from a different domain, e.g. asking the IT FAQ application about the weather,

- Questions in the domain, but not in the scope of the application, e.g. the IT FAQ might be able to help you get a VPN account, but not a Jira account.

- "Adversarial" questions, that is intentially trying to break the system, e.g. "Can you eat VPN?" and "What do you look like".

The choice of the domain and scope in a commercial system is defined largely by the customer but not always clear to the end users, who may think the IT FAQ can help them get any kind of account or the app can answer the same things as Siri.

In the finance domain we used a 100 utterance OOD test set and introduced a new intent for classifying these utterances as "None". The "None" category had 28 training utterances, which was about average for the categories in V1. The second set in Figure 2 combines the in and out of domain test sets and the third set shows results on

No. Iter	No. Sents	Intent Acc.	
		Orig. Test	Aug. Test
0 (orig)	2296	72.8	69.9
1	3086	73.5	73.9
2	4789	74.2	76.1
3	7528	73.0	76.9
4	10719	71.8	76.5

Table 3: Results of data augmentation on the standard test set.

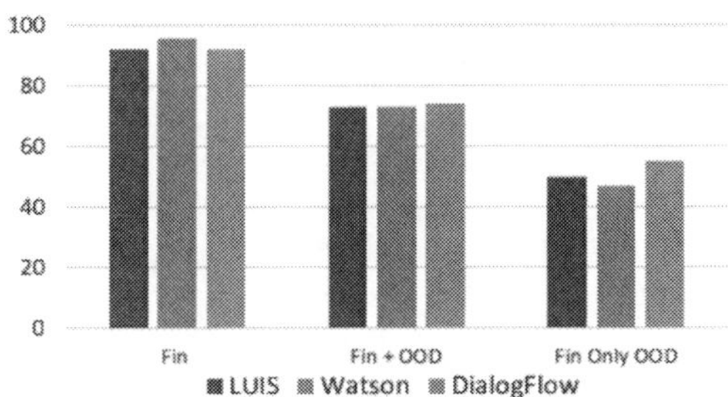

Figure 2: Intent Accuracy In and out of domain

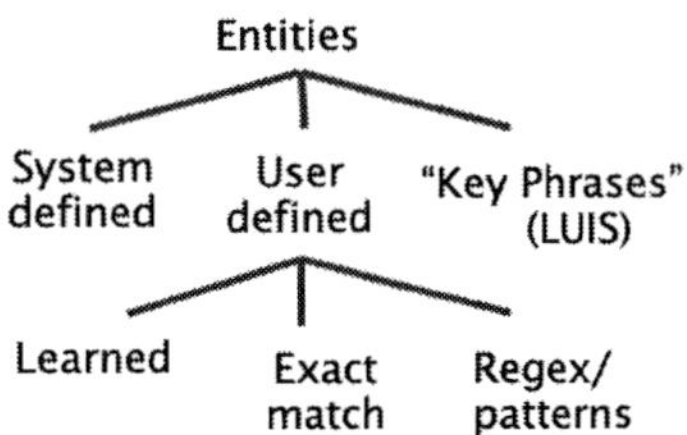

Figure 4: Entity Types

just OOD. It is clear that performance drops significantly in all the tools due to the OOD effect.

Figure 3 shows the correct accept vs. correct-reject curves for each of the tools as we threshold the response based on confidence scores. The Watson score has better confidence scores than the other tools.

While overall we find the tools quite good at classifying in-scope intents, their performance is poor on detecting out of domain and scope, which are admittedly difficult to model with a classifier. However, on the positive side, the tools allowed us to get a system into the hands of users quickly without having to start with a massive data collection effort. As we get more user data to help identify kinds of out of domain and out of scope questions will be asked, we will be able to improve on the base performance.

2.3 Entities

All three tools allow entities to be defined in multiple ways, as shown in Figure 4. System entities are common types, such as time and currency that have been built and trained by the creators of the

tools. Regular expressions can be defined by application developers to capture structured strings, like order numbers. The most interesting distinction is between learned and exact match entities. Machine learned entities are able to identify synonyms without having to predefine them. For example, if "passphrase" is used in the same context as "password" the system should be able to recognize it as a synonym.

In Dialogflow, the predominant method of defining entities is exact match, which defines entity types with values and synonyms. Learned entities appear to be fairly limited and used for things like items on a shopping list.

In LUIS, exact match entities are "List" entities, which also has a type, values and synonyms. Machine learned entities, which take context into account, are call "simple". In order to capture type and values, you can use "hierachical" entities. For example, in the IT domain, the "Investment Account" entity has as its children the five different investment accounts. The accounts had fairly complex names which were frequently reduced, for example the "Membership Contribution Pension Fund" could be referred to as the "Membership Fund", "Membership Contribution Fund", "Pension", etc. We implemented these both as list and learned entities, as shown in Table 4. List had better performance, but required listing all the variations. Learned requires annotation, which is also a cost, but it is not the case that every variant has to be accounted for.

Watson has a beta feature that lets you annotate entities in context, including annotating counter

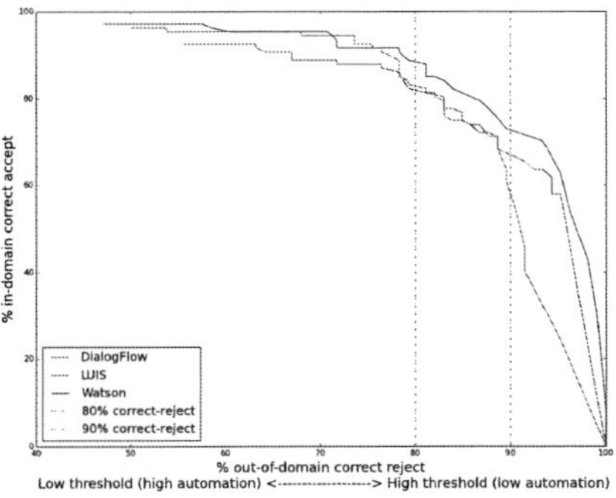

Figure 3: Confidence Scores

	Train	**Test**	**List**	**Learned**
Account	228	61	96.3%	93.8%
Slot	102	26	100%	91.5%

Table 4: Test for Entities and Slots

examples, which may be able to be used to improve performance, though due to bandwidth we were not able to do a comparison.

2.3.1 Slot filling

Slot filling is a core capability in NLU: recognizing not just that an entity occurred, but which parameter or "slot" it is filling. In most cases, which slot is being filled can be determined by the type of the entity, so as long as it is correctly identified, the slot is filled correctly. However in some cases one entity type can fill two different slots, as in transferring funds from Account A to Account B.

As with entity recognition, all three tools provide slot filling functionality we found that more rule based methods of identifying slots was more accurate than learned slot filling (see Table 4).

2.3.2 Recognizing new entities

Anything that does not match an entity is ignored. While this simplifies understanding, it can lead to false positives. For example, the question "What's my balance" in the finance app applies to the entire portfolio if no specific account is mentioned. However, if an account is mentioned but not accurately recognized, the answer will be incorrect.

A notable exception of this is LUIS, which has the unique ability to find entities that haven't been predefined through "key phrases". This additional information can be used in flagging problem interpretations and used in clarification dialogs, as in the example "How do I get a Jira account?", the intent ProcedureGetAccount is triggered and a key phrase "Jira account" is found, which would allow a clarification response such as I think you're asking about how to get an account, but I don't know anything about a "Jira account".

2.4 Language Contraction

An essential part of language understanding is the ability to interpret utterances when they undergo what we might call "language contraction" where some parts are left out or replaced with pronouns or reduced forms. While as we show in Section 3, dialog structure can be used to emulate language contraction interpretation, none of the tools address the phenomenon directly. There are two kinds of constructions that need to be addressed for dialog tools to be able to effectively handle conversational dialog.

Coreference: Where a pronoun or other referring expression is directly referring to some previous entity in the sentence.

- Whats the balance in my retirement account? When does it vest?

Ellipsis: Part of the utterance is left out and can be filled in by some portion of an earlier sentence.

- What are the fees on my retirement account? How about my annuity?

While none of the tools address this directly, both Watson and Dialogflow keep track of values in context variables. For example, in Watson, once you ask about one investment account, the variable `investmentAccount` is set, so the sequence below would be answered correctly:

Whats the value of my portfolio plan?
What are the fees?
How much as it changed over the past quarter?

However, if you asked about an account it didnt understand, such as "What are the fees for my fidelity investments", it would miss that and answer based on the previous setting of the `investmentAccount` variable.

3 Dialog Management

Beyond the level of interpretation of single utterances, the tools differ significantly. In this section we look at the development of the dialog structure and the management and application of context. To illustrate the various capabilities, we use a real estate application, which has more complex interactions. We compare the approaches of Dialogflow and Watson Assistant. The Microsoft offering has three separate tools each with their own interface and would have been a steep learning curve for developers who are not already well-versed in the Microsoft landscape, so we did not pursue it further.

A significant difference between the approaches in the tools is how tightly integrated the dialog capabilities are with the NLP. In Dialogflow, the intents are the basic dialog components and both context and control are defined as part of the intent definition, whereas Watson Assistant provides a separate interface that explicitly allows dialog nodes to be defined independently from intents and entities.

Defining dialog structure independently from the intents can be advantageous. First, the condition of whether a dialog node is triggered can be

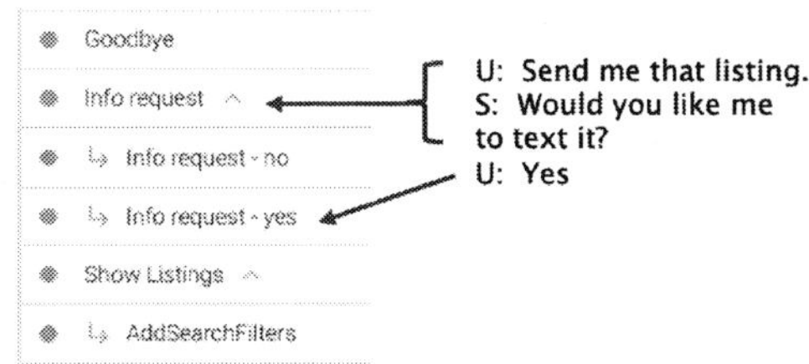

Figure 5: DialogFlow

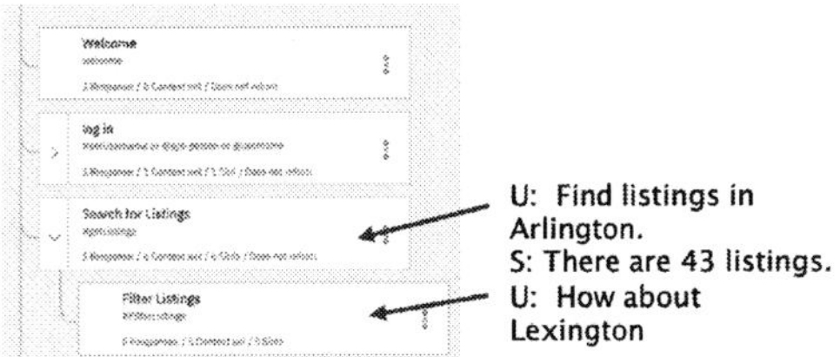

Figure 6: Watson

dependent on variables outside of the interpretation of the utterance, for example checking a context variable to determine whether a user is logged in. Second, an intent can function differently depending on where in the dialog that intent occurs.

The dialog structure allows users' answers, which are dependent on what question is asked, to be interpreted correctly, as seen in Figure 5.

Dialog structure can allow for the interpretation of coreference and ellipsis, as shown in Figure 6. Neither tool has any model of coreference or anaphora, however, careful construction of the dialog structure ensure that the utterances are interpreted correctly.

3.1 Frame-based Dialog Management

Frame-based dialog management uses the slot filling in a frame or form to control the dialog. The advantage is that it allows mixed initiative interaction: users can provide the slot values in any order and "package" them into any grouping. For example, the `CalculateMortgagePayment` intent requires an amount, term, and interest rate. The user might start by saying "What is the monthly payment for $500,000 mortgage over 30 years at 4% interest" or just "How much would the monthly payment be for $500,000". The dialog manager fills slots as the information is provided and then asks the user specifically for information that it doesn't have yet. In this example, the dialog manager might ask for a rate, but the user might choose to respond: "I am looking for a 30-year mortgage".

In contrast, a traditional procedural dialog manager covering all the possible response sequences would require complicated software development and maintenance. While only very narrow domains can be fully controlled with a frame-based mechanism, it is a very useful control structure for a range of intents which have multiple required slots to fill.

In Dialogflow, frames are defined as part of the definition of the intents. Entities are explicitly associated with the intent and any subset can be marked as "required" and the developer provides a prompt which will be asked if the entity is not filled. One downside is that the frame control can't be interrupted. For example, if the system says "What zip code would you like to search?" the user can't ask "What's the zip code for Arlington?" before answering. There is also no capability for prompting for multiple required parameters at the same time. The questions are simply strings rather than being composed dynamically, so context can't be taken into account.

Watson Assistant defines frames at the node level. The functionality is similar, allowing the app developer to add prompts for required entities. It also allows for a single prompt to be defined if none of the slots have been filled. In addition, there are "Handlers" that can interrupt the process if the user doesn't provide the required information.

3.2 Context Management

Context plays an important role in both interpretation and control of the dialog, for example the dialog manager needs to:

- Keep track of variable values that are used later, such as the user's name.

- Record that a particular action was completed, such as logging in, so that it can be checked later as a condition for another action.

- Collect information over multiple turns, such as search criteria to narrow results.

Intents in Dialogflow have input and output context variables to gate actions as well as to store the values of entities. We found some difficulties in keeping values in the context over multiple turns.

Watson assistant used the dialog structure to manage the context. While this made it clearer, there was no easy way to control what is kept in the context. However, there is a view of context variables and values in the tool interface which is useful in the design process and debugging.

3.3 Challenges in Dialog

While Watson Assistant's use of a dialog tree provides greater functionality, it still falls short when attempting to build a fully mixed initiative system. "Digressions" are allowed in Watson, but need to be defined in advance, so in the zip code example above, the application developer would need to put an explicit digression to a node for `FindZipcode` which would then return to the original dialog node. While this one seems fairly obvious, it quickly becomes difficult to predict any place the user could digress from a conversation.

4 Response Generation

Text generation is a hard problem and has gotten neither the attention nor funding that understanding and other subfields of natural language have gotten over the years. It is not surprising that it is the least developed part of the tools. Within the tools, the responses are created by the app developers, either just as word strings, mostly for prompts, or templates with variables that correspond to entities.

Both tools allow multiple responses to be created that will be chosen from randomly, creating some variability, but only Watson assistant allows the responses to be contextually dependent, based on the values of context variables.

The problem with these approaches is not just the lack of variability, but also since responses are merely strings with some parameters, there is no representation of the constituent structure or the meaning of the response. In the following exchange, "that" refers to the VP constituent corresponding to the procedure of getting an account. However, this constituent is not available for coreference.

S: In order to do save listings, you need to get an account.

U: How do I do that?

4.1 Error Recovery and Clarification

Successful dialog systems require the ability to know when the system did not understand or is not able to answer. We looked at out of domain/scope identification in Section 2.2, but the challenge is in extracting sufficient information to make an intelligent response (Stoyanchev et al., 2016). For example a "reprise question", which is a clarification that repeats a portion of the original utterance, requires that some portion of the utterance to be understood, as in the following, which would need a `ProcedureGetAccount` intent to be recognized in order to answer with one of the two reprise clarifications in the example:

U: How do I get an account on Jira?

S: How do you get what?

U: How do you get what kind of account?

Another important element in good error recovery dialog is not simply repeating the same error message over and over. Best practice in developing speech IVRs is to keep track of both the type of error (e.g. no input vs. low confidence) and the number of tries the user has made in order to vary the error message (e.g. first time, "say again", second, "try rephrasing", and third, type or just move on). While we didn't find this capability in Dialogflow, Watson allows the choice of which response to give to be based on the value of a context variable, which can be set as a counter.

Dialogflow's "Default Fallback Intent" and Watson's "Anything else" trigger when no other intent or dialog node triggers, however, without context there is no ability to tailor the response. Again, Watson's use of an explicit dialog tree allows the developer to have multiple "fallbacks". Within each subdialog, the final node can be set to fire if none of the other conditions hold.

4.2 Conclusion

We provided results and examples across a small number of domains to illustrate the challenges in developing a dialog system that supports building easy to use, natural conversational applications.

The rank-ordered accuracies of the tools varied across domains. While some differences exist among the tools in terms of how entities are handled, more significant differences among them lie in how tightly coupled the NLP and dialog components are.

At our company, we focus on inventing and implementing additional modules with enhanced complimentary features and functions to improve the utility of the three dialog systems that we presented in this paper.

References

Daniel Braun, Adrian Hernandez-Mendez, Florian Matthes, and Manfred Langen. 2017. Evaluating natural language understanding services for conversational question answering systems. In *Proceedings of the 18th Annual SIGdial Meeting on Discourse and Dialogue*, pages 174–185.

Barbara J Grosz and Candace L Sidner. 1986. Attention, intentions, and the structure of discourse. *Computational linguistics*, 12(3):175–204.

Narendra Gupta, Gokhan Tur, Dilek Hakkani-Tur, Srinivas Bangalore, Giuseppe Riccardi, and Mazin Gilbert. 2006. The at&t spoken language understanding system. *IEEE Transactions on Audio, Speech, and Language Processing*, 14(1):213–222.

Staffan Larsson. 2015. The state of the art in dealing with user answers. In *Proceedings of the 19th Workshop on the Semantics and Pragmatics of Dialogue. SEMDIAL*, pages 190–191.

Staffan Larsson. 2017. User-initiated sub-dialogues in state-of-the-art dialogue systems. In *Proceedings of the 18th Annual SIGdial Meeting on Discourse and Dialogue*, pages 17–22.

Nuance. 2002. *Advanced Developers Guide*.

Svetlana Stoyanchev, Pierre Lison, and Srinivas Bangalore. 2016. Rapid prototyping of form-driven dialogue systems using an open-source framework. In *Proceedings of the 17th Annual Meeting of the Special Interest Group on Discourse and Dialogue*, pages 216–219.

Development and Deployment of a Large-Scale Dialog-based Intelligent Tutoring System

Shazia Afzal[1], Tejas Indulal Dhamecha[1], Nirmal Mukhi[2], Renuka Sindhgatta[3]*,
Smit Marvaniya[1], Matthew Ventura[4], Jessica Yarbro[4]
[1]IBM Research - India, [2]IBM Research - Yorktown Heights, NY, USA
[3]Queensland University of Technology, Brisbane, Australia, [4]Pearson Education, USA
{shaafzal, tidhamecha, smarvani}@in.ibm.com, nmukhi@us.ibm.com
renuka.sr@qut.edu.au, {matthew.ventura, jessica.yarbro}@pearson.com

Abstract

There are significant challenges involved in the design and implementation of a dialog-based tutoring system (DBT) ranging from domain engineering to natural language classification and eventually instantiating an adaptive, personalized dialog strategy. These issues are magnified when implementing such a system at scale and across domains. In this paper, we describe and reflect on the design, methods, decisions and assessments that led to the successful deployment of our AI driven DBT currently being used by several hundreds of college level students for practice and self-regulated study in diverse subjects like Sociology, Communications, and American Government.

1 Introduction

Intelligent Tutoring Systems (ITS) have been one of the ambitions of researchers working in the fields of computer-aided education, learning sciences, and, to an extent, computational linguistics (Brusilovsky et al., 1996; Graesser et al., 1999; Evens et al., 1997). A special case of ITS is Dialog-based Tutoring (DBT) which is based on the Socratic principle of cooperative dialogue meant to stimulate critical thinking and deeper comprehension (Carbonell, 1970; Graesser et al., 1999, 2005).

Dialog-based intelligent tutoring systems (DBT) capture the effectiveness of expert human teacher-learner interactions by using natural language dialogue. Since articulation of a response in natural language involves recall and reflection of relevant knowledge it facilitates deeper comprehension of content. DBT consists of a sequence of mixed initiative dialogue moves in natural language to steer learners through varying levels of content granularity. A conversation is

---

*Work done while at IBM Research - India.

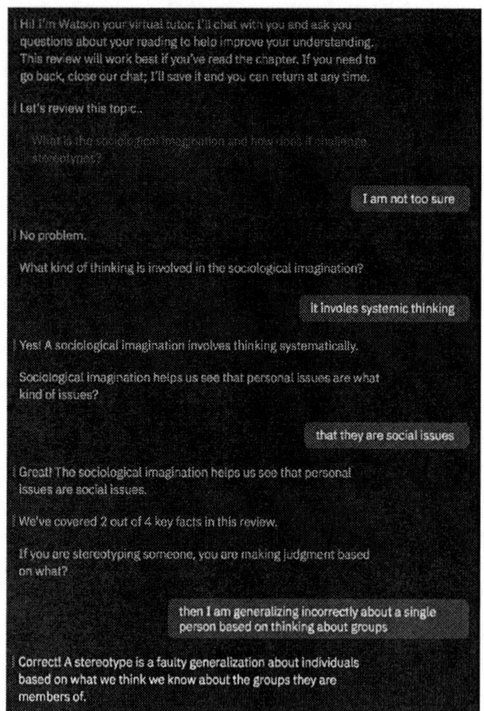

Figure 1: Screenshot of the Watson dialog-based tutor. Notice the transition from a broad question to focused question, intent classification of *I am not too sure* as need for help, and answer evaluation.

triggered when the tutor poses a question which typically leads to a series of dialog turns directed towards finer reasoning on relevant concepts. The goal is to scaffold knowledge and provide constructive remediation akin to expert one-one human tutoring. A well known example of DBT is AutoTutor (Graesser et al., 1999, 2005) while other notable systems include Why2 (VanLehn et al., 2002), CIRCSIM-Tutor (Evens et al., 1997), GuruTutor (Olney et al., 2012), DeepTutor (Rus et al., 2013), and the GIFT framework (Sottilare et al., 2012).

Proceedings of NAACL-HLT 2019, pages 114–121
Minneapolis, Minnesota, June 2 - June 7, 2019. ©2019 Association for Computational Linguistics

Building a DBT is a challenging task as it involves balancing of conversational efficiency with the tutoring goal of personalized adaptive mentoring and knowledge assessment. In spite of sustained research and development efforts there are major challenges that prohibit their vast adoption in educational practice. Some crucial challenges can be identified as:

1.1 Student Response Analysis

Natural language classification is a critical component of any DBT and is the very basis for driving an effective conversation. Performing a context-based interpretation of a student utterance is even more challenging owing to the diversity of human language, differences in vocabulary and nuances. Consequently, current NLP and AI techniques have limitations when applied in an open-response scenario like interaction with a DBT. As machine learning techniques rely on good training data to deliver good performance, the considerable subjectivity inherent in training-data annotation, benchmarking, and reaction to misclassification errors further impacts the classification accuracy.

1.2 Content Design and Creation

Extensive content authoring is required to drive any efficient DBT. The content needs to be structured in a way that drives the tutoring agenda while ensuring that knowledge elements render naturally in a conversational flow. This requires a tremendous amount of manual and semi-automated effort from subject matter experts. Content schema is also closely tied to the nature of a domain as different subjects would have their respective challenges. For example, creating content for a factual subject like Maths or Physics is substantially different to a subject like Psychology.

1.3 Dialog Strategy

Devising a meaningful conversational strategy is a non-trivial aspect as it directly impacts learner engagement and therefore learning outcomes. There should be sufficient flexibility and variation in responses to cater dynamically to the state and requirements of individual students. Additionally, there should be scope to implement interventions and scaffolds in order to keep the learner motivated. For example, surfacing relevant examples from a textbook when a student struggles or displays lack of knowledge during interaction.

1.4 Evaluation

The overall efficacy of a learning system is primarily determined by the learning gains achieved. However, the overall learning experience is significantly impacted by other dimensions such as classification accuracy, response time, style of feedback, variation in language, robustness and usability issues. Evaluation should therefore involve a holistic assessment of all factors that eventually lead to improved learning outcomes.

1.5 Scalability and robustness

The underlying algorithm design is impacted by both the domain engineering effort involved in scaling the tutor across titles as well as the ability to handle several concurrent users. Existing architectures are more often monolithic, thereby limiting the scope of improvements and scale.

In the context of the above challenges we now describe the development and refinement of our Watson dialog-based tutoring system that has so far been used by over 2,000 college students in the domains of Sociology, Communications, and American Government. Development of this system involved creating AI modules for language understanding, designing system architecture for modularity and scalability, and a significant effort to update various designs and algorithms to incorporate student feedback received at various milestones. Our DBT differs from existing systems in terms of domain and load scalability. We approach the issue of scaling across domains using a semi-automated pipeline for authoring, validation and improvisation of content. Scaling to load is enabled by designing tutor modules as cloud-based REST micro-services.

In the following sections we describe the architecture and iterative refinement of our2 tutor followed by some qualitative and quantitative evaluations from field experiments.

2 Design and Architecture

Our Watson dialog-based tutor provides remediation to learners through natural language discourse. Systematic turn-taking engages learners in a conversation style assessment of their mastery on domain knowledge. The tutor tracks the learners progress during the course of interaction and launches appropriate interventions according to pre-defined dialog strategies. The main components of the tutor are shown in Figure 2. The

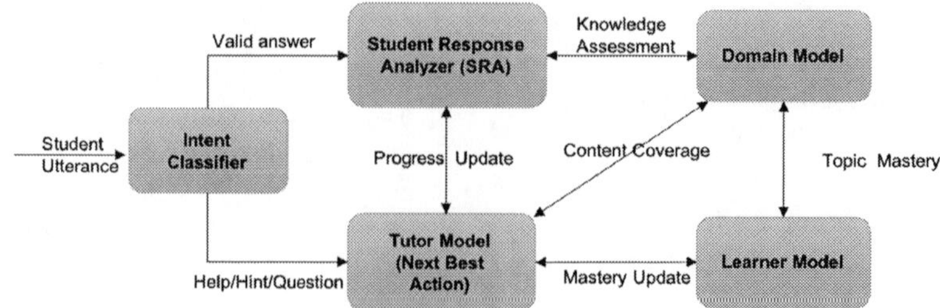

Figure 2: Simplified architecture of the tutor system.

most significant module of the tutor is the Natural Language Response Classifier comprising of two primary sub-components: the Intent Classifier and the Student Response Analyzer (SRA).

The Intent Classifier maps a student utterance to one of about 25 possible intent classes. The two main intent classes are: 1) a `valid on-topic answer` and 2) a `valid question`. Other intent classes include requests for help, requests for a hint, an expression of boredom, an insult, a greeting, and so on. This level of response classification is crucial to the effective working of the tutor as an error at this stage can have cascading effects on the entire dialog flow. This module is designed as a hierarchical classifier, going from broad intents to finer intents. The `valid on-topic answer` category requires domain/subject specific training whereas many meta-cognitive intents can be classified in domain agnostic manner.

Student Response Analysis (SRA) is the task of labeling student answers with categories that can help a dialog system to generate appropriate and effective feedback on errors. It is modeled as a classifier with underlying techniques similar to Textual Entailment (Dzikovska et al.), Semantic Textual Similarity (Agirre et al.), and Short Answer Grading (Mohler and Mihalcea, 2009). It takes the valid student answer and evaluates it against the model reference answer into one of 3 categories: `correct`, `partially correct`, and `incorrect` (Saha et al., 2018; Marvaniya et al., 2018). The SRA in our DBT thus makes use of state of art machine learning techniques to perform classification with macro-average F1 within 7% of that of human agreements; newer models (not reported here) have yielded results within 5% of human agreements. It uses an ensemble of semantic and syntactic features obtained from the tuple comprising of the question, student answer and the reference answer. This design makes it suitable for unseen-questions and, potentially for unseen-domains too. For a new domain or textbook, if student answers for training are not available, the existing base model can be used in *unseen-domain* setting. However, if the training data is available, the classification module can utilize it to improve the grading performance. In addition to response classification, SRA also performs a gap analysis on the student answer against the expected model answer to generate fill-in-the-blank (FITB) style prompts dynamically. The output of the Natural Language Response Classifier is used to drive the tutor strategy by continuous evaluation against the domain model and estimates of mastery from the learner model. The core of the tutoring framework is the domain model which is constructed by content experts as a hierarchy of learning objectives (LOs). Each LO is further structured into a sequence of assertions along with corresponding Hints and common misconceptions, if any. This formulation of content is designed to elicit knowledge gradually and allow fine-grained evaluation. With this domain model design schema, the broad task of evaluating student's understanding is broken down into set of more focused short answer evaluation.

This domain model design also enables conversational dialogue on a topic and micro-adaptation of tutorial strategy while allowing step-based assessment of learners mastery. Mastery is represented in the Learner Model which is updated on the basis of knowledge assessment on students' answers. The learner model also drives macro-adaptation between topics or LOs as defined in the pedagogical model. The pedagogical model formalizes the dialog response strategy and next-best action plan of the tutor using principles of formative feedback, hinting tactics and content coverage. Currently we use a rule-based dialog strategy instantiated for each student based on their current mastery and interaction history. (Shute,

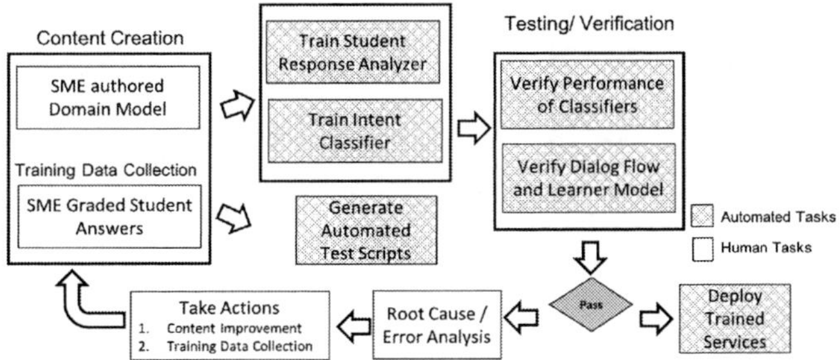

Figure 3: Sequence of tasks carried out to deploy the tutor for a new subject or domain

2008; Hume et al., 1996). The interface model is the front-end that triggers the UI to enable Tutor-Learner interaction in natural language. As our DBT is conceived to be used as a supplement to digital learning content, it is made strategically available to students for revision and practice.

3 Deployment and Scalability

All modules of the tutor are functionally isolated and are manifested as RESTful microservice APIs. This decoupling is important for scalable design. The overarching framework of Orchestration connects all the services. It is implemented in OpenWhisk (Mukhi et al., 2017) which follows a serverless computing based cloud-computing execution model. The front-end communicates with the Orchestration via broadly abstracted tutor APIs only. Depending on the functionality, some modules are domain agnostic (e.g. learner model, next-best-action), whereas others are not. For the domain dependent modules, a set of microservice instances are spawned per domain. In terms of the storage facility, NoSQL IBM Cloudant®, in-memory data structure store Redis, and Cloud Object Storage System™ are employed. Relatively small and structured data (e.g. domain content) is maintained in Cloudant; high frequency update data (e.g. student progress) is cached in Redis; whereas large AI models are stored in Cloud Object Storage. To cater to computational and traffic load, horizontal (in terms of processor and memory) and vertical (in terms of number of instances) scaling is facilitated by Kubernetes and Nginx API Gateway. Specifically in the context of commercial ITS systems, scalability has two aspects: development & load management.

3.1 Scalable to Develop

This corresponds to the ability to scale the tutor to new subjects/domains. The overall turnaround time to make the tutor usable for a new subject should be reasonably low. Figure 3 shows key tasks required to have the tutor system support a new subject such as creation of the domain model, retraining/transfer-learning of AI/NLP modules, testing the dialog and AI module performance, configuration tuning, and deploying the system. Some of these, such as domain model creation, evaluating and fine tuning the model are human labor intensive, whereas others have been automated. By design, all of these are distributable across multiple humans and machines which significantly helps formulate a *factory model* for preparing the tutor for a new subject. The training and deployment time for a new subject ranges between 6 hours - 72 hours, depending on the amount of refinement needed in the scoring models.

One of the key design elements for development scalability is re-usability of AI/NLP components with minimal modifications across various subjects. The SRA module uses a base model that can be used across all subjects. The SRA with only the base model yields a modest accuracy; it is extended with domain specific unstructured (text) and structured (student answers) to transfer it to the subject/domain. This facilitates *bootstrapping* the module and solves the problem of *cold start* often encountered in industry AI product development.

3.2 Scalable to Load

This refers to the runtime load tolerance of the tutor including simultaneous access to possibly several hundred students. Moreover, student enrollments may vastly differ per subjects and student activity may be very high during certain periods (e.g. prior to tests), and limited at other times (e.g. breaks). All these aspects require dynamic allocation of resources to various tutor modules.

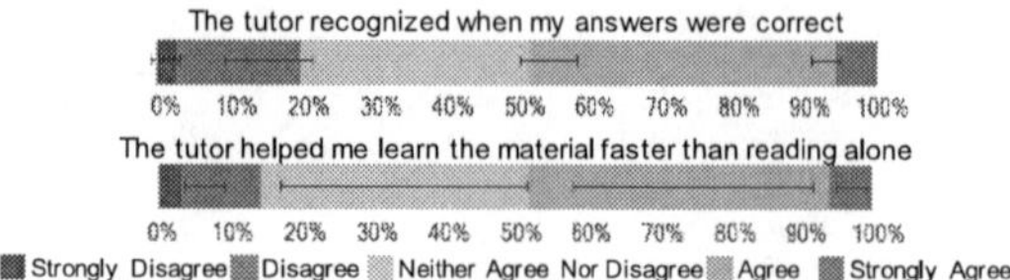

Figure 4: Response classification related survey question results illustrating positive impacts of tutor.

Some number crunching heavy modules benefit more from vertical scaling by virtue of inherent parallelization whereas gating/orchestrating modules typically benefit more from horizontal scaling. Our tutor can support 600 concurrent users (corresponding to $\sim$ 300K students using the tutor regularly over a semester) with error rate $< 0.5\%$ and response time $< 3s$ on average. The error rates and response times are much better for more typical loads ($5 - 50$ concurrent students) observed in current deployments.

4 Iterative Improvement of the System: Development Life Cycle

Various micro-experiments were done after every few internal releases to receive feedback from potential end users (sub-sampled student population). These micro-experiments helped evaluate the product features and robustness. Following are some of the key improvisations.

4.1 Evolution of the Response Classifier

Originally, the response classification was binary: `correct` or `incorrect`. A misclassification therefore resulted in either severe penalty or leniency. To mitigate this risk, the module was retrained to a three-way classifier, with the low-risk third class as `partially correct`. Doing so, indeed reduced the chance of `correct`-to-`incorrect` and vice-versa misclassification. However, in later trials we observed that if a student's answer is misclassified, it is better to suggest a finer follow up activity, than just providing partial grade. For example, by performing a gap analysis on the students answer against the expected one we dynamically generate fill-in-the-blank (FITB) style prompts or use encouragement pumps based on mastery.

4.2 Content Revision

During trials, we encountered cases, where student answers were correct in context of the text-book, but were wrong as per the authored content. This called for a need to update/enrich the authored content based on the actual student answers. As a solution, the students were given the option to rate the tutor's response using a thumbs up/down sign. These ratings are tracked to draw an SME (subject matter expert)'s attention to improve/rectify the content. This semi-automated approach allows for continuous user feedback and incremental training of the underlying modules.

4.3 Improvising the Conversation Tone

Feedback from trials was also leveraged to fine tune the tone of the tutor responses to make it more motivating, less pedantic, personable and more transparent. For example, if a student answer was classified as incorrect, the prompts `That's incorrect!`, `That seems to be a wrong answer` and `That does not match with what I have` convey the same message but with different levels of critique and encouragement. Similarly, variation in the feedback language was personalized according to students ability level and punctuation was strategically used to give a sense of enthusiasm and positivity. The overall persona and the personalized behavior were carefully revised and tuned according to situational needs. See (Afzal et al., 2019) for more details on the design and evolution of the tutor personality.

4.4 Dialog Flow Refinement

The dialog flow is essentially the entire orchestration of a tutoring goal, personalized for each student depending on their progress and mastery on specific content. Although, our initial dialog flow included two main activities of student answering questions and asking questions, we added additional activities to the dialog to adapt it to student mastery and improve engagement. These included recommending question asking based on questions asked by peers, presenting simpler binary true/false questions or presenting a fill-in-the-blank question if the computed hint question difficulty is high and student mastery is low for the topic.

5 Evaluation

As of August 2018, the Watson dialog-based tutor is available with 3 titles commercially, with a number of additional titles in development (Ventura

		Human-2		
		C	P	I
Human-1	C	57.6	20.2	22.2
	P	5.8	27.2	67.0
	I	3.1	5.3	91.6
Macro-F1: 60.2%				

		Tutor		
		C	P	I
Human-1	C	64.8	19.5	15.7
	P	31.9	23.4	44.7
	I	5.7	20.8	73.5
Macro-F1: 53.2%				

		Tutor		
		C	P	I
Human-2	C	69.0	17.4	13.6
	P	32.0	34.4	33.6
	I	11.4	13.8	74.8
Macro-F1: 55.9%				

Table 1: Confusion matrices (values in percentage) of Human-1 vs Human-2 and Humans vs Tutor for response classification during a learning experiment. C, P, and I represent `correct`, `partially correct`, and `incorrect` grade.

et al., 2018). During the fall 2018 semester, the commercially available titles were used by over 2000 students across more than 200 higher education institutions (Pearson, 2018). The system is expected to be used across a multitude of higher education institutions in the USA and will be piloted on five additional titles.

Here, we present our initial results gathered from two controlled learning experiments (LE) conducted 7 months apart. The first LE was conducted with 39 students while the second LE had 102 students. The demographic profile was similar with average GPA of ~ 3.5 and 70% female ratio. Here we discuss some relevant results on the following key dimensions:

5.1 Classification

For our two-level classification system - at intent and answer assessment level (SRA), we observed that intent classification of student utterances is 95% accurate, and the SRA system for scoring answers is within 7% of human inter-rater reliability for 3 of the 4 learning objectives tested. Figure 4 shows the student responses to survey questions that measure the efficacy of the tutor while Table 1 illustrates the evaluation of classification through formal metrics. The confusion matrices are reported for 50 transcripts pertaining to total of 1,065 student responses. Note that, `I`-to-`C` misclassification is 2.6-8.3% higher than that of human disagreement; whereas `C`-to-`I` misclassification rate is better than human disagreement.

User's feedback on how well the tutor understood their responses showed a statistically significant across the two LEs.

5.2 Validity

The tutor's estimate of student mastery scores was found to correlate significantly with the student's self-perception ($r = 0.32, p < 0.05$) and actual post–test learning measures ($r = 0.53, p < 0.001$). This is a strong indicator of the validity of the tutor's mastery measurement. Note that this validity is crucial as it is the basis for adjusting the dialog strategy to enable true personalization of the tutoring experience.

5.3 Dialog Quality

This was estimated by surveying the SMEs and students who used the system. The SMEs manually scored 236 conversational transcripts and took a survey after each transcript. In these surveys, the tutor was rated as providing an effective tutoring conversation 70% of the time, transitioning effectively through the conversation 75% of the time and providing appropriate feedback 66% of the time. Students' self–report was also fairly positive about the overall experience, feedback, value and usability of the tutor.

5.4 Iterative Improvement

Figure 5 reports the improvements observed across the two LEs on some survey items. These improvements are attributed to content refinement, response and intent classification improvement, and dialog refinement.

Perhaps more gratifying than the generally positive results are the expressions of enthusiasm, interest and engagement from students working with the Watson dialog-based tutor. Comments such as *"I wasn't having to go over reading material and lecture material over and over to understand it more fully because I grasped it the first time. I could take that time to devote to another subject, or my family"* was evidence of the truly beneficial societal impact that such a system could have, if applied the right way.

6 Discussion: Human Subjectivity

We observed that the subjectivity inherent in human language impacts the content authoring, creation of training data and, eventually, the end user experience. The domain model authoring raises

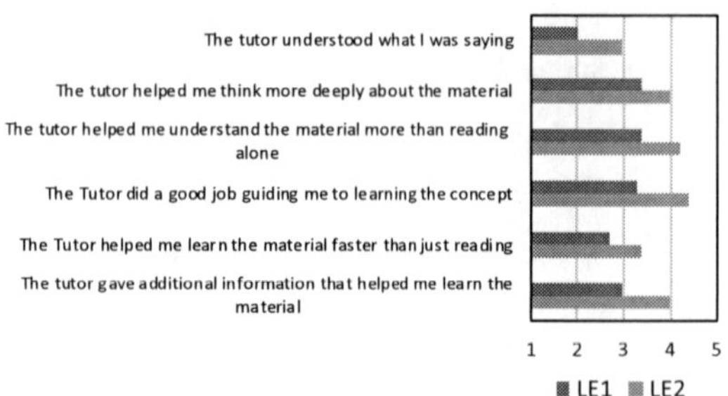

Figure 5: Comparison of LE1 & LE2 on survey items scored on 1-5 scale.

issues pertaining to the granularity of content and the resulting ambiguity expected in responses. For example (See Figure 6a), we observe that *recall* type question with WHAT interrogative pronouns are more likely to be answered correctly compared to HOW questions which may be ambiguous due to relative openness of expected answers. This implies that classification accuracy can be improved if a more standardized vocabulary is followed to limit the variation in content creation. However, this is a debatable proposition since it undervalues the richness of domain knowledge and may not be practical for non-factual domains.

Additionally, given a domain authored content like a QA pair, it is hard even for experts to determine the boundaries of correctness in student responses with respect to a reference model answer. This poor inter-rater agreement directly impacts the effectiveness of training the underlying scoring modules. To give an estimate, in one of our training data sets, three groundtruth labels were obtained from domain experts for each student answer. There was disagreement on 50% of the answers marked as partially correct by experts! Although this is a classical problem in ML/NLP, the consequences of scoring a correct answer incorrectly or vice-versa are more profound in a learning system. Human teachers are more flexible and sometimes abstract in their evaluation of an open-ended answer which is difficult to replicate in an AI system.

Finally, it is the delivery of an overall engaging and valuable experience that matters to human end users. Even here, there is remarkable subjectivity in users' perception and tolerance to the type and timing of tutor misclassifications (Afzal et al., 2018). We cannot measure efficacy solely in terms of absolute and restrictive metrics like accuracy and macro-average F1. Our best proxies, then, are

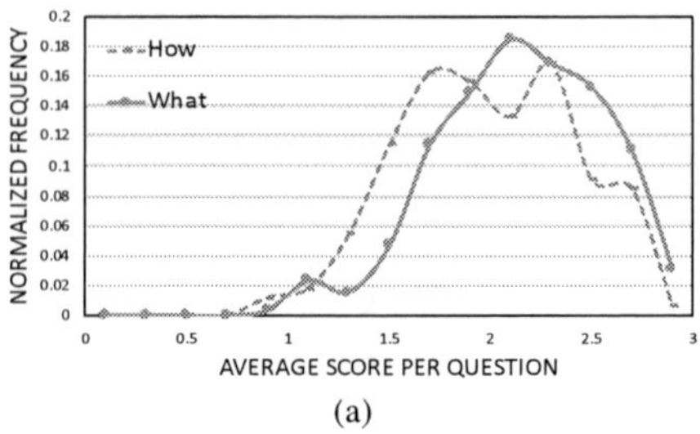

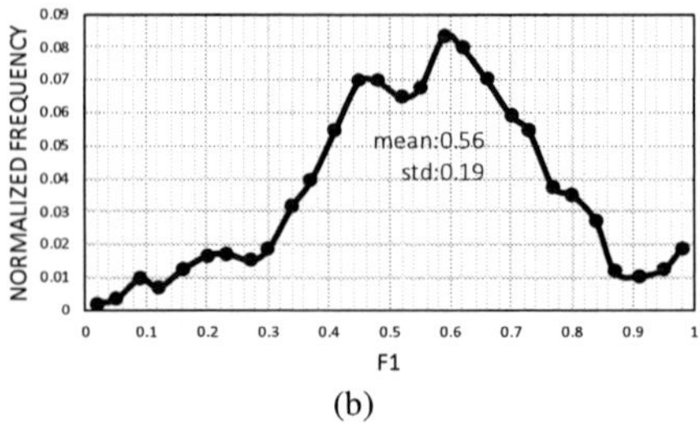

Figure 6: Quantifying issues related to human subjectivity: (a) ambiguity in answer correctness as function of question type, (b) poor inter-annotator agreement.

qualitative, detailed and timely feedback from the end users to learn and improvise over time.

7   Summary

Conversational tutoring is an important form of next-generation personalized adaptive educational technology. In this paper we have described the design and iterative development of Watson dialog-based tutor – a large-scale DBT that is optimized to scale across domain/subjects as well as usage. Its modules are functionally isolated to facilitate development and runtime scalability. We have described various challenges related to content creation and design including their impact on classification performance, refinement of feedback phrasing and tone, and dialog strategy. We have highlighted issues that arise from the inherent diversity of human language and how they impact the functioning of the tutor and the generated learning experiences. On the design side, automation of content extraction techniques can significantly speed up the content scaling process and allow building of richer domain models by making use of learning material from additional sources. On the experience side, substantial effort is needed to accurately understand natural language and use it strategically to deliver a naturalistic conversational interface that replicates the effectiveness of human teacher-learner interactions.

References

Shazia Afzal, Bryan Dempsey, Cassius D'Helon, Nirmal Mukhi, Milena Pribic, Aaron Sickler, Peggy Strong, Mira Vanchiswar, and Lorin Wilde. 2019. The personality of ai systems in education: Experiences with the watson tutor, a one-on-one virtual tutoring system. *Childhood Education*, 95(1):44–52.

Shazia Afzal, Vinay Shashidhar, Renuka Sindhgatta, and Bikram Sengupta. 2018. Impact of tutor errors on student engagement in a dialog based intelligent tutoring system. In *ITS*, pages 267–273. Springer.

Eneko Agirre, Mona Diab, Daniel Cer, and Aitor Gonzalez-Agirre. Semeval-2012 task 6: A pilot on semantic textual similarity. In *SemEval-2012*, pages 385–393. ACL.

Peter Brusilovsky, Elmar Schwarz, and Gerhard Weber. 1996. ELM-ART: an intelligent tutoring system on world wide web. In *ITS*, pages 261–269.

Jaime R Carbonell. 1970. AI in CAI: An artificial-intelligence approach to computer-assisted instruction. *IEEE TMMS*, 11(4):190–202.

Myroslava Dzikovska, Rodney Nielsen, Chris Brew, Claudia Leacock, Danilo Giampiccolo, Luisa Bentivogli, Peter Clark, Ido Dagan, and Hoa Trang Dang. Semeval-2013 task 7: The joint student response analysis and 8th recognizing textual entailment challenge. In *SemEval-2013*, volume 2, pages 263–274. ACL.

Martha W Evens, Ru-Charn Chang, Yoon Hee Lee, Leem Seop Shim, Chong Woo Woo, Yuemei Zhang, Joel A Michael, and Allen A Rovick. 1997. Circsim-tutor: An intelligent tutoring system using natural language dialogue. In *ANLP: Descriptions of system demonstrations and videos*, pages 13–14. ACL.

Arthur C Graesser, Patrick Chipman, Brian C Haynes, and Andrew Olney. 2005. Autotutor: An intelligent tutoring system with mixed-initiative dialogue. *IEEE ToE*, 48(4):612–618.

Arthur C Graesser, Katja Wiemer-Hastings, Peter Wiemer-Hastings, Roger Kreuz, Tutoring Research Group, et al. 1999. AutoTutor: a simulation of a human tutor. *Cognitive Systems Research*, 1(1):35–51.

Gregory Hume, Joel Michael, Allen Rovick, and Martha Evens. 1996. The use of hints by human and computer tutors: the consequences of the tutoring protocol. In *ICLS*, pages 135–142.

Smit Marvaniya, Swarnadeep Saha, Tejas I Dhamecha, Peter Foltz, Renuka Sindhgatta, and Bikram Sengupta. 2018. Creating scoring rubric from representative student answers for improved short answer grading. In *CIKM*, pages 993–1002. ACM.

Michael Mohler and Rada Mihalcea. 2009. Text-to-text semantic similarity for automatic short answer grading. In *EACL*, pages 567–575. ACL.

Nirmal K Mukhi, Srijith Prabhu, and Bruce Slawson. 2017. Using a serverless framework for implementing a cognitive tutor: experiences and issues. In *ACM WoSC*, pages 11–15.

Andrew M Olney, Natalie K Person, and Arthur C Graesser. 2012. Guru: designing a conversational expert intelligent tutoring system. In *Cross-disciplinary advances in applied natural language processing: Issues and approaches*, pages 156–171. IGI Global.

Pearson. 2018. Revel with watson. https://www.pearson.com/us/higher-education/products-services-teaching/digital-learning-environments/revel-with-watson.html.

Vasile Rus, Sidney DMello, Xiangen Hu, and Arthur Graesser. 2013. Recent advances in conversational intelligent tutoring systems. *AI magazine*, 34(3):42–54.

Swarnadeep Saha, Tejas I Dhamecha, Smit Marvaniya, Renuka Sindhgatta, and Bikram Sengupta. 2018. Sentence level or token level features for automatic short answer grading?: Use both. In *AIED*, pages 503–517.

Valerie J Shute. 2008. Focus on formative feedback. *Sage RER*, 78(1):153–189.

Robert A Sottilare, Keith W Brawner, Benjamin S Goldberg, and Heather K Holden. 2012. The generalized intelligent framework for tutoring (GIFT). *Orlando, FL: US Army Research Laboratory–Human Research & Engineering Directorate*.

Kurt VanLehn, Pamela W Jordan, Carolyn P Rosé, Dumisizwe Bhembe, Michael Böttner, Andy Gaydos, Maxim Makatchev, Umarani Pappuswamy, Michael Ringenberg, Antonio Roque, et al. 2002. The architecture of Why2-Atlas: A coach for qualitative physics essay writing. In *ITS*, pages 158–167.

Matthew Ventura, Maria Chang, Peter Foltz, Nirmal Mukhi, Jessica Yarbro, Anne Pier Salverda, John Behrens, Jae-wook Ahn, Tengfei Ma, Tejas I Dhamecha, et al. 2018. Preliminary evaluations of a dialogue-based digital tutor. In *AIED*, pages 480–483.

Learning When Not to Answer:
A Ternary Reward Structure for Reinforcement
Learning based Question Answering

Fréderic Godin
Ghent University
Ghent, Belgium
frederic.godin@ugent.be

Anjishnu Kumar
Amazon Research
Cambridge, United Kingdom
anjikum@amazon.com

Arpit Mittal
Amazon Research
Cambridge, United Kingdom
mitarpit@amazon.co.uk

Abstract

In this paper, we investigate the challenges of using reinforcement learning agents for question-answering over knowledge graphs for real-world applications. We examine the performance metrics used by state-of-the-art systems and determine that they are inadequate for such settings. More specifically, they do not evaluate the systems correctly for situations when there is no answer available and thus agents optimized for these metrics are poor at modeling confidence. We introduce a simple new performance metric for evaluating question-answering agents that is more representative of practical usage conditions, and optimize for this metric by extending the binary reward structure used in prior work to a ternary reward structure which also rewards an agent for not answering a question rather than giving an incorrect answer. We show that this can drastically improve the precision of answered questions while only not answering a limited number of previously correctly answered questions. Employing a supervised learning strategy using depth-first-search paths to bootstrap the reinforcement learning algorithm further improves performance.

1   Introduction

A number of approaches for question answering have been proposed recently that use reinforcement learning to reason over a knowledge graph (Das et al., 2018; Lin et al., 2018; Chen et al., 2018; Zhang et al., 2018). In these methods the input question is first parsed into a constituent question entity and relation. The answer entity is then identified by sequentially taking a number of steps (or 'hops') over the knowledge graph (KG) starting from the question entity. The agent receives a positive reward if it arrives at the correct answer entity and a negative reward for an incorrect answer entity. For example, for the question

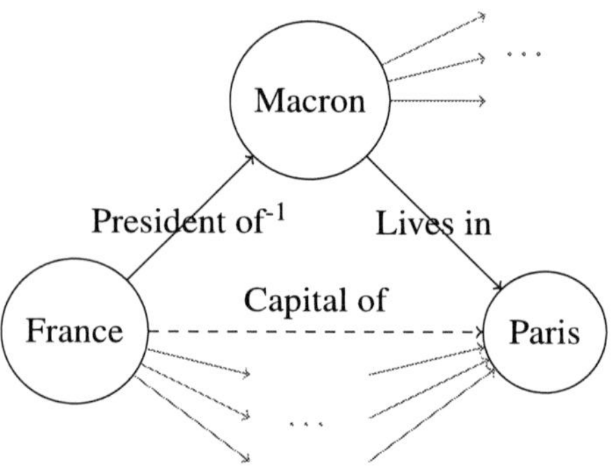

Figure 1: Fictional graph for the the question "What's the capital of France?". The relation ($Capital\ of$) does not exist in the graph and thus an alternative path needs to be used that leads to the correct answer.

"What is the capital of France?", the question entity is ($France$) and the goal is to find a path in the KG which connects it to ($Paris$). The relation between the answer entity and question entity in this example is ($Capital\ of$) which is missing from the KG and has to be inferred via alternative paths. This is illustrated in Figure 1. A possible two-hop path to find the answer is to use the fact that ($Macron$) is the president of ($France$) and that he lives in ($Paris$). However, there are many paths that lead to the entity ($Paris$) but also to other entities which makes finding the correct answer a non-trivial task.

The standard evaluation metrics used for these systems are metrics developed for web search such as Mean Reciprocal Rank (MRR) and hits@k, where k ranges from 1 to 20. We argue that this is not a correct evaluation mechanism for a practical question-answering system (such as Alexa, Cortana, Siri, etc.) where the goal is to return a single answer for each question. Moreover it is assumed that there is always an answer entity that could be

Proceedings of NAACL-HLT 2019, pages 122–129
Minneapolis, Minnesota, June 2 - June 7, 2019. ©2019 Association for Computational Linguistics

reached from the question entity in limited number of steps. However this cannot be guaranteed in a large-scale commercial setting and for all KGs. For example, in our proprietary dataset used for the experimentation, for 15.60% of questions the answer entity cannot be reached within the limit of number of steps used by the agent. Hence, we propose a new evaluation criterion, allowing systems to return 'no answer' as a response when no answer is available.

We demonstrate that existing state-of-the-art methods are not suited for a practical question-answering setting and perform poorly in our evaluation setup. The root-cause of poor performance is the reward structure which does not provide any incentive to learn not to answer. The modified reward structure we present allows agents to learn not to answer in a principled way. Rather than having only two rewards, a positive and a negative reward, we introduce a ternary reward structure that also rewards agents for not answering a question. A higher reward is given to the agent for correctly answering a question compared to not answering a question. In this setup the agent learns to make a trade-off between these three possibilities to obtain the highest total reward over all questions.

Additionally, because the search space of possible paths exponentially grows with the number of hops, we also investigate using Depth-First-Search (DFS) algorithm to collect paths that lead to the correct answer. We use these paths as a supervised signal for training the neural network before the reinforcement learning algorithm is applied. We show that this improves overall performance.

2 Related work

The closest works to ours are the works by Lin et al. (2018), Zhang et al. (2018) and Das et al. (2018), which consider the question answering task in a reinforcement learning setting in which the agent always chooses to answer.[1] Other approaches consider this as a link prediction problem in which multi-hop reasoning can be used to learn relational paths that link two entities. One line of work focuses on composing embeddings (Neelakantan et al., 2015; Guu et al., 2015; Toutanova et al., 2016) initially introduced for link prediction, e.g., TransE (Bordes et al., 2013), ComplexE

(Trouillon et al., 2016) or ConvE (Dettmers et al., 2018). Another line of work focuses on logical rule learning such as neural logical programming (Yang et al., 2017) and neural theorem proving (Rocktäschel and Riedel, 2017). Here, we focus on question answering rather than link prediction or rule mining and use reinforcement learning to circumvent that we do not have ground truth paths leading to the answer entity.

Recently, popular textual QA datasets have been extended with not-answerable questions (Trischler et al., 2017; Rajpurkar et al., 2018). Questions that cannot be answered are labeled with 'no answer' option which allows for supervised training. This is different from our setup in which there are no ground truth 'no answer' labels.

3 Background: Reinforcement learning

We base our work on the recent reinforcement learning approaches introduced in Das et al. (2018) and Lin et al. (2018). We denote the knowledge graph as $\mathcal{G}$, the set of entities as $\mathcal{E}$, the set of relations as $\mathcal{R}$ and the set of directed edges $\mathcal{L}$ between entities of the form $l = (e_1, r, e_2)$ with $e_1, e_2 \in \mathcal{E}$ and $r \in \mathcal{R}$. The goal is to find an answer entity e_a given a question entity e_q and the question relation r_q, when (e_q, r_q, e_a) is not part of graph $\mathcal{G}$.

We formulate this problem as a Markov Decision Problem (MDP) (Sutton and Barto, 1998) with the following states, actions, transition function and rewards:

States. At every timestep t, the state s_t is defined by the current entity e_t, the question entity e_q and relation r_q, for which $e_t, e_q \in \mathcal{E}$ and $r_q \in \mathcal{R}$. More formally, $s_t = (e_t, e_q, r_q)$.

Actions. For a given entity e_t, the set of possible actions is defined by the outgoing edges from e_t. Thus $A_t = \{(r', e')|(e_t, r', e') \in \mathcal{G}\}$.

Transition function. The transition function δ maps s_t to a new state s_{t+1} based on the action taken by the agent. Consequently, $s_{t+1} = \delta(s_t, A_t) = \delta(e_t, e_q, r_q, A_t)$.

Rewards. The agent is rewarded based on the final state. For example, in Das et al. (2018) and Lin et al. (2018) the agent obtains a reward of 1 if the correct answer entity is reached as the final state and 0 otherwise (i.e., $R(s_T) = \mathbb{I}\{e_T = e_a\}$).

---

[1] An initial version of this paper has been presented at the Relational Representation Learning Workshop at NeurIPS 2018 as Godin et al. (2018).

(a) History LSTM

(b) Policy network at timestep t

Figure 2: Figure 2a illustrates the LSTM which encodes history of the path taken. The output at timestep t is used as input to the policy network, illustrated in Figure 2b, to determine which action to take next.

3.1 Training

We train a policy network π using the REIN-FORCE algorithm of Williams (1992) which maximizes the expected reward:

$$J(\boldsymbol{\theta}) = \mathbb{E}_{(e_q, r_q, e_a) \in \mathcal{G}} \mathbb{E}_{a_1, \ldots, a_T \sim \pi}[R(s_T | e_q, r_q)] \tag{1}$$

in which a_t is the action selected at timestep t following the policy π, and $\boldsymbol{\theta}$ are the parameters of the network.

The policy network consists of two parts: a Long Short-Term Memory (LSTM) network which encodes the history of the traversed path, and a feed-forward neural network to select an action (a_t) out of all possible actions. Each entity and relation have a corresponding vector $e_t, r_t \in \mathbb{R}^d$. The action $a_t \in A_t$ is represented by the vectors of the relation and entity as $a_t = [r_{t+1}; e_{t+1}] \in \mathbb{R}^{2d}$. The LSTM encodes the history of the traversed path and updates its hidden state each timestep, based on the selected action:

$$h_t = LSTM(\boldsymbol{h}_{t-1}, \boldsymbol{a}_{t-1}) \tag{2}$$

This is illustrated in Figure 2a.

Finally, the feed-forward neural network (f) combines the history $\boldsymbol{h}_t$, the current entity representation e_t and the query relation r_q. Using softmax, we compute the probability for each action by calculating the dot product between the output of f and each action vector $\boldsymbol{a}_t$:

$$\pi(a_t | s_t) = softmax(\boldsymbol{A}_t f(\boldsymbol{h}_t, \boldsymbol{e}_t, \boldsymbol{r}_q)) \tag{3}$$

in which $\boldsymbol{A}_t \in \mathbb{R}^{|A_t| \times 2d}$ is a matrix consisting of rows of action vectors $\boldsymbol{a}_t$. This is illustrated in Figure 2b. During training, we sample over this probability distribution to select the action a_t, whereas during inference, we use beam search to select the most probable path.

4 Evaluation

User-facing question answering systems inherently face a trade-off between presenting an answer to a user that could potentially be incorrect, and choosing not to answer. However, prior work in knowledge graph question-answering (QA) only considers cases in which the answering agent always produces an answer. This setup originates from the link prediction and knowledge base completion tasks in which the evaluation criteria are hits@k and Mean Reciprocal Rank (MRR), where k ranges from 1 to 20. However, these metrics are not an accurate representation of practical question-answering systems in which the goal is to return a single correct answer or not answer at all. Moreover, using these metrics result in the problem of the model learning 'spurious' paths since the metrics encourage the models to make wild guesses even if the path is unlikely to lead to the correct answer.

We therefore propose to measure the fraction of questions the system answers (Answer Rate) and the number of correct answers out of all answers (Precision) to measure the system performance. We combine these two metrics by taking the harmonic mean and call this the QA Score. This can be viewed as a variant of the popular F-Score metric, with answer rate used as an analogue to recall in the original metric.

5 Proposed method

In this section, we will first introduce the supervised learning technique we used to pretrain the neural network before applying the reinforcement learning algorithm. Next we will describe the ternary reward structure.

5.1 Supervised learning

Typically in reinforcement learning, the search space of possible actions and paths grows exponentially with the path length. Our problem is no exception to this. Hence an imitation learning approach could be beneficial here where we provide a number of expert paths to the learning algorithm to bootstrap the learning process. This idea has been explored previously in the context of link and fact prediction in knowledge graphs where Xiong et al. (2017) proposed to use a Breadth-First-Search (BFS) between the entity pairs to select a set of plausible paths. However BFS favours identification of shorter paths which could bias the learner. We therefore use Depth-First-Search (DFS) to identify paths between question and answer entities and sample up to 100 paths to be used for the supervised training. If no path can be found between the entity pair we return a 'no answer' label. Following this, we train the network using reinforcement learning algorithm which refines it further. Note that it is not guaranteed that the set of paths found using DFS are all most efficient. However as we show in our experiments, bootstrapping with these paths provide good initialization for the reinforcement learning algorithm.

5.2 Ternary reward structure

As mentioned previously, we encounter situations when the answer entity cannot be reached in the limited number of steps taken by an agent. In such cases, the system should return a special answer 'no answer' as the response. We can achieve this by adding a synthetic 'no answer' action that leads to a special entity $e_{NOANSWER}$. This is illustrated in Figure 3. In the framework of Das et al. (2018) a binary reward is used which rewards the learner for the answer being wrong or correct. Following a similar protocol, we could award a score of 1 to return 'no answer' when there is no answer available in the KG. However, we cannot achieve reasonable training with such reward structure. This is because there is no specific pattern for 'no answer' that could be directly learned. Hence, if we reward a system equally for correct or no answer, it learns to always predict 'no answer'. We therefore propose a ternary reward structure in which a positive reward is given to a correct answer, a neutral reward when $e_{NOANSWER}$ is selected as an answer, and a negative reward for an

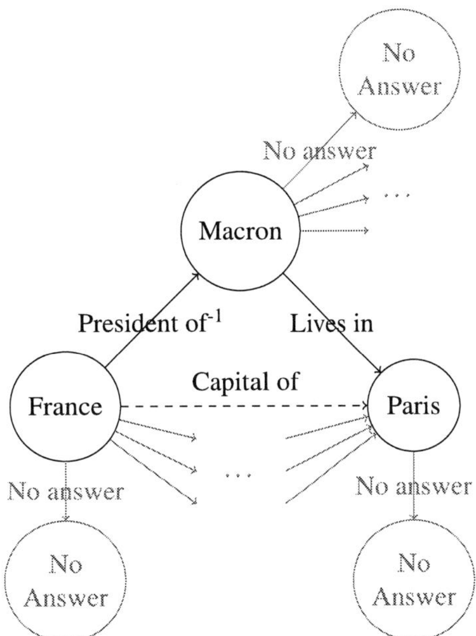

Figure 3: Fictional graph for the the question "What's the capital of France?". The relation ($Capital\ of$) does not exist in the graph and thus an alternative path needs to be used that leads to the correct answer. To avoid that the agent returns an incorrect answer when not finding the correct answer, a 'no answer' relation is added between every entity node and a special 'no answer' node, to be able to return 'no answer'.

incorrect answer. More formally:

$$
R(s_T) = \begin{cases} r_{pos} & \text{if } e_T = e_a, \\ 0 & \text{if } e_T = e_{NOANSWER}, \\ r_{neg} & \text{if } e_T \notin \{e_a, e_{NOANSWER}\} \end{cases}
\tag{4}
$$

with $r_{pos}>0$ and $r_{neg}<0$. The idea is that the agent receives a larger reward for a correct answer compared to not answering the question, and a negative reward for incorrectly answering a question compared to not answering the question. In the experimental section, we show that this mechanism provides better performance.

6 Experimental setup

We evaluate our proposed approach on a publicly available dataset, FB15k-237 (Toutanova and Chen, 2015) which is based on the Freebase knowledge graph and a proprietary dataset Alexa69k-378 which is a sample of Alexa's proprietary knowledge graph. Both the public dataset and the proprietary dataset are good examples of

Model	Hits@1	Hits@10	MRR	Precision	Answer Rate	QA Score
(Das et al., 2018)	0.217	0.456	0.293	0.217	1	0.357
(Lin et al., 2018)	0.329	0.544	0.393	0.329	1	0.495
RL	0.2475	0.4032	0.2983	0.2475	1	0.3968
Supervised	0.2474	0.4929	0.3276	0.2474	1	0.3967
Supervised + RL	0.2736	0.5015	0.3469	0.2736	1	0.4296
No Answer RL	0.2345	0.3845	0.2831	0.4011	0.5847	0.4758
All	0.2738	0.4412	0.3286	**0.4835**	0.5663	**0.5216**

Table 1: Results on FB15k-237 dataset.

Model	Hits@1	Hits@10	MRR	Precision	Answer Rate	QA Score
(Das et al., 2018)	0.1790	0.2772	0.2123	0.1790	1	0.3036
(Lin et al., 2018)	0.1915	0.3184	0.2358	0.1915	1	0.3214
RL	0.1677	0.2716	0.2031	0.1677	1	0.2872
Supervised	0.1471	0.3142	0.203	0.1471	1	0.2565
Supervised + RL	0.1937	0.3045	0.2312	0.1937	1	0.3245
No Answer RL	0.1564	0.2442	0.1858	**0.3892**	0.4019	0.3955
All	0.1865	0.294	0.2229	0.3454	0.5401	**0.4213**

Table 2: Results on Alexa69k-378 dataset.

#ent	#rel	#facts	#queries	
			valid	test
FB15k-237				
14,505	237	272,115	17,535	20,466
Alexa69k-378				
69,098	378	442,591	55,186	55,474

Table 3: Statistics of the datasets.

real-world general-purpose knowledge graphs that can be used for question answering. FB15k-237 contains 14,505 different entities and 237 different relations resulting in 272,115 facts. Alexa69k-378 contains 69,098 different entities and 378 different relations resulting in 442,591 facts. We follow the setup of Das et al. (2018), using the same train/val/test splits for FB15k-237. For Alexa69k-378 we use 10% of the full dataset for validation and test. For both datasets, we add the reverse relations of all relations in the training set in order to facilitate backward navigation following the approach of previous work. Similarly, a 'no op' relation is added for each entity between the entity and itself, which allows the agent to loop/reason mul-

tiple consecutive steps over the same entity. An overview of both datasets can be found in Table 3.

We extend the publicly available implementation of Das et al. (2018) for our experimentation. We set the size of the entity and relation representations d at 100 and the hidden state at 200. We use a single layer LSTM and train models with path length 3 (tuned using hyper-parameter search). We optimize the neural network using Adam (Kingma and Ba, 2015) with learning rate 0.001, mini-batches of size 256 with 20 rollouts per example. During the test time, we use beam search with the beam size of 100. Unlike Das et al. (2018), we also train entity embeddings after initializing them with random values. Reward values are set as $r_{pos} = 10$ and $r_{neg} = -0.1$ after performing a coarse grid search for various reward values on the validation set. For all experiments, we selected the best model with the highest QA Score on the corresponding validation set.

7 Results

The results of our experiments for FB15k-237 and Alexa69k-378 are given in Table 1 and Table 2 respectively.

Supervised learning For FB15k-237, we see that the model trained using reinforcement learning (RL) scores as well as the model trained using supervised learning. This makes supervised learning using DFS a strong baseline system for question answering over knowledge graphs, and for FB15k-237 in particular. On Alexa69k-378, models trained using supervised learning score lower on all metrics compared to RL. When combining supervised learning with RL overall performance increases.

No answer When we train RL system with our ternary reward structure (No Answer RL), the precision and QA score increase significantly on both datasets. For FB15k-237, our No Answer RL model decided not to answer over 40% of the questions, with an absolute hits@1 reduction of only 1.3% over standard RL. Moreover, of all the answered questions, 40.11% were answered correctly compared to 24.75% of the original question-answering system: an absolute improvement of over 15%. This resulted in the final QA Score of 47.58%, around 8% higher than standard RL and 12% higher than Das et al. (2018).

Similarly, 60% of the questions did not get answered on Alexa69k-378. This resulted in hits@1 decrease of roughly 1% but compared to standard RL, the precision increased from 16.77% to 38.92%: an absolute increase of more than 20%. The final QA Score also increased from 28.72% to 39.55%, and also significantly improved over Das et al. (2018) and Lin et al. (2018). The results indicate that using our method allows us to improve the precision of the question-answering system by choosing the right questions to be answered by not answering many questions that were previously answered incorrectly. This comes at the expense of not answering some questions that previously could be answered correctly.

All Finally, all methods were combined in a single method. First the model was pretrained in a supervised way. Then the model was retrained using RL algorithm with ternary reward structure. This jointly trained model obtained better QA scores than any individually trained model. On FB15k-237, a QA score of 52.16% is obtained which is an absolute improvement of 4.58% over the best individual model and 2.66% over Lin et al. (2018). Similarly, on Alexa69k-378, an absolute improvement of 2.57% over the best individual result is

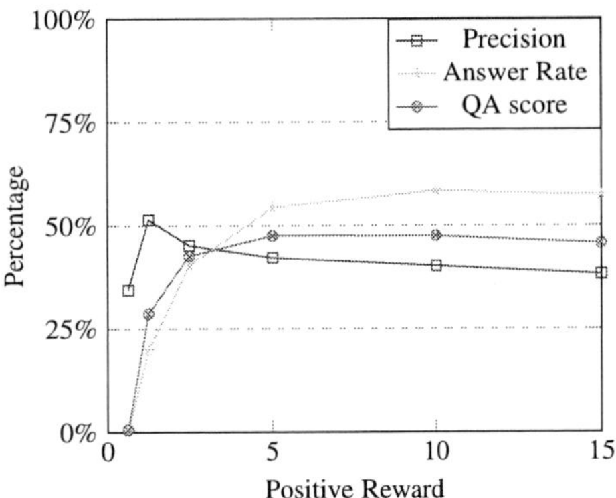

Figure 4: Influence of changing the positive reward for FB15k-237. The negative reward is fixed at $r_{neg} = -0.1$ and the neutral reward is fixed at $r_{neutral} = 0$.

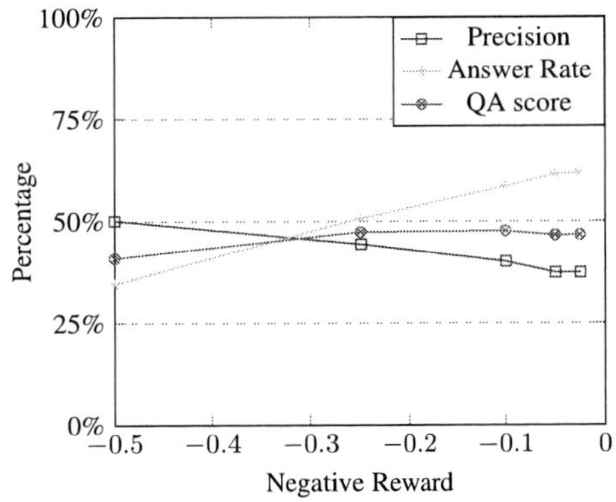

Figure 5: Influence of changing the negative reward for FB15k-237. The positive reward is fixed at $r_{pos} = 10$ and the neutral reward is fixed at $r_{neutral} = 0$.

obtained, almost 10% absolute improvement over Lin et al. (2018). Sample results from our method are given in Table 4 and Table 5.

Reward tuning An important part of increasing the QA score is to select the right combination of rewards. Therefore, we ran additional experiments where we varied either the positive or negative reward, keeping the other rewards fixed. In Figure 4, the precision, answer rate and QA score are shown when varying the positive reward and keeping the neutral and negative rewards fixed. When, the positive reward is very small ($r_{pos} = 0.625$), almost no question is answered. When the positive reward r_{pos} is 1.25, roughly 20% of the questions are answered with a 50% precision. After that, the precision starts declining and the answer rate

Question: e_q = Bruce Broughton, r_q = Profession. Answer: e_a = Music Composer

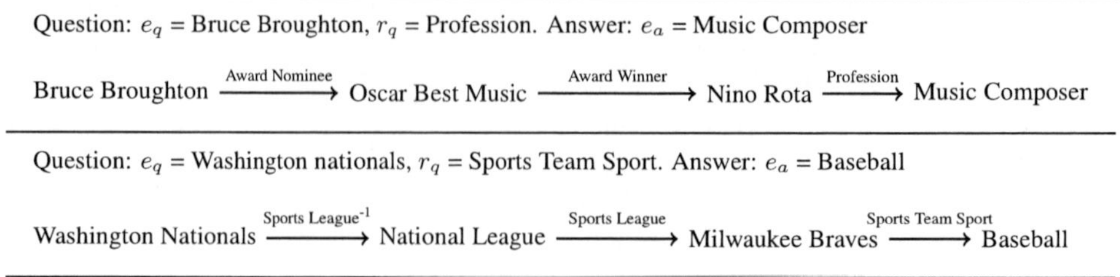

Question: e_q = Washington nationals, r_q = Sports Team Sport. Answer: e_a = Baseball

Washington Nationals —Sports League⁻¹→ National League —Sports League→ Milwaukee Braves —Sports Team Sport→ Baseball

Table 4: Example paths of correctly answered questions on FB15k-237. Note that the fact (e_q, r_q, e_a) is not part of the KG.

Question: e_q = Sherlock holmes (movie), r_q = Story By. Answer: e_a = Conan Doyle

Sherlock holmes (movie) —Film Crew Role→ Wardrobe Supervisor —No op→ Wardrobe Sup. —No op→ Wardrobe Sup.

Sherlock holmes (movie) —Film Crew Role→ Wardrobe Supervisor —No answer→ No answer —No answer→ No answer

Table 5: Example question from FB15k-237, incorrectly answered by (Das et al., 2018) and not answered by our system. Note that the fact (e_q, r_q, e_a) is not part of the KG.

---

starts increasing, resulting in an overall increase in QA score. The QA score plateaus between 5 and 10 and then starts decreasing slowly. In Figure 5, the precision, answer rate and QA score are shown when varying the negative reward and keeping the neutral and positive rewards fixed. In this case, the highest QA score is achieved when the negative reward is between -0.25 and -0.1. As long as the negative reward is lower than zero, a wrong answer gets penalized and the QA score stays high.

8 Conclusions

In this paper, we addressed the limitations of current approaches for question answering over a knowledge graph that use reinforcement learning. Rather than only returning a correct or incorrect answer, we allowed the model to not answer a question when it is not sure about it. Our ternary reward structure gives different rewards for correctly answered, incorrectly answered and not answered questions. We also introduced a new evaluation metric which takes these three options into account. We showed that we can significantly improve the precision of answered questions compared to previous approaches, making this a promising direction for the practical usage in knowledge graph-based QA systems.

References

Antoine Bordes, Nicolas Usunier, Alberto Garcia-Duran, Jason Weston, and Oksana Yakhnenko. 2013. Translating embeddings for modeling multi-relational data. In *Advances in Neural Information Processing Systems (NIPS)*.

Wenhu Chen, Wenhan Xiong, Xifeng Yan, and William Yang Wang. 2018. Variational knowledge graph reasoning. In *Proceedings of the Conference of the North American Chapter of the Association for Computational Linguistics: Human Language Technologies (NAACL-HTL)*.

Rajarshi Das, Shehzaad Dhuliawala, Manzil Zaheer, Luke Vilnis, Ishan Durugkar, Akshay Krishnamurthy, Alexander J. Smola, and Andrew McCallum. 2018. Go for a walk and arrive at the answer: Reasoning over paths in knowledge bases using reinforcement learning. *International Conference on Learning Representations (ICLR)*.

Tim Dettmers, Minervini Pasquale, Stenetorp Pontus, and Sebastian Riedel. 2018. Convolutional 2d knowledge graph embeddings. In *Proceedings of the 32th AAAI Conference on Artificial Intelligence (AAAI)*.

Fréderic Godin, Anjishnu Kumar, and Arpit Mittal. 2018. Using ternary rewards to reason over knowledge graphs with deep reinforcement learning. In *Workshop on Relational Representation Learning (NeurIPS)*.

Kelvin Guu, John Miller, and Percy Liang. 2015. Traversing knowledge graphs in vector space. In *Proceedings of the Conference on Empirical Methods in Natural Language Processing (EMNLP)*.

Diederik P. Kingma and Jimmy Ba. 2015. Adam: A method for stochastic optimization. *In Proceedings of the International Conference on Representation Learning (ICLR).*

Xi Victoria Lin, Richard Socher, and Caiming Xiong. 2018. Multi-hop knowledge graph reasoning with reward shaping. In *Proceedings of the 2018 Conference on Empirical Methods in Natural Language Processing (EMNLP).*

Arvind Neelakantan, Benjamin Roth, and Andrew McCallum. 2015. Compositional vector space models for knowledge base completion. In *Proceedings of the Annual Meeting of the Association for Computational Linguistics and the International Joint Conference on Natural Language Processing (ACL-IJCNLP).*

Pranav Rajpurkar, Robin Jia, and Percy Liang. 2018. Know what you don't know: Unanswerable questions for squad. In *Proceedings of the Annual Meeting of the Association for Computational Linguistics (ACL).*

Tim Rocktäschel and Sebastian Riedel. 2017. End-to-end differentiable proving. In *Advances in Neural Information Processing Systems (NIPS).*

Richard S. Sutton and Andrew G. Barto. 1998. *Introduction to Reinforcement Learning*, 1st edition. MIT Press, Cambridge, MA, USA.

Kristina Toutanova and Danqi Chen. 2015. Observed versus latent features for knowledge base and text inference. In *3rd Workshop on Continuous Vector Space Models and Their Compositionality (ACL).*

Kristina Toutanova, Victoria Lin, Wen-tau Yih, Hoifung Poon, and Chris Quirk. 2016. Compositional learning of embeddings for relation paths in knowledge base and text. In *Proceedings of the Annual Meeting of the Association for Computational Linguistics (ACL).*

Adam Trischler, Tong Wang, Xingdi Yuan, Justin Harris, Alessandro Sordoni, Philip Bachman, and Kaheer Suleman. 2017. Newsqa: A machine comprehension dataset. In *Proceedings of the 2nd Workshop on Representation Learning for NLP (ACL).*

Théo Trouillon, Johannes Welbl, Sebastian Riedel, Éric Gaussier, and Guillaume Bouchard. 2016. Complex embeddings for simple link prediction. In *Proceedings of the International Conference on Machine Learning (ICML).*

Ronald J. Williams. 1992. Simple statistical gradient-following algorithms for connectionist reinforcement learning. *Machine Learning.*

Wenhan Xiong, Thien Hoang, and William Yang Wang. 2017. Deeppath: A reinforcement learning method for knowledge graph reasoning. In *Proceedings of the 2017 Conference on Empirical Methods in Natural Language Processing (EMNLP).*

Fan Yang, Zhilin Yang, and William W. Cohen. 2017. Differentiable learning of logical rules for knowledge base reasoning. In *Advances in Neural Information Processing Systems (NIPS).*

Yuyu Zhang, Hanjun Dai, Zornitsa Kozareva, Alexander J. Smola, and Le Song. 2018. Variational reasoning for question answering with knowledge graph. In *Proceedings of the AAAI Conference on Artificial Intelligence (AAAI).*

Extraction of Message Sequence Charts from
Software Use-Case Descriptions

Girish K. Palshikar   Nitin Ramrakhiyani   Sangameshwar Patil
Sachin Pawar   Swapnil Hingmire
{gk.palshikar,nitin.ramrakhiyani}@tcs.com
{sangameshwar.patil,sachin7.p,swapnil.hingmire}@tcs.com
TRDDC, TCS Research and Innovation, India

Vasudeva Varma
vv@iiit.ac.in
IIIT Hyderabad, India

Pushpak Bhattacharyya
pb@cse.iitb.ac.in
IIT Patna, India

Abstract

Software Requirement Specification documents provide natural language descriptions of the core functional requirements as a set of use-cases. Essentially, each use-case contains a set of actors and sequences of steps describing the interactions among them. Goals of use-case reviews and analyses include their correctness, completeness, detection of ambiguities, prototyping, verification, test case generation and traceability. Message Sequence Charts (MSC) have been proposed as an expressive, rigorous yet intuitive visual representation of use-cases. In this paper, we describe a linguistic knowledge-based approach to extract MSCs from use-cases. Compared to existing techniques, we extract richer constructs of the MSC notation such as timers, conditions and alt-boxes. We apply this tool to extract MSCs from several real-life software use-case descriptions and show that it performs better than the existing techniques.

1   Introduction

Software Development Life Cycle (SDLC) processes generate large and complex natural language text documents, which provide a rich playground for NLP tecnhiques. In particular, NLP techniques have been extensively applied to analyze requirements specifications for early detection of problems such as ambiguity and incompleteness during reviews and inspections; e.g., (Gervasi and Zowghi, 2005; Chantree et al., 2006; Kiyavitskaya et al., 2008; Yang et al., 2011; Ferrari et al., 2017a; Rosadini et al., 2017). Another line of research is concerned with automatically translating software requirements in natural language to various formal models, in order to provide assistance in downstream SDLC tasks like prototyping, verification, test case generation and traceability. Specifically, use-cases provide a textual description of the core functional requirements as sequences of interactions among actors. Hence, Message Sequence Charts (MSC) have been proposed as an expressive, rigorous yet intuitive visual representation of use-cases (Feijs, 2000; Kof, 2008; Yue et al., 2015).

In extracting the MSC from a use-case description, we have to first identify *actors*, which refer to human users, physical objects, systems, subsystems and components. Next, we need to identify *interactions* among the actors in the form of messages of the MSC. The actor which initiates an interaction i.e. sends a message is called the sender and the actors which receive (or experience) the interaction are called receivers. NLP techniques face various challenges in these steps. Firstly, an actor (or an interaction) may be referred in different ways (actor or event co-reference). Secondly, since there is no standardized way of writing use-cases, there is tremendous variety in expressing various aspects of the functionality; e.g., main and alternate flows. While restrictions such as templates or structured English have been imposed for writing use-cases e.g., (Arora et al., 2015), we assume that a use-case is written as a sequence of numbered steps in the main flow, and an alternate flow for any steps in the main flow is specified separately. We impose no linguistic restriction in writing each step in the use-case. Finally, MSC is a rich notation with many complex facilities apart from representing actors and messages. Some of these include alt-boxes, conditions

Proceedings of NAACL-HLT 2019, pages 130–137
Minneapolis, Minnesota, June 2 - June 7, 2019. ©2019 Association for Computational Linguistics

Use Case: Move to Station	
Actors: Supervisory System, AGV system, motor, vehicle, arrival sensor, robot arm	
Main Flow:	
1. The Supervisory System sends a message to the AGV system requesting it to move to a factory station and load a part.	
2. The AGV System commands the motor to start moving.	
3. The motor notifies the AGV System that the vehicle has started moving.	
4. The AGV System sends a Departed message to the Supervisory System.	
5. The arrival sensor notifies the AGV System that it has arrived at factory station.	
6. The AGV System determines that this station is the destination station and commands the motor to stop moving.	
7. The motor notifies the AGV System that the vehicle has stopped moving.	
8. The AGV System commands the robot arm to load the part within 10 seconds.	
9. The arm notifies the AGV System that the part has been loaded.	
10. The AGV System sends an Arrived message to the Supervisory System.	
Alternate Flow:	
1. Step 6 to Step 10: If the vehicle arrives at a different station from the destination station , the vehicle passes the station without stopping and sends a Passed factory station without stopping message to the Supervisory System.	

Table 1: Sample use-case description

and timers. It is challenging to detect appropriate parts of the input text which can be mapped to these constructs. Table 1 shows an example use-case and Figure 1 shows the corresponding MSC.

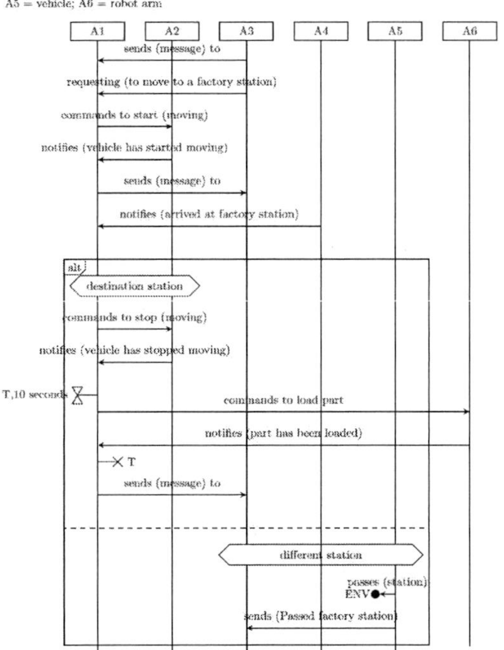

Figure 1: MSC corresponding to the use-case description in Table 1

In this paper, we describe our approach to extract MSCs from use-cases based on Open Information Extraction (OpenIE) (Mausam, 2016). OpenIE extracts structured information from a sentence in the form of relation tuples representing a relation between its subject and one or more objects. We use OpenIE to extract candidate messages and their senders / receivers. We further use WordNet and dependency parsing[1] for filtering the OpenIE candidates and obtaining the final set of messages to be depicted on the MSC.

The MSC representation supports richer constructs such as *timers*, *conditions* and *alt-boxes*. *Timers* represent start and end of specific time durations related to the messages and are shown by hourglass shaped markers. For instance, to capture the information that part loading should be completed in 10 seconds (Step 8 in Table 1), a timer can be used. Accordingly, Figure 1 shows a timer of duration 10 seconds on the timeline of the actor "the AGV system". *Conditions* represent state or situation of one or more actors and are shown as text labels inside hexagonal boxes. In Figure 1, a condition is shown on the timeline of the actors - "the AGV system" and "the motor" denoting the state of the system to be at the destination station. *Alt-boxes* are used to represent an alternate control flow with respect to a certain condition applicable to a set of actors. They are denoted using demarcating lines separating the normal and alternate set of messages. In the example (Table 1), based on the condition of the station at which the vehicle has arrived, the step mentioned as alternate flow or the steps 6 to 10 of the normal flow need to be followed. This branching is depicted using the alt-

---

[1]In this paper, we use the Stanford CoreNLP (Manning et al., 2014) pipeline for dependency parsing.

box shown in Figure 1.

The paper is organized as follows. Section 2 covers the related work; Section 3 describes the MSC extraction approach; Section 4 describes the experiments and discusses one of the use-cases in detail; Section 5 concludes the paper.

2   Related Work

Feijs (2000) studies the relationship between natural language use cases and message sequence charts. He uses context-free generative grammars for natural language description of use-cases that use object-oriented system development methods. However, this study focuses on simple sentences and sentences with coordination and subordination. Moreover, this study does not discuss empirical evaluation of the use-case to MSC conversion.

Kof (2007a) proposes a method for representing a software requirement document using a MSC. This method takes a software requirement document and a list of valid actors as its inputs. For a verb in a sentence it generates a message such that the valid actor appearing before the verb is identified as the sender, the valid actor appearing immediately after the verb is identified as the receiver and the text starting from the verb and ending before the receiver is identified as the message label. Kof (2007b) further extends this approach to include sentences with multiple verbs, conjunctions and passive voice. Kof (2007a) also proposes a set of heuristics to handle missing sender or receiver of a message. A key limitation of this method is that it ignores syntactic as well as semantic relations between the verb and its corresponding sender or receiver. Hence it is possible that some of the <sender, message label, receiver> tuples may not be valid semantically. It is important to note that Kof (2007a; 2007b) do not focus on other features of MSC such as conditions, timers and alt-boxes.

3   MSC Extraction

In this section, we describe our approach for creation of an MSC for a given use-case description. The approach involves running OpenIE based extraction on the input use-case text and processing it further for extracting the MSC elements namely actors and messages. Additionally, the approach applies a set of linguistic rules to extract conditions, alt boxes and timers.

Processing input using OpenIE: Use-case descriptions generally use well-written English. Over such text, generation of candidate messages requires a simple relation and argument extractor. We thus propose use of the OpenIE framework which provides tuples of the form (left_argument, relation, right_argument_1, right_argument_2, ...) along with confidence scores with each tuple. We first process the input use-cases through the OpenIE technique described in (Mausam et al., 2012; Mausam, 2016) and obtain a list of candidate messages.

Defining Actors in Software Engineering Use-Cases: In general (Bedi et al., 2017; Patil et al., 2018; Palshikar et al., 2019), the notion of actors in MSC is based on named entities of the types - PERSON, LOCATION and ORGANIZATION. However, in the software requirements domain, these may not be the only entities interacting with each other. This criteria is extended and is proposed to include:

- PERSONS (Human SYSTEM users), ORGANIZATIONS and LOCATIONS

- SYSTEMS (such as Supervisory System, Library System)

- Persistent components of SYSTEMS (such as servers, databases, customer accounts)

- Persistent processes in the SYSTEM (such as schedulers, daemons)

- SYSTEM components (GUI elements like buttons, menus, and similar)

Also, as part of the definition of actors, it is important to exclude the following entities seen in software requirements text.

- Attributes of the above entities (such as usernames, passwords)

- Transient entities and business processes (such as requests, responses, registration process)

To realize this definition of actors we propose a WordNet based approach and check if a candidate actor is a valid actor. We refer to this verification while identifying messages.

We consider all noun phrases as candidate actors and then filter them based on two criteria. If the head word of the noun phrase has certain specific senses as part of its WordNet hypernym hierarchy, we consider it as a valid actor. These specific senses are gathered manually through observation and consist of "Physical Object" (sense 1), "thing" (sense 4 and sense 12), "matter" (sense 3), "substance" (sense 1 and 4) and "Causal agent" (sense 1). This filters out abstract entities which are not actors such as `request`, `response` and `message`.

To allow computer and system related nouns which are abstract in nature and have none of the above specified senses in their hypernym path, we apply the second criteria. We allow nouns with head words having the following senses in their hypernym hierarchy: "Computer", "Computer File" and "database".

Identifying Messages: For identifying messages, we begin by considering output of the OpenIE tool on the use-case text which gives us a set of tuples in each sentence. These candidate message tuples are given input to the message identification approach and the list of filtered messages with their senders and receivers are obtained as output. The message identification approach is described in Algorithm 1.

The algorithm iterates over the set of OpenIE tuples. For each tuple, it checks if the left argument is a valid actor which is the sender of the message. The valid actor check is based on the proposed definition of actors. If the left argument is not a valid actor the tuple is ignored. This ensures that each message has a valid sender.

For each right argument, if it has a single dependency subtree and is a valid actor, the tuple is regarded as a valid message. If the subtree is not a valid actor but is dependent to the relation it is appended to the relation string. In the case when there are multiple subtrees in a right argument, subtrees with their head words as valid actors are considered receivers of the message.

Extracting Conditions: We consider a text fragment in a use-case as a *condition*, if it denotes a state or property and the set of associated actors are those that are "involved" in that condition. A condition text is often either a verb phrase (VP) (`has stopped moving`), a noun phrase (NP) (`power failure`) or an adjective phrase (ADJP), though sometimes a prepositional phrase (PP) is also observed. Since not all VPs or NPs are

---

Algorithm 1: *identify_messages*

Input: T = Set of tuples given by OpenIE for a sentence. T = t; t_confidence >= threshold where each t = (left argument, rel, right arguments...)

Output: set of messages M with each message m having three attributes: sender, message label (msg_label) and set of receivers

```
 1  foreach tuple t ∈ T do
 2  │   m := ()
 3  │   if t.left_arg is a valid actor then
 4  │   │   m.sender := t.left_arg
 5  │   else
 6  │   │   continue
 7  │   m.msg_label := t.rel
 8  │   foreach arg ∈ t.right_arguments do
 9  │   │   if arg contains only one dependency
    │   │        subtree then
10  │   │   │   if arg is a valid actor then
11  │   │   │   │   m.receivers ∪ arg
12  │   │   │   else if head of t.rel is governor
    │   │   │        of head of arg then
13  │   │   │   │   m.msg_label := append(m.msg_label,
    │   │   │   │        arg)
14  │   │   else
15  │   │   │   foreach dep_st ∈ arg's
    │   │   │        disjoint dependency subtrees do
16  │   │   │   │   if dep_st headed by a noun
    │   │   │   │        and is valid actor then
17  │   │   │   │   │   m.receivers ∪ arg
18  │   │   │   │   else
19  │   │   │   │   │   if head of t.rel is governor of
    │   │   │   │   │        head of dep_st then
20  │   │   │   │   │   │   m.msg_label =
    │   │   │   │   │   │        append(m.msg_label,
    │   │   │   │   │   │        dep_st)
21  │   foreach r in m.receivers do
22  │   │   new_tuple := (m.sender, m.msg_label, r)
23  │   │   M = M ∪ (new_tuple)
24  return M
```

---

conditions, we have designed a set of linguistic rules to identify conditions: (1) Any ADJP connected to a copula (or copula-like) verb and also to an actor through **nsubj** dependency relation (`The valve is open`). (2) Any VP connected to a copula (or copula-like) verb through **auxpass** dependency relation and also connected to an actor through **nsubjpass** dependency relation (`The page is refreshed`). (3) Any VP connected to a copula-like verb v (e.g., `remains`) through an **xcomp** dependency and v is connected to an actor through **nsubj** (`The engine remains idling`). (4) A VP V connected to cue phrases like `if`, `upon`, `in case of`, where the head verb of V has an actor as a part of its dependency subtree (`If power to the pump fails`). (5) If a NP is predicative nominal of another NP, the text segment comprising these NPs is considered as a condition (`This station is the destination station.`)

Extracting Alt-Boxes: Alt boxes in the MSC representation are useful to represent paths alternate to the normal flow of events. This is an important construct especially for use-case descriptions as alternate steps of action occur frequently with software systems. For identifying these alternate paths and representing them as alt boxes in MSCs, we harness the structure of use-case descriptions. As per our observation, there are generally two styles in which alternate paths are specified in use-case descriptions. In one format, the alternate flow is specified separately from the normal. The alternate flow provides a pointer to the set of steps in the normal flow to which it is alternate to. We use this structural information and capture messages from the alternate flow to be shown in "alt" to the corresponding normal flow messages. In another format, the alternate step is specified just after the normal flow step marked by a set of conditional prepositions such as `if` or prepositional phrases such as `in case`, `in the event of` or adverbs such as `else`, `otherwise`. We identify these markers with the help of regular expression based patterns and separate the alternate step from the normal step. The later format however, does not provide scope information of alternate steps. Based on observation of multiple use-cases of real software systems, we make an assumption that the scope of the alternate flow begins at the normal flow step with which it is specified and lasts till the last step in the normal flow.

Extracting Timers: MSC supports an important construct - the "timer", to capture interactions which must happen in a time-bound manner. A timer may be attached to an actor's time-line or a condition. Timers in a use-case description are extracted through two steps. Firstly, we identify the durative time expressions in the input use-case description using regular expression based patterns such as $[0 - 9] + (milliseconds|seconds|minutes|hours|days)$ (numbers followed by time period expressions like milliseconds, seconds, minutes, hours, days). Secondly, using the OpenIE output, we identify the relation for which the time expressions iden-

tified in the previous step appears as a temporal argument. We attach a timer to time-line around the message.

4 Experimentation Details

4.1 Dataset and Evaluation

We report results in this paper on a set of 4 use-cases obtained from publicly available Software Requirement Specifications (SRS) of real life software systems (Ferrari et al., 2017b). These use-cases are AGV (Automated Guided Vehicle System), G6 & G16 (gamma-j web order system) and EMS (Electronic Monitoring System). Additionally, we use one more use-case (TRAIN) from an internal project dealing with Automatic Train Control systems.

We manually create the gold standard MSC for each use-case and use them to evaluate our extraction system. As part of the evaluation, we compare the performance of our system with a baseline technique proposed in (Kof, 2007a,b).

We evaluate the proposed approach on five levels of increasing complexity starting from actor identification to complete message extraction:

1. Actors : At this level we evaluate the predicted actors with respect to the gold actors. A predicted actor is a true positive if its complete phrase is present exactly in the set of gold actors. False positives and false negatives are accordingly computed.

2. Message label : At this level we evaluate only the message label of each predicted message with respect to labels of gold messages. A predicted message label from a sentence is considered as a true positive if the main verb of the label matches the main verb of a gold message from the same sentence. False positives and false negatives are accordingly computed.

3. Message label + Sender : At this level we evaluate the combination of message label and sender of each predicted message with respect to the same combination for gold messages. A predicted combination from a sentence is considered as a true positive if it matches the combination from a gold message from the same sentence.

4. Message label + Receiver : At this level we evaluate the combination of message label and

Dataset		Actors	Message Label	Sender	Receiver	Complete Message
AGV	B	0.552	0.083	0.080	0.071	0.071
	M	0.800	0.741	0.741	0.581	**0.581**
G6	B	0.667	0.667	0.667	0.571	0.571
	M	0.778	0.947	0.947	0.727	**0.727**
G16	B	0.667	0.769	0.769	0.571	0.571
	M	0.800	1.000	1.000	0.933	**0.933**
EMS3	B	0.727	0.333	0.333	0.333	0.333
	M	0.909	0.750	0.750	0.750	**0.750**
TRAIN	B	0.556	0.667	0.444	0.526	0.421
	M	0.941	0.800	0.800	0.706	**0.706**

Table 2: Comparative performance for MSC Extraction. M: Our approach described in Algorithm 1. B: Baseline approach based on Kof (2007a; 2007b)

receiver of each predicted message with respect to the same combination for gold messages. We compute F1-measure on similar lines as above.

5. Message label + Sender + Receiver : At this level we evaluate the complete message i.e. combination of message label, sender and receiver with respect to the complete gold messages. We compute F1-measure on similar lines as above.

As each level's performance, we report the F1-measure in Table 2. Our approach outperforms the baseline on all datasets on all evaluation levels.

For extraction of the complex constructs like conditions, alt-boxes and timers, we employ a set of simple rules described earlier. The baseline technique proposed in (Kof, 2007a,b) does not focus on identifying these constructs.

4.2 Analysis

It is important to note that performance of the proposed approach is dependent on the performance of tools in the NLP processing backend (which are WordNet, Stanford CoreNLP and OpenIE in this case). We highlight a few error cases to explain the NLP challenges encountered.

OpenIE fails to identify any relation in some sentences. For example, in the sentence `System stores order confirmation and order details.`, OpenIE does not generate any relation of the form `<System, stores, order confirmation>`, because it identifies "stores" as a noun. Hence our approach fails to identify the messages in this sentence.

In the context of use-case description texts, there are multiple words which have domain specific senses which are not captured by resources like WordNet, e.g., "flag", "ticket", "turnkey", etc. As our approach depends on WordNet to identify valid actors, it may identify certain spurious messages. For example, in the sentence `System appends cookie with flag for completed checkout process.`, our approach identifies "flag" as a valid actor even though in this context it is not. Hence, it creates an incorrect message with sender as "System" and "flag" as receiver.

In use-cases we frequently observe that the actors are part of multiple interactions and a single actor is referred by multiple lexical mentions. Hence, it is necessary to perform coreference resolution to group multiple mentions of an actor and represent it using a canonical mention in the MSC. However, we observed that performing coreference resolution to group coreferring actor mentions together, degrades the performance. The average (over all use-cases) complete message identification performance degrades from an F1 of 74% to 45%. This is because of several incorrect coreference links identified by the Stanford CoreNLP toolkit. E.g., consider the following extract from a use-case: `The Supervisory System sends a message to the AGV system requesting it to move to a factory station and load a part. The AGV System commands the motor to start moving.` Here, Stanford CoreNLP incorrectly identifies `The Supervisory System` in the first sentence and `The AGV System` in the second sentence as coreferences.

These examples point out the NLP challenges faced in automated extraction of MSC and the need for further research.

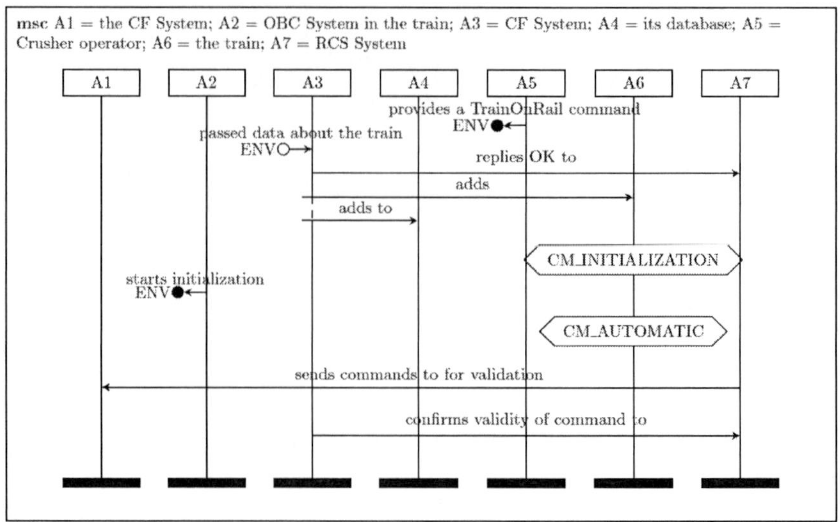

Figure 2: MSC for sample use-case about addition of a new train in the automated train system

4.3 Discussion on the TRAIN Use-Case

We have used the MSC to analyze the software use-cases for an industrial computer-controlled automated train system. It is used to move ores from mines. The automated train system has following key components: (i) the Railway Controller Software (RCS) system, (ii) the Checker Functionality (CF) system, (iii) the On-Board Computer (OBC) system. The locomotive train is controlled by the RCS. This system is used by various operators such as the crusher operator, etc. A brief use-case about addition of a new locomotive train into the the set of trains already under control of the RCS is described below:-

```
1. Crusher operator provides a
   TrainOnRail command.

2. The data about the train is passed
   to CF System.

3. CF System replies OK to RCS System.

4. CF System adds the train to its
   database.

5. At the beginning the state of the
   train is CM_INITIALIZATION.

6. OBC System in the train starts
   initialization.

7. After initialization, the state of
   the train becomes CM_AUTOMATIC.

8. RCS System sends commands to the CF
   System for validation.

9. CF System confirms validity of
   command to the RCS System.
```

Figure 2 shows the MSC for this use-case. Using the MSC, we are able to identify the gaps in the use-case specification as well as generate test-cases from the use-case. For instance, in the above use-case, the expected behaviour of the automated train system is not specified if the RCS sends a command while the train is still in the CM_INITIALIZATION state. The domain expert then clarified that the RCS should never send the commands till the train state becomes CM_AUTOMATIC. Based on the tools and techniques (Alur et al., 1996) developed for verifying MSC properties, it can be verified that such a sequence of infeasible actions is not specified in the set of given use-cases. Also, it can be verified that there are no contradictions in the given set of use-cases. It is also possible to develop test-case outlines using the MSCs prepared from the use-case descriptions. Such test-case generation is part of our future work.

5 Conclusions

We explored automatic extraction of Message Sequence Charts (MSC) from use-case descriptions in Software Requirement Specification documents. In this paper, we described an Open IE based approach which uses linguistic knowledge such as dependency parsing and WordNet hypernyms to extract MSCs from use-cases. Compared to existing techniques, we also extracted richer constructs of the MSC notation such as timers, conditions and alt-boxes. Our approach outperforms the baseline on a dataset of five real-life use-cases.

References

Rajeev Alur, Gerard J Holzmann, and Doron Peled. 1996. An analyzer for message sequence charts. In *International Workshop on Tools and Algorithms for the Construction and Analysis of Systems*, pages 35–48. Springer.

Chetan Arora, Mehrdad Sabetzadeh, Lionel C. Briand, and Frank Zimmer. 2015. Automated Checking of Conformance to Requirements Templates Using Natural Language Processing. *IEEE Trans. Software Eng.*, 41(10):944–968.

Harsimran Bedi, Sangameshwar Patil, Swapnil Hingmire, and Girish K. Palshikar. 2017. Event Timeline Generation from History Textbooks. In *Proceedings of the 4th Workshop on Natural Language Processing Techniques for Educational Applications, NLP-TEA@IJCNLP 2017, Taipei, Taiwan, December 1, 2017*, pages 69–77.

Francis Chantree, Bashar Nuseibeh, Anne N. De Roeck, and Alistair Willis. 2006. Identifying Nocuous Ambiguities in Natural Language Requirements. In *14th IEEE International Conference on Requirements Engineering (RE 2006), 11-15 September 2006, Minneapolis/St.Paul, Minnesota, USA*, pages 56–65.

Loe M. G. Feijs. 2000. Natural language and message sequence chart representation of use cases. *Information & Software Technology*, 42(9):633–647.

Alessio Ferrari, Felice Dell'Orletta, Andrea Esuli, Vincenzo Gervasi, and Stefania Gnesi. 2017a. Natural Language Requirements Processing: A 4D Vision. *IEEE Software*, 34(6):28–35.

Alessio Ferrari, Giorgio Oronzo Spagnolo, and Stefania Gnesi. 2017b. PURE: A Dataset of Public Requirements Documents. In *25th IEEE International Requirements Engineering Conference, RE 2017, Lisbon, Portugal, September 4-8, 2017*, pages 502–505.

Vincenzo Gervasi and Didar Zowghi. 2005. Reasoning About Inconsistencies in Natural Language Requirements. *ACM Trans. Softw. Eng. Methodol.*, 14(3):277–330.

Nadzeya Kiyavitskaya, Nicola Zeni, Luisa Mich, and Daniel M. Berry. 2008. Requirements for tools for ambiguity identification and measurement in natural language requirements specifications. *Requir. Eng.*, 13(3):207–239.

Leonid Kof. 2007a. Scenarios: Identifying Missing Objects and Actions by Means of Computational Linguistics. In *15th IEEE International Requirements Engineering Conference (RE 2007)*, pages 121–130.

Leonid Kof. 2007b. Treatment of Passive Voice and Conjunctions in Use Case Documents. In *Natural Language Processing and Information Systems*, pages 181–192, Berlin, Heidelberg. Springer Berlin Heidelberg.

Leonid Kof. 2008. From textual scenarios to message sequence charts: inclusion of condition generation and actor extraction. In *6th IEEE international requirements engineering conference, (RE'08)*, pages 331–332.

Christopher D. Manning, Mihai Surdeanu, John Bauer, Jenny Rose Finkel, Steven Bethard, and David McClosky. 2014. The Stanford CoreNLP Natural Language Processing Toolkit. In *Proceedings of the 52nd Annual Meeting of the Association for Computational Linguistics, ACL 2014, June 22-27, 2014, Baltimore, MD, USA, System Demonstrations*, pages 55–60.

Mausam. 2016. Open Information Extraction Systems and Downstream Applications. In *Proceedings of the Twenty-Fifth International Joint Conference on Artificial Intelligence, IJCAI 2016, New York, NY, USA, 9-15 July 2016*, pages 4074–4077.

Mausam, Michael Schmitz, Stephen Soderland, Robert Bart, and Oren Etzioni. 2012. Open Language Learning for Information Extraction. In *Proceedings of the 2012 Joint Conference on Empirical Methods in Natural Language Processing and Computational Natural Language Learning, EMNLP-CoNLL 2012, July 12-14, 2012, Jeju Island, Korea*, pages 523–534.

Girish K. Palshikar, Sachin Pawar, Sangameshwar Patil, Swapnil Hingmire, Nitin Ramrakhiyani, Harsimran Bedi, Pushpak Bhattacharyya, and Vasudeva Varma. 2019. Extraction of Message Sequence Charts from Narrative History Text. In *Proceedings of the Workshop on Narrative Understanding*.

Sangameshwar Patil, Sachin Pawar, Swapnil Hingmire, Girish K. Palshikar, Vasudeva Varma, and Pushpak Bhattacharyya. 2018. Identification of Alias Links among Participants in Narratives. In *ACL 2018*.

Benedetta Rosadini, Alessio Ferrari, Gloria Gori, Alessandro Fantechi, Stefania Gnesi, Iacopo Trotta, and Stefano Bacherini. 2017. Using NLP to Detect Requirements Defects: An Industrial Experience in the Railway Domain. In *Requirements Engineering: Foundation for Software Quality - 23rd International Working Conference, REFSQ 2017, Essen, Germany, February 27 - March 2, 2017, Proceedings*, pages 344–360.

Hui Yang, Anne N. De Roeck, Vincenzo Gervasi, Alistair Willis, and Bashar Nuseibeh. 2011. Analysing anaphoric ambiguity in natural language requirements. *Requir. Eng.*, 16(3):163–189.

Tao Yue, Lionel C. Briand, and Yvan Labiche. 2015. aToucan: An Automated Framework to Derive UML Analysis Models from Use Case Models. *ACM Trans. Softw. Eng. Methodol.*, 24(3):1–52.

Improving Knowledge Base Construction from Robust Infobox Extraction

Boya Peng[*] **Yejin Huh** **Xiao Ling** **Michele Banko**[*]

Apple Inc.
1 Apple Park Way
Cupertino, CA, USA

Sentropy Technologies

{yejin.huh,xiaoling}@apple.com {emma,mbanko}@sentropy.io[*]

Abstract

A capable, automatic Question Answering (QA) system can provide more complete and accurate answers using a comprehensive knowledge base (KB). One important approach to constructing a comprehensive knowledge base is to extract information from Wikipedia infobox tables to populate an existing KB. Despite previous successes in the Infobox Extraction (IBE) problem (*e.g.*, DBpedia), three major challenges remain: 1) Deterministic extraction patterns used in DBpedia are vulnerable to template changes; 2) Over-trusting Wikipedia anchor links can lead to entity disambiguation errors; 3) Heuristic-based extraction of unlinkable entities yields low precision, hurting both accuracy and completeness of the final KB. This paper presents a robust approach that tackles all three challenges. We build probabilistic models to predict relations between entity mentions directly from the infobox tables in HTML. The entity mentions are linked to identifiers in an existing KB if possible. The unlinkable ones are also parsed and preserved in the final output. Training data for both the relation extraction and the entity linking models are automatically generated using distant supervision. We demonstrate the empirical effectiveness of the proposed method in both precision and recall compared to a strong IBE baseline, DBpedia, with an absolute improvement of 41.3% in average F_1. We also show that our extraction makes the final KB significantly more complete, improving the completeness score of list-value relation types by 61.4%.

1 Introduction

Most existing knowledge bases (KBs) are largely incomplete. This can be seen in Wikidata (Vrandečić and Krötzsch, 2014), which is a widely used knowledge graph created largely by human editors. Only 46% of person entities in Wikidata have birth places available [1]. An estimate of 584 million facts are maintained in Wikipedia, not in Wikidata (Hellmann, 2018). A downstream application such as Question Answering (QA) will suffer from this incompleteness, and fail to answer certain questions or even provide an incorrect answer especially for a question about a list of entities due to a closed-world assumption. Previous work on enriching and growing existing knowledge bases includes relation extraction on natural language text (Wu and Weld, 2007; Mintz et al., 2009; Hoffmann et al., 2011; Surdeanu et al., 2012; Koch et al., 2014), knowledge base reasoning from existing facts (Lao et al., 2011; Guu et al., 2015; Das et al., 2017), and many others (Dong et al., 2014).

Wikipedia (https://wikipedia.org) has been one of the key resources used for knowledge base construction. In many Wikipedia pages, a summary table of the subject, called an infobox table, is presented in the top right region of the page (see the leftmost table in Figure 1 for the infobox table of The_Beatles). Infobox tables offer a unique opportunity for extracting information and populating a knowledge base. An infobox table is structurally formatted as an HTML table and therefore it is often not necessary to parse the text into a syntactic parse tree as in natural language extraction. Intra-Wikipedia anchor links are prevalent in infobox tables, often providing unambiguous references to entities. Most importantly, a significant amount of information represented in the infobox tables are not otherwise available in a more traditional structured knowledge base, such as Wikidata.

We are not the first to use infobox tables

---

[*] Work performed at Apple Inc.

[1] as of June 2018

Proceedings of NAACL-HLT 2019, pages 138–148
Minneapolis, Minnesota, June 2 - June 7, 2019. ©2019 Association for Computational Linguistics

for knowledge base completion. The pioneering work of DBpedia (Auer et al., 2007; Lehmann et al., 2015)[2] extracts canonical knowledge triples (`subject`, *relation type*, `object`) from infobox tables with a manually created mapping from Mediawiki [3] templates to relation types. Despite the success of the DBpedia project, three major challenges remain. First, deterministic mappings are sensitive to template changes. If Wikipedia modifies an infobox template (*e.g.*, the attribute "birthDate" is renamed to "dateOfBirth"), the DBpedia mappings need to be manually updated. Secondly, while Wikipedia anchor links facilitate disambiguation of string values in the infobox tables, blindly trusting the anchor links can cause errors. For instance, both "Sasha" and "Malia," children of `Barack Obama`, are linked to a section of the Wikipedia page of `Barack_Obama`, rather than their own pages. Finally, little attention has been paid to the extraction of unlinkable entities. For example, `Larry King` has married seven women, only one of which can be linked to a Wikipedia page. A knowledge base without the information of the other six entities will provide an incorrect answer to the question "How many women has Larry King married?"

In this paper, we present a system, RIBE, to tackle all three challenges: 1) We build probabilistic models to predict relations and object entity links. The learned models are more robust to changes in the underlying data representation than manually maintained mappings. 2) We incorporate the information from HTML anchors and build an entity linking system to link string values to entities rather than fully relying on the anchor links. 3) We produce high-quality extractions even when the objects are unlinkable, which improves the completeness of the final knowledge base.

We demonstrate that the proposed method is effective in extracting over 50 relation types. Compared to a strong IBE baseline, DBpedia, our extractions achieve significant improvements on both precision and recall, with a 41.3% increase in average F_1 score. We also show that the extracted triples add a great value to an existing knowledge base, Wikidata, improving an average recall of list-value relation types by 61.4%.

To summarize, our contributions are three-fold:

- RIBE produces high-quality extractions, achieving higher precision and recall compared to DBpedia.
- Our extractions make Wikidata more complete by adding a significant number of triples for 51 relation types.
- RIBE extracts relations with unlinkable entities, which are crucial for the completeness of list-value relation types and the question answering capability from a knowledge base.

2   Related Work

Auer and Lehmann (2007) proposed to extract information from infobox tables by pattern matching against Mediawiki templates and parsing and transforming them into RDF triples. However, relation types of the triples remain lexical and can be ambiguous. Lehmann et al. (2015) introduced an ontology to reduce the ambiguity in relation types. A mapping from infobox attributes to the ontology [4] is manually created, which is brittle to template changes. In contrast, RIBE is much more robust. It trains statistical models with distant supervision from Wikidata to automatically learn the mapping from infobox attributes to Wikidata relation types. RIBE properly parses infobox values into separate object mentions, instead of relying on existing Mediawiki boundaries as in (Auer and Lehmann, 2007; Lehmann et al., 2015). The RIBE entity linker learns to make entity link predictions rather than a direct translation of anchor links (Auer and Lehmann, 2007; Lehmann et al., 2015) vulnerable to human edit errors. While there is other relevant work, due to space constraints, it is discussed throughout the paper and in the appendices as appropriate.

3   Problem Definition

We define a **relation** as a triple (e_1, r, e_2) or $r(e_1, e_2)$, where r is the **relation type** and e_1, e_2 are the **subject** and the **object** entities respectively [5]. We define an **entity mention** m as the surface form of an entity, and a **relation mention**

---

[2]Throughout the paper, we use "DBpedia" to refer to its infobox extraction component rather than the DBpedia knowledge base unless specified. We use Wikidata as the baseline knowledge base for our experiments since it is updated more frequently. The last release DBpedia knowledge base was in 2016.

[3]Mediawiki is a markup language that defines the page layout and presentation of Wikipedia pages.

[4]DBpedia Mappings Wiki at `http://mappings.dbpedia.org`.

[5]e_2 can also be a literal value such as a number or a time expression unless specified.

as a pair of entity mentions (m_1, m_2) for a relation type r. We denote the set of infobox tables by $T = \{t_1, t_2, ..., t_n\}$ where t_i appears in the Wikipedia page of the entity e_i [6]. The Infobox Extraction problem studied in this paper aims at extracting a set of relation triples $r(e_1, e_2)$ from an input of Wikipedia infobox tables T.

4 System Overview

We describe the RIBE system in this section. Wikidata (Vrandečić and Krötzsch, 2014) is employed as the base external KB. We draw distant supervision from it by matching candidate mentions against Wikidata relation triples for training statistical models. We also link our mentions to Wikidata entities [7] and compare our extractions to it for evaluation (Tables 4, 8). The final output of RIBE is a set of relation triples $R = \{r_i(e_1^i, e_2^i)\}$.

4.1 Relation Extraction

Figure 1 depicts an overview of the relation extractor. It extracts relation mentions $r(m_1, m_2)$ from each infobox table in T in four stages: entity mention generation, feature generation, distant supervision, and model training and inference.

4.1.1 Mention Generation

We parse each infobox table rendered in HTML, instead of the raw Mediawiki template, to generate object mentions. As the infobox templates evolve over time, different Mediawiki templates have been used to describe the same type of things. Despite the difference in templates, the rendered infobox tables in HTML displays a surprisingly consistent format: each row contains an attribute cell and an attribute value cell.

We chunk the text of each attribute value cell and generate object mentions using a few heuristics such as HTML tag boundaries. Table 5 in Appendix A shows the heuristics. Each pair of subject and object mentions becomes one relation mention candidate. Note that an off-the-shelf noun phrase chunker (Sang and Buchholz, 2000) or a Named Entity Recognition (NER) tagger (Finkel et al., 2005) doesn't work well in this case as they are often trained on grammatical sentences instead of the textual segments seen in infobox tables.

4.1.2 Feature Generation

For each relation mention, we generate features similar to the ones from Mintz et al. (2009), with some modifications. Since the subject of a relation mention is outside the infobox, most generated features focus on the object (*e.g.*, the word shape of the object mention), and its context (*e.g.*, the infobox attribute value). Table 6 in Appendix A lists the complete set of features.

4.1.3 Distant Supervision

Instead of manually collecting training examples, we use distant supervision (Craven and Kumlien, 1999; Bunescu and Mooney, 2007; Mintz et al., 2009) from Wikidata to automatically generate training data for relation extraction. We assume that a pair of mentions (m_{e_1}, m_2) expresses the relation type r if we are able to match m_2 to e_2 where $r(e_1, e_2)$ is a Wikidata relation. Since the object mention m_2 is non-canonical, we do a string match between the entity name and the mention text or a direct entity match if an anchor link exists for the mention. We construct the negative training data for a relation type r by combining positive examples of other relation types and a random sample of the unlabeled entity mention pairs.

4.1.4 Model Training and Inference

We train a binary logistic regression classifier (Friedman et al., 2001) for each relation type. The classifier predicts how likely a pair of entity mentions is to express a relation type r. We only output relations with probabilities higher than a threshold θ (0.9 is used empirically). Otherwise, a mention pair is deemed to not express any relation type. We choose one binary classifier for each type rather than a single multi-class classifier because one pair of mentions can express multiple relation types. For example, the mention pair ("The Beatles", "England") under the attribute "Origin" (see Fig. 1) expresses two relation types: *country of origin* and *location of formation*.

4.2 Entity Linking & Normalization

Figure 2 provides an overview of the entity linker in four stages: candidate generation, feature generation, distant supervision, and model training and inference. The subject m_{e_i} of each extracted relation mention $r(m_{e_i}, m_2)$ is trivially linked to the subject entity e_i. The entity linker links the object mention to a Wikidata entity unless no corresponding entity exists, in which case we mark

---

[6]We assume that only one representative infobox table is available on each page.

[7]Note that each Wikipedia page has a corresponding Wikidata entry. Exceptions exist but are negligible. In this paper, we use "Wikipedia entity" and "Wikidata entity" interchangeably for the same real-world entity.

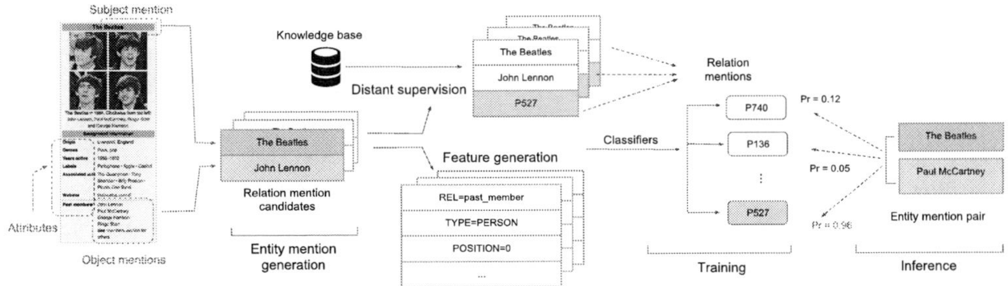

Figure 1: Relation Extractor Overview

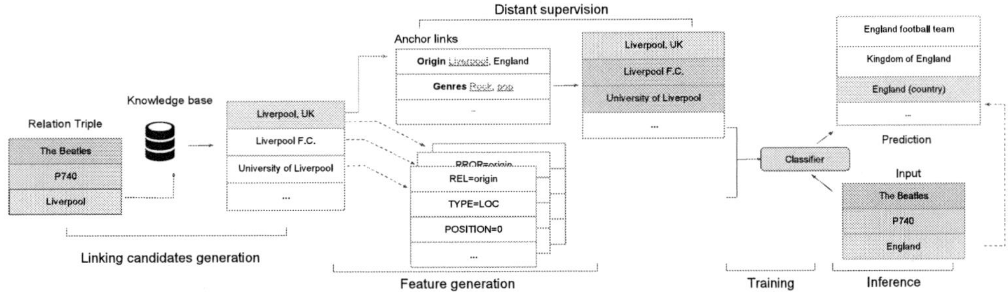

Figure 2: Entity Linker Overview

m_2 an unlinkable entity. We normalize the literal values when m_2 is not an entity reference.[8]

4.2.1 Candidate Generation

We generate candidate entities $\{\tilde{e}_2^i\}$ for m_2 in each $r(m_{e_1}, m_2)$ extracted. Candidate entities are generated from the anchor link associated with the mention if present, matching the surface form text of anchor links harvested from other pages for the same relation type r, and type-aware name matching with Wikidata entities. We determine the entity type(s) of the object for a relation type r from the statistics of existing relation triples in Wikidata. In this work, we use a set of coarse-grained entity types: person, band, school, organization, location, event, creative work, and award.[9]

4.2.2 Feature Generation

We generate features for each candidate entity of m_2, including lexical features of m_2, textual similarity between the entity name and m_2, how the candidate entity is generated (*e.g.*, anchor link or name matching), and for name matching, the kind of names the mention is matched against (*e.g.*, har-

vested surface form text or an entity alias). Contextual information surrounding m_2 in the same infobox is also used for disambiguation.[10]

4.2.3 Distant Supervision

Similar to Sec. 4.1.3, we use Wikidata to distantly supervise the entity linker. We compare each $r(m_{e_1}, \tilde{e}_2^i)$ triple with all $r(e_1, e_2)$ triples from Wikidata. The candidate entity in which $\tilde{e}_2^i = e_2$ is labeled as a positive example, while the rest of the candidate entities are considered negative examples. Note that the supervision is noisy because there may be multiple valid or very similar canonical entities for the same $r(m_{e_1}, m_2)$, especially for relation types such as *genre*. Additional heuristic rules are used to denoise the supervision (cf. *labeling functions* in Ratner et al. (2016)).

4.2.4 Model training & Inference

We use a logistic regression model to predict the probability of each candidate for a mention. The candidate entity with the highest probability for a mention is chosen. If the highest probability does not meet a threshold (0.5 is chosen empirically), we mark a mention an unlinkable entity. For location-type objects, we make a collective prediction that the entity choices of neighboring mentions are decided altogether (see Appendix B.2).

---

[8]For relation types with quantity objects such as *population* and *height*, date objects such as *birth date*, or string values such as *website*, we normalize them into a canonical form with respect to each data type.

[9]When the required entity type is absent from this set (*e.g.*, an object value of the *language spoken* relation type), no candidate is provided from type-aware name matching.

[10]See feature examples in Table 7 of Appendix A.

5 Experiments

In this section, we conduct experiments to answer the following questions:

- Does RIBE produce high-quality extractions? (Sec. 5.2)
- Are these extractions a significant addition to Wikidata? (Sec. 5.3)
- How does the extraction with unlinkable entities affect the quality of the KB especially for the list-valued relation types? (Sec. 5.4)

5.1 Data

We use Wikipedia infobox tables and Wikidata [11] to construct our training and evaluation data set. We test RIBE on both coarse-grained entity types such as *person*, *location* and *event* as well as fine-grained ones such as *band* and *school*. We denote the set of entity types ET. A set of 51 Wikidata relation types RT is used as extraction targets, a sample of which is shown in Table 4 [12].

To assign types to entities, we first recursively traverse Wikidata to collect all sub-types of a target entity type $t \in ET$ via the *subclass of* relation. For example, both *city* and *state* are subclasses of type *location*. Next, we use the *instance of* relation type to identify types for entities. An entity is deemed type t if and only if it appears as the subject of an *instance of* relation, where the object is one of the sub-types of t. Around 1.2 million infobox tables remain after a subject type filtering. Table 1 displays a type breakdown.

5.2 Extraction Quality

We compare RIBE with a strong IBE baseline, DBpedia (Lehmann et al., 2015). We obtain extractions from DBpedia by running their extractor[13] on the same set of 1.2 million infobox tables. We identified 74 mappings of relation types between DBpedia and Wikidata from the DBpedia ontology[14]. 23 of them overlap with our target relation set RT (see Table 3). We divide DBpedia relation types by subject types. For instance, we create two sub-types *person:record_label* and *band:record_label* from the DBpedia relation type *recordLabel*, where the first one includes *record-Label* relations with subject type *person*, and the second one with *band*. Table 2 lists the complete

Subject entity type	Percentage (%)
Person	81.5
Event	10.4
Location	3.3
Band	2.7
School	1.9

Table 1: Infobox subject entity type breakdown.

Subject:Relation type	Wikidata	DBpedia
per:team	P54	team
per:place_of_birth	P19	birthPlace
per:date_of_birth	P569	birthDate
per:occupation	P106	occupation
per:place_of_death	P20	deathPlace
per:date_of_death	P570	deathDate
per:educated_at	P69	almaMater
band:has_member	P527	bandMember formerBandMember currentMember pastMember
per:spouse	P26	spouse
per:award	P166	award
per:child	P40	child
per:political_party	P102	party
per:partner	P551	residence
per:record_label	P264	recordLabel*
per:parent	K206	parent
band:genre	P136	genre
per:instrument	P1303	instrument
band:record_label	P264	recordLabel*
per:employer	P108	employer
per:burial_place	P119	placeOfBurial
school:student_count	P2196	numberOfStudents
band:country	P17	country
event:country	P17	country
loc:largest_city	K223	largestCity
loc:ethic_group	P172	ethnicGroup*

Table 2: Mappings from Wikidata relation types to DBpedia ones. The relation types followed by * are missing from the output generated by the DBpedia extraction code but present in the latest public DBpedia data release. We use the latter for those relation types for a fair comparison.

mappings of relation types from Wikidata to DBpedia.

5.2.1 Evaluation Methodology

We evaluate the extraction quality for each relation type $r \in RT$ using four metrics: yield, precision, recall, and F_1 score. **Yield** (Y) is defined as the number of all uniquely extracted relations $r(e_1, e_2)$. To compute precision and recall, we first collect a ground truth set of relations $G = \{G_r | r \in RT\}$. [15] We create a union of extractions from RIBE and DBpedia, and randomly sample around 100 entities with at least one relation extracted from either system. This is similar to the pooling methodology used in the TAC KBP evaluation process (TAC, 2017). The sampled extractions are graded by human annotators.

---

[11] An 11/2018 Wikipedia and a 06/2018 Wikidata dump.

[12] The full list is provided in Table 8 in Appendix C

[13] https://github.com/dbpedia/extraction-framework/

[14] https://wiki.dbpedia.org/Downloads2014#h395-1

[15] If both systems have low true recall, this ground truth set will have low recall as well. While we leave a better estimate of recall for future work, anecdotally we see that that is not the case here.

Subject	Relation Type	Yield		P / R / F_1 (%)		C (%)	
		RIBE	DBpedia	RIBE	DBpedia	RIBE	DBpedia
person	team	1,606,179	27598	97.9 / 99.4 / 98.6	42.8 / 0.8 / 1.5	97.6	1.1
person	place of birth	1,222,396	733498	99.3 / 80.5 / 88.9	100.0 / 51.6 / 68.0	74.0	39.4
person	date of birth	878,537	478383	100.0 / 98.1 / 99.0	100.0 / 48.6 / 65.4	-	-
person	occupation	541,901	355723	99.4 / 98.9 / 99.1	34.4 / 16.5 / 22.3	97.8	13.9
person	place of death	445,128	226721	98.7 / 97.5 / 98.1	98.8 / 54.0 / 69.8	95.6	45.0
person	birth name	325,594	89574	98.9 / 97.0 / 97.9	100.0 / 25.0 / 40.0	97.0	25.0
person	date of death	317,489	187762	100.0 / 98.0 / 98.9	100.0 / 57.6 / 73.0	-	-
person	educated at	279,661	100916	93.3 / 96.2 / 94.7	100.0 / 36.9 / 53.9	94.0	32.6
band	has member	186,090	49485	97.6 / 98.8 / 98.1	97.4 / 19.2 / 32.0	92.7	11.4
person	spouse	156,984	40312	96.6 / 98.3 / 97.4	92.5 / 21.4 / 34.7	97.8	17.3
person	award	119,136	91158	91.5 / 92.6 / 92.0	73.6 / 58.3 / 65.0	85.7	52.3
person	child	115,582	30441	97.6 / 96.2 / 96.8	98.1 / 25.5 / 40.4	93.4	25.0
person	political party	111,061	45528	100.0 / 96.0 / 97.9	100.0 / 36.6 / 53.5	95.5	31.4
person	partner	94,541	57354	100.0 / 89.8 / 94.6	100.0 / 56.7 / 72.3	87.7	51.1
person	record label	82,478	46440	99.1 / 96.2 / 97.6	100.0 / 52.8 / 69.1	90.7	38.1
person	parent	79,497	36105	98.0 / 94.4 / 96.1	93.6 / 36.9 / 52.9	92.6	33.6
band	genre	78,742	66843	99.2 / 98.8 / 99.0	99.1 / 76.7 / 86.4	96.9	84.6
person	instrument	69,816	42150	100.0 / 94.2 / 97.0	96.1 / 40.9 / 57.3	91.8	36.7
band	record label	64,148	37883	98.5 / 97.2 / 97.8	97.6 / 59.2 / 73.7	93.4	46.7
person	employer	62,183	8726	93.2 / 96.8 / 94.9	92.5 / 16.1 / 27.4	95.7	20.0
person	place of burial	54,430	1141	98.6 / 98.7 / 98.6	100.0 / 4.0 / 7.6	97.8	4.3
school	student count	20,410	24624	98.6 / 79.6 / 88.1	98.7 / 83.9 / 90.7	-	-
event	country	12,625	9028	100.0 / 89.3 / 94.3	50.0 / 23.8 / 32.2	88.7	23.7
location	largest city	914	3205	100.0 / 24.5 / 39.3	100.0 / 89.8 / 94.6	-	-
location	ethnic group	753	147	91.1 / 90.8 / 90.9	83.9 / 16.8 / 27.9	84.1	18.8
	Average			**97.9 / 91.9 / 93.8**	89.9 / 40.3 / 52.5	**92.4**	31.0

Table 3: Comparison with DBpedia. $P/R/F_1$ denotes Precision/Recall/F1 measures. C denotes the completeness score for list-value relation types. An asterisk marks the relation types that are missing from the output generated by the DBpedia extraction code but present in the last public DBpedia release at `https://wiki.dbpedia.org/develop/datasets/dbpedia-version-2016-10`. We use the latter for those relation types to conduct a fair comparison.

According to our annotation guidelines, we mark an extraction incorrect if one of the the the following is met.

- The relation is not expressed in the infobox.

- The object entity has an incorrect identifier.

- The object of a relation triple is unlinked by the system but should be linked in the ground truth. For instance, a string "United States" not linked to its entity identifier in Wikidata is considered incorrect.

- The object is incorrectly parsed. For example, "Sasha and Malia" would be an incorrect extraction for the *child* relation of `Barack Obama`.

The final set G_r consists of all correct relations of the sampled entities from both approaches. The number of labels varies from 83 for *event:country* to 557 for *band:has_member*, resulting in a total of 4,858 labels on triples and an average of 194 per relation type. The **Precision** (P) of a system s, RIBE or DBpedia, is computed as $P_r^s = \frac{|U_r^s \cap G_r|}{|U_r^s|}$, where U_r^s is the set of all extracted relations of r by system s. An absolute **Recall** (R) of the universe is difficult to compute. We compute an estimated recall $R_r^s = \frac{|U_r^s \cap G_r|}{|G_r|}$ w.r.t the ground truth set. The standard **F1 Score** (F_1) is computed as a harmonic mean of P_r and R_r.

5.2.2 Results

Table 3 shows that RIBE achieves better precision, recall, F_1, and yield for almost all relation types. The DBpedia extractor underperforms for two reasons. First, the extraction fully relies on Wikipedia anchor links for entity linking, which not only hurts the precision due to erroneous links, but also results in a low linked ratio since mentions without anchor links will not be linked. Secondly, it treats each row in an infobox table as one mention without proper chunking in the absence of anchor links. This approach hurts both precision and recall, since an extracted string value of "Sasha and Malia" for *child* not only misses the correct entities for both `Sasha` and `Malia`, but also provides false information that "Sasha and Malia" represents one single person. In contrast, RIBE identifies object mentions from infobox rows and predicts entity links even when no anchor link exists. Also, RIBE is able to consistently link to entities whose types are compatible to the target relation type. For example, we consistently link to an occupation object (*e.g.*, `Lawyer`) for *occupation* rather than to a discipline (*e.g.*, `Law`).

Relation type (Wikidata ID)	Wikidata yield	RIBE yield	+Yield (%)	Linked (%)	Precision (%)
student count (P2196)	1,325	23,440	1758.5	N/A	94.78
doctoral student (P185)	2,998	9,131	263.0	78.8	97.96
has part (P527)*	105,825	185,804	166.2	18.9	100.00
recurring date (P837)	785	1,282	126.5	89.4	95.65
instrument (P1303)	56,877	69,800	93.3	98.6	100.00
member of sports team (P54)	1,190,242	1,600,285	51.3	95.0	96.69
unmarried partner (P451)	5,263	3,108	44.5	53.1	98.97
doctoral advisor (P184)	14,300	10,688	35.2	73.9	97.12
destination point (P1444)	4,942	1,824	19.1	98.8	100.00
award received (P166)	498,505	118,509	16.3	77.4	93.18
official website (P856)	525,496	100,623	11.0	N/A	100.00
population (P1082)	695,577	53,071	4.9	N/A	100.00
sibling (P3373)	188,328	12,129	4.1	75.4	100.00
country of citizenship (P27)	2,687,600	239,798	2.4	98.6	100.00

Table 4: Comparison with Wikidata for a sample of relation types. See Table 8 in Appendix C for the full list. The column *Wikidata yield* shows the total number of relation triples in Wikidata per relation type. RIBE *yield* shows the total number of relation triples extracted by RIBE. *+Yield* represents the number of relation triples we extract that are not in Wikidata divided by Wikidata counts. Data is added to Wikidata organically by editors and the source is not limited to infoboxes. Therefore yield comparison shows that extractions from infoboxes may complement Wikidata to construct a better knowledge graph.*Linked (%)* shows that the percentage of relation triples with their objects linked to Wikidata entities ("N/A" if the object type is a literal value). ∗ We use P527 to represent *band has member* where the subject entity is a band and the object entity is a current or past member of the band.

5.3 Complement to Wikidata

We compare RIBE to Wikidata using the same subject type filter on Wikidata relation types. Table 4 shows the evaluation for a sample of relation types (see Table 8 in Appendix C for the complete list). To evaluate the quality of extra yield, we compute per-relation-type precision by randomly sampling 100 relation triples that do not exist in Wikidata (around 5.1k labels in total). The predictions are graded by human annotators and precision is computed as described in Sec. 5.2.1. RIBE achieves a significant increase in yield over Wikidata (17 out of 51 relation types have 100%+ increase), while maintaining higher than 95% precision for almost all relation types. This indicates that the extracted triples are high-quality and a critical complement to Wikidata.[16] We observe that relation types with person object type have a lower linked ratio since not all objects have corresponding entities in Wikidata (*e.g.*, children of celebrities).

5.4 Completeness of list-value relation types

A list-value relation type allows multiple objects for the same subject (*e.g.*, a person can have multiple children). In order to measure the completeness of extractions for list-value relation types, we define a completeness score C for each relation type r using a set equality by comparing the extracted set of object values for each subject entity to the ground truth set. To compute C_r, we average the completeness scores over the sampled subject entities. The "C (%)" column of Table 3 shows that RIBE consistently produces substantially more complete extractions than DBpedia does.

6 Conclusion and Future Directions

We proposed a novel system, RIBE, that extracts knowledge triples from Wikipedia infobox tables. The proposed system produces high-quality data and improves the average F_1 score over 51 relation types by 41.3% compared to a strong IBE system, DBpedia. We also empirically show the added value of the extracted knowledge with respect to Wikidata. Additionally, RIBE takes into account unlinkable entities, dramatically improving the completeness of list-value relation types.

In future work, we would like to investigate its effectiveness and robustness in a cross-lingual setting. We would like to work on Entity Discovery (Hoffart et al., 2014; Wick et al., 2013) to discover and disambiguate the unlinkable entities. We would also like to jointly model the relation extractor and the entity linker to improve the model performance.

Acknowledgments

We would like to thank Mike Cafarella, Pablo Mendes, Stephen Pulman, Chris DuBois, Lawrence Cayton, Matthias Paulik, Madian Khabsa, and Jo Daiber for providing valuable feedback and discussion, Mark Biswas for proofreading our manuscript, Thomas Semere for leading the annotation project, and Eric Chahin, Vivek Raghuram, and Eric Choi for the engineering support. We also appreciate the comments from the anonymous reviewers.

---

[16]Wikidata is mostly curated by human edits and therefore the Wikidata yield and RIBE yield is not directly comparable.

References

Sören Auer, Christian Bizer, Georgi Kobilarov, Jens Lehmann, Richard Cyganiak, and Zachary G. Ives. 2007. Dbpedia: A nucleus for a web of open data. In *Proceedings of the 6th International Semantic Web Conference and 2nd Asian Semantic Web Conference (ISWC/ASWC-2007)*, pages 722–735.

Sören Auer and Jens Lehmann. 2007. What have innsbruck and leipzig in common? extracting semantics from wiki content. In *ESWC*.

Razvan Bunescu and Raymond Mooney. 2007. Learning to extract relations from the web using minimal supervision. In *Annual meeting-association for Computational Linguistics*, volume 45, page 576.

M. Craven and J. Kumlien. 1999. Constructing biological knowledge bases by extracting information from text sources. In *Proceedings of the Seventh International Conference on Intelligent Systems for Molecular Biology, August 6-10, 1999, Heidelberg, Germany*, pages 77–86. AAAI.

S. Cucerzan. 2007. Large-scale named entity disambiguation based on wikipedia data. In *Proceedings of EMNLP-CoNLL*, volume 2007, pages 708–716.

Rajarshi Das, Arvind Neelakantan, David Belanger, and Andrew McCallum. 2017. Chains of reasoning over entities, relations, and text using recurrent neural networks. In *EACL*.

Xin Dong, Evgeniy Gabrilovich, Geremy Heitz, Wilko Horn, Ni Lao, Kevin Murphy, Thomas Strohmann, Shaohua Sun, and Wei Zhang. 2014. Knowledge vault: a web-scale approach to probabilistic knowledge fusion. In *KDD*.

J.R. Finkel, T. Grenager, and C. Manning. 2005. Incorporating non-local information into information extraction systems by gibbs sampling. In *Proceedings of the 43rd Annual Meeting on Association for Computational Linguistics*, pages 363–370. Association for Computational Linguistics.

Jerome Friedman, Trevor Hastie, and Robert Tibshirani. 2001. *The elements of statistical learning*, volume 1. Springer series in statistics New York, NY, USA:.

Kelvin Guu, John Miller, and Percy Liang. 2015. Traversing knowledge graphs in vector space. In *EMNLP*.

Sebastian Hellmann. 2018. Wikidata Adoption in Wikipedia. https://lists.wikimedia.org/pipermail/wikidata/2018-December/012681.html.

Johannes Hoffart, Yasemin Altun, and Gerhard Weikum. 2014. Discovering emerging entities with ambiguous names. In *Proceedings of the 23rd international conference on World wide web*, pages 385–396. International World Wide Web Conferences Steering Committee.

Raphael Hoffmann, Congle Zhang, Xiao Ling, Luke Zettlemoyer, and Daniel S Weld. 2011. Knowledge-based weak supervision for information extraction of overlapping relations. In *Proceedings of the 49th Annual Meeting of the Association for Computational Linguistics: Human Language Technologies*, volume 1, pages 541–550.

Mitchell Koch, John Gilmer, Stephen Soderland, and Daniel S Weld. 2014. Type-aware distantly supervised relation extraction with linked arguments. In *EMNLP*.

Sayali Kulkarni, Amit Singh, Ganesh Ramakrishnan, and Soumen Chakrabarti. 2009. Collective annotation of Wikipedia entities in web text. In *Proceedings of the 15th ACM SIGKDD international conference on Knowledge discovery and data mining*, pages 457–466. ACM.

Ni Lao, Tom M. Mitchell, and William W. Cohen. 2011. Random walk inference and learning in a large scale knowledge base. In *EMNLP*.

Jens Lehmann, Robert Isele, Max Jakob, Anja Jentzsch, Dimitris Kontokostas, Pablo N Mendes, Sebastian Hellmann, Mohamed Morsey, Patrick Van Kleef, Sören Auer, et al. 2015. Dbpedia–a large-scale, multilingual knowledge base extracted from wikipedia. *Semantic Web*, 6(2):167–195.

Xiao Ling, Sameer Singh, and Daniel S. Weld. 2015. Design challenges for entity linking. *TACL*, 3:315–328.

Mike Mintz, Steven Bills, Rion Snow, and Dan Jurafsky. 2009. Distant supervision for relation extraction without labeled data. In *Proceedings of the Joint Conference of the 47th Annual Meeting of the ACL and the 4th International Joint Conference on Natural Language Processing of the AFNLP: Volume 2 - Volume 2*, ACL '09, pages 1003–1011, Stroudsburg, PA, USA. Association for Computational Linguistics.

Alexander Ratner, Christopher De Sa, Sen Wu, Daniel Selsam, and Christopher Ré. 2016. Data programming: Creating large training sets, quickly. *Advances in neural information processing systems*, 29:3567–3575.

Erik F. Tjong Kim Sang and Sabine Buchholz. 2000. Introduction to the conll-2000 shared task chunking. In *CoNLL/LLL*.

Mihai Surdeanu, Julie Tibshirani, Ramesh Nallapati, and Christopher D Manning. 2012. Multi-instance multi-label learning for relation extraction. In *Proceedings of the 2012 Joint Conference on Empirical Methods in Natural Language Processing and Computational Natural Language Learning*, pages 455–465. Association for Computational Linguistics.

TAC. 2017. Cold start knowledge base population at tac 2017 task description. Technical report.

Denny Vrandečić and Markus Krötzsch. 2014. Wikidata: A free collaborative knowledgebase. *Commun. ACM*, 57(10):78–85.

Michael Wick, Sameer Singh, Harshal Pandya, and Andrew McCallum. 2013. A joint model for discovering and linking entities. In *Proceedings of the 2013 workshop on Automated knowledge base construction*, pages 67–72. ACM.

Fei Wu and Daniel S. Weld. 2007. Autonomously semantifying wikipedia. In *Proceedings of the International Conference on Information and Knowledge Management (CIKM-2007)*, pages 41–50.

A Mention Generation Heuristics and Example Features

We present the heuristics used in mention generation of the relation extractor in Table 5 and example features in Table 6 and 7 for the relation extractor and the entity linker respectively.

B Implementation Details

In this appendix, we describe a few implementation details in addressing the noise from distant supervision and making collective entity link prediction.

B.1 Denoise Distant Supervision

Distant supervision for relation extraction assumes that every occurrence of two entities that participate in a known relation expresses the relation. However, the assumption does not always hold. For example, in the infobox table of `John Lennon` (`https://en.wikipedia.org/wiki/John_Lennon`), the object mention "Yoko Ono" appears under both `Spouse(s)` and `Associated acts`. Both occurrences of ("John Lennon", "Yoko Ono") will be labeled as positive instances of the *spouse* relation type in Wikidata, despite the second occurrence being unrelated. Therefore, we introduce a whitelist A_r of normalized infobox attributes [17] if the relation type r is vulnerable to noise. A relation mention $r(m_1, m_2)$ (e.g., the second occurrence of `John Lennon` and `Yoko Ono`) will be removed if the attribute a (*e.g.*, `associated_act`) is not in A_r (*e.g.*, {`spouse`, `wife`, `husband`}).

B.2 Collective Entity Linking

Locations are often presented in multiple levels, such as "San Jose, CA, USA". There are many candidate cities named "San Jose" in Wikidata. One candidate `San Jose, CA` has a relation *located in* [18] with `California`, which is a candidate for the mention "CA". Another candidate `San Jose, Costa Rica` does not have such a relation with the neighboring mention and therefore is less likely to be the correct entity. Similarly, if two cities are mentioned together, the candidate entities that are in the same country are more likely to be the correct prediction at the same time. This

---

[17]We normalize a raw infobox attribute by singularizing and converting all tokens to lower case.

[18]It is equivalent to the Wikidata relation type P131, located in the administrative territorial entity.

Heuristic	Input example	Output example
Keep anchor linked text intact	Earnest & Young	`[Earnest & Young]`
Split and reconstruct dates	`Jan 12-14th, 2013`	`[2013-01-12, 2013-01-14]`
Split on special characters	`Monday/Tuesday`	`[Monday, Tuesday]`
Split on stop words	`Alice, and Bob`	`[Alice, Bob]`

Table 5: Heuristics used for mention generation in the relation extractor.

Feature Type	Feature	Example
Lexical	Normalized infobox attribute of the object mention	`PROP=member`
Lexical	Position of the mention in the list of object values	`POS=0`
Lexical	Head and tail tokens of the object mention	`t_0=Paul`
Lexical	Window of k tokens to the left of the object mention	`t-1=Lennon`
Lexical	Window of k tokens to the right of the object mention	`t+1=George`
Lexical	Word shape of the object mention	`NUM:ALL`
Lexical	Type of the object mention	`TYPE:LOC`
Lexical	Whether all tokens in the mention are upper-cased	`OBJ_UPPER`
Conjunctive	Conjunction of two features	`PROP=member&POS=0`

Table 6: Example features used in the relation extractor.

Feature Type	Feature	Example
CandGen	Source of the candidate entity	`source=anchor_link`
CandGen	Match key between entity and mention phrase	`match_key=alias`
CandGen	Conjunctive Source and Match key	`P740:s=link^mk=phrase`
CandGen	Candidate Generator	`P740:link_match_w_phrase`
Type	Object entity type	`P740:LOC`
Phrase	Coarse-grained similarity score	`fuzzy_score=3`
Context	Entity and neighboring phrases	`Q5355602^phrase1=england`
Context	Overlap in page links and Wikidata triples	`has_connection_P413`

Table 7: Example features used in the entity linker.

also applies to relation types such as *educated at*, which expects schools as object entities. A location mention following the school name may help disambiguate.

We perform this collective entity linking approach (Cucerzan, 2007; Kulkarni et al., 2009; Ling et al., 2015) in the following way: for candidate entities e_i and e_j of two neighboring mentions, we represent the relation between the two by r_{ij}. From this we calculate the normalized score (NS) for a location phrase with token length ℓ defined as

$$\text{NS} = \begin{cases} \alpha \sum_i^\ell p_i & (\ell = 1) \\ \frac{1}{\ell} \sum_i^\ell p_i + \frac{1}{\binom{\ell}{2}} \sum_{i,j}^\ell r_{i,j} & (\ell > 1) \end{cases}, \quad (1)$$

where

$$r_{ij} = \begin{cases} 1.0 & \texttt{located\_in}(e_i, e_j) \\ 0.5 & \texttt{same\_country}(e_i, e_j) \end{cases}, \quad (2)$$

p_i is the local probability of e_i being the correct entity and α is a hyperparameter empirically set to

1.5. For $\ell > 1$, the maximum NS allowed is 2. A score larger than 1 implies a presence of either *located in* or *same country* relation. If NS is above a threshold, say 1.3, we sort by (ℓ, NS) in descending order and choose the top set of entities. While we prefer entities that are consistent with a longer phrase, the threshold accounts for the incompleteness of the relation *located in*. If there is no candidate with a NS above the threshold, we choose the candidate with the highest NS.

Conceptually the same method (with different link types r_{ij}) can be applied to all object types. However in practice we found that for non-location entities the impact was small and not worth the increased computation.

C Supplementary Experimental Results

In this appendix, we present the complete version of Table 4 in Table 8.

Relation name (Wikidata ID)	Wikidata yield	RIBE Yield	+Yield (%)	Linked (%)	Precision (%)
student count (P2196)	1,325	23,440	1758.5	N/A	94.78
work period (start) (P2031)	11,154	157,273	1384.6	N/A	100.00
statistical leader (P3279)	1,699	20,637	1125.1	90.6	98.08
allegiance (P945)	4,725	37,497	721.7	99.7	98.82
largest city ***	242	919	279.7	99.9	100.00
doctoral student (P185)	2,998	9,131	263.0	78.8	97.96
record label (P264)	46,900	146,259	236.7	66.4	97.20
location (P276)	52,320	128,419	216.0	95.6	99.17
has part (P527) *	105,825	185,804	166.2	18.9	100.00
winner (P1346)	28,182	52,016	156.7	97.9	100.00
spouse (P26)	91,458	155,795	137.2	25.8	98.98
end time (P582)	19,762	33,682	136.0	N/A	98.95
recurring date (P837)	785	1,282	126.5	89.4	95.65
genre (P136)	134,712	228,276	123.6	98.2	96.77
start time (P580)	20,611	31,557	121.9	N/A	100.00
residence (P551)	61,040	94,003	121.3	97.6	100.00
instrument (P1303)	56,877	69,800	93.3	98.6	100.00
location of formation (P740)	23,405	30,878	84.5	99.8	98.10
consecrator (P1598)	4,934	5,315	83.8	92.1	98.35
child (P40)	147,599	115,621	61.2	28.7	96.91
member of sports team (P54)	1,190,242	1,600,285	51.3	95.0	96.69
place of burial (P119)	88,068	53,584	49.6	80.9	100.00
conflict (P607)	92,886	73,931	49.2	98.5	98.15
dissolved (P576)	32,589	16,409	48.8	N/A	99.04
unmarried partner (P451)	5,263	3,108	44.5	53.1	98.97
place of death (P20)	637,832	441,445	41.7	96.2	97.12
musical conductor (P3300)	340	236	40.3	60.3	100.00
place of birth (P19)	1,685,695	1,218,098	37.1	96.5	100.00
doctoral advisor (P184)	14,300	10,688	35.2	73.9	97.12
parent **	141,409	79,372	33.9	48.7	100.00
family (P53)	22,245	14,590	33.6	84.6	88.78
student (P802)	12,665	3,813	26.3	68.1	100.00
destination point (P1444)	4,942	1,824	19.1	98.8	100.00
start point (P1427)	5,115	1,912	18.6	99.1	98.95
employer (P108)	247,406	61,741	17.1	90.9	95.54
member of political party (P102)	238,962	110,263	16.6	97.7	95.96
award received (P166)	498,505	118,509	16.3	77.4	93.18
religion (P140)	54,654	9,519	14.4	99.2	98.99
educated at (P69)	752,542	277,301	14.3	95.1	93.16
point in time (P585)	164,951	34,960	13.4	N/A	98.95
official website (P856)	525,496	100,623	11.0	N/A	100.00
occupation (P106)	3,624,331	539,557	8.5	93.4	98.99
inception (P571)	349,012	49,202	8.0	N/A	98.98
population (P1082)	695,577	53,071	4.9	N/A	100.00
date of birth (P569)	2,685,493	876,610	4.6	N/A	100.00
sibling (P3373)	188,328	12,129	4.1	75.4	100.00
date of death (P570)	1,309,427	315,381	3.9	N/A	99.00
country of citizenship (P27)	2,687,600	239,798	2.4	98.6	100.00
country (P17)	1,690,459	34,707	1.6	99.9	95.90
languages (P1412)	611,498	6,891	0.4	99.4	98.90
sport (P641)	689,697	5,466	0.2	100.0	100.00

Table 8: Comparison with Wikidata. The column *Wikidata yield* shows the total number of relation triples in Wikidata per relation type. RIBE *yield* shows the total number of relation triples extracted by RIBE. *+Yield* shows the number of relation triples we extract that are not in Wikidata. *Linked (%)* shows that the percentage of relation triples with their objects linked to Wikidata entities. * We use P527 to represent *band has member* where the subject entity is a band and the object entity is a current or past member of the band. Note that *parent* and *largest city* in Table 8 do not currently exist in Wikidata. ** We combine relations for Wikidata predicates *father* (P22) and *mother* (P25) to form the *parent* relation type. *** We collect all the cities located in every location entity, e, in Wikidata that contains cities and use the city with the largest and latest population number as the largest city of e. This way, we construct a total of 242 *largest city* relations from Wikidata.

A k-Nearest Neighbor Approach towards Multi-level Sequence Labeling

Yue Chen
Interactions LLC
Indiana University
ychen@interactions.com
yc59@indiana.edu

John Chen
Interactions LLC
jchen@interactions.com

Abstract

In this paper we present a new method for spoken language understanding to support a spoken dialogue system handling complex dialogues in the food ordering domain. Using a small amount of authentic food ordering dialogues yields better results than a large amount of synthetic ones. The size of the data makes this approach amenable to cold start projects in the multi-level sequence labeling domain. We used windowed word n-grams, POS tag sequences and pre-trained word embeddings as features. Results show that a heterogeneous feature set with the k-NN learner performs competitively against the state-of-the-art results and achieve an F-score of 60.71.

1 Introduction

Handling complex dialogues between customers and agents is hard, especially in the food ordering domain where there are a lot of hesitations and noise involved. A sample dialogue with only the customer side available is shown in Figure 1. The agent side is not available since our software setup does not include an Automatic Speech Recognition (ASR) component on the agent side. The complexity stems from the fact that food ordering dialogues are mixed initiative, and individual customer utterances may contain multiple intents and refer to food items with complex structure. For example, a customer might say "Can I get a deluxe burger with large fries and oh put extra mayo on the burger would you?" Since essentially we are trying to give each word an IOB tag with some sub-label referring to a specific class, it is natural that we approach this task as a multi-level sequence labeling problem. Additionally, this must be performed with limited authentic training data, since we are starting from scratch and not many dialogues have been collected from our customers yet.

```
uh give me a medium order of
onion rings and i 'd like to
have them well done

no tartar no lettuce but
i 'd like to have uh mustard
pickles on

yes that 's it
```

Figure 1: A Sample Dialogue with only the Customer Side Available

Both traditional methods such as Hidden Markov Models (HMMs), Maximum Entropy Markov Models (MEMMs), or Conditional Random Fields (CRFs) and newer methods like Deep Neural Networks (DNNs) or Bi-directional Long Short-Term Memories (BiLSTMs) typically use only homogeneous feature sets. Here homogeneous feature set refers to the type of feature set within which there is only one type of feature, for example, the presence/absence word n-grams. Heterogeneous feature set, on the other hand, refers to the type of feature set within which at least more than one type of feature are used, for example, the presence/absence of word n-grams and pre-trained word embeddings, one being symbolic and the other being vectorized. Newer methods perform better but also require considerably more data. Previous research has synthesized data to obtain the required amounts for training.

We use a k-NN learner with a heterogeneous feature set. Instead of using a massive amount of synthetic dialogues, we are able to achieve superior results by annotating less than 1% of the authentic ones. This is within a reasonable budget of time and effort for a cold start project. To incorporate traditional linguistic knowledge and distributional word representation, we used windowed

Proceedings of NAACL-HLT 2019, pages 149–156
Minneapolis, Minnesota, June 2 - June 7, 2019. ©2019 Association for Computational Linguistics

word n-grams, POS tag sequences and pre-trained word embeddings as features. We performed experiments comparing the use of synthetic and authentic customer data while also performing semi-supervised self-training to obtain additional labeled data.

2   Related Work

Many techniques from slot filling and information retrieval have been adopted for the understanding task in dialogues. For example, (Xu and Sarikaya, 2013) implement a CNN-CRF that performs joint intent detection and slot filling over user utterances in the ATIS corpus. (Hakkani-Tür et al., 2016) explore the use of bi-directional RNNs for extraction of domain type, intent, and slot-fillers from the users of a virtual assistant when they booked flights. (El Asri et al., 2017) implement a pipeline of DNNs to perform intent and slot filler extraction over user utterances in the Frames corpus for a travel planning task. Unlike the current work, the understanding task is simpler. Whereas we focus on hierarchical structure, previous work has focused on fillers for flat structures.

Traditional methods like HMMs, MEMMs or CRFs mostly typically take only homogeneous feature set where only one type of feature (e.g., words or POS tags) can be used. The accuracy of such methods is also no longer the state of the art. Newer methods like DNNs and BiLSTMs make use of the recent advances in feature representation, like word embeddings, but are usually confined to use homogeneous features, since using heterogenous features would go against the design philosophy of DNNs of not needing feature engineering. They also require a much larger training data set that sometimes we do not have to achieve the state-of-the-art accuracy.

A lack of a large amount of hand annotated data hampers the effectiveness of these methods. Even leaving aside the matter of annotated data, for certain applications, it is difficult to even obtain a set of raw utterances. In this kind of situation, one approach that is still feasible is to synthesize data from hand generated templates, an instantiation of which has been applied to sentence planning (Walker et al., 2001).

We use TiMBL as the implementation of the k-NN classifier (Daelemans et al.). It is one of the most widely-used k-NN classifiers. The implemented algorithms have in common that they store some representation of the training set explicitly in memory. During testing, new cases are classified by extrapolation from the most similar stored cases. For over fifteen years TiMBL has been mostly used in natural language processing as a machine learning classifier component. Due to its particular decision-tree-based implementation, TiMBL is in many cases far more efficient in classification than a standard k-nearest neighbor algorithm would be.

3   Methodology

3.1   Data Set

In this project, we the (Chen et al., 2018) data set. In that paper, an annotation scheme is described that is suitable for describing food ordering intents for a target restaurant, but can also be customized to describe ordering at other types of restaurants or even to describe ordering products in general. The annotation scheme is applied to a corpus of human-human dialogs in the food ordering domain from an undisclosed restaurant location. The resulting data set consists of 95 dialogs out of which all of the customer utterances, 462 of them, have been annotated with food item mentions and intents.

This data set has been annotated with three levels of annotation: entity, item and intent. Entities are atomic elements of orderable food items. One or more entities can be composed into an item, representing something that may be ordered by the customer. In general, intents represent the communicative goals of the customer. For our domain, these primarily involve adding, modifying, and removing food items from the customer's order.

Figure 2 is an example of an utterance labeled with the three levels of our annotation scheme. In this example, there are two items, a sausage cheese croissant and a medium hash brown, which can be decomposed into five entities, sausage, cheese, croissant, medium, and hash brown. Thus, it shows the compositional nature of of food item specification in this annotation scheme.

Generally intent analysis is perceived as a classification task because most existing dialog corpora contain one intent per utterance (Hemphill et al., 1990). However, as around 42.2% of our data contain more than one intent per utterance, we define this intent analysis task as a sequence labeling task. We assume any consecutive N-word span in one utterance can be labeled as one

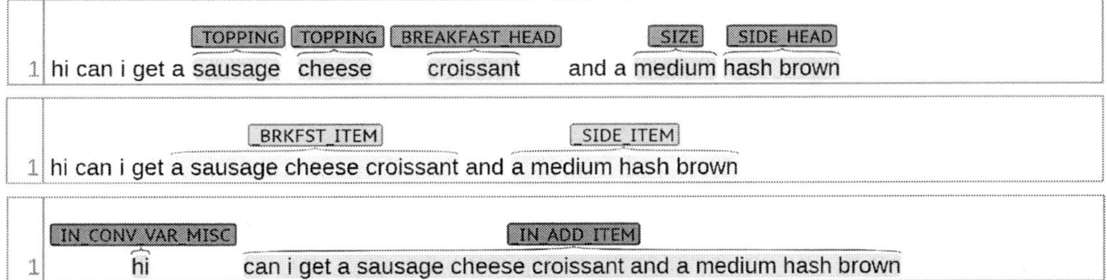

Figure 2: Annotation on the Three Levels

entity/item/intent and it is possible, even likely, that there is more than one span in each utterance. For example, in Figure 2, the example utterance contains two intents, `_IN_CONV_MISC` and `_IN_ADD_ITEM`.

3.2 Synthetic Data Set

The synthetic data generator consists of a context free grammar that generates not only customer utterances but also the entities, items, and intents that go with each utterance. The grammar consists of rules each having nonzero positive integer weights. Rules to generate entities correspond to menu items and ways to specify variations of menu items (e.g. small versus large). Customer utterances are generated by randomly selecting rules from the grammar, simulating a context free derivation.

There are 170 rules to generate intent sequences, 1275 rules to generate items, and 450 rules to generate entities. For our experiments, the data generator was run so that 55,000 synthetic utterances were generated.

3.3 Sequence Labeling as a Classification Task

Sequence labeling can be treated as a set of independent classification tasks, one per member of the sequence. We acknowledge that the accuracy is generally improved by making the optimal label for a given element dependent on the choices of nearby elements, using special algorithms to choose the globally best set of labels for the entire sequence at once (Erdogan, 2010).

However, we would like to present our k-NN classification appproach. With the help of post-processing, our approach yields better results compared to classic MEMMs, CRFs or neural networks.

In our approach, each word in the utterance is labeled independently. Post-processing is performed for each utterance after all the words are labeled. The post-processing step contains two actions:

1. If an N-word span does not begin with a beginning (B-) tag, correct it to be a beginning tag.

2. In an N-word span, if several entities/items/intents are identified, perform a majority vote to unify the entities/items/intents.

Table 1 is a comparison between the predicted labels and the labels after post-processing. For example, the predicted label for a certain span may look like the second column in Table 1. There are two obvious prediction mistakes we can systematically correct without introducing new ones. The first IOB tag can be corrected from "I-" to "B-" since it is the beginning of the chunk. Since there is a two-to-three split in the item labels, we can also unify the labels by taking a majority vote to make them all "_BURGER_ITEM".

We will show in Section 4 that post-processing will improve upon the classification results.

3.4 Experiment Setup

Our series of experiment contains four subsets of experiments. The results are presented in Section 4 and discussed in Section 5.

The first set of experiments uses synthesized training data provided by the synthetic data generator and both human transcribed (HT) and automatic speech recognition (ASR) customer-generated test data. In the second set of experiments, we switched from using synthesized training data to using human transcribed training data.

Words	Predicted Labels	Labels after Post-processing
a	I-_BURGER_ITEM	B-_BURGER_ITEM
double	I-_MEAL_ITEM	I-_BURGER_ITEM
burger	I-_BURGER_ITEM	I-_BURGER_ITEM
with	I-_BURGER_ITEM	I-_BURGER_ITEM
cheese	I-_MEAL_ITEM	I-_BURGER_ITEM

Table 1: Predicted and Post-processed Labels

We tested on both human transcribed and ASR data.

In the third set of experiments, we investigate how semi-supervised training can help with the classification task. We obtained additional unannotated but human transcribed data only one eighth the size of our synthesized data. We used the annotated human transcribed data, which is identical to the training set in the second set, as our seeding data and performed prediction on our additional data set. We use the distance as a confidence measure, so we could set multiple thresholds and add the prediction as additional training data to our training set. The thresholds were set at the first, second and third quartile. We also experimented with only using the predictions of the additional data as our training set. In this experiment setting, all the predictions that have a distance of zero, which is a confidence of 100%, are also removed to increase the diversity of the training set as this kind of predictions are simply exact matches to the seeding training set.

In the fourth set of experiments, we moved back to using only the annotated human transcribed training data. However, with the help of ASR improvement, we tested on a more accurate test set. We performed post-processing in this set of experiments as well.

In experiments comparing TiMBL with the use of other classifiers, we specifically compare against MEMM (McCallum et al., 2000) and BiLSTM-CRF with ELMO embeddings (Peters et al., 2018). For the BiLSTM-CRF we use the Baseline open source software package (Pressel et al., 2018).

All experiments include parameter optimization in reported results.

3.5 Features

Most machine learning models prefer homogeneous data. We usually use data of the same type in one feature matrix. For example, in bag-of-words (BOW) approach towards text classification, we fill in every cell of the matrix with a Boolean value (present/absent) of a certain word or character n-gram. Another example would be, for image classification, we pass the raw pixel value to a deep neural network. Such vector representations of words and sentences are also common among recent works in natural language processing. Word2vec, GloVe and ELMO word embeddings are especially popular in recent years. These kind of vector representations are generally used with a neural network classifier too (Peters et al., 2018).

To the best of our knowledge, no previous research has investigated using both symbolic features and vector representations in a single k-NN classifier for sequence labeling. We present this new feature vector, the concatenation of two types of features. In our approach, we use three kinds of features, two of them being symbolic and one of them being a vector representation. Our features are:

1. Windowed left and right 5 word unigrams

2. Windowed left and right 5 part-of-speech (POS) tag unigrams

3. 25-dimensional GloVe word embedding vectors

Windowed word unigrams refer to a sequence of words like this: For a given word w, the windowed word unigrams are w-4, w-3, w-2, w-1, w, w+1, w+2, w+3, and w+4. Here we are using the window size of 5. This parameter was optimized in our pilot study.

We tag the utterances with the Maximum Entropy POS tagger (maxent_treebank_pos_tagger) provided by NLTK (Bird and Loper, 2004). The tagset we used is the standard Penn Treebank POS tagset (Marcus et al., 1993). Like the windowed word unigrams, windowed POS tag unigrams are also of the window size 5.

GloVe vectors are designed to capture a word as its relation to its co-occurrent words in the global corpus (Pennington et al., 2014). Since k-NN classifiers are better at handling fewer number of symbolic and abstract features, we chose the 25-dimensional word vector. This is also under the consideration that k-NN classifier will weigh features and we would like to maintain enough weight for our symbolic features. We also did pilot study to determine the best dimensionality and the result is consistant with our observation. All hyper-parameters of the classifier are optimized using leave-one-out method on the training set.

4 Results

In this section we present our evaluation results. All the numbers are calculated using the labeled bracketed score. For example, if a n-word span is labeled as N, the predictions need to match both the left and the right boundaries and the label N unanimously to be counted as one correct prediction. If the predictions have the wrong word span or at least one wrong label, the entire chunk is considered incorrect.

4.1 Experiment Results

The results are shown in Table 3.

In the Experiment I, using synthesized training data and human transcribed (HT in Table 3) test data produced the best result. Overall we achieved an F-score of 41.25.

In the Experiment II, the leave-one-out experiment performed on human transcribed data is used to show the upper bound of the task (italicized in Table 3). This is the ideal situation in which we do not introduce errors from automatic speech recognition. The distribution of training set and the test set is identical. In this best scenario, our classifier achieved an F-score of 61.33.

In the Experiment III, we have two different settings. One of them is to use both human transcribed data and additional self-training labeled data, the other is to only use human transcribed data as the seed while the training set itself is the sole self-training labeled data. The second setting is closer to real world scenario especially when we are dealing with situations like a cold start. In this set, human transcribed data plus additional self-training labeled data reached an F-score of 48.30, outperforming only the additional data by slightly over four points.

In the Experiment IV, we show that with the accuracy improvement from ASR, our F-score is improving as well. By performing post-processing, which is a process that is designed strictly to correct errors without compromising the performance in the long run, we manage to achieve close to upper bound performance with an F-score of 60.71.

4.2 Multilevel Results

The best performance for all levels is achieved when we have improved ASR output and perform post-processing to correct the errors caused by the nature of classification.

However, the results in the third set of experiment show some interesting trends. When training with human transcribed data, the best performance is achieved with the least additional data. Meanwhile, when training without human transcribed data, the best performance is achieved with the most additional data. Even this cannot produce comparable results to the experiments with human transcribed data.

4.3 Results of Using Other Classifiers

Overall we achieve 60.71 F measure on ASR input using TiMBL. In comparison, as shown in Figure 4, two previous systems, MEMM and BiLSTM-CRF, achieved 48.26 and 47.75 respectively. When hand transcribed text is input, BiLSTM-CRF performs the best, 69.15 F, followed by MEMM and TiMBL at 67.37 F and 61.3 F, respectively.

4.4 Running Times

The running times for different classifiers are shown in Figure 5. It can be seen that while the BiLSTM-CRF may be a better classifier than the MEMM in terms of accuracy, there is a trade-off in terms of running time. It may be noted, however, that degradation of performance at test time for BiLSTM-CRF is not as severe as the performace drop during training.

5 Discussion

In this section we discuss our findings from our experiments.

5.1 Experiment I

The purpose of this set of experiment is to show that errors introduced early on in the pipeline will propagate through to cause performance decrease

	Training Set	Size	Test Set	Size
Experiment I	Synthesized	464,675	Human Transcription (HT)	3,610
	Synthesized	464,675	Automatic Speech Recognition	3,336
Experiment II	Human Transcription	3,610	HT leave-one-out	3,610
	Human Transcription	3,610	Automatic Speech Recognition	3,336
Experiment III (1)	HT + 25% Additional	17,134	Automatic Speech Recognition	3,336
	HT + 50% Additional	30,657	Automatic Speech Recognition	3,336
	HT + 75% Additional	44,180	Automatic Speech Recognition	3,336
	HT + 100% Additional	57,703	Automatic Speech Recognition	3,336
Experiment III (2)	Seeded 25%	14,617	Automatic Speech Recognition	3,336
	Seeded 50%	29,223	Automatic Speech Recognition	3,336
	Seeded 75%	43,849	Automatic Speech Recognition	3,336
	Seeded 100%	58,465	Automatic Speech Recognition	3,336
Experiment IV	Human Transcription	3,715	Automatic Speech Recognition	3,509
	Human Transcription	3,715	ASR + Post-processing	3,509

Table 2: Experiment Setup

	Training / Test	Entity	Item	Intent	All
Experiment I	Synthesized / HT	**65.59**	**23.24**	**33.60**	**41.25**
	Synthesized / ASR	51.14	12.81	19.39	27.51
Experiment II	HT leave-one-out	*80.11*	*43.25*	*53.30*	*61.33*
	HT / ASR	66.53	37.70	38.07	48.76
Experiment III (1)	HT + 25% / ASR	66.26	**37.06**	**37.65**	**48.30**
	HT + 50% / ASR	65.60	36.55	37.08	47.75
	HT + 75% / ASR	**66.31**	35.31	36.71	47.44
	HT + 100% / ASR	66.26	35.38	37.18	47.68
Experiment III (2)	Seeded 25% / ASR	48.53	20.71	32.07	35.59
	Seeded 50% / ASR	60.04	27.10	33.39	41.89
	Seeded 75% / ASR	62.95	30.52	**33.87**	43.91
	Seeded 100% / ASR	**64.29**	**30.70**	33.61	**44.28**
Experiment IV	HT / Better ASR	75.39	51.37	45.03	57.87
	HT / ASR + Post-processing	**75.46**	**52.84**	**49.66**	**60.71**

Table 3: Experiment Results (F-score)

later. Compared to testing on human transcribed data, testing on ASR data performed much worse with a decrease of almost fourteen points in terms of F-score. Human transcribed data tend to be more grammatical and relevant. As we can see in our first example, ASR data has a lot more noise. The word sequences occurred in the sentence are also less common. Words that sound similar can be mistaken from each other. However, this poses some difficulty on the POS tagger when it tries to tag the words based on the left and right context. We believe this is one of the reasons we saw a big performance difference here.

5.2 Experiment II

The leave-one-out experiment with the human transcribed data serves as the upper bound, the ideal situation where the distribution is identical and no error is introduced externally. However, it is unlikely to achieve such result in real life scenario since user input is noisy and external errors will be introduced along the pipeline inevitably.

What is interesting is the second experiment. In this particular experiment, we used human transcribed data as our training set and ASR data as our test set. This is a more realistic scenario. While we only had less than 1% of the data compared to the previous experiments in Experiment I, we achieved a much better F-score. We believe

Model	Training / Test	Entity	Item	Intent	All
MEMM	HT 10-fold CV	73.22	55.22	67.21	67.37
	HT / Better ASR	60.87	32.97	42.92	**48.26**
BiLSTM-CRF	HT 10-fold CV	77.16	59.12	66.54	**69.15**
	HT / Better ASR	62.97	33.90	39.45	47.57

Table 4: Comparable Results (F-score)

Model	Training Time	Test Time
MEMM	18.00 seconds	10.00 seconds
BiLSTM-CRF	1 hour	27.80 seconds
TiMBL	0.19 second	3.05 seconds

Table 5: Times taken to train and test different classifiers over one fold of the test corpus.

this shows that with very little training data we can still achieve rather decent results. The closer the distribution of both data sets have, the more likely we can achieve higher accuracy. Having just a little bit of human transcribed and annotated data is a reasonable cost for higher quality prediction.

5.3 Experiment III

This is a set of experiment that is rather a reinforcement of the second experiment. Though the F-score dropped minimally due to the added noise from the additional data, it is still obvious that by using real world data we are improving the accuracy.

The second half of this set of experiment provides a potential alternative to our approach. As much as the result is not as good as the first half of this experiment or the second set of experiments, it is still even more accurate than the first set of experiments. With better ASR quality we believe semi-supervised self-training can and should help.

5.4 Experiment IV

This is our best and state-of-the-art result of this task. With the help from ASR quality improvement, the classifier receives a significant boost in performance from an F-score of 48.76 to 57.87.

It is especially worth noticing that by post-processing we achieve 3 points even more. Post-processing is strictly used to correct the inconsistency in the predictions as each individual decision is made independent of each other. It will not hurt the performance in the long run.

5.5 Using Other Classifiers

It is interesting to note that the BiLSTM-CRF performs the worst on ASR input, perhaps because the ELMO embeddings that are used by the BiLSTM-CRF are sensitive to the context of the whole utterance, and this context can differ quite a lot between the training utterances which are hand transcribed and the test utterances which are provided by ASR.

6 Conclusion

In this paper we present a new method to perform multi-level sequence labeling. We show that this method actually outperforms other state-of-the-art methods for this task, showing k-NN is competitive with other methods in the not infrequent situation where only a small amount of training data is available.

We achieved labeled bracketed F-scores of 75.46, 52.84 and 49.66 for the three levels of sequence labeling. Overall we achieved 60.71 at all levels.

7 Future Work

We believe that the pipeline should be fully automated for production purposes. We could automate how the rules are obtained, or extend the rules to correct more mistakes.

As a future research direction for conversational AI, we think that to train and test a k-NN model for predicting which dialog move to take will be beneficial as well.

References

Steven Bird and Edward Loper. 2004. Nltk: the natural language toolkit. In *Proceedings of the ACL 2004 on Interactive poster and demonstration sessions*, page 31. Association for Computational Linguistics.

John Chen, Rashmi Prasad, Svetlana Stoyanchev, Ethan Selfridge, Srinivas Bangalore, and Michael Johnston. 2018. Corpus and annotation towards nlu for customer ordering dialogs. In *Proceedings of IEEE SLT 2018 Workshop on Spoken Language Technology*, Athens, Greece.

Walter Daelemans, Jakub Zavrel, Kurt Van Der Sloot, and Antal Van den Bosch. Timbl: Tilburg memory-based learner.

Layla El Asri, Hannes Schulz, Shikhar Sharma, Jeremie Zumer, Justin Harris, Emery Fine, Rahul Mehrotra, and Kaheer Suleman. 2017. Frames: A corpus for adding memory to goal-oriented dialogue systems. In *Proceedings of the SIGDIAL 2017 Conference*, pages 207–219, Saarbrücken, Germany.

Hakan Erdogan. 2010. Sequence labeling: Generative and discriminative approaches. iCMLA.

Dilek Hakkani-Tür, Gokhan Tür, Asli Celikyilmaz, Yun-Nung Vivian Chen, Jianfeng Gao, Li Dung, and Ye yi Wang. 2016. Multi-domain joint semantic frame parsing using bi-directional rnn-lstm. In *Proceedings of The 17th Annual Meeting of the International Speech Communication Association (INTER-SPEECH 2016)*.

Charles T Hemphill, John J Godfrey, and George R Doddington. 1990. The ATIS spoken language systems pilot corpus. In *Speech and Natural Language: Workshop Proceedings*, Hidden Valley, Pennsylvania.

Mitchell P Marcus, Mary Ann Marcinkiewicz, and Beatrice Santorini. 1993. Building a large annotated corpus of english: The penn treebank. *Computational linguistics*, 19(2):313–330.

Andrew McCallum, Dayne Freitag, and Fernando CN Pereira. 2000. Maximum entropy markov models for information extraction and segmentation. In *Icml*, volume 17, pages 591–598.

Jeffrey Pennington, Richard Socher, and Christopher Manning. 2014. Glove: Global vectors for word representation. In *Proceedings of the 2014 conference on empirical methods in natural language processing (EMNLP)*, pages 1532–1543.

Matthew E Peters, Mark Neumann, Mohit Iyyer, Matt Gardner, Christopher Clark, Kenton Lee, and Luke Zettlemoyer. 2018. Deep contextualized word representations. *arXiv preprint arXiv:1802.05365*.

Daniel Pressel, Sagnik Ray Choudhury, Brian Lester, Yanjie Zhao, and Matt Barta. 2018. Baseline: A library for rapid modeling, experimentation and development of deep learning algorithms targeting NLP. In *Proceedings of Workshop for NLP Open Source Software*, pages 34–40.

Marilyn A. Walker, Owen Rambow, and Monica Rogati. 2001. SPoT: A trainable sentence planner. In *Proceedings of the second meeting of the North American Chapter of the Association for Computational Linguistics on Language technologies*.

Puyang Xu and Ruhi Sarikaya. 2013. Convolutional neural network based triangular crf for joint intent detection and slot filling. In *Automatic Speech Recognition and Understanding (ASRU)*, pages 78–83.

Train One Get One Free: Partially Supervised Neural Network for Bug Report Duplicate Detection and Clustering

Lahari Poddar[1,2] Leonardo Neves[2] William Brendel[2]
Luis Marujo[2] Sergey Tulyakov[2] Pradeep Karuturi[2]

[1]School of Computing, National University of Singapore
lahari@comp.nus.edu.sg
[2]Snap Research
{lneves, willb, luis.marujo}@snap.com
{stulyakov, pradeep.karuturi}@snap.com

Abstract

Tracking user reported bugs requires considerable engineering effort in going through many repetitive reports and assigning them to the correct teams. This paper proposes a neural architecture that can jointly (1) detect if two bug reports are duplicates, and (2) aggregate them into latent topics. Leveraging the assumption that learning the topic of a bug is a sub-task for detecting duplicates, we design a loss function that can jointly perform both tasks but needs supervision for only duplicate classification, achieving topic clustering in an unsupervised fashion. We use a two-step attention module that uses self-attention for topic clustering and conditional attention for duplicate detection. We study the characteristics of two types of real world datasets that have been marked for duplicate bugs by engineers and by non-technical annotators. The results demonstrate that our model not only can outperform state-of-the-art methods for duplicate classification on both cases, but can also learn meaningful latent clusters without additional supervision.

1 Introduction

User feedback is a key part of the development and improvement of software products. Each piece of feedback needs to be manually reviewed and assigned to the correct engineer responsible for maintaining the feature mentioned in the report. On online platforms with millions of users, different users tend to report the same issue, yielding a large number of duplicate reports. Sorting through these massive volumes of bug reports incur a significant amount of engineering time and cost. Additionally, these services are constantly releasing new product features. Therefore, we cannot rely on static annotated data for product feature classification because they rapidly become outdated. This motivates us to develop a framework that can automatically identify duplicate bug reports and cluster them without requiring additional labels.

Previous research in the software engineering domain has addressed duplicates detection and product feature identification as two separate problems framed as independent fully-supervised classification tasks (Nguyen et al., 2012; Budhiraja et al., 2018b; Jonsson et al., 2016; Mani et al., 2018). However, we observe that users generally report issues when accessing certain features of a product, e.g., 'app crashed when opening camera', 'chat won't load' and so on (here, camera and chat are the product features, respectively). Hence, two reports should *at least* discuss the same feature to be considered as duplicates. Therefore, we hypothesize that determining the feature discussed in a report is a *sub-task* of detecting whether or not a report is a duplicate to another one.

Inspired by the effectiveness of Siamese architectures for modeling pairs of texts (Tan et al., 2015; Bowman et al., 2015), we use a shared Recurrent Neural Network (RNN) to encode the two reports. We note that the latent vectors, learned by an RNN for a sequence of words, encode a multitude of semantic information; all of which may not be necessary to understand the topic of the report. We decompose the latent semantic vectors in order to distill only the topical information in a few designated dimensions. This allows us to perform the sub-task of feature-based clustering using only a subset of dimensions, and use the complete vector for the duplicate classification task. We propose a partially supervised learning framework that uses the label for duplicity through a similarity loss on the designated topic dimensions of the latent representation to learn topic clusters.

We use a two-step attention module, since the same words are often not crucial for both tasks. We first learn a self-attention for topic similarity

Proceedings of NAACL-HLT 2019, pages 157–165
Minneapolis, Minnesota, June 2 - June 7, 2019. ©2019 Association for Computational Linguistics

modeling and learn a conditional attention using a memory vector for duplicate classification.

To summarize, we present a systematic study of a classic problem in the software industry. The work has three major contributions.

- We propose a neural model for multi-task learning that requires supervision for only one of the tasks.

- The model uses semantic space decomposition and a hierarchical-conditional attention module to perform the tasks of duplicate detection and topic based clustering.

- We present the challenges we faced during our experience obtaining labels from non-technical annotators, and conduct extensive experiments on both engineer labeled and non-technical labeled datasets.

2   Related Work

The software engineering community has conducted some research work for detecting duplicate bugs. In Minh (2014), a combination of n-gram features and cluster shrinkage algorithm is used for duplicate classification, whereas, in Sun et al. (2011) the BM-25 based scoring has been used akin to information retrieval engines. A combination of tf-idf and topics learned by LDA have also been used (Nguyen et al., 2012; Budhiraja et al., 2018b). Recently, word embeddings have been used to compute similarity of two reports(Yang et al., 2016; Budhiraja et al., 2018a). However, in these approaches, the sequence information of a natural language sentence is not captured.

Among the NLP community, the closest line of applicable work are the generic approaches of textual similarity (Cer et al., 2017; Wang et al., 2017; Neculoiu et al., 2016; Yin et al., 2016). They predominantly employ Siamese architecture (Mueller and Thyagarajan, 2016; Severyn and Moschitti, 2015) and more recently, attention mechanism (Wang et al., 2017; Shen et al., 2018; Wang et al., 2018; Tran and Niedereé, 2018). Inspired by these approaches, we propose a solution for duplicate detection while utilizing the partial supervision to achieve a sub-task of clustering *for free*.

Solving owner attribution of a report has been approached using feature-based methods (Jonsson et al., 2016; Xuan et al., 2012) and very recently using deep learning solutions (Mani et al., 2018).

However, the connection between these two problems have not been explored and they require supervision for product feature identification.

3   Annotation Challenges

We consider a dataset consisting of user reported bugs collected from the Snapchat app. The bugs have been submitted by beta-testers using a bug-tracking functionality named Shake2Report(S2R) within the app. In S2R a user can submit a small textual description of the bug and attach a screenshot of the app while experiencing the issue. In this work, we only consider the textual descriptions of the reports.

Following previous work of duplicate bug tracking (Lazar et al., 2014), we first studied 500 pairs of reports marked as duplicates by engineers. However, these pose several challenges. Firstly, we realized that engineers often needed additional meta-data such as stack-traces and timestamps to accurately determine whether or not a pair of reports referred to the same problem. On the other hand, such additional meta-data cannot be made available to external crowd-sourced annotators due to legal and user privacy restrictions. Finally, the total amount of reports was far beyond what an engineering team could tackle, hence the need for our classification system, which helps scaling the bug report load while maintaining the annotation quality.

Our task is to automatically classify report pairs, and to add engineers to the loop only when pairs are textually ambiguous. We asked non-expert annotators to label the pairs only according to their semantic similarity (no metadata). The annotators had a high agreement among themselves with a Krippendorff's alpha (Krippendorff, 1970) score of 0.78. After adding engineers to the annotation pool, the score dropped to 0.58. To understand this disparity, consider the pairs:

- *"Crashed when posting story from memories"* and *"Crashed while exporting from memories"*
- *"Stuck on typing notification"* and *"Did not get notification for this group chat"*

Although not marked as duplicates by non-experts, they referred to the same underlying problem from the engineering side. While out-of-scope for this paper, we plan to conduct a dedicated study to explore these differences in future work.

As mentioned in the introduction, bug▸team assignments become rapidly outdated as the app product features (and therefore the teams working on them) are constantly evolving. Also, non-expert annotators cannot be assumed to have any knowledge of these assignments, so we treat bug▸ team assignments as an unsupervised task.

4 Proposed Method

We now describe the proposed learning framework as shown in Figure 1. Given a pair of reports P and Q, the system uses a single binary label $r(P, Q)$ (1 if the reports are duplicate, 0 otherwise) to supervise both tasks: duplicate classification and topic similarity modeling.

4.1 Text Encoder

This component takes a bug report represented as a sequence of words $\{w_1, w_2, \cdots, w_n\}$ as input and encodes it to latent vectors $\{\mathbf{h}_1, \mathbf{h}_2, \cdots, \mathbf{h}_n\}$.

We first use word embeddings to transform all words in a text into finite d-dimensional vectors $\{\mathbf{v}_1, \mathbf{v}_2, \cdots, \mathbf{v}_n\}$. The vectors are then fed to a Gated Recurrent Unit (GRU) layer (Chung et al., 2014). We use bi-directional GRU units to encode the context information around a word. For a word w_i, outputs from the forward and backward GRUs are latent vectors of dimension g and denoted as $\mathbf{h}_i^f$ and $\mathbf{h}_i^b$, respectively. We concatenate these two vectors to form a single latent representation of the word as, $\mathbf{h}_i = \mathbf{h}_i^f \oplus \mathbf{h}_i^b$.

4.2 Semantic Space Decomposition

A word's encoded representation $\mathbf{h}_i$ has various information intertwined in an abstract way within the vector dimensions. It is difficult to interpret individual dimensions and meaningfully use a subset of dimensions for a different sub-task.

We aim to distill the coarser topical information into designated dimensions within the vector, storing other finer pieces of information in remaining dimensions. Such disentanglement allows us to do the topic similarity modeling using only the designated dimensions and ignore the rest.

To this end, we force the network to learn topical information about each word in the first k dimensions of its latent vector space. For a bi-directional GRU, we have two encoded representations for the ith word from the forward and backward passes i.e., $\mathbf{h}_i^f$, and $\mathbf{h}_i^b$. We define the topic vector of a word i as,

$$\boldsymbol{\theta}_i = \mathbf{h}_i^f[1:k] \oplus \mathbf{h}_i^b[1:k] \tag{1}$$

where $\mathbf{h}_i^f[1:k]$ and $\mathbf{h}_i^b[1:k]$ denote the first k dimensions in the GRU encoded latent vectors from the forward and backward passes respectively.

4.3 Topic Similarity Modeling

We aggregate the topic vectors of the constituent words to represent the topic of a report, and use a self-attention layer to learn the weights of the words important in determining the topic:

$$\mathbf{z}_i = \tanh(\mathbf{W} \cdot \mathbf{h}_i + \mathbf{b}_i) \tag{2}$$

$$\boldsymbol{\alpha}_i = \frac{\exp(\mathbf{z}_i)}{\sum_i \exp(\mathbf{z}_i)}, \tag{3}$$

$$\boldsymbol{\theta} = \sum_{i=1}^{n} \boldsymbol{\alpha}_i \cdot \boldsymbol{\theta}_i. \tag{4}$$

where $\boldsymbol{\alpha}_i$ is the weight for word w_i and $\boldsymbol{\theta}$ is the topic vector of the report. Note that only the designated topical dimensions of the words contribute to representing the topic vector of the report.

In order to learn the semantic space of topic vectors, we need to constrain them in such a way that if two reports (P and Q) have similar topics (e.g., both are talking about *camera*), their $\boldsymbol{\theta}^P$ and $\boldsymbol{\theta}^Q$ values should be closer and vice-versa. Since only the ground-truth label for duplicity is available, we consider this signal as *partially* observed for the topic modeling task. Following our hypothesis that determining the topic of a report is a sub-task for duplicate detection, there can be three possible cases for a pair of reports:

Case 1: Duplicates from the same topic;
Case 2: Non-duplicates from different topics;
Case 3: Non-duplicates from the same topic.

Since for duplicate tickets (P, Q) their topics are bound to be same, we reduce the distance between $\boldsymbol{\theta}^P$, and $\boldsymbol{\theta}^Q$ in our loss. However, non-duplicate pairs may or may not be from the same topic (Case 2, and 3).

We do not include Case 3 in the loss, as inferring it is difficult without explicit labels. We assume that if a pair of non-duplicate reports have no word overlap (apart from stopwords), then only they belong to different topics i.e., Case 2. For such pairs we wish to increase the distances between their topic vectors. We imbue this principle in the network through the following loss function:

$$\mathcal{L}_{\text{sim}} = r(P, Q) \cdot S_{\text{C}}(\boldsymbol{\theta}^P, \boldsymbol{\theta}^Q) \tag{5}$$
$$- (1 - r(P, Q)) \cdot S_{\text{C}}(\boldsymbol{\theta}^P, \boldsymbol{\theta}^Q)$$

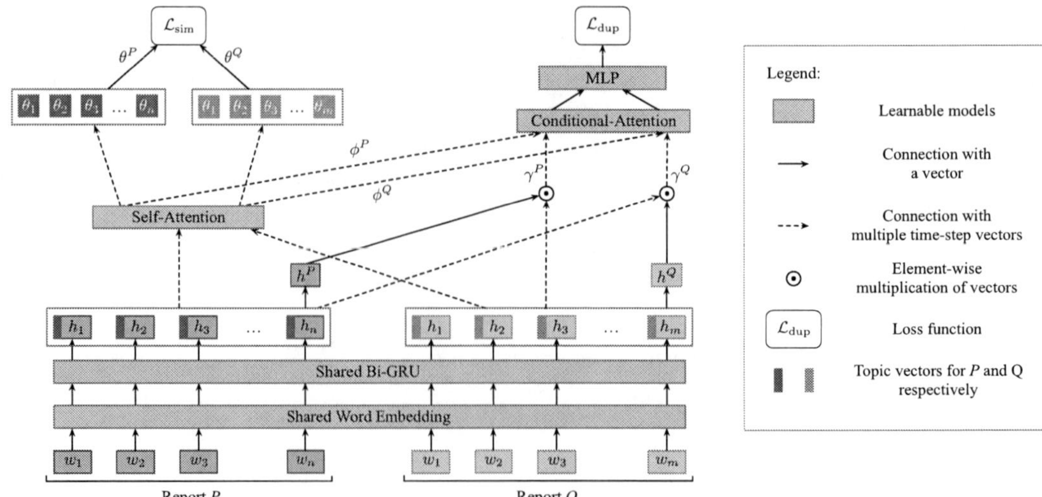

Figure 1: **The proposed partially supervised learning framework.** The framework takes two user reports P and Q as inputs. The left branch performs topic clustering with self-attention mechanism using topic dimensions. The right branch performs duplicates detection with conditional attention taking a pair of encoded reports as inputs.

where $r(P, Q)$ is the ground-truth duplicity label (0 or 1), S_C is cosine similarity. A careful reader might observe that the function minimizes distance of duplicates pairs ($r(P, Q) = 1$), while exhibiting the exact opposite behaviour for non-duplicates ($r(P, Q) = 0$). To account for the skewed distribution of duplicate vs. non-duplicates, we normalize the loss using proportional class weights.

4.4 Duplicate Classification

The final component of the network considers the complete latent vectors of the words for the task of duplicate classification. We use another attention layer for this component to allow the network to focus on important words. However, it is not necessary that the same words will be important for both the tasks. For example, consider the following pair of tickets: *"Can't import these pics from camera roll to memories"* and *"No pics in memory"*. In order to determine the product feature, the self attention module needs to focus on the words *memories* and *memory* in the reports, respectively. However, to decide whether they are duplicates or not, the second attention module needs to focus on the specific error, i.e. *Can't import pics* and *No pics* in the two reports respectively. For report P, we create a memory vector ϕ^P to guide this attention layer using the hidden representations of the words as well the previously

learned self-attention weights for topic modeling.

$$\phi^P = \sum_i \alpha_i^P \cdot \mathbf{h}_i^P + \sum_i \mathbf{h}_i^P \tag{6}$$

We also note that unlike the self-attention used for topic similarity modeling, for duplicate classification we need to use a form of conditional attention. For determining whether a report (P) is duplicate to another one (Q), the words that are important in P are dependent on the words in Q. Therefore, for each word position i in P we compute its relevance to the report Q as,

$$\gamma_i^P = \mathbf{h}_i^P \odot \mathbf{h}^Q \tag{7}$$

where $\mathbf{h}_i^P$ is the hidden state of the ith word in report P, $\odot$ denotes element-wise multiplication, and $\mathbf{h}^Q$ is the representation of report Q obtained using averaging the hidden states of all words in Q i.e. $\mathbf{h}^Q = \mathrm{Avg}(\mathbf{h}_1, \mathbf{h}_2, \cdots, \mathbf{h}_m)$, m is the number of words in Q.

We now use this conditional representation γ_i^P and the memory vector ϕ^P to learn the conditional attention weights (β) and compute the weighted representation $\mathbf{c}^P$ as,

$$\mathbf{c}_i^P = \tanh(\mathbf{W}_1 \cdot \gamma_i^P) \cdot \tanh(\mathbf{W}_2 \cdot \phi^P) \tag{8}$$

$$\beta_i^P = \frac{\exp(\mathbf{c}_i^P)}{\sum_i \exp(\mathbf{c}_i^P)} \tag{9}$$

$$\mathbf{c}^P = \sum_{i=1}^{n} \beta_i^P \cdot \mathbf{c}_i^P \tag{10}$$

160

We concatenate the weighted representations of P and Q as $\mathbf{c}^{PQ} = \mathbf{c}^{P} \oplus \mathbf{c}^{Q}$. We pass this concatenated vector through a Multi-Layer Perceptron, the final layer of which outputs a prediction $\hat{r}(P, Q)$ whether they are duplicates or not. We use binary cross-entropy loss to train this objective.

$$\mathcal{L}_{\text{dup}} = H(r(PQ), \hat{r}(PQ)), \qquad (11)$$

where H is binary cross-entropy. The overall loss for the whole network is a weighted combination of the two losses.

$$\mathcal{L} = \lambda \mathcal{L}_{\text{sim}} + (1 - \lambda)\mathcal{L}_{\text{dup}} \qquad (12)$$

In our experiments, we use $\lambda = 0.5$ but it can be varied depending on the importance of the tasks. We optimize the network using Adam optimizer and train in an end-to-end fashion through back-propagation.

5   Evaluation

5.1   Dataset

We experiment on four real-world datasets.

(1) Snap S2R : Composed of bugs reported through an in-app tool. The data was labeled as duplicate or not by non-technical annotators (described in section 3).

(2-4). Open Source Projects [1] : Repository of bugs submitted for the open-source projects of **Eclipse Platform**, **Mozilla Firefox** and **Eclipse JDT**. Each report consists of a short title and a longer description which often describes the steps to reproduce the issue. We only consider the title of the report in our experiments. The reported bugs have been marked for duplicates by engineers while resolving them.

We augment the S2R data with randomly sampled negative pairs to resemble a positive to negative ratio that is estimated in production. For the Eclipse and Firefox datasets, we randomly sample negative pairs, keeping the positive to negative ratio close to what was previously mentioned (Lazar et al., 2014). Table 1 shows the statistics of the four datasets. These datasets were selected to capture different training sizes and variations of vocabulary used.

5.2   Experimental Settings

We initialize the words using pre-trained Glove embeddings (Pennington et al., 2014) of 300 dimensions but tune it during training to capture the

---

[1] https://github.com/logpai/bugrepo

Dataset	#pairs	#vocab	%dups	#reports	avg #words /report
Snap S2R	66,945	7763	9%	17,255	14.6
Eclipse Platform	170,312	29,702	12%	83,608	7.9
Eclipse JDT	90,592	17,228	14%	44,670	8.1
Firefox	231,628	34,590	26%	113,262	10.0

Table 1: Statistics of the datasets used

intrinsic features of the specific task and dataset at hand. For the GRU layers we use 150 dimensions and the first 20 dimensions of them are used for topic representation. For the MLP in duplicate classification we use 2 layers of fully connected layers of 100 hidden neurons each, with $relu$ activation and 20% dropout rate. For fair comparison we use the same number of parameters in all baselines. The learning rate is set to 0.003 and a batch size of 128 samples is used while training all the models.

5.3   Evaluating Duplicate Classification

We first start evaluating the proposed approach for detecting duplicate bug reports. We compare with the following six baselines:

- **Logistic Regression** uses a bag of n-grams representation with n ranging from one to three words. Tf-idf scores are used for feature weighting.

- **Siamese CNN** (Severyn and Moschitti, 2015) encodes the texts with a shared convolution network followed by an MLP for classification.

- **Siamese Bi-GRU** uses a shared bidirectional GRU for encoding text.

- **Siamese Bi-GRU with Attention** uses an attention layer on top of the GRU outputs to encode the texts

- **DWEN** (Budhiraja et al., 2018a) is the state-of-the-art deep learning approach for duplicate bug detection using word embeddings.

- **BiMPM** (Wang et al., 2017) is the state-of-the-art sentence similarity modeling that uses multi-perspective symmetric matching for a pair of texts.

We report results after averaging five independent trials using 80% data for training, 10% for

Method	Snap S2R			Eclipse Platform			FireFox			Eclipse JDT		
	P	R	F1	P	R	F1	P	R	F1	P	R	F1
Logistic Regression	0.67	0.63	0.65	0.71	0.88	0.78	0.92	0.95	0.94	0.76	0.88	0.81
Siamese CNN (2015)	0.67	0.63	0.65	0.81	0.81	0.81	0.93	0.94	0.93	0.79	0.79	0.79
Siamese Bi-GRU	**0.76**	0.61	0.68	**0.86**	0.84	0.85	**0.95**	0.93	0.94	0.85	0.84	0.84
Siamese Bi-GRU w Att	**0.76**	0.62	0.68	**0.86**	0.86	0.86	**0.95**	0.94	0.94	0.84	0.84	0.84
DWEN (2018a)	0.69	0.55	0.62	0.83	0.74	0.78	0.93	0.92	0.93	0.81	0.71	0.76
BiMPM (2017)	0.73	0.65	0.69	**0.86**	0.82	0.84	0.94	0.92	0.93	0.85	0.79	0.82
Our Method	0.73	**0.67***	**0.70**	0.84	**0.91***	**0.87***	0.94	**0.96***	**0.95***	**0.86**	**0.90***	**0.88***

Table 2: Comparison of different methods for duplicate classification task on multiple datasets. * denotes statistical significance with the runner up for $p\text{-}value < 0.01$

validation, and 10% for testing. Due to the imbalanced class distribution, we use precision, recall and F1-score of the positive class as evaluation metrics.

From the results in Table 2 we see that our proposed method largely outperforms all other models in terms of recall and in most cases on F1 score as well. Using a sequence encoder like GRU boosts the performance significantly compared to using n-grams as in Logistic Regression or CNN. We note that the overall scores on Eclipse and Firefox datasets are much higher than the scores on Snap S2R data. One of the reasons could be the difference in data size where the Snap S2R dataset is much smaller in size compared to others. Noisy labels from non-technical annotators could also be a potential reason. Manually examining the posts we also note that the bug reports submitted for the open projects are often by engineers, who use concrete technical terms to describe the problem. In contrast, for the Snap S2R dataset, the reports are submitted by end-users using free text with non-technical terms that make it harder for a machine learning model to disambiguate.

5.4 Evaluating Clusters

A major advantage of our model is its ability to perform clustering of the bug reports to aid in ownership attribution. In this set of experiments, we show that our model is able to learn a semantic space so that nearby reports in the space indeed belong to the same product feature.

We use the topic vector (θ) of a report learned by our model and run an off-the-shelf clustering algorithm K-means[2]. Ideally, there should be a one-to-one mapping between the obtained clusters and the actual project features. For comparison,

we use one of the most popular unsupervised topic model, LDA (Blei et al., 2003) to learn latent topics from the bug reports. For implementation of LDA we use the Gensim library[3]. We perform standard pre-processing steps, and remove stopwords before training the LDA model. We evaluate the learned latent clusters by comparing them to the ground truth project features, as have been marked by users while submitting reports for S2R dataset. For fair comparison, we use the same (20) number of clusters for both methods, which is close to the actual number of product features.

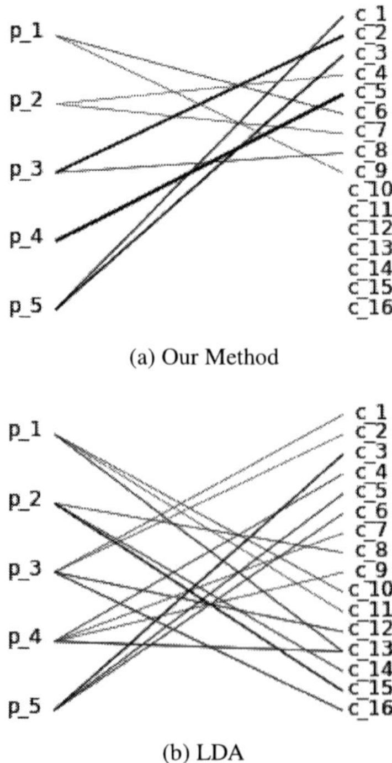

(a) Our Method

(b) LDA

Figure 2: Mapping between the learned latent clusters and top-5 product features for Snap S2R dataset.

[2]https://scikit-learn.org/stable/modules/generated/sklearn.cluster.KMeans.html

[3]https://radimrehurek.com/gensim/models/ldamodel.html

Figure 2 shows the mapping between learned latent clusters and top-5 ground truth product features for the proposed model and LDA. To reduce the effect of noisy labels, we consider a cluster-product feature mapping only if more than 10 reports about a product feature are assigned to a cluster. The width of the connecting edge is proportional to the number of times a cluster-product feature association is observed.

Firstly, we observe that LDA requires more clusters to represent the same number of features. This demonstrates that LDA over-clusters, failing to identify reports that talk about the same product feature and assigns them to different clusters. Secondly, some clusters in LDA (e.g., c_13) are connected to multiple product features denoting impurity of the cluster. Finally, for most features, their mappings to a cluster are much stronger in our model as demonstrated by the width of the edges in the graph. This shows that with partial supervision from duplicity labels, we are able to learn clusters that better correspond to ground truth product features.

Cluster 1	Cluster 2	Cluster 3	Cluster 4	Cluster 5
video	load	lens	app	specs
audio	long	lenses	map	spec
videos	story	carousel	viewing	importing
playback	time	preview	crashed	v2
sync	taking	applied	navigating	unpaired

Table 3: Top Words according to their tf-idf scores from few clusters learned by our model.

Table 3 shows top words according to their tf-idf scores appearing in bug reports assigned to a cluster. The learned clusters are coherent and represent specific product features. For example, *Cluster 1* talks about issues regarding `video` or `audio`, while *Cluster 2* is mostly about issues related to loading of a `story` (a feature in the app). In *Cluster 3* reports related to various `lenses` and `filters` are placed, while *Cluster 4* seems to be about `maps` and `navigation` features. It is also interesting to note that generic issues like *'crashed'* appear in some of the clusters. Although one could identify most of the bugs as crashes, this indicates that users have a specific vocabulary when referring to a particular product feature.

5.5 Analyzing Attention Weights

Finally, we present case studies of the attention weights learned by our proposed model. As we have two-steps of attention layers optimized by the

two objectives, they can learn to focus on words that are important for the specific tasks.

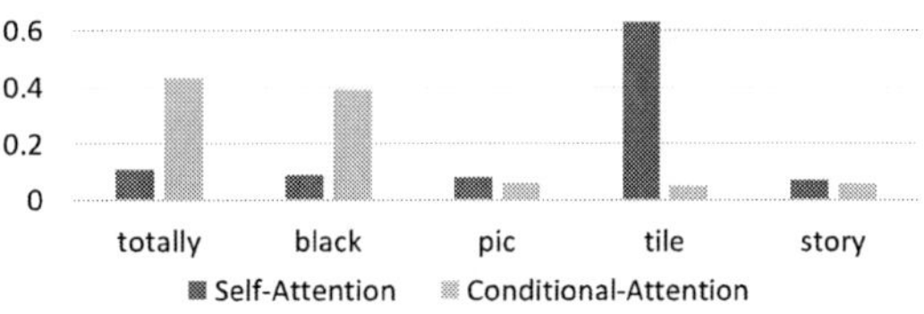

(a) bug report: *totally black pic for **tile** story*

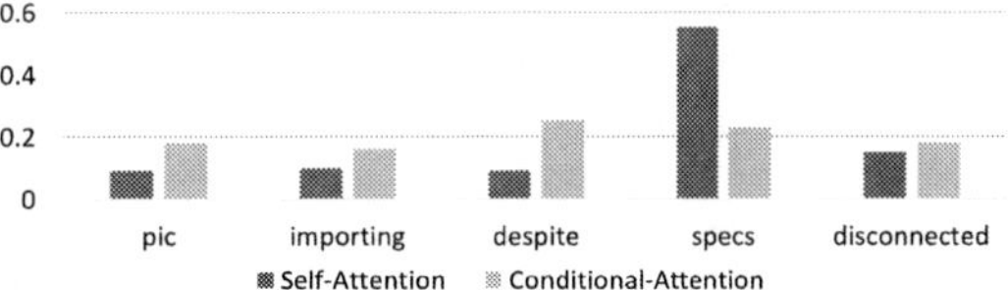

(b) bug report: *pic importing despite **specs** disconnected*

Figure 3: Visualization of the attention weights learned by the two attention modules on few sample bug reports

Figure 3 shows the attention weights for two sample bug reports from Snap S2R dataset. We observe that the two attention modules tend to focus on different parts of the text. The self-attention gives more weight to the words that determine the overall topic of the report (*tile* in Figure 3a, *specs* in Figure 3b). In contrast, the conditional-attention focuses on the set of words describing the specific issue to aid in detecting duplicates.

6 Conclusion

In this paper we have studied bug-tracking, which is a widespread problem in the software industry. We develop a neural architecture that can learn to classify duplicates and cluster them into meaningful latent topics without additional supervision. The architecture decomposes the latent semantic space of a word to only distill the topical information into a few designated dimensions, and uses a two-step attention module to focus on different textual parts for the two tasks. We share the challenges of annotating a user reported bug dataset with non-technical annotators, as opposed to using annotations from engineers. This is a direction we plan to further explore in future work. Experimental results on different types of datasets indicate that the proposed approach is promising compared to existing techniques for both tasks. Most importantly, our model's construction is generic and presents new possibilities in various domains for modeling sub-tasks for free, with partial supervision from another task.

References

David M Blei, Andrew Y Ng, and Michael I Jordan. 2003. Latent dirichlet allocation. *Journal of machine Learning research*, 3(Jan):993–1022.

Samuel R Bowman, Gabor Angeli, Christopher Potts, and Christopher D Manning. 2015. A large annotated corpus for learning natural language inference. *Conference on Empirical Methods in Natural Language Processing*.

Amar Budhiraja, Kartik Dutta, Raghu Reddy, and Manish Shrivastava. 2018a. Dwen: deep word embedding network for duplicate bug report detection in software repositories. In *Proceedings of the 40th International Conference on Software Engineering: Companion Proceeedings*, pages 193–194. ACM.

Amar Budhiraja, Raghu Reddy, and Manish Shrivastava. 2018b. Lwe: Lda refined word embeddings for duplicate bug report detection. In *Proceedings of the 40th International Conference on Software Engineering: Companion Proceeedings*, pages 165–166. ACM.

Daniel Cer, Mona Diab, Eneko Agirre, Inigo Lopez-Gazpio, and Lucia Specia. 2017. Semeval-2017 task 1: Semantic textual similarity-multilingual and cross-lingual focused evaluation. *arXiv preprint arXiv:1708.00055*.

Junyoung Chung, Caglar Gulcehre, Kyunghyun Cho, and Yoshua Bengio. 2014. Empirical evaluation of gated recurrent neural networks on sequence modeling. In *NIPS Workshop on Deep Learning and Representation Learningp, December*.

Leif Jonsson, Markus Borg, David Broman, Kristian Sandahl, Sigrid Eldh, and Per Runeson. 2016. Automated bug assignment: Ensemble-based machine learning in large scale industrial contexts. *Empirical Software Engineering*, 21(4):1533–1578.

Klaus Krippendorff. 1970. Estimating the reliability, systematic error and random error of interval data. *Educational and Psychological Measurement*, 30(1):61–70.

Alina Lazar, Sarah Ritchey, and Bonita Sharif. 2014. Generating duplicate bug datasets. In *Proceedings of the 11th working conference on mining software repositories*, pages 392–395. ACM.

Senthil Mani, Anush Sankaran, and Rahul Aralikatte. 2018. Deeptriage: Exploring the effectiveness of deep learning for bug triaging. *arXiv preprint arXiv:1801.01275*.

Phuc Nhan Minh. 2014. An approach to detecting duplicate bug reports using n-gram features and cluster chrinkage technique. *Int. J. Sci. Res. Publ.(IJSRP)*, 4(5):89–100.

Jonas Mueller and Aditya Thyagarajan. 2016. Siamese recurrent architectures for learning sentence similarity. In *AAAI*, volume 16, pages 2786–2792.

Paul Neculoiu, Maarten Versteegh, and Mihai Rotaru. 2016. Learning text similarity with siamese recurrent networks. In *Proceedings of the 1st Workshop on Representation Learning for NLP*, pages 148–157.

Anh Tuan Nguyen, Tung Thanh Nguyen, Tien N Nguyen, David Lo, and Chengnian Sun. 2012. Duplicate bug report detection with a combination of information retrieval and topic modeling. In *Proceedings of the 27th IEEE/ACM International Conference on Automated Software Engineering*, pages 70–79. ACM.

Jeffrey Pennington, Richard Socher, and Christopher Manning. 2014. Glove: Global vectors for word representation. In *Proceedings of the 2014 conference on empirical methods in natural language processing (EMNLP)*, pages 1532–1543.

Aliaksei Severyn and Alessandro Moschitti. 2015. Learning to rank short text pairs with convolutional deep neural networks. In *Proceedings of the 38th international ACM SIGIR conference on research and development in information retrieval*, pages 373–382. ACM.

Chenlin Shen, Changlong Sun, Jingjing Wang, Yangyang Kang, Shoushan Li, Xiaozhong Liu, Luo Si, Min Zhang, and Guodong Zhou. 2018. Sentiment classification towards question-answering with hierarchical matching network. In *Proceedings of the 2018 Conference on Empirical Methods in Natural Language Processing*, pages 3654–3663.

Chengnian Sun, David Lo, Siau-Cheng Khoo, and Jing Jiang. 2011. Towards more accurate retrieval of duplicate bug reports. In *Proceedings of the 2011 26th IEEE/ACM International Conference on Automated Software Engineering*, pages 253–262. IEEE Computer Society.

Ming Tan, Cicero dos Santos, Bing Xiang, and Bowen Zhou. 2015. Lstm-based deep learning models for non-factoid answer selection. *arXiv preprint arXiv:1511.04108*.

Nam Khanh Tran and Claudia Niedereée. 2018. Multi-hop attention networks for question answer matching. In *The 41st International ACM SIGIR Conference on Research & Development in Information Retrieval*, pages 325–334. ACM.

Lu Wang, Shoushan Li, Changlong Sun, Luo Si, Xiaozhong Liu, Min Zhang, and Guodong Zhou. 2018. One vs. many qa matching with both word-level and sentence-level attention network. In *Proceedings of the 27th International Conference on Computational Linguistics*, pages 2540–2550.

Zhiguo Wang, Wael Hamza, and Radu Florian. 2017. Bilateral multi-perspective matching for natural language sentences. *IJCAI*.

Jifeng Xuan, He Jiang, Zhilei Ren, and Weiqin Zou. 2012. Developer prioritization in bug repositories. In *Software Engineering (ICSE), 2012 34th International Conference on*, pages 25–35. IEEE.

Xinli Yang, David Lo, Xin Xia, Lingfeng Bao, and Jianling Sun. 2016. Combining word embedding with information retrieval to recommend similar bug reports. In *2016 IEEE 27th International Symposium on Software Reliability Engineering (ISSRE)*, pages 127–137. IEEE.

Wenpeng Yin, Hinrich Schütze, Bing Xiang, and Bowen Zhou. 2016. Abcnn: Attention-based convolutional neural network for modeling sentence pairs. *Transactions of the Association of Computational Linguistics*, 4(1):259–272.

Robust Semantic Parsing with Adversarial Learning for Domain Generalization

Gabriel Marzinotto[1,2], Géraldine Damnati[1], Frédéric Béchet[2], Benoît Favre[2]
(1) Orange Labs / Lannion France
(2) Aix Marseille Univ, CNRS, LIS / Marseille France
gabriel.marzinotto@orange.com, geraldine.damnati@orange.com
frederic.bechet@lis-lab.fr, benoit.favre@lis-lab.fr

Abstract

This paper addresses the issue of generalization for Semantic Parsing in an adversarial framework. Building models that are more robust to inter-document variability is crucial for the integration of Semantic Parsing technologies in real applications. The underlying question throughout this study is whether adversarial learning can be used to train models on a higher level of abstraction in order to increase their robustness to lexical and stylistic variations. We propose to perform Semantic Parsing with a domain classification adversarial task without explicit knowledge of the domain. The strategy is first evaluated on a French corpus of encyclopedic documents, annotated with FrameNet, in an information retrieval perspective, then on PropBank Semantic Role Labeling task on the CoNLL-2005 benchmark. We show that adversarial learning increases all models generalization capabilities both on in and out-of-domain data.

1 Introduction

For many NLP applications, models that perform well on multiple domains and data sources are essential. As data labeling is expensive and time consuming, especially when it requires specific expertise (FrameNet, Universal Dependencies, etc.), annotations for every domain and data source are not feasible. On the other hand, domain biases are a major problem in almost every supervised NLP task. Models learn these biases as useful information and experience a significant performance drop whenever they are applied on data from a different source or domain. A recent approach attempting to tackle domain biases and build robust systems consists in using neural networks and adversarial learning to build domain independent representations. In the NLP community, this method has been mostly used in crosslingual models to transfer information from

English to low resource languages in problems and recently in various monolingual tasks in order to alleviate domain bias of trained models.

In the context of Semantic Frame Parsing, we address in this paper the generalization issue of models trained on one or several domains and applied to a new domain. We show that adversarial learning can be used to improve the generalization capacities of semantic parsing models to out of domain data. We propose an adversarial framework based on a domain classification task that we use as a regularization technique on state-of-the-art semantic parsing systems. We use unsupervised domain inference to obtain labels for the classification task.

Firstly we perform experiments on a large multi-domain frame corpus (Marzinotto et al., 2018a) where only a relatively small number of frames where annotated, corresponding to possible targets in an Information Extraction applicative framework. We evaluate our adversarial framework with a semantic frame parser we developed on this corpus and presented in (Marzinotto et al., 2018b). Secondly we checked the genericity of our approach on the standard PropBank Semantic Role Labeling task on the CoNLL-2005 benchmark, with a tagging model proposed by (He et al., 2017). We show that in both cases adversarial learning increases all models generalization capabilities both on in and out-of-domain data.

2 Related Work

2.1 Domain-Adversarial Training

Domain Independence can be approached from different perspectives. A popular approach that emerged in image processing (Ganin et al., 2016) consists in optimizing a double objective composed of a task-specific classifier and an adversarial domain classifier. The latter is called adver-

Proceedings of NAACL-HLT 2019, pages 166–173
Minneapolis, Minnesota, June 2 - June 7, 2019. ©2019 Association for Computational Linguistics

sarial because it is connected to the task-specific classifier using a gradient reversal layer. During training a saddle point is searched where the task-specific classifier is good and the domain classifier is bad. It has been shown in (Ganin and Lempitsky, 2015) that this implicitly optimizes the hidden representation towards domain independence.

In NLP problems this approach has successfully been used to train cross-lingual word representations (Conneau et al., 2017) and to transfer learning from English to low resource languages for POS tagging (Kim et al., 2017) and sentiment analysis (Chen et al., 2016). These approaches introduce language classifiers with an adversarial objective to train task-specific but language agnostic representations. Besides the cross-lingual transfer problem, there are few studies of the impact of domain-adversarial training in a monolingual setup. For instance, (Liu et al., 2017) successfully uses this technique to improve generalization in a document classification task. It has also been used recently for varied tasks such as transfer learning on Q&A systems (Yu et al., 2018) or duplicate question detection (Shah et al., 2018) and removal of protected attributes from social media textual data (Elazar and Goldberg, 2018).

2.2 Robustness in Semantic Frame Parsing

In Frame Semantic Parsing, data is scarce and classic evaluation settings seldom propose out-of-domain test data. Despite the existence of out-of-domain corpora such MASC (Passonneau et al., 2012) and YAGS (Hartmann et al., 2017) the domain adaptation problem has been widely reported (Johansson and Nugues, 2008; Søgaard et al., 2015) but not extensively studied. Recently, (Hartmann et al., 2017) presented the first in depth study of the domain adaptation problem using the YAGS frame corpus. They show that the main problem in domain adaptation for frame semantic parsing is the frame identification step and propose a more robust classifier using predicate and context embeddings to perform frame identification. This approach is suitable for cascade systems such as SEMAFOR (Das et al., 2014), (Hermann et al., 2014) and (Yang and Mitchell, 2017). In this paper we propose to study the generalization issue within the framework of a sequence tagging semantic frame parser that performs frame selection and argument classification in one step.

3 Semantic parsing model with an adversarial training scheme

3.1 Semantic parsing model: `biGRU`

We use in this study a sequence tagging semantic frame parser that performs frame selection and argument classification in one step based on a deep bi-directional GRU tagger ($biGRU$). The advantage of this architecture is its flexibility as it can be applied to several semantic parsing schemes such as PropBank (He et al., 2017) and FrameNet (Yang and Mitchell, 2017).

More precisely, the model consists of a 4 layer bi-directional Gated Recurrent Unit (GRU) with highway connections (Srivastava et al., 2015). This model does not rely solely on word embeddings as input. Instead, it has a richer set of features including syntactic, morphological and surface features. (see (Marzinotto et al., 2018b) for more details).

Except for words where we use pre-trained embeddings, we use randomly initialized embedding layers for categorical features.

3.2 Sequence encoding/decoding

For all experiments we use a BIO label encoding. To ensure that output sequences respect the BIO constrains we implement an A* decoding strategy similar to the one proposed by (He et al., 2017). We further apply a coherence filter to the output of the tagging process. This filter ensures that the predicted semantic structure is acceptable. Given a sentence and a word w that is a Lexical Unit (LU) trigger, we select the frame F as being the most probable frame among the ones that can have w as a trigger. Once F is determined, we then mask all FEs that do not belong to F and perform constrained A* decoding. Finally, we improve this strategy by introducing a parameter $\delta \in (-1; 1)$ that is added to the output probability of the *null* label $P(y_t = O)$ at each time-step. By default, with $\delta = 0$ the most probable non-null hypothesis is selected if its probability is higher than $P(y_t = O)$. Varying $\delta > 0$ (resp. $\delta < 0$) is equivalent to being more strict (resp. less strict) on the highest non-null hypothesis. By doing so we can study the precision/recall (P/R) trade-off of our models. This δ parameter is tuned on a validation set and we either provide the P/R curve or report scores for the $Fmax$ setting.

3.3 Adversarial Domain Classifier

In order to design an efficient adversarial task, several criteria have to be met. The task has to be related to the biases it is supposed to alleviate. And furthermore, the adversarial task should not be correlated to the main task (i.e semantic parsing here), otherwise it may harm the model's performances. Determining where these biases lay is not easy, although this is critical for the success of our method. We propose to use a domain classification adversarial task.

Given two data-sets (X1, Y1) and (X2, Y2) from different domains. The expected gains from introducing an adversarial domain classifier are proportional to how different X1 and X2 are (the more dissimilar the better) and proportional to how similar the label distributions Y1 and Y2 are (higher similarity is better). Otherwise, if X1 and X2 are very similar, there is no need to transfer learning from one domain to another. Under this condition, The adversarial domain classifier will not be able to recognize domains and give proper information on how to build better representations. If Y1 and Y2 are extremely dissimilar, to the point where Y cannot be predicted without explicit domain information, using adversarial learning may be harmful. In our case, prior probabilities for both frame distribution and word senses are correlated to the thematic domains. However, adversarial learning can still be useful because most of the LUs are polysemous even within a domain. Therefore, the model needs to learn word sense disambiguation through a more complex process than simply using the domain information.

Our adversarial domain classifier is an extension of (Ganin and Lempitsky, 2014) to recurrent neural networks. We start from our *biGRU* semantic parser and on the last hidden layer, we stack another neural network that implements a domain classifier (called adversarial task). The domain classifier is connected to the *biGRU* using a gradient reversal layer. Training consists in finding a saddle point where the semantic parser is good and the domain classifier is bad. This way, the model is optimized to be domain independent.

The architecture is shown in Figure 1. The adversarial task can be implemented using a CNN, a RNN or a FNN. In this paper we use CNN as they yield the best results on preliminary experiments.

This architecture is trained following the guidelines of (Ganin and Lempitsky, 2014). During

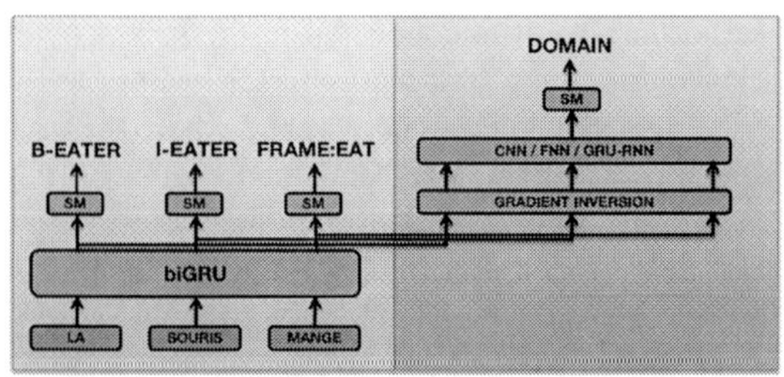

Figure 1: Adversarial Domain Classifier model

training, the adversarial classifier is trained to predict the target class (*i.e.* to minimize the loss L_{adv}) while the main task model is trained to make the adversarial task fail (*i.e.* to minimize the loss $L_{frame} - L_{adv}$). In practice, in order to ensure stability when the parameters of the shared network are updated, the adversarial task gradient magnitude is attenuated by a factor λ as shown in (1). Here ∇L represents the gradients w.r.t the weights θ for either the frame classifier loss or the adversarial loss, θ are the model's parameters being updated, and μ is the learning rate. This λ factor increases on every epoch following (2), where p is the progress, starting at 0 and increasing linearly up to 1 at the last epoch.

$$\theta \leftarrow \theta - \mu * (\nabla L_{frame} - \lambda \nabla L_{adv}) \quad (1)$$

$$\lambda = \frac{2}{1 + \exp(-10 \cdot p)} - 1 \quad (2)$$

3.4 Unsupervised domain inference

The originality of our approach lies in the design of an adversarial task in an unsupervised way. Our purpose is to design a general method that could easily and efficiently apply in any realistic conditions, independently of the fact that the training sentences can be linked to an *a priori* explicit domain or topic. To this end, an unsupervised clustering algorithm is used to partition the training corpus into *clusters* that are supposed to reflect topics, lexical or stylistic variation within the corpus, depending on the metric used for the clustering. In a first attempt for our experiments, we use K-means, in the `sklearn` implementation, to cluster training sentences. For clustering purpose, sentences are represented by the average of their word embedding vectors. K-means with a euclidean distance is then used to group these representations into K clusters. We use a standard *Kmeans++* initialization. The clustering process is repeated 10 times and the one that produces the

Document Source	# Sentence	# Frame	# FE
D1 Wikipedia WW1	30994	14227	32708
D2 Wikipedia ARCH	27023	9943	19892
D3 Vikidia ANC	5841	85034	3246

Table 1: Description of the CALOR-Frame corpus

minimal intra-cluster inertia is kept. Eventually, the resulting clusters are used as classes that the CNN will be trained to recognize for each corresponding training sentence. The underlying assumption is that the clustering process will capture domain-related regularities and biases that will be harnessed by the adversarial task in order to increase the model's generalization capacities.

4 Evaluation setting

To create an experimental setting that shows the effect of domain on the semantic parsing task, we run experiments on the CALOR-Frame corpus (Marzinotto et al., 2018a), which is a compilation of French encyclopedic documents, with manual FrameNet annotations (Baker et al., 1998). The CALOR-Frame corpus has been designed in the perspective of Information Extraction tasks (automatic filling of Knowledge Bases, document question answering, semantically driven reading comprehension, etc.). Due to the *partial parsing* policy, the CALOR corpus presents a much higher amount of occurrences per Frame (504) than the FrameNet 1.5 corpus (33).

We selected three subsets from the corpus, each one from a different source and/or thematic domain: Wikipedia World War 1 portal (D1), Wikipedia Archeology portal (D2) and Vikidia[1] Ancient history portal (D3). These sources allow to study the impact of both style changes (associated to differences on syntactic structures) and thematic changes (associated to lexical differences).

For the study, we focus on a set of 53 Frames that occur in all the three sub-corpora. Each partition has a different prior on the Frames and lexical units (LUs) distributions. Figure 2 shows the normalized Frame distributions for the three subsets, illustrating the thematic domain dependence. Frames such as *Attack* and *Leadership* are frequent in D1 while *Age* and *Scrutiny* are characteristic Frames for D2. The same analysis can be done using LUs, yielding similar conclusions. We also observe that D2 and D3 are more similar but the difference between these sub-corpora lie more in

---

¹Vikidia is an encyclopedia for children vikidia.org

the syntactic structure of sentences and in the polysemic use of some LU, as will be discussed in the experiments.

5 Results

In these experiments we evaluate the impact of our adversarial training scheme on the semantic frame parser presented in section 3.1. The parser is trained on 80% of the $D1$ and $D2$ corpora and evaluated on the remaining 20%, considered here as *in-domain* data, as well as the whole $D3$ corpus for the *out-of-domain* data. For the domain inference, we use the method presented in section 3.4. Several experiments were made, varying the number of clusters K ($K = 2$, $K = 5$ and $K = 10$). The performance obtained were very similar, the influence of K being negligible in our experiments, therefore we report here only those done with $K = 5$.

We report results using *precision/recall/f-measure* metrics at the *Target*, *Frame* and *Argument identification* levels. The errors are cumulative: to obtain a correct argument identification, we need to have both its frame and target correct. Moreover we use a hard-span metric for argument identification, meaning that both the label and the span have to be correct for an hypothesis to be considered as correct.

Results are given in figure 3 where the precision/recall curve on argument identification is given with and without adversarial training for the in-domain corpus $D1$ and the out-of domain corpus $D3$. Table 2 presents F-measure (F-max) for the 3 identification tasks (target, frame, argument) for $D1$, $D2$ and $D3$.

Figure 3 clearly illustrates the drop in performance between in-domain and out-of-domain corpora. The difference is significant, it accumulates at each step resulting on a 9 points drop in F-max for the argument identification task as shown in table 2. When applying our adversarial method during model training, we clearly increase the generalization capabilities of our model on out-of-domain data ($D3$), as the $biGRU + AC$ curve outperforms the $biGRU$ curve at every operating point in figure 3. This is confirmed on the F-max values for each level in table 2.

Interestingly our adversarial training method not only improves parser performance on out-of-domain data, but also on in-domain data, as shown for $D1$ in figure 3. This improvement is mainly

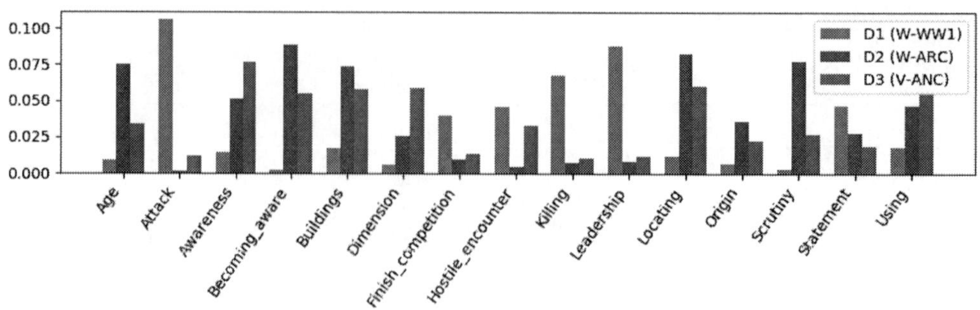

Figure 2: Most frequent frames and their normalized distribution for each partition (from left to right: W-WW1 (D1), W-ARC (D2) and V-ANC (D3))

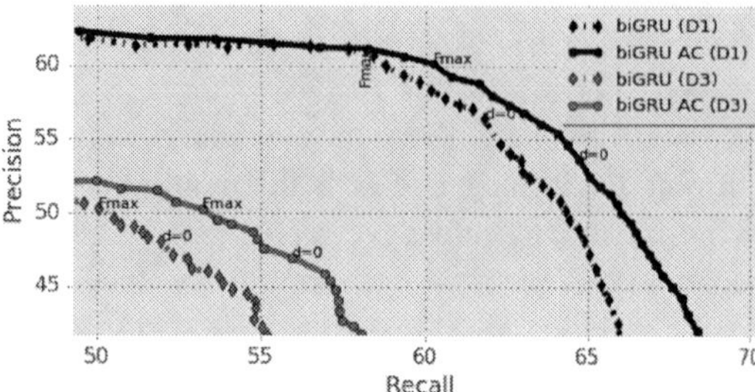

Figure 3: Precision/Recall trade-off with ($biGRU+AC$) and without ($biGRU$) adversarial training on $D1$ (in-domain) and $D3$ (out-of-domain)

due to a gain in recall, and is confirmed on the F-max measures for $D1$ and $D2$ in table 2.

We believe that, since domains are correlated with the lexicon, the adversarial objective pushes the model to rely less on lexical features and to give more importance to features such as syntax and part-of-speech. This is inline with the observation that most of the improvement comes from a higher recall. This can also explain the performance gains on in-domain data. The high dimensionality of word embeddings may have lead to some over-fitting on our initial $biGRU$ model. On the other hand, adversarial learning can act as a regularization technique that makes the model rely as much as possible on domain independent features.

In order to have a better understanding of the behavior of our method we performed two additional contrastive experiments where we used firstly *gold domain labels* instead of inferred ones, and secondly a single domain corpus for training rather than a multi-domain one.

Gold domain labels. We consider here the *true* domain labels for $D1$ and $D2$ as the classes for our adversarial classifier. Therefore only two domains are considered in the adversarial training process. Results are presented in the second part of table 2, in line *biGRU+AC-gold*. As we can see results are very similar to those obtained with automatic clustering ($biGRU+AC$). With an average difference of only 0.3pts (Fmax) for the argument identification task across the different domains. This confirms that our unsupervised clustering approach is as efficient as a supervised domain classification for adversarial learning. Moreover, our approach has the advantage that it can be applied in situations where no domain information is available.

Single-thematic corpus: This contrastive experiment consists in using as training a single-domain corpus. We want to check if the gains obtained on both in and out-of-domain corpora in table 2 hold when the training corpus does not explicitly contain several domains. Here, the models are trained only on the training set from $D1$. We evaluate them on $D1$ (in-domain) and $D2$, $D3$ (out-of-domain). The adversarial task is obtained by running our domain inference algorithm only on $D1$ training set. Here again, we have chosen to partition training data into 5 clusters. Alternative experiments not reported in this paper using only $D2$ as in-domain training data have also been performed and yielded similar conclusions. F-max values reported in table 3 are lower than those of table 2. This is expected as the training corpus considered here is much smaller (only $D1$), however performances follow the same trend: some gains are obtained for all 3 levels both for in and out-of-domain corpora. This is a very interesting result as it shows that there is no need for an explicitly multi-thematic training corpus in order to run the adversarial training and to obtain some

| | Target Identification | | | Frame Identification | | | Argument Identification | | |
| | in-domain | | out-of-domain | in-domain | | out-of-domain | in-domain | | out-of-domain |
	D1	D2	D3	D1	D2	D3	D1	D2	D3
biGRU	97.1	97.5	94.2	93.4	95.4	91.0	59.2	56.3	50.2
biGRU+AC	97.3	98.7	94.7	94.2	95.9	91.9	60.0	57.0	51.7
biGRU+AC-gold	97.7	98.2	94.9	94.9	95.9	92.0	60.1	56.7	51.3

Table 2: F-measure (Fmax) on target, frame and argument identification with (*biGRU+AC*) and without (*biGRU*) adversarial training. Clustering with exact domain labels is given in line *biGRU+AC-gold*

gains in terms of model generalization.

5.1 Error Analysis

5.1.1 Target and Frame Identification

When looking carefully at the generalization capabilities of the initial model, we observed that the frames with the highest performance drops on D3 are those associated to LUs that are polysemous in a general context, but are unambiguous given a thematic domain. For example, *installer (to install)* triggers the frame *Installing* in both D1 and D2, but triggers *Colonization* in D3. Sometimes the confusion comes from changes in the writing style. For example *arriver (to arrive)* means *Arriving* in both D1 and D2, but in D3 it is used as a modal verb (*arriver à* meaning *to be able to*) triggering no frame.Under these circumstances, a model trained on a single domain underestimates the complexity of the frame identification task, mapping the LU to the frame without further analysis of its sense.

When we apply $biGRU + AC$, the gains observed on Frame Identification are not constant across LUs. To analyze the impact of the adversarial approach, we compare for each LU the distribution across clusters of the sentences containing the given LU. This is done separately for D1 and D3 (for D3, sentences are projected into the clusters by choosing the less distant cluster centroid). In table 4, we present the LUs for which the cluster distribution on D1 and D3 are the most dissimilar. These are also the LUs that are the most positively affected by the adversarial strategy.

This means that whenever a LU has similar distribution of context words across the different domains this context information is already exploited by the system to perform frame disambiguation. On the other hand, when the context words of a LU depend on the domain, the model can take advantage of adversarial learning to build a higher level representation that abstracts as much as possible from the lexical variations of the words surrounding the LU.

5.1.2 Argument identification

In this section, we focus on the Frame Argument (or FE for Frame Element) Identification level, and propose contrastive experiments following the complexity factors analysis proposed by (Marzinotto et al., 2018b). In this study, the authors have shown that FE identification is performing better for verbal LU triggers than for nominal ones, and for triggers that are at the root of the syntactic dependency tree. We want to see here how these complexity factors are affected by the adversarial learning strategy. Additionally, we want to see if the system behaves equivalently over core and non-core Frame Elements. Actually, in the usual evaluation Framework of the Framenet 1.5 shared task, non-core FEs are assigned a 0.5 weight for the F-measure computation, reducing the impact of errors on non-core FEs. In this paper, all FEs are rated equally, but here we separate them to observe their behaviour. As we can see in table 5, adversarial training consistently improves the FE identification results, in all conditions. Moreover, bigger gains are observed for the *difficult* conditions.

6 Generalization to PropBank Parsing

We further show that this adversarial learning technique can be used on other semantic frameworks such as Propbank. In PropBank Semantic Role Labeling, CoNLL-2005 uses Wall Street Journal (WSJ) for training and two test corpora. The in-domain (ID) test set is derived from WSJ and the out-of-domain (OOD) test set contains 'general fiction' from the Brown corpus. In published works, there is always an important gap in performances between ID and OOD. Several studies have tried to develop models with better generalization capacities (Yang et al., 2015), (FitzGerald et al., 2015). In recent works, PropBank SRL systems have evolved and span classifier approaches have been replaced by current state of the art sequence tagging models that use recurrent neural networks (He et al., 2017) and neural atten-

	Target Identification			Frame Identification			Argument Identification		
	in-domain	out-of-domain		in-domain	out-of-domain		in-domain	out-of-domain	
	D1	D2	D3	D1	D2	D3	D1	D2	D3
biGRU	97.6	95.5	93.3	93.8	93.4	90.9	58.2	46.1	43.6
biGRU+AC	97.6	95.6	94.3	95.3	94.5	91.2	60.0	47.1	45.2

Table 3: Frame semantic parsing performances (Fmax). Models trained on D1. Adversarial learning with inferred domains $biGRU + AC$.

LU	*biGRU*		*biGRU + AC*	
	D1	D3	D1	D3
arriver	88.2	63.4	91.8	70.0
écrire	96.5	73.3	97.8	88.4
expression	49.8	66.6	56.5	92.4

Table 4: Frame Identification score for LUs with the highest variation in cluster distribution

D3	*biGRU*	*biGRU + AC*
overall	50.2	51.7 (+3%)
core FE	56.5	57.0 (+0.9%)
non-core FE	48.9	50.4 (+3.1%)
verbal trigger	53.4	54.9 (+2.8%)
nominal trigger	34.6	39.0 (+12.7%)
root trigger	59.5	61.3 (+3.0%)
non-root trigger	45.4	47.2 (+4.0%)

Table 5: Frame Element Identification results according to complexity factors on D3 (Fmax)

	ID WSJ	OOD BROWN
(He et al., 2017)	82.4	71.7
(He et al., 2017)+ *AC*	83.0	72.3

Table 6: SRL performance (Fmax) on CoNLL-2005, based on (He et al., 2017) model

tion (Tan et al., 2017; Strubell et al., 2018). However, these parsers still suffer performances drops of up to 12 points in F-measure on OOD with respect to ID. For this experiment we have applied the same adversarial approach over a state-of-the-art Propbank parser (He et al., 2017) using a single straight classifier model. As there is no explicit domain partitions in the training corpus, we apply our inferred domain adversarial task approach, running the clustering algorithm with 5 clusters. We were not able to reproduce the same results as the one published in the paper, we hence provide the results obtained running the downloaded system in our lab. Similarly to the previous FrameNet parsing model, we vary a threshold on the output probabilities of Semantic Roles in order to optimize the F-measure and we provide F-max values, computed using the official evaluation script. We observe in table 6 that the adversarial approach outperforms the original system on both the ID and OOD tests sets.

7 Conclusion

We have presented a study on improving the robustness of a frame semantic parser using adversarial learning. Results obtained on a multi-domain publicly available benchmark, called *CALOR-Frame*, showed that domain adversarial training can effectively be used to improve the generalization capacities of the tagging models, even without prior information about domains in the training corpus. We showed that our technique can be applied to other semantic models, by implementing it into a state-of-the-art PropBank parser and showing some consistent gains. This positive result suggests that our approach could apply successfully to more NLP tasks.

References

Collin F Baker, Charles J Fillmore, and John B Lowe. 1998. The berkeley framenet project. In *Proceedings of the 36th Annual Meeting of the Association for Computational Linguistics and 17th International Conference on Computational Linguistics-Volume 1*, pages 86–90. Association for Computational Linguistics.

Xilun Chen, Yu Sun, Ben Athiwaratkun, Claire Cardie, and Kilian Weinberger. 2016. Adversarial deep averaging networks for cross-lingual sentiment classification. *ArXiv e-prints*.

Alexis Conneau, Guillaume Lample, Marc'Aurelio Ranzato, Ludovic Denoyer, and Hervé Jégou. 2017. Word translation without parallel data. *arXiv preprint arXiv:1710.04087*.

Dipanjan Das, Desai Chen, André FT Martins, Nathan Schneider, and Noah A Smith. 2014. Frame-semantic parsing. *Computational linguistics*, 40(1):9–56.

Yanai Elazar and Yoav Goldberg. 2018. Adversarial removal of demographic attributes from text data. In *EMNLP*.

Nicholas FitzGerald, Oscar Täckström, Kuzman Ganchev, and Dipanjan Das. 2015. Semantic role labeling with neural network factors. In *Proceedings of the 2015 Conference on Empirical Methods in Natural Language Processing*, pages 960–970.

Yaroslav Ganin and Victor Lempitsky. 2014. Unsupervised domain adaptation by backpropagation. *arXiv preprint arXiv:1409.7495*.

Yaroslav Ganin and Victor Lempitsky. 2015. Unsupervised domain adaptation by backpropagation. In *International Conference on Machine Learning*, pages 1180–1189.

Yaroslav Ganin, Evgeniya Ustinova, Hana Ajakan, Pascal Germain, Hugo Larochelle, François Laviolette, Mario Marchand, and Victor Lempitsky. 2016. Domain-adversarial training of neural networks. *Journal of Machine Learning Research*, 17(59):1–35.

Silvana Hartmann, Ilia Kuznetsov, Teresa Martin, and Iryna Gurevych. 2017. Out-of-domain framenet semantic role labeling. In *Proceedings of the 15th Conference of the European Chapter of the Association for Computational Linguistics: Volume 1, Long Papers*, volume 1, pages 471–482.

Luheng He, Kenton Lee, Mike Lewis, and Luke Zettlemoyer. 2017. Deep semantic role labeling: What works and what's next. In *Proceedings of the Annual Meeting of the Association for Computational Linguistics*.

Karl Moritz Hermann, Dipanjan Das, Jason Weston, and Kuzman Ganchev. 2014. Semantic frame identification with distributed word representations. In *ACL (1)*, pages 1448–1458.

Richard Johansson and Pierre Nugues. 2008. The effect of syntactic representation on semantic role labeling. In *Proceedings of the 22nd International Conference on Computational Linguistics (Coling 2008)*, pages 393–400. Association for Computational Linguistics.

Joo-Kyung Kim, Young-Bum Kim, Ruhi Sarikaya, and Eric Fosler-Lussier. 2017. Cross-lingual transfer learning for pos tagging without cross-lingual resources. In *Proceedings of the 2017 Conference on Empirical Methods in Natural Language Processing*, pages 2832–2838. Association for Computational Linguistics.

Pengfei Liu, Xipeng Qiu, and Xuanjing Huang. 2017. Adversarial multi-task learning for text classification. *CoRR*, abs/1704.05742.

Gabriel Marzinotto, Jeremy Auguste, Frédéric Béchet, Géraldine Damnati, and Alexis Nasr. 2018a. Semantic Frame Parsing for Information Extraction : the CALOR corpus. In *LREC 2018*, Miyazaki, Japan.

Gabriel Marzinotto, Frédéric Béchet, Géraldine Damnati, and Alexis Nasr. 2018b. Sources of Complexity in Semantic Frame Parsing for Information Extraction. In *International FrameNet Workshop 2018*, Miyazaki, Japan.

Rebecca J Passonneau, Collin Baker, Christiane Fellbaum, and Nancy Ide. 2012. The masc word sense sentence corpus. In *Proceedings of LREC*.

Darsh J. Shah, Tao Lei, Alessandro Moschitti, Salvatore Romeo, and Preslav Nakov. 2018. Adversarial domain adaptation for duplicate question detection. In *EMNLP*.

Anders Søgaard, Barbara Plank, and Hector Martinez Alonso. 2015. Using frame semantics for knowledge extraction from twitter. In *AAAI*, pages 2447–2452.

Rupesh Kumar Srivastava, Klaus Greff, and Jürgen Schmidhuber. 2015. Training very deep networks. In *NIPS 2015*, pages 2377–2385, Montral, Qubec, Canada.

Emma Strubell, Patrick Verga, Daniel Andor, David Weiss, and Andrew McCallum. 2018. Linguistically-informed self-attention for semantic role labeling. *arXiv preprint arXiv:1804.08199*.

Zhixing Tan, Mingxuan Wang, Jun Xie, Yidong Chen, and Xiaodong Shi. 2017. Deep semantic role labeling with self-attention. *CoRR*, abs/1712.01586.

Bishan Yang and Tom Mitchell. 2017. A joint sequential and relational model for frame-semantic parsing. In *Proceedings of the 2017 Conference on Empirical Methods in Natural Language Processing*, pages 1247–1256. Association for Computational Linguistics.

Haitong Yang, Tao Zhuang, and Chengqing Zong. 2015. Domain adaptation for syntactic and semantic dependency parsing using deep belief networks. *Transactions of the Association for Computational Linguistics*, 3:271–282.

Jianfei Yu, Minghui Qiu, Jing Jiang, Jun Huang, Shuangyong Song, Wei Chu, and Haiqing Chen. 2018. Modelling domain relationships for transfer learning on retrieval-based question answering systems in e-commerce. In *Proceedings of the Eleventh ACM International Conference on Web Search and Data Mining*, pages 682–690. ACM.

TOI-CNN: A Solution of Information Extraction on Chinese Insurance Policy

Lin Sun
Zhejiang University City College
50 Huzhou Street, Hangzhou, China
sun1@zucc.edu.cn

Kai Zhang *
Zhejiang University City College
50 Huzhou Street, Hangzhou, China
31601102@stu.zucc.edu.cn

Fule Ji
Zhejiang University City College
50 Huzhou Street, Hangzhou, China
31601087@stu.zucc.edu.cn

Zhenhua Yang
Shanghai Fortune FIS Co., Ltd.
1687 Changyang Road, Shanghai, China
yangzhenhua@fc18.com.cn

Abstract

Contract analysis can significantly ease the work for humans using AI techniques. This paper shows a problem of Element Tagging on Insurance Policy (ETIP). A novel Text-Of-Interest Convolutional Neural Network (TOI-CNN) is proposed for the ETIP solution. We introduce a TOI pooling layer to replace traditional pooling layer for processing the nested phrasal or clausal elements in insurance policies. The advantage of TOI pooling layer is that the nested elements from one sentence could share computation and context in the forward and backward passes. The computation of backpropagation through TOI pooling is also demonstrated in the paper. We have collected a large Chinese insurance contract dataset and labeled the critical elements of seven categories to test the performance of the proposed method. The results show the promising performance of our method in the ETIP problem.

1 Introduction

Automatic contract analysis can gain immediate insight into the content of specific contractual documents in legal or financial areas (Moens et al., 2000). Compared to the traditional method of manually reviewing hundreds of contracts, it is helpful not only manage and access contracts but also significantly free knowledge workers from menial, laborious and often error-prone tasks. The insurance policy is a legal contract that outlines the rights and obligations of the insured and insurer. It consists of a wide variety of different types of insurance coverages to meet specific needs, although most insurance policies are somewhat standardized. Understanding the various types of insurance coverage is time-consuming and error-prone. This paper shows a problem of Element

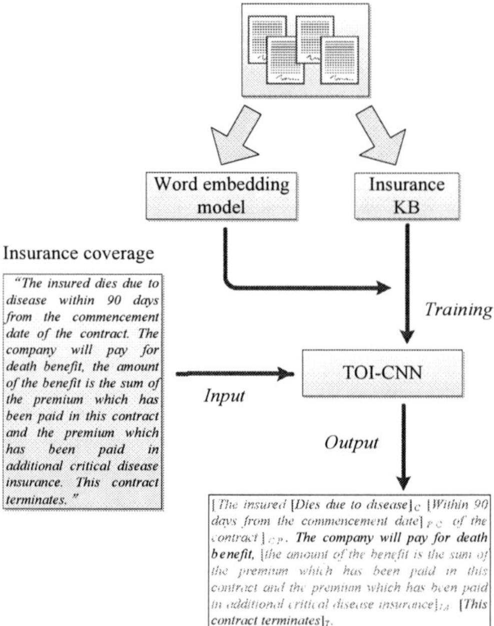

Figure 1: The processing architecture for ETIP.

Tagging on Insurance Policy (ETIP). It can automatically convert a massive amount of insurance policies into structural archives for management and comparison. Due to the vital information highlighted by ETIP, it can also timely provide insurance staff valuable insight into policies, quickly locate requested information and speed up claim processing.

The processing architecture for ETIP is shown in Fig. 1. We have built a large Chinese insurance contract corpus. There are two usages of the corpus. One is for learning word embeddings. In Sec. 5.3, we show the advantage of the insurance-specific corpus over other general language corpora for the training of word embeddings. Another usage of the corpus is to create insurance knowl-

---

Proceedings of NAACL-HLT 2019, pages 174–181
Minneapolis, Minnesota, June 2 - June 7, 2019. ©2019 Association for Computational Linguistics

edge base (KB). Insurance KB, which consists of seven categories of the elements manually labeled by the insurance employees, provides the training data for TOI-CNN model. Specifically, the contributions of this paper can be summarized as follows:

- To our best knowledge, this is the first work on semantic-specific tagging on insurance contracts. Compared to nested NER, not only the type of the elements varies from a short phrase to a long sentence, but also a phrase or clause element could be embedded in other elements.

- We propose a novel TOI-CNN model for the ETIP solution. The advantage of TOI pooling layer is that the elements from the same sentence could share computation and context in the forward and backward passes.

- We have collected 500 Chinese insurance contracts of 46 insurance companies and published the dataset. The experimental results show that the overall performance of TOI-CNN is promising for practical application.

2 Related Work

The work of contract analysis is typically divided into two categories, segmentation and information extraction (IE). Segmentation (Hasan et al., 2008; Loza Mencía, 2009) aims to outline the structure of a conventional text format by annotating title, section, subsection, and so on. Information extraction (Cohen and McCallum, 2004; Piskorski and Yangarber, 2013) focuses on the classification of words, phrases or sentences. Recent works of contract information extraction have addressed recognition of some essential elements in legal documents (Curtotti and Mccreath, 2010; Indukuri and Krishna, 2010). Chalkidis et al. (2017) extracted the contract element, types of which are contract title, contracting parties, date, contract period, legislation refs and so on. The extraction method was based on Logistic Regression, SVM (Chalkidis et al., 2017) and BILSTM (Chalkidis and Androutsopoulos, 2017) with POS tag embeddings and hand-crafted features. García-Constantino et al. (2017) presented the system called CLIEL for extracting information from commercial law documents. CLIEL identified five element categories similar to the literature mentioned in (Chalkidis

et al., 2017) by rule-based layout detection. Azzopardi et al. (2016) developed a mixture extraction method of regular expressions and named entity to extract information from contract clauses, and provided an intelligent contract editing tool to lawyers. Previous works of contract information extraction always focused on title, date, layout, contracting party, etc.. They are not directly related to the semantics of contracts, and could not provide deep insight into contract understanding. The insurance policies are formal legal documents and usually have general elemental compositions, e.g., coverage, payment, and period. In this paper, we investigate how to interpret insurance clauses. Some examples of ETIP are shown in Sec. 3.

The tasks of information extraction could be Named Entity Recognition (NER) (Nadeau and Sekine, 2007; Ritter et al., 2011), Information Extraction by Text Segmentation (IETS) (Cortez and Da Silva, 2013; Hu et al., 2017), etc.. NER typically recognizes persons, organizations, locations, dates, amounts, etc.. IETS identifies attributes from semi-structured records in the form of continuous text, e.g., product description and ads. The previous IE works on contracts (Azzopardi et al., 2016; Chalkidis et al., 2017) are similar to NER.

Recently researchers pushed the field of NER towards nested representations of named entities. Muis and Lu (2017) incorporated mention separators to capture how mentions overlap with one another. Both of two works relied on hand-crafted features. Ju et al. (2018) designed a sequential stack of flat NER layers that detects nested entities. One bidirectional LSTM layer represented word sequences and CRF layer on top of the LSTM layer decoded label sequences globally. Katiyar and Cardie (2018) presented a standard LSTM-based sequence labeling model to learn the nested entity hypergraph structure for an input sentence. Our ETIP problem is a variant of nested NER, called lengthy nested NER. The type of nested entities varies from phrase to clause. However, in the previous nested NER datesets (Kim et al., 2003; Doddington et al., 2004), the type of nested entities only contains short phrase and the average length is approximately three words.

3 ETIP Problem Statement

In this section, we first give the definition of elements tagging on insurance policy (ETIP) problem. Given an insurance coverage $C =$

$(s_1, s_2, ..., s_n)$, where s_i is the ith sentence in C. $s_i = (w_{i,1}, w_{i,2}, ..., w_{i,m})$, where $w_{i,j}$ is the jth word in sentence s_i. An element e in the coverage C is continuous words in one sentence, denoted as $e = \{(w_{i,s}, w_{i,s+1}, ..., w_{i,t}), l\}$, where l is the category label of the element e. The goal of ETIP is to find the element e of category l in the coverage C. We define seven categories of insurance clauses listed as follows,

- Cover (C)
- Waiting Period (WP)
- Period of Coverage (PC)
- Insured Amount (IA)
- Exclusion (E)
- Condition for Payment (CP)
- Termination (T).

Here we give a coverage example in ETIP and translate it for English reading paper. One category is represented by one kind of font color.

> "被保险人于本合同生效之日90天内因疾病身故，本公司给付身故保险金，其金额为本保险实际交纳的保险费与本合同所附的重大疾病保险实际交纳的保险费二者之和，本合同终止。"
>
> *The insured dies due to disease within 90 days from the commencement date of the contract. The company will pay for death benefit, the amount of the benefit is the sum of the premium which has been paid in this contract and the premium which has been paid in additional critical disease insurance. This contract terminates.*

The extractable elements in the example are listed as follows,

- **C**: *dies due to disease*

- **PC**: *within 90 days from the commencement date*

- **CP**: *The insured dies due to disease within 90 days from the commencement date of the contract*

- **IA**: *the amount of the benefit is the sum of the premium which has been paid in this contract and the premium which has been paid in additional critical disease insurance*

- **T**: *This contract terminates.*

In this example, the sentence of CP in red contains the other two elements which are C in purple and PC in green respectively. It is the challenge of ETIP, a general element tagging problem, which allows that the elements of various length could be overlapped. We demonstrate other examples in ETIP along with English translation as follows, where $[\,]_{tag}$ is a category tag labeling the range of an element.

1. [我们向您退还 [本合同终止时]$_T$ 的现金价值]$_{IA}$
   [We refund you the cash value when [this contract terminates]$_T$]$_{IA}$

2. [等待期是指本合同生效后 [平安人寿不承担保险责任]$_E$ 的一段时间]$_{WP}$
   [The waiting period refers to the period of [no obligation for insurance benefits from Ping An life insurance]$_E$ after the contract takes effect]$_{WP}$

3. [若被保险人在本合同生效之日起180日 ([这180日的时间段称为"等待期"]$_{WP}$) 内 [身故]$_C$]$_{CP}$
   [If [the insured died]$_C$ within 180 days ([this 180-day period is called "waiting period"]$_{WP}$) from the commencement date of the contract]$_{CP}$

4. [主合同的保险费 [自给付保险金后的首个保险费约定支付日起]$_{CP}$ 将按被保险人投保年龄的费率及基本保险金额支付]$_{IA}$
   [The insurance benefits of the main contract will be paid [from the date of the first premiums paid after the payment of the insurance benefits]$_{CP}$ according to the premiums rate of the insured's age and the basic insurance amount]$_{IA}$

To illustrate phrasal level of an element, we define a metric, called Element Length Ratio (ELR),

$$ELR = \frac{element\_length}{sentence\_length}. \tag{1}$$

For example, $ELR(C) = 4/16 = 0.25$, $ELR(PC) = 7/16 = 0.44$, $ELR(CP) = 1$ in the previous example. Tab. 1 in experiment section will list the statistics of ELR.

4   TOI-CNN Architecture

Fig. 2 illustrates the TOI-CNN architecture. TOI-CNN takes as input an entire sentence and a set of elements. The network first processes the whole sentence with one convolutional layer (Conv+Relu in Fig. 2) to yield 36 feature maps. Then for each element, the TOI pooling layer extracts a fixed-length feature vector from the feature map. Each feature vector is fed into a sequence of fully connected (fc1) layer that finally connects the output layer, which produces softmax probability estimates over K element classes plus a non-element class.

4.1   The Convolutional Layer

We use the CNN model (Kim, 2014) with pre-trained word embedding (Mikolov et al., 2013) for the convolutional layer. w_i is i-th word in the sentence and is represented as the k-dimensional word embedding vector. The dimension of the input layer is $n \times k$ (padding zeros when the length of the sentence is less than n). Our neural network

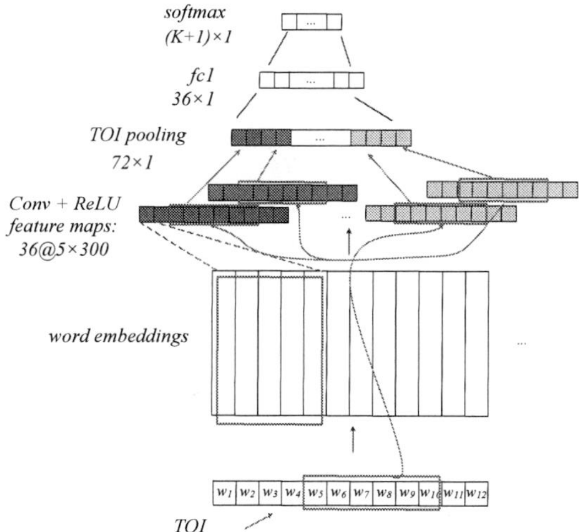

Figure 2: TOI-CNN architecture.

consists of one convolution layer with ReLU activation and one TOI pooling layer, which replaces the max pooling layer of CNN in general. The convolution layer has a set of filters of size $h \times k$ and produces p feature maps of size $(n-h+1) \times 1$.

4.2 The TOI Pooling Layer

The TOI pooling layer uses max pooling to convert the features inside any valid region of an interesting window into a small feature map with a fixed length of L (e.g., $L = 2$ in Fig. 2). Fig. 2 describes the TOI pooling in detail using red lines and rectangles. The TOI pooling layer extracts text region of the elements from the feature maps of the convolutional layer. The TOI region is shown as a red rectangle in the input sentence, shown in Fig. 2. The corresponding TOI window in the feature maps is connected by red curved lines. The length of the TOI window becomes shorter because of the narrow convolution.

TOI max pooling works by dividing the TOI window of length rl into L sub-windows of size $\lfloor rl/L \rfloor$ and then max-pooling the values in each sub-window into the corresponding cell of TOI pooling layer. For example, $rl = 6$ in Fig. 2 and hence the sub-window of size $6/2 = 3$ produce a cell of the pooling layer. Pooling operator is applied independently in each feature map channel. The pooling results of all feature maps are sequentially arranged into a vector, which is followed by the fully connected layer ($fc1$).

4.3 Training Samples of TOI-CNN

In TOI-CNN, training samples include two categories: 1) TOI ground truths, 2) negative sliding windows. A sliding window is defined as negatives, or called non-element class, if IoU (Intersection over Union) with all ground truths of a sentence is less than a threshold th_s. Function $IoU(a, b)$, measuring how much overlap occurs between two text strings a and b, is defined as,

$$IoU(a, b) = \frac{length(a \cap b)}{length(a \cup b)}. \tag{2}$$

4.4 Backpropagation through TOI Pooling Layer

The network is modified to take two data inputs: a set of sentences and a list of training samples in those sentences. Each training sample is given as a one-hot encoding label $p = (0, ..., p_j = 1, ..., 0)$ with a class j . The cross entropy loss L is,

$$L = -log\, p_j^*, \tag{3}$$

where p^* is the output of the softmax layer. Then, we present the derivative rules in backpropagation through the TOI pooling layer.

Let x_i be the i-th activation input into the TOI pooling layer and let $y_{s,j}$ be the layer's j-th output from the s-th training sample. The TOI pooling layer computes $y_{s,j} = max(x_i), x_i \in \mathcal{W}_{s,j}$, where $\mathcal{W}_{s,j}$ is the j-th input sub-window over which max-pooling outputs $y_{s,j}$. Due to overlaps between training samples, a single x_i may be assigned to several different outputs $y_{s,j}$. Let $\mathcal{M}(x_i)$ be the set of $y_{s,j}$ that x_i activates in the TOI pooling layer.

Finally, the TOI pooling layer's backwards function computes partial derivative of the loss function with respect to input variable x_i as follows,

$$\frac{\partial L}{\partial x_i} = \sum_s \sum_j \frac{\partial L}{\partial y_{s,j}}, \quad y_{s,j} \in \mathcal{M}(x_i). \tag{4}$$

The partial derivative $\partial L/\partial y_{s,j}$ is accumulated if $y_{s,j}$ is activated by x_i in TOI max-pooling. In backpropagation, the partial derivatives $\partial L/\partial y_{s,j}$ are already computed by the backwards function of the layer on top of the TOI pooling layer.

5 Experiments

5.1 ETIP Dataset

We collected 500 Chinese insurance contracts, which include life, disability, health, property, home, and auto insurance, where 350 contract-s are regarded as the corpus for training word embeddings (Mikolov et al., 2013) and the other 150 contracts are manually labeled for element tagging testing. The maximum nested level is three in ETIP. The dataset is available online (https://github.com/ETIP-team/ETIP-Project/) without author information. This project cooperated with an information solution provider of China Pacific Insurance Co., Ltd. (CPIC). Tab. 1 shows the number (N), average length ($\overline{L}$) and average element length ratio ($\overline{ELR}$) of seven categories in ETIP dataset. CP and IA are the two largest categories in the dataset. $\overline{ELR}$ of C, PC and E are 0.12, 0.63 and 0.76 respectively, which means that they are usually a phrase or clause embedded in a sentence and C is a 2-3 word phrase. $\overline{ELR}$ of CP, IA, and T are nearly 1.0, which denotes that they are always sentences.

Category ID	N	$\overline{L}$	$\overline{ELR}$
Cover (C)	618	2.6	0.12
Waiting Period (WP)	21	17.6	0.91
Period of Coverage (PC)	186	20.0	0.63
Condition for Payment (CP)	1295	25.5	0.98
Insured Amount (IA)	1068	27.3	0.99
Exclusion (E)	25	12.9	0.76
Termination (T)	398	9.2	0.97

Table 1: Statistics of seven categories in ETIP.

5.2 Experimental Settings

Chinese texts are tokenized with Jieba (Jieba, 2017) or NLPIR (NLPIR, 2018). 300-dimensional word vectors are trained on our insurance corpus. The size of the input layer in the CNN model is 60×300, and zeros are padded if the length of the training sample is less than 60. The kernel size of the convolution layer is 5×300, and the size of the feature maps is 36. the fixed length of TOI pooling layer output is $72 = 2 \times 36$.

The 150 labeled contracts are split into five equal folds, and we use the evaluation procedure in 5-fold cross-validation. Dealing with imbalanced data, the small categories, e.g., WP, E, and PC, are oversampled. The size of mini-batches is 4 sentences, randomly sampling up to 48 negative sliding windows from each sentence. We implement TOI-CNN using PyTorch and run Adam (Kingma and Ba, 2014) optimizer for 50 training epochs with the learning rate of 0.0001.

In the detection, we apply a greedy non-maximum suppression within and between classes simultaneously if two sliding windows positionally intersect but they have no inclusion relation. In within-class suppression, a sliding window is rejected if its length is shorter than the other one. In between-class suppression, a sliding window is rejected if its softmax score is lower than the other one. In performance evaluation, a sliding window is recognized as true positive if IoU over a ground truth is larger than th_p and the predicted label is the same as the ground truth.

5.3 Word Embedding Comparison

350 contracts in ETIP Dataset are regarded as the corpus for training word embeddings (Mikolov et al., 2013). The augmented word2vec model trained by our insurance contract corpus can improve the similarities of the insurance synonyms compared to the models trained by other corpora, e.g., Baidu Encyclopedia (Baidu, 2018), Wikipedia_zh (Wikipedia, 2018), People's Daily News (People's_Daily, 2018). Cosine similarity between word vectors of insurance synonyms is shown in Tab. 2. The Chinese words are translated into English by Google Translate. Tab. 2 shows that the insurance corpus can greatly improve the word embedding similarity between insurance synonyms compared with other corpora.

5.4 Performance of TOI-CNN on ETIP

Tab. 3 shows the confusion matrix computed by TOI-CNN with Jieba word segmentation, where $th_s = 0.5$ and $th_p = 0.8$ The confusion matrix has eight categories, where seven of them are the categories shown in Tab. 1 and the eighth one is negative. Each row of the matrix corresponds to an actual class, and each column of the matrix corresponds to a predicted class. The neg. in the rightmost column denote the ground truths which have been removed from the final candidates, i.e., false negatives. The neg. in the bottom row denote those final candidates who are not the real elements of seven categories, i.e., false positives. PC is more susceptible to negative sliding windows than other categories because PC is always a kind of time description and easily disturbed by other time descriptions in the insurance contracts. Condition for Payment (CP) and Insured Amount (IA) could be confused with each other, because CP sometimes includes coverage amount descriptions like IA.

Tab. 4 shows the results of precision (P), recall (R) and F1 score on seven categories when $th_p =$

	ETIP	Baidu Encyclopedia	Wikipedia_zh	People's Daily News
缴纳(pay) vs 交付(deliver)	0.786	0.457	0.344	0.457
解除(release) vs 撤销(cancel)	0.701	0.347	0.311	0.408
期间(period) vs 有效期(validity period)	0.475	0.247	0.249	0.215
投保人(insured) vs 您(you)	0.752	0.355	0.384	0.247
成立(established) vs 生效(effective)	0.555	0.354	0.335	0.426

Table 2: Examples of word embedding similarity between insurance synonyms.

	C	WP	PC	CP	IA	E	T	neg.
C	519	0	0	0	0	0	0	99
WP	0	11	5	2	0	0	0	3
PC	0	0	108	1	0	0	0	77
CP	0	0	3	1171	33	0	0	89
IA	0	0	0	31	982	1	0	54
E	0	0	0	0	4	16	0	5
T	0	0	0	3	0	1	380	14
neg.	118	0	46	82	9	2	21	/

Table 3: Confusion matrix result of TOI-CNN.

0.8 and word segmentation={Jieba, NLPIR}. The overall performance of Jieba and NLPIR are approximately equal in TOI-CNN model. In TOI-CNN training, we create negative sliding windows using IoU threshold th_s (see Sec. 4.3). Fig. 3 shows F1 score comparison of negative samples generated with varied th_s when $th_p = 0.8$. The performance of $th_s = 0.5$ is better than that of others and close to that of $th_s = 0.6$.

	Jieba			NLPIR		
	P	R	F1	P	R	F1
C	0.811	0.834	0.823	0.30	0.807	0.819
WP	1.00	0.524	0.688	1.00	0.476	0.645
PC	0.667	0.581	0.621	0.659	0.586	0.620
CP	0.908	0.902	0.905	0.910	0.901	0.905
IA	0.955	0.920	0.937	0.951	0.924	0.937
E	0.800	0.640	0.711	0.762	0.640	0.696
T	0.945	0.954	0.950	0.941	0.930	0.936
Avg.	0.887	0.878	**0.883**	0.890	0.866	**0.878**

Table 4: Evaluation results of TOI-CNN on seven categories.

Tab. 5 shows the comparison of F1 scores with nested NER models, where $th_p = 0.8$. We use Jieba for word segmentation and POS tagging. We compare with two public nested NER models, Muis and Lu (2017) and Ju et al. (2018). We have tuned the hyper-parameters of the baselines for the best performance. We chose the best hyper-parameters via Bayesian optimization provided by (Ju et al., 2018). We set the l2-regularization parameter ($\lambda = 0.01$) and the number of Brown clusters ($n = 140$) in (Muis and Lu, 2017). Our TOI-CNN outperforms other models in C, CP, E, and T, and get an excellent result in the overall performance.

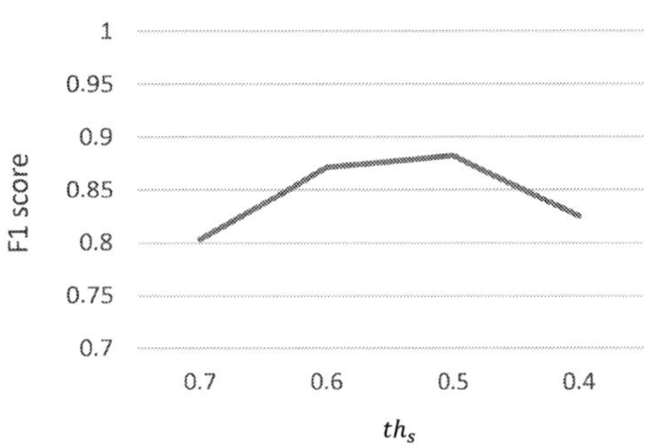

Figure 3: Comparison of negative samples generated with varied th_s.

6 Conclusion

This paper has presented a way of how to tag insurance policies. Seven critical elemental categories in the insurance policy are identified. We collected a large Chinese insurance contract corpus, labeled the samples with seven categories and published the dataset. The proposed TOI-CNN method can effectively solve the overlapping elements extraction problem. The overall performance of TOI-CNN is better than that of the probabilistic graphical models, especially for the overlapped phrases and clauses. Our method can accurately extract the vast majority of Chinese insurance policies according to the pre-defined categories.

7 Acknowledgments

This work was supported by Zhejiang Provincial Natural Science Foundation of China (No.

	C	WP	PC	CP	IA	E	T	Avg.
Muis and Lu (2017)	0.612	0.645	0.759	0.805	**0.947**	**0.711**	0.933	0.832
Ju et al. (2018)	0.808	**0.757**	**0.788**	0.886	0.783	0.664	0.906	0.854
TOI-CNN	**0.823**	0.688	0.621	**0.905**	0.937	**0.711**	**0.950**	**0.883**

Table 5: F1 score comparison with other models.

LY17F020008).

References

Shaun Azzopardi, Albert Gatt, and Gordon J Pace. 2016. Integrating natural language and formal analysis for legal documents. In *10th Conference on Language Technologies and Digital Humanities*, volume 2016.

Baidu. 2018. Baidu encyclopedia. https://baike.baidu.com/.

Ilias Chalkidis and Ion Androutsopoulos. 2017. A deep learning approach to contract element extraction. In *JURIX*, pages 155–164.

Ilias Chalkidis, Ion Androutsopoulos, and Achilleas Michos. 2017. Extracting contract elements. In *Proc. of the 16th Int. Conf. on Artificial Intelligence and Law*, pages 19–28.

William Cohen and Andew McCallum. 2004. Information extraction and integration: an overview. In *SIGKDD Conference*.

Eli Cortez and Altigran S Da Silva. 2013. *Unsupervised information extraction by text segmentation*. Springer.

Michael Curtotti and Eric Mccreath. 2010. Corpus based classification of text in australian contracts.

George R Doddington, Alexis Mitchell, Mark A Przybocki, Lance A Ramshaw, Stephanie Strassel, and Ralph M Weischedel. 2004. The automatic content extraction (ace) program-tasks, data, and evaluation. In *LREC*, volume 2, page 1.

Matías García-Constantino, Katie Atkinson, Danushka Bollegala, Karl Chapman, Frans Coenen, Claire Roberts, and Katy Robson. 2017. Cliel: context-based information extraction from commercial law documents. In *Proceedings of the 16th edition of the International Conference on Articial Intelligence and Law*, pages 79–87. ACM.

Ismael Hasan, Javier Parapar, and Roi Blanco. 2008. Segmentation of legislative documents using a domain-specific lexicon. In *Database and Expert Systems Application, 2008. DEXA'08. 19th International Workshop on*, pages 665–669. IEEE.

Meng Hu, Zhixu Li, Yongxin Shen, An Liu, Guanfeng Liu, Kai Zheng, and Lei Zhao. 2017. Cnn-iets: A cnn-based probabilistic approach for information extraction by text segmentation. In *Proceedings of the 2017 ACM on Conference on Information and Knowledge Management*, pages 1159–1168. ACM.

Kishore Varma Indukuri and P Radha Krishna. 2010. Mining e-contract documents to classify clauses. In *Proceedings of the Third Annual ACM Bangalore Conference*, page 7. ACM.

Jieba. 2017. https://github.com/fxsjy/jieba. Accessed: 2018-05-28.

Meizhi Ju, Makoto Miwa, and Sophia Ananiadou. 2018. A neural layered model for nested named entity recognition. In *Proceedings of the 2018 Conference of the North American Chapter of the Association for Computational Linguistics: Human Language Technologies, Volume 1 (Long Papers)*, volume 1, pages 1446–1459.

Arzoo Katiyar and Claire Cardie. 2018. Nested named entity recognition revisited. In *Proceedings of the 2018 Conference of the North American Chapter of the Association for Computational Linguistics: Human Language Technologies, Volume 1 (Long Papers)*, volume 1, pages 861–871.

J-D Kim, Tomoko Ohta, Yuka Tateisi, and Jun'ichi Tsujii. 2003. Genia corpus—a semantically annotated corpus for bio-textmining. *Bioinformatics*, 19(suppl_1):i180–i182.

Yoon Kim. 2014. Convolutional neural networks for sentence classification. *arXiv preprint arXiv:1408.5882*.

Diederik P Kingma and Jimmy Ba. 2014. Adam: A method for stochastic optimization. *arXiv preprint arXiv:1412.6980*.

Eneldo Loza Mencía. 2009. Segmentation of legal documents. In *Proceedings of the 12th International Conference on Artificial Intelligence and Law*, pages 88–97. ACM.

Tomas Mikolov, Kai Chen, Greg Corrado, and Jeffrey Dean. 2013. Efficient estimation of word representations in vector space. *arXiv preprint arXiv:1301.3781*.

Marie-Francine Moens, Caroline Uyttendaele, and Jos Dumortier. 2000. Intelligent information extraction from legal texts. *Information & Communications Technology Law*, 9(1):17–26.

Aldrian Obaja Muis and Wei Lu. 2017. Labeling gaps between muis2017labelingwords: Recognizing overlapping mentions with mention separators.

In *Proceedings of the 2017 Conference on Empirical Methods in Natural Language Processing*, pages 2608–2618.

David Nadeau and Satoshi Sekine. 2007. A survey of named entity recognition and classification. *Lingvisticae Investigationes*, 30(1):3–26.

NLPIR. 2018. `https://github.com/NLPIR-team/NLPIR`. Accessed: 2018-05-28.

People's_Daily. 2018. News data from people's daily. `http://data.people.com.cn/`.

Jakub Piskorski and Roman Yangarber. 2013. Information extraction: Past, present and future. In *Multi-source, multilingual information extraction and summarization*, pages 23–49. Springer.

Alan Ritter, Sam Clark, Oren Etzioni, et al. 2011. Named entity recognition in tweets: an experimental study. In *Proceedings of the conference on empirical methods in natural language processing*, pages 1524–1534. Association for Computational Linguistics.

Wikipedia. 2018. Chinese wikipedia. `https://dumps.wikimedia.org/`.

Cross-lingual Transfer Learning for Japanese Named Entity Recognition

Andrew Johnson
Saarland University
Saarbrücken, Germany
ajohnson@coli.uni-saarland.de

Penny Karanasou
Amazon
Cambridge, UK
pkarana@amazon.co.uk

Judith Gaspers
Amazon
Aachen, Germany
gaspers@amazon.de

Dietrich Klakow
Spoken Language Systems
Saarland University
Saarbrücken, Germany
dietrich.klakow@lsv.uni-saarland.de

Abstract

This work explores cross-lingual transfer learning (TL) for named entity recognition, focusing on bootstrapping Japanese from English. A deep neural network model is adopted and the best combination of weights to transfer is extensively investigated. Moreover, a novel approach is presented that overcomes linguistic differences between this language pair by romanizing a portion of the Japanese input. Experiments are conducted on external datasets, as well as internal large-scale real-world ones. Gains with TL are achieved for all evaluated cases. Finally, the influence on TL of the target dataset size and of the target tagset distribution is further investigated.

1 Introduction

Due to the growing interest in voice-controlled devices, such as Amazon Alexa-enabled devices or Google Home, porting these devices to new languages quickly and cheaply has become an important goal. One of the main components of such a device is a model for Named Entity Recognition (NER). Typically, NER models are trained on large amounts of annotated training data. However, collecting and annotating the required data to bootstrap a large-scale NER model for an industry application with reasonable performance is time-consuming, costly, and it doesn't scale to a growing number of new languages.

Aiming to reduce the time and costs needed for bootstrapping an NER model for a new language, we leverage existing resources. In particular, we explore *cross-lingual transfer learning*, in which weights from a trained model in the source language are transferred to a model in the target language. Transfer learning (TL) has been shown previously to improve performance for target models (Yang et al., 2017; Lee et al., 2017; Riedl and Padó, 2018). However, work related to cross-lingual transfer learning for NER has mainly focused on rather similar languages, e.g. transferring from English to German or Spanish. In contrast, we focus on transferring between dissimilar languages, i.e. from English to Japanese.

We present experimental results on external, i.e. publicly available, corpora, as well as on internally gathered large-scale real-world datasets. First, a deep neural network model is developed for NER, and we extensively explore which combinations of weights are most useful for transferring information from English to Japanese. Furthermore, aiming to overcome the linguistic and orthographic dissimilarity between English and Japanese, we propose to romanize the Japanese input, i.e. convert the Japanese text into the Latin alphabet. This results in a common character embedding space between the two languages, and intuitively should allow for more efficient transfer learning at the character level.

Gains with TL are achieved on all evaluated target datasets, even large-scale industrial ones. Moreover, the effect of TL on the target dataset size and of the target tagset distribution is investigated. Finally, we show that similar gains are achieved when applying the proposed approach from English to German, indicating the possibility to generalize it both to European and non-European target languages.

The author Andrew Johnson conducted the work for this paper during an internship at Amazon, Aachen, Germany.

Proceedings of NAACL-HLT 2019, pages 182–189
Minneapolis, Minnesota, June 2 - June 7, 2019. ©2019 Association for Computational Linguistics

2   NER model

The growth in neural approaches spurred a push towards "NLP from scratch", that is, without engineering task- or language-specific features by hand (Collobert et al., 2011). Currently, mainly recurrent and/or convolutional neural networks are applied. In Chiu and Nichols (2015), the authors combined a Bi-LSTM to learn long-distance relationships with a CNN to generate character-level representations. A Bi-LSTM-CNN-CRF showed state-of-the-art performance on NER (Ma and Hovy, 2016). CNNs have been shown to be less useful for languages like Japanese, in which average NEs are quite short at around two characters on average (Misawa et al., 2017). Bi-LSTM-CRF models without any CNN layer have also performed well on NER (Huang et al., 2015; Lample et al., 2016). Using this architecture with a novel type of embeddings termed "contextual string embeddings" has recently led to state-of-the-art results (Akbik et al., 2018).

For our baseline NER system we use a Bi-LSTM architecture that takes word and character embeddings as input. The same architecture is used both for the source and the target languages to allow for transfer of weights when the cross-lingual TL is applied. This architecture largely resembles the model in Lample et al. (2016), except for the final CRF layer. For every token, word and character embeddings are generated. The latter are passed through a character Bi-LSTM, the output of which is concatenated with the word embeddings. This combined representation is then passed into the word Bi-LSTM, followed by a dense layer and a final softmax layer. An example for English is presented in Figure 1. Note that the character level inputs in this figure are unigrams, but in practice we use bigrams, i.e. "Ye" and "es" for "Yes".

Although including a CRF as the final layer tends to raise scores overall (Reimers and Gurevych, 2017; Huang et al., 2015), others have demonstrated that transferring CRF weights does not contribute to meaningful gain in the context of TL (Lee et al., 2017). In this work, a CRF layer is not included in the baseline. In another recent work, monolingual Japanese models have used "character-based models", with labels assigned to each individual character (Misawa et al., 2017). We do not employ this approach since our source model in English is not character-based.

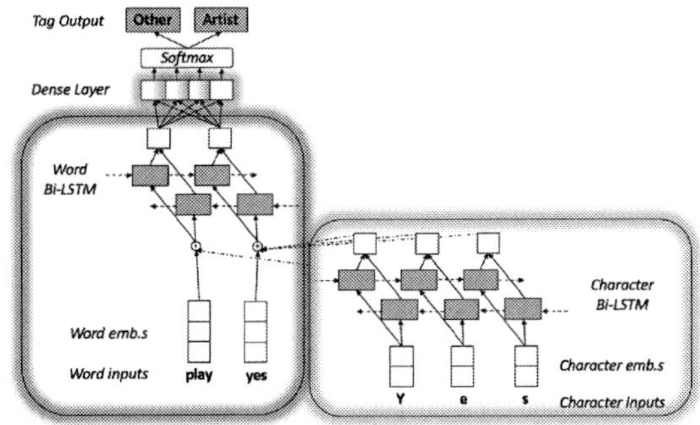

Figure 1: NER model: an English example

3   Transfer Learning

Cross-lingual TL is applied to transfer knowledge from the source to the target language. Working with neural network-based models, this is achieved by initializing some layers of the target network using the weights of the source network, which is assumed to be already trained using a (large) available annotated training corpus.

3.1   Related work

One of the first works on cross-lingual TL for NER that did not rely on parallel corpora used a CRF and included hand-crafted features (Zirikly and Hagiwara, 2015). Currently, most work on TL is done with neural models. Because neural models often consist of multiple layers, one important design decision is which layers to transfer from source to target. Much related work involves only transferring a single layer or specific combination of layers. In Lee et al. (2017) the authors present more thorough results combining lower and higher layers, without transferring intermediate layers though. In Yang et al. (2017) it is suggested to transfer only the character embeddings and the character RNN weights between languages. The reason for this is likely that many languages written in the Latin alphabet have a large charset overlap, but far less vocabulary overlap.

Another question of interest concerns the pair of languages between which TL can be achieved. Past work has shown transferring to a related language to help more than to an unrelated one for NER, POS tagging, and NMT (Zirikly and Hagiwara, 2015; Kim et al., 2017; Dabre et al., 2017). In Yang et al. (2017) it is mentioned that without additional resources, it is "very difficult for transfer learning between languages with disparate alphabets". This background suggests TL from English to Japanese to be non-trivial.

Finally, another consideration with TL is the size of the target dataset. For one NER task, TL gains were shown to decrease to nearly zero as the size of the target training data increased to around 50k tokens (Lee et al., 2017). Similarly, for domain adaptation, a "phase transition" was observed in the amount of used target data, such that using source data was not effective when the target model was trained on 3.13k or more target instances (Ben-David et al., 2010).

3.2 Specificities of Japanese language

Transferring between English and Japanese is more challenging and less explored than transferring between languages with the same alphabet. Japanese is written using an unsegmented mixture of two syllabaries as well as thousands of Chinese characters, which encode semantic information.

A process that we explore in this work to overcome the orthographic dissimilarity is the "romanization" of Japanese text, i.e. the process of transcribing Japanese text into the Latin alphabet. However, when applying romanization we lose the disambiguating effect that characters have. In fact, due to its small phonemic inventory, Japanese contains many homophones. Consider the homophone pairs in Table 1, actual examples taken from our external Japanese dataset. In their original written forms, there is no ambiguity, as there are different characters representing each meaning. This information, which is crucial here to determining which is the NE, is lost after romanization. Empirical results for sentiment classification have confirmed that romanizing Japanese text hurts performance for a monolingual model (Zhang and LeCun, 2017).

押収	欧州	加盟	亀井
oushuu	*oushuu*	*kamei*	*kamei*
to seize	Europe	to join	Kamei [surname]

Table 1: Japanese Homophones

3.3 Proposed model

Since we explore transferring weights from a source network, an important design decision is which layers to transfer. Addressing this question, we evaluate different combinations of layers to find the best one for our task. We group our weights together as shown in Figure 1 (grouped layers in boxes): character embeddings and character Bi-LSTM weights form the "character weights", word embeddings and word Bi-LSTM weights form the "word weights", and dense layer weights form the "dense weights". All possible combinations of these three groups are explored. To account for the incomplete overlap when transferring embeddings, we only update the vectors that correspond to char n-grams or words observed in both the source and target training data. This is a limitation that could be overcome if multi-lingual embeddings were used which we leave for future work.

For transferring to a target language with a different writing system than the source one we propose the *Mixed Orthographic Model* (MOM). Specifically, the character layer inputs are romanized while the word layer inputs are kept in their original Japanese text. This allows for transfer of character information from a source to a target language with originally different writing systems by creating a common and overlapping character embedding space. At the same time, keeping the original Japanese text in the word level allows us to keep the capacity to disambiguate homophones, which is lost via the romanizing process as explained in the previous section (Section 3.2).

Here is an example of the MOM for the utterance "play jazz":

Raw utterance	"ジャズを流して"
Word input	["ジャズ", "を", "流して"]
Character input	["jazu", "wo", "nagashite"] [1]

4 Experimental setup

In this section, the datasets as well as the details of the developed NER model are presented.

4.1 Datasets

For our experiments we make use of datasets in three languages. First, an English dataset is used to train the source NER model. Then, a target language dataset, which is smaller in size than the source dataset, is used to build a target NER model. This serves as the target baseline. The weights transferred from the source model are used to initialize this target model, which is then trained with the available target data, resulting in a new target model. As mentioned before, the focus of this paper is TL between dissimilar languages, and thus the main experiments use a Japanese dataset as the target corpus. However, for the sake

---

[1] Shown prior to conversion into character n-grams

Language	Dataset	Train	Test	Dev
EN	ConLL 2003	14,987	3,684	3,466
JP	BCCWJ	3,600	325	324
	CRF-KNBC	2,940	980	979

Table 2: Number of utterances per external dataset

Language	Dataset	Train	Test	Dev
EN	Large	5M	200k	200k
JP	Large	1M	255k	255k
	Medium	381k	47k	47k
	Small	49.3k	6.2k	6.2k
DE	Large	1M	143.6k	143.6k
	Medium	99.4k	12.4k	12.4k

Table 3: Number of utterances per internal dataset

of comparison, we also conducted some experiments using a German target dataset, thus transferring between more similar languages, i.e. both belonging to the indo-European family, and evaluating the generalization power of the adopted approach.

We evaluate our approach both on external and internal datasets. External datasets are composed of company data and are mainly used for comparing our monolingual models to the state-of-the-art, while internal datasets are composed of publicly available data and are used to explore potential data reductions in a real-world large-scale industry setting.

Segmentation and romanization of Japanese text are performed with the open source Japanese text analyzer MeCab[2].

4.1.1 External data

As external English data, we use the English CoNLL 2003 NER dataset (Tjong Kim Sang and De Meulder, 2003) which contains four named entity (NE) categories.

We make use of three external datasets for Japanese NER. The first one is the Balanced Corpus of Contemporary Written Japanese (BCCWJ) (Iwakura et al., 2016), containing a variety of writing types, such as blogs and magazine articles. In addition, we created a dataset by combining two small Japanese datasets annotated with NEs: i) a small dataset included in the CRF++ tool, and ii) the Kyoto University and NTT Blog Corpus (KNBC) with data from blogs on topics such as tourism, sports, and technology. We are referring to this dataset as "CRF-KNBC".

Most Japanese NER datasets use IREX tags. Similar to CoNLL 2003, IREX 1999 was a shared task for NER and contains eight tags, three of which are the same as in CoNLL. The remaining tags can be viewed as an expansion of ConLL's fourth category, and hence can be grouped together to have the same tagset as CoNLL. We do this to facilitate TL from English.

See Table 2 for details on the external datasets.

<hr>

[2]http://taku910.github.io/mecab/

4.1.2 Internal data

We are mainly interested in exploring TL and the resulting potential data reduction in a large-scale industry setting with different amounts of target data being available, as target data amounts typically increase over time due to continuous data collection. Internal datasets comprise utterances which are representative of user requests to voice-controlled devices and are annotated with NEs. To explore the benefit of TL during different stages of system development, i.e. with availability of different data sources, we include different datasets in our experiments which we distinguish by their size. In particular, we shall refer to any dataset containing over one million utterances as "Large", anything with fewer than one million but more than one hundred thousand as "Medium", and anything with fewer than one hundred thousand utterances as "Small". Note the difference in scale from the external data, the largest of which would still be well below the threshold defined here as small. Following this convention, we have the internal datasets presented in Table 3. None of the smaller datasets are subsets of the larger ones; each is an entirely separate dataset. However, each dataset includes the same kind of data and largely shares the same tagset.

Another major difference from the external datasets is the size of the tagset. Internal data, including both source and target, use over two hundred distinct tags, which are not evenly distributed. In fact, Figure 2 (in log-log scale) shows a very long tail, with the most frequently observed tags belonging to a very small subset of all possible tags. This characteristic makes the internal data a challenging case.

4.2 Model setup

For optimizing our NER models we used Adam (Kingma and Ba, 2014) over cross entropy loss. To avoid overfitting, a dropout layer was used before the Word Bi-LSTM. We lowercase all word-level input. However, since capitalization is a

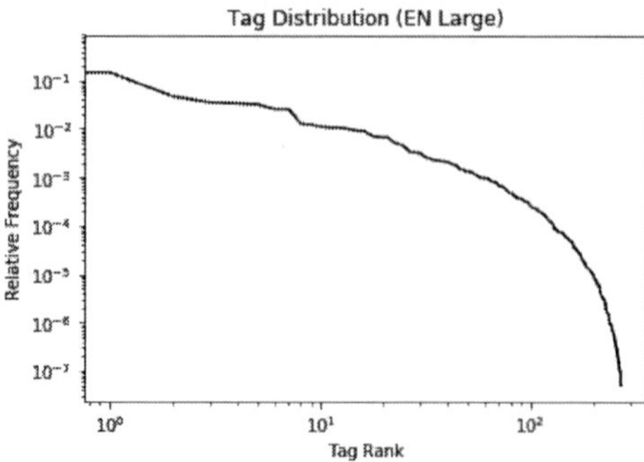

Figure 2: Tag distribution-EN internal training data in log-log scale

| Layers | Corpora | | |
Transferred	BCCWJ	CRF-KNBC	Med.-10k
No TL	65.50	50.48	81.64
Char	+0.34	-2.63	-1.62
Word	+1.50	+0.86	+1.14
Dense	-1.54	+2.86	**+3.77**
Char+Word	-0.09	+1.33	-0.39
Word+Dense	+0.63	**+4.69**	+1.95
Char+Dense	**+3.86**	+3.74	+3.72
Char+Word +Dense	+2.35	+3.92	-0.02

Table 4: Absolute gains on JP datasets by transferring different layer combinations

feature that strongly predisposes a word to be an NE, we did not lowercase the character-level input. No pre-trained word embeddings were used with internal datasets, while external datasets used Polyglot word embeddings (Al-Rfou et al., 2013). The word embedding dimensionality was 50, except where Polyglot pre-trained embeddings were used, in which case it was 64. The word LSTM size was set to 300. Character embeddings were 50-dimensional and character bigrams were used. The character LSTM was of size 100 for external datasets and 30 for internal ones. Dropout was set to 0.5. We used the evaluation script from the CoNLL shared task to compute F1 score.

During the parameter tuning phase, development set performance stabilized after 10 epochs for external models and 20 epochs for internal models. Therefore, we conduct experiments on the test set by training for these respective number of epochs. The scores reported for each model reflect the highest F1 value among all epochs.

5 Results

5.1 Layer combinations for TL

We first investigate which layer combination yields best results when being transferred. The layer groups defined in Section 3.3 are combined and experiments are conducted on the two external JP datasets as well as on a subset of the JP "Medium" internal one. The results are presented in Table 4 as absolute gains against the baseline without TL. Approximate randomization is used for each experiment (Noreen, 1989; Yeh, 2000), and all TL gains were found to be significant to p<0.001. The results reported are the average of running experiments five times with different random seeds. In all experiments, the system configuration detailed in Section 4.2 is followed and the

MOM (see Section 3.3) is applied.

The best performing combination (in bold) varies between datasets. However, the "Char+Dense" combination seems to be the most reliable one, providing consistent and significant TL gains over all three evaluated corpora. This combination is different than what was previously reported in litterature (Yang et al., 2017), where it was suggested that transferring character level weights suffices. This might be because of the specific nature of our task on transferring weights between languages with dissimilar alphabets. In our case transferring word weights actually performs better than transferring character weights (compare rows "Word" and "Char"). In addition, combining the weights at word or character levels with the next dense layer weights improves further the results (rows "Word+Dense" and "Char+Dense") indicating that this dense layer still captures some language-independent information.

Due to these results, we use the "Char+Dense" combination in the following experiments.

5.2 Effect of romanization of Japanese on TL

The effect of romanization of Japanese is evaluated on one external ("BCCWJ") and a subset of an internal ("Med.-10k") JP dataset. Results are presented in Table 5 with and without romanization before and after TL, and consistent gains are shown when MOM is used with TL. In addition, there are significant gains when used without TL in the case of the internal dataset ("Med.-10k"). To the best of our knowledge, this is the first work introducing the MOM and comparing these approaches for Japanese in the context of TL. Since this model gives consistently improved results with TL, all the remaining results on Japanese data will employ this approach.

Dataset		No roman.	MOM
BCCWJ	No TL	**67.31**	65.50
	With TL	69.08	**69.36**
Med.-10k	No TL	80.65	**81.64**
	With TL	84.12	**85.36**

Table 5: Romanization of Japanese - Effect on TL

Dataset	No TL	With TL	Rel. gain
BCCWJ	65.50	**69.36**	+5.89
CRF-KNBC	50.48	**54.22**	+7.41
Small	83.15	**84.85**	+2.04
Medium	91.64	**92.20**	+0.61
Large	91.66	**92.21**	+0.60
DE Medium	87.82	**88.86**	+1.18
DE Large	89.24	**89.63**	+0.44

Table 6: Results with TL over full JP and DE datasets

5.3 TL on external and internal datasets

Applying the best configuration established previously, i.e. transfer "Char+Dense" layers and use of MOM, the results before and after TL on the full JP datasets are presented in Table 6. Gains with TL are achieved in all evaluated datasets. Moreover, with MOM and TL, we achieve state-of-the-art NER results on BCCWJ, outperforming Ichihara et al. (2015) (reported F1 score 67.68% vs. ours 69.36%). In addition, important relative gains are achieved by TL in the small external datasets, making our method particularly suited for bootstrapping a new language with very limited available annotated data. Another interesting outcome is that we still see gains in the large internal datasets (i.e. up to 1M training utterances in the internal "Large" set). This will be investigated further in the next section (Section 5.4).

Results on DE internal datasets are presented for sake of comparison and show the same trends as JP internal datasets, thus revealing the generalization of our approach for cross-lingual TL both to European and non-European target languages.

5.4 Effect of target dataset size on TL

To further investigate how the size of the target datasets influences the performance of TL, we conducted experiments on different sizes of the internal data. This was done by training on subsets of the original "Large" JP internal training set, with sizes varying from 10k to 1M utterances. Note that the source English training data is still used in full each time. The results are presented in Figure 3. As expected, larger gains are observed for smaller splits. However, TL still produces statistically significant gains for all split sizes. Note

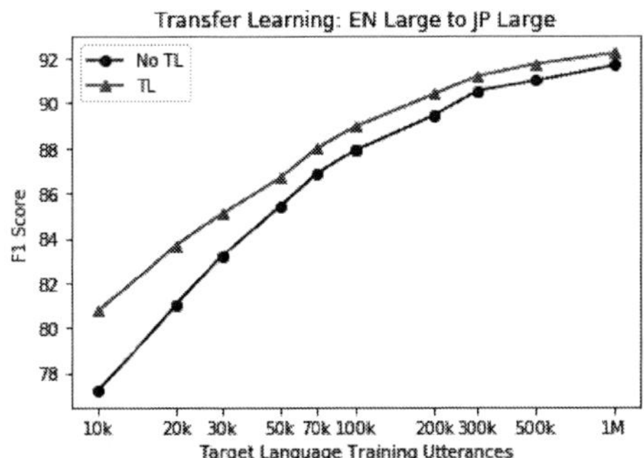

Figure 3: Applying TL on varying target training size

also that training, for example, on 500k utterances with TL is better than training on 1M utterances without TL, indicating the possibility of reducing data requirements with TL even in large-scale industrial systems.

A further analysis of the results on the internal datasets showed that the frequency of a tag class in the target training data correlated the most with TL gain. This is visualized in Figure 4 for a subset of the JP "Small" dataset. An arrow is used for each tag class with the tail of the arrow indicating the F1 score without TL and the point indicating the F1 score of that same class with TL. Thus, classes with gains point upward (blue arrows), while those that performed worse point downwards (red arrows). Classes that showed no change are indicated as circles. These mostly cluster along the bottom as classes that have an F1 score of zero before and after TL. The tags are arranged along the x axis based on their frequency in the target training dataset.

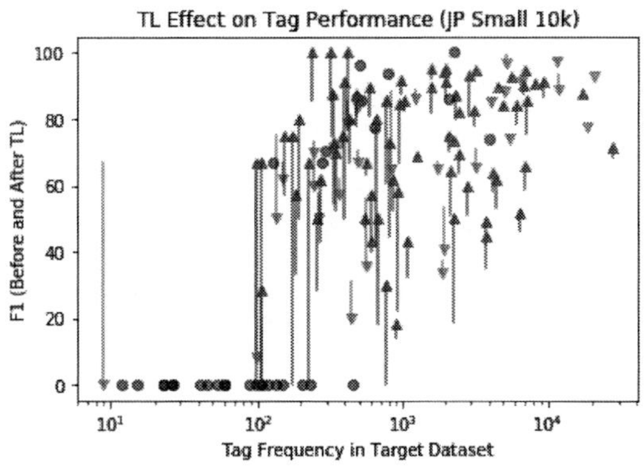

Figure 4: Gains by tag

This figure indicates that frequent tags (rightmost part of the figure) gain less by TL, probably because they already perform well. Tag classes generally begin to show gains from TL only after they pass a certain *minimum frequency threshold* in the target dataset, which appears to be around 100. This may be the reason why we have TL gains even with large target datasets. As infrequent tag classes are observed more and more in larger splits, they begin to cross this threshold and gain from TL. Real-world data generally have long-tailed distributions, thus even very large target datasets are likely to have tag classes with few data which can benefit from TL.

6 Conclusions

A cross-lingual transfer learning approach for NER was proposed, focusing on dissimilar languages, i.e. English and Japanese. A deep neural network model was adopted and the best layer combination to transfer was extensively investigated. To overcome the orthographic dissimilarity between source and target languages a novel method, the MOM, was proposed that romanizes part of the Japanese input. Gains with TL were consistently achieved on external and large-scale real-world datasets showing that it is possible to transfer knowledge between dissimilar languages, even for large target corpora.

In the future, the proposed approach could be applied to other dissimilar language pairs, e.g. English and Chinese. Other possible extensions include using multi-lingual embeddings that could complement the currently transferred weights.

References

Alan Akbik, Duncan Blythe, and Roland Vollgraf. 2018. Contextual string embeddings for sequence labeling. In *Proceedings of the 27th International Conference on Computational Linguistics*, pages 1638–1649.

Rami Al-Rfou, Bryan Perozzi, and Steven Skiena. 2013. Polyglot: Distributed word representations for multilingual nlp. In *Proceedings of the Seventeenth Conference on Computational Natural Language Learning*, pages 183–192. Association for Computational Linguistics.

Shai Ben-David, John Blitzer, Koby Crammer, Alex Kulesza, Fernando Pereira, and Jennifer Wortman Vaughan. 2010. A theory of learning from different domains. *Machine learning*, 79(1-2):151–175.

Jason PC Chiu and Eric Nichols. 2015. Named entity recognition with bidirectional lstm-cnns. *arXiv preprint arXiv:1511.08308*.

Ronan Collobert, Jason Weston, Léon Bottou, Michael Karlen, Koray Kavukcuoglu, and Pavel Kuksa. 2011. Natural language processing (almost) from scratch. *Journal of Machine Learning Research*, 12(Aug):2493–2537.

Raj Dabre, Tetsuji Nakagawa, and Hideto Kazawa. 2017. An empirical study of language relatedness for transfer learning in neural machine translation. In *Proceedings of the 31st Pacific Asia Conference on Language, Information and Computation*, pages 282–286.

Zhiheng Huang, Wei Xu, and Kai Yu. 2015. Bidirectional lstm-crf models for sequence tagging. *arXiv preprint arXiv:1508.01991*.

Masaaki Ichihara, Kanako Komiya, Tomoya Iwakura, and Maiko Yamazaki. 2015. Error analysis of named entity recognition in bccwj. *Recall*, 61:2641.

Tomoya Iwakura, Kanako Komiya, and Ryuichi Tachibana. 2016. Constructing a japanese basic named entity corpus of various genres. In *Proceedings of the Sixth Named Entity Workshop*, pages 41–46.

Joo-Kyung Kim, Young-Bum Kim, Ruhi Sarikaya, and Eric Fosler-Lussier. 2017. Cross-lingual transfer learning for pos tagging without cross-lingual resources. In *Proceedings of the 2017 Conference on Empirical Methods in Natural Language Processing*, pages 2832–2838.

Diederik P Kingma and Jimmy Ba. 2014. Adam: A method for stochastic optimization. *arXiv preprint arXiv:1412.6980*.

Guillaume Lample, Miguel Ballesteros, Sandeep Subramanian, Kazuya Kawakami, and Chris Dyer. 2016. Neural architectures for named entity recognition. *arXiv preprint arXiv:1603.01360*.

Ji Young Lee, Franck Dernoncourt, and Peter Szolovits. 2017. Transfer learning for named-entity recognition with neural networks. *arXiv preprint arXiv:1705.06273*.

Xuezhe Ma and Eduard Hovy. 2016. End-to-end sequence labeling via bi-directional lstm-cnns-crf. *arXiv preprint arXiv:1603.01354*.

Shotaro Misawa, Motoki Taniguchi, Yasuhide Miura, and Tomoko Ohkuma. 2017. Character-based bidirectional lstm-crf with words and characters for japanese named entity recognition. In *Proceedings of the First Workshop on Subword and Character Level Models in NLP*, pages 97–102.

Eric W Noreen. 1989. *Computer-intensive methods for testing hypotheses*. Wiley New York.

Nils Reimers and Iryna Gurevych. 2017. Optimal hyperparameters for deep lstm-networks for sequence labeling tasks. *arXiv preprint arXiv: 1707.06799*.

Martin Riedl and Sebastian Padó. 2018. A named entity recognition shootout for german. In *Proceedings of the 56th Annual Meeting of the Association for Computational Linguistics (Volume 2: Short Papers)*, volume 2, pages 120–125.

Erik F Tjong Kim Sang and Fien De Meulder. 2003. Introduction to the conll-2003 shared task: Language-independent named entity recognition. In *Proceedings of the seventh conference on Natural language learning at HLT-NAACL 2003-Volume 4*, pages 142–147. Association for Computational Linguistics.

Zhilin Yang, Ruslan Salakhutdinov, and William W Cohen. 2017. Transfer learning for sequence tagging with hierarchical recurrent networks. *arXiv preprint arXiv:1703.06345*.

Alexander Yeh. 2000. More accurate tests for the statistical significance of result differences. In *Proceedings of the 18th conference on Computational linguistics-Volume 2*, pages 947–953. Association for Computational Linguistics.

Xiang Zhang and Yann LeCun. 2017. Which encoding is the best for text classification in chinese, english, japanese and korean? *arXiv preprint arXiv:1708.02657*.

Ayah Zirikly and Masato Hagiwara. 2015. Cross-lingual transfer of named entity recognizers without parallel corpora. In *Proceedings of the 53rd Annual Meeting of the Association for Computational Linguistics and the 7th International Joint Conference on Natural Language Processing (Volume 2: Short Papers)*, volume 2, pages 390–396.

Neural Text Normalization with Subword Units

Courtney Mansfield†, Ming Sun‡, Yuzong Liu⋆, Ankur Gandhe⋆, Björn Hoffmeister⋆
†University of Washington, Seattle, WA, USA
`coman8@uw.edu`
‡Amazon Alexa AI, Seattle, WA, USA
`suming@amazon.com`
⋆Amazon Alexa Speech, Seattle, WA, USA
`{liuyuzon,aggandhe,bjornh}@amazon.com`

Abstract

Text normalization (TN) is an important step in conversational systems. It converts written text to its spoken form to facilitate speech recognition, natural language understanding and text-to-speech synthesis. Finite state transducers (FSTs) are commonly used to build grammars that handle text normalization (Sproat, 1996; Roark et al., 2012). However, translating linguistic knowledge into grammars requires extensive effort. In this paper, we frame TN as a machine translation task and tackle it with sequence-to-sequence (seq2seq) models. Previous research focuses on normalizing a word (or phrase) with the help of limited word-level context, while our approach directly normalizes full sentences. We find subword models with additional linguistic features yield the best performance (with a word error rate of 0.17%).

1 Introduction

Non-standard words (NSWs) include expressions such as time or date (e.g., 4:58AM, 08-02, 8/2/2018), abbreviations (e.g., ft.) and letter sequences (e.g., IBM, DL) (Sproat et al., 2001). They commonly appear in written texts such as websites, books and movie scripts. *Written* form of non-standard words can be normalized/verbalized to a *spoken* form, e.g., "August second".

Although there is no incentive for human users to transcribe NSWs into spoken form, it plays an integral role in spoken dialog systems. As shown in Figure 1, automatic speech recognition (ASR), natural language understanding (NLU) and text-to-speech synthesis (TTS) components all involve written-to-spoken form normalization or its inverse process, spoken-to-written text normalization (ITN). ASR normalizes the training corpus before building its language model. Among many benefits, such a model can reduce the size of the required vocabulary and address data sparsity issues. NLU might adopt ITN to recover the written text from ASR in run-time (e.g., "five p m " → "5:00PM"). In text-to-speech synthesis, for example, in order to pronounce "221B Baker St", TTS needs to first convert the text to "two twenty one b baker street" and then generate the audio signal.

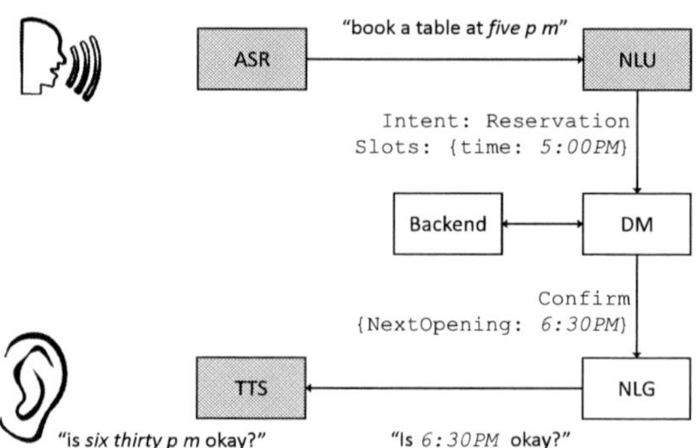

Figure 1: Text normalization in spoken dialog systems. Grey boxes involve text normalization or inverse text normalization.

Normalizing the written form text to its spoken form is difficult due to the following bottlenecks:

1. Lack of supervision — there is no incentive for people to produce spoken form text. Thus, it is hard to obtain a supervised dataset for training machine learning models;

2. Ambiguity — for written text, a change in context may require a different normalization. For example, "2/3" can be verbalized as a date or fraction depending on the meaning of the sentence.

Traditionally, the task of NSW normalization has been approached by manually authoring grammars in the form of finite-state transducers (Sproat, 1996; Roark et al., 2012) such

Proceedings of NAACL-HLT 2019, pages 190–196
Minneapolis, Minnesota, June 2 - June 7, 2019. ©2019 Association for Computational Linguistics

as integer grammars (e.g., "26" → "twenty six") or time grammars (e.g., "5:26" → "five twenty six"). Constructing such grammars is time consuming and error-prone and requires extensive linguistic knowledge and programming proficiency. Recently, with the rise of machine learning and especially deep learning techniques, researchers are starting to bring more data-driven approaches to this field (Sproat and Jaitly, 2016).

In this paper, we present our approach to non-standard text normalization via machine translation techniques, where the source and target are written and spoken form text, respectively.

2 Related work

2.1 Finite state transducer

Normalizing written-form text to its spoken form has been approached by authoring weighted finite state transducer (WFST) grammars to handle individual categories of NSW (e.g., time, date) and subsequently join them together (Sproat, 1996; Roark et al., 2012). One bottleneck to this approach is the heavy demand of translating linguistic knowledge into WFSTs. A second problem is a lack of context awareness. For example, "dr." may refer to "doctor" or "drive" in different contexts. We have observed accuracy improvements by using an n-gram LM to re-rank hypotheses generated by WFSTs. However, an n-gram LM's context awareness is limited.

2.2 Data-driven approaches

Recently, methods based on neural networks have been applied to TN and ITN (Sproat and Jaitly, 2016; Pusateri et al., 2017; Yolchuyeva et al., 2018). To overcome one of the biggest problems — a lack of supervision, WFSTs have been used to transform large amounts of written-form text to its spoken form. Researchers hope a vast amount of such data can counteract the errors inherited in WFST-based models.

Recent data-driven approaches examine window-based sequence-to-sequence (seq2seq) models and convolutional neural networks (CNN) to normalize a central piece of text with the help of context (Sproat and Jaitly, 2016; Yolchuyeva et al., 2018). Window-based methods have the advantage of limiting the output vocabulary size, as most tokens that do not need to be transformed are labeled with a special <self> token.

Hybrid neural/WFST models have also been proposed and applied to the text normalization problem (Pusateri et al., 2017; Yolchuyeva et al., 2018). Tokens in the input are first tagged with labels using machine learned models whereupon a handcrafted grammar corresponding to each label conducts conversion. In both methods, a tagger is needed to first segment/label the input tokens and conversion must be applied to each segment to normalize a full sentence. Our seq2seq model does not require the aforementioned tagger (although could benefit from the tagger as we will show later) and directly translates a written-form sentence to its spoken form without grammars.

3 Model

3.1 Baseline models

Following Sproat and Jaitly (2016), we implement a seq2seq model trained on window-based data. Table 1 illustrates the window-based model's training examples corresponding to one sentence "wake me up at 8 AM ." which is broken down into 6 pairs. <n> and </n> indicate the center of the window. A window center might contain 1 or more words (e.g., "8 AM") and the grouping is provided by the dataset where each input sentence is segmented into chunks corresponding to labels such as TIME, DATE, ORDINAL (Sproat and Jaitly, 2016). The model outputs tokens which correspond to the center of the window.

Table 1: In the window-based configuration, <n> and </n> denote the center of the window. <self> indicates transforming the central piece to itself. This example illustrates a window size of 1.

Input	Output
<n> wake </n> me	<self>
wake <n> me </n> up	<self>
me <n> up </n> at	<self>
up <n> at </n> 8AM	<self>
at <n> 8 AM </n> .	eight a m
AM <n> . </n>	<sil>

The model architecture is similar to Chan et al. (2016) and uses attention to align the output tokens with input characters as in Bahdanau et al. (2014). The encoder takes character sequences as input. Otherwise, sequences of numbers or dates (e.g., 2018-08-04) are hard to interpret. On the output side, we believe various granularities such as character, word or word fragments can be suitable. Following the literature, we used a word level decoder.

A window-based seq2seq model, although able to attend well to a central piece of text, is not practical for applying over a whole sentence. To extend the model to full sentences, we break source sentences into segments. We then apply the model to one segment after another and concatenate their output tokens to produce full sentences.

As our second baseline, a seq2seq model is trained with full sentence data. As a result, it does not require any pre-processing step to generate windows of text. It directly translates a sentence to its spoken form. Again, the encoder works at the character level while the decoder output sequences of words while attention is used to align the input and output sequences.

3.2 Proposed model

There are several issues with the baseline seq2seq models. First of all, although there is no out-of-vocabulary (OOV) problem on the input side since it is modeled as a sequence of characters, the decoder has an OOV issue–we cannot model every possible token. The window-based seq2seq adopts a special output token <self> that significantly reduces the output vocabulary size. This is not practical in the full sentence baseline as it requires the additional step of mapping each <self> in the output to a word in the input.

Subwords have been shown to work well in open-vocabulary speech recognition and machine translation tasks (Sennrich et al., 2015; Qin et al., 2011). Subwords (i.e., a grouping of one or more characters) capture frequently co-occurring character combinations. For example, the word "subword" might be decomposed into two parts: "_sub" and "word", where "_" indicates the start of a word. An extreme case of the subword model is a character model. Compared with only characters, we believe segmenting input/output into subwords eases a seq2seq model's burden of modeling long-distance dependencies.

3.2.1 Linguistic features

Sennrich and Haddow (2016) have shown that the addition of linguistic features can improve the quality of neural machine translation models. We observe that features such as casing and part-of-speech tags can also provide helpful insights into how a NSW should be normalized. For example, "US" should be normalized to "u s" instead of "us". Similarly, part-of-speech tags can help the model decide how to verbalize ambiguous forms such as "resume", which is kept as-is as a verb or read out as "résumé" as a noun. In regards to subwords, it is important to know where the fragment comes from — beginning, middle, end of a word or the full word. For example, "id" should be normalized as "id" if it comes from the beginning of a word like "idea". However, it could also be verbalized as "i d" when taken as a standalone word.

In this paper, we explore linguistic features that are inexpensive to compute such as casing, POS, and positional features. We also use the edit labels from Google's dataset (e.g., TIME, DATE) although we acknowledge these labels are expensive and often times not accessible.

4 Experiments and results

4.1 Dataset

The data for the window-based seq2seq model and full sentence seq2seq were generated from the publicly available release of parallel written/speech formatted text from Sproat and Jaitly (2016). The set consists of Wikipedia text which was processed through Google TTS's Kestrel text normalization system relying primarily on hand-crafted rules to produce speech-formatted text.

Although a large parallel dataset is available for English, we consider the feasibility of developing neural models for other languages which may not have text normalization systems in place. Therefore, we choose to scale the training data size to a limited set of text which could be generated by annotators in a reasonable time frame. As summarized in Table 2, both window-based and sentence-based models are trained with 500K training instances.

Our datasets were randomly sampled from a set of 4.9M sentences in the training data portion of the Sproat and Jaitly (2016) data release and split into training, validation, and test data. However, the training data for window-based and sentence-based models are not identical due to differences in input configurations. While the window-based model uses 500K randomly sampled windows, the sentence-based models use 500K sentences. For testing, 62.5K identical test sentences are used across all models. In order to decode sentences with the window-based model, sentences are first segmented into windows before inference.

Among 16 edit labels available in the dataset release, we found the normalization target for

Table 2: Size of training, validation, and test datasets. For the window-baseline, the data are pairs of windows and the normalization of the central piece of the window. For the sent-baseline and subword models, the data are pairs of sentences but in different formats — sent-baseline: (character sequence, word sequence); subword: (subword sequence, subword sequence). All models are evaluated on the same set of 62.5K sentences.

Model	Train	Valid	Test
Window-baseline	500K	62.4K	62.5K
Sent-baseline	500K	62.5K	62.5K
Subword	500K	62.5K	62.5K

ELECTRONIC text is not suitable for our system as it primarily reads out URLs letter by letter, e.g., "Forbes.com" → "f␣o␣r␣b␣e␣s␣dot␣c␣o␣m" (as opposed to "forbes dot com"). Therefore, we exclude ELECTRONIC data in our experiments. There are large numbers of <self> tokens present in the dataset. We follow Sproat and Jaitly (2016) in down-sampling window-based training data to constrain the proportion of "<self>" tokens to 10% of the data.

For training sentence-based models, the source sentence is segmented into characters while the target sentence is broken into tokens. For the subword model, both the source and target sentences are segmented into subword sequences. Subword units are concatenated to words for evaluation.

4.2 Baseline model setup

Our first approach replicates the window-based seq2seq model of Sproat and Jaitly (2016). The model encodes the central piece of text (1 or more tokens) including its context of N previous and following tokens at the character level. The output is a target token or a sequence of tokens. The input vocabulary consists of 250 common characters including letters, digits and symbols (e.g., $). The decoder vocabulary consists of 1K tokens including <self> and <sil>, the latter of which is used to normalize punctuation.

Following Chan et al. (2016), we use a stacked (2-layer) bi-directional long short term memory network (bi-LSTM) as encoder and a stacked (2-layer) LSTM as decoder. We use 512 hidden states for the (bi-)LSTM. A softmax output distribution is computed over output vocabulary at each decoding step. Decoding uses the attention mechanism from Bahdanau et al. (2014) and a beam size of 5.

Word and character embeddings are trained from scratch.

We use the OpenNMT toolkit (Klein et al., 2017) to train our models on a single P2.8xlarge Amazon EC2 instance. Models were trained with Stochastic Gradient Descent (SGD) on 200K timesteps (approximately 13 epochs). Approaching 200K timesteps, a significant decay in accuracy and plateau in perplexity of the validation set occurred for all models. Validation occurred every 10K timesteps and the number of timesteps was chosen based on maximum accuracy on the validation data. The learning rate was tuned to 1.0 for the window-based model and 0.5 for sentence-based models to achieve optimal performance. Learning rate decayed at a rate of 0.5 if perplexity on the validation set did not decrease or after 50K steps. A dropout of 0.3 was used across all models.

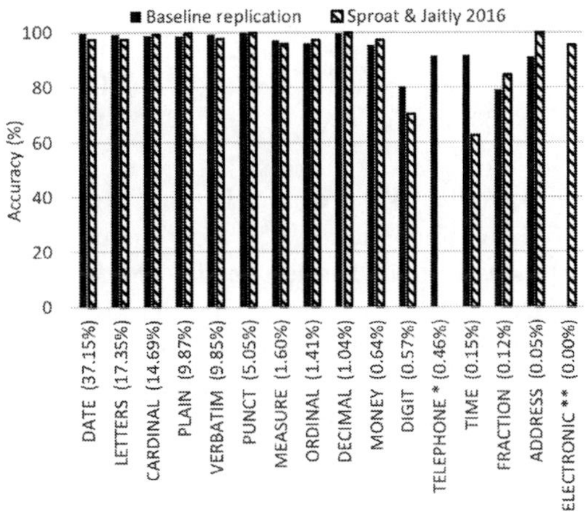

Figure 2: Evaluation of the window-based model. Categories are sorted by frequency. * TELEPHONE is not reported in Sproat and Jaitly (2016) but included in the dataset; ** we removed ELECTRONIC category.

As shown in Figure 2, our replicated window-based model achieves reasonable performance compared with Sproat and Jaitly (2016), considering our training set is much smaller. There are 16 different edit labels shown. Data with TELEPHONE labels were not included in the initial analysis of Sproat and Jaitly (2016), but were made available in the dataset release.

For our second baseline model which operates on whole sentences, on the input side, we still use 250 common characters. However, due to the removal of the <self> token, the output space is drastically extended from 1K tokens to 45K tokens. Thus, it becomes increasingly difficult for the model to learn and predict.

4.3 Subword inventory

A subword inventory can be populated by data-driven approaches such as Byte Pair Encoding (BPE) (Sennrich et al., 2015). Text is first split into character sequences and the most frequently co-occurring units are greedily merged into one subword unit. This procedure continues until the desired subword inventory size is reached. Here, we enforce that two units cannot be merged if they cross a word boundary.

Table 3: Performance of different subword inventory sizes on validation set.

Inventory size	SER (%)	WER (%)
16K	3.56	0.92
8K	3.49	0.92
4K	3.34	0.90
2K	3.20	**0.87**
1K	**3.17**	0.90
500	3.53	1.01

To avoid OOV words, we also populate the subword inventory with the 250 most common characters used in the baseline model and digits 0-9. In data preparation, we force the subword model to split digits into a single subword piece (e.g., "1234" $\rightarrow$ "_1 _2 _3 _4"), regardless of whether a certain combination of numbers co-occur frequently (e.g., "19"). Tokenizing digits is beneficial when interpreting large sequences of numbers where every digit must be read out (e.g., 1,342 $\rightarrow$ "one thousand three hundred and forty two"). In this work, we use the SentencePiece toolkit[1] and vary the inventory size. One can imagine that a larger subword inventory may contain longer subword entries. For example, the word "anthology" is split into "_an th ology" by a subword model of 2K size and "_anth ology" by a model of 8K size. Our experiments find that an inventory size between 1K and 2K yields the best WER and SER (see Table 3). For the rest of the paper, we use 2K.

4.4 Overall performance

Table 4 summarizes the performance of each model. We report sentence-error-rate (SER), word-error-rate (WER), BLEU score (Papineni et al., 2002) and latency (millisecond per input

---

[1] https://github.com/google/sentencepiece

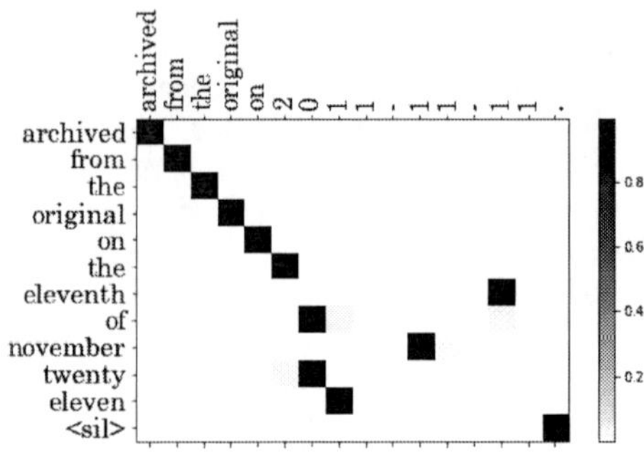

Figure 3: Attention visualization: x-axis is the input; y-axis is the output.

sentence), measured on the test set. We also report number of parameters and training time.

For the identity model, we replaced all non-alphanumerical characters in the source data with "<sil>", except for spaces. As expected, this model generates a large number of errors. When evaluated on full sentences, the window-based model yields a reasonable accuracy, although it leverages a limited context. On the other hand, although the sentence baseline is directly trained on full sentences, its WER and SER are both worse than the window-based approach. The expansion of the output space significantly increases the trainable parameters from 10M to 55M, leading to more difficulties in training and inference.

As shown in Table 4, the subword model significantly outperforms baseline models in both accuracy and inference speed. Due to the source of the dataset (i.e., Wikipedia), test set and training set have an overlap of about 27%. For instance, several source citations were commonly found in Wikipedia articles and appeared in training and test (e.g., *"IUCN Red List of Threatened Species."*). We found that, for sentences that were not seen by the subword model in training, our model still produces reliable outputs with a SER of 4.59% and WER of 1.09%.

Figure 3 demonstrates that the attention mechanism can effectively learn the non-monotonous nature of the text normalization problem as "eleventh", "November" and "eleven" correspond to the third, second and first "11" in the input.

4.5 Linguistic features

We use the following linguistic features: 1) *capitalization*: upper, lower, mixed, non-alphanumerical, foreign characters; 2) *position*:

Table 4: Comparison of models on test set.

Model	SER (%)	WER (%)	BLEU	Params (M)	Train Time (hours)	Latency (ms/sent)
Identity	99.39	32.70	51.74	N/A	**0**	N/A
Window-based	12.74	3.75	94.55	10	3.9	238
Sentence-based	48.67	9.26	82.28	55	8.0	159
Subword	**3.31**	**0.91**	**98.79**	12	10.0	**88**
Subword + Feat. w/o label	2.77	0.78	98.98	12	13.5	89
Subword + Feat. w/o casing	0.96	0.23	99.66	12	12.8	**88**
Subword + Feat. w/o POS	0.79	0.18	99.71	12	10.4	**88**
Subword + Feat. w/o position	0.80	**0.17**	**99.73**	12	13.0	**88**
Subword + All Feat.	**0.78**	**0.17**	**99.73**	12	15.4	89

beginning, middle, end, singleton; 3) *POS tags*: 44 Penn Treebank tags; 4) *labels*: 15 edit labels. Among these four types of features, capitalization and position are the least computationally expensive. POS tags are automatically predicted using an Averaged Perceptron Tagger from the Natural Language Toolkit (Bird et al., 2009). Edit labels are the most expensive to obtain in real life. Our labels are generated directly from the Google FST (Sproat and Jaitly, 2016). Each type of feature is represented by a one-hot encoding.

To combine linguistic features with subword units, one can add or concatenate each subword's embedding with its corresponding linguistic feature embedding and feed a combined embedding to the bi-LSTM encoder. Or, a multi-layer perceptron (MLP) can be applied to combine information in a non-linear way. Our experiments find that concatenation outperforms the other two methods.

In Table 4 we can see that the subword model with linguistic features produces the lowest SER (0.78%) and WER (0.17%). In addition, results from the ablation study show that each feature makes a positive contribution to the model. However, edit labels seem to make the strongest contribution. We acknowledge that edit labels may not always be readily available. The model which utilizes all linguistic features except for edit labels still shows a 16% relative SER reduction and 14% WER reduction over the subword model without linguistic features.

5 Discussion

Errors from the subword model are presented in Table 5. Severe errors are shown in the first two rows. While these types of errors are infrequent, they change or obscure the meaning of the utterance for a user. For example, the currency "nok" (e.g., "norwegian kroner") was verbalized as "euros", reflecting a bias in the training data. While "euros" appeared 88 times, "norwegian kroner" appeared just 10 times.

Another type of error does not change the sentence meaning but can be unnatural. For example, "alexander iii" was predicted as "alexander three" rather than "alexander the third". In this case, the referent of the sentence would likely be understandable given context. Examples such as "5' 11''" reflect the variety of natural readings which a human might produce. "Five foot eleven inches", "five foot eleven", and "five eleven" may all refer to a person's height. Here the reference and model have produced different but acceptable variations.

Table 5: Errors from the subword model with linguistic features.

Input	Reference	Prediction
un nok 3 billion	u n three billion norwegian kroner	un three billion euros
alexander iii 2000 gb	alexander the third two thousand gigabytes	alexander three two thousand g b
5' 11''	five foot eleven	five eleven

A fundamental problem is the lack of supervised data for training and evaluation, particularly data which reflects the variety of acceptable readings of non-standard text. The pairs in this study (and in other text normalization research) are generated by a system which does not have the full capability to verbalize sentences in different but natural ways. Our system's normalization WER and SER may not translate proportionally to ASR's WER and SER, simply because real users will read non-standard text in a variety of ways. It remains a challenge for the academic community to come up with better data solutions.

6 Conclusion

In this paper, we investigate neural approaches to text normalization which directly translate a written-form sentence to its spoken counterpart without the need of a tagger or grammar. We show that the use of subwords can effectively reduce the OOV problem of a baseline seq2seq model with character inputs and token outputs. The addition of linguistic features including casing, word position, POS tags, and edit labels leads to further gains. We empirically test the addition of each linguistic feature revealing that all features make a contribution to the model, and combining features results in the best performance. Our model is an improvement over both window-based and sentence-based seq2seq baselines, yielding a WER of 0.17%.

References

Dzmitry Bahdanau, Kyunghyun Cho, and Yoshua Bengio. 2014. Neural machine translation by jointly learning to align and translate. *arXiv preprint arXiv:1409.0473*.

Steven Bird, Ewan Klein, and Edward Loper. 2009. *Natural language processing with Python: analyzing text with the natural language toolkit.* " O'Reilly Media, Inc.".

William Chan, Navdeep Jaitly, Quoc Le, and Oriol Vinyals. 2016. Listen, attend and spell: A neural network for large vocabulary conversational speech recognition. In *Acoustics, Speech and Signal Processing (ICASSP), 2016 IEEE International Conference on*, pages 4960–4964. IEEE.

Guillaume Klein, Yoon Kim, Yuntian Deng, Jean Senellart, and Alexander M Rush. 2017. OpenNMT: Open-source toolkit for neural machine translation. *arXiv preprint arXiv:1701.02810*.

Kishore Papineni, Salim Roukos, Todd Ward, and Wei-Jing Zhu. 2002. Bleu: a method for automatic evaluation of machine translation. In *Proceedings of the 40th annual meeting on association for computational linguistics*, pages 311–318. Association for Computational Linguistics.

Ernest Pusateri, Bharat Ram Ambati, Elizabeth Brooks, Ondrej Platek, Donald McAllaster, and Venki Nagesha. 2017. A mostly data-driven approach to inverse text normalization. *Proc. Interspeech 2017*, pages 2784–2788.

Long Qin, Ming Sun, and Alexander Rudnicky. 2011. OOV detection and recovery using hybrid models with different fragments. In *Twelfth Annual Conference of the International Speech Communication Association*.

Brian Roark, Richard Sproat, Cyril Allauzen, Michael Riley, Jeffrey Sorensen, and Terry Tai. 2012. The openGrm open-source finite-state grammar software libraries. In *Proceedings of the ACL 2012 System Demonstrations*, pages 61–66. Association for Computational Linguistics.

Rico Sennrich and Barry Haddow. 2016. Linguistic input features improve neural machine translation. *arXiv preprint arXiv:1606.02892*.

Rico Sennrich, Barry Haddow, and Alexandra Birch. 2015. Neural machine translation of rare words with subword units. *arXiv preprint arXiv:1508.07909*.

Richard Sproat. 1996. Multilingual text analysis for text-to-speech synthesis. *Natural Language Engineering*, 2(4):369–380.

Richard Sproat, Alan W. Black, Stanley Chen, Shankar Kumar, Mari Ostendorf, and Christopher Richards. 2001. Normalization of non-standard words. *Computer Speech & Language*, 15:287–333.

Richard Sproat and Navdeep Jaitly. 2016. RNN approaches to text normalization: A challenge. *arXiv preprint arXiv:1611.00068*.

Sevinj Yolchuyeva, Géza Németh, and Bálint Gyires-Tóth. 2018. Text normalization with convolutional neural networks. *International Journal of Speech Technology*, pages 1–12.

Audio De-identification: A New Entity Recognition Task

Ido Cohn, Itay Laish, Genady Beryozkin, Gang Li, Izhak Shafran,
Idan Szpektor, Tzvika Hartman, Avinatan Hassidim, Yossi Matias
Google
Tel Aviv, Israel
{idoc,itaylaish,leebird,tzvika}@google.com

Abstract

Named Entity Recognition (NER) has been
mostly studied in the context of written text.
Specifically, NER is an important step in
de-identification (de-ID) of medical records,
many of which are recorded conversations between a patient and a doctor. In such recordings, audio spans with personal information
should be redacted, similar to the redaction of
sensitive character spans in de-ID for written
text. The application of NER in the context of
audio de-identification has yet to be fully investigated. To this end, we define the task of
audio de-ID, in which audio spans with entity
mentions should be detected. We then present
our pipeline for this task, which involves Automatic Speech Recognition (ASR), NER on the
transcript text, and text-to-audio alignment. Finally, we introduce a novel metric for audio de-ID and a new evaluation benchmark
consisting of a large labeled segment of the
Switchboard and *Fisher* audio datasets and
detail our pipeline's results on it.

1 Introduction

Personal data in general, and clinical records data
in particular, is a major driving force in today's sci-
entific research. Despite its abundance, the presence of Personal Health Identifiers (PHI) hinders
data availability for researchers. Therefore, data
de-identification (de-ID) is a critical component in
any plan to make such data available. However,
the amount of data involved makes it prohibitively
expensive to employ domain experts to tag and
redact PHI manually, providing a good opportunity for automatic de-identification tools. Indeed,
high performance tools for the de-identification of
medical text notes have been developed (Dernoncourt et al., 2017a; Liu et al., 2017).

Due to the rise of tele-medicine (Weinstein
et al., 2014), clinical records consist of many other
types of data, such as audio conversations (Chiu
et al., 2017), scanned documents, video, and im-

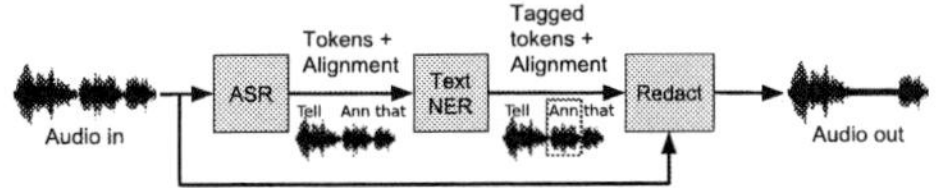

Figure 1: High level audio de-ID pipeline

ages. In this work, we direct our attention towards
the task of de-identifying clinical audio data. This
task is expected to become increasingly more important, as Machine Learning applications in tele-
medicine are growing in popularity. Given an input
audio stream, the objective is to produce a modified audio stream, where all PHI is redacted, while
the rest of the stream is kept unchanged. To the
best of our knowledge, de-identifying audio is a
new task, requiring a new benchmark.

We define and publish[1] a benchmark consisting of the following: 1. A large labeled subset of
the *Switchboard* (Godfrey et al., 1992) and *Fisher*
(David et al., 2004) conversational English audio
datasets, denoted as *SWFI*. 2. A new evaluation
metric, measuring how well the PHI words in the
input audio were identified and redacted, and how
well the rest of the audio was preserved.

To better understand the challenges of the
audio de-id task, we evaluate it both end-to-end
and by breaking it down and solving it using
individual components. Our pipeline (Fig. 1) first
produces transcripts from the audio using ASR,
proceeds by running text-based NER tagging, and
then redacts PHI tokens, using the aligned token
boundaries determined by ASR. Our tagger relies
on the state-of-the-art techniques for solving the
audio NER problem of recognizing entities in
audio transcripts (Lample et al., 2016; Ma and
Hovy, 2016). We leverage the available Automatic
Speech Recognition (ASR) technology, and use
its component of alignment back to audio.

---

[1] https://g.co/audio-ner-annotations-data

197

Proceedings of NAACL-HLT 2019, pages 197–204
Minneapolis, Minnesota, June 2 - June 7, 2019. ©2019 Association for Computational Linguistics

Finally, we evaluate our pipeline and describe its performance, both end-to-end and per-component. Although results on audio are worse than NER performance on text, the pipeline achieves better results than expected despite the compounding pipeline errors. Last, we analyze our performance and provide insights for next steps.

2 Related Work

2.1 NER for Speech

Prior work addressed entity recognition for audio recordings via the *audio NER* task: the detection of entities in the text transcript of the audio input. The majority of these works used a pipeline approach, in which ASR is first applied to the audio and then NER is applied on the noisy textual output of the ASR. These works include discriminative models (Sudoh et al., 2006), incorporating OOV word indicators (Parada et al., 2011), hierarchical structure (Raymond, 2013), and conditional random fields (Hatmi et al., 2013).

Many audio NER works learn from and measure performance on French datasets, such as **ESTER** (Galliano et al., 2009) and **ETAPE** (Galibert et al., 2014). This may indirectly affect the overall quality of these systems because the ASR component, which is crucial in the pipeline approach but is typically used "off-the-shelf", has lower performance in languages other than English.

An alternative end-to-end approach was proposed by Ghannay et al. (2018), in which the model accepts audio as input and outputs a tagged word sequence which consists of normal words and the NER labels in HTML-like tag encoding. Their model did not attain reasonable performance, perhaps due to the small training set.

We emphasize that both pipeline and end-to-end approaches output tagged word sequences, and do not propagate the recognized entity labels back for redaction on the audio itself, which is the end goal of our proposed audio de-ID task.

2.2 De-identification in the Health Domain

Previous efforts of de-ID in health care focused on redaction of textual medical records. The main approach involves applying NER techniques to the text, including rule-based (Ruch et al., 2000; Neamatullah et al., 2008) and machine learning (Guo et al., 2006; Yang and Garibaldi, 2015) methods.

Adoption of neural network models boosted the performance of NER on text without requiring hand-crafted rules and complex feature engineering (Collobert et al., 2011; Huang et al., 2015; Lample et al., 2016; Ma and Hovy, 2016; Dernoncourt et al., 2017a). Dernoncourt et al. (2017b) applied the model proposed in Lample et al. (2016) to medical de-ID, achieving state-of-the-art performance on the I2B2-2014 (Stubbs and Uzuner, 2015) de-ID challenge dataset. We have chosen this architecture for the NER component of our pipeline method (Section 5).

3 The Audio De-identification Task

The goal of the Audio de-ID task is to convert an input audio stream into a modified audio stream where the PHI words are redacted. In essence, the goal of the task is to limit the ability of a listener to identify the entities of the conversation while leaving as much information as possible in order to keep the audio understandable.

Formally, the input audio stream is a function $A(t)$ of time, that can be transcribed into a sequence of words $W = \{w_j\}$, where w_j is mapped to the time interval in the audio $T_j = [t_j^{start}, t_j^{end})$. We consider each word to be either PHI or non-PHI, and let I denote the set of PHI words $\{j : w_j$ is PHI$\}$.

The output of an audio de-ID algorithm is a zero-one redaction function $R(t)$, indicating which parts of the audio stream are to be redacted, where a value of zero indicates PHI information at time t. The redacted audio stream can be obtained by zeroing out the redacted part of the stream, $A_{redacted}(t) = R(t)A(t)$.

To evaluate the performance of a de-ID algorithm, we term w_j as *fully-covered* if $R(t)$ is zero for all $t \in T_j$, and define a corresponding indicator function $covered(w_i)$. This in turn defines the following standard NER metrics for the audio de-ID task:

$$TruePositives\ (TP) = \sum_{j \in I} covered(w_j),$$

$$FalsePositives\ (FP) = \sum_{j \notin I} covered(w_j),$$

$$FalseNegatives\ (FN) = \sum_{j \in I} 1 - covered(w_j)$$

$$Precision = \frac{TP}{TP + FP}\ ,\ Recall = \frac{TP}{TP + FN}$$

Finding the exact time interval corresponding to a word is not a trivial task, while redacting

Dataset	Medium	# Notes	# Tokens	% PHI
I2B2'14 train	Text	521	336,422	3.5
AMC'17 train	Audio	4,629	8,348,899	0.02
SWFI train	Audio	468	710,348	1.8
SWFI test		108	158,923	2.0

Table 1: Dataset statistics for train and test sets, showing the number of notes (written or spoken), token count, and percent of tokens which are PHI.

PHI Labels %	*I2B2'14*	*AMC'17*	*SWFI* train / test
Name	0.84%	0.12%	0.22% / 0.23%
Age	0.24%	0.01%	0.12% / 0.1%
Date	1.56%	0.03%	0.1% / 0.12%
Hospital	0.28%	0.004%	-
Pharmacy	-	0.01%	-
Organization	0.025%	0.003%	0.48% / 0.59%
Location (General)	0.001%	0.004%	0.24% / 0.29%
State	0.07%	-	0.15% / 0.16%
City	0.08%	0.003%	0.25% / 0.29%
Country	0.02%	-	0.23% / 0.27%
Profession	0.04%	-	0.23% / 0.27%
Holiday	-	-	0.12% / 0.07%
Season	-	-	0.04% / 0.03%

Table 2: Statistics for PHI labels as percent of total tokens per dataset. Tags in **bold** are common to all datasets and are used in Section 7

most of the interval T_j results in a similar de-ID effect as fully covering all the interval. To this end, we extend $covered(w_i)$ into the indicator $\rho - covered(w_j)$ that is true iff $R(t)$ is zero on at least ρ proportion of interval T_j.

With this indicator function we further extend the aforementioned NER metrics to TP_ρ, FP_ρ, and FN_ρ, and correspondingly define $Recall_\rho$ and $Precision_\rho$. When $\rho = 1$ these metrics equal the strict metrics. When $\rho < 1$ the new metrics determine the quality of the system with respect to redacting at least ρ of each audio interval in PHIs.

We note that the proposed metrics only evaluate the redaction function $R(t)$ on the word intervals.

4 Datasets

To create a benchmark for the audio de-ID task, we use three datasets from two distinct domains: *conversational English* and *medical records*. We summarize the main dataset statistics in Table 1. Importantly, we did not perform text normalization specific to each domain.

Word Type	WER	Well Aligned	Extended Alignment	Shortened Alignment
PHI	41.8	86%	5%	9%
non-PHI	38.3	81%	8%	12%

Table 3: ASR WER and token-audio alignment distribution on sample conversations from the *SWFI* dataset.

In the domain of medical datasets, we use *I2B2'14* (Stubbs and Uzuner, 2015), which consists of identified textual medical notes with PHI tagging, and the Audio Medical Conversations dataset from (Chiu et al., 2017), denoted *AMC'17*, which contains de-identified audio of doctor-patient conversations and their corresponding manual transcripts. Processing the *AMC'17* conversations was facilitated by the fact that it is a de-identified dataset, which provides us with the locations of the PHI in the audio and the transcripts. Three PHI types: names, dates and ages were redacted, preserving type information, and synthetic data was generated using dictionaries and context-aware rules. First names were drawn from the US Social Security Administration babies names registry[2] and last names were drawn from the Frequently Occurring Surnames list from the 1990's US Census[3]. Human annotators used surrounding context to resolve the other PHI types and filled in fake appropriate identifiers.

Notably, neither of the above-mentioned medical datasets could serve as a benchmark for the audio de-ID task, as *I2B2'14* is text-based, and *AMC'17* contains only redacted audio conversations and is not publicly available. Therefore, we focused on the conversational English domain, where we generated a combined dataset *SWFI* from the *Switchboard* (Godfrey et al., 1992) and *Fisher* (David et al., 2004) datasets. These datasets include hundreds of conversations in English about a variety of subjects, along with their transcripts. To enable proper training and evaluation for the audio de-ID task, we annotated all 250 *Switchboard* conversations, and 326 from *Fisher*. Annotation included named PHI labels, and the time intervals $T_j = [t_j^{(start)}, t_j^{(end)})$ matching each named PHI back into the audio. This dataset is publicly available[1] to allow for standardized evaluation of novel approaches to this task.

The annotation process began by tokenization of the transcripts provided in both datasets using white-space separators, removing special transcript characters and keeping word capitalization in its original form. Following that, PHI word annotation was performed manually. The results can be seen in Table 2.

---

[2]https://www.ssa.gov/oact/babynames/
[3]https://www.census.gov/topics/population/genealogy/data/1990_census.htmlcensus_namefiles.html

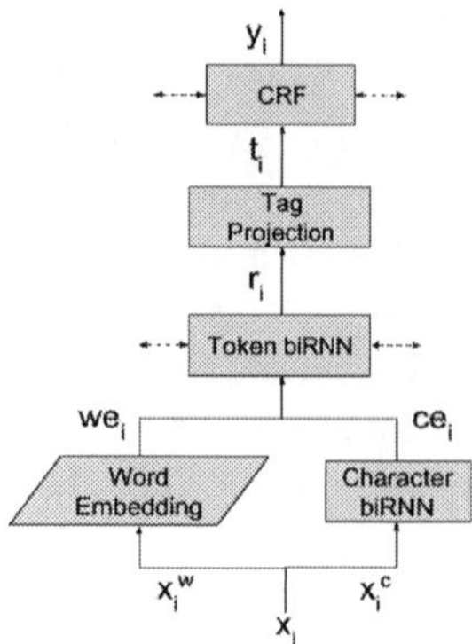

Figure 2: Neural architecture for text de-ID

As performing temporal labeling manually is an arduous process, we opt for a semi-automatic ASR-based procedure. To this end, we determine word start and end times by aligning the manual transcripts to audio intervals. We assess the quality of this semi-automatic labeling scheme using human evaluation. For a random sample of 6 **SWFI** conversations (3 **Switchboard** and 3 **Fisher**), we slice the audio according to the aligned interval times per transcript word, and measure both the quality of the transcription, and that of the alignment. Table 3 shows the distribution of alignment errors of the tokens from the sample conversations. These are denoted as good alignment, short (i.e. ASR interval is shorter than actual word) and extended (i.e. interval is longer than expected) where all alignment errors are in the scale of 30-60ms (1-2 audio frames).

5 Pipeline Models

We next describe the models we trained and evaluated to gain insights on the types of challenges this task presents. We chose to use the pipeline approach as an audio de-ID benchmark due to the ubiquity and maturity of the ASR technology, and abundance of training data for text NER. Our pipeline models contain three main components:

1. An ASR system, which transcribes the audio into text.

2. A NER tagger, which tags the transcript with the required labels.

3. An alignment component, which maps each word in the transcript back to its time interval in the audio.

For the ASR component, we use Google Cloud's Speech API[4] with the *command_and_search* model, which gave us the best transcription accuracy on the data. For each conversation, which usually contains two different speakers, we send the entire audio to the service to obtain the transcript. The API also returns alternative hypotheses for the corresponding text and their confidence. We incorporate these alternative hypotheses by taking the top-k ASR hypotheses and feeding them into the next two stages. We then take the logical OR of the detections on all of the hypotheses. Unless stated otherwise, $k = 1$.

For the NER tagger component, our models use the architecture described in Lample et al. (2016), depicted in Fig. 2. This is a neural network model using pre-trained GloVe word embeddings[5] (Pennington et al., 2014) and a character-based bidirectional RNN to generate token embeddings, followed by a bidirectional RNN, tag projection, and CRF layers. We define three models, where each model has a NER tagger trained on a different dataset. The models are:

M_{AMC} – Trained using the training data from the **AMC'17** dataset.

M_{SWFI} – Trained using the training data from the **SWFI** dataset.

M_{I2B2} – Trained using the training data from the **I2B2'14** dataset.

The M_{AMC} and M_{SWFI} models were trained using the conversation transcripts. We use data augmentation in order to increase robustness to ASR errors, in particular to word deletion, insertion, substitution, and inconsistent capitalization. Data augmentation is carried out in several stages. First we create an ASR transcript from the audio, align it back to the reference transcript by minimizing the word-level edit distance, and transfer the labels to the new transcript. For each of the two transcripts, we then generate three additional transcripts by changing word capitalization to camel, lower and upper case. Finally, each of the augmented transcripts is broken down into segments of 20 speaker turns with a step of 10 turns, to resemble the utterance structure of the ASR output. We include the three variants of the M_{SWFI} model: $M_{SWFIReg}$ uses no augmentations,

200

$M_{SWFI\_MixCase}$ uses mix-case augmentations only, and $M_{SWFI\_MixCase+Asr}$ uses all mix-case and ASR augmentations.

The M_{I2B2} model is tuned to achieve state-of-the-art results on textual medical notes, such as in Dernoncourt et al. (2017a); Liu et al. (2017). It should be stressed that the model was used as is, without an attempt to adapt it to the domain of ASR output. M_{AMC} and all M_{SWFI} models are both trained on conversational data, and should be better adapted to the task. M_{AMC} is trained on data originating from the medical domain, as opposed to M_{SWFI} models which train on data from the English conversation target domain. This is offset by the fact that M_{AMC} is trained on a significantly larger training set.

Finally, for the alignment component we add a padding hyperparameter allowing a variable number of mismatched frames at either side of the identified intervals. This slack in interval size is used to compensate for alignment errors.

6   Experimental Settings

To test the performance of our models on the audio de-ID task, we conducted a number of experiments, described next. Section 7 then details our results. We report *Recall*, *Precision*, and $F1$ scores for all experiments, which are significantly more informative than accuracy due to a low PHI/non-PHI ratio. We report results on the **SWFI** test set using the tags which are shown in bold in Table 2. We evaluate our performance against the coverage threshold $\rho \in [0, 1]$ which is defined in Section 3. Specifically, we focus on type-less metrics, as we care more about the tokens' redaction than their type classification.

Our first experiment evaluates the performance of M_{AMC}, M_{SWFI}, and M_{I2B2} on the **SWFI** test set. First, to decouple their tagging performance from the other pipeline errors, we measure their tagging performance on the manually annotated transcripts (referred to as *NER score*). NER errors may arise due to train-test disparity, where the train and test data are from different domains or different mediums (e.g. text vs. audio), which results in different discriminative models. Additionally, we measure their overall end-to-end score. We analyze the complex behavior of the models' precision by inspecting the coverage distribution of PHI and non-PHI tokens.

Our second experiment evaluates the effect

Model	NER Recall / Precision / F1	$F1$ (ρ)
M_{I2B2}	0.37 / 0.48 / 0.41	0.37 (0.4)
M_{AMC}	0.18 / 0.98 / 0.3	0.23 (0.35)
$M_{SWFIReg}$	0.82 / 0.92 / 0.87	0.41 (0.4)
$M_{SWFI\_MixCase}$	0.87 / 0.92 / 0.89	0.46 (0.4)
$M_{SWFI\_MixCase+Asr}$	0.88 / 0.92 / 0.9	0.51 (0.4)

Table 4: NER score of the different NER models, and their end-to-end $F1$ in their optimal choice of ρ.

Error type	Count	% of total
ASR Transcription errors	152	45.24
NER errors	168	50
Alignment errors	14	4.17
Manual Transcription errors	2	0.6

Table 5: Error analysis of a sample of M_{SWFI} FN errors, including errors from all components across the pipeline and even occasional manual transcription errors which contribute to both FP and FN errors.

of two significant hyperparameters on pipeline performance using the **SWFI** test set:

- The number of alternative hypotheses passed on from the ASR to the NER tagger.

- The amount of padding added around each detection by the alignment component.

7   Results

In Table 3 we report the Word Error Rate (WER) of our ASR component on the **SWFI** dataset, which was computed by comparing the manual and ASR transcripts of the entire audio. For WER of PHI words, we removed all the non-PHI words from manual ASR transcripts before computing the WER. WER of non-PHI words was computed similarly. We see that both WERs are substantial, and can be thought of as an upper-bound on our pipeline's end-to-end performance.

Next, Table 4 shows the NER and their end-to-end performance of each model for its $F1$ optimal choice of coverage threshold ρ. We can also see that the M_{SWFI} surpasses the others in performance due to its training set being in-domain and in the same medium. Additionally, the $M_{SWFI\_MixCase+Asr}$ variant does not display any advantage over its other variants when running on manual transcripts, but gets significantly better performance on the end-to-end scenario. The difference between NER and end-to-end scores is apparent, and may be attributed to additional pipeline components of ASR and alignment. Interestingly, in the case of $M_{SWFIReg}$, compounding

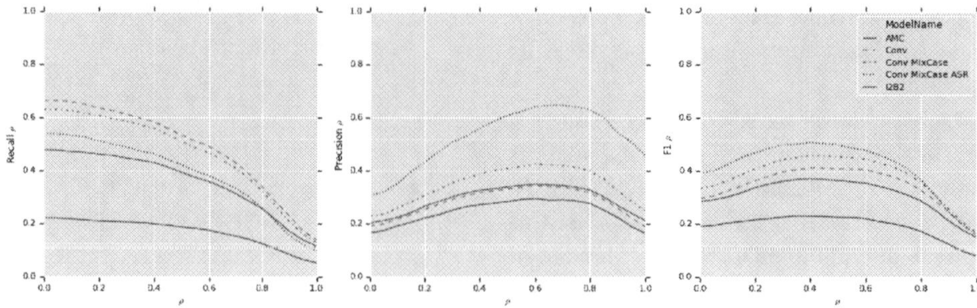

Figure 3: End-to-end performance comparison of NER models – Recall (left), Precision (middle) and F1 (right).

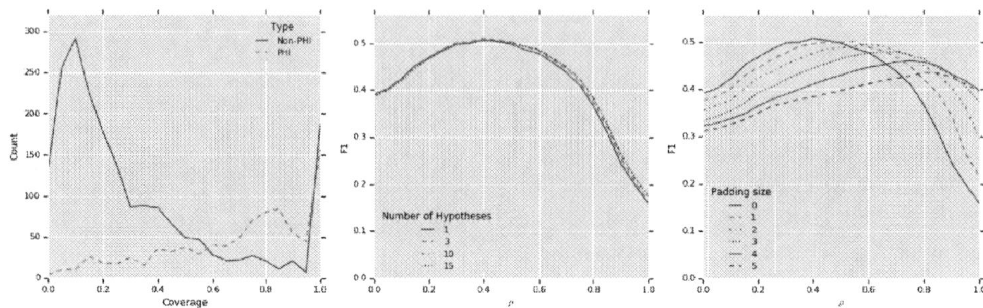

Figure 4: Coverage distribution between PHI and non-PHI tokens (left) and End-to-end performance for different pipeline parameters – number of hypotheses (center) and padding (right).

the WER and alignment error rate from Table 3 and the NER from Table 4 leads to an expected *Recall* of approximately 0.44, yet the end-to-end *Recall* at $\rho = 0.5$ is 0.53. This implies a non-trivial co-dependence between errors in the different components of the pipeline.

Figure 3 presents the end-to-end evaluation of the different models with respect to the coverage threshold ρ. As expected, *Recall* is monotonically non-increasing with respect to the threshold. Meanwhile, *Precision* (and consequently $F1$) are not monotonic and have more complex behavior. This behavior is due to difference in the distribution of the coverage between PHI and non-PHI, which we see in Figure 4 (left). An interesting insight is that most PHI words have more than half their length redacted by the pipeline while non-PHI words' coverage is bi-modal, one mode close to 0, and the other close to 1. A plausable explanation for this behavior is that the FPs are derived from alignment errors in low coverage, while the high coverage FPs occur due to classification errors, either due to ASR transcription mistakes or due to model NER errors.

Finally, we show the end-to-end evaluation of the pipeline using $M_{SWFI\_MixCase+Asr}$ with differ-

ent choices of the pipeline parameters. In Figure 4 (center) the performance of the pipeline slightly increases when using additional alternative hypotheses, while a different experiment shows that when using alternative hypotheses with $M_{SWFI\_MixCase}$ performance decreases. This decrease is consistent with the hypotheses' decreasing confidence scores, which can be alleviated with ASR training data but is not addressed by the naive OR approach described in Section 5. This leads us to seek new ways to utilize the additional ASR artifacts, such as the hypotheses confidence scores and speech lattice. In Section 8 we discuss possible directions to improve the pipeline's robustness to ASR errors. Last, Figure 4 (right) shows that the choice of padding size does not improve performance, but rather alters the value of the optimal coverage threshold.

8   Conclusions

We introduced the audio de-ID task, an important prerequisite for protecting privacy when processing sensitive audio datasets in the medical domain as well as other domains. To this end, we created and made available a new test set benchmark derived from annotating the **Switchboard** and **Fisher** audio datasets. We also presented new metrics for the task, $Recall_\rho$ and $Precision_\rho$, as extensions of standard $Recall$ and $Precision$ where words are considered de-identified when at least a portion ρ of their audio signal is redacted. Finally, we detailed our algorithm for this task, a pipeline approach consisting of three components: ASR, NER on transcripts and a novel alignment from tagged transcripts to audio for the actual redaction.

We showed that ASR performance is the main impedance towards achieving results comparable to text de-ID. In future work, we plan to address this through several directions, including end-to-end de-ID (Ghannay et al., 2018), lattice-based techniques (Ladhak et al., 2016), and diarization and segmentation of the audio as part of the transcription process (Cerva et al., 2013).

9 Acknowledgements

The authors would like to thank Oren Gilon, Shlomo Hoory, Amir Feder, Debby Cohen, Amit Markel, and Ronit Slyper for their generous help in the writing of this paper.

Deidentified clinical records used in this research were provided by the i2b2 National Center for Biomedical Computing funded by U54LM008748 and were originally prepared for the Shared Tasks for Challenges in NLP for Clinical Data organized by Dr. Ozlem Uzuner, i2b2 and SUNY.

References

Petr Cerva, Jan Silovsky, Jindrich Zdansky, Jan Nouza, and Ladislav Seps. 2013. Speaker-adaptive speech recognition using speaker diarization for improved transcription of large spoken archives. *Speech Communication*, 55(10):1033–1046.

Chung-Cheng Chiu, Anshuman Tripathi, Katherine Chou, Chris Co, Navdeep Jaitly, Diana Jaunzeikare, Anjuli Kannan, Patrick Nguyen, Hasim Sak, Ananth Sankar, et al. 2017. Speech recognition for medical conversations. *arXiv preprint arXiv:1711.07274*.

Ronan Collobert, Jason Weston, Léon Bottou, Michael Karlen, Koray Kavukcuoglu, and Pavel Kuksa. 2011. Natural language processing (almost) from scratch. *JMLR*, 12(Aug):2493–2537.

Christopher Cieri David, David Miller, and Kevin Walker. 2004. The fisher corpus: a resource for the next generations of speech-to-text. In *in Proceedings 4th International Conference on Language Resources and Evaluation*, pages 69–71.

Franck Dernoncourt, Ji Young Lee, Ozlem Uzuner, and Peter Szolovits. 2017a. De-identification of patient notes with recurrent neural networks. *J. Am Med Inform Assoc*, 24(3):596–606.

Franck Dernoncourt, Ji Young Lee, Ozlem Uzuner, and Peter Szolovits. 2017b. De-identification of patient notes with recurrent neural networks. *Journal of the American Medical Informatics Association*, 24(3):596–606.

Olivier Galibert, Jeremy Leixa, Gilles Adda, Khalid Choukri, and Guillaume Gravier. 2014. The etape speech processing evaluation. In *LREC*, pages 3995–3999. Citeseer.

Sylvain Galliano, Guillaume Gravier, and Laura Chaubard. 2009. The ester 2 evaluation campaign for the rich transcription of french radio broadcasts. In *Tenth Annual Conference of the International Speech Communication Association*.

Sahar Ghannay, Antoine Caubrière, Yannick Estève, Antoine Laurent, and Emmanuel Morin. 2018. End-to-end named entity extraction from speech. *arXiv preprint arXiv:1805.12045*.

John J. Godfrey, Edward C. Holliman, and Jane McDaniel. 1992. Switchboard: Telephone speech corpus for research and development. In *Proceedings of the 1992 IEEE International Conference on Acoustics, Speech and Signal Processing - Volume 1*, ICASSP'92, pages 517–520, Washington, DC, USA. IEEE Computer Society.

Yikun Guo, Robert Gaizauskas, Ian Roberts, George Demetriou, Mark Hepple, et al. 2006. Identifying personal health information using support vector machines. In *i2b2 workshop on challenges in natural language processing for clinical data*, pages 10–11. Citeseer.

Mohamed Hatmi, Christine Jacquin, Emmanuel Morin, and Sylvain Meignier. 2013. Named entity recognition in speech transcripts following an extended taxonomy. In *First Workshop on Speech, Language and Audio in Multimedia*.

Zhiheng Huang, Wei Xu, and Kai Yu. 2015. Bidirectional lstm-crf models for sequence tagging. *arXiv:1508.01991*.

Faisal Ladhak, Ankur Gandhe, Markus Dreyer, Lambert Mathias, Ariya Rastrow, and Bjrn Hoffmeister. 2016. Latticernn: Recurrent neural networks over lattices. In *Interspeech 2016*, pages 695–699.

Guillaume Lample, Miguel Ballesteros, Sandeep Subramanian, Kazuya Kawakami, and Chris Dyer. 2016. Neural architectures for named entity recognition. In *ACL*.

Zengjian Liu, Buzhou Tang, Xiaolong Wang, and Qingcai Chen. 2017. De-identification of clinical notes via recurrent neural network and conditional random field. *J. Biomed. Inf.*, 75:34–42.

Xuezhe Ma and Eduard Hovy. 2016. End-to-end sequence labeling via bi-directional lstm-cnns-crf. In *ACL*.

Ishna Neamatullah, Margaret M Douglass, H Lehman Li-wei, Andrew Reisner, Mauricio Villarroel, William J Long, Peter Szolovits, George B Moody, Roger G Mark, and Gari D Clifford. 2008. Automated de-identification of free-text medical records. *BMC medical informatics and decision making*, 8(1):32.

Carolina Parada, Mark Dredze, and Frederick Jelinek. 2011. Oov sensitive named-entity recognition in speech. In *Twelfth Annual Conference of the International Speech Communication Association*.

Jeffrey Pennington, Richard Socher, and Christopher Manning. 2014. Glove: Global vectors for word representation. In *EMNLP*.

Christian Raymond. 2013. Robust tree-structured named entities recognition from speech. In *Acoustics, Speech and Signal Processing (ICASSP), 2013 IEEE International Conference on*, pages 8475–8479. IEEE.

Patrick Ruch, Robert H Baud, Anne-Marie Rassinoux, Pierrette Bouillon, and Gilbert Robert. 2000. Medical document anonymization with a semantic lexicon. In *Proceedings of the AMIA Symposium*, page 729. American Medical Informatics Association.

Amber Stubbs and Özlem Uzuner. 2015. Annotating longitudinal clinical narratives for de-identification: The 2014 i2b2/uthealth corpus. *J. Biomed. Inf.*, 58:20–29.

Katsuhito Sudoh, Hajime Tsukada, and Hideki Isozaki. 2006. Incorporating speech recognition confidence into discriminative named entity recognition of speech data. In *Proceedings of the 21st International Conference on Computational Linguistics and the 44th annual meeting of the Association for Computational Linguistics*, pages 617–624. Association for Computational Linguistics.

Ronald S Weinstein, Ana Maria Lopez, Bellal A Joseph, Kristine A Erps, Michael Holcomb, Gail P Barker, and Elizabeth A Krupinski. 2014. Telemedicine, telehealth, and mobile health applications that work: opportunities and barriers. *The American journal of medicine*, 127(3):183–187.

Hui Yang and Jonathan M Garibaldi. 2015. Automatic detection of protected health information from clinic narratives. *Journal of biomedical informatics*, 58:S30–S38.

In Other News: A *Bi-style* Text-to-speech Model
for Synthesizing Newscaster Voice with Limited Data

Nishant Prateek, Mateusz Łajszczak, Roberto Barra-Chicote, Thomas Drugman,
Jaime Lorenzo-Trueba, Thomas Merritt, Srikanth Ronanki, Trevor Wood

Amazon Research Cambridge, UK

`nprateek@amazon.co.uk`

Abstract

Neural text-to-speech synthesis (NTTS) models have shown significant progress in generating high-quality speech, however they require a large quantity of training data. This makes creating models for multiple styles expensive and time-consuming. In this paper different styles of speech are analysed based on prosodic variations, from this a model is proposed to synthesise speech in the style of a newscaster, with just a few hours of supplementary data. We pose the problem of synthesising in a target style using limited data as that of creating a bi-style model that can synthesise both neutral-style and newscaster-style speech via a one-hot vector which factorises the two styles. We also propose conditioning the model on contextual word embeddings, and extensively evaluate it against neutral NTTS, and neutral concatenative-based synthesis. This model closes the gap in perceived style-appropriateness between natural recordings for newscaster-style of speech, and neutral speech synthesis by approximately two-thirds.

1 Introduction

Newscasters have a clearly identifiable dynamic style of speech. As more people are using virtual assistants, in their mobile devices and home appliances, for listening to daily news, synthesising newscaster-style of speech becomes commercially relevant. A newscaster-style of speech gives users a better experience when listening to news as compared to news generated in the neutral-style speech, which is typically used in text-to-speech synthesis. In addition, synthesising news using text-to-speech is more cost-effective and flexible than having to record new snippets of news with professional newscasters every time a new story breaks in.

Recent advances in neural text-to-speech (NTTS) synthesis (Van Den Oord et al., 2016;

Wang et al., 2017; Shen et al., 2018; Merritt et al., 2018) have enabled researchers to generate high-quality speech with a wide range of prosodic variations. For many years, concatenative-based speech synthesis (Black and Campbell, 1995; Taylor, 2006; Qian et al., 2013; Merritt et al., 2016; Wan et al., 2017) has been the industry standard. Concatenative-based speech synthesis methods can produce high-quality speech, but are limited by the coverage of units in its database. When it comes to more expressive styles of speech, this problem is aggravated by the many hours of speech data that would be needed to cover an acceptable range of prosodic variations present in a particular style of speech. The concatenative approaches also require extensive hand-crafting of relevant low-level features, and arduous engineering efforts.

Recently proposed models based on sequence-to-sequence (seq2seq) architecture (Wang et al., 2017; Shen et al., 2018; Ping et al., 2017) attempt to alleviate some of these issues by transforming the low-level feature representation into a learning task. These models function as acoustic models which take text, in the form of characters or phonemes as input, and output low-level acoustic features that can be then converted into speech waveform using one of the several 'vocoding' techniques (Perraudin et al., 2013; Shen et al., 2018; Lorenzo-Trueba et al., 2018). Seq2seq models also allow us to condition the model on additional observed or latent attributes that help in improving the flexibility (modelling different speaker, and styles), and naturalness (Ping et al., 2017; Jia et al., 2018; Wang et al., 2018; Skerry-Ryan et al., 2018; Stanton et al., 2018). Li et. al. (2018) have explored transformer networks for context generation. This improves training efficiency while capturing long-range dependencies. Even though transformers have enabled parallel training, they still suffer from slow inference due to autoregres-

Proceedings of NAACL-HLT 2019, pages 205–213
Minneapolis, Minnesota, June 2 - June 7, 2019. ©2019 Association for Computational Linguistics

sion. LSTM-based seq2seq architectures, having lesser number of trainable parameters, allow for faster inference.

Several works have explored the "controllability" of style in synthesised speech through latent-variable modelling techniques (Akuzawa et al., 2018; Henter et al., 2018; Hsu et al., 2018). These models not only enable us to jointly model different styles, but also allow the user to control the style through modification of disentangled latent variable during the inference. Although flexible, these models usually require a large amount of data to capture the idiosyncrasies of speaking styles, and to disentangle the characteristics of speech (pitch, duration, amplitude etc.) Additionally, these models are slow to train and are potentially overly complex for modelling styles of speech that are expressive but do not display large prosodic variations. During inference, the user would need to input the latent variables to synthesise, which is not ideal for production systems.

Conventional seq2seq models for NTTS rely on a single encoder for linguistic inputs (phonemes/character embeddings). This encoder cannot be solely relied upon to capture higher-level text characteristics like syntax or semantics. The relation between syntax, semantics and prosody is complex. Many linguistic theories try to tie these phenomena but they struggle to explain some edge cases and are mutually inconsistent (Taylor, 2009) . Thus, it might be unsatisfactory to apply linguistic knowledge directly to prosody modelling by conditioning the model on manually selected features. Recent advances in representation learning for text (Peters et al., 2018; Devlin et al., 2018) have allowed us to come up with linguistic representations that not only capture the semantics of a word, but are also context-dependent as a function of the entire sentence. Contextual word embeddings (CWE) can be used to present to the model additional conditioning features that can help model the prosodic variations in each word, based on the context in which it is present.

Latorre et. al (2018) investigated the effect of data reduction on seq2seq acoustic models. They train a multispeaker model with limited data from several speakers. Chung et. al (2018) pre-train the decoder of their acoustic model on a large amount of unpaired data where the decoder learns the task of predicting the next frame. They also propose conditioning the model on traditio-

nal word-vectors like GloVe and Word2vec (Pennington et al., 2014; Mikolov et al., 2013) to provide additional linguistic information. Both these works don't look at varying prosody or speaking-style. There has been a growing interest in adaptive techniques for voice cloning (Arik et al., 2018; Chen et al., 2019), and style adaptation (Bollepalli et al., 2018) with limited data. However, these models require extensive fine-tuning. Additional investigation is needed on the performance of such adaptive models on more multi-style setting.

The contribution of this work is two-fold: (1) We propose a *'bi-style'* model that is capable of generating both a distinct newscaster style of speech, and neutral style of speech, trained only on few hours of supplementary newscaster-style data, (2) we explore the use of CWE as an additional conditioning input for prosody modelling.

2   Data Exploration

This section aims at understanding the prosodic variability in neutral-style, and newscaster-style corpora. For this purpose, we study the average variance in the natural logarithm of fundamental frequency (*lf0*) for each utterance in the two styles. The values are reported in Table 1. For contrast, we also study per-utterance *lf0* in a mixed-expressive corpus from the same speaker. We notice that among the three corpora, the neutral-style utterances have the lowest mean variance per utterance, making it more tractable and easier to model with NTTS than the other two corpora. Newscaster-style has a slightly higher mean variance given greater expressiveness, and the mixed-expressive corpus has the highest mean variance. Latent-variable models (Akuzawa et al., 2018; Hsu et al., 2018; Wang et al., 2018; Henter et al., 2018; Stanton et al., 2018) tackle the problem of modelling varied expressive corpora. As we have already discussed, these models are slow to train, and require prediction or manual injection of continuous latent variables during inference. These might not be well-suited for the task of modelling newscaster-style, which even though is expressive, has much lower mean variance per utterance than the mixed-expressive corpus.

Latorre et. al. (2018) found that a minimum of ∼ 15000 utterances (approximately 15 hours of data) are required to train a seq2seq acoustic model from scratch. Gathering 15 hours of data

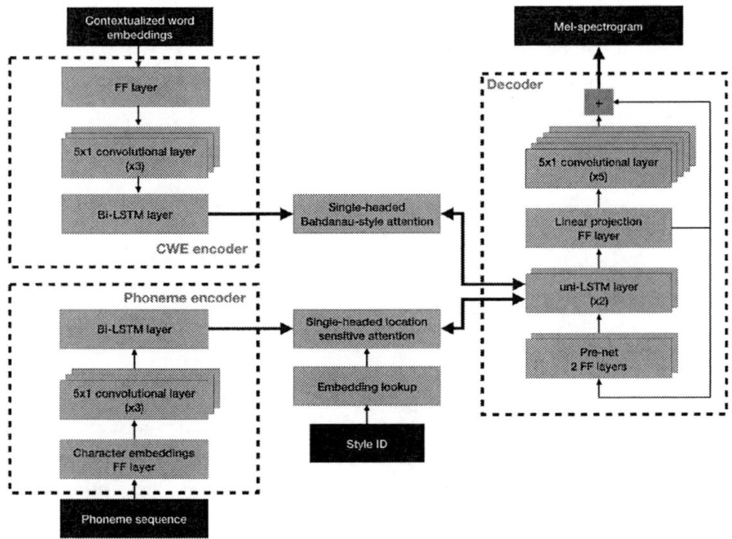

Figure 1: Context Generation Module

Corpus	Variance	Range
Neutral	6.32	5.66
Newscaster	6.33	5.68
Mixed expressive	6.79	5.71

Table 1: Analysis of mean prosodic variations based on *lf0* per utterance

for each new style is both expensive and time-consuming. Given that the mean variance for the newscaster-style utterances is marginally higher than that of neutral-style utterances, we propose jointly modelling both the neutral-style and the newscaster-style, with a one-hot *'style ID'* to differentiate between the two styles. We hypothesise that the style ID will be able to effectively factorise the neutral and newscaster styles, and generate style-appropriate samples for both. This will also alleviate the problem of prediction, and injection of continuous latent variables, that might introduce additional latency in the system. During inference, the style ID can be set by modification of simple binary flags.

From our internal corpus of female US-English voice, we use $\sim$ 20 hours of neutral-style utterances. For the newscaster-style, we use additional recordings from the same voice talent, approximating the style of American newscasters. For experiments in this paper, the amount of data used for the newscaster-style is one-fifth that of neutral-style. Using both these utterances to train a bi-style model provides us with enough overall data to train the acoustic model, and also help the model learn to factorise the two styles with the style ID input.

3 Model Description

Our proposed model is composed of two modules - Context Generation and Waveform Synthesis. The context generation module takes phonemes as inputs, and predicts temporal acoustic features, e.g. mel-spectrograms. The predicted acoustic features are then converted to time-domain audio waveforms by the Waveform Synthesis module. We provide additional inputs to the context generation module, in the form of 'style ID' and contextual word embeddings, for better prosody modelling.

3.1 Context Generation

The context generation module is an extension of the seq2seq-based acoustic model proposed by Latorre et al. (2018), and is shown in Figure 1. We propose multi-scale encoder conditioning, with the acoustic model processing phoneme-level inputs, and an additional CWE encoder that processes word-level inputs.

3.1.1 Acoustic Model

The acoustic model consists of the *phoneme encoder*, style ID input, a single-headed location-sensitive attention block, and the decoder module. The style ID is a two-dimensional one-hot vector (representing whether the input utterance belongs is in the neutral-style or newscaster-style), which is projected into continuous space by an embedding lookup layer to produce a *style embedding*. The style embedding is concatenated at each step of the output of the phoneme encoder. Single-headed location-sensitive attention (Chorowski et al., 2015) is applied to the concatenated outputs. A unidirectional LSTM-layer takes the concatenated vector of the output vector of the attention block and the pre-net layer as an input. The decoder, in each step, predicts blocks of 5 frames of 80-dimensional mel-spectrograms. We define a frame as a $50ms$ sequence, with an overlap of $12.5ms$. The last frame of the previous outputs is passed to the pre-net layer as input for generating the next set of frames.

3.1.2 CWE Encoder

We use *Embeddings from Language Models* (ELMo), introduced by Peters et al. (2018) for obtaining the contextual word embeddings for the input utterance. ELMo takes advantage of unsupervised language modelling task to learn rich text representations on a large text corpus. These representations can then be transferred to downstream tasks that often require explicit labels. ELMo embeddings bring a significant improvement for a variety of Natural Language Processing (NLP) tasks. They are able to capture both semantic and syntactic relations between words (Perone et al., 2018). As such, they seem to be a good fit for modelling prosody.

For each sentence in the training set we extract ELMo features using publicly available CLI tool (Gardner et al., 2018). This model is pre-trained on the 1 Billion Word Benchmark dataset (Chelba et al., 2014). We only use hidden states from the top layer of bi-directional Language Model (biLM). This produces a sequence of 1024-dimensional vectors, one for each word in a sentence. During training these vectors are fed to *CWE encoder*. CWE encoder has a similar topology to the phoneme encoder.

Encoded ELMo embeddings are passed to the decoder through Bahdanau-style attention (Bahdanau et al., 2015). It operates independently of location sensitive attention for phoneme encodings. It can attend to encodings of words that are not focused by location sensitive attention. We hypothesise that this can help the decoder to consider a broader context.

3.2 Waveform Synthesis

We use the pre-trained speaker-independent RNN-based "neural vocoder" proposed by Lorenzo-Trueba et. al. (2018) to convert the mel-spectrograms predicted by our context generation module into high-fidelity audio waveforms.

4 Experimental Protocol

4.1 Training

The news stories are on an average longer than neutral-style utterances, and consist of multiple sentences. Seq2seq models have a tendency to lose attention and have misalignment in longer input sequences during inference. To alleviate this, we split the news stories into individual sentences in both the training and the test sets. Splitting into individual sentences also enables us to train the model on larger batch size, helping the model to converge faster and with lesser perturbation of the training loss. To convert the utterances into phoneme sequences, we use our internal grapheme-to-phone mapping tool, which encodes the phonemes, stress marks, and punctuations as one-hot vectors.

We train the model using an L1 loss in the decoder output for mel-spectrogram prediction. To indicate when to stop predicting the decoder outputs, we have a linear stop token generator at the decoder outputs, trained jointly with the context generation module. The stop token generator is trained with an L2 loss. During training, the stop token is linearly increased from 0 at the beginning of the sentence to 1 at the end.

ADAM optimizer (Kingma and Ba, 2014) is used to minimise the training loss, with learning rate decay. The model is trained with teacher-forcing on the decoder outputs. The attention weights are normalised to add up to 1 using a softmax layer.

We use mel-spectrogram distortion (Kubichek, 1993) to monitor the input-output alignment, and the training loss to get a rough estimation on the convergence of our model. We also synthesise some held-out sentences to monitor the segmental quality and the prosody of our system, as the perceptual quality of the generated samples does not always align with the lower training and validation losses, and spectrogram distortion metrics.

System	Description
Concatenative	Concatenative-based unit selection system driven by state-level statistical parametric predictions
Neutral	Neutral-style NTTS speech
News w/o CWE	Newscaster-style NTTS speech without CWE conditioning
News with CWE	Newscaster-style NTTS speech with CWE conditioning
Recordings	Natural speech waveforms

Table 2: Systems present in the MUSHRA evaluation

4.2 Setup for Evaluation

4.2.1 Objective Metrics

We compare acoustic parameters extracted from the synthesised sentences, and the natural recordings for the analysis of prosody and segmental quality. To match the predicted sequence length to the reference sequence length for all comparisons, we use the dynamic time warping (DTW) algorithm (Bellman and Kalaba, 1959).

We use Mel-spectrogram Distortion to assess the segmental quality of the synthesised sentences.

Mel-spectrogram distortion (MSD) (Kubichek, 1993) measures the distortion between predicted and extracted (from natural speech) mel-spectrogram coefficients and is defined as:

$$MSD = \frac{\alpha}{T} \sum_{t=1}^{T} \sqrt{\sum_{d=1}^{D-1} (c_d(t) - \hat{c}_d(t))^2} \quad (1)$$

$$\alpha = \frac{10\sqrt{2}}{ln10} \quad (2)$$

where $c_d(t)$, $\hat{c}_d(t)$ are the d-th mel-spectrogram coefficient of the t-th frame from reference and predicted. T denotes the total number of frames in each utterance and D is the dimensionality of the mel-spectrogram coefficients. For our experiments, we use 80 coefficients per speech frame. The zeroth coefficient (overall energy) is excluded from MSD computation, as shown in equation 1.

For evaluating prosody, we use the following metrics calculated on $lf0$:

F0 Root Mean Square Error (FRMSE) is defined as:

$$FRMSE = \sqrt{\frac{\sum_{t=1}^{T} (x_t - \hat{x}_t)^2}{T}} \quad (3)$$

where x_t and $\hat{x}_t$ in our work denote $lf0$ extracted from reference and predicted audio respectively.

F0 Linear Correlation Coefficient (FCORR) is the measure of the direct linear relationship between the predicted $lf0$ and the reference $lf0$. It is expressed as:

$$\frac{T \sum (x_t \hat{x}_t) - (\sum x_t)(\sum \hat{x}_t)}{\sqrt{T(\sum x_t^2) - (\sum x_t)^2}\sqrt{T(\sum \hat{x}_t^2) - (\sum \hat{x}_t)^2}} \quad (4)$$

If x_t and $\hat{x}_t$ have a strong positive linear correlation, FCORR is close to +1.

Gross pitch error (GPE) (Nakatani et al., 2008) is measured as percentage of voiced frames whose relative $lf0$ error is more than 20%. Relative $lf0$ error is defined as:

$$\frac{|x_t - \hat{x}_t|}{x_t} \times 100 \quad (5)$$

Fine pitch error (FPE) (Krubsack and Niederjohn, 1991) is measured as standard deviation of the distribution of relative $lf0$ errors, for which relative $lf0$ error is less than 20%.

Since we don't explicitly predict $lf0$, we use $lf0$ extracted from natural recordings, and synthesised sentences for computation of the objective metrics described above.

4.2.2 Subjective Evaluations

Even though the objective metrics give us a general indication on the prosody and segmental quality of synthesised speech, the metrics may not directly correlate to the perceptual quality. We conduct additional subjective evaluations with human listeners and consider these as the final outcome of our experiments.

For subjective evaluations, we concatenate the synthesised news-style sentences into full news stories, to capture the overall experience of our intended use-case. Each utterance is 3-5 sentences long, and the average duration is $33.47 seconds$. We test our system with 10 expert listeners with native linguistic proficiency in English, using the

MUltiple Stimuli with Hidden Reference and Anchor (MUSHRA) methodology (ITUR Recommendation, 2001). The systems used in this evaluation are described in Table 2. The listeners are asked to rate the appropriateness of each system as a newscaster voice on a scale of 0 to 100. For each utterance, 5 stimuli are presented to the listeners side-by-side on the same screen, representing the 5 test systems in a random order. Each listener rates 51 screens.

5 Results

5.1 Analysis of Objective Metrics

The scores for the objective metrics are shown in Table 3. We observe that both of our newscaster-style models obtain consistently better scores on all metrics, than neutral NTTS and concatenative-based system. Furthermore, we also observe that conditioning the newscaster-style model with CWE helps improve the prosody of the synthesised utterances.

There's a slight loss in segmental quality when conditioning the model with CWE, but it appears to be imperceptible to human listeners.

5.2 Analysis of MUSHRA Scores

The listener responses from the subjective evaluation are shown in Figure 2. In Table 4 the descriptive statistics for the MUSHRA evaluation are reported. The proposed model closes the gap between concatenative-based synthesis for newsreading, which is still largely the industry standard, and the natural recordings by 69.7%. The gap compared with the neutral NTTS voice is also closed by 60.9%. All of the systems present in the MUSHRA test are statistically significant from each other at a p-value of 0.01. This significance is observed across the listener responses using a t-test. Holm-Bonferroni correction was applied due to the number of condition pairs to compare. This significance is also observed over the MUSHRA responses in terms of the rank order awarded by listeners. For this a Wilcoxon signed-rank test applying Holm-Bonferroni correction was used.

The concatenative-based system is prone to audible artefacts at the concatenation-points, primarily due to abrupt changes in fundamental frequency in voiced phonemes. This reduces the perceived naturalness of synthesised speech. The neutral-style system is unable to model the prosody that is distinct to the newscaster-style of spe-

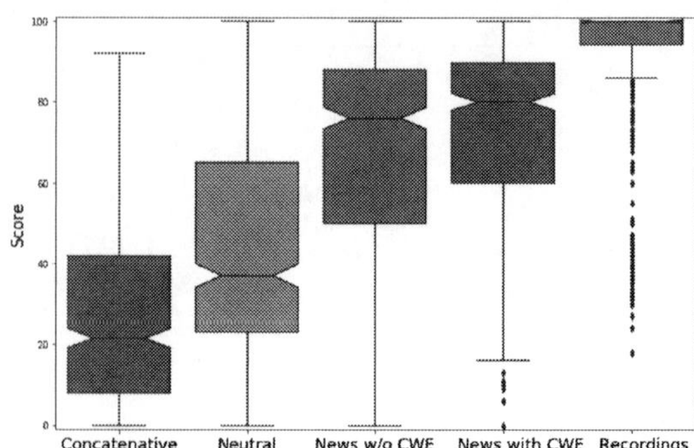

Figure 2: Boxplot of the listener responses in the MUSHRA evaluation

ech. A higher score for the newscaster-style model with CWE conditioning with respect to the model without, provides evidence supporting the hypothesis that we made in Section 1 that CWE features help model the prosodic variation better given the additional information on the syntactic context of words in the sentence.

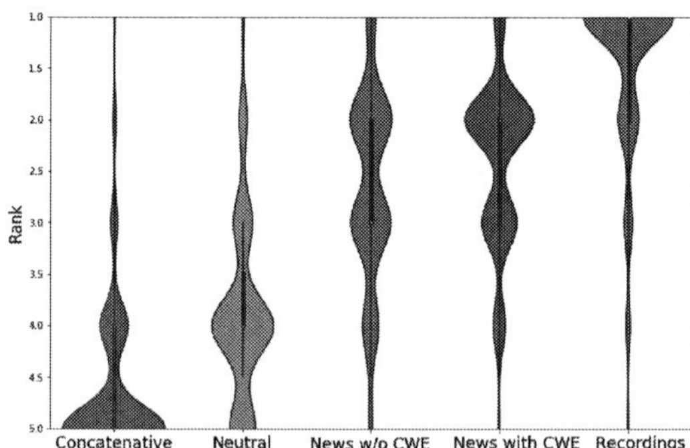

Figure 3: Violin plot of the rank-order awarded by listeners

We also generated a violin plot (Figure 3) depicting the distribution of the rank-order awarded to the systems in the test. We notice that for some of the utterances, the listeners have ranked our newsreader voice (both with and without CWE) higher than the natural recordings, showing that our context generation module is able to closely mimic the recordings in terms of prosody and naturalness.

5.3 Effect of Contextual Word Embeddings on Prosody Modelling

To further reinforce the effect of CWE on prosody modelling for newscaster-style, a preference test was conducted comparing newscaster-style with and without CWE conditioning, using 10 expert

	Segmental Quality	Prosody			
System	MSD (dB)	FRMSE (Hz)	FCORR	GPE (%)	FPE (cents)
Concatenative	6.07	44.85	0.28	33.58	5.68
Neutral	5.27	44.81	0.30	32.02	5.63
News w/o CWE	**4.52**	42.90	0.35	28.89	5.57
News with CWE	4.54	**42.14**	**0.36**	**27.59**	**5.55**

Table 3: Objective metrics for analysis of prosody and segmental quality. High FCORR indicates better prosody. For all other metrics, lower value indicates better performance.

System	Mean score	Median score	Mean Rank	Median Rank
Concatenative	28.31	21.5	4.60	5
Neutral	42.44	37.0	3.86	4
News w/o CWE	68.15	76.0	2.67	3
News with CWE	72.4	80.0	2.41	2
Recordings	91.61	100.0	1.45	1

Table 4: Listener ratings from the MUSHRA evaluation

listeners. Listeners were informed to rate the systems in terms of their naturalness, and were asked to choose between News with CWE, News w/o CWE, or indicate *No Preference*(NP).

Preference	Votes
News with CWE	43.2%
News w/o CWE	31%
No Preference	25.8%

Table 5: Preference test between systems with and without CWE conditioning

The listener responses are shown in Table 5. The samples conditioned on contextual word embeddings are shown to be significantly preferred (43.2%) over the samples generated without (31%), with $p < 0.01$. A binomial test was used to detect statistical significance.

5.4 Analysis of Speech Tempo

We define speech tempo of a corpus as the average number of phonemes present per second. Speech tempo is a crucial aspect in differentiating between the neutral and the newscaster styles. The newscaster-style is more dynamic than the neutral-style utterances, with higher speech tempo. In Table 6 we report the speech tempo in the neutral-style, and the newscaster-style for natural recordings, and compare those with our models with and without CWE. We observe that the model conditioned on CWE can better model the speech tempo in both styles. This gives us additional evidence that conditioning the model on CWE helps us synthesise samples that are not only more style-appropriate, but are also better in naturalness with respect to natural recordings. Analysis of speech

System	Neutral	Newscaster
Recordings	11.63	14.02
with CWE	10.12	13.88
w/o CWE	10.11	13.65

Table 6: Speech tempo: recordings vs test systems

tempo also shows us that the model is able to factorise, and replicate during inference, both styles using just a one-hot style ID.

6 Conclusions

We proposed a bi-style model for generating neutral and newscaster styles of speech. We also proposed multi-scale encoder conditioning, focusing on phoneme-level and word-level inputs. Our proposed model is shown to be able to generate high-quality newsreader voice, which is significantly preferred over the neutral-style voice. We showed that the two styles can be factorised using a one-hot style ID. We also showed that the introduction of CWE conditioning significantly improves the prosody modelling ability of our context generation module, and hope that this result inspires more research into the use of NLP features in NTTS.

References

Kei Akuzawa, Yusuke Iwasawa, and Yutaka Matsuo. 2018. Expressive speech synthesis via modeling expressions with variational autoencoder. In *Interspeech*, pages 3067–3071.

Sercan Arik, Jitong Chen, Kainan Peng, Wei Ping, and Yanqi Zhou. 2018. Neural voice cloning with a few samples. In *Advances in Neural Information Processing Systems*, pages 10040–10050.

Dzmitry Bahdanau, Kyunghyun Cho, and Yoshua Bengio. 2015. Neural machine translation by jointly learning to align and translate. In *ICLR*.

Richard Bellman and Robert Kalaba. 1959. On adaptive control processes. *IRE Transactions on Automatic Control*, 4(2):1–9.

Alan W Black and Nick Campbell. 1995. Optimising selection of units from speech databases for concatenative synthesis.

Bajibabu Bollepalli, Lauri Juvela, and Paavo Alku. 2018. Speaking style adaptation in text-to-speech synthesis using sequence-to-sequence models with attention. *CoRR*.

Ciprian Chelba, Tomas Mikolov, Mike Schuster, and Qi Ge. 2014. orsten brants, phillipp koehn, and tony robinson. 2014. one billion word benchmark for measuring progress in statistical language modeling. INTERSPEECH.

Yutian Chen, Yannis Assael, Brendan Shillingford, David Budden, Scott Reed, Heiga Zen, Quan Wang, Luis C. Cobo, Andrew Trask, Ben Laurie, Caglar Gulcehre, Aäron van den Oord, Oriol Vinyals, and Nando de Freitas. 2019. Sample efficient adaptive text-to-speech. In *International Conference on Learning Representations*.

Jan K Chorowski, Dzmitry Bahdanau, Dmitriy Serdyuk, Kyunghyun Cho, and Yoshua Bengio. 2015. Attention-based models for speech recognition. In *Advances in neural information processing systems*, pages 577–585.

Yu-An Chung, Yuxuan Wang, Wei-Ning Hsu, Yu Zhang, and RJ Skerry-Ryan. 2018. Semi-supervised training for improving data efficiency in end-to-end speech synthesis. *CoRR*, abs/1808.10128.

Jacob Devlin, Ming-Wei Chang, Kenton Lee, and Kristina Toutanova. 2018. Bert: Pre-training of deep bidirectional transformers for language understanding. *CoRR*, abs/1810.04805.

Matt Gardner, Joel Grus, Mark Neumann, Oyvind Tafjord, Pradeep Dasigi, Nelson F. Liu, Matthew Peters, Michael Schmitz, and Luke S. Zettlemoyer. 2018. AllenNLP: A deep semantic natural language processing platform. In *ACL workshop for NLP Open Source Software*.

Gustav Eje Henter, Jaime Lorenzo-Trueba, Xin Wang, and Junichi Yamagishi. 2018. Deep encoder-decoder models for unsupervised learning of controllable speech synthesis. *CoRR*, abs/1807.11470.

Wei-Ning Hsu, Yu Zhang, Ron J. Weiss, Heiga Zen, Yonghui Wu, Yuxuan Wang, Yuan Cao, Ye Jia, Zhifeng Chen, Jonathan Shen, Patrick Nguyen, and Ruoming Pang. 2018. Hierarchical generative modeling for controllable speech synthesis. *CoRR*, abs/1810.07217.

ITUR Recommendation. 2001. Method for the subjective assessment of intermediate sound quality (mushra). *ITU, BS*, pages 1543–1.

Ye Jia, Yu Zhang, Ron J Weiss, Quan Wang, Jonathan Shen, Fei Ren, Zhifeng Chen, Patrick Nguyen, Ruoming Pang, Ignacio Lopez Moreno, et al. 2018. Transfer learning from speaker verification to multispeaker text-to-speech synthesis. In *Advances in neural information processing systems*.

Diederik P Kingma and Jimmy Lei Ba. 2014. Adam: Amethod for stochastic optimization. In *Proc. 3rd Int. Conf. Learn. Representations*.

David A Krubsack and Russell J Niederjohn. 1991. An autocorrelation pitch detector and voicing decision with confidence measures developed for noise-corrupted speech. *IEEE Transactions on signal processing*, 39(2):319–329.

R Kubichek. 1993. Mel-cepstral distance measure for objective speech quality assessment. In *Proceedings of IEEE Pacific Rim Conference on Communications Computers and Signal Processing*, volume 1, pages 125–128. IEEE.

Javier Latorre, Jakub Lachowicz, Jaime Lorenzo-Trueba, Thomas Merritt, Thomas Drugman, Srikanth Ronanki, and Viacheslav Klimkov. 2018. Effect of data reduction on sequence-to-sequence neural tts. *CoRR*, abs/1811.06315.

Naihan Li, Shujie Liu, Yanqing Liu, Sheng Zhao, Xiukun Lin, and Ming Zhou. 2018. Close to human quality tts with transformer. *CoRR*, abs/1809.08895.

Jaime Lorenzo-Trueba, Thomas Drugman, Javier Latorre, Thomas Merritt, Bartosz Putrycz, and Roberto Barra-Chicote. 2018. Robust universal neural vocoding. *CoRR*, abs/1811.06292.

Thomas Merritt, Robert AJ Clark, Zhizheng Wu, Junichi Yamagishi, and Simon King. 2016. Deep neural network-guided unit selection synthesis. In *ICASSP)*, pages 5145–5149. IEEE.

Thomas Merritt, Bartosz Putrycz, Adam Nadolski, Tianjun Ye, Daniel Korzekwa, Wiktor Dolecki, Thomas Drugman, Viacheslav Klimkov, Alexis Moinet, Andrew Breen, et al. 2018. Comprehensive evaluation of statistical speech waveform synthesis. In *SLT*.

Tomas Mikolov, Ilya Sutskever, Kai Chen, Greg S Corrado, and Jeff Dean. 2013. Distributed representations of words and phrases and their compositionality. In *Advances in neural information processing systems*, pages 3111–3119.

Tomohiro Nakatani, Shigeaki Amano, Toshio Irino, Kentaro Ishizuka, and Tadahisa Kondo. 2008. A method for fundamental frequency estimation and voicing decision: Application to infant utterances recorded in real acoustical environments. *Speech Communication*, 50(3):203–214.

Jeffrey Pennington, Richard Socher, and Christopher Manning. 2014. Glove: Global vectors for word representation. In *Proceedings of the 2014 conference on empirical methods in natural language processing (EMNLP)*, pages 1532–1543.

Christian S Perone, Roberto Silveira, and Thomas S Paula. 2018. Evaluation of sentence embeddings in downstream and linguistic probing tasks. *CoRR*, abs/1806.06259.

Nathanaël Perraudin, Peter Balazs, and Peter L Søndergaard. 2013. A fast griffin-lim algorithm. In *Applications of Signal Processing to Audio and Acoustics (WASPAA), 2013 IEEE Workshop on*, pages 1–4. IEEE.

Matthew E. Peters, Mark Neumann, Mohit Iyyer, Matt Gardner, Christopher Clark, Kenton Lee, and Luke Zettlemoyer. 2018. Deep contextualized word representations. In *Proc. of NAACL*.

Wei Ping, Kainan Peng, Andrew Gibiansky, Sercan O. Arik, Ajay Kannan, Sharan Narang, Jonathan Raiman, and John Miller. 2017. Deep voice 3: Scaling text-to-speech with convolutional sequence learning.

Yao Qian, Frank K Soong, and Zhi-Jie Yan. 2013. A unified trajectory tiling approach to high quality speech rendering. *IEEE transactions on audio, speech, and language processing*, 21(2):280–290.

Jonathan Shen, Ruoming Pang, Ron J Weiss, Mike Schuster, Navdeep Jaitly, Zongheng Yang, Zhifeng Chen, Yu Zhang, Yuxuan Wang, Rj Skerrv-Ryan, et al. 2018. Natural tts synthesis by conditioning wavenet on mel spectrogram predictions. In *2018 IEEE International Conference on Acoustics, Speech and Signal Processing (ICASSP)*, pages 4779–4783. IEEE.

R. J. Skerry-Ryan, Eric Battenberg, Ying Xiao, Yuxuan Wang, Daisy Stanton, Joel Shor, Ron J. Weiss, Rob Clark, and Rif A. Saurous. 2018. Towards end-to-end prosody transfer for expressive speech synthesis with tacotron. In *ICML*.

Daisy Stanton, Yuxuan Wang, and R. J. Skerry-Ryan. 2018. Predicting expressive speaking style from text in end-to-end speech synthesis. *CoRR*, abs/1808.01410.

Paul Taylor. 2006. The target cost formulation in unit selection speech synthesis. In *Ninth International Conference on Spoken Language Processing*.

Paul Taylor. 2009. *Text-to-speech synthesis*, pages 111–112. Cambridge university press.

Aäron Van Den Oord, Sander Dieleman, Heiga Zen, Karen Simonyan, Oriol Vinyals, Alex Graves, Nal Kalchbrenner, Andrew W Senior, and Koray Kavukcuoglu. 2016. Wavenet: A generative model for raw audio. In *SSW*, page 125.

Vincent Wan, Yannis Agiomyrgiannakis, Hanna Silen, and Jakub Vit. 2017. Google's next-generation real-time unit-selection synthesizer using sequence-to-sequence lstm-based autoencoders. In *Proc. Interspeech*, pages 1143–1147.

Yuxuan Wang, R. J. Skerry-Ryan, Daisy Stanton, Yonghui Wu, Ron J. Weiss, Navdeep Jaitly, Zongheng Yang, Ying Xiao, Zhifeng Chen, Samy Bengio, Quoc V. Le, Yannis Agiomyrgiannakis, Rob Clark, and Rif A. Saurous. 2017. Tacotron: A fully end-to-end text-to-speech synthesis model. *CoRR*, abs/1703.10135.

Yuxuan Wang, Daisy Stanton, Yu Zhang, R. J. Skerry-Ryan, Eric Battenberg, Joel Shor, Ying Xiao, Ye Jia, Fei Ren, and Rif A. Saurous. 2018. Style tokens: Unsupervised style modeling, control and transfer in end-to-end speech synthesis. In *ICML*.

Generate, Filter, and Rank: Grammaticality Classification for Production-Ready NLG Systems

Ashwini Challa[*]   Kartikeya Upasani[*]   Anusha Balakrishnan   Rajen Subba

Facebook Conversational AI
{ashwinichalla, kart, anushabala, rasubba}@fb.com

Abstract

Neural approaches to Natural Language Generation (NLG) have been promising for goal-oriented dialogue. One of the challenges of productionizing these approaches, however, is the ability to control response quality, and ensure that generated responses are acceptable. We propose the use of a generate, filter, and rank framework, in which candidate responses are first filtered to eliminate unacceptable responses, and then ranked to select the best response. While acceptability includes grammatical correctness and semantic correctness, we focus only on grammaticality classification in this paper, and show that existing datasets for grammatical error correction don't correctly capture the distribution of errors that data-driven generators are likely to make. We release a grammatical classification and semantic correctness classification dataset for the weather domain that consists of responses generated by 3 data-driven NLG systems. We then explore two supervised learning approaches (CNNs and GBDTs) for classifying grammaticality. Our experiments show that grammaticality classification is very sensitive to the distribution of errors in the data, and that these distributions vary significantly with both the source of the response as well as the domain. We show that it's possible to achieve high precision with reasonable recall on our dataset.

1 Introduction

In recent years, neural network-based approaches have been increasingly promising in the context of goal-oriented Natural Language Generation (NLG). These approaches can effectively learn to generate responses of desired complexity and detail from unaligned data. Additionally, these approaches can be scaled with relatively low effort

to new domains and use cases. However, they are less robust to mistakes and have poor worst case performance. Consistently achieving acceptable response quality in a customer facing product is an immediate blocker to using such models widely.

Controlling quality at generation time in these models is challenging, and there are no guarantees that any of the generated responses are suitable to surface to an end user. Additionally, quality is hard to enforce at data collection time, given the increasingly widespread dependence on large pools of untrained annotators. As a result, classifying acceptability with high precision is extremely desirable. It can be used to establish safe fallbacks to acceptable, but potentially less ideal, responses that are generated by more traditional NLG systems like templates. Such responses are likely to be grammatically and semantically correct, but may sacrifice detail, variety, and naturalness; this trade-off may sometimes be necessary in a consumer-facing product. For example, the system could respond with "Here's your weather forecast", and show a card with relevant weather information, rather than generate an incoherent weather forecast.

Some key aspects of acceptability are **grammaticality** and **semantic correctness**. A grammatical response is one that is well-formed, and a semantically correct response is one that correctly expresses the information that needs to be conveyed. Systems that generate ungrammatical or incorrect responses run the risk of seeming unreliable or unintelligent. Another important facet of acceptability is the **naturalnesss** (or human likeness) of the response, that can improve the usability of chatbots and other dialogue systems.

In this paper, we first propose the inclusion of a filtering step that performs acceptability classification in the more widely used generate & rank framework (Generate, Filter, and Rank). Then,

Proceedings of NAACL-HLT 2019, pages 214–225
Minneapolis, Minnesota, June 2 - June 7, 2019. ©2019 Association for Computational Linguistics

---

[*]Equal contribution

we narrow our focus to grammaticality classification, and show how this problem calls for datasets of a different nature than typical grammatical error correction (GEC) datasets. We also show that state-of-the-art GEC models trained on general corpora fail to generalize to this problem. Finally, we introduce a dataset of system-generated grammatical errors for the **weather** domain, and demonstrate the performance of some strong baselines for grammatical classification on this data. This dataset can also be used for further research on semantic correctness classification. Our experiments also reinforce the need for the new framework we propose.

2 Generate, Filter, and Rank

In this section, we first review the pros and cons of the traditional generate & rank framework, and then propose a "filter" step that addresses some of its downsides.

The generate & rank framework has been proposed and widely used in several prior works on goal-oriented dialogue (Walker et al. (2001), Langkilde-Geary and Knight (1998)). In NLG systems, the typical use of this framework involves generating multiple candidate responses (often using various different surface realization techniques), and then reranking these using statistical models (most commonly language models). More recent works have also proposed reranking to optimize for certain personality traits or user engagement (Fang et al. (2017)). The input to the generators is usually a structured representation of what the system needs to convey.

This setup allows for the use of multiple generator models, as proposed in Serban et al. (2017) and Pichl et al. (2018), among others. This greatly increases the number of possible responses that can be surfaced, which can improve both diversity and naturalness. The use of statistical rerankers also allows systems under this framework to optimize for naturalness as well as acceptability (primarily grammaticality), since typical statistical models should easily be able to downrank potentially ungrammatical candidates. However, there are a few practical concerns that arise with using this framework in production:

1. Data sparsity: The space of unseen named entities like locations, datetimes, etc., and other sparse token types is potentially very large. This can result in suboptimal language modeling behaviors, in which language models downrank valid candidates with sparse surface forms.

2. Statistical models that are typically used for reranking cannot capture semantic correctness without conditioning on the goal and arguments. They also run the risk of accidentally biasing towards more likely (but semantically incorrect) responses. This is particularly tricky for ML-based generators, where the generated responses can easily leave out important information. For example, the best models from Nayak et al. (2017) have error rates between 2-5%.

3. There is a significant risk that none of the responses generated by data-driven models is acceptable. For example, in the dataset that we release in this work, there were no grammatical responses generated for around 12% of the scenarios (see Section 4).

The common thread in these issues is that the generate & rank framework conflates acceptability, which is objective, with naturalness and other traits, which are subjective. To address, we propose the addition of a high-precision "filter" step that eliminates any unacceptable responses before the ranking stage, allowing the reranker to focus on optimizing for naturalness and other desirable properties. Since we found grammaticalness to be a more serious issue than semantic correctness in our dataset (Table 2), we explore methods to implement a grammaticality "filter" in the following sections.

	CoNLL 2014	Our dataset
# grammatical	53426	18494
# ungrammatical	21638	14511
% scenarios with no grammatical responses	N/A	12%
Avg. length	22.8	17.9
Vocab size	28180	5669
# goals	N/A	2
# semantically correct	N/A	28475
# semantically incorrect	N/A	4530

Table 2: Comparison of weather responses dataset against the NUCLE corpus

Error Category	Examples
Repeated words like "with", "and".	In Grand Prairie , it 's 100 degrees fahrenheit **with** cloudy skies **with** snow showers.
Agreement	Friday, September 15 in Branford , it'll be cloudy with a high of 73 degrees fahrenheit with **an 61** percent chance of snow showers .
Dangling modifiers	In Tongan Qu on Monday, May 22 **will be** scattered clouds with Patches of Fog , with a high of 18 degrees celsius and a low of 7 degrees .
Incorrect word choice	In Larne on Thursday, November 23 , **it'll be scattered clouds** with Fog , with a high of 46 and a low of 35 degrees fahrenheit.
Ungrammatical n-grams	In Funabashi-shi on Monday, March 20 , there will be a low of 31 with a high of 47 degrees fahrenheit with **scattered clouds skies** and a Light Drizzle
Missing contextual words, like "degrees"	In Caloocan City , expect a temperature of **3 celsius** with mostly sunny skies and Fog Patches
Linking words/phrases	Right now in Arrondissement de Besancon , it 's 2 degrees fahrenheit **with sunny and Light Fog**

Table 1: Mistakes involving grammatical errors and other cases of unacceptability in model-generated weather responses

Generator	Train		Eval		Test	
	# gr	**# ungr**	**# gr**	**# ungr**	**# gr**	**# ungr**
SC-LSTM Lex	4957	2386	1565	882	1712	757
SC-LSTM Delex	1083	2078	365	679	377	657
IR	1530	2513	532	839	493	833
Gen LSTM	3614	1624	1133	600	1247	549

Table 3: Distribution of positive and negative examples in weather responses dataset. # gr and # ungr denote number of grammatical and ungrammatical samples respectively.

3 Mismatched Error Distributions

The CoNLL-2014 shared task on grammatical error correction (Ng et al. (2014)) released the NUCLE corpus for grammatical error correction (GEC), written by students learning English. Ungrammatical sentences in this dataset contain annotations and corrections of each individual error. From a classification perspective, each original ungrammatical utterance in the dataset is a negative example, and the final corrected utterance (obtained by applying all of the corrections to the original ungrammatical utterance) is a positive example. Additionally, sentences without any corrections are positive examples as well.

These positive and negative samples can then be directly used to train the grammaticality filter described in previous sections. In the runtime of the goal-oriented NLG system, this filter would be used to filter out ungrammatical responses that are generated by **models** - even though the filter was trained on human-written responses. This signals the possibility of a data mismatch.

To better understand the nature of this difference, we collected a corpus of system-generated responses for the **weather** domain (see Section 4) and manually inspected 200 of these responses to identify common categories of model mistakes (see Table 1). Interestingly, we found that the most common mistakes made by our models, like repeated words and missing contextual words, don't match any of the error categories in NUCLE (see Table 1 from Ng et al. (2014)). There are also qualitative differences stemming from the domains in these datasets. Our corpus has a large number of mentions of sparse entities (particularly locations), dates, and weather-specific constructs like temperatures, while the NUCLE corpus is open-ended and spans a variety of topics.

In order to quantify this difference, we measure the performance of open-domain GEC models on our corpus by evaluating a model that achieves state-of-the-art performance on the CoNLL-2014 test set (Chollampatt and Ng, 2018). We found that this model failed to generalize well to our dataset (see section 6), and missed several classes of errors. For example, the model failed to catch any of the errors in Table 1 (see Appendix A for more examples).

Intuitively, this suggests that training models for response filtering demands datasets very different in distribution from publicly available datasets that only reflect human mistakes. We show this empirically through experiments in section 6, and describe the process for collecting our dataset in the next section.

4 Dataset

We first collected a dataset of human-generated responses for the weather domain, using a process similar to the one used in Novikova et al. (2017). Each of the collected responses is conditioned on a **scenario**, consisting of a goal (the intent to be expressed) and arguments (information to be expressed). In collecting the dataset, we restricted ourselves to the goals `inform_current_condition` and `inform_forecast`.

An example scenario is

"requested_location": "London",

"temp": "32",

"temp_scale": "fahrenheit",

"precip_summary": "Heavy Blowing Snow"

A possible response for this scenario is `In London, it's currently 32 degrees Fahrenheit with heavy snow.`.

We then trained some standard NLG models on this corpus. Two of these (`sc-LSTM Lex` and `sc-LSTM Delex`) are semantically conditioned LSTMs as described in Wen et al. (2015); the `genLSTM` model is a vanilla LSTM decoder; and `IR` is a simple retrieval-based generator. The details of these are described in Appendix A.1. We generated $n = 3$ responses from each of these models for each scenario in a held out data set, and deduped generated candidates that differed by a single character (often punctuation). We then asked crowdworkers to judge the grammaticality of these responses. Our final dataset[1] consists of 33K model-generated responses with grammaticality and semantic correctness judgments. Table 3 shows a detailed breakdown of grammatical and ungrammatical responses per model.

[1] github.com/facebookresearch/momi

5 Approach

Preprocessing We made the assumption that the specific values of arguments such as locations, dates, and numbers do not affect sentence framing. We therefore replaced locations and dates with placeholder tokens. Numbers are replaced with either __num__, __num_vowel__ if the number begins with a vowel sound (example, 80), or __num_one__ if the number is 1. Hence the sentence *"There is an 85 percent chance of rain in New York on Wednesday, August 25"* would become *"There is an __num_vowel__ percent chance of rain in __location__ on __date__"*. In case of `sc-LSTM delex`, all remaining arguments (such as weather conditions) are also delexicalized.

To maintain class balance in the train set, for each response source, the class with fewer samples is upsampled to match the number of samples of the other class. When training on samples from multiple generators, the samples of each generator in train set are upsampled to match those of generator with highest number of samples. Upsampling is not done for validation or test sets.

Features from Language Model	
Geometric mean: $(\Pi_{i=1}^{m} p_i)^{(1/m)}$	Arithmetic mean: $\sum_{i=1}^{m} p_i/m$
$\min P_x$	$\max P_x$
Median: $\tilde{p}$	Std Dev: σ_{P_x}
$C_{P_x}(0, 0.1), C_{P_x}(0.1, 0.2), ... C_{P_x}(0.9, 1.0)$	

Table 4: Features derived from Language Model. $P_x = p_1, p_2, ...p_m$ is the set of all n-gram probabilities from an n-gram LM for a sentence x. $C_{P_x}(a, b) \in [0, 1]$ is the ratio of n-gram probabilities $p_i \in P_x$ for which $a \leq p_i < b$.

Gradient Boosted Decision Tree Using LM Features (LM-GBDT) Language models (Brown et al. (1992)) can effectively capture n-gram patterns that occur in grammatical data, making features derived from them good candidates to distinguish between grammatical and ungrammatical responses. We train a 7-gram LM[2] on human-written weather responses described in Section 4. The trained LM is then used to extract features listed in Table 4 for each model-generated response. Finally, we feed these features into a

---

[2] We found that 7 gram LM performed slightly better than other lower n-gram LMs. LM with larger n-grams may be better at catching model mistakes that require looking at long-range dependencies.

Model	Training Data	Test Data	R@P98	R@P
Chollampatt and Ng (2018)	NUCLE	Weather	-	75 @ 64
CNN	NUCLE	NUCLE	62.4	-
		Weather	-	80 @ 56.8
	NUCLE + Weather	Weather	52.5	-
CNN	Weather	Weather	71.9	-
CNN + source	**Weather**	**Weather**	**72.8**	-
LM-GBDT	Weather	Weather	63.8	-

Table 5: Training on NUCLE and weather data

gradient boosted decision tree (GBDT) (Friedman (2001)) to classify the model-generated response as grammatical or not.

CNN-based Classification Model We used a convolutional neural network (CNN) for sentence classification in an approach similar to Kim (2014). After pooling convolutional features along the time dimension, the result can be optionally concatenated with additional features. A one-hot vector of length 4 encoding the source of the response (IR, `GenLSTM`, `sc-LSTM delex`, `sc-LSTM lex`) is passed as an additional feature when training on responses from multiple sources.

6 Experiments

We try different combinations of NUCLE corpus and our dataset as train and test sets to learn a grammaticality classifier for model-generated weather responses. Table 5 and 7 lists the results of these experiments described above. As discussed before, since the goal is to build a classifier for use in production systems, we report the recall of models for grammatical class when the precision is very high (98%). In cases where the model does not achieve this precision, we report recall at the highest precision achieved by the model.

`CNN + source` represents the case when the source of response is passed as an additional feature to the CNN. We used filters with widths 2, 3, 4, 5 for the CNN. Performance did not change with different number and sizes of filters.

	Ungrammatical	Semantically incorrect
Ranker	29.4%	8.2%
Filter + Ranker	2.4%	0.75%

Table 6: Comparison of number of times the top ranked response is unacceptable with and without filtering.

6.1 Ranker vs Filter + Ranker

In order to validate the Generate, Filter, and Rank framework, we used our trained n-gram language model[3] (from Section 4) to rank all the responses for each scenario in our dataset. We then measured the % of times the top ranked candidate is ungrammatical, to understand how many times the final response would be ungrammatical in a traditional generate & rank framework. We repeat the experiment with our proposed framework, by filtering ungrammatical responses using a CNN-based filter with 98% precision before the ranking step. The results are shown in Table 6.

The filtering step increases the overall response quality, but comes at the cost of losing genuine grammatical candidates because of slightly lower recall, 72.8%, (the best recall we achieved on the weather data set). This is a fundamental trade-off of our proposed framework; we sacrifice recall for the sake of precision, in order to ensure that users of the system very rarely see an unacceptable response. The semantic correctness also improves, but this doesn't indicate that grammatical filter is enough to solve both grammaticalness and correctness problems.

6.2 Performance of filters on NUCLE and weather data

Table 5 compares performance of CNN, LM-GBDT, and the GEC model used by Chollampatt and Ng (2018). The GEC model is adopted for binary classification by checking whether the model makes a correction for an ungrammatical sentence, and doesn't make any corrections for a grammati-

---

[3] an n-gram based language model is a simple baseline. It is possible to use more sophisticated rankers (such as RNN-LMs) to achieve better results. However, ranking approaches will still fail over filters when there are no grammatical candidates at all.

Model	Training Data	Test Data	R@P98	R@P
CNN + source	Weather	IR	9.8	-
	IR	IR	23.2	-
	Weather	GenLSTM	95.5	-
	GenLSTM	GenLSTM	92.2	-
	Weather	SC-LSTM Delex	25.2	-
	SC-LSTM Delex	SC-LSTM Delex	-	45.9@80
	Weather	SC-LSTM Lex	96.8	-
	SC-LSTM Lex	SC-LSTM Lex	94.6	-
LM-GBDT	Weather	IR	-	8@95.5
	IR	IR	18	-
	Weather	GenLSTM	83.4	-
	GenLSTM	GenLSTM	76	-
	Weather	SC-LSTM Delex	2	-
	SC-LSTM Delex	SC-LSTM Delex	-	65.5@70.5
	Weather	SC-LSTM Lex	90.6	-
	SC-LSTM Lex	SC-LSTM Lex	88.4	-

Table 7: Performance of filter for individual generators

cal sentence [4]. This model achieves poor precision and recall on our dataset, and we found that it fails to generalize adequately to the novel error types in our data.

We also train the CNN on NUCLE data and find that it similarly achieves poor recall when classifying weather responses. This is attributed to the fact that the domain and category of errors in both datasets are different. Comparing Table 1 in Ng et al. (2014) and Table 1 of this work further supports this observation.

The CNN and LM-GBDT are trained and tested on our weather dataset. We report the performance of these models on the **complete** weather test set, not just on individual generators, since this is closest to the setting in which such models would be used in a production system. The CNN consistently has better recall than LM-GBDT at the same precision. CNN + source performs better than the CNN, indicating that information regarding source helps in classifying responses from multiple generators.

Augmenting the weather responses with NUCLE corpus while training the CNN did not help performance.

6.3 Performance of filter for individual generators

Table 7 presents results on test sets of each generator for classifiers trained together on all generators and trained on individual generators. Models trained individually on IR and SC-LSTM Delex responses perform poorly compared to GenLSTM and SC-LSTM Lex as the training set size is much smaller for former. The recall for individual generators is higher when training is done on data from all generators, indicating that the approach generalizes across sources. An exception to this is IR which does better when trained just on IR responses. This may be due to errors of retrieval based approach being different in nature compared to LSTM-based approach.

Tables 8 and 9 in Appendix shows the errors in responses from different generators. Some errors occur more frequently with one generator than another, for example, the problem of repeating words (like *with* and *and*) is dominant in responses generated by the LSTMs, but very rarely seen in IR since it is a retrieval based approach.

6.4 Comparison of LM-GBDT and CNN

The recall of CNN is slightly better than LM-GBDT consistently across experiments. Both approaches do well in catching types of errors listed in Table 1. One difference between the two is the ability of CNN-based models to successfully catch errors such as "1 degrees", while the LM-

---

[4]We assume that the GEC model has classified the response as ungrammatical if an edit is made. This does not account for cases in which the edited response is still ungrammatical. As a result, the precision of this model in the true setting would be lower than that reported in this setting.

GBDT fails to do so. On further inspection, we noticed that the human generated weather responses, which were used as training data for the language model, contained several instances of "1 degrees". The LM-GBDT has a heavy dependency on the quality of features generated by LM (which in turn depends on the quality of the LM training corpus), and this is a disadvantage compared to the CNNs.

7   Related Work & Conclusion

Several previous works have established the need for a generate & rank framework in a goal-oriented NLG system (Walker et al. (2001), Langkilde-Geary and Knight (1998)). Recent work on the Alexa prize (Ram et al. (2018)) has demonstrated that this architecture is beneficial for systems that bridge the gap between task-oriented and open-ended dialogue (Serban et al. (2017), Fang et al. (2017), Pichl et al. (2018)). In such systems, the ranker needs to choose between a much more diverse set of candidates, and potentially optimize for other objectives like personality or user satisfaction. To make such systems practical for production-scale usage, our work proposes the inclusion of a high precision filter step that precedes ranking and can mark responses as acceptable. Our experiments show that this filter with sufficient fallbacks guarantees response quality with high precision, while simply reranking does not (Section 6.1).

In this work, we focus specifically on filtering ungrammatical responses. Previous work in this space has focused on classifying (and sometimes correcting) errors made by humans (Ng et al. (2014)) or synthetically induced errors (Foster (2007)). We found, however, that the domain and error distribution in such datasets is significantly different from that of typical data-driven generation techniques. To address this gap, we release grammatical and semantic correctness classification data generated by these models, and present a reasonable baseline for grammatical classification. The approaches we present are similar to work on grammatical classification using features from generative models of language, like language models (Wagner et al. (2009)). One future direction is to explore modeling semantic correctness classification with the datatset we release.

We compare the performance of two approaches for classifying grammaticality: CNNs, and GBDTs with language model features. Both are standard classifiers that are easy to deploy in production systems with low latency. An interesting future direction would be to explore model architectures that scale better to new domains and generation approaches. This could include models that take advantage of existing GEC data consisting of human responses, as well as datasets similar to ours for other domains. Models that successfully make use of these datasets may have a more holistic understanding of grammar and thus be domain- and generator-agnostic.

A drawback of the generate-filter-rank framework is the increased reliance on a fallback response in case no candidate clears the filtering stage. This is an acceptable trade-off when the goal is to serve responses in production systems where the standards of acceptability are high. One way to alleviate this is to do grammatical error correction instead of simply removing unacceptable candidates from the pipeline. Correcting errors instead of rejecting candidates can be of value for trivial mistakes such as missing articles or punctuation. However, doing this with high precision and correcting semantic errors remains a challenge.

References

Peter F Brown, Peter V Desouza, Robert L Mercer, Vincent J Della Pietra, and Jenifer C Lai. 1992. Class-based n-gram models of natural language. *Computational linguistics*, 18(4):467–479.

Shamil Chollampatt and Hwee Tou Ng. 2018. A multilayer convolutional encoder-decoder neural network for grammatical error correction. In *Proceedings of the Thirty-Second AAAI Conference on Artificial Intelligence*.

Hao Fang, Hao Cheng, Elizabeth Clark, Ariel Holtzman, Maarten Sap, Mari Ostendorf, Yejin Choi, and Noah A Smith. 2017. Sounding board–university of washingtons alexa prize submission. *Alexa Prize Proceedings*.

Jennifer Foster. 2007. Treebanks gone bad. *International Journal of Document Analysis and Recognition (IJDAR)*, 10(3-4):129–145.

Jerome H Friedman. 2001. Greedy function approximation: a gradient boosting machine. *Annals of statistics*, pages 1189–1232.

Yoon Kim. 2014. Convolutional neural networks for sentence classification. In *Proceedings of the 2014 Conference on Empirical Methods in Natural Language Processing*, pages 1746–1751.

Irene Langkilde-Geary and Kevin Knight. 1998. Generation that exploits corpus-based statistical knowledge. In *COLING-ACL*.

Neha Nayak, Dilek Hakkani-Tur, Marilyn Walker, and Larry Heck. 2017. To plan or not to plan? discourse planning in slot-value informed sequence to sequence models for language generation. In *INTERSPEECH*.

Hwee Tou Ng, Siew Mei Wu, Ted Briscoe, Christian Hadiwinoto, Raymond Hendy Susanto, and Christopher Bryant. 2014. The conll-2014 shared task on grammatical error correction. In *Proceedings of the Eighteenth Conference on Computational Natural Language Learning: Shared Task*.

Jekaterina Novikova, Ondej Due, and Verena Rieser. 2017. The e2e dataset: New challenges for end-to-end generation. In *Proceedings of the SIGDIAL 2017 Conference*, pages 201–206.

Jan Pichl, Petr Marek, Jakub Konrád, Martin Matulík, Hoang Long Nguyen, and Jan Sedivý. 2018. Alquist: The alexa prize socialbot. *CoRR*, abs/1804.06705.

Ashwin Ram, Rohit Prasad, Chandra Khatri, Anu Venkatesh, Raefer Gabriel, Qing Liu, Jeff Nunn, Behnam Hedayatnia, Ming Cheng, Ashish Nagar, et al. 2018. Conversational ai: The science behind the alexa prize. *arXiv preprint arXiv:1801.03604*.

Iulian Vlad Serban, Chinnadhurai Sankar, Mathieu Germain, Saizheng Zhang, Zhouhan Lin, Sandeep Subramanian, Taesup Kim, Michael Pieper, Sarath Chandar, Nan Rosemary Ke, Sai Mudumba, Alexandre de Brébisson, Jose Sotelo, Dendi Suhubdy, Vincent Michalski, Alexandre Nguyen, Joelle Pineau, and Yoshua Bengio. 2017. A deep reinforcement learning chatbot. *CoRR*, abs/1709.02349.

Joachim Wagner, Jennifer Foster, and Josef van Genabith. 2009. Judging grammaticality: Experiments in sentence classification. In *CALICO Journal*, pages 474–490.

Marilyn A. Walker, Owen Rambow, and Monica Rogati. 2001. Spot: A trainable sentence planner. In *NAACL*.

Tsung-Hsien Wen, Milica Gasic, Nikola Mrksic, Pei-Hao Su, David Vandyke, and Steve Young. 2015. Semantically conditioned lstm-based natural language generation for spoken dialogue systems. In *EMNLP*.

A   Appendices

A.1   NLG Models for Generating Weather Responses

The dataset we present in this paper consists of responses generated by 4 model types:

1. `sc-LSTM delex`: An sc-LSTM trained on fully delexicalized human responses, where delexicalization refers to the process of replacing spans corresponding to specific arguments by placeholder strings.

2. `sc-LSTM lex`: An sc-LSTM trained on partly delexicalized human responses. For this model, we only delexicalize locations, dates, and temperatures, thus allowing the model to freely choose surface forms for any other arguments.

3. `GenLSTM`: A vanilla LSTM-based decoder model, where the decoder hidden state is initialized using embeddings of the goal and arguments. This model is also trained on fully delexicalized responses.

4. `IR`: A simple retrieval approach in which n random candidates that satisfy the given goal and arguments are retrieved. The retrieved candidates are delexicalized, and any candidates that contain the right arguments (regardless of argument value) are considered valid.

For all models, the final response is obtained by replacing argument placeholders by the canonical values of those arguments in the scenario.

Since our goal was just to get responses from a diverse set of data-driven generators with a reasonable distribution of errors, we did not experiment too much with improving `IR` and `genLSTM`, which are much weaker than the sc-LSTM models.

A.2   Model-Generated Responses: Error Analysis

Tables 8 and 9 show errors made by different generators. While there is an overlap in the category of grammatical errors made by different generators, the frequency of the errors is largely different. There are also a few generator-specific errors. For example, the problem of repeating words (like *with* and *and*) is dominant in responses generated by `GenLSTM`, `sc-LSTM delex`, `sc-LSTM lex`, but very rarely seen in `IR`. This is because human responses themselves are unlikely to have repeating words, however the LSTM-based generators tend to make these mistakes while trying to fit all information into the response. Ungrammatical n-grams like *scattered clouds skies* are very infrequent in `sc-LSTM lex` responses while more commonly seen with other generators. This is because the `sc-LSTM lex` generator directly produces surface forms of weather conditions. LSTM models doesn't tend to generate responses with out of vocabulary words, but it is something common with IR responses usually because of spelling mistakes in templates.

A.3 General GEC Model Performance

Table 10 shows examples of ungrammatical responses that the general GEC model ((Chollampatt and Ng, 2018)) failed to correct, and Table 11 shows examples of ungrammatical responses that the model correctly edited. The model corrects mistakes that are much more likely to occur in the GEC data (like verb agreement), but fails to catch model-specific error types like stuttering and other ungrammatical n-grams.

Generator	Error Category	Examples
SC-LSTM Lex	Repeating words like "with", "and".	In Grand Prairie , it 's 100 degrees fahrenheit **with** cloudy skies **with** snow showers.
	Poor choice of words to connect 2 phrases	Right now in Medford , **with** a temperature of -10 degrees celsius .
	Wrong Plurals/singulars	In Yushu , it's **1 degrees** celsius and cloudy .
	Missing words that forms incomplete sentences	In Tongan Qu on Monday, May 22 **will be** scattered clouds with Patches of Fog , with a high of 18 degrees celsius and a low of 7 degrees . ... May 22 there will be scattered clouds ... Right now in East Liverpool it is **-3 fahrenheit** with Heavy Rain. *missing word degrees*
	Wrong articles	Friday, September 15 in Branford , it'll be cloudy with a high of 73 degrees fahrenheit with **an 61** percent chance of snow showers .
	Wrong pronouns	In Larne on Thursday, November 23 , **it'll be scattered clouds** with Fog , with a high of 46 and a low of 35 degrees fahrenheit. *there'll be scattered clouds*
SC-LSTM Delex	Repeating words like "with", "and"	In Chengtangcun on Wednesday, April 12 expect a high of 2 degrees and a low of -10 degrees celsius **with** cloudy skies **with** Snow Showers .
	Wrong word choices Wrong articles	In Funabashi-shi on Monday, March 20 , there will be a low of 31 with a high of 47 degrees fahrenheit with **scattered clouds skies** and a Light Drizzle In Newbury on Tuesday, February 07 , there will be **an 46** percent chance of Heavy Rain Showers with a high of 5 degrees celsius with overcast skies .
	Wrong Pluarals/Singulars	In Shiselweni District on Tuesday, March 21 , it will be overcast with a high of 8 degrees celsius and a low of **1 degrees** .
	Missing contextual words like "degrees"	In Caloocan City , expect a temperature of **3 celsius** with mostly sunny skies and Fog Patches

Table 8: Some more examples of grammatical errors made by different generation models in our dataset.

Generator	Error Category	Examples
Gen LSTM	Repeating words like "with", "and"	Right now in Wojewodztwo Maopolskie , it 's sunny **with** Light Thunderstorms **with** Hail and a temperature of 13 degrees fahrenheit .
	Poor word choices	Right now in Franklin Square , it 's 96 degrees fahrenheit with **scattered clouds skies** .
	Wrong articles	On Friday, November 17 in San-Pedro , expect a low of 44 and a high of 68 degrees fahrenheit with **an 41** percent chance of Flurries .
	Wrong Plurals/Singulars	Right now in Minnetonka Mills , it 's **1 degrees** celsius with sunny skies .
	Wrong pronouns	On Monday, July 03 in Himeji Shi , **it'll be scattered clouds** with a high of 48 degrees fahrenheit. *there'll be scattered clouds*
	Wrong connecting words	Right now in Arrondissement de Besancon , it 's 2 degrees fahrenheit **with sunny and Light Fog** *... and sunny with light fog ... would make it grammatical*
IR	Wrong articles	In Shiraki Marz on Thursday, November 09, there will be **an 51** percent chance of Heavy Blowing Snow and a high of 39 degrees fahrenheit
	Wrong ordinal indicators	On Friday, June **02th** in Selma there will be a low of 82 degrees fahrenheit with Light Thunderstorms with Hail
	Wrong Plurals/Singulars	On Tuesday, June 13, in Wilayat-e Paktiya, there will be Heavy Snow Showers and the high will be **1 degrees** celsius.
	Wrong helping verbs (Plural versus singular)	N/A
	Wrong Pronoun	On Wednesday, October 18, in Reus, **it'll be scattered clouds** and 3 degrees celsius. *... there'll be scattered clouds ...*
	Poor templates like one with repeating words, spelling mistakes, missing words like degrees	In Rudraprayag on Tuesday, November Tuesday, June 13 temp is **-8 to 0 celsius** with Low Drifting **Snow Snow** Showers and overcast cloud
	Out of vocabulary words	It's currently -15 degrees fahrenheit **t** and mostly clear with gentle breeze in Dammam

Table 9: Some more examples of grammatical errors made by different generation models in our dataset.

Response	Error type
On Friday, February 17 in Changwat Samut Songkhram, expect **a likely of heavy rain showers** and a high of 15 degrees celsius.	Agreement
Currently in Maastricht there is fog and is -3 Fahrenheit.	Missing "degrees"
Right now in Westminster it is **1 degrees** Fahrenheit with partly cloudy skies.	Numerical agreement
In Ayacucho on Wednesday, February 22, **with a** high of 83 degrees fahrenheit **with a** 98 percent chance of light snow.	Repeated "with", and missing linking words
In kajiado on Thursday, January 12, expect a high of 82 degrees and a low of 61 degrees Fahrenheit **with mostly sunny**.	Incomplete response

Table 10: Mistakes involving grammatical errors and other cases of unacceptability in model-generated weather responses

Original Response	Corrected Response
The weather for Wednesday, December 27 in Oak Hill will includes a high of 14 Celsius and a 37 percent chance of heavy freezing rain.	The weather for Wednesday, December 27 in Oak Hill **will include** a high of 14 Celsius and a 37 percent chance of heavy freezing rain.
In Ocean County, it is 34 degrees Fahrenheit with sunny.	In Ocean County, it is 34 degrees Fahrenheit with sunny **weather**.
In Bim Son, it is 1 degrees fahrenheit with funnel cloud.	In Bim Son, it is 1 degrees fahrenheit with **funnel clouds**.

Table 11: Mistakes involving grammatical errors and other cases of unacceptability in model-generated weather responses

Content-based Dwell Time Prediction Model for News Articles

Heidar Davoudi[1], Aijun An[1], Gordon Edall[2]
[1]Department of Electrical Engineering and Computer Science, York University, Canada
[2]The Globe and Mail, Canada
{davoudi,aan}@cse.yorku.ca, GEdall@globeandmail.com

Abstract

The article dwell time (i.e., expected time that users spend on an article) is among the most important factors showing the article engagement. It is of great interest to news agencies to predict the dwell time of an article before its release. It allows online newspapers to make informed decisions and publish more engaging articles. In this paper, we propose a novel content-based approach based on a deep neural network architecture for predicting article dwell times. The proposed model extracts emotion, event and entity-based features from an article, learns interactions among them, and combines the interactions with the word-based features of the article to learn a model for predicting the dwell time. We apply the proposed model to a real dataset from a national newspaper showing that the proposed model outperforms other state-of-the-art baselines.

1 Introduction

For online newspapers, it is desirable to predict how user-engaging an article is before publishing it so that editors have an idea about the prosperity of the article. This will help editors select more engaging articles to publish and also make smarter decisions to increase revenue (e.g., displaying more advertisements with an engaging article). Most of the previous studies focus on predicting the page views (i.e., user clicks) as the sole indicator of user engagement and article success (Kim et al., 2016; Ioannidis et al., 2016). However, click-based engagement modeling can be quite noisy (e.g., when a user clicks on a wrong article) and may not show the actual user engagement or satisfaction (Yi et al., 2014). Alternatively, it is shown that the time that a user spends on a page, known as the *dwell time*, is one of the most significant indicators of user engagement (Claypool et al., 2001; Fox et al., 2005; Kim et al., 2014). Thus, we consider dwell time as an engagement measure and design an effective model to predict the dwell time of an article based on its content.

There are some studies on dwell time prediction. Most of them predict dwell time for web-pages instead of news articles. Liu et al. (Liu et al., 2010) use regression trees to predict the Weibull distributions of webpage dwell time using keywords and page size. Yi et al. (Yi et al., 2014) predict web content dwell time using support vector regression based on the content length and topic category across different devices. Kim et al. (Kim et al., 2014) use a regression model to estimate the Gamma distributions of page dwell time based on the topic of the page, its length and its readability level. To our knowledge, none of the studies focuses on news articles nor investigates whether high-level features such as events, entities and emotions play an important role in the user engagement of an article measured by dwell time. We believe such high level features are important factors for dwell time prediction.

In this paper we focus on news articles and consider *events*, *emotions* as well as *people* and *organizations* as main contributors to the article dwell time. Both low-level (e.g., word-based) and high level features (e.g., people) are used in our prediction model. However, features such as people and organizations have a very high dimensionality resulting in sparse data representations. In addition, interactions between such features matter. For example, articles mentioning two celebrities (e.g., Prince Harry and Meghan Markle) may be more engaging than articles mentioning only one of them. To address such issues, we propose a model based on the wide and deep neural network architecture (Cheng et al., 2016) which *memorizes* the low order interactions between the sparse features (e.g., people in articles), and at the same

Proceedings of NAACL-HLT 2019, pages 226–233
Minneapolis, Minnesota, June 2 - June 7, 2019. ©2019 Association for Computational Linguistics

time *generalizes* word-based content through the deep component. In order to learn the interactions between features, we adopt the factorization machine (Guo et al., 2017), which extracts feature interactions automatically, as the wide component in the proposed model. Our main contributions are as follows. First, we design a novel framework for predicting the dwell time of a news article based on its content. Second, we propose an effective deep neural network model that combines the low-order interactions between high-level factors (i.e., events, emotions and entities) and word-based abstract features for article dwell time prediction. Third, we apply the proposed model to a real dataset from the Globe and Mail[1] and show the effectiveness of the proposed model and the usefulness of event, emotion and entity based features and their interactions for dwell time prediction.

2 Problem Definition

Assume that $\mathcal{D} = \{a_i\}_{i=1}^{N}$ is a set of articles, and $\mathcal{T}_i = \{t_j\}_{j=1}^{N_i}$, is a set of dwell times of article $a_i \in \mathcal{D}$ (based on different users visits), and N_i is the number of visits which article a_i has. To see which type of distribution is most appropriate for modeling article dwell time, we fit the dwell times of articles into different distributions and calculate the average log likelihood among all the articles as the fitness scores. The negative log likelihood of Normal, Exponential and Weibull distributions for our real dataset from the Globe and Mail dataset are 5100.57, 4447.62, and 4306.89 respectively. Therefore, Weibull distribution is selected for modeling article dwell times. Thus, we define the *dwell time* of article a_i, denoted by y_i, as the expected value of the Weibull distribution of dwell times in $\mathcal{T}_i$. We utilize y_i as the target value and build a model to predict it.

PROBLEM STATEMENT: Given a set of articles $\mathcal{D} = \{a_i\}_{i=1}^{N}$ and their respective dwell times, the goal is to learn a model so that it can be used to predict the dwell time of a new article.

3 Detecting High Level Content Factors

3.1 Article-level Emotion Detection

Emotion detection from text has been widely studied in different contexts (Mohammad and Turney, 2013). However, it is not been investigated for the dwell time prediction task. We consider 6 basic emotions (i.e., *happiness, sadness, disgust, anger, surprise,* and *fear*) which are widely used in the emotion detection (Ekman, 1992; Agrawal et al., 2018). We utilize a publicly available emotion lexicon (Mohammad and Turney, 2010) as the seed words of different emotions. Given an article $a_i \in \mathcal{D}$, and the word $w \in a_i$, the emotion vector of word w is defined as: $\boldsymbol{em}(w) = [emw_j]$, where emw_j is the average similarity[2] between the pre-trained embedding vector of word w (Mikolov et al., 2013) and those of the seed words of emotion j. The emotion vector for article a_i is calculated as:

$$X_{EM}^i = \frac{1}{|\sum_{w \in a_i} \boldsymbol{em}(w)|_1} \sum_{w \in a_i} \boldsymbol{em}(w) \qquad (1)$$

where the denominator is for the scaling purpose.

3.2 Article-level Event Detection

News and events are closely related to each other. Most of the time, a news article reports one central event and a mixture of associated subsidiary events (Chakraborty et al., 2016). The central and subsidiary events manifest themselves in the article content through the event trigger words. Despite the importance of events in news analytics applications (Agrawal et al., 2016), to the best of our knowledge, no study has considered them in article dwell time analysis.

We adapt the method proposed in (Yang and Mitchell, 2016) to extract the events at the article level. The method learns event structures and relations from a corpus and trains a Conditional Random Field (CRF) to extract events. The learned probabilistic models are integrated into a single model to jointly extract events and entities (e.g., people and organizations) from a document. We train the model on the ACE 2005 corpus[3] (Walker et al., 2006). We follow the same setting as (Yang and Mitchell, 2016). We define the event vector for each word w in article a_i as follows: $\boldsymbol{ev}(w) = [evw_j]$, where evw_j is 1 if w is assigned to the $j'th$ event, otherwise 0. The article level event vector X_{EV}^i for article a_i is defined as:

$$X_{EV}^i = \frac{1}{|\sum_{w \in a_i} \boldsymbol{ev}(w)|_1} \sum_{w \in a_i} \boldsymbol{ev}(w) \qquad (2)$$

We compute the entity vector for word w in a similar fashion: $\boldsymbol{en_k}(w) = [enw_j]$, where enw_j is 1 if w is the $j'th$ instance of entity k (where

---

[1] https://www.theglobeandmail.com

[2] We use the positive cosine similarity (i.e., max{0,cosine similarity}) as the similarity measure.

[3] https://catalog.ldc.upenn.edu/LDC2006T06

k is a type of entity, i.e., person or organization), otherwise 0. For article a_i, the article level entity vector $X^i_{EN_k}$ is defined as:

$$X^i_{EN_k} = \frac{1}{|\sum_{w \in a_i} en_k(w)|_1} \sum_{w \in a_i} en_k(w) \qquad (3)$$

We extract 31 events, 87083 people, and 79143 organizations from the the Globe and Mail dataset.

4 Content-based Correlation Analysis

In this section, we study how different factors of an articles (i.e., entities, emotions, and events) impact the dwell time of the article. We define the *engagement score* of factor c as follows:

$$Score(c) = \frac{1}{df(c)} \sum_i \mathbb{I}[c \in a_i] \times y_i \qquad (4)$$

where $\mathbb{I}$ is the indicator function and $df(c)$ is the number of articles containing c. The intuition is that if a factor c appears exclusively in some articles with high dwell time (i.e., y_i), it should have a high engagement score. For example, if *Barak Obama* appears in articles with high dwell time, it should receive a high engagement score.

To investigate the extend to which the engagement score of each article factor could explain the variability of the dwell time of articles, we do a Pearson correlation analysis. In particular, we estimate the predicted dwell time of article a_i by averaging the engagement scores of all individual factors of the same type in the article a_i, and then calculate the Pearson correlation coefficient between an article's actual dwell time and its predicted value. Figure 1 shows the Pearson correlation scores between the actual dwell times and the predicted ones for each type of factor. As illustrated, the emotions (EMO) involved in the articles show the most correlation with the article dwell time. Moreover, location (LOC) and time (TIME) have the least correlation with dwell times. This observation motivates us to use emotion (EMO), event (EVENT), person (PER) and organization (ORG) as the *augmented features* in building the dwell time prediction model.

5 Deep Dwell-time Prediction Model

To learn a dwell time prediction model, we represent an article using both the words in the article and its augmented features (i.e., emotions, events, people and organizations). However, the people and organization features are sparse and high-dimensional. Thus, special attention should

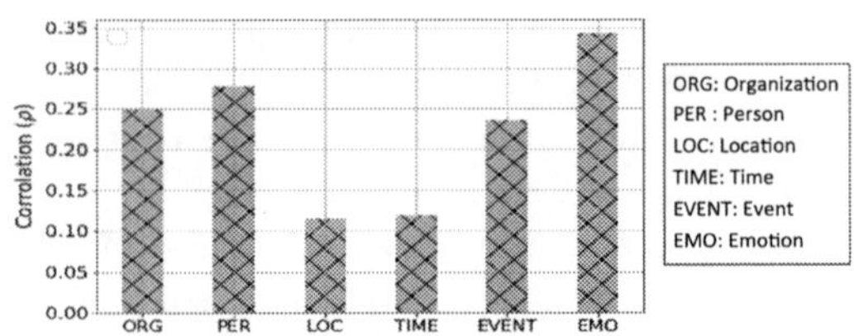

Figure 1: Correlation between the true dwell time and predicted dwell time based on different factors.

be paid to deal with such input features. *Deep neural networks* can learn feature representations and alleviate need for feature engineering by embedding sparse features into a low-dimensional dense space. However, the embedding space may be over-generalized and produce poor results in prediction tasks, when the interactions between high-dimensional features are sparse (Cheng et al., 2016). But such interactions are important for predicting dwell time. For example, an article about two celebrities attending the same event is more likely attracting more readers. Thus, we propose a deep neural network architecture which leverages the augmented features and their interactions in combination with the document (i.e., article) representation to predict the article dwell time.

Inspired by (Guo et al., 2017), we utilized the factorization machine (Rendle, 2010) to capture the augmented feature interactions. However, the proposed model is different from (Guo et al., 2017) in the following aspects: (1) we augment the article content with emotion, event and entity features (2) our model allows multiple factorization machines (each feature is represented with multiple embedding vectors in the factorization layer).

5.1 The Architecture

Figure 2 shows the proposed architecture for the article dwell time engagement prediction task. The architecture consists of two main components: the *deep* and the *factorization machine* components. While the deep competent learns the high order feature interactions and generalizes the article content through a multilayer encoder, the factorization machine captures the low order interactions among the highly sparse augmented features. In particular, suppose that each article is represented by the *TFIDF* (Salton and McGill, 1986) vector X_c, which is fed into the deep component, and augmented vector $X_f = [X_{EV}; X_{EM}; X_{EN}]$, which goes to the factorization machine component, where X_{EV}, X_{EM}, and

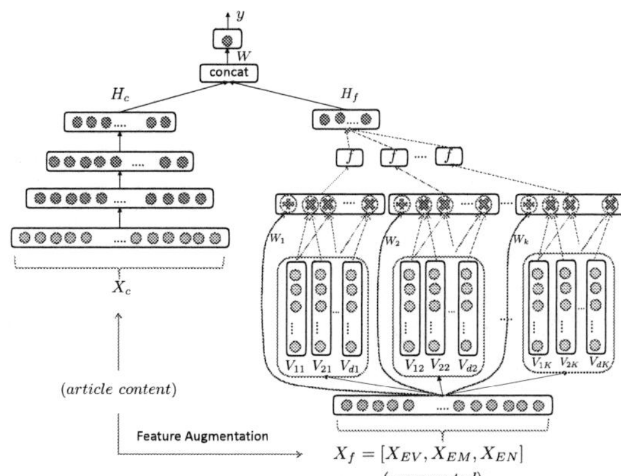

Figure 2: The architecture for article dwell time engagement prediction (left side is deep component and right side is the factorization machine).

$X_{EN} = [X_{EN_{PER}}; X_{EN_{ORG}}]$ are event, emotion, and entity vectors respectively. The whole model is specified by the following equation:

$$H = Concat(Hc, H_f) \qquad (5)$$
$$y = WH + b \qquad (6)$$

where H_c, H_f are the latent vectors learned by deep and the factorization machine components, H is the concatenation of these two vectors, and W, and b are weight and bias parameters.

5.1.1 Factorization Machine Component

A simple strategy to capture the interactions between features is to learn a weight for each combination of two features. However, this naive approach does not work when the input feature space is sparse. Factorization machine solves the problem by modeling the pairwise feature interactions as the inner product of low dimensional vectors.

The first layer in the factorization machine component is the embedding layer. Given the sparse (augmented) input vector $X_f = [x_i]_{d \times 1}$, it learns multiple vectors $V_{ik} = [v_{ikl}]_{M \times 1}$ ($k = 1 \ldots K$) for each input dimension, where V_{ik} is the $k'th$ vector for dimension i, and v_{ikl} is the $l'th$ elements of V_{ik}. Then, these factors are fed into the interaction layer to capture the first order and the second order interactions. The interaction layer operation along with the $k'th$ dimension can be formalized as follows:

$$hf_k = f(\underbrace{b_k + W_k \cdot X_f}_{\oplus} + \sum_{i=1}^{d} \sum_{j=i+1}^{d} \underbrace{V_{ik} \cdot V_{jk} x_i x_j}_{\otimes}) \qquad (7)$$

where hf_k is the $k'th$ elements of factorization machine component output $H_f = [hf_k]_{K \times 1}$, $W_k = [w_{km}]_{d \times 1}$ (w_{km} is the $m'th$ element of W_k) and b_k

are the parameter vector and the bias to be learned and f is the activation function. The $\oplus$ and $\otimes$ symbols in Figure 2 refer to the first order and the second order interaction operations respectively. In fact, factorization machine replaces the interaction weights between feature x_i and x_j with the inner product of respective embedding vectors (i.e., $V_{ik} \cdot V_{jk}$). From modeling perspective, this is powerful since each feature ends up in an embedding space where similar features in this space are close to each other.

5.1.2 Deep Component

In the proposed architecture, the deep component is a dense feed-forward neural network. Each article is vectorized using the *TFIDF* approach (after removing stop words), then is fed into this component. The feed-forward layers convert this sparse vector into low-dimensional dense real-valued vectors.

6 Empirical Evaluation

6.1 Dataset and Set up

All the experiments are conducted on a real dataset from the Globe and Mail dataset. The data collection platform in this company records a timestamp whenever an article page is requested. The difference between two consecutive page click timestamps is used to calculate the articles dwell times. As usual in web analytics the last article in a visit is ignored as we cannot estimate the dwell time for it. Clickstream data is usually noisy. Thus, as a cleaning step, the articles with less than 10 views and dwell time more than 30 minutes are removed resulting in 28502 articles published over period of 2014-01 to 2014-07. Moreover, all the experiments in this section are based on the 10-fold cross validation. We set M and K in the proposed model to 100 and 10 respectively. We used the code in (Pedregosa et al., 2011) with default parameter setting for non-neural networks, and neural network models are implemented using Keras with tensorflow backend (Chollet et al., 2015).

6.2 Baselines

We compare the proposed model with the following baselines including both shallow and deep models as well as Random Forest based models.

Linear Regression (LR): This is a simple baseline used the topics or document vectors as the features and the linear regression method to predict article dwell times. We extract the articles topics based on the LDA approach (Blei et al., 2003). We set the number of topics to 70 based on the best coherence scores proposed in (Röder et al., 2015). Moreover, we learn the vector representation of each article using the doc2vec method proposed in (Le and Mikolov, 2014). We set the vector size to 100 in all experiments.

Random Forest Regression (RF): Random Forest regression performs well in many applications. It trains an ensemble of uncorrelated decision trees (10 trees in our experiments, which is the default setting in the sklearn code (Pedregosa et al., 2011)), and outputs the average result in the prediction. We used the topic or doc2vec vectors as the input to the Random Forest regression model.

Word Embedding + CNN: We adopt the approach proposed in (Kim, 2014) for the dwell time prediction task. The architecture is comprised of one layer of convolution on top of word vectors pre-trained from an unsupervised neural language model. We use the word vectors[4] trained on 100 billion words of Google News (Mikolov et al., 2013) to initialize the embedding vectors, then fine tuned them in the learning phase. We change the last layer of the architecture (i.e., softmax) to a fully connected (i.e., dense) layer for our task. The final architecture includes convolution, max pooling and fully connected layers.

LSTM + Attention: This is the attention mechanism on top of LSTM layer. The attention layer is designed according to (Raffel and Ellis, 2015). The input of the LSTM are word vectors initialized to pre-trained vectors in (Mikolov et al., 2013). We use a fully connected layer on top of the attention layer to produce the final output.

Multilayer Perception (MLP): This is the multilayer feed-forward network with 3 fully connected (dense) hidden layers. In the model architecture we set 300, 200, and 100 as the hidden layer sizes respectively. This is the deep component in the proposed deep and wide model.

6.3 Evaluation Metrics

We utilize the following metrics to evaluate the performance of different models. Given the actual dwell time y_i and predicted dwell time $\hat{y}_i$ for article a_i ($i = 1, 2, \ldots N$). We calculate the *Mean Square Error* (*MSE*) as follows:

$$MSE = \frac{1}{N} \sum_{i=1}^{N} (y_i - \hat{y}_i)^2 \qquad (8)$$

---

[4] Available at: https://code.google.com/archive/p/word2vec/

Method	MSE	RAE (%)
LR +LDA	4835.74	90.75
LR + Doc2Vec	4857.26	91.21
RF + LDA	4750.10	87.96
RF + Doc2Vec	4566.38	86.44
Word2Vec+CNN	4564.80	85.58
LSTM + Attention	4553.85	90.66
MLP	4122.35	80.79
MLP+Flat Augmented Features (without FM)	4483.34	85.77
Proposed Model (MLP+Augmented Features+FM)	**3883.13**	**78.51**

Table 1: Evaluation of different methods.

Moreover, we calculate the *Relative Absolute Error* (*RAE*) as:

$$RAE = \frac{\sum_{i=1}^{N} |y_i - \hat{y}_i|}{\sum_{i=1}^{N} |y_i - \bar{y}_i|} \qquad (9)$$

where $\bar{y}_i = \frac{1}{N} \sum_{i=1}^{N} y_i$. Note that $RAE \in [0, \infty)$.

6.4 Experimental Results

Table 1 shows the MSEs and RAEs of different baseline approaches as well as the proposed model. As shown, the proposed model outperforms all the baselines. For shallow (i.e., LR-based) and RF-based models we learn the features using LDA or Doc2Vec approaches and then train the model with Linear Regression (LR) and Random Forest (RF) respectively. As shown, among such models RF+Doc2Vec performs the best.

Among the deep neural network based baselines, we observe that MLP performs better than the other two. One reason could be that our dataset is not very big (with 28502 articles) and as a result the complex models such as CNN and LSTM may overfit to the training data.

To investigate the effect of learning feature interactions with factorization machines, we created another baseline that use MLP with both words and augmented features as input without using factorization machines (denoted as 'MLP + Flat Augmented features" in Table 1). We choose MLP because it is the best among the baselines. As can be seen, the naive approach of adding the augmented features to MLP without using factorization machines leads to poor results.

Table 2 shows the effect of different types of augmented features on the performance of the proposed model. As we observe, using all the augmented features in the proposed model results in the best performance.

6.5 Hyper parameter study

Figure 3 shows the model performance in terms of the number of hidden vectors per feature dimension. We increase the number of hidden vectors

Augmented Features	MSE	RAE (%)
PER	3966.15	79.49
PER+ORG	3963.55	79.36
PER+ORG+EVENT	3933.71	79.10
PER+ORG+EVENT+EMO	**3883.13**	**78.51**

Table 2: Effect of different augmented features.

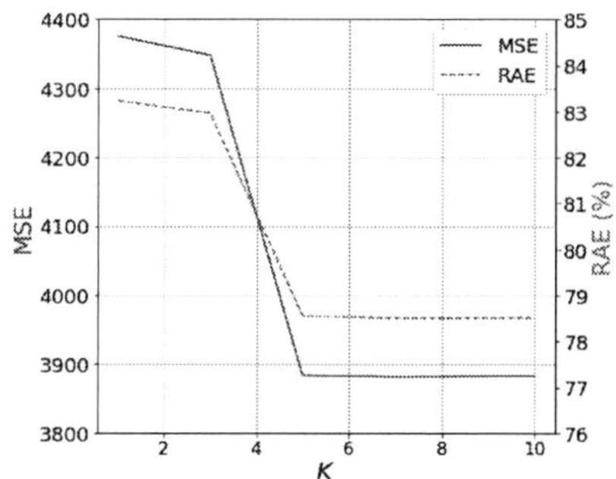

Figure 3: The number of hidden vectors.

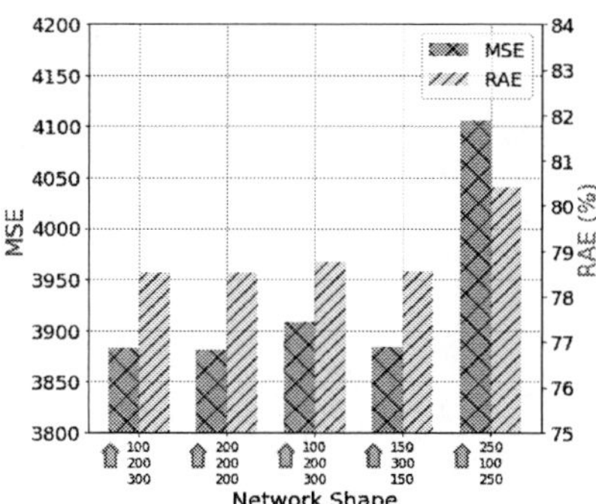

Figure 4: The architecture shapes.

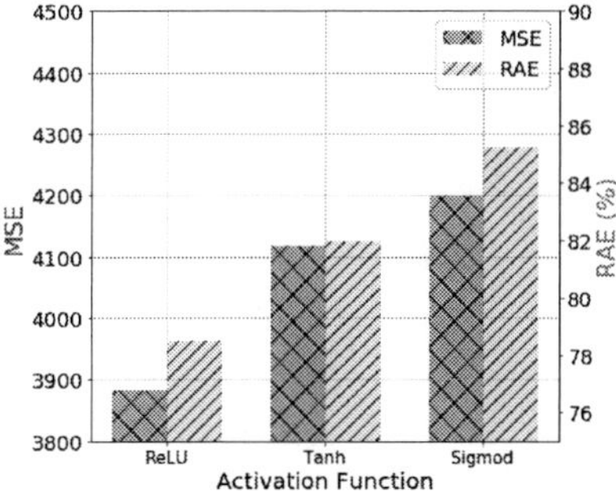

Figure 5: The activation functions.

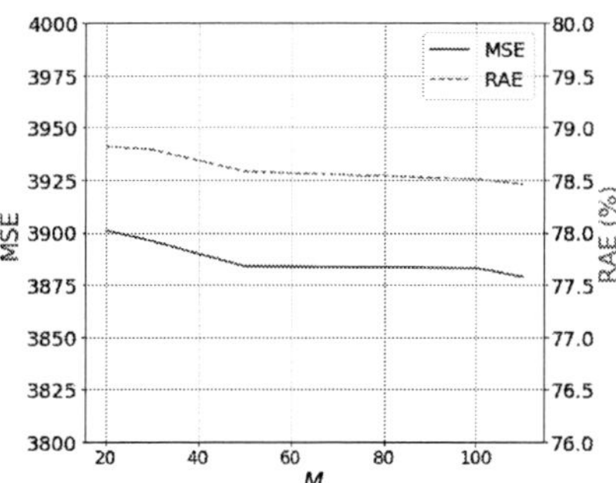

Figure 6: The hidden vector size.

(i.e., K) in the factorization machine component and calculate the errors accordingly. As can be observed, the errors decrease significantly by increasing K from 1 to 5, then becomes stable. This suggests that a value between 5 to 10 would be a good choice for this parameter.

To see the effect of different deep component architecture shapes on the error measures, we keep the number of nodes constant (i.e., 600), and change the number of nodes in the hidden layers. Figure 4 shows the effect of selecting different architectures on the errors. As can be seen, the 250-100-250 is the worst among all architecture and 300-200-100 is slightly better than the others.

In order to study the effect of activation functions on the overall errors, we keep the last layer activation function to ReLU (as it outputs a dwell time value which is always a positive real number) and change the other activation functions to $Tanh$

and $Sigmoid$, and then $ReLU$. Figure 5 shows the model errors for different activation functions. Among these activation functions, $ReLU$ gives the best performance and $Simod$ performs considerably worse than the others.

Figure 6 shows the effect of the hidden vector size (i.e., M) of factorization machine component on the overall errors. We observe that errors slightly decrease by increasing hidden vector size form 20 to 40, and then does not show any significant improvement for M between 40 to 100. As such, the proposed model is not sensitive to vector size and this parameter can be set with a value between 40 to 100. Figure 7 shows the prediction errors for different numbers of layers of the deep component. As can be seen, the errors decrease as we increase the number of hidden layers from 1 to 2 and is the best when it is 3.

In order to study the effect of neurons on prediction errors. We start from $300 - 200 - 100$ architecture and increase the hidden layer size by a certain percentage (i.e., 10%, 20%,...), then calculate the errors for each architecture. Figure 8 shows the performance of the model for different percentage of node number increase. We observe that the errors remain almost at the same levels

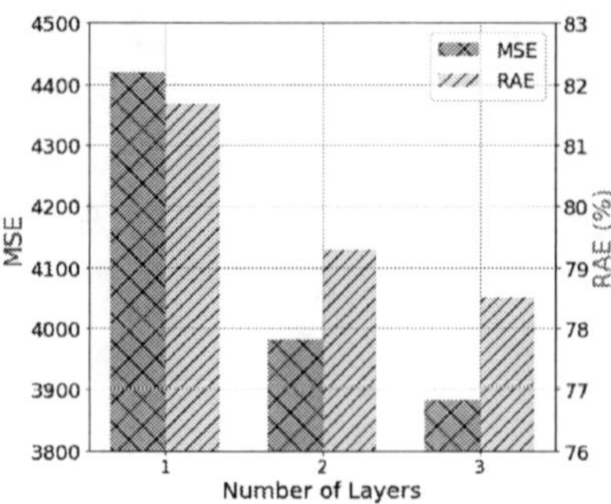

Figure 7: The number of layers.

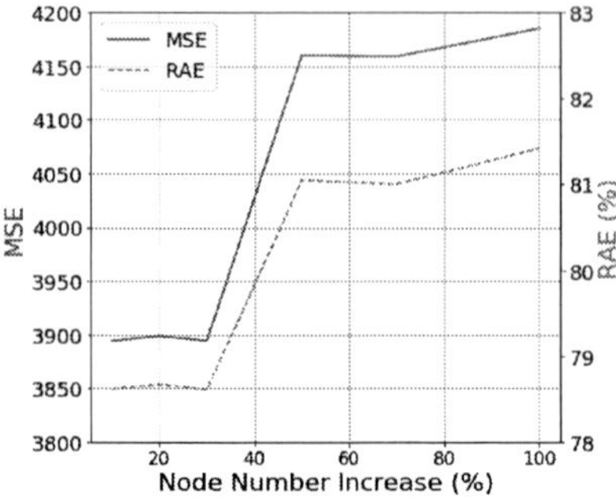

Figure 8: The number of nodes.

when the node numbers in each layer increase by 30%, then starts to get worse from 30% to 100%. This could be due to the overfitting problem.

7 Conclusion

We proposed a novel model to predict the dwell time of a news article based on its content. We first extracted events, emotions, people and organizations from news articles, and then used a deep and wide neural network architecture to learn a prediction model from both the word-based features (via the deep model) and the interactions among the pre-extracted features (via factorization machines). We applied the proposed model to a real dataset from a national newspaper, and showed that using events, emotions, people and organizations and their interactions as features greatly improves article dwell time prediction. The performance of our model is better than using only the deep models for learning abstract features from document representations such as topics, word embedding or TFIDF-based features. As dwell time is a commonly used article engagement measure, the proposed method is of great practical value for news agencies. In addition, the proposed model can be used for other text regression tasks (e.g., predicting revenues from reviews).

Acknowledgments

This work is funded by Natural Sciences and Engineering Research Council of Canada (NSERC), The Globe and Mail, and the Big Data Research, Analytics and Information Network (BRAIN) Alliance established by the Ontario Research Fund-Research Excellence Program (ORF-RE). We would also like to thank Amin Omidvar for his collaboration at the early stage of this work.

References

Ameeta Agrawal, Aijun An, and Manos Papagelis. 2018. Learning emotion-enriched word representations. In *Proceedings of the 27th International Conference on Computational Linguistics, COLING 2018, Santa Fe, New Mexico, USA, August 20-26, 2018*, pages 950–961.

Ameeta Agrawal, Raghavender Sahdev, Heidar Davoudi, Forouq Khonsari, Aijun An, and Susan McGrath. 2016. Detecting the magnitude of events from news articles. In *Web Intelligence (WI), 2016 IEEE/WIC/ACM International Conference on*, pages 177–184. IEEE.

David M Blei, Andrew Y Ng, and Michael I Jordan. 2003. Latent dirichlet allocation. *Journal of machine Learning research*, 3(Jan):993–1022.

Sunandan Chakraborty, Ashwin Venkataraman, Srikanth Jagabathula, and Lakshminarayanan Subramanian. 2016. Predicting socio-economic indicators using news events. In *Proceedings of the 22nd ACM SIGKDD International Conference on Knowledge Discovery and Data Mining*, pages 1455–1464. ACM.

Heng-Tze Cheng, Levent Koc, Jeremiah Harmsen, Tal Shaked, Tushar Chandra, Hrishi Aradhye, Glen Anderson, Greg Corrado, Wei Chai, Mustafa Ispir, et al. 2016. Wide & deep learning for recommender systems. In *Proceedings of the 1st Workshop on Deep Learning for Recommender Systems*, pages 7–10. ACM.

François Chollet et al. 2015. Keras. https://keras.io.

Mark Claypool, Phong Le, Makoto Wased, and David Brown. 2001. Implicit interest indicators. In *Proceedings of the 6th international conference on Intelligent user interfaces*, pages 33–40. ACM.

Paul Ekman. 1992. An argument for basic emotions. *Cognition & emotion*, 6(3-4):169–200.

Steve Fox, Kuldeep Karnawat, Mark Mydland, Susan Dumais, and Thomas White. 2005. Evaluating implicit measures to improve web search. *ACM Transactions on Information Systems (TOIS)*, 23(2):147–168.

Huifeng Guo, Ruiming Tang, Yunming Ye, Zhenguo Li, and Xiuqiang He. 2017. Deepfm: a factorization-machine based neural network for ctr prediction. *arXiv preprint arXiv:1703.04247*.

Stratis Ioannidis, Yunjiang Jiang, Saeed Amizadeh, and Nikolay Laptev. 2016. Parallel news-article traffic forecasting with admm. In *SIGKDD Workshop on Mining and Learning from Time Series*. ACM.

Joon Hee Kim, Amin Mantrach, Alejandro Jaimes, and Alice Oh. 2016. How to compete online for news audience: Modeling words that attract clicks. In *Proceedings of the 22nd ACM SIGKDD International Conference on Knowledge Discovery and Data Mining*, pages 1645–1654. ACM.

Yoon Kim. 2014. Convolutional neural networks for sentence classification. In *Proceedings of the 2014 Conference on Empirical Methods in Natural Language Processing (EMNLP)*, pages 1746–1751.

Youngho Kim, Ahmed Hassan, Ryen W White, and Imed Zitouni. 2014. Modeling dwell time to predict click-level satisfaction. In *Proceedings of the 7th ACM international conference on Web search and data mining*, pages 193–202. ACM.

Quoc Le and Tomas Mikolov. 2014. Distributed representations of sentences and documents. In *International Conference on Machine Learning*, pages 1188–1196.

Chao Liu, Ryen W White, and Susan Dumais. 2010. Understanding web browsing behaviors through weibull analysis of dwell time. In *Proceedings of the 33rd international ACM SIGIR conference on Research and development in information retrieval*, pages 379–386. ACM.

Tomas Mikolov, Ilya Sutskever, Kai Chen, Greg S Corrado, and Jeff Dean. 2013. Distributed representations of words and phrases and their compositionality. In *Advances in neural information processing systems*, pages 3111–3119.

Saif M Mohammad and Peter D Turney. 2010. Emotions evoked by common words and phrases: Using mechanical turk to create an emotion lexicon. In *Proceedings of the NAACL HLT 2010 workshop on computational approaches to analysis and generation of emotion in text*, pages 26–34. Association for Computational Linguistics.

Saif M Mohammad and Peter D Turney. 2013. Crowdsourcing a word–emotion association lexicon. *Computational Intelligence*, 29(3):436–465.

F. Pedregosa, G. Varoquaux, A. Gramfort, V. Michel, B. Thirion, O. Grisel, M. Blondel, P. Prettenhofer, R. Weiss, V. Dubourg, J. Vanderplas, A. Passos, D. Cournapeau, M. Brucher, M. Perrot, and E. Duchesnay. 2011. Scikit-learn: Machine learning in Python. *Journal of Machine Learning Research*, 12:2825–2830.

Colin Raffel and Daniel PW Ellis. 2015. Feedforward networks with attention can solve some long-term memory problems. *arXiv preprint arXiv:1512.08756*.

Steffen Rendle. 2010. Factorization machines. In *Data Mining (ICDM), 2010 IEEE 10th International Conference on*, pages 995–1000. IEEE.

Michael Röder, Andreas Both, and Alexander Hinneburg. 2015. Exploring the space of topic coherence measures. In *Proceedings of the eighth ACM international conference on Web search and data mining*, pages 399–408. ACM.

Gerard Salton and Michael J. McGill. 1986. *Introduction to Modern Information Retrieval*. McGraw-Hill, Inc., New York, NY, USA.

Christopher Walker, Stephanie Strassel, Julie Medero, and Kazuaki Maeda. 2006. Ace 2005 multilingual training corpus. *Linguistic Data Consortium, Philadelphia*, 57.

Bishan Yang and Tom Mitchell. 2016. Joint extraction of events and entities within a document context. *arXiv preprint arXiv:1609.03632*.

Xing Yi, Liangjie Hong, Erheng Zhong, Nanthan Nan Liu, and Suju Rajan. 2014. Beyond clicks: dwell time for personalization. In *Proceedings of the 8th ACM Conference on Recommender systems*, pages 113–120. ACM.

Author Index